Comparative CSR and Sustainability

This book breaks new ground by providing a structured and cohesive set of contributions on the actions, developments, problems and theories of corporate social responsibility (CSR). With new case studies from the UN's Least Developed Countries (LDCs), contributors in this book investigate how firms in Eastern and Western countries are responding to and making use of evolving CSR guidelines.

The book addresses the following questions: is CSR simply greenwashing or an authentic commitment to responsible corporate citizenship? Has globalization drawn CSR conduct in LDCs closer to that of industrialized countries? Stakeholder theory, actor–network theory and a new orbital theory of accountability are applied to give coherence to the case studies. Other chapters address greenwashing in reports, the impact of CSR in socially stigmatized occupations, an analysis on what responsibility precisely entails in CSR, and the interface between law and CSR. The book also considers the impact of COVID-19 on the hospitality industry, and includes a contribution from Ukrainian scholars, one written while their city of Kharkiv was under attack by Russian forces.

This book will be a useful reference to those interested in discussions on crises, climate change, and SDGs and realizing sustainable goals through CSR.

Gabriel Donleavy is a Professor of Accounting at the University of New England, Australia.

Carlos Noronha is an Associate Professor of Accounting at the University of Macau, Macau SAR, China.

Routledge Research in Sustainability and Business

Corporate Social Responsibility in the Arctic
The New Frontiers of Business, Management, and Enterprise
Gisele M. Arruda and Lara Johannsdottir

The New Corporate Climate Leadership
Edward Cameron and Emilie Prattico

Supply Chain Sustainability in Small and Medium Sized Enterprises
Edited by Prasanta Kumar Dey, Soumyadeb Chowdhury, and Chrisovalantis Malesios

Corporate Regulation for Climate Change Mitigation in Africa
A Case for Dilute Interventionism
Kikelomo O. Kila

The Role of Business in Global Sustainability Transformations
Edited by Dalia D'Amato, Anne Toppinen and Robert Kozak

Understanding Sustainability Performance in Business Organizations
Implications for the Sustainability Service Industry
Jean-Pierre Imbrogiano

Comparative CSR and Sustainability
New Accounting for Social Consequences
Edited by Gabriel Donleavy and Carlos Noronha

Environmental Disclosure
Critical Issues and New Trends
Luigi Lepore and Sabrina Pisano

For more information about this series, please visit: www.routledge.com/Routledge-Research-in-Sustainability-and-Business/book-series/RRSB

Comparative CSR and Sustainability

New Accounting for Social Consequences

Edited by
Gabriel Donleavy and Carlos Noronha

Routledge
Taylor & Francis Group
LONDON AND NEW YORK

First published 2023
by Routledge
4 Park Square, Milton Park, Abingdon, Oxon OX14 4RN

and by Routledge
605 Third Avenue, New York, NY 10158

Routledge is an imprint of the Taylor & Francis Group, an informa business

British Library Cataloguing-in-Publication Data
A catalogue record for this book is available from the British Library

Library of Congress Cataloging-in-Publication Data
Names: Donleavy, G. D. (G. Douglas) editor. | Noronha, Carlos, editor.
Title: Comparative CSR and sustainability: new accounting for social consequences/edited by Gabriel Donleavy and Carlos Noronha.
Description: New York, NY: Routledge, 2023. | Series: Routledge research in sustainability and business | Includes bibliographical references and index. |
Identifiers: LCCN 2022034015 (print) | LCCN 2022034016 (ebook) | ISBN 9781032228686 (hardback) | ISBN 9781032228709 (paperback) | ISBN 9781003274575 (ebook)
Subjects: LCSH: Social responsibility of business. | Sustainable development reporting.
Classification: LCC HD60 .C5957 2023 (print) | LCC HD60 (ebook) | DDC 658.4/08--dc23/eng/20220804
LC record available at https://lccn.loc.gov/2022034015
LC ebook record available at https://lccn.loc.gov/2022034016

ISBN: 9781032228686 (hbk)
ISBN: 9781032228709 (pbk)
ISBN: 9781003274575 (ebk)

DOI: 10.4324/9781003274575

Typeset in Galliard
by Deanta Global Publishing Services, Chennai, India

Contents

Figures

Tables

Contributors

Cristina Sales Baptista is a Senior Assistant Professor at ISEG, Lisbon School of Economics and Management, University of Lisbon, Portugal.

Teresa Burguete is a Senior Consultant Mining Engineer in Portugal and holds a PhD in Economic Sociology.

Ariana Chang is an Assistant Professor in the Interdisciplinary Studies Program (BPIS) at Fu Jen Catholic University, Taiwan, R.O.C.

Nadine Chorão is a Project Manager at ARCTEL-CPLP, Portugal.

Taras Danko is a Professor of International Business at the National Technical University Kharkiv Polytechnic Institute, Ukraine.

Gabriel Donleavy is a Professor of Accounting at the University of New England, Australia.

Anisur R. Faroque is an Associate Professor of International Business at the School of Business and Management, LUT University, Finland.

Limin Fu is a Lecturer (Assistant Professor) in Management at the University of Newcastle, Australia.

Mohammad Osman Gani is a doctoral student at the Graduate School of Humanities and Social Sciences, Hiroshima University, Japan.

Paulo Almeida Gonçalves is an Assistant Professor at ISEG, Lisbon School of Economics and Management, University of Lisbon, Portugal.

Jieqi Guan is an Assistant Professor at the Macao Institute for Tourism Studies, Macau SAR, China.

Denis De Castro Halis is an Associate Professor of Law at UNESA/Rio de Janeiro and External Associate Professor of CECS, Faculty of Law, University of Copenhagen.

Pui San Ip is an Adjunct Faculty Member of Accounting at the Macao Institute for Tourism Studies, Macau SAR, China.

Pirooz Tohidi Khiavi is a doctoral student of industrial engineering and management at LUT University, Finland.

Nataliia Krasnokutska is a Professor of Management and International Business and the Director of the Educational and Scientific Institute of Economics, at the National Technical University Kharkiv Polytechnic Institute, Ukraine.

Cindia, Ching Chi Lam is an Assistant Professor at the Macao Institute for Tourism Studies, Macau SAR, China.

Weng Si Lei is an Assistant Professor at the Macao Institute for Tourism Studies, Macau SAR, China.

Tiffany Cheng-Han Leung is an Assistant Professor at the City University of Macau, Macau SAR, China.

Kim Ieng Loi is the Vice President at the Macao Institute for Tourism Studies, Macau SAR, China.

Fernando Lourenço is an Assistant Professor at the Macao Institute for Tourism Studies, Macau SAR, China.

Constâncio Augusto Machanguana is an Assistant Professor of Sociology at the Zambeze University, Mozambique.

Md Tapan Mahmud is an Assistant Professor of Accounting at Bangladesh University of Professionals (BUP), Bangladesh.

Pedro Verga Matos is a Senior Associate Professor at ISEG, Lisbon School of Economics and Management, University of Lisbon, Portugal.

Sina Mortazavi is a post-doctoral researcher at the LUT School of Business and Management, LUT University, Finland.

Carlos Noronha is an Associate Professor of Accounting at the University of Macau, Macau SAR, China.

Esnaina Quader is a Lecturer in the Department of Management at North South University, Bangladesh.

Markus Raatikainen is a Project Researcher at the Department of Business of the University of Eastern Finland, Finland.

Idalina Dias Sardinha is an Invited Professor and a Senior Researcher at Lisbon School of Economics and Management (ISEG), University of Lisbon, Portugal.

Sam Sarpong is an Associate Professor of Management and Marketing at Xiamen University-Malaysia, Malaysia.

Sandy Hou In Sio is the President of the Administrative Council of the Macau Institute for Corporate Social Responsibility in Greater China (MICSRGC), Macau SAR, China.

Duane Windsor is the Lynette S. Autrey Professor of Management at Rice University's Jesse H. Jones Graduate School of Business, Houston, USA.

You Shi Xiang is a Doctor of Business Administration candidate at the City University of Macau, Macau SAR, China.

Ruopiao Zhang is an Assistant Professor of Accounting at the Macau University of Science and Technology, Macau SAR, China.

Foreword

As I suspect is true for most of my colleagues engaged in research related to issues of corporate social responsibility (CSR), the goal of my endeavors is to help improve the social and environmental impacts of the world's organizations. A crucial step in that process is a better understanding of the concept of CSR itself and how organizations are, or are not, addressing the relevant issues.

In this book, Editors Gabriel Donleavy and Carlos Noronha bring together an interesting mix of contemporary studies exploring CSR through both conceptual and empirical investigations, with the latter including studies across both CSR actions and CSR disclosures. A real strength of the compilation is its substantial, although not exclusive, focus on CSR in Eastern and developing countries, areas much in need of rich investigation. The book is also very timely in that several of the contributions examine and reflect on how the COVID-19 pandemic may be having influences on a variety of CSR issues.

Although academic interest in CSR dates back more than 50 years, how organizations are impacting the issues of concern – environmental degradation, community health, worker safety and so many others – remains a critical avenue for further investigation. To this end, *Comparative CSR and Sustainability: New Accounting for Social Consequences* offers new insights on where we stand and where we need to go.

Dennis M. Patten
Emeritus Distinguished Professor of Accounting
Illinois State University

1 Introduction

CSR at the Peak of the Globalisation Movement

Gabriel Donleavy and Carlos Noronha

Overview of the Field

Corporate social responsibility (CSR) emerged as the name for the age-old idea that all institutions have a role as part of the society in which they operate. Milton Friedman (1970) notoriously expressed the resentment of the Chicago School of economics against the idea when he said that the social responsibility of business was to increase its profits, a sentiment echoed by UK Prime Minister Thatcher's equally notorious claim in a 1987 interview in *Woman's Own* that there is no such thing as society (*The Guardian*, 2013). Public consciousness of climate change, the corporate role in pollution and the political dimensions of legal clothing in one corporate personality, the nexus of contracts constituting modern business, all started to become more centre stage through the 1980s. The end of the cold war with the fall of the Berlin Wall in 1989 and the disbanding of the Soviet Union in 1991 opened the door for green to become ahead of red as the colour of issues at the forefront of democratic concern (Jasanoff, 2004; Dunn, 2012). A series of scandals around oil spills from tankers carrying the oil of the Seven Sisters, the fact and mismanagement of the Chernobyl nuclear explosion in 1986, the perceived increasing volatility and unreliability of capital markets with the emergence of derivatives in the 1990s, of the dotcom bubble at the turn of the century and of the global financial crisis of 2008 all converged to raise public consciousness of CSR as a real and important issue of concern which has only increased ever since. Ed Freeman's (1984) normative stakeholder theory provided much of the conceptual framework for transitioning between the raw and financialised capitalism defended by Milton Friedman to a more socially responsible capitalism in which corporate citizenship has a noblesse oblige implication no longer much in dispute. Freeman's (1984) stakeholder theory has been adopted by the international accounting standard setting community to lift, in 2022, integrated accounting to the same level of validation, approval and professional backing as has always been enjoyed by traditional financial accounts (IFRS, 2021a). The announcement by the IFRS that its new subsidiary, the ISSB, will take over the Value Reporting Foundation which itself had only a year earlier absorbed the International Integrated Reporting Council, certifies this assertion. Freeman (1984) holds that business in the long term is a positive sum game creating value and any short- or

DOI: 10.4324/9781003274575-1

medium-term contraindication by way of zero sum appropriation or diversion of value cannot last. By such a declaration, capitalism is saved to fight another day as the major leader of human progress. Against this view, the Global Reporting Initiative (GRI) has declared it will try and converge with the ISSB on sustainability accounting, but it has issued new guidelines in 2022 (IFRS, 2021b) stressing a new requirement for firms to report on their human impacts, especially their impacts on human rights; but the GRI has lost the battle for sustainability accounting dominance with the IFRS move to espouse integrated accounting, as integrated accounting retains the sovereignty of the equity shareholder over all other stakeholders, so any zero-sum gaming in the short or medium term is apt to be resolved in favour of shareholders as against any other stakeholder group.

In parallel with the real-world developments summarised above, management and accounting theory has developed, albeit in a lagged rather than a leading fashion. Normative stakeholder theory has been a major framework used by CSR researchers from the beginning. A theory that has been even more dominant is not really a theory at all but rather a characterisation of CSR "dimensions"; Carroll's (1979, 1991, 2016) and Carroll and Shabana's (2010) specification is the most cited of all theoretical frameworks in CSR scholarship. It postulates four dimensions of CSR activity: economic, political, philanthropic and promotional. These dimensions are often used to discuss motivations for firm engagement in CSR activity and CSR reporting. It has come under increasing criticism in the last ten years but not to the point where an alternative model threatens to displace it in the near future. Not even invented when CSR scholarship began, institutional theory (DiMaggio and Powell, 1983; Meidinger, 1987) has become progressively more widely employed to explain CSR behaviour both in action and in reporting. Institutional theory has a dominant construct of isomorphism, whereby three alternative but not mutually exclusive forces act to drive a convergence between organisations that begin from quite different structures, policies and patterns of activity. It is often used to describe how globalisation drove an increase in CSR activity. The other major construct in institutional theory is even more widely employed in CSR research: decoupling. This is a term for the failure of CSR actions to match or back up CSR words – greenwashing is one particular form of it (De Freitas Netto et al., 2020). As isomorphism pressures increase, so does decoupling as firms respond to such pressure in words ahead of compliance in actions.

The next section summarises the state of CSR research to 2008 according to contributions to the *Oxford Handbook on Corporate Social Responsibility* (Crane et al., 2008). Then the following section outlines major CSR scholastic developments since the publication of the Handbook. Finally, the contributions to the present book are introduced.

Highlights of CSR Research to 2008

The first wave of research on CSR focused on the consequences of CSR implementation on financial performance rather than on comparative CSR as a rapidly developing business strategy by way of response to globalisation (Williams and Aguilera, 2008).

An early example of government leadership of CSR cited by Williams and Aguilera (2008) is Prime Minister Tony Blair's requiring the trustees of occupational pension funds to adopt Statements of Investment Principles detailing the way social and environmental information is taken into account in constructing investment portfolios. This law had an important effect on the behaviour of the largest pension funds, causing them to ask questions of asset managers about their CSR records, and in turn fuelling greater interest in, and investment in, socially responsible investment. Twenty years ago, comparative studies cited by Williams and Aguilera (2008) showed that companies in the United Kingdom had higher rates of stakeholder engagement and social reporting than companies in every other European country except Norway.

In developing countries, a concern was then that governments ignore corporate irresponsibility and refuse to enforce protective labour or environmental standards in the law in order to encourage foreign investment (Aman, 2001). Chappel and Moon (2005) found that CSR in Asia was related to the extent to which domestic companies engage in international trade. Thus, the isomorphic pressures of globalisation were a factor in rising levels of CSR activity.

Corporate governance scholars tended to divide the world into the Anglo-American "outsider" system versus the Continental European and Japanese "insider" systems. Yet, a number of studies show that legal developments and institutional contexts in Britain concerning CSR show important similarities with Europe, and related contrasts with the United States: "[s]ome institutional investors are beginning to use their influence to monitor performance by companies across a range of social and environmental issues that impact upon stakeholders" (Armour et al., 2003, 545). Matten and Moon (2004) compared CSR in Europe versus in the United States. They defined explicit CSR as that seen in the United States, where companies volunteer to address important social and economic issues through their CSR policies, in significant part because of less stringent legal requirements than in Europe for such things as health care provision, employees' rights, environmental protection and the like. In contrast, in Europe and the United Kingdom, responsibility for these issues is undertaken as part of a company's legal responsibilities, and thus CSR is "implicit" in the way the company does business. Legal factors included more required disclosure of social and environmental information by publicly listed companies in the United Kingdom than in the United States; and the required disclosure by pension fund trustees of the extent to which social and environmental issues are considered in constructing their investment portfolios (Williams and Conley, 2005). Institutional factors included: (a) differences in the composition of institutional investors in the two markets, with a higher percentage of institutional investors in the United Kingdom being pension funds and insurance companies with longer time-horizons for investment than the mutual funds that have dominated in the United States; (b) "soft law" encouragement in the United Kingdom by the highly influential Cadbury Commission of institutional investor engagement with portfolio companies; and (c) encouragement of attention to CSR issues by the Institutional Shareholders Committee, which represents over 80% of institutional investment in the United Kingdom.

There is, according to Williams and Aguilera (2008), an extensive literature on why managerial attitudes towards CSR are likely to have a strong influence on firm-level CSR outcomes. It tends to show that individual and organisational values are much more significant predictors of CSR managerial behaviour than the national cultural dimensions identified by Hofstede (1980, 2001) so long ago. There is extensive evidence showing that top management teams behave differently across countries because they are highly influenced by the national cultural norms of work in which they are embedded. We know, however, from the business ethics literature that there is a strong relationship between the likelihood that a manager will engage in corrupt business behaviour and the extent to which managers operate in countries with high power distance, masculinity and uncertainty (Husted, 1999).

Cullen et al. (2004) found significant nation-level effects, for instance, that industrialisation weakens social norms and triggers a win-at-all-cost mentality, or that in societies with strong cultural values such as universalism and materialism managers tend to engage in more egoistic ethical reasoning.

Orpen (1987) conducted a survey among senior managers in South Africa and the United States to uncover their attitude towards CSR and found that US managers hold a much more positive attitude to CSR activities than South African managers; and that US managers felt more pressure to get involved in CSR strategies than their counterparts in South Africa.

Maignan and Ralston's (2002) cross-national study showed that businesses' communication about CSR in 1999 in France, the Netherlands, the United Kingdom and the United States, varies significantly. They concluded that US and UK firms tended to be more eager to show that they "cared" about CSR issues, at least on the surface, whereas Dutch and French firms were more likely to include CSR issues in their websites only as a response to stakeholders' scrutiny and pressures. Communities and consumers were the primary stakeholder drivers in the United Kingdom while customers and regulators were more salient in France and the Netherlands.

Brazil scores high in institutional collectivism and China scores high in power distance; Waldman et al. (2006) showed that managers in countries which esteem institutional collectivism traits, such as obtaining gratification for addressing long-term concerns, and devalue high power distance traits are more likely to manifest managerial behaviours positively associated with CSR. In addition, they showed that managers in wealthier countries are mostly concerned with shareholder/owner CSR issues, that is, CSR strategies that maximise economic returns.

Egri et al. (2006) analysed what influences corporate responsibility outcomes across countries. In addition to reporting that personal values have a direct relationship with the type of CSR that managers are likely to support in different countries, they show that managers in traditional cultures that promote ethical idealism and communitarian norms, and tend to have a Roman Catholic heritage (e.g., Colombia and Italy) were more supportive of social CSR than environmental or economic CSR. Secular-rational and survival societies such as ex-Communist countries (e.g., Croatia and Hungary) or Confucian-oriented societies (e.g., Taiwan and Hong Kong) were more likely to support economic CSR initiatives. Such studies reflect the continuing dominance of the Hofstede paradigm of national managerial values in cross-national studies, and this has only recently been challenged, as the next section will describe.

Consumers are stakeholders who can become problematic for companies, as Nike experienced when it came under attack over labour practices in Asia, or as Royal Dutch Shell experienced with the Brent Spar mismanagement. It is clear that corporate social performance information can affect consumer purchase intentions. It is important to note that while there are societies that place a lot of emphasis on the consumer's voice and have in place direct mechanisms where they can express their concerns such as in France, this is not the case in other societies such as Japan, where the consumer movement has been relatively weak (Wokutch, 1990).

Studies consistently found that sustainability reporting rates were highest in Europe, followed by Japan, and with the United States showing the lowest rates of reporting. Kolk's (2003) study shows that 90% of European companies in the Fortune Global 250 publish sustainability reports, followed by 83% of Japanese companies, as contrasted with 35% of American companies. It must be noted that Europe requires social and environmental reporting; the fact that Europe requires some aspects of sustainability reporting can also be understood as evidence of its leadership on CSR. Kolk found that about 60% of sustainability reports now discuss the corporate governance of sustainability within the organisation, while surveys of similar sets of companies only a few years ago (2002 reports) did not discuss this. Kolk also finds that European and Japanese companies are more specific than US companies about "the organizational aspects and responsibilities for sustainability". As Kolk recognised, American disclosure patterns and lack of verification may reflect the greater concern with litigation in the United States, and the difficulties of a purely voluntary approach to expanded sustainability disclosure in such a context.

Meek et al. (1995) conducted a study of voluntary annual report disclosure by US, UK and continental European multinational firms. They showed that the country of origin has a significant effect not only on the degree of voluntary disclosure but also on what type of information (i.e., strategic, non-financial and financial) is most likely to be covered in these MNCs' annual reports.

Strike et al. (2006) produced empirical evidence that international diversification of firms increases not only CSR reporting but also "corporate irresponsibility", presumed to be on account of the difficulties of managing semi-autonomous subsidiaries in different countries across the different subsidiaries of a given MNC. Husted and Allen (2006) investigated how CSR was managed within MNCs, and studied the relationship between global and local (country-specific) CSR. Local CSR issues are those that respond to the specific needs and concerns of particular communities, such as HIV-AIDS in Africa. It is an issue that every company doing business in Africa needs to address, but has not become part of the global CSR agenda. Husted and Allen (2006) surveyed firms in Mexico, and found that the firms followed different patterns of management of global and local CSR issues depending on whether they were firms with many, semi-autonomous subsidiaries (multi-domestic); were organised from a central office with lean subsidiaries (global); or combined elements of central organisation and local responsiveness (transnational).

In sum, the picture in 2008 was of strong differences between countries in their CSR reporting and action behaviours – reliance on the Hofstede paradigm to explain them, widespread decoupling and the use of the Freeman stakeholder theory to justify concern with sustainability reporting issues and a continuing reliance on the triple bottom line framework of sustainability and CSR reporting norms – in the period before the introduction of integrated accounting and the GRI. In analysing CSR activities themselves, the Carroll (1979) dimensions were used in the vast majority of published studies.

CSR Research since 2008

The Global Financial Crisis of 2008 with its bail out of banks and its punishment of such deeply indebted economies as Greece and Spain, facilitated a wider adoption of CSR perspectives within the major capitalist economies and became a dominant narrative of justification for the Chinese Communist Party regime too. The GRI and the IIRC were established in the five years after the crisis and immediately dominated the sustainability reporting space. Both paid lip service to triple bottom line reporting and the salience of all stakeholder groups. Only GRI, however, expressly treated all stakeholders as having prima facie equal salience, whereas integrated reporting (IR) has never deviated from its postulate that suppliers of capital are the primary audience for their reports and by implication are the primary stakeholders. The consolidation of earlier and later sustainability accounting boards in 2021 and 2022 greatly reinforces the dominance of the integrated accounting approach. Its major advance on traditional reporting is the opening out of the concept of capital from the purely financial to include manufactured, intellectual, human, relationship and natural capitals as all being stores of long-term value and all being valid attributions of the concept of value itself. The integrated accounting revolution may well preserve capitalist structures and shareholder primacy, but is still revolutionary in making reports long-term oriented rather than short-term, in extending the idea of value to five non-traditional stores of value and in accepting that most of these other stores can be described but cannot be precisely measured or enumerated. This reflects Keynes' dictum that it is better to be roughly right than to be precisely wrong, but such reflection is unlikely to have been in the minds of the standard setters.

Least Developed Countries

CSR in least developed countries (LDCs) had been seen as discretionary in Carroll's schema and mostly greenwashing, but Sorour et al. (2021) say it is changing to greater manifestation of authentic commitment to real CSR; for example, in Egypt since its 2011 revolution, especially political CSR where firms fill public sector vacuums to provide public goods. UN Global Compact 2019 is associated with a significant number of firms becoming involved in solving social and economic problems. Scott's (2014) neo-institutional theory "elides" the distinction between institution and its environments by focusing on processes.

Kusyk (2021) challenges the applicability of the Carroll dimensions to SMEs. Only 30% of the CSR research reviewed from 1984 to 2019 fit Carroll's dimensions, but SMEs are 90% of the biz population, 79% of its employment and 55% of global GDP per WTO in 2016 (see WTO, 2016).

More often in LDCs intentions for CSR were formed by economic and proprietorial philanthropic orientation dimensions. Aquif and Wahab (2021) review LDC CSR practices over the last ten years. Pizzi et al. (2020) show competition is a factor driving CSR performance. Atiq et al. (2014) see internationalisation; but Ali et al. (2017) show pollution and environment are still not such major concerns for LDCs.

In sum, in the ten years of globalisation and internationalisation up to the COVID-19 pandemic (which stopped, then arguably began to reverse the international isomorphism), the distinction found in earlier periods between LDCs and developed countries in all aspects of CSR were converging.

Employee Commitment

For Lebanon, El Kassar et al.'s (2017) study showed employee identification moderates the effect of CSR on commitment but also vice versa. Chen et al. (2019) confirmed that the result in other countries is that CSR does affect employee relationships, especially for ethical CSR which is immune from a pre-existing sense of fit by the employee to the employer that is not very high. However, Donia et al. (2019) found that employee fit was an important mediator on CSR effects on employee performance as part of a wider moderating effect of employee attitudes. Ahmad et al. (2021) further show that environmental CSR affects both employee commitment and organisational reputation more widely. Before these studies, interaction of CSR and employee motivation had not been examined, and the studies are the more important now that GRI 102's new guideline requires much new information on this aspect of CSR impacts.

Behavioural Aspects

Pope and Waerass' (2016) model indicates five joint conditions needed for greenwashing to work on customers: (1) consumers demand CSR activities; (2) consumers support CSR practices; (3) firms must advertise their CSR activities; (4) consumers are aware of CSR announcements and disclosures; and (5) firms actually do decouple. Empirical evidence they allege to be good for 2 and 3 but not for 4, so the model is not fully supported by the facts. Chen et al. (2018) show that customers respond more to value-creating CSR than to promotional or philanthropic CSR. Kim et al. (2019) apply the Hofstede framework to show that individualism is associated with scepticism toward CSR activities. Ulke and Schons (2016) demonstrate that firms with bad reputations benefit more from engaging in CSR than firms with good ones. As a prelude to or accompaniment of decoupling, Jeriji and Louhichi (2021) show how poor sustainability performers disclose low quality hard negative information. Fehre and Weber (2016) report an inverse relationship between the seriousness of a crisis facing the firm, in Germany, and disclosure of CSR matters.

Two Further Aspects of Global Convergence

El-Bassioury et al. (2019) show institutional theory is born out by the effects on CSR disclosure of foreign owners and directors in Egypt, Germany and the United States, while government regulation and promotion of CSR vary greatly between the three countries.

Buhman (2016) shows that juridification and legislation on CSR has been steadily growing, facilitated by such international declarations as the OECD (2011) guidelines for MNEs, the UN guiding principles on business which uses the term "social licence to operate" and the ISO 26000 social responsibility guidance standard. Transnationalisation of law allows for shifts of legal norms of conduct across boundaries. This is strong confirmation of an international convergence in the second decade of the century, which coincidentally exemplifies the orbital theory's postulate that CSR pressure is to move from the outer orbits of accountability to the inner one where law is the driving force (Donleavy, Chapter 14, in this book).

The Chapters in This Collection

All the contributions of the book were written while convergence and globalisation were still apparent, even if slowing down in response to COVID-19. The Russian war on Ukraine began in February 2022 and quickly restored the world of the Cold War as regards economic blocks and serious confrontation between them, thereby reversing the convergences of the previous decade or so. The contributions in this book are a mix of closely focused case studies of CSR in very particular contexts, some broader empirical research and some rethinking of the theoretical underpinning of CSR, both positive and normative. The chapters are loosely grouped by common coverage areas but they should be read individually to do them justice rather than as threads cohering with each other in any systematic or deliberate manner. If reversal of globalisation continues well through the 2020s, it can be predicted that the editors of a follow up book in ten years' time will contrast dramatically with the somewhat optimistic tone of the present work.

Chapter 1: Introduction

This is the present chapter.

Part 1: CSR – Extinction, Disasters and the New Paradigm

Advancing knowledge of changing CSR characteristics in China, Zhang in Chapter 2 begins by presenting current practices of biodiversity disclosure in China through documentary analysis of the CSR reports of Chinese enterprises listed on the Fortune Global 500. This analysis explains the necessity to switch from biodiversity accounting to extinction accounting, using the example of the critically endangered Chinese sturgeon.

Machanguana in Chapter 3 focusses on CSR in a particular LDC in a particular context of resettlement. Resettlement often leads to tensions between those resettled, the investors and the governments. His research reviews processes to plan, initiate and guide to minimise tensions and conflicts. He concludes that although the affected community knows how resettlement should be managed to avoid tensions, the attitude of the Chinese company and the inertia of the government shift the victims to the margins of concern.

The study in Chapter 4 by Ip and Noronha investigates the effect of COVID-19 on sustainability reporting in the hospitality industry. Data were collected from the sustainability reports and official online resources of the top hotel chains worldwide. The findings demonstrate that COVID-19 does not have significant influence on the sustainability reporting performance.

In Chapter 5, Lei et al. illustrate the nature of the CSR activities of the major enterprises in Macau through the use of stakeholder theory. They find that many CSR actions in Macau are reciprocal in nature but also that the local government has triggered CSR practices beyond mere compliance.

Chang in Chapter 6 explores the role of social responsibility in socially stigmatised occupations. She describes how social responsibility practices can be exercised in a stigmatised industry to advance sustainable development goals. The anecdotal evidence presented in this chapter suggests that socially responsible practices are even more relevant for stigmatised groups in times of crisis. Responsible leadership can help mitigate the impact of COVID-19 on stigmatised workers as they encounter profoundly contested identities.

Part 2: CSR Challenges in Developing and Least Developed Countries

Faroque et al. in Chapter 7 critically review the role of nongovernmental organisations in shaping CSR. Changes in NGOs' structure and operation have altered how CSR is perceived in the nations in which they operate. They compare the role of NGOs as major practitioners and facilitators of CSR in developing and developed nations. NGOs with strong global and national presences in developing countries (e.g., Bangladesh and China) and developed countries (e.g., the United States and the United Kingdom) were selected. Differences and similarities are found in this study.

Mortazavi et al. in Chapter 8 draw on evidence from one case study of Nokia, to offer an explanation of the process of inclusive innovation (ININ) creation in India and to identify the constraints on survival and growth in India's low-income markets. The study shows that MNEs utilise market-specific strategies to overcome constraints and create social empowerment in these target markets.

Matos et al. in Chapter 9 consider how internet access and new information technologies are increasingly being presented as an important tool to support economic and social developments. They analyse the implementation of the Sustainable Villages for Development (SV4D) project in Mozambique.

Using actor–network theory, Noronha and Zhang in Chapter 10 explore CSR reporting in the information and communication technology sector within China's Belt and Road Initiative.

Part 3: CSR – Greenwashing and Window-Dressing

Fu in Chapter 11 reviews the positive contributions of green initiatives to the circular economy along with the rampant use of window-dressing. She also explores how these different elements of green initiatives interact with organisational processes and motives, and the consequences.

Mahmud in Chapter 12 discusses the motivation of the Japanese IR publishers using institutional theory. The contribution of coercive mechanism to the motivation of the Japanese IR publishers is low, whereas normative and mimetic mechanisms have greater explanatory power.

Windsor's Chapter 13 provides a conceptual framework for defining corporate social responsibility (CSR) avoidance and engagement in contrast to corporate social irresponsibility (CSIR). The framework is a more precise formulation than the general distinction between CSR and CSIR found in the extant literature. The proposed framework identifies a set of four general strategies for business executives in addressing responsibilities of the profit-seeking business sector toward society. These four strategies are located along a simple continuum from socially "bad" (CSIR) to socially "good" (CSR engagement) as defined externally to the firm. CSR engagement is good corporate citizenship.

Part 4: CSR and New Underlying Assumptions

The orbital theory of accountability, presented by Donleavy in Chapter 14, is a positive theory of accountability compatible with, but differently anchored from, the Carroll model. It postulates that accountability manifests in different ways in the inner juridification orbit from the model of socially interactive action and from the outer or one-way travel orbit, of which accountability to posterity looms large and therefore the accountability process occurs. The chapter explains how orbital theory predicts that CSR will manifest in each of the three different accountability orbits. It concludes with a research agenda anchored on hypotheses.

Halis in Chapter 15 investigates the political and legal responsibilities of companies as a new frontier of CSR in times of digital technologies. CSR is no longer just linked to the marketing strategies of companies; it is now regulated via rules with legal force.

Sarpong in Chapter 16 explores whether responsibilities are more intrinsic, as opposed to obligations, and questions whether businesses have a responsibility or an obligation to society or both.

The focus of Chapter 17 by Burguete et al. uses an interdisciplinary approach to analyse stakeholder relationships. Their model claims to be appropriate for the understanding of the development of long-term relationships in the mining industry.

Part 5: Sustainability Goals and ESG

Guan et al. in Chapter 18 discuss the stages of development of sustainability goals in China and identify the challenges and obstacles during the implementation process. In-depth interviews were conducted to examine the perspectives of industry practitioners, scholars and key opinion leaders. They found that mention of social development goals in CSR reports in China have almost doubled in recent years. However, the disclosed information is still fragmented, accompanied by weak verification and supervision.

Leung and You in Chapter 19 focus on Hong Kong's history and prospects in developing Environmental, Social and Governance (ESG) guidelines up to 2020. The Hong Kong Stock Exchange (HKEX) takes step-by-step actions to regulate local ESG reporting practice, gradually raising the overall compliance level of the Guide from voluntary to mandatory. HKEX tends to emphasise board governance, stakeholder engagement and materiality assessment.

Ukrainian academics, Krasnokutska and Danko make a heroic contribution in Chapter 20, given the wartime conditions afflicting Kharkiv at the time of writing their piece. They use an institutional theory perspective to build a strategic options typology of sustainable practices transfer across national borders.

Concluding Remarks: Comparative CSR and Sustainability Research – An Axial Analysis

In the concluding Chapter 21, Donleavy and Noronha firstly review the development of the field of comparative management in order to mirror the notion of comparative CSR and sustainability. The chapters in this collection are then analysed in detail through looking into their research philosophy over a continuum from "conventional" to "critical". Four axial diagrams are formed using this continuum to combine with four other continua, namely from theory-building to theory-confirming, from high to low non-standard conformance, from global to local, and from forward-looking to retrospective. The chapters are then positioned in the axial diagrams to identify possible research opportunities. Donleavy and Noronha finally advocate a new concept of "phenomenon *grande*" which is much in need for the future development of comparative CSR studies at the new Anthropocene level. They indicate that avenues for further research in this area are expected and very much welcome.

References

Ali, W., Frynas, J.G. and Mahmood, Z. (2017). Determinants of corporate social responsibility (CSR) disclosure in developed and developing countries: A literature review. *Corporate Social Responsibility and Environmental Management*, 24(4), 273–294.

Ahmad, N., Ulah, Z., Arshad, M.Z., Kamran, H., Scholz, M. and Han, H. (2021). Relationship between corporate social responsibility at the micro level and environmental performance: The mediating role of employee pro-environmental behavior and the moderating role of gender. *Sustainable Production and Consumption*, 27, 1131–1148.

Aman, A., Jr. (2001). Privatization and the democracy problem in globalisation: Making markets more accountable through administrative law. *Fordham Urban Law Journal*, 28, 1477–1506.

Aqif, T. and Wahab, A. (2021). Developing an understanding of the determinants, disclosures, and outcomes of CSR practices – A focus on developed and developing countries: A past review of 10 years. *Journal of Global Responsibility*, 12(3), 289–316.

Armour, J., Deakin, S. and Konzelmann, S.J. (2003). Shareholder primacy and the trajectory of UK corporate governance. *British Journal of Industrial Relations*, 41(3), 531–555.

Atig, H., Boubarkri, M. and Ghoul, S. (2014). Firm internationalization and corporate social responsibility. *Journal of Business Ethics*, 134(2), 171–197.

Buhmann, K. (2016). Public regulators and CSR: The 'social licence to operate' in recent United Nations instruments on business and human rights and the juridification of CSR. *Journal of Business Ethics*, 136(4), 699–714.

Carroll, A.B. (1979). A three-dimensional conceptual model of corporate performance. *Academy of Management Review*, 4(4), 497–505.

Carroll, A.B. (1991). The pyramid of corporate social responsibility: Toward the moral management of organizational stakeholders. *Business Horizons*, 34(4), 39–48.

Carroll, A.B. (2016). Carroll's pyramid of CSR: Taking another look. *International Journal of Corporate Social Responsibility*, 1(3), 1–8.

Carroll, A.B. and Shabana, K.M. (2010). The business case for corporate social responsibility: A review of concepts, research and practice. *International Journal of Management Reviews*, 12(1), 85–105.

Chapple, W. and Moon, J. (2005). Corporate social responsibility (CSR) in Asia: A seven-country study of CSR. *Business and Society*, 44(4), 415–441.

Crane, A., McWilliams, A., Matten, D., Moon, J. and Siegel, D.S. (Eds.). (2008). *The Oxford Handbook of Corporate Social Responsibility*. Oxford: Oxford University Press.

Cullen, J.B., Parboteeah, K.P. and Hoegl, M. (2004). Cross-national differences in managers' willingness to justify ethically suspect behaviors: A test of institutional anomie theory. *Academy of Management Journal*, 47, 411–421.

Chen, X., Huang, R., Yang, Z. and Dube, L. (2018). CSR types and the moderating role of corporate competence. *European Journal of Marketing*, 52(7), 1358–1386.

Chen, Z.F., Cheng, H. and Occa, A. (2019). How different CSR dimensions impact organization-employee relationships: The moderating role of CSR-culture fit. *Corporate Communications*, 24(1), 63–78.

De Freitas Netto, S.V., Sobral, M.F.F., Ribeiro, A.R.B. and da Luz Soares, G.R. (2020). Concepts and forms of greenwashing: A systematic review. *Environmental Sciences Europe*, 32(1), 19. https://doi.org/10.1186/s12302-020-0300-3

DiMaggio, P.J. and Powell, W.W. (1983). The iron cage revisited: Institutional isomorphism and collective rationality in organizational fields. *American Sociological Review*, 48(2), 147–160.

Donia, M.B.L., Ronen, S., Carol-Ann, T.S. and Bonaccio, S. (2019). CSR by any other name? The differential impact of substantive and symbolic CSR attributions on employee outcomes. *Journal of Business Ethics*, 157(2), 503–523.

Dunn, J. (2012). The aftermath of communism and the vicissitudes of public trust. In Markova, I. (Ed.), *Trust and Democratic Transition in Post-communist Europe*. London: British Academy.

Egri, C.P., Ralston, D.A., Milton, L., Casado, T., Palmer, I., Ramburuth, P., Wangenheim, F., Fu, P.P., Kuo, M.H., Carranza, M.T.G., Girson, I., Dabic, M., Butt, A., Srinvasan, N., Furrer, O., Hallinger, P., Dalgic, T., Richards, M., Rossi, A.M., Danis, W., Gutirez, J.R., Reynaud, E., Brock, D., Molteni, M., Starkus, A., Castro, F., Chia, H.B., Darder, F.L., Wallace, A., Naoumova, I., Ansari, M., Riddel, L., Potocan, V.V. and Thanh, H.V. (2006). The influence of personal values and national contexts on attitudes towards corporate responsibilities. Third B.C. Organizational Behaviour Conference, Vancouver, Canada.

El-Bassiouny, D. and El-Bassiouny, N. (2019). Diversity, corporate governance and CSR reporting: A comparative analysis between top-listed firms in Egypt, Germany and the USA. *Management of Environmental Quality*, 30(1), 116–136.

El-Kassar, A., Messarra, L.C. and El-Khalil, R. (2017). CSR, organizational identification, normative commitment, and the moderating effect of the importance of CSR. *The Journal of Developing Areas*, 51(3), 409–424.

Fehre, K. and Weber, F. (2016). Challenging corporate commitment to CSR: Do CEOs keep talking about corporate social responsibility (CSR) issues in times of the global financial crisis? *Management Research Review*, 39(11), 1410–1430.

Friedman, M. (1970). The social responsibility of business is to increase its profits. *New York Times*, 13 September, 17.

Freeman, R.E. (1984). *Strategic Management: A Stakeholder Perspective*. Englewood Cliffs, NJ: Prentice Hall.

Hofstede, G. (1980). *Culture's Consequences: International Differences in Work-Related Values*. Beverly Hills, CA: Sage.

Hofstede, G. (2001). *Culture's Consequences: Comparing Values, Behaviours, Institutions, and Organizations across Nations*, 2nd edition. Thousand Oaks, CA: Sage.

Husted, B. and Allen, D.B. (2006). Corporate social responsibility in the multinational enterprise: Strategic and institutional approaches. *Journal of International Business Studies*, 37(6), 838–849.

Husted, B.W. (1999). Wealth, culture and corruption. *Journal of International Business Studies*, 30(2), 339–360.

IFRS. (2021a). Value reporting foundation. Available at: https://www.ifrs.org/sustainability/value-reporting-foundation/

IFRS. (2021b). Exposure draft and comment letters: General sustainability-related disclosures. Available at: https://www.ifrs.org/projects/work-plan/general-sustainability-related-disclosures/exposure-draft-and-comment-letters/

Jasanoff, S. (2004). *States of Knowledge: The Co-production of Science and the Social Order*. New York: Routledge.

Jeriji, M. and Louhichi, W. (2021). The relationship between poor CSR performance and hard, negative CSR information disclosures. *Sustainability Accounting, Management and Policy Journal*, 12(2), 410–436.

Sorour, K., Shrives, P.J., El-Sakhawy, A.A. and Soobaroyen, T. (2021). Exploring the evolving motives underlying corporate social responsibility (CSR) disclosures in developing countries: The case of "political CSR" reporting. *Accounting, Auditing and Accountability Journal*, 34(5), 1051–1079.

Kim, M., White, C. and Kim, C. (2019). Examining relationships among cultural factors and expectations of CSR. *Journal of Communication Management*, 23(4), 427–443.

Kolk, A. (2003). Trends in sustainability reporting by the Fortune Global 250. *Business Strategy and the Environment*, 12(5), 279–291.

Kusyk, S. (2021). Carroll's CSR pyramid: An empirical investigation of SME CSR orientation. *Journal of Leadership, Accountability and Ethics*, 18(4), 100–115.

Maignan, I. and Ralston, D. (2002). Corporate social responsibility in Europe and the US: Insights from businesses' self-presentations. *Journal of International Business Studies*, 33(3), 497–514.

Matten, D. and Moon, J. (2004). "Implicit" and "explicit" CSR: A conceptual framework for understanding CSR in Europe. In Habisch, A., Jonker, J., Wegner, M. and Schmidpeter, R. (Eds.), *CSR Across Europe*. Berlin: Springer-Verlag.

Meek, G., Roberts, C. and Gray, S. (1995). Factors influencing voluntary annual report disclosures by U.S., U.K. and continental European multinational corporations. *Journal of International Business Studies*, 26(3), 555–573.

Meidinger, E. (1987). Regulatory culture: A theoretical outline. *Law and Policy*, 9(4), 355–382.

OECD. (2011). *OECD Guidelines for Multinational Enterprises*. OECD Publishing. Available at: http://dx.doi.org/10.1787/9789264115415-en

Orpen, C. (1987). The attitudes of US and South African managers to corporate social responsibility. *Journal of Business Ethics*, 6(2), 89–96.

Pizzi, S., Caputo, A., Corvino, A. and Venturelli, A. (2020). Management research and the UN sustainable development goals (SDGs): A bibliometric investigation and systematic review. *Journal of Cleaner Production*, 276, 124033.

Pope, S. and Wæraas, A. (2016). CSR-washing is rare: A conceptual framework, literature review, and critique. *Journal of Business Ethics*, 137(1), 173–193.

Scott, W.R. (2014). *Institutions and Organizations: Ideas, Interests and Identities*. Thousand Oaks, CA: Sage Publications.

Strike, V.M., Gao, J. and Bansal, P. (2006). Being good while being bad: Social responsibility and the international diversification of US firms. *Journal of International Business Studies*, 37(6), 850–862.

The Guardian. (2013). Margaret Thatcher: A life in quotes – Key comments from Britain's first female prime minister. *The Guardian*, 8 April, 2013. Available at: https://www.theguardian.com/politics/2013/apr/08/margaret-thatcher-quotes

Ulke, A. and Schons, L.M. (2016). CSR as a selling of indulgences: An experimental investigation of customers' perceptions of CSR activities depending on corporate reputation. *Corporate Reputation Review*, 19(3), 263–280.

Waldman, D.A., Siegel, D.S. and Javidan, M. (2006). Components of CEO transformational leadership and corporate social responsibility. *Journal of Management Studies*, 43(8), 1703–1725.

Williams, C. and Aguilera, R.V. (2008). Corporate social responsibility in a comparative perspective. In Crane, A., Matten, D., McWilliams, A., Moon, J. and

Siegel, D.S. (Eds.), *Oxford Handbook of Corporate Social Responsibility*. Oxford: Oxford University Press.
Williams, C.A. and Conley, J. (2005). An emerging third way? The erosion of the Anglo-American shareholder value construct. *Cornell International Law Journal*, 38(2), 493–551.
Wokutch, R.E. (1990). Corporate social responsibility Japanese style. *Academy of Management Executive*, 42, 56–74.
WTO. (2016). *World Trade Report 2016: Levelling the Trading Fields for SMEs*. Geneva: WTO.

Part 1

CSR – Extinction, Disasters, and the New Paradigm

2 The Transition from Biodiversity to Extinction Accounting in the Chinese Context

Ruopiao Zhang

Accounting for Biodiversity in China

Biodiversity, which includes genetic, species, and ecosystem diversity, provides ecological and food security for a global population of nearly 7.6 billion people, and it is a condition on which human survival depends. Biodiversity is also the basis for sustainable economic and social development (Atkins et al., 2014). According to a *New Economics of Nature* report, a total of approximately US$44 trillion of the global economy is moderately or highly dependent on nature, accounting for about half of the global gross domestic product (GDP) (Roberts et al., 2021). China is one of the most biodiverse countries in the world, with 13.7% of total vertebrate species and the third-largest inventory of vascular land plant species (Ministry of Environmental Protection, 2020; UN-CBD, 2021). However, its rapid industrial and urban expansion, which has resulted in heavy pollution, inefficient resource utilization, and ill health expenses, is driving species and habitat loss (Ali et al., 2018; Wang et al., 2020). In the face of these environmental threats, China has initiated a slew of biodiversity conservation projects, many of which have already yielded impressive results. These include the world's fastest-growing forest resources, and ongoing improvements to the integrity of marine ecosystems (Jiang et al., 2015; Liu et al., 2019). Nevertheless, the country's biodiversity resources are still declining (Meng et al., 2019). This loss of biodiversity poses an irreversible threat to ecosystems, preventing China from achieving its strategic goal of constructing a prosperous society and an ecological civilization (Cao et al., 2017; Fan et al., 2020).

The Convention on Biological Diversity (CBD), one of the most important biodiversity treaties in the world, came into effect in 1993 following ratification by 196 countries, including members of the European Union. It aims to safeguard plant and animal species in various ecosystems, promote sustainable use of natural resources, and ensure equal distribution of the benefits associated with the use of genetic resources. It encourages the creation of biodiversity policy frameworks and promotes the inclusion of ecosystem services and biodiversity accounting disclosures in decision making (Jones, 2003). In 1996, the third Conference of the Parties (COP3) to the CBD first identified enterprises as essential stakeholders and encouraged firms to take action to promote biodiversity, which led to

DOI: 10.4324/9781003274575-3

the emergence of corporate biodiversity accounting (Jones, 1996, 2003; Xue et al., 2012). Enterprises that enhance their knowledge and understanding of, and make timely disclosures of their progress on biodiversity may gain recognition from stakeholders, and may even become more competitive (Boiral, 2016).

As an emerging field, biodiversity accounting has attracted increasing attention over the last decade (Jones and Solomon, 2013; Weir, 2018; Zhao and Atkins, 2021). The term "biodiversity reporting" refers to the process through which a business informs its stakeholders of its impact on biodiversity (Jones, 1996, 2003; Jones and Solomon, 2013). Biodiversity reporting documents are multifunctional texts for stakeholders that establish points of interaction and interchanges between businesses and public forums with diverse motivations and expectations (Jones and Solomon, 2013). To account for biodiversity and involve policymakers and businesses, ecological and economic indicators such as the Global Reporting Initiative (GRI) framework and ISO 26000: A Guide to Social Responsibility (2010) are being established as reporting metrics (Cuckston, 2018a).

In 2010, China issued its *China Biodiversity Conservation Strategy and Action Plan (2011–2030)*, which has ten priority areas for action, one of which is to establish public participation mechanisms and partnerships for biodiversity conservation (Wang and Shen, 2016). In June 2015, the General Administration of Quality Supervision, Inspection and Quarantine and the State Standardization Administration of China jointly issued *Guidelines for the Preparation of Social Responsibility Reports* (GB/T36001-2015) and *Guidelines for the Classification of Social Responsibility Performance* (GB/T36002-2015), which include contents relating to biodiversity. Furthermore, biodiversity conservation and ecological restoration and management are reporting indicators in corporate social responsibility (CSR) 4.0, issued by the Chinese Academy of Social Science in 2017, and in October 2017, a report by the 19th Party Congress proposed building ecological corridors and biodiversity protection networks to safeguard ecosystems (Tian et al., 2020). The 15th meeting of the COP to the CBD was held in Kunming, China in October 2021. As the country advances its construction of an ecological civilization, more Chinese enterprises are becoming aware of the importance of biodiversity conservation and are making it an essential element of fulfilling their social responsibility and implementing sustainable development goals (Sun et al., 2021).

There are five main theoretical underpinnings of biodiversity accounting. First, stakeholder theory positions the natural environment as a critical stakeholder and proposes that companies' disclosures on natural resource protection have a legitimate and ethical stance (Laine, 2010; Stead and Stead, 2000). Second, legitimacy theory suggests that companies may take action to redress biodiversity loss in order to prove their legitimacy (Bhattacharyya and Yang, 2019; Rimmel and Jonäll, 2013). Third, environmental stewardship theory relates to demonstrating shared responsibility for environmental quality by all whose actions affect the environment (Jones, 2003; Ridings, 2018; Siddiqui, 2013). Fourth, resource dependence theory argues that companies are more likely to engage in biodiversity accounting if they see biodiversity as a material or reputational concern

(Adler et al., 2018; Haque and Jones, 2020). Finally, deep ecology theory recognizes that nature has an inherent value and that humans are deeply connected with it and are part of it (Drengson, 1995; Naess, 1973, 1993; Jacob, 1994). However, some studies suggest that accounting for biodiversity is fundamentally anthropocentric, focusing on a certain group of species that people care about, and that it therefore has limited emancipatory potential (Jones and Solomon, 2013; Atkins et al., 2014).

Despite a trend toward biodiversity accounting, most previous studies take a pessimistic view on the state of the world and the role of various types of corporate reporting in reversing extinction trends (Tregidga et al., 2014). Previous literature criticizes current corporate biodiversity disclosures as "fossil records" for display purposes, simply benchmarking the past and the present (Atkins and Maroun, 2018). For example, although the GRI Standards encourage firms to report information on vulnerable and endangered species affected by their current business activities, the relevant principles are heavily criticized in the accounting literature (e.g., Atkins and Atkins, 2019; Atkins and Maroun, 2018; Jones and Solomon, 2013). Specifically, scholars criticize the GRI for not precisely defining the terms "sustainability" and "sustainable development" and for being silent on how corporations should integrate biodiversity management into their risk assessment, strategy, and operational processes. The current reporting guidelines on biodiversity impacts appear to be fairly broad, and firms may perceive them as disclosure checklists rather than as a framework for lowering biodiversity risks or averting extinction. In other words, superficial and general biodiversity disclosures do little to help organizations offer forward-looking and future-oriented demonstrations of how they treat "natural capital" and prevent extinctions in areas in which they operate (Atkins and Atkins, 2019; Atkins and Maroun, 2018; Fuentes, 2011; Tregidga, 2013).

Although various environmental regulations address biodiversity concerns at regional and international levels, most guidance on biodiversity disclosures is voluntary in nature, providing only a range of guiding principles rather than mandatory and detailed implementation guidelines or disclosure frameworks. Table 2.1 summarizes the major biodiversity disclosure guidelines for Chinese firms.

This chapter explores four major themes of biodiversity disclosures: evaluations of operational impacts on biodiversity, measures to reduce those impacts, ecosystem protection initiatives, and actions to restore ecosystems. These were identified through exploratory documentary analysis of CSR reports (or sustainability reports, environmental reports, and integrated reports) of Chinese enterprises listed on the Fortune Global 500 from the agriculture, forestry, fishing, and animal husbandry (7 sample firms), mining (8 firms), coal (15 firms), metals (51 firms), construction (28 firms), transportation (23 firms), and utilities (32 firms) industries in 2020. These four major themes of disclosure are in line with current regional and international reporting guidelines relating to biodiversities, such as GRI and CASS-CSR 4.0. Table 2.2 presents typical biodiversity themes in the content of Chinese firms' reports.

Table 2.1 Major Biodiversity Disclosure Guidelines for Chinese Firms

Biodiversity accounting guidelines	*Indicators*	*Disclosure contents*
GRI 304: BIODIVERSITY	Disclosure 304-1	Operational sites owned, leased, managed in, or adjacent to, protected areas and areas of high biodiversity value outside protected areas
	Disclosure 304-2	Significant impacts of activities, products, and services on biodiversity
	Disclosure 304-3	Habitats protected or restored
	Disclosure 304-4	International Union for Conservation of Nature (IUCN) Red List species and national conservation list species with habitats in areas affected by operations
ISO26000	Environment: Issue 4	Protection of the environment, biodiversity, and restoration of natural habitats
CASS-CSR 4.0	E3.3	Ecological restoration and management
	E3.4	Biodiversity conservation

This evidence reveals that the majority of Chinese companies present over-simplified reports on their efforts to promote biodiversity, without detailed data, records, or assessment mechanisms. For example, some companies disclose information on initiatives relating to biodiversity conservation, but do not disclose specific data on their inputs, outputs, and performance in operationalizing these plans. Moreover, the biodiversity sections of their reports typically use identical wording and repeat narratives from year to year. Although some companies do disclose biodiversity-related data, their data sources are mostly single projects rather than company-wide data, lacking comparability across years. Some leading Chinese enterprises disclose their biodiversity conservation efforts in their CSR reports, but biodiversity accounting remains a very new concept for most Chinese firms (GoldenBee, 2021). These findings are in line with the objection of many critical theorists that biodiversity accounting is not immediately understandable, sounds academic, and may fail to convey a sense of responsibility for species and animals and the urgency of species extinction. It is therefore a barrier to achieving the goal of species reporting and emancipatory accounting (Fuentes, 2011; Jones and Solomon, 2013; Tregidga, 2013)

Extinction Crisis in China

As previously discussed, Chinese enterprises' disclosures of their efforts to promote biodiversity are superficial, and lack detailed data, transparency, and

Table 2.2 Typical Contents of Chinese Firms' Biodiversity Reports

Themes of biodiversity disclosure	*Examples from annual reports*
Evaluations of operational impacts on biodiversity	"Zijin Mining conducts biodiversity status surveys and assessments within the mine area and in areas that may be affected by various mining activities. We prepare environmental impact assessment reports before mining projects, assess the biodiversity impacts in the area of influence, and propose management measures" (Zijin Mining, 2020, 42).
Measures to reduce the impacts of operations on biodiversity	"the Group attaches great importance to interactions between the enterprise and the ecological system of the place where it operates, and has formulated management measures to reduce the impact of business operations on local biodiversity. The group prohibits production activities within the ecological red line control area. All new projects are scientifically constructed in accordance with the requirements of site selection and environmental impact assessment" (China International Marine Containers, 2020, 52).
Ecosystem protection initiatives	"China Three Gorges Corporation conducts surveys of wild plant resources in the Yangtze River basin and relocates, protects and breeds rare plants on a regular basis. By 2020, the Company effectively protects 1,181 species of Yangtze River cherished plants" (China Three Gorges Corporation, 2020, 55).
Actions to restore ecosystems	"All of our mining sites have a Mine Geological Environmental Protection and Land Reclamation Plan. In the early stage, we will try to restore and rebuild by restoring topsoil and planting local endemic trees. In the later stage, we will gradually increase biodiversity and enhance the stability of the ecosystem through a reasonable mix of trees and shrubs" (Zijin Mining, 2020, 42).

follow-up. For example, they tend to focus on rescuing flora and fauna that are perceived to have high economic value. However, the planet's food chain and ecological chain are an organic whole, and enterprises must take a holistic view of species protection in the interests of the entire ecological community. Chinese enterprises' reporting and accounting methods for flora and fauna protection can be regarded as a way to discharge their accountability to interested parties and stakeholders. Furthermore, their disclosures focus mainly on reversing the negative impacts that they have already had on the environment in order to defend their social legitimacy, rather than taking proactive steps toward a gradual emancipatory outcome for species protection and preservation (Zhao and Atkins,

2021). Thus, the current reporting form is not effective for protecting species and often fails to save species from extinction.

The case of the Chinese sturgeon illustrates the extinction dilemma in China. This is an ancient and rare fish that has existed for more than 140 million years and can be found in both freshwater and marine environments along China's coast. However, the population of wild Chinese sturgeon has declined dramatically in recent years. In 2015, the total number of adults was assessed to be 2,569, down from 6,000 in 2010 and 32,260 prior to 1981 (Huang and Wang, 2018). China began to control sturgeon fishing in the 1970s when the breeding population had been reduced to barely 10,000. This move spared the species from extinction. However, an even greater existential threat has emerged in recent decades from the construction of numerous dams (Zhou et al., 2020), which impair river connectivity, separate watersheds, and reduce species richness by disrupting fish migration (Yi et al., 2010). The reproductive output of the local population plummeted by more than 75% after the Gezhouba Dam was built on the upper streams of the Yangtze River, and the Three Gorges Dam was built across the Yangtze in 2003 without any fish transit devices. Since then, the Xiangjiaba Dam and Xiluodu Dam have also been completed. The Chinese sturgeon population stagnated as each new structure divided the river into smaller and smaller areas. Dams generate layers of changing water temperatures within the river, which may further disrupt the aquatic ecology of the sturgeon.

The China Three Gorges Project Corporation (CTG) was established in September 2009, with the consent of the State Council, to build the Three Gorges Project and develop the Yangtze River. Since then, CTG has collaborated with other parties to protect endangered species along the Three Gorges and prevent extinction. For example, it set up the Chinese Sturgeon Research Institute to increase the number of wild Chinese sturgeon. However, scarcely any have survived, and the institute's efforts have been inadequate and unsustainable, focusing mainly on the sturgeons' migration, artificial propagation, and oxytocic activities. These initiatives are not designed to promote genuine biodiversity and save species from extinction. They simply tinker around the edges after weighing up the various economic benefits, lacking any emancipatory element. In recent years, detailed initiatives and data on the conservation of the Chinese sturgeon have no longer been disclosed in CTG's CSR reports. As numbers of wild Chinese sturgeon continue to plummet, disclosures on this species are likely to gradually disappear from CSR reports, as if the species had never existed. Sadly, current practices do not provide effective protection even for a national treasure like the Chinese sturgeon, let alone other rare species

Extinction Prevention from the Perspective of Chinese Philosophical Traditions

Our planet is facing a global extinction disaster unprecedented in human history (Atkins and Atkins, 2019; Atkins and Maroun, 2018, 2020). Recent research has explored the possibility of encapsulating emancipatory elements in CSR that demonstrate intentions to be transformative, in the sense of enhancing biodiversity protection and preventing species extinctions (Atkins et al., 2018; Atkins and Maroun, 2018). This marks a new era of CSR reporting for Chinese companies, moving from biodiversity disclosures towards more comprehensive and emancipatory reporting that accounts for extinction prevention (Atkins and Maroun, 2018). However, without a business case based on financial risk and materiality, businesses and investors are unlikely to acknowledge the necessity for extinction accounting (Atkins and Maroun, 2020; Zhao and Atkins, 2021). Traditional Chinese philosophies such as Confucianism, Daoism, and Buddhism encompass a plethora of ethical beliefs about human–nature interactions. In linking species protection with Chinese philosophical traditions, this section explains the importance of extinction accounting in the Chinese context.

Confucianism, Daoism, and Buddhism are the three primary faiths or traditional philosophies in China. They all place a premium on mutual respect, societal peace, and interconnectedness with nature and the environment, all of which align with the goal of sustainable development while nourishing the natural environment. Confucianism advocates humanism and integration of man and nature. One famous saying from the Analects of Confucius is "*jǐ suǒ bù yù, wù shī yú rén*" (do not do to others what you do not wish to be done to yourself), which applies not only to people but also to the natural environment and species around the globe. That is to say, humans should not impose the risk of extinction on other species because we would not wish it to happen to ourselves. Furthermore, Confucianism preaches a cosmic triad consisting of Heaven, Earth, and Humanity, which are interconnected and fused into a single whole (Berthrong, 2003; Tianchen, 2003). Unlike the prevailing anthropocentrism, which views humans as distinct from and superior to nature, Confucianism maintains that no single component of the triad dominates (Birkin et al., 2021; Guo et al., 2017; Li et al., 2019).

Daoism focuses on the goal of achieving the Dao, or the Way of Heaven, Earth, and Humanity (Xing and Starik, 2017; D'Ambrosio, 2013). It argues that humans and the natural environment are mutually enhancing, and that protecting different kinds of species allows sustainable flourishing. Daoism has a distinctive conception of worth, in that it measures prosperity by the diversity of species (Miller, 2003; Miller and Cline, 2004). A phrase in the *Dao De Jing* (Book of the Way and its Power, one of the classic documents of Daoism) states: "Humanity follows the Earth, the Earth follows Heaven, Heaven follows the Dao, and the Dao follows what is natural". This implies that humanity as a whole should place a premium on the Earth and adhere to its laws of motion, and that those who have only a rudimentary knowledge of humanity's relationship with nature will carelessly exploit it. Daoism contends that communities will be rich if all creatures in the universe grow well (Nelson, 2020). Furthermore, in Daoism, everything is composed of two opposing energies known as Yin (the dark swirl connected with the trough of a wave, shadow, and femininity) and Yang (the light swirl connected with brightness, enthusiasm, and growth), and the energy of life is created when Yin and Yang achieve equilibrium. The philosophical and spiritual basis of

Daoism opposes hurting endangered species, as harming or causing pain to other creatures will disturb the balance of Yin and Yang.

Buddhism sees all things as interdependent, with various elements in the universe interacting mutually, entangled in a web of cause-and-effect linkages. Several core values of Buddhism, such as the Theories of Causality (Karma) and the Theory of Equality for All Things, support a harmonious and nature-friendly lifestyle (Clooney, 1989; Thathong, 2012; Yeh, 2014). In this regard, humans will suffer if they continue to degrade the environment (Abeydeera et al., 2016; Danial, 2007; Hanh, 2001; Suriyankietkaew and Kantamara, 2019). In addition, the Four Noble Truths of the Buddha's basic teaching emphasize the need to overcome attachments and appetites such as greed, ill-will, and illusion which, if not mastered, fuel a never-ending cycle of suffering (Buswell and Lopez, 2013; Harvey, 2013). This observation is especially important in light of the unsustainable development paradigm mirrored in the over-consumerism and over-materialism of the prevailing economic, social, and cultural order. Buddhism argues that all species, including human beings, are a part of nature and have importance in their own existence. Thus, humans should respect life and quell their desire to conquer and plunder nature.

These Chinese philosophical traditions illustrate distinct perspectives on sustainability that have institutional implications for harmonious development and biodiversity protection. These core ideas are of great significance even in modern times. Humans and businesses must be held accountable for their influence on nature and species and must seek to coexist harmoniously. Understanding the connections between global principles of sustainability and local values, culture, and belief systems offers a holistic approach to the broader application of extinction accounting in thought and action.

From Passive to Proactive Disclosure: Toward Extinction Accounting in China

Having hosted the 15th COP at the CBD, China, aims to work with the international community to build a global ecological civilization and contribute to conserving global biodiversity (Li et al., 2020). The CBD has also brought new opportunities for the development of emancipatory biodiversity accounting in China. Atkins and Atkins (2019) emphasize the importance of tackling the planet's ongoing mass extinction issue and seeking solutions from the corporate world. Therefore, an evolutionary form of biodiversity accounting, that of extinction accounting, is needed to enable enterprises to address the variety of challenges emerging from the changing environment and the impact of human activities. Extinction accounting strives to help stakeholders better understand how companies' actions affect natural capital and how businesses evaluate the impact of extinction on their operations and prospects (Atkins and Maroun, 2018; Atkins and Thomson, 2014; Cuckston, 2018a, 2018b).

Previous research has established an extinction accounting framework (EAF) (see Atkins and Maroun, 2018; Atkins et al., 2019; Atkins and Maroun, 2020) that incorporates the crucial element of "emancipation" into an innovative governance framework. There are five elements in the proposed EAF (Atkins and Atkins, 2019; Atkins and Maroun, 2018, 2020). Element 1 includes the disclosure topics recommended by the GRI Principles, elements 2 and 3 are concerned with proactive reporting on extinction prevention, and elements 4 and 5 include detailed reviews of whether or not extinction prevention targets have been met, any challenges encountered, and changes to plans or strategies adopted to ensure that extinction disclosures are comprehensive. Although extinction accounting is critical, CSR reports rarely include it explicitly. The complicated nature of biodiversity, widespread misconceptions of the value of biodiversity to organizations, and a dearth of information all contribute to this omission (Boiral, 2016; Syarifuddin and Damayanti, 2019). The next sections provide critical insights into how different parties might contribute to the development of extinction accounting, and what disclosure items should be incorporated in the case of China.

The Role of Regulatory Bodies and NGOs

Chinese companies face challenges such as lack of pressure from stakeholders (e.g., government and community), lack of detailed regulations and monitoring of biodiversity reporting, and lack of understanding of the importance and benefits of biodiversity to the business (Adler et al., 2018; Atkins and Thomson, 2014; Cuckston, 2018a, 2018b, 2019; Zhao and Atkins, 2021). Regional and international CSR reporting guidelines relating to biodiversity are voluntary in nature and provide limited guidance on and illustrations of biodiversity accounting (and extinction accounting). Therefore, it is suggested that regulatory bodies should encourage firms to adhere to the "Corporate Biodiversity Commitment" proposed by the UN-CBD and incorporate the UN's 2030 Sustainable Development Goals (SDGs) into their business operations. Regulatory bodies must also play a role in establishing standardized frameworks and measurements, and potentially in setting up subsidies and incentive mechanisms for enterprises. In addition, further regulations and guidelines should be devised to promote biodiversity conservation to multiple stakeholders, including suppliers, consumers, and employees. For example, many enterprises try to track their direct and indirect impacts on biodiversity and extinction prevention, but encounter difficulties in gathering critical information from their supply chains and downstream markets. This may hamper them from reporting on the full scope of their impacts. Therefore, in order to promote traceability, it is recommended that data sharing and cooperative research and development in terms of biodiversity and extinction prevention be encouraged among various parties along the entire industry chain.

In addition to working with businesses, the Secretariat of the CBD has established relevant mechanisms to promote action by NGOs and greater public participation in biodiversity conservation. Many NGOs participated actively in the process of developing the post-2020 global biodiversity framework, and may have accumulated specialist wisdom on the ground (Arenas et al., 2009). This will enable them to contribute new perspectives on the formulation of accords, beyond the viewpoints of official delegations, through discussions of biodiversity that take account of the interests of local communities. Therefore, establishing closer connections between NGOs and Chinese enterprises might provide further insights and corporate solutions to prevent extinctions.

The Role of Green Finance

Under-development of the finance and biodiversity agendas is an unfortunate reality (Narain et al., 2020). Green finance is helpful in directing and providing funds to environmentally friendly rather than polluting projects (Wang and Zhi, 2016), and further efforts to include the private sector in biodiversity protection, sustainable use, and equitable benefit sharing would be beneficial in China. Increased private investment in biodiversity projects would have the greatest impact on enterprises in developing countries, where the conservation budget gap is highest and many critically endangered species and habitats are now safeguarded. For example, the EU's Biodiversity Strategy for 2030 commits to providing at least €20 billion to be spent on nature through green finance (Maes et al., 2016).

Similarly, financial institutions in China are increasingly seeing the importance of expanding their emphasis beyond climate change to include the hazards associated with nature and biodiversity conservation. For example, the *Opinions on Strengthening the Protection of Biodiversity*, released in October 2021 by the General Office of the Communist Party of China and the General Office of the State Council, touches on international cooperation mechanisms such as the Belt and Road Initiative (BRI) and South–South Cooperation in order to safeguard biodiversity through green finance (Hughes, 2019; Narain et al., 2020). Green finance from both public and private sectors is critical to assist businesses, and especially small and medium-sized enterprises (SMEs), in becoming involved in and disclosing more biodiversity-related and extinction prevention initiatives. Closer cooperation between financial institutions and Chinese enterprises will intensify efforts to bridge the current chasm between the financial sector and advocates of nature stewardship (Callaghan and Hubbard, 2016).

Incorporating Chinese Characteristics into the EAF

In the *Opinions of the State Council on Strengthening Major Environmental Protection Work* released in 2011, the Chinese government formally advocated Ecological Conservation Redline (ECR) designation as a major aspect of national environmental protection policy. Over the past decade, methods of delineating ECRs have undergone several rounds of modification and have gradually become unified. Since the end of 2020, all ECRs in China have been officially demarcated. The country's administrative boundaries have been broken down to connect existing nature reserves, and there are now 35 priority zones for biodiversity conservation. The ECRs have been established following the examination of a variety of factors, including biodiversity, erosion susceptibility, critical ecosystem services, and resilience to natural disasters. In order to make the proposed EAF more applicable in China, it is suggested that disclosures of whether business operations are located in or close to any ECR should be incorporated (see Element 1g of Table 2.3). Furthermore, details should be presented on the direct and indirect impacts of business operations on ECRs (see Element 1h of Table 2.3). In addition, Chinese enterprises should disclose how they engage in environmental stewardship to promote biodiversity within ECR zones, such as being involved in or sponsoring extinction prevention initiatives or conducting related research and development projects (see Element 2b of Table 2.3).

Another concern relating to biodiversity and extinction accounting practices lies in the mega-globalization of Chinese enterprises (Asmussen and Fosfuri, 2019). China has been one of the world's largest sources of outbound foreign direct investment (OFDI) since 2003. Encouraged by various policies of the Chinese government, a very large number of Chinese multinational enterprises (MNEs) have ventured abroad. Therefore, biodiversity concerns about Chinese foreign direct investment (FDI) are garnering greater attention from global stakeholders. Conservationists are particularly concerned about places where Chinese MNEs' overseas infrastructure projects intersect with biodiversity hotspots around the globe. Thus, it is critical to ensure that the business implications of and reliance on biodiversity are factored into decision making when investing abroad (Baik and Park 2019). Several specific reporting topics are needed in the EAF to encourage MNEs to scale up their contributions to biodiversity conservation and extinction prevention overseas (see Elements 1i, 1j, 2c, and 3b of Table 2.3).

Concluding Remarks

Enterprises significantly influence biodiversity and ecosystems through their direct and indirect business operations (Maroun and Atkins, 2018). However, current reporting guidelines on biodiversity allow enterprises to explain only how they respond to the negative impacts of biodiversity arising from their business operations, as well as their mitigation and restoration initiatives. In this chapter, it has been argued that the concept of extinction accounting adds value to the current form of biodiversity accounting and has more effective and transformative emancipatory potential (Maroun and Atkins, 2018: 106).

Chinese researchers have paid little attention to corporate accounting and accountability for specific species on the verge of extinction (Dunsmoor et al., 2015). This chapter has presented the background and status quo of Chinese firms' reports on biodiversity and species protection by analyzing CSR reports and giving thought-provoking examples of dam projects along the Yangtze River. It has also explored the rationale for extinction accounting from the perspective of Chinese philosophical traditions, and has discussed the efforts required to promote such disclosure practices in China. It has revealed a need for more standardized disclosure requirements, involvement of regulatory bodies and NGOs, and dialogues between the public and private sectors to encourage uptake of extinction prevention initiatives at the country level.

Table 2.3 Incorporating Chinese Characteristics into the Extinction Accounting Disclosure Framework

Element	*Topic*	*Disclosure content*
1: Current extinction accounting under GRI	a	Record a list of plant and animal species, identified as endangered by the IUCN Red List, whose habitats are affected by the company's activities.
	b	Report where, geographically, the company's activities pose a threat to endangered plant and animal species, as identified by the IUCN Red List and assess habitat status.
	c	Report potential risks/impacts on these specific species arising from the company's operations.
	d	Incorporate images of threatened species which are affected by the company's operations and which the company needs to protect and explain how have these been integrated into the company's internal control system, business model, business strategy, and operational plans.
	e	Report full details (narrative as well as financial figures) relating to any fines or ongoing claims relating to endangered species legislation including the names of species and a summary of losses suffered with causes identified.
	f	Report corporate expressions of moral, ethical, and/or emotional motivations for preserving species and preventing extinction with consideration of ecosystem-level effects, including normative reflective self-accounts of the company's impact on threatened and endangered species.
	g	Report where, geographically, the company's operational sites owned, leased, managed on are adjacent to Ecological Conservation Redlines in China.
	h	Report significant impacts of activities, products, and services on nearby Ecological Conservation Redlines in China.
	i	Environmental compliance in terms of biodiversity laws and regulations in overseas host countries (for Chinese MNEs).
	j	Report significant impacts of activities, products, and services on biodiversity in overseas host countries (for Chinese MNEs).
2: Reporting of actions	a	Report actions/initiatives taken by the company to avoid harm to, and to prevent the extinction of endangered plant and animal species.

(*Continued*)

Table 2.3 (Continued)

Element	*Topic*	*Disclosure content*
	b	Report actions/initiatives taken by the company to promote biodiversity and extinction prevention within Ecological Conservation Redlines of China.
	c	Report actions/initiatives taken by the company to promote biodiversity and extinction prevention in overseas host countries (for Chinese MNEs).
3: Reporting of partnerships	a	Report partnerships between wildlife/nature/conservation organizations and the company which aim to address corporate impacts on endangered species and report the outcome/impact of engagement/ partnerships on endangered species as well as the outcome of engagement with the responsible investment community (respecting investor confidentiality where appropriate).
	b	Report enrollments in global sustainable development organizations/alliances to uptake extinction prevention in overseas host countries (for Chinese MNEs).

Many developing countries are biodiverse, but are struggling to mitigate urgent biodiversity losses in tandem with strong economic growth. The transition from traditional biodiversity to extinction accounting in China opens up research avenues relating to the potential to apply extinction accounting in other emerging economies. It has been argued that international cooperation may provide a solid foundation for biodiversity conservation and extinction prevention, as well as better environmental stewardship and management across nations. It is hoped that this chapter will inspire further research on the broader applications and impacts of extinction disclosures.

References

Abeydeera, S., Kearins, K. and Tregidga, H. (2016). Buddhism, sustainability and organizational practices: Fertile ground? *Journal of Corporate Citizenship*, 61(61), 44–70.

Adler, R., Mansi, M. and Pandey, R. (2018). Biodiversity and threatened species reporting by the top Fortune Global companies. *Accounting, Auditing and Accountability Journal*, 31(3), 787–825.

Ali, M., Kennedy, C.M., Kiesecker, J. and Geng, Y. (2018). Integrating biodiversity offsets within Circular Economy policy in China. *Journal of Cleaner Production*, 185, 32–43.

Arenas, D., Lozano, J.M. and Albareda, L. (2009). The role of NGOs in CSR: Mutual perceptions among stakeholders. *Journal of Business Ethics*, 88(1), 175–197.

Asmussen, C.G. and Fosfuri, A. (2019). Orchestrating corporate social responsibility in the multinational enterprise. *Strategic Management Journal*, 40(6), 894–916.

Atkins, J. and Atkins, B. (2019). *Around the World in 80 Species: Exploring the Business of Extinction*. London: Routledge.

Atkins, J., Gräbsch, C. and Jones, M. (2014). Corporate biodiversity reporting: Exploring its anthropocentric nature. In Jones, M. (Ed.), *Accounting for Biodiversity*. London: Routledge.

Atkins, J. and Maroun, W. (2018). Integrated extinction accounting and accountability: Building an ark. *Accounting, Auditing and Accountability Journal*, 31(3), 750–786.

Atkins, J. and Maroun, W. (2020). The naturalist's journals of Gilbert White: Exploring the roots of accounting for biodiversity and extinction accounting. *Accounting, Auditing and Accountability Journal*, 33(8), 1835–1870.

Atkins, J., Maroun, W., Atkins, B.C. and Barone, E. (2018). From the Big Five to the Big Four? Exploring extinction accounting for the rhinoceros. *Accounting, Auditing and Accountability Journal*, 31(2), 674–702.

Atkins, J. and Thomson, I. (2014). Accounting for biodiversity in nineteenth century Britain: William Morris and the defence of the fairness of the Earth. In Jones, M. (Ed.), *Accounting for Biodiversity*. London: Routledge.

Baik, Y. and Park, Y. (2019). Managing legitimacy through corporate community involvement: The effects of subsidiary ownership and host country experience in China. *Asia Pacific Journal of Management*, 36(4), 971–993.

Berthrong, J. (2003). Confucian views of nature. In Selin, H. (Ed.), *Nature Across Cultures: Views of Nature and the Environment in Non-western Cultures*. London: Kluwer Academic Publishers.

Bhattacharyya, A. and Yang, H. (2019). Biodiversity disclosure in Australia: Effect of GRI and institutional factors. *Australasian Journal of Environmental Management*, 26(4), 347–369.

Birkin, F., Margerison, J. and Monkhouse, L. (2021). Chinese environmental accountability: Ancient beliefs, science and sustainability. *Resources, Environment and Sustainability*, 3, 100017.

Boiral, O. (2016). Accounting for the unaccountable: Biodiversity reporting and impression management. *Journal of Business Ethics*, 135(4), 751–768.

Buswell, R.E. and Lopez, D.S. (2013). *The Princeton Dictionary of Buddhism*. Princeton, NJ: Princeton University Press.

Callaghan, M. and Hubbard, P. (2016). The Asian infrastructure investment bank: Multilateralism on the silk road. *China Economic Journal*, 9(2), 116–139.

Cao, S., Shang, D., Yue, H. and Ma, H. (2017). A win-win strategy for ecological restoration and biodiversity conservation in Southern China. *Environmental Research Letters*, 12(4), 044004.

China International Marine Containers. (2020). Annual CSR Report. Available at: http://www.cimc.com/uploadfile/2020/0327/20200327083501318.pdf

China Three Gorges Corporation. (2020). Annual CSR Report. Available at: https://www.ctgfoundation.org.cn/sxjjh/_644196/_644208/index.html

Clooney, F.X. (1989). Evil, divine omnipotence, and human freedom: Vedānta's theology of karma. *The Journal of Religion*, 69(4), 530–548.

Cuckston, T. (2018a). Making accounting for biodiversity research a force for conservation. *Social and Environmental Accountability Journal*, 38(3), 218–226.

Cuckston, T. (2018b). Making extinction calculable. *Accounting, Auditing and Accountability Journal*, 31(3), 849–874.

Cuckston, T. (2019). Seeking an ecologically defensible calculation of net loss/gain of biodiversity. *Accounting, Auditing and Accountability Journal*, 32(5), 1358–1383

D'Ambrosio, P. (2013). Rethinking environmental issues in a Daoist context: Why daoism is and is not environmentalism. *Environmental Ethics*, 35(4), 407–417.

Daniel, M. (2007). Jung's affinity for Buddhism: Misunderstandings and clarifications. *Psychological Perspectives*, 50(2), 220–234.

Drengson, A. (1995). The deep ecology movement. *The Trumpeter*, 12(3), 2–7.

Dunsmoor, J.E., Niv, Y., Daw, N. and Phelps, E.A. (2015). Rethinking extinction. *Neuron*, 88(1), 47–63.

Fan, P.F., Yang, L., Liu, Y. and Lee, T.M. (2020). Build up conservation research capacity in China for biodiversity governance. *Nature Ecology and Evolution*, 4(9), 1162–1167.

Fuentes, M. (2011). Economic growth and biodiversity. *Biodiversity and Conservation*, 20(14), 3453–3458.

GoldenBee. (2021). *Golden Bee Research on Corporate Social Responsibility Reporting in China 2020. Beijing, China*. Available at: https://www.pishu.com.cn/skwx_ps/initDatabaseDetail?siteId=14andcontentId=12362831andcontentType=literatureandtype=%25E6%258A%25A5%25E5%2591%258A

Guo, X., Krempl, S. and Marinova, D. (2017). Economic prosperity and sustainability in China: Seeking wisdom from Confucianism and Taoism. In Zacher, L.W. (Ed.), *Technology, Society and Sustainability*. Cham: Springer.

Hanh, T.N. (2001). *Thich Nhat Hanh: Essential Writings*. Maryknoll, NY: Orbis Books.

Haque, F. and Jones, M.J. (2020). European firms' corporate biodiversity disclosures and board gender diversity from 2002 to 2016. *The British Accounting Review*, 52(2), 100893.

Harvey, P. (2013). Dukkha, non-self, and the teaching on the four "Noble Truths". In Emmanuel, S.M. (Ed.), *A Companion to Buddhist Philosophy*. Chichester: Wiley.

Huang, Z. and Wang, L. (2018). Yangtze dams increasingly threaten the survival of the Chinese sturgeon. *Current Biology*, 28(22), 3640–3647.

Hughes, A.C. (2019). Understanding and minimizing environmental impacts of the Belt and Road Initiative. *Conservation Biology*, 33(4), 883–894.

Jacob, M. (1994). Sustainable development and deep ecology: An analysis of competing traditions. *Environmental Management*, 18(4), 477–488.

Jiang, Z., Qin, H., Liu, Y., Ji, L. and Ma, K. (2015). Protecting biodiversity and promoting sustainable development: In memory of the releasing of Catalogue of Life China 2015 and China biodiversity Red List on the International Day for Biological Diversity 2015. *Biodiversity Science*, 23(3), 433.

Jones, M. (1996). Accounting for biodiversity: A pilot study. *The British Accounting Review*, 28(4), 281–303.

Jones, M.J. (2003). Accounting for biodiversity: Operationalising environmental accounting. *Accounting, Auditing and Accountability Journal*, 16(5), 762–789.

Jones, M.J. and Solomon, J.F. (2013). Problematising accounting for biodiversity. *Accounting, Auditing and Accountability Journal*, 26(5), 668–687.

Laine, M. (2010). The nature of nature as a stakeholder. *Journal of Business Ethics*, 96(1), 73–78.

Li, F., Wang, X. and Kashyap, R. (2019). Socially responsible practice and CSR orientation of Chinese managers: The role of Confucian ethics and Confucian dynamism. *Sustainability*, 11(23), 6562.

Li, L., Hu, R., Huang, J., Bürgi, M., Zhu, Z., Zhong, J. and Lü, Z. (2020). A farmland biodiversity strategy is needed for China. *Nature Ecology and Evolution*, 4(6), 772–774.

Liu, J., Coomes, D.A., Gibson, L., Hu, G., Liu, J., Luo, Y., Wu, C. and Yu, M. (2019). Forest fragmentation in China and its effect on biodiversity. *Biological Reviews of the Cambridge Philosophical Society*, 94(5), 1636–1657.

Maes, J., Liquete, C., Teller, A., Erhard, M., Paracchini, M.L., Barredo, J.I., Grizzetti, B., Cardoso, A., Somma, F., Petersen, J., Meiner, A., Gelabert, E.R., Zal, N., Kristensen, P., Bastrup-Birk, A., Biala, K., Piroddi, C., Egoh, B., Degeorges, P., Fiorina, C., Santos-Martín, F., Naruševičius, V., Verboven, J., Pereira, H.M., Bengtsson, J., Gocheva, K., Marta-Pedroso, C., Snäll, T., Estreguil, C., San-Miguel-Ayanz, J., Pérez-Soba, M., Grêt-Regamey, A., Lillebø, A.I., Malak, D.A., Condé, S., Moen, J., Czúcz, B., Drakou, E.G., Zulian, G. and Lavalle, C. (2016). An indicator framework for assessing ecosystem services in support of the EU biodiversity strategy to 2020. *Ecosystem Services*, 17, 14–23.

Maroun, W. and Atkins, J. (2018). The emancipatory potential of extinction accounting: Exploring current practice in integrated reports. *Accounting Forum*, 42(1), 102–118.

Meng, H.H., Zhou, S.S., Li, L., Tan, Y.H., Li, J.W. and Li, J. (2019). Conflict between biodiversity conservation and economic growth: Insight into rare plants in tropical China. *Biodiversity and Conservation*, 28(2), 523–537.

Miller, J. (2003). Daoism and nature. In Selin, H. (Ed.), *Nature Across Cultures: Views of Nature and the Environment in Non-western Cultures*. Dordrecht: Kluwer Academic Publishers.

Miller, J. and Cline, E.M. (2004). Daoism: A short introduction. *Journal of Chinese Philosophy*, 31(4), 547–549.

Ministry of Environmental Protection China. (2020). *National Ecological Quality Profile in 2020*. Beijing: Environmental Science Press. Available at: http://www.xinhuanet.com/energy/2021-03/03/c_1127160268.htm

Naess, A. (1973). The shallow and the deep: Long-range ecology movement: A summary. *Inquiry*, 16(1–4), 95–99.

Naess, A. (1993). Beautiful action: Its function in the ecological crisis. *Environmental Values*, 2(1), 67–71.

Narain, D., Maron, M., Teo, H.C., Hussey, K. and Lechner, A.M. (2020). Best-practice biodiversity safeguards for Belt and Road Initiative's financiers. *Nature Sustainability*, 3(8), 650–657.

Nelson, E.S. (2020). *Daoism and Environmental Philosophy: Nourishing Life*. London: Routledge.

Ridings, P. (2018). Redefining environmental stewardship to deliver governance frameworks for marine biodiversity beyond national jurisdiction. *ICES Journal of Marine Science*, 75(1), 435–443.

Rimmel, G. and Jonäll, K. (2013). Biodiversity reporting in Sweden: Corporate disclosure and preparers' views. *Accounting, Auditing and Accountability Journal*, 26(5), 746–778.

Roberts, L., Hassan, A., Elamer, A. and Nandy, M. (2021). Biodiversity and extinction accounting for sustainable development: A systematic literature review and future research directions. *Business Strategy and the Environment*, 30(1), 705–720.

Siddiqui, J. (2013). Mainstreaming biodiversity accounting: Potential implications for a developing economy. *Accounting, Auditing and Accountability Journal*, 26(5), 779–805.

Stead, J.G. and Stead, E. (2000). Eco-enterprise strategy: Standing for sustainability. *Journal of Business Ethics*, 24(4), 313–329.

Sun, Y., Ip, P.S., Jones, M., Wang, J.J. and An, Y. (2021). Determinants of animal welfare disclosure practices: Evidence from China. *Sustainability*, 13(4), 2200.

Suriyankietkaew, S. and Kantamara, P. (2019). Business ethics and spirituality for corporate sustainability: A Buddhism perspective. *Journal of Management, Spirituality and Religion*, 16(3), 264–289.

Syarifuddin, S. and Damayanti, R.A. (2019). Biodiversity accounting: Uncover environmental destruction in Indonesia. *Social Responsibility Journal*, 16(6), 809–825.

Thathong, K. (2012). A spiritual dimension and environmental education: Buddhism and environmental crisis. *Procedia-Social and Behavioral Sciences*, 46, 5063–5068.

Tian, Z., Tian, Y., Chen, Y. and Shao, S. (2020). The economic consequences of environmental regulation in China: From a perspective of the environmental protection admonishing talk policy. *Business Strategy and the Environment*, 29(4), 1723–1733.

Tianchen, L. (2003). Confucian ethics and the environment. *Culture Mandala*, 6(1), 5856.

Tregidga, H. (2013). Biodiversity offsetting: Problematisation of an emerging governance regime. *Accounting, Auditing and Accountability Journal*, 26(5), 806–832.

Tregidga, H., Milne, M. and Kearins, K. (2014). (Re) presenting 'sustainable organizations'. *Accounting, Organizations and Society*, 39(6), 477–494.

UN-CBD. (2021). *Country Profiles: China*. Available at: https://www.cbd.int/countries/profile/?country=cn.

Wang, W., Feng, C., Liu, F. and Li, J. (2020). Biodiversity conservation in China: A review of recent studies and practices. *Environmental Science and Ecotechnology*, 2, 100025.

Wang, Y. and Shen, N. (2016). Environmental regulation and environmental productivity: The case of China. *Renewable and Sustainable Energy Reviews*, 62, 758–766.

Wang, Y. and Zhi, Q. (2016). The role of green finance in environmental protection: Two aspects of market mechanism and policies. *Energy Procedia*, 104, 311–316.

Weir, K. (2018). The purposes, promises and compromises of extinction accounting in the UK public sector. *Accounting, Auditing and Accountability Journal*, 31(3), 875–899.

Xing, Y. and Starik, M. (2017). Taoist leadership and employee green behaviour: A cultural and philosophical microfoundation of sustainability. *Journal of Organizational Behavior*, 38(9), 1302–1319.

Xue, D., Wu, J. and Zhao, F. (2012). Actions, progress and prospects in implementation of the Convention on Biological Diversity during the past 20 years in China. *Biodiversity Science*, 20(5), 623.

Yeh, E.T. (2014). Reverse environmentalism: Contemporary articulations of Tibetan culture, Buddhism and environmental protection. In Miller, J., Yü, D.S. and van der Veer, P. (Eds.), *Religion and Ecological Sustainability in China*. London: Routledge.

Yi, Y., Wang, Z. and Yang, Z. (2010). Impact of the Gezhouba and Three Gorges Dams on habitat suitability of carps in the Yangtze River. *Journal of Hydrology*, 387(3–4), 283–291.

Zhao, L. and Atkins, J. (2021). Assessing the emancipatory nature of Chinese extinction accounting. *Social and Environmental Accountability Journal*, 41(1–2), 8–36.

Zhou, X., Chen, L., Yang, J. and Wu, H. (2020). Chinese sturgeon needs urgent rescue. *Science*, 370(6521), 1175–1175.

Zijin Mining. (2020). Annual CSR Report. Available at: https://www.zjky.cn/upload/pdfjs/web/viewer.html?file=/upload/file/2021/04/26/b1e025cc515144409cff4492c61a7a62.pdf

3 Responsive Approaches to Community Involvement in Resettlement Schemes to Prevent Conflict

A Case Study in the Chibuto District, Mozambique

Constâncio Augusto Machanguana

Introduction

Resettling communities for mining purposes often leads to tensions between those resettled, the investors, and governments. Factors such as environmental impacts, non-participation of the community, extra-local alliances, and distrust towards the State and extractive companies tend to increase resistance and tension (Chivangue, 2017; Conde and Le Billon, 2017). Economic marginalization, corporate social responsibility (CSR) activities, remoteness, and attachment to a place have mixed effects on shaping the communities within the resettlement zones (Conde and Le Billon, 2017). It is a fact that the mining industry provokes deep transformation where it operates (Bebbington et al., 2008; Lillywhite et al., 2015). For example, for the benefit of industrial operations in residential areas, the local communities must be resettled in other locations. This gives rise to deforestation when new areas of residence do not offer fertile land for agriculture and cattle pasture, which forces the communities to look for new living alternatives. The massive arrival of multinational mining companies has brought great opportunities for development to African countries, raising expectations for rapid development in Mozambique (see Mosca and Selemane, 2011). Castel-Branco (2013) considers these discoveries a "curse" as they are susceptible to leading to potential conflict that might be instigated by major international superpowers or local leadership. The regulation framework for the management of such resources constitutes one of the weaknesses that enforce these conflicts (Osório, 2018).

In Mozambique, two arguments divide scholars in relation to the economic and social impact of multinational mining companies. According to the Extractive Industry Initiative (EITI) (2015), the increase in investments in mining exploration will serve as an anchor for strategic public works, power infrastructures, and logistics and for the creation of other funding. On the other hand, the pessimistic argument is centered on mistrust. CIP (2013) disapproves the idea that the contribution of the mining industry will be proportional to the improvement of life conditions of local communities, especially in job generation and business

DOI: 10.4324/9781003274575-4

opportunities for local entrepreneurs. We must consider the benefits that those multinational companies have, and the poor capacity of national entities to effectively control, explore, and export resources, in the context of State fragility.

Since the arrival of extractive multinationals in Mozambique, the society's concern has been about the benefits they bring to the communities (José and Sampaio, 2011; Mosca and Selemane, 2011, 2012) and their potential to generate income. Conflicts, marginalization, and impoverishment of the natives (Chivangue, 2017; Machanguana and Dias Sardinha, 2021) have been other concerns. The discovery of minerals in the province of Gaza since 2009 with the arrival of the multinational BHP Billiton in the district of Chibuto had raised the expectation of "wealth" with compensation for land expropriation, formal job creation, and the construction of water and electricity and health and education infrastructures within the scope of its social responsibility. However, this project did not proceed due to lack of funding. And then, a new Chinese company arrived and the expectations of the local communities rose again: promotion of employment, good compensation derived from resettlements, and the construction of social infrastructures and other social responsibility activities that promoted the acceptance of the mining project in Chibuto.

Since the mining operations began in 2016, the communities, the Chinese company, and the local government have been in a latent conflict. The community claims the promises made initially; the mining company avoids direct dialogue with the communities and has not yet concluded the process of compensating the resettled families; the government is unable to bring the parties together, and shows weakness in providing responses to the people's complaints. At least three strikes against the Chinese company have taken place. Nowadays, people are frustrated and feel betrayed. What constructive resettlement models should be adopted to prevent tensions? To what extent should the community be involved in the process? What contribution would CSR have or, according to Zheng (2020), which "corporate social justice" would be implemented after the resettlement to promote peacebuilding in the community? This study seeks to show the ways used to reduce tension and build consensus between communities and mining companies.

This chapter argues that, on the one hand, in order to get the so-called "social license to operate" thus preventing conflict with local communities, there should be established mechanisms that enforce the involvement of locals during the resettlement process, so that peacebuilding foundations are consolidated. On the other hand, after the resettlement, the Chinese company should implement CSR actions rooted in the needs and aspirations of the community. This is a case study on a specific community affected by mining operations in Chibuto, Mozambique. The chapter starts by discussing the problems around the extractive industry in developing countries. It highlights its contribution to development processes and stresses the impacts on the host communities, especially in Mozambique. Additionally, it maps mining conflicts and their causes, for instance, the most documented conflicts that took place in Tete Province (Mozambique) in Vale Company. Resettlement schemes linked to mining operations are discussed to understand their dynamics and impacts on the community lives (losses and gains of the process). Finally, the chapter presents CSR or "corporate social justice" as a responsive approach to resettlement processes that prevents conflict among the parties (community, company, and the government).

Literature Review

This section addresses the main concepts related to the topic of this chapter: the extractive industry and its dynamics in the host communities (Auty, 2006; Castel-Branco, 2010; Conde and Le Billon, 2017; Eweje, 2006; Mosca and Selemane, 2011, 2012). It also addresses the conflicts generated by the mining action and ways to promote peacebuilding (Abuya, 2016; Arbeláez-Ruiz, 2021; Bebbington et al., 2008; Bond, 2014), the resettlement schemes and how the communities are affected (Bennett and McDowell, 2012; Downing, 2002; Vanclay, 2017; Varia, 2013; Wickeri, 2010), and lastly, the main idea of CSR or "corporate social justice" and its potentiality to harmonize the relationship among the resettled, the company, and the local government (Jamali et al., 2015; Jamali and Mirshak, 2007; Zheng, 2020).

The Extractive Industry and Its Controversies in Developing Countries

The extractive multinationals (Barreto and Barsted, 2005) were attracted by the recent discoveries of huge hydrocarbon deposits on the Indian coast (cf. Augé, 2014). Their spread and the urgency to boost rural development with their contribution puts CSR on the agenda of the government. However, it is recognized that extractive multinationals, when operating in developing countries, are often associated with a series of problems in the host communities. In fact, they have the power to negatively affect community values and customs and to stimulate the emergence of conflicts among the local people (Chivangue, 2017; Kemp et al., 2017; Onyewuchi and Obumneke, 2013). In Nigeria and South Africa, host communities view multinational mining companies as not acting correctly, which contributes to the degradation of the communities' quality of life (Conde and Le Billon, 2017). This problem contributes to mobilization and violence against the mining industry (Bebbington et al., 2008; Chivangue, 2017; Middeldorp et al., 2016). There is criticism of mining companies that are viewed as provoking political instability between them and the hosting States, already weakened (Auty, 2006), which raises doubts about the economic benefits of these companies to local communities. More specifically, in the case of Mozambique (Castel-Branco, 2013), large mining businesses have had an adverse impact on sovereignty. Those who criticize mining companies' actions in developing countries (Ali and O'Faircheallaigh, 2007; Blowfield and Frynas, 2005; Frynas, 2005) are skeptical about the real contribution to transforming the communities positively (Eweje, 2006; Székely and Knirsch, 2005), and they present various arguments. Eweje (2006) argues that host communities view mining corporations as not acting correctly. The majority of these communities expect higher benefits from those companies (Frynas, 2005).

Mining Conflicts

Conflicts between communities and mining companies resulting from land expropriation have been growing all over the world between 2000 and 2013 (Andrews et al., 2017; Bond, 2014). These growing conflicts are also observed in the majority of developing countries with natural resources and mining projects. The presence of mining companies in developing countries brings social changes in the host communities that may generate conflicts between the communities and mining companies (Arbeláez-Ruiz, 2021). In fact, it is worth being reminded of the dimension of mining conflict concept given by Bond (2014, 60–61):

> Conflict is not a bad thing, per se. Non-physically violent conflict can be an indication that an opportunity for change is emerging. However, the outcomes from conflict have the potential to be either positive or negative for the parties involved. Change is an integral characteristic of mining as a large, disruptive activity in competition for land, water and other resources. Conflict continues to occur in the mining company-community space as a response to both potential and actual mining-related change in the environment as well as within/between communities. Negative outcomes from conflict between mining companies and communities can be costly both financially and otherwise: damaged property, loss of life, injury, relational rupture, reputational damage, legal procedures, loss of income and of development opportunities.

Abuya (2016) explains that conflicts related to mining are justified by: (a) landownership; (b) unfair compensations; (c) unfair resource distribution; (d) environmental degradation; (e) worsening of poverty conditions induced by mining; (f) conflicts related to human rights abuse perpetuated by the mining companies. In fact, this tension may be diminished by the adoption of dialogue mechanisms and building consensus (Anguelovski, 2011), and a profound engagement between the companies and communities to obtain what Dare et al. (2014) and Prno (2013) call "a social license to operate". Machanguana and Dias Sardinha (2021) showed that the institutional regulation and the fragility within governing structures in developing countries lead to conflicts between mining companies and host communities. In Mozambique, mining companies face: (1) weakness of public institutions demonstrated by the inability to negotiate and enforce contract concessions in a sustainable way (Castel-Branco, 2010, 2013); (2) a strong dependence on foreign aid, which makes local government incapable of negotiating concession contracts with major revenue benefits for the local economy, not to mention the excessive benefits of concession contracts (Selemane, 2009); and (3) excessive promiscuity and involvement of national elites in business (Augé, 2014; Cohen et al., 2014; Selemane, 2009), which further weakens the power of institutions to conduct the exploitation of resources for the benefit of the national economy.

In Mozambique, examples of mining conflicts found in Tete Province (Vale Company) show more aggressiveness. The Vale Company is Brazilian and was founded in 1942. It became the largest diversified mining company in the Americas and the second largest in the world. It operates in 13 Brazilian states and on five continents. It employs more than 100,000 people, including its own employees and those outsourced. Vale is quoted on the stock exchanges of São Paulo (Bovespa), New York (NYSE), Madrid (Latibel), and Hong Kong (HKSE). Chivangue (2017) conducted a study of local communities' protests in Tete, as Vale Company was not honoring its commitments related to job promises and betterment of local life conditions. The study shows evidence of tension between the company and the communities. For their part, Coutinho (2019) and Machanguana and Dias Sardinha (2021) demonstrated that the company did not present a clear plan to compensate or promote the development of local communities, and that local public authorities are incapable of protecting the rights of these communities, which makes this tension more visible in people's behavior.

Mining Resettlement

Mining resettlement is the extensive process of planning and relocating people, households, and communities from one site affected by mining projects to another. It comprises, in addition, all the associated activities such as the provision of compensation, livelihood restoration, and the improvement of the social conditions of the affected communities (Vanclay, 2017). However, giving money to people or just moving them to new housing places is not enough. According to The Human Rights Watch report, a great part of resettlement practice has to do only with providing cash compensation or replacement housing, without giving adequate attention to other necessities of the resettled (Varia, 2013). Other socio-economic determinants should be respected during the people removal process. The land, rivers, trees, and places have symbolic meanings and belonging sentiments and identities for communities (Wickeri, 2010). So, if some determinants are not observed during the process, a bad resettlement can provoke emotional pain and other social impacts (Bennett and McDowell, 2012), including the feeling of abandonment.

A study by Gukurume and Tombindo (2021) in rural interior Zimbabwe concludes that the creation of mining enclaves fostered a feeling of exclusion and dispossession, and caused multiple forms of precariousness marked by physical displacement of populations and socio-emotional damage. Owen and Kemp (2015) explain that when displaced people have minimal control over the circumstances that result in their displacement, the potential for negative impacts, including trauma, can be high. The most common problems related to resettlements are chaotic resettlement planning; inadequate/unfair compensation; not taking advantage of the benefits of exploiting the resources; violation of people's social, economic, and cultural rights; disruption of local values and customs; loss of irreplaceable values such as memorial/sacred places; violation of housing rights and foundational human rights (e.g. poor chances of accessing schools, hospitals, police stations, water sources); marginalization and discrimination of the most vulnerable groups (such as indigenous populations, tribal groups, women and children); and lack of a social support system for people resettled in new areas of residence (Downing, 2002; Terminski, 2012). However, whilst Cernea (2008) considers that some people can benefit from the resettlements or at least through CSR projects, like training for self-employment or business opportunities, in Tete, according to Zacarias (2016) and Bihale (2016), people felt excluded from the benefits of mineral resources extraction. Besides that, they lost their farmland, they were disconnected from their cultural and religious symbols such as graveyards, trees, water sources, etc., which has led to the sentiment of disruption from their ancestors (Lillywhite et al., 2015).

The Need for Corporate Social Responsibility (CSR) and Peacebuilding

One central idea of CSR is to assure that the negative effects of the displacement are controlled and the positive ones are boosted in order to enhance the quality of life. It should be done in an ethical, moral, and legal way, whilst responding to the needs and expectations of the stakeholders along the value chain of the project (see Jamali et al., 2015). The need for CSR initiatives is probably more urgent in developing countries where the legal and institutional framework does not assure the protection of the local communities' interests. The idea of CSR becomes meaningless if not rooted in the need of the locals. Despite this, it is recognized that promoting peacebuilding in Africa is paramount (Hudson, 2016) and it should be boosted by all parties. In addition, in front of violent or non-violent conflict over the possession of resources or over the demand for social recognition of the minorities and the underprivileged, the issue of building concessions remains the priority of the main social actors and public entities (Murithi, 2006).

In most developing countries with weak legal institutions, bureaucratic inconsistency, poor property rights, and corruption (see Liu, 2016; Tvedten and Picardo, 2018), CSR may get a very different dynamic (Jamali and Mirshak, 2007). In these countries, the fragilities cause mining companies to replace CSR with compensation resulting from the displacements (see Machanguana and Dias Sardinha, 2021). However, a well-designed CSR plan should go beyond a mere compensation plan, it should include providing basic needs for development and sustainability, such as water, economic and social infrastructure, health services and education, human rights, gender equality, democracy, and freedom. Indeed, the company is responsible for providing substantial improvement in the people's quality of life (Luetkenhorst, 2004). The need for CSR, or ultimately, "corporate social justice", has become more apparent over the last few years. Over CSR, corporate social justice is a framework regulated by the trust between a company and its employees, customers, shareholders, and the broader community, with the goal of explicitly doing good to all of them (Zheng, 2020). Corporate social justice is a reformulation of CSR based on the measurability of the programs in the communities affected by the company's operations.

Research Methodology

This study used a qualitative research framework, encompassing various methods and sources of information. The process was sequenced to provide the researcher with an appropriate context for fieldwork on January 10 and 11, 2022. The primary research tool was the interviews of key informants – the resettled people. Community leaders participated in the process of negotiation with the Chinese company. Therefore, three focus group sessions of three hours each were held. Each session was attended by 17–22 participants, where 21 were men and 37 women. These sessions aimed at capturing the perception of the already resettled communities and those in the process of resettlement about their vision of the resettlement process. They were focused on the economic and socio-cultural aspects, and they also discussed with each other who had experienced other models of negotiations aiming at avoiding tensions and conflicts with the Chinese company and the local government. To prevent people from concentrating in the same place (under trees), and to observe the measures against COVID-19, a relatively reduced sample was chosen, of which each participant represented a family, according to Table 3.1.

The documentary research and the structured interviews with the affected community leaders and the government provided additional information, which served to confirm and consolidate the results of the focus groups. A literature review was foundational to providing information about the policies and development planning, as well as providing examples of cases of success and failure in resettlement processes, land dispute, socio-environmental crisis, and the building of consensus between communities and companies.

Before going into the details of the case study, a piece of background information is provided here. The government and the mining project have been spreading a narrative that Chibuto has one of the largest reserves of heavy sands in Africa. Recently, the Chinese mining company built an airport and offered it to

Table 3.1 Distribution of Participants per Session

First session – January 10, 09:00–11:30			*Second session – January 10, 14:00–17:30*			*Third session – January 11, 09:00–11:30*		
Mabecuane and Mudumeia neighborhoods			*Savene and Mutsicuana neighborhoods*			*Mudada neighborhood*		
Total	*Men*	*Women*	*Total*	*Men*	*Women*	*Total*	*Men*	*Women*
17	3	14	22	9	13	19	9	10

the government. There is a plan to construct a railway line of about 100 km and a port in Xai-xai – all these infrastructures bring expectations of rapid development.

The Case Study

The Chibuto Heavy Sands Exploration Project

The first bid for the exploration of Chibuto heavy sands was made to the Australian company Corridor Sands, Ltd which later sold the project to BHP Billiton, which in turn, after several prospecting and testing works, abandoned the project in 2009 as it lacked the adequate technology to carry out the project. After BHP Billiton, a Canadian company was granted a concession which later had its exploration license canceled because it failed to meet the deadlines (Estudos, 2016). In 2013, a mining license (for ilmenites), was granted to a Chinese company called Anhui Foreign Economic and Yunnan Xinli in consortium with the Ministry of Mineral Resources and Energy of Mozambique (MIREM). This was to operate in an area of 10,840 ha, in the same location. The heavy sands exploration project 7054C in Chibuto had an investment of USD 500,000,000. The first surveys carried out for the infrastructure indicated that 324 families (see Table 3.2) would be resettled and their properties removed: housing, tents, garages, churches, cemeteries, water sources, and trees among others. The affected infrastructure of the communities was estimated at USD 2,663,013.70. In addition to building houses, compensation of USD 29,165,445.21 will be made for fruit trees and crops, support infrastructure, pens, and exhumation of graves in the mining area, as well as in the host areas.

Findings

Perception of the Economic and Socio-cultural Rupture

The expectation regarding people's removal to a new area of residence created some ruptures in their socio-cultural dynamics as their relationship with the land is very strong. With the displacement, the communities lose some economic and

Table 3.2 Communities and Families Affected (Resettlement Plan Report, 2016)

Community	*No. of families*
Mabecuane	21
Mudada	115 (yet to be resettled)
Mudumeia	41
Savene	104
Mutsicuane	43
Total	324

cultural practices developed in their previous home. The new neighborhood does not offer the conditions to pursue the same activities as before, and the places (rivers, lagoons, fields of cultivation) are more distant. The respondents explained that in their old neighborhoods they did fishing, gathered firewood, and cut reeds for sale at the Chibuto market (the sellers were exclusively women) and agriculture. These activities ensured their livelihood and education for their children. In the new neighborhood, these activities have become a challenge, as the distance to the place for agriculture has reduced their productivity. During the fruit season, the communities harvested cashews and nuts for eating, and prepared and sold alcoholic beverages (also used in celebration ceremonies and cultural events). These trees were cut down and no replanting was provided in the new neighborhoods. Agriculture was the main livelihood activity for the communities. After chestnuts and seasonal fruits commerce (cashew nuts and mangoes), livestock farming was hugely practiced – raising chickens, ducks, goats, pigs, and cattle, although these were not intended for sale.

> We had space for each one to raise domestic animals in their backyard ... the animals could graze inside my backyard at will, without invading the neighbor's backyard. But here it is not possible. The space we have is not enough to raise our animals.
>
> (Community leader)

In the resettlement neighborhood, in Muwamuza, the economic and livelihood activities are limited. The farms are located far away. They also have to get up at around 3 a.m. to start work at 6 a.m., which affects their income, as they must return home before 12 o'clock to care for the children and prepare food. Besides, they must pay a fee to use the land for cultivation.

> There is no work here; there are no places to cut reeds and firewood as we used to do. No place for livestock farming. However, before displacement, we were promised land and place for grazing, something that has not fulfilled to date.
>
> (Woman, resident at Muwamuza)

> The land given to us for farming is distant. We sometimes go there, but when it rains, we work in the fields of local residents that charge a rent. Most of the time, we sit here without work.
>
> (Woman, resident at Muwamuza)

In short, the community's general perception of the resettlement process is that they lost much, especially their affection to the land, ancestors, traditional habits, and customs. Therefore, during the fruit season, these communities are allowed to return to their former lands (not yet explored), to collect fruits from their old trees. But some trees and crops have been destroyed by the mining operations. The grazing of cattle and agriculture are not allowed because of the risk derived from the mining activities in the concession area.

Displacement: Positive and Negative Changes

It is not just losses that the community reports as a result of their displacement. The social infrastructure (schools and hospitals) did not exist in their former residence which forced them to travel more than 40 km to the city of Chibuto and schools only offered primary education. In the new neighborhood, however, schools and hospitals exist but they do not comply with the Ministry of Education's building standards. Apart from that, secondary schools are found only 5 km away. The water sources used to be far away. In the new neighborhood, a supply system has been built to provide free potable water to the entire community. In Muwamuza, there is also a police station and all the houses have electricity.

At the cultural level, previously, there were many instances of witchcraft. But now the new urban configuration has sorted out that problem thanks to the access to information through TV, the internet, interaction with other people, and religion in the surrounding neighborhoods. The issue of religion was ignored during the resettlement process.

> We were given only one place to build our churches, but we come from different denominations and it is not possible to build church halls in a row. There are many who come to ask for space to build churches here in Muwamuza neighborhood, but we don't have any more plots.
>
> (Man, community leader)

Furthermore,

> In the past, we used to bury our dead in our backyard and this has a great significance in our spirituality, but here, in Muwamuza, we have a common cemetery. And we were not properly compensated for the removal of our graves. The Chinese company reduced the compensation amount without justification, we don't know why.
>
> (Man, resident at Muwamuza)

Other typical problems of growing urban areas are the diseases, such as malaria. This disease is caused by mosquitos which are abundant in stagnated waters and damp places. The existence of water ponds is justified by major water availability and its misuse by families.

The Origin of Tensions/Conflicts

The first two focus groups of Muwamuza complained that the Chinese company did not fulfill its promises, and the local government did little to negotiate with the company. Thus, they sought to meet up directly with the managers to demand their rights. For example, although most of them were displaced from small houses, they demanded houses for their children, now grown up; says one of the residents:

> Our tradition enforces an adult son to sleep in a separate house from his parents, even though there are free bedrooms. The best is for him to build his own house inside or outside the family's backyard. We wish the Chinese company had taken this into consideration.
>
> (Man, resident at Muwamuza)

Another resident at Mudada (a community which awaits resettlement) added that:

> Our demand before the resettlement is for the Chinese company to build us better houses, and consider that our adult children must have their own houses too, separate from their parents'. We are from Machagana tribe, and it is not right for an adult child to sleep in the same house with his parents.
>
> (Man, resident at Mudada)

The feeling of rejection by the community in Muwamuza is evident among the people interviewed:

> We were just evicted, and they never came to know how we are.
>
> (Woman, resident at Muwamuza)

Residents claimed that representatives of the Chinese company made several promises (employment and fair compensation, as per signed agreements). The company assured that it would create jobs for the resettled people or for their children, but "instead, other people are hired, some coming from Maputo … the locals are disqualified for unknown reasons" (man, resident in Muwamuza). Families also stated that they were not notified about the displacement date.

> Compositions were not fair. They promised to compensate us before our displacement but suddenly we were told to leave our houses … we wanted to take some goods but they did not give us enough time. They had promised to pay USD 100Mt for each fruit tree, but that did not happen.
>
> (Woman, resident at Muwamuza)

Furthermore:

> The district administrator promised to provide a monthly basic food allowance for the people after the displacement … he didn't yet, nor visited us here.
>
> (Woman, resident at Muwamuza)

Among other reported frustrations by the communities, the Chibuto resettlement process experienced some moments of tension. The community made violent demonstrations in front of the Chinese company and the government buildings. People demanded the rights they had been promised.

In 2018, prior to the beginning of the resettlement, the Mudumeia community rose up against the Chinese company because it had interrupted compensating for the trees. The first agreement was to pay USD 410 but this amount was reduced to USD 100 without a clear explanation. Wielding sticks and blocking access, the community blocked the Chinese company's work for five hours until the police force came to disperse the protesters. The community vandalized two Chinese company vehicles. Consequently, the company and the government representatives previously appointed to coordinate the resettlement process were dismissed. To reach a solution, a memorandum was signed in which the community was forced to agree to receive USD 100 per tree.

> We were forced to sign this memorandum, not least because the police were called to the scene and the government persuaded us to consent to the Chinese company's proposal.
>
> (Man, community leader, Muwamuza)

Then the people complained that an office should be created to manage the communities' demands throughout the resettlement process in order to prevent further incidents. The office would be responsible for forwarding the communities' concerns to the Chinese company and local government. The local community had gone through other resettlement processes with Corridor Sands Ltd during the prospecting phase that paid "better". Furthermore, recently, there had been a process of resettlement for the installation of a power transmission line to Maputo by Electricidade de Moçambique, which was making "good" compensation: "even the trees are well compensated" explained one of the residents of Muwamuza. However, with this Chinese company, the "promises of compensation were not kept".

In September 2021, the communities again went on strike, complaining about the delay in completion of the compensation process. According to residents, "there are many people who have not even been paid their first compensation" but have already been displaced to Muwamuze. Representatives of the resettled communities said that another popular uprising was in sight if the agreement was not honored.

Lessons and Responsive Approaches to Avoid Conflicts in Mining Resettlements

For focus group participants (Muwamuza and Mudada) tension and conflicts could be avoided if the Chinese company deepened community consultations, involved more people, and considered their opinions:

> They do not want to hear our voices. After the displacement we are no longer valuable. We are not welcome even by our local government.
>
> (Man, resident at Muwamuza)

The compliance of the compensation plan should be enforced by the local government in order to assure fairness and justice. Furthermore, the Chinese company should not have been allowed to displace the families before compensation was complete:

> That was our mistake … because we accepted the displacement without being compensated. Now it is difficult to get our rights back because the Chinese company closed itself to us.
>
> (Man, resident at Muwamuza)

Another approach to minimize the displaced people's suffering, like in Tete, was the onset by the community of an effective Corporate Social Responsibility Plan in order to promote continuous improvement of people's living conditions, as recommended in the Corporate Social Responsibility Regulation of the mining industry:

> As you can see nothing is done for us, not any help. There are people who are left for their luck. Elderly people (living alone) who had small farms in their backyards, now have no space to continue … They cannot even raise small animals because there is no space here. They are suffering, without assistance or income alternatives.
>
> (Woman, resident at Muwamuza)

Discussion

As in any situation of people's displacement, social structure and lifestyle change. Such transformation can be negative, like trauma (see Owen and Kemp, 2015). It can take place at a local or global level. It can be social or environmental (see Conde and Le Billon, 2017) and economic (see EITI, 2020). The existing model of resettlement plan seems to follow the same logic as the previous experiences in Tete (Bihale, 2016; Chivangue, 2017; Mosca and Selemane, 2012), but it is no different from those of other developing countries (Andrews et al., 2017; de Abreu Coutinho, 2019; Lillywhite et al., 2015): unfair compensation, broken agreements, non-post resettlement assistance, sudden disruption of the lifestyle of the rural communities, and loss of land and their cultural values. The communities are not deeply involved and do not have access to essential information about the project nor about their future lives after the displacement. Like in Tete (see CIP, 2013; Machanguana and Dias Sardinha, 2021), in the neighborhood of Muwamuza, the communities feel abandoned by the Chinese company, which causes frustration and the will to protest.

In fact, for Muwamuza residents, this resettlement process has benefited the Chinese company and the government more. Being already poor people, their social and economic conditions have worsened considerably. Now they cannot carry out subsistence activities because in the urbanized areas there are few livelihood alternatives other than formal employment and businesses. The occupation of their lands has given rise to disruption of their cultural objects and symbols. Cultural events, ceremonies, and celebrations have been diluted in Muwamuza. However, it is undeniable that life has improved in Muwamuza, which was unthinkable: a school, a hospital, and a police station are now much closer to their homes than before. Drinkable water and electricity have never been more available.

Muwamuza residents understand that they have been misled by the Chinese company and poorly protected by the local government. Some important lessons are underlined in this research. Conflicts and tensions (see Chivangue, 2017) can be avoided if the companies create mechanisms to obtain a social license from the affected communities (Moffat et al., 2016; Zhang and Moffat, 2015). Thus, good CSR programs (see Jamali and Mirshak, 2007) can help minimize adverse effects in resettlement camps. A good CSR plan, in addition to compensation (not yet completed) could eventually minimize the community complaints. An important step for the Chinese company would be to program initiatives that develop capacities and skills for locals to develop self-employment, agriculture, and livestock. The involvement of the community in the design of this plan is fundamental for their long-term survival in the new neighborhood.

Conclusion

This study sought to discuss responsive approaches to mining resettlement processes that prevent tensions and conflicts. Fieldwork based on focus groups and semi-structured interviews with key actors was carried out in two communities affected by the Chibuto heavy sands exploration project (Muwamuza, resettled; and Mudada, yet to be resettled). I collected data that allowed me to understand that, on the one hand, the community is clearly aware of its interest and desire in a resettlement process. On the other hand, people recognize the way in which the process should be conducted in order to avoid tension and conflicts with the Chinese mining company. Empirical data collected in the fieldwork allowed us to conclude that a resettlement process seeking to avoid tensions and conflicts should, necessarily, prioritize compensation before the removal of the communities. Additionally, it should establish and monitor a post resettlement monitoring committee to ensure that community concerns arising from displacement are promptly addressed. Finally, a CSR plan must be implemented to ensure that the community regenerates and adapts to a new lifestyle with different livelihood activities. I finally argue that when the resettlements linked to mining activities are characterized by conflicts between communities and the companies, the company must assume full responsibility for the implementation of CSR plans in case of negative impacts. It will then move to "corporate social justice", if there are human rights issues over the economic gains of the Chinese company. Good social plans can contribute to the enhancement of people's lives. So, I recommend the local government take on its role of safeguarding and protecting the local communities' rights, and act as an interlocutor between the community and the Chinese company. Finally, the government should ensure compliance with approved national plans and rules.

Acknowledgment

This publication was made possible by support from the African Peacebuilding Network of the Social Science Research Council, with funds provided by Carnegie Corporation of New York. I would like to express my special thanks to my colleagues: Nélio Candido and Paulo Muando, Petra Penninkhoff, and Géssica Macamo who lent their knowledge and support during all the stages of this research, especially during the fieldwork in Chibuto. I am really grateful to them.

References

Abuya, W.O. (2016). Mining conflicts and corporate social responsibility: Titanium mining in Kwale, Kenya. *The Extractive Industries and Society*, 3(2), 485–493.

Ali, S.H. and O'Faircheallaigh, C.S. (2007). Introduction: Extractive industries, environmental performance and corporate social responsibility. *Greener Management International*, 52(52), 5–16.

Amós Zacarias. (2016). Famílias ainda aguardam reassentamento da Vale em Moatize. Available at: http://www.dw.com/pt-002/famílias-ainda-aguardam-reassentamento-da-vale-em-moatize/a-19104541

Andrews, T., Elizalde, B., Le Billon, P., Oh, C.H., Reyes, D. and Thomson, I. (2017). *The Rise in Conflict Associated with Mining Operations: What Lies Beneath.* Vancouver, BC: Canadian International Resources and Development Institute (CIRDI).

Anguelovski, I. (2011). Understanding the dynamics of community engagement of corporations in communities: The iterative relationship between dialogue processes and local protest at the Tintaya copper mine in Peru. *Society and Natural Resources*, 24(4), 384–399.

Arbeláez-Ruiz, D.C. (2021). Indigenous resistance to mining in post-conflict Colombia. *The Extractive Industries and Society*, 9, 100953.

Augé, B. (2014). *Gas in Mozambique, a High-risk Economic Revolution.* Paris and Brussells: IFRI.

Auty, R. (2006). Mining enclave to economic catalyst: Large mineral projects in developing countries. *The Brown Journal of World Affairs*, 13(1), 135–145.

Barreto, P. and Barsted, D.F. (2005). *Responsabilidade Social e Multinacionais em Países em Desenvolvimento.* Available at: https://www.ifri.org/sites/default/.../auge_gas_in_mozambique

Bebbington, A., Humphreys Bebbington, D., Bury, J., Lingan, J., Muñoz, J.P. and Scurrah, M. (2008). Mining and social movements: Struggles over livelihood and rural territorial development in the Andes. *World Development*, 36(12), 2888–2905.

Bennett, O. and McDowell, C. (2012). *Displaced: The Human Cost of Development and Resettlement.* New York: Springer.

Bihale, D. (2016). *Indústria Extractiva em Moçambique: Perspectivas para o Desenvolvimento do País.* Washington, DC: Friedrich Ebert Stifung.

Blowfield, M. and Frynas, J.G. (2005). Setting new agendas: Critical perspectives on corporate social responsibility in the developing world. *International Affairs*, 81(3), 499–513.

Bond, C.J. (2014). Business, peace and mining: A literature review. *Business, Peace and Sustainable Development*, 4(4), 59–83.

Castel-Branco, C.N. (2010). *Economia Extractiva e Desafios de Industrialização em Moçambique*. Maputo: Instituto de Estudos Sociais e Económicos (IESE).

Castel-Branco, C.N. (2013). Economia extractiva e desafios de industrialização : para além de rendas dos recursos naturais. Estrutura da Apresentação. Conferência Internacional sobre a Governação da Economia Extractiva "Recursos Naturais: Benção ou Maldição?". 22 de Maio de 2013.

Cernea, M.M. (2008). Compensation and benefit sharing: Why resettlement policies and practices must be reformed. *Water Science and Engineering*, 1(1), 89–120.

Chivangue, A. (2017). Emergente contra a indústria extractive em Tete: renegociando instituições através de protestos populares? *Working Paper CeSA, CSG 150/2017.*

CIP. (2013). *Primeiros Grandes Projectos do Sector Extractivo Frustram as Expectativas dos Moçambicanos*. Maputo: CIP.

Cohen, E., Selemane, T. and Umarji, M. (2014). *The State's Engagement in Business in Mozambique*. Maputo: USAID.

Conde, M. and Le Billon, P. (2017). Why do some communities resist mining projects while others do not? *The Extractive Industries and Society*, 4(3), 681–697.

Dare, M., Schirmer, J. and Vanclay, F. (2014). Community engagement and social licence to operate. *Impact Assessment and Project Appraisal*, 32(3), 188–197.

de Abreu Coutinho, C. (2019). Política mineira e a integração sócio-cultural e sustentável dos reassentados em Cateme-Mocambique: 2009–2017. *Revista Brasileira de Estudos Africanos*, 4(8), 95–114.

Downing, T.E. (2002). Avoiding new poverty: Mining-induced displacement and resettlement. MMSD No 58. IIED and WBCSD.

EITI. (2020). Relatório Independente da Iniciativa de Transparência na Indústria Extractiva Ano de 2019. Available at: http://itie.org.mz/index.php/download/nono-relatorio-itie/?wpdmdl=3092andrefresh=5fdb4f87084921608208263

Estudos, E. (2016). *Relatório do PAR-Plano de Reassentamento: Projecto de Exploração da Ilmenite no Depósito de Areias Pesadas de Chibuto, Província de Gaza, Moçambique.*

Eweje, G. (2006). The role of MNEs in community development initiatives in developing countries: Corporate social responsibility at work in Nigeria and South Africa. *Business and Society*, 45(2), 93–129.

Frynas, J.G. (2005). The false developmental promise of corporate social responsibility: Evidence from multinational oil companies. *International Affairs*, 81(3), 581–598.

Gukurume, S. and Tombindo, F. (2021). Post-displacement livelihoods in mining communities: The politics of precarity and everyday uncertainty in Marange, Zimbabwe. *The Extractive Industries and Society*, 8(4), 100992.

Hudson, H. (2016). Decolonizing the mainstreaming of gender in peacebuilding: Toward an Agenda for Africa. African Peacebuilding Network (APN) Working Paper No. 8. Social Science Research Council.

ITIE Moçambique. (2015). *Sexto Relatório da ITIEM – Anos de 2013 e 2014*. Maputo: Intellica.

Jamali, D., Karam, C. and Blowfield, M. (2015). Introduction: Corporate social responsibility in developing countries: A development-oriented approach. In Jamali, D., Karam, C. and Blowfield, M. (Eds.), *Development-Oriented Corporate Social Responsibility: Volume 2 - Locally Led Initiatives in Developing Economies.* London: Routledge.

Jamali, D. and Mirshak, R. (2007). Corporate Social Responsibility (CSR): Theory and practice in a developing country context. *Journal of Business Ethics*, 72(3), 243–262.

José, D.S. and Sampaio, C.H. (2011). *Estado da Arte da Mineração em Moçambique: Caso Carvão de Moatize, Tete.* Brasil: Universidade Federal Do Rio Grande Do Sul-RS.

Kemp, D., Owen, J.R. and Collins, N. (2017). Global perspectives on the state of resettlement practice in mining. *Impact Assessment and Project Appraisal*, 35(1), 22–33.

Lillywhite, S., Kemp, D. and Sturman, K. (2015). *Mining, Resettlement and Lost Livelihoods: Listening to the Voices of Resettled Communities in Mualadzi, Mozambique.* Melbourne: Oxfam.

Liu, X. (2016). Corruption culture and corporate misconduct. *Journal of Financial Economics*, 122(2), 307–327.

Luetkenhorst, W. (2004). Corporate social responsibility and the development agenda: The case for actively involving small and medium enterprises. *Intereconomics*, 39(3), 157.

Machanguana, C.A. and Dias Sardinha, I. (2021). Exploring mining multinational resettlements and corporate social responsibility in emerging economies: The case of the company VALE, SA in Mozambique. *Sustainability Accounting, Management and Policy Journal*, 12(3), 591–610.

Middeldorp, N., Morales, C. and van der Haar, G. (2016). Social mobilisation and violence at the mining frontier: The case of Honduras. *The Extractive Industries and Society*, 3(4), 930–938.

Moffat, K., Lacey, J., Zhang, A. and Leipold, S. (2016). The social licence to operate: A critical review. *Forestry: An International Journal of Forest Research*, 89(5), 477–488.

Mosca, J. and Selemane, T. (2011). *El Dorado Tete: Os Mega Projectos de Mineração.* Maputo: CIP.

Mosca, J. and Selemane, T. (2012). Mega-projectos no meio rural, desenvolvimento do territorio e pobreza: O caso de Tete. In de Brito, L., Castel-Branco, C., Chichava, S., Forquilha, S. and Francisco, A. (Eds.), *Desafios para Moçambique 2012.* Maputo: IESE.

Murithi, T. (2006). African approaches to building peace and social solidarity. *African Journal on Conflict Resolution*, 6(2), 9–33.

Onyewuchi, G. and Obumneke, E. (2013). Multinational corporations and the Nigerian economy. *International Journal of Academic Research in Business and Social Sciences*, 3(4), 360–371.

Osório, C. (2018). Conluios para a exclusão social: empresas mineradoras e agentes de regulação estatal. Projeto: "Empoderamento Das Raparigas e Mulheres Em Zonas de Exploração Mineira" 2016–2017-2018. Available at: http://www.wlsa.org.mz/conluios-para-a-exclusao-social-2/

Owen, J.R. and Kemp, D. (2015). Mining-induced displacement and resettlement: A critical appraisal. *Journal of Cleaner Production*, 87, 478–488.

Prno, J. (2013). An analysis of factors leading to the establishment of a social licence to operate in the mining industry. *Resources Policy*, 38(4), 577–590.

Selemane, T. (2009). *Alguns Desafios na Indústria Extractiva em Moçambique*. Maputo: Centro de Integridade Pública (CIP).

Székely, F. and Knirsch, M. (2005). Responsible leadership and corporate social responsibility: Metrics for sustainable performance. *European Management Journal*, 23(6), 628–647.

Terminski, B. (2012). Mining-induced displacement and resettlement: Social problem and human rights issue. Genf: SSOAR. Available at: https://www.ssoar.info/ssoar/handle/document/32777

Tvedten, I. and Picardo, R. (2018). 'Goats eat where they are tied up': Illicit and habitual corruption in Mozambique. *Review of African Political Economy*, 45(158), 541–557.

Vanclay, F. (2017). Project-induced displacement and resettlement: From impoverishment risks to an opportunity for development? *Impact Assessment and Project Appraisal*, 35(1), 3–21.

Varia, N. (2013). "What is a house without food?": Mozambique's coal mining boom and resettlements. Human Rights Watch. Available at: https://www.hrw.org/report/2013/05/23/what-house-without-food/mozambiques-coal-mining-boom-and-resettlements

Wickeri, E. (2010). Land is life, land is power: Landlessness, exclusion, and deprivation in Nepal. *Fordham International Law Journal*, 34, 930–1041.

Zhang, A. and Moffat, K. (2015). A balancing act: The role of benefits, impacts and confidence in governance in predicting acceptance of mining in Australia. *Resources Policy*, 44, 25–34.

Zheng, L. (2020). We're entering the age of corporate social justice. *Harvard Business Review*, June 15. Available at: https://hbr.org/2020/06/were-entering-the-age-of-corporate-social-justice

Legislations

Resolution No. 21/2014, of 16 May, May 1st Series, No. 40, which approves the Corporate Social Responsibly policy for the Mining Sector. Boletim da República Imprensa Nacional de Mozambique, Maputo.

Decree No. 21/2012, of 08 of August - Regulation on the Resettlement Process Resulting from Economic activity.

4 Sustainability Reporting during COVID-19

A Study of the Hospitality Industry

Pui San Ip and Carlos Noronha

Introduction

According to the definition by the World Bank (2004), sustainability is a commitment for organizations to contribute to economic development in a continuous manner. On the other hand, Dyllick and Hockerts (2002, 131) define corporate sustainability as "meeting the needs of a firm's direct and indirect stakeholders such as shareholders, employees, clients, pressure groups, communities, etc., without compromising its ability to meet the needs of future stakeholders as well". Sustainability is an important concept in tourism industry development; Richards and Derek (2000) propose that tourism positively affects the local and regional development if companies are managed according to the principles of sustainability. However, tourism may have a negative impact on the community; for instance, tourism may lead to unstable job status and inflation, cause negative effects on the environment, and force local people to leave the place they normally live because of their jobs (Agarwal, 2002).

The revenue of the hospitality and tourism industry accounts for 10% of global GDP and has been increasing at a faster rate than the overall global economic development (World Economic Forum, 2017). Tourism is an important source of employment, revenue, and foreign exchange (Dodds and Kuehnel, 2010). However, willingness to travel can be affected by various factors such as political stability, economic conditions, environment, and weather, as well as crises or disasters (Okumus et al., 2005; Cró and Martins, 2017). At the time of conducting this study, 219 countries and territories were affected by the COVID-19 pandemic, with around 120 million cases recorded, causing 2.6 million deaths (Worldometers, 2021). The estimated number of job losses in the Asia Pacific region alone was 48.7 million (Statista, 2020). COVID-19 has already been regarded as a disaster (Bertrand and Lecarpentier, 2021) as it cannot be avoided due to its unpredictability and has an impact on the survival of humans (Faulkner, 2001).

Similar to SARS, COVID-19 can be transmitted through human contact (Chan et al., 2020; Shereen et al., 2020). Thus, changes of tourist behaviours in previous studies may also be applicable to COVID-19. For instance, tourists now tend to do more information research (Fuchs and Reichel, 2011) and

DOI: 10.4324/9781003274575-5

purchase travel insurance (Fuchs and Reichel, 2006, Lo et al., 2011, Mitchell and Vassos, 1998). This study intends to investigate how COVID-19 specifically affects the sustainability reporting behaviour of the hospitality industry as there may be a change in the amount of information demanded by stakeholders and the resources available in reporting sustainability information.

This study proposes to use a framework that includes the economic, environmental, and social dimensions, plus an additional dimension, namely the "pandemic dimension". This framework provides a more comprehensive way to examine and evaluate the sustainability disclosure performance of the hospitality industry during the COVID-19 pandemic. By investigating the extent of sustainability disclosure of the seven largest hotel chains, this study provides implications for other hotels and chains on what sustainability information to disclose during the COVID-19 disaster. The study can also act as a reference for governments and sustainability reporting standard-setting bodies to consider the possibility of making sustainability reporting compulsory or to reconsider the need to amend sustainability reporting standards. Finally, the research framework can also serve to explore how COVID-19 has changed hotel chains' sustainability disclosure behaviours. The remainder of the chapter is structured as follows. We begin by presenting a brief review of the literature. Next, the research methodology is explained and the hypotheses are developed. Then, the research findings are presented and discussed. Lastly, a conclusion is drawn and suggestions are proposed.

Literature Review

Sustainability in the Hospitality Industry

Currently, stakeholders are demanding more information such as ecological and social policies rather than only financial information from corporations (Herremans et al., 2016). To meet such demands, organizations start to develop corporate sustainability reports which incorporate both the expectations of external and internal stakeholders in their decision making (Qi et al., 2013). Different researches on sustainability have been conducted at the global level (de Grosbois, 2012; Font et al., 2012; Franzoni and Avellino, 2019; Guix et al., 2019; Jones et al., 2014; Roblek et al., 2016), country level (Jayawardena et al., 2013; Pérez and Rodríguez del Bosque, 2014), and regional level (Khatter et al., 2019).

Hotels are found to monitor sustainability in three areas, namely, economic, environmental, and social sustainability (Roblek et al., 2016) which are referred to as the triple bottom line (TBL) framework (Elkington, 1997). Prarie (2012) finds that the hotel industry is in the midst of a sustainability awakening. The progress of sustainability development is not satisfactory (Tonne, 2021) and hotels are recommended to improve their sustainability reporting (Franzoni and Avellino, 2019). Moreover, hotels are found to invest in environmental sustainability for immediate or short-term returns (Khatter et al., 2021) and sustainability reporting of hotels is regarded as a way to build legitimacy only (Guix et al., 2018). Hotels are found to mainly focus on environmental issues such as energy and water management which allow cost savings (Jones et al., 2014). However, some studies suggest hotels use their environmental practices as a tool for greenwashing – hotels that use signs like "save the planet: re-use towels" give customers the impression of greenwashing as they are trying to reduce the use of water to save on laundry expenses (Garza, 2011).

Benefits and Issues of Sustainability Reporting

Sustainability reporting is a process that assists organizations in setting goals, measuring performance, and managing change towards a sustainable global economy (Global Reporting Initiative, 2013). Disclosure on sustainability is an important part of strategic management in hotels and it is used to communicate information that is desired by the stakeholders (Roblek et al., 2016) and demonstrate organizations' commitment to sustainability which allows them to gain competitive advantage (Jones et al., 2014). Hotels that disclose social responsibility and sustainability information are found to be more likely to attract capital, business partners, and customers (Roblek et al., 2016). Moreover, showing care for the environment allows hotels to enjoy better revenue and higher customer loyalty (Roblek et al., 2016).

Sustainability reporting is expected to provide value-relevant information to both external and internal stakeholders (Brockett and Rezaee, 2012). There are three dominant sustainability frameworks, namely the Global Reporting Initiative (GRI), the International Integrated Reporting Council (IR) Framework, and the Sustainability Accounting Standards Board (SASB) guidelines (Landrum and Ohsowski, 2018). However, there is no unique standardized sustainability reporting standard (Adams and Evans, 2004) and there are calls for reducing the number of sustainability reporting frameworks (Hume and Sanderson, 2020; Tett, 2020). Organizations may use this insufficiency in standardized sustainability reporting to mislead stakeholders for image-building and some hotels use corporate social responsibility (CSR) as a marketing tool (de Grosbois, 2012). Low transparency and inaccurate decision-making criteria in sustainability responsiveness give rise to the question of whether sustainability reporting is only a way to build legitimacy or a means of greenwashing (Guix et al., 2018). Sustainability reporting in hotels also shows signs of omissions of important information, implying reports are prepared in favour of the hotels themselves rather than in the interests of stakeholders (Guix et al., 2019). Customers of hotels are aware of such greenwashing measures which negatively affect their willingness to revisit the hotel (Rahman et al., 2015).

Disaster and Sustainability

COVID-19 has affected the tourism industry in both supply and demand sides negatively (Li et al., 2020). Suppliers are suffering from decrease in revenue while tourists are concerned about their safety and thus are less willing to travel (Simon, 2009). The main concerns of tourists during disease outbreaks are safety (Simon, 2009; Wen et al., 2021) and health risks (Lepp and Gibson, 2003; Cameron and Shah, 2015; Cassar et al., 2017).

Different studies have been conducted on disaster management, of which management-oriented theories guide a majority of these studies in the tourism and hospitality industry (Hao et al., 2020). Several frameworks provide a comprehensive overview of a disaster situation at each stage (Wang and Ritchie, 2011). For example, Le and Phi (2021) propose a strategic framework of hotel pandemic crisis management which is guided by an integrated crisis management framework in other studies (Faulkner, 2001; Novelli et al., 2018; Ritchie, 2004). The framework includes the pre-event and early symptom phase, emergency phase, crisis phase, and recovery phase. In the pre-event and early symptom phase proposed by Le and Phi (2021), hotels mostly employ a saving strategy through selling assets and freeing up working capital. When the number of local cases and cancellations of bookings keep on increasing, hotels are in the emergency phase and employ cost-cutting measures. In the crisis phase when the disease is so widespread that lockdown or strict regulations are imposed, hotel chains may be forced to stop operation or have to provide quarantine facilities. When the situation eases, hotels step into the recovery phase. The strategic crisis management tools of hotels include marketing and sales strategies, as well as health and safety measures. By disclosing sustainability and health (COVID-19) information, hotels may be able to differentiate themselves from other competitors as proposed by signalling theory (Carpenter and Boyle, 2011).

Objective of the Study

This study aims to explore the performance of sustainability reporting in the hospitality industry during the COVID-19 pandemic by employing a comprehensive framework. The main concerns of tourists during disease outbreaks are safety (Simon, 2009; Wen et al., 2021) and health risks (Lepp and Gibson, 2003). Customers may be more risk-averse as suggested by the promoting effect (Cameron and Shah, 2015; Cassar et al., 2017) and demand more information. Hotel groups may communicate health information to stakeholders using digital media such as websites (Liu, 2020). As the information demand during the COVID-19 pandemic is expected to be higher and organizations may want to describe and inform potential risks to their target groups through risk communication (Uğur and Akbıyık, 2020), we expect hotel chains to disclose more information on sustainability during the outbreak. Thus, the first research question is proposed as follows.

RQ1: Do hotel chains disclose more sustainability information during COVID-19?

As COVID-19 can be transmitted through human contact (Chan et al., 2020; Shereen et al., 2020) and impose significant risk on guests, tourists are more concerned about their health risks (Lepp and Gibson, 2003) and their safety (Simon, 2009; Wen et al., 2021). Therefore, it is necessary for hotel chains to disclose enough information to customers and other stakeholders to improve transparency and enhance confidence towards the hotel chains. During the SARS outbreak, transparency was documented to be able to assist the management in dealing with fear and uncertainty (Menon and Goh, 2005). It is thus important for hotel chains to disclose sufficient information, especially information related to COVID-19 to their stakeholders. To meet the information demand of stakeholders, hotel chains are expected to disclose all available information on the pandemic dimension. Hence, the second research question is developed as below.

RQ2: Do hotel chains disclose all available information on the pandemic dimension during COVID-19?

Research Methodology

This research uses content analysis as suggested by other studies (Bohdanowicz and Zientara, 2009, Font et al., 2012; Gröschl, 2011; Holcomb et al., 2007). Content analysis is defined as "a technique for gathering and analysing the content of text" (Neuman, 2003, 219) and it allows repeatability and valid inferences from data gathered (Krippendorff, 1980). The top ten hotel chains indicated in *Hotel Magazine 2019* according to the total number of rooms are investigated. Three of the ten hotel chains, Jin Jiang International (Holdings) Co. Ltd, Huazhu Group Ltd, and BTG Hotels (Group) Co. Ltd did not provide enough information in English. Due to the lack of manpower for translation, these three hotel chains were excluded. The list of hotel chains examined is shown in Table 4.1. We analysed the most updated information and reports available on the official websites of the hotel chains at the time of the study.

The Global Reporting Initiative (GRI) guidelines are the most widely used standards for measuring sustainability (Goswami and Lodhia, 2014; Luque-Vílchez and Larrinaga, 2016); hence, the framework of this study is based on the most updated GRI G4 guidelines. This study develops a sustainability disclosure framework which incorporates the dimensions proposed by the guidelines plus a pandemic dimension which is inspired by the study of Ikram et al. (2020). The sustainability reports and official websites of the hotel chains from February to July 2021 were analysed using content analysis. The data collection period is more than one year after the outbreak of COVID-19, allowing hotel chains enough time to disclose information related to COVID-19. The latest sustainability reports and resources available on the official websites at the time of the study were examined. In total, five sustainability reports and seven company official websites were analysed.

The framework consists of 32 indicators categorized into four dimensions and there are 3, 6, 10, and 13 indicators in the economic, environmental, social,

Table 4.1 Seven of the Top 10 International Hotel Groups

Hotel groups	*Headquarters*	*Number of countries operating in 2019*	*Number of hotels in 2019*	*Number of rooms in 2019*	*Legal form*	*Sustainability report*	*Year of data reported in sustainability report*
Marriott International, Inc. (Marriott)	US	131	7,163	1,348,532	Public	2020 Serve 360 Report	2019
Oyo Room (Oyo)	India	80	45,600	1,054,000	Private	N/A	N/A
Hilton Worldwide Holdings Inc. (Hilton)	US	119	6,110	971,780	Public	2020 Environmental, Social, and Governance (ESG) Report	2020
InterContinental Hotels Group (IHG)	UK	Over 100	5,903	883,563	Public	March 2021 Environmental, Social, and Governance Databook	2020
Choice Hotels International, Inc. (Choice)	US	Over 40	9,280	831,025	Public	2020 Environmental, Social, and Governance Report	2020
Wyndham Hotels and Resorts (Wyndham)	US	Over 90	5,036	739,537	Public	2020 Social Responsibility Report	2019
Accor Hotels (Accor)	France	110	7,153	590,897	Public	N/A	N/A

and pandemic dimensions, respectively. The codes are shown in the first column of Table 4.2. An open coding system was used. We analysed the information based on the disclosure guidelines of GRI. The binary scoring system was used for coding. "1" was assigned when related information was found and "0" was assigned otherwise. This coding system is regarded as being simple and can reduce subjectivity (Fonseca et al., 2011; Sánchez et al., 2015). The score of each sub-category represents the number of hotel chains that reported the item. For instance, in the economic dimension, if one indicator was present, a score of 1 was given. If two were present then a total score of 2 was given. If three were present, then a maximum score of 3 was allotted. A relative score was then calculated to compare the score of individual hotel groups to the hotel group which obtained the highest score in each dimension. Qualitative analysis on the extract of sustainability reports or information available on the official websites of the hotel chains was also conducted to provide more detailed information on the sustainability disclosure.

Findings

The profiles of the hotel groups investigated are outlined in Table 4.1. Of the seven hotel chains investigated, their headquarters are in different continents, four are from the United States, and the others are from the United Kingdom, France, and India respectively. Five of the hotel chains have "stand-alone" sustainability reports though the hotels do not include "sustainability report" in their report names. The information of sustainability reports of Hilton, IHG, and Choice is from 2020 and that of Marriott and Wyndham are based on 2019 information. All hotel chains are publicly traded and operate in different countries except for the third largest hotel, Oyo, which is a privately owned enterprise.

Economic Dimension Performance

Marriott, Hilton, IHG, Wyndham, and Accor performed best in the economic dimension, receiving a score of 2. All hotel groups disclosed their economic performance; specifically, Marriott, Hilton, IHG, and Wyndham included economic performance information in their stand-alone sustainability reports. For example, Marriott reported in its sustainability report the following.

> In 2019, over $20.9 billion in revenue was generated ... We contribute to tax-qualified retirement plans for the benefit of U.S. associates who meet certain eligibility requirements and choose to participate in the plans. Participating associates specify the percentage or amount of salary they wish to contribute from their compensation.

No hotels reported any information on market presence. Most of the hotel chains disclosed information on indirect economic impacts except Oyo and

Table 4.2 Descriptive Statistics of Content Analysis

	Marriott	*Oyo*	*Hilton*	*IHG*	*Choice*	*Wyndham*	*Accor*	*Total*
Economic (maximum score 3)								
Economic performance	1	1	1	1	1	1	1	7
Market presence	0	0	0	0	0	0	0	0
Indirect economic impacts	1	0	1	1	0	1	1	5
Total	**2**	**1**	**2**	**2**	**1**	**2**	**2**	**12**
% out of maximum score	**0.67**	**0.33**	**0.67**	**0.67**	**0.33**	**0.67**	**0.67**	**0.57**
Relative to highest score (1.00)	**1.00**	**0.50**	**1.00**	**1.00**	**0.50**	**1.00**	**1.00**	–
Environment (maximum score 6)								
Materials	0	0	0	0	0	0	0	0
Energy	1	0	1	1	0	1	1	5
Water and effluents	1	1	1	1	0	1	1	6
Biodiversity	1	0	1	1	0	0	1	4
Emissions	1	0	1	1	0	1	1	5
Effluents and waste	1	0	1	1	1	1	0	5
Total	**5**	**1**	**5**	**5**	**1**	**4**	**4**	**25**
% out of maximum score	**0.83**	**0.17**	**0.83**	**0.83**	**0.17**	**0.67**	**0.67**	**0.60**
Relative to highest score (1.00)	**1.00**	**0.20**	**1.00**	**1.00**	**0.20**	**0.80**	**0.80**	–
Social (maximum score 10)								
Employment	1	1	1	1	1	1	0	6
Labour/management relations	0	0	0	0	0	0	0	0
Training and education	1	1	1	1	1	1	1	7
Diversity and equal opportunity	1	0	1	1	0	1	1	5
Child labour	0	0	1	1	1	1	0	4
Forced or compulsory labour	0	0	1	1	1	1	0	4
Supplier social assessment	1	0	1	1	0	1	0	4

(*Continued*)

Table 4.2 (Continued)

	Marriott	*Oyo*	*Hilton*	*IHG*	*Choice*	*Wyndham*	*Accor*	*Total*
Local communities	1	1	1	1	1	1	1	7
Procurement practices	1	1	1	1	0	0	0	4
Customer health and safety (unrelated to COVID-19)	1	0	0	1	1	1	1	5
Total	**7**	**4**	**8**	**9**	**6**	**8**	**4**	**46**
% out of maximum score	**0.70**	**0.40**	**0.80**	**0.90**	**0.60**	**0.80**	**0.40**	**0.66**
Relative to highest score (1.00)	**0.78**	**0.44**	**0.89**	**1.00**	**0.67**	**0.89**	**0.44**	–
Pandemic (maximum score 13)								
Emergency response plan	0	1	1	0	0	0	0	2
Employee safety protection	1	1	1	1	1	1	1	7
Social distancing	1	1	1	1	1	1	1	7
Donation of masks	1	0	1	1	1	1	0	5
Provision of rooms for quarantine or medical staff	0	1	1	1	1	0	1	5
Saving strategy	1	0	0	0	0	0	0	1
Cost-cutting strategy	0	1	0	0	0	0	0	1
Layoff	0	0	0	0	0	0	0	0
Reskill programme	0	0	0	0	0	0	0	0
Rehire offer	0	1	1	0	0	0	0	2
Mental health of employees	0	1	0	0	0	0	0	1
Employee vaccination	1	1	1	0	0	0	1	4
COVID-19 test	1	0	1	1	1	0	1	5
Total	**6**	**8**	**8**	**5**	**5**	**3**	**5**	**40**
% out of maximum score	**0.46**	**0.62**	**0.62**	**0.38**	**0.38**	**0.23**	**0.38**	**0.44**
Relative to highest score (1.00)	**0.75**	**1.00**	**1.00**	**0.63**	**0.63**	**0.38**	**0.63**	–

Choice. Wyndham mentioned in its 2020 Social Responsibility Report the following.

> Wyndham Hotels and Resorts supported various charitable programs including youth and education, military, community and environmental programs in 2019 by donating $1,369,591.

Environment Dimension Performance

Marriott, Hilton, and IHG performed the best in the environment dimension by disclosing information on all environmental indicators except for the materials indicator which was not reported by any of the seven hotel chains. Marriott, Hilton, IHG, and Accor included information on biodiversity online. For instance, Marriott stated in its sustainability report the following.

> We have … commitment to support and enhance natural capital with projects and initiatives such as the Juma REDD+ … project in Brazil's Amazon rainforest, mangrove and coral restoration as well as reforestation efforts, and participating in fishery improvement projects in South America and Asia Pacific.

Five hotel chains reported information on energy, emissions, and effluents and waste. For instance, Hilton reported total energy consumption, total energy use intensity, and scope 1 to scope 3 emissions in its sustainability report. Water and effluents information indicator performed the best – six out of the seven hotel chains disclosed such information. Specifically, Hilton even reported water withdrawal (105,841 megalitres) and water withdrawal intensity (1,568 litres/ m^2) figures.

Determining Report Content: Social Dimension

The hotel group that performed the best in the social dimension was IHG which scored 9 and the hotel chains that obtained the least scores were Oyo and Accor, both with only 4 out of 10. Training and education, and local communities were the best performed indicators, with all hotels disclosing such information. The staff at Marriott can have their tuition fee reimbursed and have flexible schedules to attend school and training. Hotel chains also pay great effort on local communities. Hilton in the UK runs a special charity program called Springboard to provide "training and support to unemployed people … needed an influx of volunteers to assist trainees in the wake of COVID-19".

Five hotel chains disclosed in their websites or reports information on diversity and equal opportunity. Marriott reported that at the end of 2019, the board of directors was comprised of nine men and five women, while the proportion of females on the board of directors in Hilton was 44%. Four hotel chains emphasized the CSR of suppliers as this may have a social impact on society. Wyndham stated in its report that "In 2019 … had greater than 25% of procurable spend with suppliers that meet the Responsible Supplier criteria".

Pandemic Dimension Performance

Oyo and Hilton performed the best in the pandemic dimension, receiving a score of 8, followed by Marriott, with a score of 6; while IHG and Wyndham scored the least, with only 3. No hotel chains reported any information on layoffs and on reskill programs offered to existing or laid-off staff. Marriott was the only hotel chain that disclosed its saving strategy that "on March 18, 2020, Marriott disclosed that it had deferred renovations". Oyo declared "the next four Wednesdays, the 12th, 19th, and 26th of May 2021 and the 2nd of June 2021 as company holidays" as a way to cut the cost to deal with the effect of COVID-19. Two hotel chains disclosed their emergency plan regarding COVID-19. Hilton stated that it "developed and implemented Disaster Response Playbook", which "support[s] emergency preparedness before disaster strikes, provide[s] immediate aid in the aftermath of a disaster to our impacted Team Members".

The hotel chains paid a lot of attention to securing the health of customers. All of them disclosed information on how they maintained social distancing. For example, Oyo Rooms mentioned that customers may "use the OYO App or the link sent on your booking SMS to upload your ID ... seamlessly check-in even before you arrive ... enables social distancing" and Hilton offered "contactless food delivery by providing designated pick-up spots".

Five out of the seven hotel chains disclosed information on the donation of masks, provision of rooms for quarantine, and provision of COVID-19 tests. Hilton and IHG donated free rooms for medical professionals. Choice and Accor offered special rates to workers and volunteers serving the communities during the pandemic. Marriott, Hilton, IHG, Choice, and Accor offered COVID-19 testing on site at the hotels. In particular, Choice offered free COVID-19 tests to guests who stayed for at least three nights. Of the hotel chains investigated, four disclosed their support for the vaccination of employees. Marriott had a Vaccination Care Program which awarded vaccinated employees four hours of pay and provided flexible scheduling for vaccination appointments. Oyo even covered the vaccination costs of its staff and their families. Since COVID-19 greatly affects the revenue of the hospitality industry and has a severe effect on unemployment (United Nations, 2020), Oyo and Hilton provided re-employment opportunities to formal employees affected by COVID-19.

Discussion

The results indicate that the sustainability disclosure level of the hospitality industry was average. The social dimension was the most well-performed dimension with 0.66 (out of 100%), followed by the economic and environmental dimensions with 0.60 and 0.57, respectively. Unexpectedly, information disclosure related to COVID-19 performed the worst, obtaining only 0.44. The results do not support the hypothesis that COVID-19 has a positive impact on the sustainability disclosure level in the hospitality industry. The findings contradict our expectation that hotel chains tend to actively disclose more information to increase transparency to their stakeholders in order to maintain the legitimacy of their operations (Cho and Patten, 2007; Darrell and Schwartz, 1997) through sustainability reporting practices (Assaf et al., 2012; de Grosbois, 2012) during COVID-19.

As suggested by the "promoting effect", individuals who have been exposed to disasters before regarding the world as a more dangerous place (Cameron and Shah, 2015). With a fear of uncertainty and lack of control (Lerner and Keltner, 2001), they are more sensitive to risk and are therefore more risk-averse (Callen et al., 2014; Cassar et al., 2017). With the experience of infectious diseases such as SARS and MERS, we expected individuals to be more risk-averse and require hotel groups to reveal more information so as to reduce personal uncertainty. However, the findings suggested a consistent disclosure level in sustainability before and during the COVID-19 pandemic, suggesting the hotel groups did not perceive stakeholders to be solely dominated by the promoting effect. The results may imply another effect, namely the "inhibiting effect", which may also have a certain degree of influence. Regarding the inhibiting effect, individuals who compare current risk occurrences to past disaster experiences may conclude the current events to be less significant and hence are more inclined to take risks (Ben-Zur and Zeidner, 2009). Furthermore, past experiences in disasters may increase one's confidence to deal with high-risk situations (Aldwin, 2007).

As COVID-19 imposes significant risks on health and the economy, risk communication between hotel chains and stakeholders is important to disclose potential risks and to increase transparency. The findings did not support our expectation that hotel chains would report more information on the pandemic dimension to meet the information demand of stakeholders. Hotel chains rarely reported saving strategies and were also reluctant to disclose their cost-cutting measures and layoff information. However, one or two hotel groups reported their cost-cutting measures, suggesting that the hotel chains were in the pre-event and early symptom phase of the strategic framework of pandemic crisis management proposed by Le and Phi (2021). An alternative explanation for the lack of disclosure of saving and cost-cutting strategies could be that hotel chains were reluctant to disclose negative information to their stakeholders as this may affect their image (bad news). Negative corporate news has an adverse effect on the affinity of consumers toward their favourite brands (Sago and Hinnenkamp, 2014). On the other hand, the majority of the hotel chains disclosed their availability of free rooms to medical staff and donation of masks to the community. The hotel chains appeared to be more willing to report positive information as such disclosure could allow them to build a reputation and signal their high-quality products or services (Beatty and Ritter, 1986). This coincides with the findings that large companies tend to report selective information in their sustainability reports (Global Reporting Initiative, 2013) and hotel chains prepare sustainability reports for their own interests (Guix et al., 2019). Furthermore, the unsatisfactory sustainability disclosure performance may also be explained by the disempowerment of the sustainability teams of the hotel chains and the lack of knowledge, skills, or time to engage with and respond to stakeholders' needs (Guix et al., 2019).

Conclusion

The sustainability reporting level in the hospitality industry during the COVID-19 pandemic and the disclosure performance of different dimensions were examined through content analysis. The results indicated that the disclosure level of sustainability reporting was only average. The hotel chains did not show obvious signs that they were disclosing more sustainability information during the pandemic. The hotel chains appeared to have no intention to use online resources to communicate risks to their stakeholders or respond to the increasing transparency demanded by the stakeholders (Font et al., 2012), even during the COVID-19 crisis.

This study answers the call of Andrades et al. (2021) for the use of G4 guidelines for analysing sustainability reporting during the COVID-19 pandemic. The framework in this study incorporates the pandemic dimension which enables future studies to investigate the effect of COVID-19 on sustainability reporting. This study also allows standard-setters and governments to consider amending sustainability guidelines or the possibility of imposing legal requirements of sustainability reporting to improve the quality of information reported and prevent selective disclosure.

Finally, some limitations have to be mentioned. First, the framework used in this study was applied to a rather limited research context with only seven hotel chains investigated. In order to obtain better insight into sustainability reporting, future studies could be conducted with larger samples. Second, this study has only provided the sustainability reporting level during the COVID-19 pandemic. Future studies may investigate the long-term impact of the disease on sustainability disclosure in the industry. Third, the scoring system in this study merely indicates the presence of sustainability information but fails to investigate the depth of the reporting. More thorough examinations of the performance measurement systems employed in the hospitality industry are therefore recommended.

References

Adams, C.A. and Evans, R. (2004). Accountability, completeness, credibility and the audit expectations gap. *Journal of Corporate Citizenship*, 14(14), 97–115.

Agarwal, S. (2002). Restructuring seaside tourism: The resort lifecycle. *Annals of Tourism Research*, 29(1), 25–55.

Aldwin, C.A. (2007). *Stress, Coping, and Development: An Integrative Perspective.* New York: The Guilford Press.

Andrades, J., Larrán, M., Muriel, M.J., Calzado, M.Y. and Lechuga Sancho, M.P. (2021). Online sustainability disclosure by Spanish hospitals: An institutionalist approach. *International Journal of Public Sector Management*, 34(5), 529–545.

Assaf, A.G., Josiassen, A. and Cvelbar, L.K. (2012). Does Triple Bottom Line reporting improve hotel performance? *International Journal of Hospitality Management*, 31(2), 596–600.

Beatty, R.P. and Ritter, J.R. (1986). Investment banking, reputation, and the underpricing of initial public offerings. *Journal of Financial Economics*, 15(1), 213–232.

Ben-Zur, H. and Zeidner, M. (2009). Threat to life and risk-taking behaviors: A review of empirical findings and explanatory models. *Personality and Social Psychology Review*, 13(2), 109–128.

Bertrand, C. and Lecarpentier, E. (2021). COVID-19: A disaster. *Médecine de Catastrophe - Urgences Collectives*, 6(1), 45–48.

Bohdanowicz, P. and Zientara, P. (2009). Hotel companies' contribution to improving the quality of life of local communities and the well-being of their employees. *Tourism and Hospitality Research*, 9(2), 147–158.

Brockett, A.M. and Rezaee, Z. (2012). The future of business sustainability: Sustainability reporting and assurance. In Brockett, A.M. and Rezaee, Z. (Eds.), *Corporate Sustainability: Integrating Performance and Reporting*. Hoboken, NJ: John Wiley and Sons.

Callen, M., Isaqzadeh, M., Long, J.D. and Sprenger, C. (2014). Violence and risk preference: Experimental evidence from Afghanistan. *American Economic Review*, 104(1), 123–148.

Cameron, L. and Shah, M. (2015). Risk-taking behavior in the wake of natural disasters. *Journal of Human Resources*, 50(2), 484–515.

Carpenter, B.W. and Boyle, D.M. (2011). Testing goodwill for impairment: An optional consideration of qualitative factors. *The CPA Journal*, 8(11), 36–39.

Cassar, A., Healy, A. and Kessler, C. (2017). Trust, risk, and time preferences after a natural disaster: Experimental evidence from Thailand. *World Development*, 94, 90–105.

Chan, J.F., Yuan, S., Kok, K.H., To, K.K., Chu, H., Yang, J., Xing, F., Liu, J., Yip, C.C., Poon, R.W., Tsoi, H.W., Lo, S.K., Chan, K.H., Poon, V.K., Chan, W.M., Ip, J.D., Cai, J.P., Cheng, V.C., Chen, H., Hui, C.K. and Yuen, K.Y. (2020). A familial cluster of pneumonia associated with the 2019 novel coronavirus indicating person-to-person transmission: A study of a family cluster. *The Lancet*, 395(10223), 514–523.

Cho, C.H. and Patten, D.M. (2007). The role of environmental disclosures as tools of legitimacy: A research note. *Accounting, Organizations and Society*, 32(7–8), 639–647.

Cró, S. and Martins, A. (2017). Structural breaks in international tourism demand: Are they caused by crises or disasters? *Tourism Management*, 63, 3–9.

Darrell, W. and Schwartz, B.N. (1997). Environmental disclosures and public policy pressure. *Journal of Accounting and Public Policy*, 16(2), 125–154.

de Grosbois, D. (2012). Corporate social responsibility reporting by the global hotel industry: Commitment, initiatives and performance. *International Journal of Hospitality Management*, 31(3), 896–905.

Dodds, R. and Kuehnel, J. (2010). CSR among Canadian mass tour operators: Good awareness but little action. *International Journal of Contemporary Hospitality Management*, 22(2), 221–244.

Dyllick, T. and Hockerts, K. (2002). Beyond the business case for corporate sustainability. *Business Strategy and the Environment*, 11(2), 130–141.

Elkington, J. (1997). *Cannibals with Forks, the Triple Bottom Line of 21st Century Business*. Oxford: Capstone Publishing.

Faulkner, B. (2001). Towards a framework for tourism disaster management. *Tourism Management*, 22(2), 135–147.

Fonseca, A., Macdonald, A., Dandy, E. and Valenti, P. (2011). The state of sustainability reporting at Canadian universities. *International Journal of Sustainability in Higher Education*, 12(1), 22–40.

Font, X., Walmsley, A., Cogotti, S., McCombes, L. and Häusler, N. (2012). Corporate social responsibility: The disclosure–performance gap. *Tourism Management*, 33(6), 1544–1553.

Franzoni, S. and Avellino, M. (2019). Sustainability reporting in international hotel chains. *Emerging Issues in Management*, 1(1), 96–107.

Fuchs, G. and Reichel, A. (2006). Tourist destination risk perception: The case of Israel. *Journal of Hospitality and Leisure Marketing*, 14(2), 83–108.

Fuchs, G. and Reichel, A. (2011). An exploratory inquiry into destination risk perceptions and risk reduction strategies of first time vs. repeat visitors to a highly volatile destination. *Tourism Management*, 32(2), 266–276.

Garza, N.L. (2011). Effect of ecolabels in context on perceived sustainability. *Undergraduate Honors College*. Corvallis, OR: Oregon State University.

Global Reporting Initiative. (2013). *G4 Sustainability Reporting Guidelines*. Amsterdam: GRI.

Goswami, K. and Lodhia, S. (2014). Sustainability disclosure patterns of South Australian local councils: A case study. *Public Money and Management*, 34(4), 273–280.

Gröschl, S. (2011). Diversity management strategies of global hotel groups. *International Journal of Contemporary Hospitality Management*, 23(2), 224–240.

Guix, M., Bonilla-Priego, M.J. and Font, X. (2018). The process of sustainability reporting in international hotel groups: An analysis of stakeholder inclusiveness, materiality and responsiveness. *Journal of Sustainable Tourism*, 26(7), 1063–1084.

Guix, M., Font, X. and Bonilla-Priego, M.J. (2019). Materiality: Stakeholder accountability choices in hotels' sustainability reports. *International Journal of Contemporary Hospitality Management*, 31(6), 2321–2338.

Hao, F., Xiao, Q. and Chon, K. (2020). COVID-19 and China's hotel industry: Impacts, a disaster management framework, and post-pandemic agenda. *International Journal of Hospitality Management*, 90, 102636.

Herremans, I.M., Nazari, J.A. and Mahmoudian, F. (2016). Stakeholder relationships, engagement, and sustainability reporting. *Journal of Business Ethics*, 138(3), 417–435.

Holcomb, J.L., Upchurch, R.S. and Okumus, F. (2007). Corporate social responsibility: What are top hotel companies reporting? *International Journal of Contemporary Hospitality Management*, 19(6), 461–475.

Hume, N. and Sanderson, H. (2020). Gold chief calls for common ESG reporting standard. *Financial Times*, 19 October, 2020.

Ikram, M., Zhang, Q., Sroufe, R. and Ferasso, M. (2020). The social dimensions of corporate sustainability: An integrative framework including COVID-19 insights. *Sustainability*, 12(20), 8747.

Jayawardena, C., Pollard, A., Chort, V., Choi, C. and Kibicho, W. (2013). Trends and sustainability in the Canadian tourism and hospitality industry. *Worldwide Hospitality and Tourism Themes*, 5(2), 132–150.

Jones, P., Hillier, D. and Comfort, D. (2014). Sustainability in the global hotel industry. *International Journal of Contemporary Hospitality Management*, 26(1), 5–17.

Khatter, A., McGrath, M., Pyke, J., White, L. and Lockstone-Binney, L. (2019). Analysis of hotels' environmentally sustainable policies and practices. *International Journal of Contemporary Hospitality Management*, 31(6), 2394–2410.

Khatter, A., White, L., Pyke, J. and McGrath, M. (2021). Barriers and drivers of environmental sustainability: Australian hotels. *International Journal of Contemporary Hospitality Management*, 33(5), 1830–1849.

Krippendorff, K. (1980). *Content Analysis: An Introduction to its Methodology*. London: Sage.

Landrum, N.E. and Ohsowski, B. (2018). Identifying worldviews on corporate sustainability: A content analysis of corporate sustainability reports. *Business Strategy and the Environment*, 27(1), 128–151.

Le, D. and Phi, G. (2021). Strategic responses of the hotel sector to COVID-19: Toward a refined pandemic crisis management framework. *International Journal of Hospitality Management*, 94, 102808.

Lepp, A. and Gibson, H. (2003). Tourist roles, perceived risk and international tourism. *Annals of Tourism Research*, 30(3), 606–624.

Lerner, J.S. and Keltner, D. (2001). Fear, anger, and risk. *Journal of Personality and Social Psychology*, 81(1), 146–159.

Li, Z., Zhang, S., Liu, X., Kozak, M. and Wen, J. (2020). Seeing the invisible hand: Underlying effects of COVID-19 on tourists' behavioral patterns. *Journal of Destination Marketing and Management*, 18, 100502.

Liu, P.L. (2020). COVID-19 information seeking on digital media and preventive behaviors: The mediation role of worry. *Cyberpsychology, Behavior, and Social Networking*, 23(10), 677–682.

Lo, A.S., Cheung, C. and Law, R. (2011). Hong Kong residents' adoption of risk reduction strategies in leisure travel. *Journal of Travel and Tourism Marketing*, 28(3), 240–260.

Luque-Vílchez, M. and Larrinaga, C. (2016). Reporting models do not translate well: Failing to regulate CSR reporting in Spain. *Social and Environmental Accountability Journal*, 36(1), 56–75.

Menon, K.U. and Goh, K.T. (2005). Transparency and trust: Risk communications and the Singapore experience in managing SARS. *Journal of Communication Management*, 9(4), 375–383.

Mitchell, V.W. and Vassos, V. (1998). Perceived risk and risk reduction in holiday purchases: A cross-cultural and gender analysis. *Journal of Euromarketing*, 6(3), 47–79.

Neuman, W.L. (2003). *Social Research Methods: Qualitative and Quantitative Approaches*. New York, NY: Allyn and Bacon.

Novelli, M., Gussing Burgess, L., Jones, A. and Ritchie, B.W. (2018). "No Ebola … still doomed" – The Ebola-induced tourism crisis. *Annals of Tourism Research*, 70, 76–87.

Okumus, F., Altinay, M. and Arasli, H. (2005). The impact of Turkey's economic crisis of February 2001 on the tourism industry in Northern Cyprus. *Tourism Management*, 26(1), 95–104.

Pérez, A. and Rodríguez del Bosque, I. (2014). Sustainable development and stakeholder relations management: Exploring sustainability reporting in the hospitality industry from a SD-SRM approach. *International Journal of Hospitality Management*, 42, 174–187.

Prarie, P. (2012). A critical look at hotel sustainability. Available at: http://www.huffingtonpost.com/pattiprairie/a-critical-look-at-hotel-_b_1471188.html

Qi, G., Zeng, S., Yin, H. and Lin, H. (2013). ISO and OHSAS certifications. *Management Decision*, 51(10), 1983–2005.

Rahman, I., Park, J. and Chi, C.G. (2015). Consequences of "greenwashing": Consumers' reactions to hotels' green initiatives. *International Journal of Contemporary Hospitality Management*, 27(6), 1054–1081.

Richards, G. and Derek, H. (2000). *Tourism and Sustainable Community Development*. London: Routledge.

Ritchie, B.W. (2004). Chaos, crises and disasters: A strategic approach to crisis management in the tourism industry. *Tourism Management*, 25(6), 669–683.

Roblek, V., Milenkovska, V. and Milojica, V. (2016). *The Impact of Corporate Sustainability in Achieving Business Goals in Hotel Industry*. University of Rijeka, Faculty of Tourism and Hospitality Management.

Sago, B. and Hinnenkamp, C. (2014). The impact of significant negative news on consumer behavior towards favorite brands. *Global Journal of Business Research*, 8(1), 65–72.

Sánchez, R.G., Bolívar, M.P.R. and Hernandez, A.M.L. (2015). Are Australian universities making good use of ICT for CSR reporting? *Sustainability*, 7(11), 14895–14916.

Shereen, M.A., Khan, S., Kazmi, A., Bashir, N. and Siddique, R. (2020). COVID-19 infection: Emergence, transmission, and characteristics of human coronaviruses. *Journal of Advanced Research*, 24, 91–98.

Simon, H. (2009). The crisis and customer behaviour: Eight quick solutions. *Journal of Customer Behaviour*, 8(2), 177–186.

Statista. (2020). Predicted employment loss in the travel and tourism industry due to the corona virus (COVID-19) pandemic world-wide in 2020, by region. Available at: www.statista.com/statistics/1104835/coronavirus-travel-tourism-employment-loss/

Tett, G. (2020). The alphabet soup of green standards needs a new recipe. *Financial Times*, 16 January.

Tonne, C. (2021). Lessons from the COVID-19 pandemic for accelerating sustainable development. *Environmental Research*, 193, 110482–110482.

Uğur, N.G. and Akbıyık, A. (2020). Impacts of COVID-19 on global tourism industry: A cross-regional comparison. *Tourism Management Perspectives*, 36, 100744.

United Nations. (2020). Reskill young people for green jobs, address COVID-19 crisis through fiscal action, secretary-general stresses at "Rebirthing the Global Economy" round table. Available at: https://www.un.org/press/en/2020/sgsm20229.doc.htm

Wang, J. and Ritchie, B. (2011). A theoretical model for strategic crisis planning: Factors influencing crisis planning in the hotel industry. *International Journal of Tourism Policy*, 3(4), 297–317.

Wen, J., Wang, W., Kozak, M., Liu, X. and Hou, H. (2021). Many brains are better than one: The importance of interdisciplinary studies on COVID-19 in and beyond tourism. *Tourism Recreation Research*, 46(2), 310–313.

World Bank. (2004). *Corporate Social Responsibility*. Available at http://www.worldbank.org

World Economic Forum. (2017). The travel and tourism competitiveness report 2017. Geneva: World Economic Forum Reports.

Worldometer. (2021). Available at: https://www.worldometers.info/coronavirus

5 The Reciprocal Nature of CSR

A Case Study of Macau

Weng Si Lei, Fernando Lourenço, and Kim Ieng Loi

Introduction

This chapter attempts to explain the corporate social responsibility (CSR) responses of companies on COVID-19 based on stakeholder theory. A case study of Macau was conducted to examine the types of CSR strategies taken up during the severe period of the pandemic in the city in 2020. CSR-related stakeholder theory (Freeman, 1984; Freeman and Evan, 1990) from the field of organisational sociology suggests that business behaviour is not always guided by rational economic decisions aiming to maximise financial benefits and it could be sometimes reciprocal in nature (Hahn, 2015). External environmental factors such as regulations, norms, values, beliefs, and traditions will influence managerial and organisational decisions and behaviours. Organisations respond to the pressures and expectations of various stakeholders because they need to gain legitimacy to be regarded as socially acceptable and appropriate (Meyer and Rowan, 1977).

According to Scott (1995), there are three pillars that provide legitimacy to an organisation's behaviour and influence its structure and practice. They are regulative, normative, and cognitive ones. Scott's framework is widely adopted to investigate how environmental factors shape organisational behaviour. Organisations respond to the pressure from these institutional constituencies and, consequently, gain legitimacy by conforming with the regulations, norms, values, beliefs, and expectations (DiMaggio and Powell, 1983; Meyer and Rowan, 1977; Scott, 1995; Zucker, 1977). In recent years, there are examples of hospitality-related studies that apply CSR theory to explain phenomena such as the adaptation of environmental management (DeBoer et al., 2017; Mensah and Blankson, 2013; Ouyang et al., 2019; Zhu et al., 2013), CSR reporting (De Grosbois, 2016), investment in experiential learning (Dice et al., 2019), anti-smoking regulations (Simons et al., 2016), and explicit and implicit CSR to engage stakeholders (Kumar et al., 2019).

In this study, the authors investigate the biggest enterprises in Macau, and examine the CSR strategies implemented by them through the lens of stakeholder theory. Through this case study, the authors aim to understand the nature of CSR activities taking place during the pandemic outbreak. A qualitative research approach is adopted to seek insights from the companies' CSR

DOI: 10.4324/9781003274575-6

strategies to cope with the pandemic. The findings reveal the genres of CSR strategies executed by the case companies and explained within the framework of stakeholder theory.

Research Background

The impact of the COVID-19 pandemic is unprecedented and worldwide, affecting all sectors. Among them, hospitality and tourism practitioners around the world have demonstrated serious concern for both survival during the pandemic and recovery and rebound afterward. It is also with this objective that the World Tourism Organization (UNWTO) published the *Global Guidelines to Restart Tourism* at the end of May 2020 (UNWTO, 2020). Macau has recorded some of the world's lowest figures of reported confirmed cases (82 cases at the time of writing). Nonetheless, the government has established the "Novel Coronavirus Response and Coordination Centre" to handle and manage related matters. The centre is actively operating daily.

On 22 January 2020 the first case of COVID-19 was confirmed in Macau. Then, the government ordered an unprecedented closure of the casinos for 15 days from 5 February 2020. It is worth noting that 86% of total government revenue originates from gaming tax revenue (Macau Statistics and Census Department, 2020b). The closure affected not only casinos but also spilled over to hotels and the entire tourism industry, in which visitor arrivals dropped by 99.7% and the average hotel occupancy rate plunged by 78.6% year-on-year in April 2020 (Macau Statistics and Census Department, 2020a, 2020c). Before the pandemic, Macau received 28 million tourists (or 71% of its total tourist arrivals) from mainland China in 2019 (Macau Statistics and Census Department, 2020c). With the COVID-19 outbreak, thousands of hotel rooms remained vacant and hotel operators struggled to continue operation while learning how to handle the pandemic, which is so different from previous disease outbreaks, such as SARS, Ebola, and Zika, all of which were concentrated in a particular region instead of the whole world. Besides, group tour visas and individual traveller schemes from mainland China to Macau were all suspended. The normally vibrant city suddenly became deserted.

Nevertheless, the tourism and hospitality industry in which the biggest corporations nested has been actively promoting CSR as seen in local newspapers throughout the pandemic period. The authors thus question this interesting phenomenon and aim to examine the rationale behind all the CSR practices seen. Even with some scattered developments of the pandemic in 2021, the number of cases in Macau is still considered to be very low and this is believed to be the result of the government's firm management of the situation. With the determined management of the local government over the pandemic and various CSR practices seen and implemented by the corporations, the authors believe that Macau offers a unique testing bed to examine CSR strategies during the pandemic situation.

Literature Review

Corporate Social Responsibility and Business Management

Corporate social responsibility has become an accepted management concept and its relevance is being recognised by companies (Doh and Guay, 2006; Husted and Salazar, 2006; Matten and Moon, 2004; Moon, 2011). The concept of CSR is still disputed from a definitional standpoint, but the core idea of managing business processes to produce a positive impact on society is generally agreed upon. The European Commission emphasises the importance of CSR, defining it as a way to include social and environmental concerns in the conduct of business and the interaction with stakeholders (European Commission, 2011a, 2014). Being responsible is argued to have the potential to enhance various common goals such as social cohesion, more rational use of natural resources, and economic competitiveness (European Commission, 2011b, 2014). The relationship between corporate social performance and financial performance has been well documented in numerous studies (Hasan et al., 2018; Martinuzzi et al., 2011; Orlitzky et al., 2003; Peloza, 2009; Podsakoff and MacKenzie, 1997; Waddock and Graves, 1997). In essence, the recent development of CSR in the management field indicates its increasing relevance and wide business acceptance.

Perspectives of Corporate of Social Responsibility

The literature section reviews the earlier view of corporate responsibility by Friedman (1962, 1970) on looking after the needs of shareholders, and later his view linking to the real concept of CSR, which he values. The literature indicates different perspectives of the concept. In the classical view of CSR, Milton Friedman demonstrates the positive link between corporate social performance and financial performance while arguing that governments should be in charge of preventing and solving social problems caused by fraudulent business practices instead of these being dealt with by individual businesses. For this reason, the only responsibility of a business is to maximise return to shareholders as long as it stays within the rules of the game, that is to engage in open and free competition without deception or fraud (Friedman, 1962, 1970). As such, if sustainability or CSR initiatives fail to maximise shareholder value and profit (i.e., *corporate altruism*) then they are seen as wasteful and detrimental to the competitiveness and efficiency of the firm (i.e., *it is irrelevant*) (Husted and Salazar, 2006; Lourenço, 2013). On the other hand, the advocates of stakeholder theory suggest that businesses should benefit not only shareholders but also a wider range of stakeholders (Freeman, 1984).

In order to clarify the variety of stakeholder perspectives, the conceptualisation of corporate environmental performance as explained in Slater and Dixon-Fowler (2010) is adopted. According to them, there are two fundamental perspectives of stakeholder theory: normative and instrumental. From the normative perspective, businesses should not allow negative externalities to affect social well-being

(Donaldson and Preston, 1995). For this reason, businesses have a moral obligation to consider their societal and environmental impact (Bowen, 1953; Carroll, 1979; Donaldson and Preston, 1995; Frederick, 1960). Therefore, activities and initiatives related to sustainable development and CSR belong to their rightful moral responsibilities and obligations (i.e., *doing right*) (Lourenço, 2013). On the other hand, the instrumental perspective of stakeholder theory has an indirect link to the classical Friedman approach because it contends that engaging in socially responsible initiatives is necessary (instrumental) to comply with minimum social expectations and avoid being sued, fined, or subject to consumer boycotts and decreased sales (Husted and Salazar, 2006) (i.e., *doing what is necessary*) (Lourenço, 2013). Eventually, a firm can strategically use sustainability and CSR initiatives to promote self-interest and use it as a form of social investment to improve productivity and profit-maximisation to benefit shareholders in return (Husted and Salazar, 2006). It is apparent that this instrumental perspective of stakeholder theory fits well with Friedman's classical view and provides business justification for responsible initiatives (Freeman and Evan, 1990; Jones, 1995; Slater and Dixon-Fowler, 2010). Nevertheless, sustainability and CSR initiatives from this avenue are not perceived as "responsibility" per se. These are only perceived as instruments to improve productivity and profit-maximisation (i.e., *doing well*) (Lourenço, 2013). In essence, regardless of the various perspectives, one can carry out CSR instrumentally (or strategically), altruistically, or egoistically towards their business interest.

A Societal Approach

van Marrewijk (2013, 647) advocates the societal approach which indicates that companies are part of and responsible to the society. This is particularly true for companies whose operations require licences, for example producing public goods or operations which are essential to the society's needs. These companies have to constantly react to changing circumstances that generate corporate challenges. There are three main reasons for companies to react: (1) they feel obliged to do it; (2) they are made to do it, and (3) they want to do it. Therefore, a balance of the triadic relationship between and among state (government), business, and civic society is proposed (van Marrewijk, 2013, 648). Each party has a role and a set of specific goals to fulfil in the society. They all operate under their configuration to perform their role and reach specific goals. van Marrewijk (2013) advocates that institutional arrangements from the past, when norms and common values were led by the government and imposed on businesses, should transform and redefine their roles and relationships with others. Values and norms realised by the civic society are to be responded to by the government and businesses together.

As the enterprises under this study are all hospitality and tourism related, the authors also reviewed CSR studies in hospitality and tourism in the past decade. There is a range of studies examining different dimensions and aspects of CSR and the stream has been growing. For example, Loi et al. (2021) and Shin et al.

(2021) examine the strategies adopted by hotel operators towards their support for various stakeholders during the COVID-19 pandemic. The study of Gu et al. (2013) examines Chinese hotel operators' actions in defending consumer and labour rights. There are studies that examine the philanthropy work conducted by hotel operators (Gard McGehee et al., 2009; Loi et al., 2021; Shin et al., 2021). The study of Chung (2020) looks at the impact of green hotel management as an important CSR and green-marketing strategy. The main motivation to promote CSR has been summarised in the work of Serra-Cantallops et al. (2018). Their systematic literature review suggests that motivation can be related to altruistic reasons and manager's personal values such as environmental protection and social commitment, ethics, and morals. Economic reasons can be related to cost reduction and branding. Engaging in CSR can also be motivated by the need to build their legitimacy and regulative pressure. The literature review provides multiple perspectives to look through the case of Macau, in particular on the CSR strategies implemented during the COVID-19 pandemic.

In summary, the literature indicates three CSR approaches: normative perspective (a moral obligation to business stakeholders), instrument/business-case perspective (a business strategy to serve multiple stakeholders), and the classical Friedman perspective (irrelevant or instrumentally adopted as a business strategy to serve shareholders). These perspectives can be plotted on a spectrum, moving from the normative to the instrument and the classical instrumental perspective. For instance, the sustainability movement has used "blame-game" and awareness-building exercises to criticise the world of commerce (Carson, 1962; Klein, 2001; Meadows et al., 1972). However, environmental concerns are viewed as additional costs and not as a way to improve economic performance, policy decisions, and daily operations (Starik et al., 2010). The recent literature is more positive and instrumental as it suggests that sustainability and CSR initiatives can be used to build competitive advantage and to improve financial performance (Hart and Milstein, 1999, 2003; Hawken, 1993; Hawken et al., 1999; van Marrewijk, 2013).

Research Method

As the situation of COVID-19 is unprecedented and there are only scant studies previously relating to the pandemic and the hospitality industry, a qualitative research approach is considered suitable to investigate and explore insights from the hoteliers on CSR strategies adopted under this situation. A constructivist approach is employed in this study (Berger and Luckmann, 1991). The approach is suitable to investigate the phenomenon in which access to participants of the situation is crucial to the investigation. Integrated resorts are the primary targets due to their scale and casino operations.

To gain insights into the strategies implemented, managerial level and above personnel from six integrated resorts (covering all six gaming concessionaires) are invited. For those who may not be familiar with the situation in Macau, the gaming industry was liberalised in 2002 with licences granted to six concessionaires who operate various integrated resorts and hotels in Macau and these resorts and hotels form the major room suppliers in the local tourism industry and are the major tax contributors. Seven respondents, who are all senior management personnel with an average of ten years of industry experience and have held executive management positions at the hotels for an average of more than three years are received. In-depth interviews are arranged to obtain insights concerning the situation. Due to the senior nature of the respondents, all of them are in a position to provide their views and experience of the construction of the situation (Berger and Luckmann, 1991). Interview questions are designed based on the research questions as well as the updated development of the pandemic situation. A chronological list of the happenings in Macau assisted the interviewer and the interviewees, particularly in inspiring questions for further discussion (Roberts, 2020). Table 5.1 shows the participants' profiles.

The interviews were mostly carried out either at the coffee shops of the informants' hotels or at their offices. Chinese or English was used to conduct the interviews and the language choice was subject to the preference of the interviewees. Interview data were transcribed verbatim and coded accordingly. Coding was first done individually by the research team members, and codes generated by each member were then compared to cross-check the inter-rater reliability. After two rounds of comparison and cross-checking, an inter-rater reliability of 0.90 was achieved. Data analysis was performed by following the steps of data reduction delineated by Huberman and Miles (2002) and data were structured according to the method of Gioia et al. (2013) which is a systematic approach to inductive research. Among the key themes generated from the data analysis, the ones most relevant to the topic of this chapter are selected and reported in the section below. They are human resources tactics, financial aids, quarantine hotels, face masks donation, and other CSR initiatives.

Table 5.1 Participants' Profiles

Participant	*Gender*	*Position*	*Years with company*	*Year(s) in current position*
H1	Female	Financial Controller (equivalent to Director of Finance)	14	4
H2	Female	Director in Human Resources Department	11	3
H3	Female	Senior Vice President in Marketing	16	1
H4	Male	Director in Human Resources	12	6
H5	Female	Director in Human Resources	14	4
H6	Male	Director in Retails (equivalent to Retail Director)	7	3
H7	Male	Vice President in Operations	5	5

Findings

Human Resources Tactics and Financial Aids

The nosedive of tourist arrivals due to the pandemic severely impacted the entire hotel and gaming industry. Fear of losing jobs among hoteliers and people engaging in related businesses was widespread. Different human resources tactics were carried out by the mega-resorts to calm down or prevent the fear of the staff. One interviewee depicted:

> Our normal occupancy is around 100% and now is 1.9%. Average above 95% per month. From 3,000 rooms, now we have 60 rooms occupied, but these people are here more on a long-term stay. So of course, for workers who are responsible for these rooms, now they are not needed. In the beginning, the staff was in denial. But for us, we have a simple four-step strategy. 1) ask you to take your annual leave, 2) take no-pay leave, and 3) reduce working hours, then 4) offer training if you are there, this is the journey. In each stage, people will resist and do not agree because everyone had planned but then accepted the reality as the whole world is in this together.
>
> (Interviewee H4)

Unfortunately, laying off staff becomes unavoidable during such difficult times. When asking about the plan to laying off staff, one interviewee responded:

> I bet all properties want to, but not many dare to do it. You know … our CE mentioned CSR, right … you will lay off unless you dare to bet on the renewal of your gaming license. Everybody knows it!
>
> (Interviewee H5)

Laying off local staff seems to be a very sensitive issue, so some hotels aim at expatriates. A director in human resources explained:

> You know, ex-pats are expensive. Although they have been here long but I think it is sensible to lay off one senior management person (an ex-pat) in which could cover … say maybe a small team of staff. I bet they won't complain and probably they are very well compensated before dismissal.
>
> (Interviewee H1)

Another interviewee expressed:

> All six operators have massive investments in Macau. Everyone wants to make sure they can continue their success. Continue to serve and do the right thing. When it comes to the decision to WHY NOT renew, we need to make sure we are doing the right things and the government also wants to make sure we operate responsibly. We have been very supportive of the

> people, people still being employed and not let go, so this meets the expectation of the Chief Executive.
>
> (Interviewee H7)

While hotels struggle to reduce manpower costs, it is interesting to learn that one hotel offered financial aid to its staff. The hotel offered MOP 1,000 (approximately USD 125) cash coupons to its 13,600 staff. The money was advised to be spent at local small-and-medium enterprises (SMEs) to further support the local economy during this tough time. Corporate social responsibility was the reason for keeping local employment intact to minimise the harm that already dampened the local economy. In addition to retaining local staff, hotels went the extra mile to boost up their sense of social responsibility by offering financial aid to staff with the aim to create an economic spill-over effect on the society (reduced financial stress and increased propensity to consume which may benefit multiple facets of the economic sectors, especially local SMEs).

This action indeed echoed very much the government's direction in launching a series of economic relief schemes, for example, electronic vouchers (USD 1,000 per citizen) for local consumption to be spent between May and December 2020. Supporting SMEs has always been a government policy consideration for the city. Even during normal times, the government implemented various supporting policies towards their survival and development. The government has reiterated the same direction during this pandemic to help SMEs sail through the challenges.

Quarantine Hotels

Corporate social responsibility is further acknowledged by a few interviewees whose hotels had been made available to house Macau citizens returning from overseas for the 14-day medical quarantine. The interviewees declared various concerns such as the potential negative impact on the hotel branding, arousing guests' anxiety, and operational difficulties. Nevertheless, they also asserted the importance of making the properties available for medical observation due to the pandemic situation as they knew that the city had limited space and insufficient hospital beds and facilities for such purposes. One interviewee expressed:

> CSR is not about donations, photo-taking, and showing off. CSR is about a genuine way to help the community ... like helping SMEs, the elderly, even animals, etc. ... it is about doing it, with genuine care, not just about photo opportunities.
>
> (Interviewee H3)

Despite the challenges, some interviewees mentioned that this could be an effective branding exercise for the hotel as well; however, the costs and benefits have to be weighed up cautiously. One interviewee shared:

> The cost is huge if your property has been used for medical observation ... sanitising, hygiene, concerns raised by staff, and future customers. Well,

> we did not avail our property so … we are not sure but I think that's great marketing.
>
> (Interviewee: H6)

In fact, volunteering to be a quarantine hotel seems to be very well received as a proper CSR act, while earning minimally to cover operating costs. One financial controller shared her view:

> Instead of idling the operation team, it could be a sensible act to volunteer to be a quarantine hotel. At least, MOP800 a night is guaranteed for each guest's stay. You know … vacant room is also costly to maintain.
>
> (Interviewee: H1)

Face Mask Donation and Other CSR Initiatives

Between February and March 2020, when face masks were in short supply, all participants' hotels donated face masks to the government, local charity organisations, schools, and non-profit-making associations. One interviewee revealed:

> Our priority is the safety of our team members e.g., preorder more face masks and gloves to protect them while they are on duty. Other than that, availing masks for donation comes second.
>
> (Interviewee: H2)

The interviewees revealed that a pandemic is a time to show their support to the society. One participant disclosed that the hotel had sourced face masks around the globe, as early as the beginning of February, to be able to make face mask donation possible to the local community. The face mask cost and freight charge were huge.

In addition to face mask donation, the participants also reported that their companies have taken CSR very seriously during this difficult time in the society. Examples as reported by interviewees include:

> Waiving monthly rental for shops in the property. Allowing retailers to operate during reduced operating hours to minimise manning costs. Organising local events inside the hotel property for SMEs to showcase their products and create business opportunities.
>
> (Interviewee: H6)

Discussion and Conclusion

CSR beyond Compliance Practice: Stakeholder Theory View

The data reveal that all six integrated resorts had done much more than expected conventionally from a CSR perspective, particularly from the stakeholder theory;

whereas, ensuring competitive advantage in order to enhance stakeholder value is the ultimate goal. In the case of Macau, implementing various human resources tactics to minimise laying off staff could be seen as abnormal especially during this tough time. When tourist arrivals dropped by more than 90% and the hotel occupancy rate was in single digits, staff retention seemed to be suicidal behaviour to many outsiders. All the integrated resorts tried their best to conduct CSR, to a point that was close to a cut-throat approach of engaging in a free-market price war. All these CSR activities were very costly. The financial aid of MOP1,000 (USD125) per staff offered by one hotel could cost MOP10 million-plus (USD1.6 million), which easily surpassed a CSR budget which is a normal 2% of net profit for a multinational corporation (KPMG, 2020). So, what was behind all these intriguing CSR activities that were taken way beyond compliance practice? One key reason may be that all these happened at the dawn of a period when the gaming concession licences were maturing and under review for renewal soon. The licences are expected to be renewed in December 2022.

Every enterprise is trying hard to meet the government expectation and wish to gain legitimacy to be regarded as socially acceptable and appropriate (Meyer and Rowan, 1977), especially during this special time – the COVID-19 pandemic. However, the government's expectation is largely inexplicit, except those listed clearly in the licensing agreement; for example, to facilitate the development of Macau to become a destination for regional tourism, leisure gaming, convention, and exhibition with international standards (Macau Gaming History, 2014). The outbreak of COVID-19 has ignited the game of CSR. Understanding the companies' behaviour is beyond the normative and instrumental perspective of stakeholder theory conventionally applied; whereas, expectations from the government, which has an upper hand in the gaming concessions, play a key role. Because of the inexplicit expectations from the government, all integrated resorts (gaming concessionaires) are trying their best to offer what they believe is socially acceptable and appropriate, such as staff retention, volunteering to provide quarantine hotels, masks donation, and organising all other activities to boost up CSR. While the government has expectations of the hotel businesses to spare resources to cooperate, simultaneously, the society also has expectations of the hotel businesses to do good.

According to the societal approach (van Marrewijk, 2013) of stakeholder theory and the findings of the case study, the authors depict the reciprocal relationship between and among the government, society, and the hotels (gaming concessionaires) in Figure 5.1.

During this global disaster of COVID-19, the society expects different levels of financial aid from the government, while it is striving hard to secure job employment. Policies include offering interest-free loans and setting up a specialised office to offer aid and support to SMEs to enhance business survival and minimise staff lay-off (DSEDT, 2022). On the other hand, the government expects various levels of CSR to be conducted by gaming operators. As reflected from the data collected, the gaming operators tried hard to conduct different CSR actions so as to earn credits towards being socially responsible. It is believed that the more

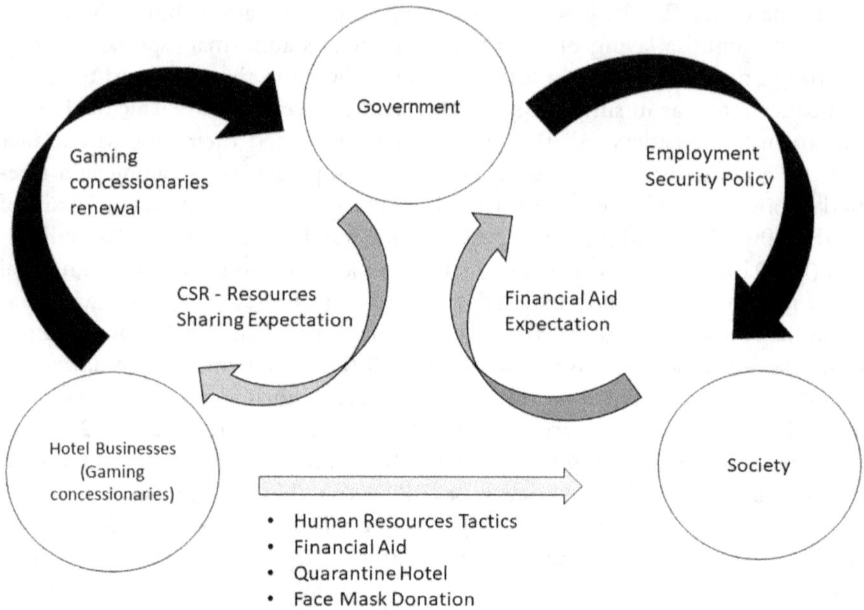

Figure 5.1 Reciprocal Nature of CSR

CSR actions made, the better the chance of securing a gaming licence renewal. As the government is still reviewing the licence renewal terms and conditions, uncertainties are there and all concessionaires are very much concerned about the new terms and conditions.

To some extent, the government is playing the game right. They are manoeuvring their regulative institution successfully, to trigger self-regulative compliance and beyond compliance acts of altruism and CSR from the gaming operators. This shows a very good case of how the government can stimulate CSR by targeting where it truly matters. But, of course, it works because of the largely lucrative gaming market here in the city of Macau. Again, the moral of the story is to target where it really matters.

This study has examined the CSR practice and rationale behind the biggest enterprises in the city of Macau during the COVID-19 outbreak. By collecting views and insights from senior personnel, the findings reveal that the reciprocal nature of CSR is taking place between the government and the private sector. Although the private sector has struggled with a significant drop in business during the pandemic, businesses have all exercised CSR beyond any explicit compliance set by the local government. The findings of the chapter could be used as a base to form further investigation to examine the connection between enterprise CSR actions and government regulation as well as various forms of institutional arrangement.

References

Berger, P.L. and Luckmann, T. (1991). *The Social Construction of Reality: A Treatise in the Sociology of Knowledge*. London: Penguin.

Bowen, H.R. (1953). *Social Responsibilities of the Businessman*. New York: Harper and Row.

Carroll, A.B. (1979). A three-dimensional conceptual model of corporate social performance. *Academy of Management Review*, 4(4), 497–505.

Carson, R. (1962). *Silent Spring (Reprinted 2000)*. London: Penguin Books.

Chung, K.C. (2020). Green marketing orientation: Achieving sustainable development in green hotel management. *Journal of Hospitality Marketing and Management*, 29(6), 722–738.

De Grosbois, D. (2016). Corporate social responsibility reporting in the cruise tourism industry: A performance evaluation using a new institutional theory based model. *Journal of Sustainable Tourism*, 24(2), 245–269.

DeBoer, J., Panwar, R. and Rivera, J. (2017). Toward a place-based understanding of business sustainability: The role of green competitors and green locales in firms' voluntary environmental engagement. *Business Strategy and the Environment*, 26(7), 940–955.

Dicen, K.B., Yodsuwan, C., Butcher, K. and Mingkwan, N. (2019). The institutional context for experiential learning investment in hospitality education: A case study from Thailand. In Liu, C. and Schanzel, H. (Eds.), *Tourism Education and Asia*. Singapore: Springer.

DiMaggio, P.J. and Powell, W.W. (1983). The iron cage revisited: Institutional isomorphism and collective rationality in organizational fields. *American Sociological Review*, 48(2), 147–160.

Doh, J.P. and Guay, T.R. (2006). Corporate social responsibility, public policy, and NGO activism in Europe and the United States: An institutional-stakeholder perspective. *Journal of Management Studies*, 43(1), 47–73.

Donaldson, T. and Preston, L.E. (1995). The stakeholder theory of the corporation: Concepts, evidence, and implications. *Academy of Management Review*, 20(1), 65–91.

DSEDT. (2022). Small and medium-sized enterprises aid scheme. Available at: https://www.dsedt.gov.mo/en_US/web/public/pg_icf_sme?_refresh=true

European Commission. (2011a). Sustainable and responsible business: Corporate social responsibility. Available at: http://ec.europa.eu/enterprise/policies/sustainable-business/corporate-social-responsibility/index_en.htm

European Commission. (2011b). Sustainable and responsible business: Corporate social responsibility and competitiveness. Available at: http://ec.europa.eu/enterprise/policies/sustainable-business/corporate-social-responsibility/competitiveness/index_en.htm#h2-1

European Commission. (2014). EU Corporate Social Responsibility policy: The Commission seeks stakeholders' views on achievements and future challenges. Available at: https://www.europa-nu.nl/id/vjjcfc1mk8z7/nieuws/eu_corporate_social_responsibility

Frederick, W.C. (1960). The growing concern over business responsibility. *California Management Review*, 2(4), 54–61.

Freeman, R.E. (1984). *Strategic Management: A Stakeholder Approach*. Boston, MA: Pitman Publishing.

Freeman, R.E. and Evan, W. (1990). Corporate governance: A stakeholder interpretation. *Journal of Behavioral Economics*, 19(4), 337–360.

Friedman, M. (1962). *Capitalism and Freedom*. Chicago, IL: The University of Chicago Press.

Friedman, M. (1970). The social responsibility of business is to increase its profits. *New York Times Magazine*, September.

Gard McGehee, N., Wattanakamolchai, S., Perdue, R.R. and Onat Calvert, E. (2009). Corporate social responsibility within the US lodging industry: An exploratory study. *Journal of Hospitality and Tourism Research*, 33(3), 417–437.

Gioia, D.A., Corley, K.G. and Hamilton, A.L. (2013). Seeking qualitative rigor in inductive research: Notes on the Gioia methodology. *Organizational Research Methods*, 16(1), 15–31.

Gu, H., Ryan, C., Bin, L. and Wei, G. (2013). Political connections, guanxi and adoption of CSR policies in the Chinese hotel industry: Is there a link? *Tourism Management*, 34, 231–235.

Hahn, T. (2015). Reciprocal stakeholder behavior: A motive-based approach to the implementation of normative stakeholder demands. *Business and Society*, 54(1), 9–51.

Hart, S.L. and Milstein, M.B. (1999). Global sustainability and the creative destruction of industries. *Sloan Management Review*, 41(1), 23–33.

Hart, S.L. and Milstein, M.B. (2003). Creating sustainable value. *Academy of Management Executive*, 17(2), 56–67.

Hasan, I., Kobeissi, N., Liu, L. and Wang, H. (2018). Corporate social responsibility and firm financial performance: The mediating role of productivity. *Journal of Business Ethics*, 149(3), 671–688.

Hawken, P. (1993). *The Ecology of Commerce: A Declaration of Sustainability*. New York: HarperBusiness Publishers.

Hawken, P., Lovins, A.B. and Lovins, L.H. (1999). *Natural Capitalism: The Next Industrial Revolution*. London: Earthscan Publications Ltd.

Huberman, A.M. and Miles, M.B. (2002). *The Qualitative Researcher's Companion*. Thousand Oaks, CA: Sage.

Husted, B.W. and Salazar, J.J. (2006). Taking Friedman seriously: Maximizing profits and social performance. *Journal of Management Studies*, 43(1), 75–91.

Jones, T.M. (1995). Instrumental stakeholder theory: A synthesis of ethics and economics. *Academy of Management Review*, 20(2), 404–437.

Klein, N. (2001). *No Logo*. London: Routledge.

KPMG. (2020). The KPMG survey of sustainability reporting 2020. Available at: https://home.kpmg/xx/en/home/insights/2020/11/the-time-has-come-survey-of-sustainability-reporting.html

Kumar, K., Boesso, G., Batra, R. and Yao, J. (2019). Explicit and implicit corporate social responsibility: Differences in the approach to stakeholder engagement activities of US and Japanese companies. *Business Strategy and the Environment*, 28(6), 1121–1130.

Loi, K.I., Lei, W.S. and Lourenço, F. (2021). Understanding the reactions of government and gaming concessionaires on COVID-19 through the neo-institutional theory–The case of Macau. *International Journal of Hospitality Management*, 94, 102755.

Lourenço, F. (2013). To challenge the world view or to flow with it? Teaching sustainable development in business schools. *Business Ethics: A European Review*, 22(3), 292–307.

Macau Gaming History. (2014). Available at: http://www.dicj.gov.mo/web/en/history/

Macau Statistics and Census Department. (2020a). Package tours and hotel occupancy rate. Available at: https://www.dsec.gov.mo/en-US/Statistic?id=403.

Macau Statistics and Census Department. (2020b). Statistics. Available at: http://www.dsec.gov.mo/TimeSeriesDatabase.aspx

Macau Statistics and Census Department. (2020c). Visitor arrivals. Available at: https://www.dsec.gov.mo/TourismDBWeb/#/main?lang=en

Martinuzzi, A., Gisch-Boie, S. and Wiman, A. (2011). Does corporate responsibility pay off? Exploring the links between CSR and competitiveness in Europe's industrial sectors. Available at: http://ec.europa.eu/enterprise/policies/sustainable-business/files/csr/documents/competitiveness/101124_csr_comp_final_report_long_version_final_en.pdf

Matten, D. and Moon, J. (2004). Corporate social responsibility education in Europe. *Journal of Business Ethics*, 54(4), 323–337.

Meadows, D.H., Meadows, D.L., Randers, J. and Behrens, C.W. (1972). *The Limits to the Growth*. New York: Universe Books Publishing Company.

Mensah, I. and Blankson, E.J. (2013). Determinants of hotels' environmental performance: Evidence from the hotel industry in Accra, Ghana. *Journal of Sustainable Tourism*, 21(8), 1212–1231.

Meyer, J.W. and Rowan, B. (1977). Institutionalized organizations: Formal structure as myth and ceremony. *American Journal of Sociology*, 83(2), 340–363.

Moon, J. (2011). *Corporate Social Responsibility: An Idea Whose Time Has Come? If so, What Idea?* Paper presented at the Management and Business: Fifty Years On (a conference in recognition of Grigor McClelland). Manchester Business School.

Orlitzky, M., Schmidt, F.L. and Rynes, S.L. (2003). Corporate social and financial performance: A meta-analysis. *Organizational Studies*, 24(3), 403–441.

Ouyang, Z., Wei, W. and Chi, C.G. (2019). Environment management in the hotel industry: Does institutional environment matter? *International Journal of Hospitality Management*, 77, 353–364.

Peloza, J. (2009). The challenge of measuring financial impacts from investments in corporate social performance. *Journal of Management*, 35(6), 1518–1541.

Podsakoff, P.M. and MacKenzie, S.B. (1997). Impact of organizational citizenship behaviour on organizational performance: A review and suggestions for future research. *Human Performance*, 10(2), 133–151.

Roberts, R.E. (2020). Qualitative interview questions: Guidance for novice researchers. *Qualitative Report*, 25(9), 3185–3205.

Scott, W.R. (1995). *Institutions and Organizations. Foundations for Organizational Science*. London: Sage.

Serra-Cantallops, A., Peña-Miranda, D.D., Ramón-Cardona, J. and Martorell-Cunill, O. (2018). Progress in research on CSR and the hotel industry (2006–2015). *Cornell Hospitality Quarterly*, 59(1), 15–38.

Shin, H., Sharma, A., Nicolau, J.L. and Kang, J. (2021). The impact of hotel CSR for strategic philanthropy on booking behavior and hotel performance during the COVID-19 pandemic. *Tourism Management*, 85, 104322.

Simons, T., Vermeulen, P.A. and Knoben, J. (2016). There's no beer without a smoke: Community cohesion and neighboring communities' effects on organizational resistance to antismoking regulations in the Dutch hospitality industry. *Academy of Management Journal*, 59(2), 545–578.

Slater, D.J. and Dixon-Fowler, H.R. (2010). The future of the planer in the hands of MBAs: An examination of CEO MBA education and corporate environmental performance. *Academy of Management Learning and Education*, 9(3), 429–441.

Starik, M., Rands, G., Marcus, A.A. and Clark, T.S. (2010). In search of sustainability in management education. *Academy of Management Learning and Education*, 9(3), 377–383.

UNWTO. (2020). Global guidelines to restart tourism. Available at https://webunwto.s3.eu-west-1.amazonaws.com/s3fs-public/2020-05/UNWTO-Global-Guidelines-to-Restart-Tourism.pdf

van Marrewijk, M. (2013). Concepts and definitions of CSR and corporate sustainability: Between agency and communion. In Michalos, A.C. and Poff, D.C. (Eds.), *Citation Classics from the Journal of Business Ethics: Celebrating the First Thirty Years of Publication* (pp. 641–655). Dordrecht: Springer Netherlands.

Waddock, S.A. and Graves, S.B. (1997). The corporate social performance-financial performance link. *Strategic Management Journal*, 18(4), 303–319.

Zhu, Q., Cordeiro, J. and Sarkis, J. (2013). Institutional pressures, dynamic capabilities and environmental management systems: Investigating the ISO 9000–Environmental management system implementation linkage. *Journal of Environmental Management*, 114, 232–242.

Zucker, L.G. (1977). The role of institutionalization in cultural persistence. *American Sociological Review*, 42(5), 726–743.

6 The Impact of COVID-19 on Social Responsibility in Stigmatized Occupations

Ariana Chang

Introduction

The impact of the COVID-19 pandemic on the global economy has been devastating and unprecedented. Every social entity, from an individual to a corporation to a government, has had to make significant changes to survive the pandemic (Donthu and Gustafsson, 2020). Prior to it, research on corporate social responsibility (CSR) had thrived and could be recognized as one of the most exhaustively examined sub-fields in management but the pandemic distinctly cast challenges on a number of CSR assumptions (Crane and Matten, 2020). The pandemic has brought business uncertainty to new heights, putting corporate agility and leadership to the test as businesses struggle to manage difficulties on both micro and global stages.

The COVID-19 pandemic has been reflected upon as a prevalent "grand challenge" that needs to be tackled with coordinated efforts from the various stakeholders (Howard-Grenville, 2021). There is no clear solution to such a grand challenge which is so complicated and difficult to solve by its nature. By addressing grand challenges, organizations and enterprises help to advance the 2030 Agenda for Sustainable Development (a set of 17 goals and 169 targets) adopted by the United Nations in 2015 to end poverty, protect the environment, and leave no one behind (George et al., 2016).

Enterprises need to cope with the "new normal" and rethink ways of operation due to the drastic effects of the pandemic (Ratten, 2020) which have greatly challenged prior CSR concepts. The pandemic has distinctively redefined the frontline workforce and who should be regarded as "essential" stakeholders of business (Crane and Matten, 2020). Thus, the economy has been propelled by frontline workers in sectors such as health care, transportation, and food services. COVID-19 is expected to exacerbate disparities and contribute to an increase in precarious employment, especially among "essential" workers (Kniffin et al., 2020).

These workers are usually economically disadvantaged (Lowrey, 2020) and have been exposed to the pandemic without the necessary protections (*The Lancet*, 2020). In many forms, precarious work refers to non-standard employment that is poorly paid, temporary, and insecure. Thus, such workers are usually

DOI: 10.4324/9781003274575-7

denied formal employee rights. Olsthoorn (2014) stated that the three components of precarious employment are insecure employment, unsupportive entitlements, and vulnerable employees. Multiple facilitating factors have affected the amount and nature of precarious work, which have evolved over time and between nations (Bobek et al., 2018).

According to the International Labor Organization (ILO), around 2 billion people work informally around the globe and 1.6 billion are barely making a living (Strauss, 2020). As a result of the pandemic, many of the services typically accessible to marginalized people living in precarious situations such as the homeless and binners (i.e., those who collect redeemable items as a living) have been shut down. In comparison to the general population, research has found that the homeless are more inclined to become infected, require intensive care treatment, and die from the virus (Kottasová, 2022).

This research extends the current literature on CSR and provides novel insights into the importance of leadership during turbulent times. The lessons learned from the crisis, particularly from a contentious industry that has been disregarded, help illuminate how social responsibility via leadership can play a critical role in assisting firms to move forward in the face of grave circumstances.

In this study, we sought to examine how social responsibility is "conducted" in the precarious and unprotected stigmatized occupations. Specifically, the havoc wreaked by the COVID-19 pandemic has had a huge impact on precarious workers. To this end, the case study approach was utilized based on interviews with workers of stigmatized occupations in Taiwan. To capture the effects during the different time periods of the pandemic (at the onset of COVID-19 and when COVID-19 was at its worst) on stigmatized workers, interviews were conducted across multiple periods.

Precarious Work and Stigma

According to Noronha et al. (2020), 61% of global employment is dependent on the informal economy. The rise of precarious employment in both emerging and developed countries have been spurred on by structural changes. Famira-Muehlberger (2014) defined precarious work as employment that is characterized by insecurity, along with social and/or economic fragility. This encompasses rather non-standard forms of work such as temporary and marginal work. In addition, the surge of indignity at work is attributed to low-paying jobs and the decline of high-paying manufacturing jobs (Berg and Frost, 2005; Kalleberg, 2009). One of the most pressing challenges in the labor force is the emergence of rising precarity in jobs. Precarious employment is becoming more widely acknowledged as a major contributor to poor health and a critical component of interactions among work, socioeconomic status, and health and well-being (Benach et al., 2014).

The workers who are trapped in precarious employment are among those most affected by the COVID-19 pandemic (Matilla-Santander et al., 2021) and the pandemic is expected to both worsen disparities and contribute to an increase in precarious work (Kniffin et al., 2020). To many of these workers, they encounter social marginalization. In addition, the discrediting of organizational members, organizational activities, and the organizations themselves is referred to as organizational stigma (Sutton and Callahan, 1987) which involves the examination of off-putting activities, work, and organizations (Hudson and Okhuysen, 2014).

In the past three decades, social science research on stigmatization has escalated rapidly (Roca, 2010). Stigmatized occupations consist of, but are not limited to, funeral, crematorium, sanitation, and sex workers. A portion of society depicts stigmatized occupation itself as "dirty work" and those with such occupations as "dirty workers" (Ashforth and Kreiner, 1999). Organizations and those who work in these industries are judged and evaluated to differing degrees by diverse audiences. With the immediate above in mind, the public usually regard stigmatized work as demeaning, distasteful, immoral, dangerous, and even disgusting (Hughes, 1958). Therefore, it can be very challenging to attract and retain employees for businesses that carry stigma.

One of the research areas that requires further exploration is how CSR initiatives are practiced by the "so-called" stigmatized businesses and industries (Austin and Gaither, 2017). Businesses in this category contribute negatively to an issue of societal concern (Gregory and Satterfield, 2002; Miller and Sinclair, 2012) and suffer from bad publicity. Often, stakeholder concerns are assuaged by firms through CSR engagement to reduce public skepticism. In deciding on how CSR initiatives should be pursued, stigmatized companies encounter various challenging questions (Austin and Gaither, 2017). Companies must grapple with how to survive in the face of the COVID-19 pandemic while also meeting public expectations and whether they should be concerned about the public's well-being during this difficult time (Lee and Cho, 2022).

Social Responsibility

For an extensive range of businesses and industries, CSR has become a ubiquitous communication strategy (Austin and Gaither, 2017). Whether a business is stigmatized or not, CSR has become a norm for most businesses (Lee and Cho, 2022). For companies, social responsibility is informed by a wide scope of concepts outside the corporate domain (Mialon and McCambridge, 2018). CSR has become a core concern in contemporary business activities (Maon et al., 2010) and CSR implementation is no longer an option but a requirement for corporations. To implement CSR initiatives is rather complex and multifaceted (Aguinis and Glavas, 2012; Garriga and Mele, 2004; Secchi, 2007) because much of it is constrained by context. One of the primary driving forces for CSR stems from the leader's personal values and internal organizational culture (Ligeti and Oravecz, 2009).

Aside from having good corporate governance, CSR extends beyond compliance with legal, regulatory, and contractual requirements, emphasizing its voluntary nature (McWilliams and Siegel, 2001; Liang and Renneboog, 2017). CSR has been a much-discussed subject (Wanderley et al., 2008) and gained immense attraction among civil society, academics, government, and media worldwide (Gatti et al., 2019). To progress societal well-being, different institutions have a role in supporting an enabling environment for CSR. By executing corporate social initiatives, businesses enact positive social changes and become more purpose-driven. According to over 80% of a sample of millennials, the primary and most important goal of a business is to provide social value, rather than to make profit, and to create a positive difference in the world (Buffet and Eimicke, 2018).

The COVID-19 pandemic has instead shown a new political economics of CSR, re-centering the government as a quintessential actor in addressing grand challenges (Crane and Matten, 2020). Thus, the government needs to take the key role of coordinating actions among sectors and all sectors have the responsibility to be involved in pandemic preparedness. Crane and Matten (2020) stated that the government is no longer the ineffective actor that is portrayed in the CSR literature, but an actor that others need to work alongside. In shaping CSR, the reintegration of the government is crucial (Wickert, 2021). During the pandemic, the social responsibility of firms is to safeguard their workers, produce useful products, and protect their stakeholders together with the government and other actors (Crane and Matten, 2020).

Social Responsibility and Stigmatized Occupations

Although CSR practices enable companies to meet the public's expectation to be good citizens and generate competitive advantages (Gürtürk et al., 2011, Park et al., 2019), it is difficult for businesses dealing with stigmatized occupations to generate favorable public responses (Lee and Cho, 2022). These businesses often contribute, through CSR activities, to a wide range of social issues that appear to be contradictory to their own business models. Responsible drinking campaigns by alcohol sellers to mitigate public concerns that are caused by their own products and services are a typical example (Lee and Cho, 2022). The general public is interested in the motivations behind CSR initiatives, questioning whether a company undertakes CSR initiatives for its own advantage or for the good of the society (Du et al., 2010). What prompts a company to engage in CSR activities can be classified into two categories, namely, social (public-serving/intrinsic) and economic (firm-serving/extrinsic) motives (Kim and Lee, 2012; Karaosmanoglu et al., 2016).

According to Vogel (2006), CSR encourages practices that improve workplace quality and go beyond what businesses are legally required to do. This research analyzes the reasons that influence social responsibility practices of the businesses of stigmatized occupations. By examining the "special industry" (entertainment venues which cater for men drinking with primarily female staff) in Taiwan, the main objective of this study is to identify the key factors that contribute to how social responsibility is managed in a controversial business dealing with stigmatized occupations. The "special industry" faces public condemnation because their products and services may harm the society and give the impression that their business philosophy is only to maximize profits solely for self-interest at the expense of the social good (Lee and Cho, 2022). Therefore, businesses in this industry need to engage not only in simple acts like charitable donations. Their social responsibility involves creating a safe and healthy work environment because the nature of this business usually concerns controversial activities.

In this “special industry”, a safe occupational environment is quintessential since the employees are more vulnerable to certain occupational dangers and health risks. In such a challenging workplace, the promotion and creation of safety for women and a responsible drinking environment are imperative. If the environment is not managed properly, intoxicated individuals, both hostesses and customers, may become targets of avoidable problems or even crime.

A note of clarification is that the current study investigates the *mai xiao* (pleasure-selling) sector of the “special industry” in Taiwan. On the grounds of urban hedonism, work in this sector occurs in a legal and modern entertainment venue in which sex work is not necessarily implied (Chen, 2008). Contrarily, the *mai shen* (body-selling) sector involves explicit sexual services that are deemed illegal.

Case Description

The severe global spread of the COVID-19 pandemic has sparked a growing debate over the trade-off between economic lockdowns and the contagion (Perugini and Vladisavljević, 2021). For many of the precarious workers across the world, they have lost their jobs practically overnight as a result of social distancing restrictions. Fearing for their livelihoods and health, some are turning to offer services online while others are seeking support from non-profit organizations. The businesses in this study included nightclubs, karaoke bars, teahouses, and saunas in Taiwan.

This study examines “dirty” work that has been tainted with multiple stigmas (physical, moral, and social). Ashforth and Kreiner (2014) found that combinations that include moral stigma are usually among the dirtiest because those associated with such occupations are blemished. The lives of dirty workers could also encounter various sources of taint such as class, race, and/or gender (Shepherd et al., 2021). In the “pleasure-selling” sector, the hostesses work to gratify clients’ demands in entertainment establishments (Chen, 2006). In this sector, which mainly caters for the more affluent politicians and businessmen, women work as entertainers and waitresses to boost men’s ego (Hwang, 2003). At these service clubs, the engagement in “flower drinking” is considered to be critical to doing business in Taiwan and supports male bonding (Bedford and Hwang, 2011). In addition, group drinking activities can be a method for men to establish masculinity (West, 2001).

The Special Industry

Although a controversial place, the red-light district in Taiwan is a subject of much fascination. With a 1980s backdrop, the 2021 Taiwanese Netflix original series *Light the Night* which focused on the various lifestyles and relationships of madams and their hostesses of a red-light district club has gained popularity among viewers worldwide. In such a context, relationships and interactions are paid for by women who are willing to listen and keep their clients' company. In the hustle and bustle of the cities in Taiwan, various kinds of *jiu dian* （酒店） are ubiquitously seen. In particular, *jiu dian* is a unique phenomenon exclusive in Taiwan, which is the apt counterpart to hostess bars or strip clubs in the West. Although *jiu dian* means hotel in Mandarin, it represents a place where men go and have drinks with women (whom they select) to keep them company in Taiwan. The women are hired for men to have a good time at the clubs and physical contact is negotiable (Bedford and Hwang, 2011). In Taiwan, there are various kinds of *jiu dian*, namely karaoke (KTV) parlors, dance halls, nightclubs, hostess bars, tea houses, bars, barbershops, dance halls, etc. In other words, they are adult entertainment establishments (licensed premises) that provide clients with a "room" with liquor and female accompaniment. For the hostesses, a main part of their job is to perform femininity and bond with their respective clients. The engagement between hostesses and customers includes fondling, kissing, and playing games such as placing ice cubes on body parts (Hwang, 1996).

Usually charged by 10-minute sessions, the hostess's job includes, but is not limited to, making her customers at ease and entertained by listening to them, talking and sitting with them, and pouring and mixing alcohol. They also need to create a pleasant atmosphere by singing and engaging in drinking games with their customers. The hostesses will make more money if more drinks are consumed by their clients. Most importantly, it is about satisfying the customers and keeping them feeling content. The majority of these businesses do not provide sexual services, although what transpires outside the businesses' immediate vicinities regarding the hostess–client relationship remains often ambiguous.

While "sexuality" is a critical element in special service clubs, one of the motivations for going to these service clubs is having the opportunity to bond with other men. The hostesses can help foster bonding, convene a group of men into playing games and such engagement can help elevate a man's self-image among his male companions and himself (Bedford and Hwang, 2011). Social rituals serve as a source of energy for all participants, providing strength and support (Collins, 1988). In this case, recreation in hostess clubs is utilized for fostering bonding and generating enjoyable moments. Micro-structural relations between individuals are influenced by expansive structural shifts (Kimmel, 1987). According to Bedford and Hwang (2011), some of the men expressed that they want to escape from feeling "incompetent" because their salary or educational level is lower than that of their girlfriends or wives.

The Effect of the COVID-19 Pandemic on Stigmatized Occupations

The "special industry" came to global attention when various media reported Taiwan's COVID-19 pandemic outbreak burst and hostess teahouses were affected (Zennie and Tsai, 2021). Since parlors and nightclubs were forced to close due to the contagion, many transitioned into other forms of businesses. For example, a prominent hostess bar in Taichung City temporarily turned into a self-service karaoke bar (which does not provide hostesses to accompany the clients) that operated during daytime so that it could resume operations (Hsu, 2021). The tea house cluster infection at the Wanhua tea parlors prompted the public's concern about hostesses and deepened already negative discussions. The Wanhua district once had a thriving sex trade (government-regulated parlors were officially abolished in the 1990s) due to the assemblage of migrant workers. Aside from the tea parlors, many brothels are operating illicitly even to this day. This district was already suffering from a negative reputation of aggressive sex workers ruining Wanhua by actively offering male pedestrians discounts, hurting Taipei City's international image (Sung and Pan, 2013).

Some of the public even referred to the virus as the "Wanhua virus". The massive COVID-19 outbreak involving tea parlors in the Wanhua district back in May 2021 also led to a nation-wide tracking of tea parlor hostesses from outside Taipei. Worse still, the mass uncalled-for discrimination was directed towards Wanhua residents in general, not just tea parlors. Due to the more advanced age of the clientele, the tea parlors were known as "grandpa shops". Especially as most such clientele go to tea parlors simply for companionship purposes, not necessarily for sexual ones.

Usually, the fees charged in these grandpa shops are fairly low and the services are not as expensive compared to the high-end services on the more affluent side (eastern side of Taipei City) of Taiwan. In these tea parlors, the customers can find on-the-spot intimacy and camaraderie. Many of these more senior clients are retired blue-collar workers. Some even spend their daily routines there because the hostesses have become more like their family members in a certain sense. In the Wanhua district, the affected are not only limited to tea parlors and supply chains but surrounding businesses including taxi drivers, fruit stands, and those who sell joss papers. To keep the "popular" hostesses, parlors have to take a lower commission or else the hostesses are headhunted by another parlor. Somewhat from a sense of loyalty, the clients will often follow wherever the hostess works too.

In these tea parlors, a lot of the workers are non-local hostesses. Some of them arrived in Taiwan to work as caregivers, but later fled from their original employers and sought work in tea parlors. Taiwan's National Immigration Agency (NIA) had to urge these foreign workers to come forward regardless of their immigration status because many feared that if tea parlor businesses were forced to close, many of them would return or move to central and southern Taiwan, furthering the massive spread of the COVID-19 infection.

In addition to coping with the impact of the pandemic, these workers also had to counter stigma, even when the outbreak restrictions were relaxed. Due to the stigma associated with the Wanhua district, the tea parlor businesses hit an all-time low and some owners even committed suicide. When business could be resumed, the owners had to go through tedious paperwork and red tape, along with finding hostesses to come back and work for them. Furthermore, they had to adhere to the abundance of restrictions and administrative work.

Research Methodology

Based on interviews conducted with informants who have been involved directly or indirectly in the stigmatized occupation (former hostesses, clients, administrative personnel, and close friends of the hostesses), cases are used to illustrate the complexities and dynamics of the relevant stakeholders. The former hostesses who took part in this study have had more than two years of experience working in urban adult entertainment establishments and none of their family members knew that they worked as hostesses. Drawing on 16 interviews with informants aged between 25 to 45 years old, face-to-face interviews lasted from 60 to 90 minutes and all of them were informed that the data would be used for research purposes only. Prior to the interviews, participants were reminded that they could refuse to talk about any subject matter or end the interview at any time. Note-taking was conducted for all the interviews. Some of the interviewees were uncomfortable having the interviews recorded because they said that they were afraid of being identified and the recorders made them uneasy, so only note-taking was conducted. However, the participants allowed the researcher to contact them for follow-ups if there was anything unclear. With the help of the first informant, the researcher was able to gain access to other informants who had insights into this industry.

Research Findings

SDGs and Dirty Work

To be achieved by 2030, the United Nations adopted the Sustainable Development Goals (SDGs) that consist of 17 goals and 169 targets. For academics, many SDGs are directly relevant to management scholars such as "good health and well-being" (SDG 3), "gender equality" (SDG 5), "decent work and economic growth" (SDG 8), and "reduced inequalities" (SDG 10) (George et al., 2016). The stigmatized occupations are uniquely positioned to address SDGs toward a more inclusive society through safeguarding the "dirty workers". Notably, socially responsible practices through responsible leadership can help contribute to "decent work and economic growth" (SDG 8). SDG 8 encourages job development as well as taking effective steps to eliminate forced labor, slavery, and human trafficking (Aerni et al., 2021). This research pinpoints four SDGs to help frame and analyze the empirical data collected.

Full of controversies, stigmatized occupations are viewed as degrading or disgusting because the society perceives such jobs to have certain characteristics that are devaluing (Hughes, 1958). Thus, the self-perception of the people who work in the stigmatized industry is affected by the resulting social rejection (Roca, 2010). Individuals are geared toward others for approval and want to think positively of themselves and the roles they have in the society (Banaji and Prentice, 1994; Leary, 2007) and it is even more imperative that workers are protected during the pandemic (Crane and Matten, 2020).

Hostess Job Description

The routine jobs of a hostess include: chatting, drinking, dancing, singing, playing games (e.g., dice-rolling, cards); expressing admiration and listening to their clients' stories; showing femininity through costumes of a particular style such as miniskirts to show off good figures (Chen, 2008).

> It might seem that we have an easy job but there are also work difficulties. The pay is inconsistent because it is very dependent on customer demand. I have to wear high heels and riveting clothings every day and this can be cumbersome. I have to make sure that I am glammed up to the max.
>
> (Confidential informant)

Good Health and Well-being (SDG 3)

Aside from greeting guests, hostesses are required to engage in chatting, feasting, singing, pouring drinks, along with displaying empathetic emotions toward the clientele. For this role, they need inter-personal skills to make sure that their clients have a positive experience from the moment they arrive until their departure. Also, it is very common that hostesses sing along to songs with their clientele. Especially, karaoke singing is one of Taiwan's most popular forms of recreation. For KTV parlors, some of the hostesses are also called "princesses". For these hostesses, they do not have to be good singers, but they have to be good entertainers instead. Since these parlors cater to men seeking drinks and company, hostesses often have to do heavy drinking. For parlors that care for their hostesses, they will put an alcohol cap limit for their hostesses and refuse service to unduly patrons.

Contested Work Identities

> Once you have worked as a hostess, it will be difficult to work in a different field due to the cash flow. Money comes too easily. Most young women delve into this industry because they want to make extra pocket money. Some enter this industry to pay off debts for their families. Furthermore, it is hard for some of these women to have normal relationships outside their career. For those who enter without high school diploma don't go back to finish their studies. To some, money symbolizes love and care. Their mindsets become somewhat too materialistic. Some of the girls do provide sexual services after their working hours and it is not something that the club can control. This also diminishes the reputation of the job. I wouldn't want my daughter to work in this industry. A hostess would never outright tell you that she is a hostess.
>
> (A former administrative staff of a nightclub)

Decent Work and Economic Growth (SDG 8)

Workers in stigmatized work groups encounter social refusal and discrimination that harm their social identity (Roca, 2010). The majority of these hostesses are of lower educational level (e.g., high school dropouts) and they state that it is hard for them to leave such an occupation because this is the only kind of work they have ever been exposed to. To manage the negative aspects of work, strategies such as recalibrating, reframing, and refocusing are used by dirty workers to normalize the social, physical, and/or moral taint of their occupation (Ashforth and Kreiner, 1999). For some workers, their employers will tell them that this job is not a good long-term career choice but just a stand-up service job that is not very dignified. Most importantly, it is a job that puts you at risk of future and long-term health problems.

> I have a loyal customer who visits the nightclub on a regular basis. All I need to do is to be a good listener, keep him company, and pour drinks for him. He mainly talks to me about his work and family problems. He knows that he can talk to me without being judged. I think my job helped me develop a feminine trait.
>
> (Confidential informant)

Moreover, many of these workers often receive lavish materialistic goods from their clients. To some extent, some of these relations have evolved into the worker herself becoming the client's long-term "companion". And once the relationship has progressed into companionship, the hostess no longer has to expand her clientele. However, the downside is being very dependent on one major single source of income. The hostesses have also been advised not to be personally and emotionally attached, especially as once work and personal life become entangled, difficulties might arise.

> I lie that I do not have a boyfriend. Some of my friends are married, yet they also lie that they are single. I do not want my relationship status to drive my customers away. You will be surprised, some of my hostess friends even have children. With the high living costs, it is hard to raise a child well. She didn't even graduate from high school; it is hard for her to find a decent job. (Confidential informant)

Even though the public would expect these women to be of lower educational background, there is a trend for educated women and young adults taking up such an occupation. To some, this is a valid career that helps them make a living or earn extra pocket money quickly that is based on straight commission.

> One of my major incomes are from the tips I receive during the evenings. The perks of the tips I receive are that they are all in cash and tax-free. The tips are one of my major sources of income. Some of my clients do not give me tips but they are very generous, they always shower me with gifts. They know that I like luxury goods so they will shower me with bags or jewelry from time to time.
>
> (Confidential informant)

Sometimes, this type of work is extremely lucrative. However, the hostesses can be lavish spenders and usually have a hard time managing their finances with no savings.

> I am not going to deny that I like luxury goods. I feel that these goods give me confidence. By having them, they boost my confidence and help me gain a better impression. (Confidential informant)

> Money is the biggest attraction of what got me into the industry. I can make five to ten times of what I would normally make. The downside is the abnormal working hours and the graveyard shifts. I tell my parents that I work at a nightclub but as an administrative employee such as a clerk. Although I make more money, I also spend considerable finances on maintaining an attractive appearance. My maintenance fees include hairdos, facials, manicures, and pedicures. I am lucky that my nightclub provides me with clothing to wear so that I do not have to spend money to buy work clothes. Everyone in this industry is physically attractive and that is why I need to keep up to par. For this job, I have more autonomy over how much I can make.
>
> (Confidential informant)

When indoor dining restrictions were eased, Taiwan's Central Epidemic Command Center (CECC) did not lift the ban on the "special industry" and more than 300 workers went onto the streets to protest in Taichung City (Oung, 2021). The workers demanded more subsidies from the government because they could not cope with supporting their families. During the initial outbreak, many such parlors refused to release their clientele list to health authorities who were conducting stringent epidemiological investigations. From a public health scope, this was quite worrisome, given that many workers and clients come in close physical and intimate contact. For example, it is common that the hostesses and their clients share the same drinking glasses. People work precariously due to a lack of work protection and such work will lead to ramifications of decent and productive work which are essential components of SDG 8 (Silaban et al., 2021).

The Impact of Responsible Leadership

> I am not scared to go to work, it is only required of me to keep these men company and provide some sort of entertainment. Some men only come to clubs to talk and discuss about business deals. My supervisors help me refuse customers that I do not want to provide services to.
>
> (Confidential informant)

Gender Equality (SDG 5), Decent Work and Economic Growth (SDG 8) and Reduced Inequalities (SDG 10)

Responsible leadership is the "the art of building and sustaining morally sound relationships with all stakeholders of an organization" (Maak and Pless, 2006,

5). This type of leadership is navigated towards the concerns of others, including accountability, appropriate moral decision making, and trust (Pless and Maak, 2011). The call for responsible leadership is not limited to scandals and irresponsibility (Brown and Trevino, 2006) but espoused from the new demands of businesses (Maak and Pless, 2006; Waldman and Galvin, 2008). For the job content of *mai xiao*, it is thus hard to draw a fine line regarding personal boundaries between what can be conducted intimately. Hence, the agent can seek to build a firm stance towards the job requirements of his/her hostesses.

> Although some of the hostesses do find their boyfriends at the nightclubs, relationships can be difficult because it is founded on a superficial level. However, some clients come to clubs to find girlfriends. Some clients can become very obsessive.
>
> (Confidential informant)

Instead of situating the hostesses in a super-competitive environment, a well-thought-out supervisor will make sure that each member has a respective partnership stake. Moreover, the club will not let its hostesses compromise their own safety after working hours.

> As an administrative staff, it is my responsibility to tell my ladies to never get serious with their customers. In our line of work, only money is real. Getting into a relationship is troublesome for all three parties. Although some of my ladies give an illusion of on-spot-intimacies, I help them screen clients to make sure they do not get into trouble.
>
> (Former administrative staff)

There are agents who recruit young women to go into the industry and some even develop relationships with these women. Some of these agents will use tactics to lure young women into the industry and have them perform duties that are outside the scope of the job. Furthermore, there are also questionable businesses that engage in outright unethical behaviors.

> We have customers of all kinds. Many are kind to us while some are sleazy. The sleazy customers like to see the hostesses get drunk and will keep on forcing us to drink. I make sure that I do not get drunk by drinking slowly. There are definitely clients who like to take little advantages of us. It really depends on if I like the client or not or if he is a regular. I make sure that my regular clients receive extra and more profound attention from me. I usually don't mind some intimacy as long as they do not go too far.
>
> (Confidential informant)

The Entertainment Worker and Hostess Union was established in 2021. One of the main objectives of this union is to protect the hostesses' employee rights and advocate a safer working environment for hostesses. The founder of this union is currently an agent for hostesses and was a former hostess herself. When perceiving CSR activities, the public is inclined to scrutinize stigmatized groups more intensely compared to non-stigmatized groups (Austin and Gaither, 2017; Kim and Lee, 2012; Yoon et al., 2006).

A more "responsible" club will make sure that the administrative team and hostesses help each other out. Although it is difficult to avoid lousy clients, a nightclub that cares for its workers will make sure that all of their employees help each other out, especially when there is a difficult client to deal with. Instead of competing for clients, the hostesses would instead befriend each other so they are not taken advantage of. In addition, the club will help hostesses deal with sexual harassment issues.

> My supervisors protect me. They make sure that my clients do not take advantage of me. For example, there should not be any inappropriate groping or touching on site. There are definitely iffy clubs out there but I make sure that I am not mingled into that.
>
> (Confidential informant)

The administration team will provide constant reminders that platonic relationships do not exist. Therefore, this means it is a way to protect their employees from being involved in complicated relationships.

> It really helps if you have supervisors who are willing to side and stand up for you. Usually, the higher-end clubs take care of their employees better.
>
> (Confidential informant)

Many of these hostesses who leave this occupation will re-enter it due to the low workforce entry barrier. It is a job that requires prior training or on-the-job training. However, if the hostess wants to excel in her work, it is important for her to develop skills outside the job. For example, many of the hostesses engage in reading and keeping up with current events so they have something to discuss with their clients. This is especially vital if they want to have clients in managerial positions. For those who would like to have a broader clientele base (e.g., international clientele), they will learn a foreign language such as English or Japanese. Before the start of the COVID-19 pandemic, there were frequent visits made by clients from overseas. With additional skills such as knowing a foreign language, the hostesses believe that they will not only attract more business opportunities but also have their identities subverted.

The Turning Point

As many Asian countries slowly begin to ease COVID-19 restrictions, the pressing social concerns that the pandemic has intensified are once again brought to the forefront of our attention. The pandemic has exposed the vulnerabilities of marginalized groups. The forced temporary closure of the "special industry" during the most intense outbreak back in May 2021 in Taiwan actually made some women who worked in tea parlors and nightclubs switch careers. They had no choice but to find temporary jobs. For the first time, many of them started to self-question their long-term career plans. Likewise, in the light of the complexities presented by the pandemic and all of its permutations, the pandemic highlighted the worst of social inequities. Given the negative socioeconomic effects of COVID-19 containment on informal businesses and workers without social protection, the government should take proactive measures to prevent the spread of infection, treat those who are infected, provide social safety nets and economic relief to both informal workers and firms (Nguimkeu and Okou, 2020).

Discussion

The impact of the COVID-19 pandemic has opened up a meaningful area of management scholarship for policymakers and practitioners seeking to develop solutions to execute social responsibility in the "special industry" and to reshape stigmatized occupations. Many of these workers do not have sufficient savings and live from one paycheck to the next. This pandemic was a huge shock for these workers and has been a very difficult transition for them since they have minimal exposure to other industries and it is extremely difficult to transition into other jobs. Even if they have found other jobs, it is a huge challenge for them because they have to work somewhat more laboriously with less pay altogether. With more persistent derogation by certain societal members, morally stigmatized occupations are often depicted as more evil than necessary (Ashforth and Kreiner, 2014).

Many of the hostesses that work in this "exquisite" industry are often reluctant to openly discuss their work. Their respective customers come from a wide array of blue- and white-collar jobs. Interestingly, many are even high-profile, well-established, and well-known members of the society. And the men who pay for such services do not usually outrightly admit that they patronize such places because that may bring negative connotations. Due to reasons of confidentiality, the hostesses need to be extremely discreet about their clientele list and the dynamics of their relationships. Any disclosure will hamper the business side of things and even attract unwanted attention from authorities. Overall, this industry has a very patronage-like environment that is also money-centric. This study hopes to open more avenues for research in stigmatized work and social responsibility since there is still a lot to unpack.

Conclusion

At this critical juncture, we are already seeing more leaders than ever step up, form partnerships, catalyze their resources and capital, to meet the Sustainable Development Goals by 2030. We look forward to seeing some notable studies in dirty work. Especially, more attention needs to be paid to how dirty work can help contribute to "good health and well-being" (SDG 3), "gender equality"

(SDG 5), "decent work and economic growth" (SDG 8), and "reduced inequalities" (SDG 10). The nature of the "dirtiness", as well as the methods by which occupational members resist it, differs by varying degrees across different settings and cultures.

As the pandemic has further widened the chasm between the wealth gap, workers thus encounter hardships and firms must step up their efforts to protect the well-being and health of their employees and the communities they serve. Especially, the far-reaching effects of the pandemic have jeopardized and compromised the livelihoods of families. Since the inception of the COVID-19 pandemic, all sectors have encountered a rather steep battle. Stigmatized industries are often situated in sites of marginalization. Likewise, the involvement in precarious work has further exacerbated the inequalities in our society. On top of coping with stigma and contestation, workers fear for their livelihoods; especially, as such workers are often prone to infections without the necessary social protection.

Due to the pandemic, precarious workers globally are experiencing hardship, a total loss of income, harassment, and increased discrimination. In businesses involving stigmatized occupations, targets of shaming are attempted from those who devalue their identities and curb their relationships, opportunities, and mobility (Ashforth and Kreiner, 1999; Galvin et al., 2004; Hughes, 1958; Simpson et al., 2012). In times of uncertainty, marginalized groups thus become even more vulnerable and encounter higher risk of poverty and social exclusion compared to other members of the society. It is even more pivotal that social responsibility is exercised in these groups as they have suffered more acutely. The COVID-19 pandemic poses a great challenge for marginalized groups and this chasm must be bridged so that we leave no one behind.

References

Aerni, P., Stavridou, M. and Schluep, I (2021). Transitioning to decent work and economic growth. In Aerni, P., Stavridou, M. and Schluep, I. (Eds.) *Transitioning to Sustainability*. Basel: MDPI.

Aguinis, H. and Glavas, A. (2012). What we know and don't know about corporate social responsibility: A review and research agenda. *Journal of Management*, 38(4), 932–968.

Ashforth, B.E. and Kreiner, G.E. (1999). 'How can you do it?' Dirty work and the challenge of constructing a positive identity. *Academy of Management Review*, 24(3), 413–434.

Ashforth, B.E. and Kreiner, G.E. (2014). Dirty work and dirtier work: Differences in countering physical, social, and moral stigma. *Management and Organization Review*, 10(1), 81–108.

Austin, L. and Gaither, B.M. (2017). Perceived motivations for corporate social responsibility initiatives in socially stigmatized industries. *Public Relations Review*, 43(4), 840–849.

Banaji, M.R. and Prentice, D.A. (1994). The self in social contexts. *Annual Review of Psychology*, 45(1), 297–332.

Bedford, O. and Hwang, S.L. (2011). Flower drinking and masculinity in Taiwan. *Journal of Sex Research*, 48(1), 82–92.

Benach, J., Vives, A., Amable, M., Vanroelen, C., Tarafa, G. and Muntaner, C. (2014). Precarious employment: Understanding an emerging social determinant of health. *Annual Review of Public Health*, 35, 229–253.

Berg, P. and Frost, A. (2005). Dignity at work for low wage, low skill service workers. *Industrial Relations*, 60(4), 657–682.

Bobek, A., Pembroke, S. and Wickham, J.J.R. (2018). *Living with Uncertainty: Social Implications of Precarious Work.* Dublin: TASC.

Brown, M.E. and Trevino, L.K. (2002). Ethical leadership: A review and future directions. *The Leadership Quaterly*, 17, 595–616.

Buffet, H.W. and Eimicke, B.W. (2018). How companies, governments, and nonprofits can create social change together. *Harvard Business Review*, May 31. Available at: https://hbr.org/2018/05/how-companies-governments-and-nonprofits-can-create-social-change-together

Chen, M.H. (2006). Selling bodies/selling pleasure: The social organization of sex work in Taiwan. In Gangoli, G. and Westmarland, N. (Eds.), *International Approaches to Prostitution: Law and Policy in Europe and Asia.* Bristol: The Polity Press.

Chen, M.H. (2008). Sex and work in sex work: Negotiating intimacy and commercial sex among Taiwanese sex workers. In Jackson, S., Liu, J. and Wu, J. (Eds.), *East Asian Sexualities: Modernity, Gender and New Sexual Cultures.* New York: Zed Books.

Collins, R. (1988). *Theoretical Sociology.* New York, NY: Harcourt Brace Jovanovich.

Crane, A. and Matten, D. (2020). COVID-19 and the future of CSR Research. *Journal of Management Studies*, 58(1), 280–284.

Donthu, N. and Gustafsson, A. (2020). Effects of COVID-19 on business and research. *Journal of Business Research*, 117, 284–289.

Du, S., Bhattacharya, C.B. and Sen, S. (2010). Maximizing business returns to corporate social responsibility (CSR): The role of CSR communication. *International Journal of Management Reviews*, 12(1), 8–19.

Famira-Muehlberger, U. (2014). Precarious work. In Michalos, A.C. (Ed.), *Encyclopedia of Quality of Life and Well-Being Research.* Dordrecht: Springer.

Galvin, T.L., Ventresca, M.J. and Hudson, B.A. (2004). Contested industry dynamics. *International Studies of Management and Organization*, 34(4), 56–82.

Garriga, E. and Melé, D. (2004). Corporate social responsibility theories: Mapping the territory. *Journal of Business Ethics*, 53(1), 51–71.

Gatti, L., Vishwanath, B., Seele, P. and Cottier, B. (2019). Are we moving beyond voluntary CSR? Exploring theoretical and managerial implications of mandatory CSR resulting from the new Indian Companies Act. *Journal of Business Ethics*, 160(4), 961–972.

George, G., Howard-Grenville, J., Joshi, A. and Tihanyi, L. (2016). Understanding and tackling societal grand challenges through management research. *Academy of Management Journal*, 59(6), 1880–1895.

Gregory, R.S. and Satterfield, T.A. (2002). Beyond perception: The experience of risk and stigma in community contexts. *Risk Analysis*, 22(2), 347–358.

Gürtürk, A., Wanderley, L.S.O. and Coolen, J. (2011). Strategic corporate social responsibility in a stigmatized industry. *Res Manageri*, 21(4), 31–44.

Howard-Grenville, J. (2021). Grand challenges, Covid-19 and the future of organizational scholarship. *Journal of Management Studies*, 58(1), 254–258.

Hsu, P. (2021). Taichung Hostess Bar turned into self-service KTV can resume operations. Available at: https://news.pts.org.tw/article/548021

Hudson, B.A. and Okhuysen, G.A. (2014). Taboo topics: Structural barriers to the study of organizational stigma. *Journal of Management Inquiry*, 23(3), 242–253.

Hughes, E.C. (1958). *Men and Their Work*. Glencoe, IL: Free Press.

Hwang, S.L. (1996). Women in sex industries: Victims, agents, or deviants. *Taiwan: A Radical Quarterly in Social Studies*, 22, 103–153.

Hwang, S.L. (2003). Masculinity and Taiwan's flower-drinking culture. *Taiwan She Hui Xue*, 5, 73.

Kalleberg, A.L. (2009). Precarious work, insecure workers: Employment relations in transition. *American Sociological Review*, 74(1), 1–22.

Kim, S. and Lee, Y.J. (2012). The complex attribution process of CSR motives. *Public Relations Review*, 38(1), 168–170.

Kimmel, M.S. (1987). Men's responses to feminism at the turn of the century. *Gender and Society*, 1(3), 261–283.

Kottasová, C. (2022). Meet the doctor on a quest to get the homeless vaccinated against Covid-19. Available at: https://www.cnn.com/2021/03/30/uk/coronavirus-homeless-vaccinations-intl-cmd-gbr/index.html

Leary, M.R. (2007). Motivational and emotional aspects of the self. *Annual Review of Psychology*, 58, 317–344.

Lee, Y.J. and Cho, M. (2022). Socially stigmatized company's CSR efforts during the COVID-19 pandemic: The effects of CSR fit and perceived motives. *Public Relations Review*, 48(2), 102180.

Liang, H. and Renneboog, L. (2017). On the foundations of corporate social responsibility. *Journal of Finance*, 72(2), 853–910.

Ligeti, G. and Oravecz, Á. (2009). CSR communication of corporate enterprises in Hungary. *Journal of Business Ethics*, 84(2), 137–149.

Lowrey, A. (2020). Don't blame Econ 101 for the plight of essential workers. The Atlantic. Available at: https://www.theatlantic.com/ideas/archive/2020/2005/why-are-americas-most-essential-workers- so-poorly-treated/611575/

Karaosmanoglu, E., Altinigne, N. and Isiksal, D.G. (2016). CSR motivation and customer extra-role behavior: Moderation of ethical corporate identity. *Journal of Business Research*, 69(10), 4161–4167.

Kim, S. and Lee, Y.J. (2012). The complex attribution process of CSR motives. *Public Relations Review*, 38(1), 168–170.

Kniffin, K.M., Narayanan, J., Anseel, F., Antonakis, J., Ashford, S.P., Bakker, A.B., Bamberger, P., Bapuji, H., Bhave, D.P., Choi, V.K., Creary, S.J., Demerouti, E., Flynn, F.J., Gelfand, M.J., Greer, L.L., Johns, G., Kesebir, S., Klein, P.G., Lee, S.Y., Ozcelik, H., Petriglieri, J.L., Rothbard, N.P., Rudolph, C.W., Shaw, J.D., Sirola, N., Wanberg, C.R., Whillans, A., Wilmot, M.P. and van Vugt, M. (2020). COVID-19 and the workplace: Implications, issues, and insights for future research and action. *American Psychologist*, 76(1), 63–77.

Maak, T. and Pless, N.M. (2006). Responsible leadership in a stakeholder society–a relational perspective. *Journal of Business Ethics*, 66(1), 99–115.

Matilla-Santander, N., Ahonen, E., Albin, M., Baron, S., Bolíbar, M., Bosmans, K., Burström, B., Cuervo, I., Davis, L., Gunn, V., Håkansta, C., Hemmingsson, T., Hogstedt, C., Jonsson, J., Julià, M., Kjellberg, K., Kreshpaj, B., Lewchuk, W.,

Muntaner, C., O'Campo, P., Orellana, C., Östergren, P.O., Padrosa, E., Ruiz, M.E., Vanroelen, C., Vignola, E., Vives, A., Wegman, D.H., Bodin, T. and All Members of the PWR Study Consortium. (2021). COVID-19 and precarious employment: Consequences of the evolving crisis. *International Journal of Health Services*, 51(2), 226–228.

Maon, F., Lindgreen, A. and Swaen, V. (2010). Organizational stages and cultural phases: A critical review and a consolidative model of corporate social responsibility development. *International Journal of Management Reviews*, 12(1), 20–38.

McWilliams, A. and Siegel, D. (2001). Profit maximizing corporate social responsibility. *Academy of Management Review*, 26(4), 504–505.

Nguimkeu, B.Y.P. and Okou, C. (2020). A tale of Africa today: Balancing the lives and livelihoods of informal workers during the COVID-19 pandemic. World Bank Group Open Knowledge Repository. Available at: http://hdl.handle.net/10986/34582

Mialon, M. and McCambridge, J. (2018). Alcohol industry corporate social responsibility initiatives and harmful drinking: A systematic review. *European Journal of Public Health*, 28(4), 664–673.

Miller, B. and Sinclair, J. (2012). Risk perceptions in a resource community and communication implications: Emotion, stigma, and identity. *Risk Analysis: An International Journal*, 32(3), 483–495.

Noronha, E., Chakraborty, S. and D'Cruz, P. (2020). 'Doing dignity work': Indian security guards' interface with precariousness. *Journal of Business Ethics*, 162(3), 553–575.

Olsthoorn, M. (2014). Measuring precarious employment: A proposal for two indicators of precarious employment based on set-theory and tested with Dutch labor market-data. *Social Indicators Research*, 119(1), 421–441.

Oung, A. (2021). MOEA to aid 'eight industries' workers. Available at: https://www.taipeitimes.com/News/biz/archives/2021/09/04/2003763744

Park, S.Y., Cho, M. and Kim, S. (2019). The effect of CSR expectancy violation: Value from expectancy violation theory and confirmation bias. *Journal of Marketing Communications*, 27(4), 365–388.

Perugini, C. and Vladisavljević, M. (2021). Social stability challenged by Covid-19: Pandemics, inequality and policy responses. *Journal of Policy Modeling*, 43(1), 146–160.

Pless, N.M. and Maak, T. (2011). Responsible leadership: Pathways to the future. *Journal of Business Ethics*, 98(S1), 3–13.

Ratten, V. (2020). Coronavirus (covid-19) and entrepreneurship: Changing life and work landscape. *Journal of Small Business and Entrepreneurship*, 32(5), 503–516.

Roca, E. (2010). The exercise of moral imagination in stigmatized work groups. *Journal of Business Ethics*, 96(1), 135–147.

Secchi, D. (2007). Utilitarian, managerial and relational theories of corporate social responsibility. *International Journal of Management Reviews*, 9(4), 347–373.

Shepherd, D.A., Maitlis, S., Parida, V., Wincent, J. and Lawrence, T.B. (2021). Intersectionality in intractable dirty work: How Mumbai ragpickers make meaning of their work and lives. *Academy of Management Journal*. Available at: https://doi.org/10.5465/amj.2019.0125

Silaban, R., Widiawaty, D. and Basir, S. (2021). The growth of platform work as precarious work that threatens Indonesia's target to meet decent work as formulated in Goal 8 of SDGs. *IOP Conference Series: Earth and Environmental Science*, 940(1), 012057.

Simpson, R., Slutskaya, N., Lewis, P. and Höpfl, H. (2012). Introducing dirty work, concepts and identities. In Simpson, R., Slutskaya, N., Lewis, P. and Hopfl, H. (Eds.), *Dirty Work: Concepts and Identities*. Basingstoke: Palgrave Macmillan.

Strauss, D. (2020). Global job losses rise sharply as coronavirus lockdowns are extended. Available at: https://www.ft.com/content/89a015d4-84d9-4b6f-880b-2720779f5531

Sung, H. and Pan, J. (2013). *Aggressive Sex Workers Ruining Wanhua, Locals Say*. Available at: https://www.taipeitimes.com/News/taiwan/archives/2013/09/23/2003572817

Sutton, R.I. and Callahan, A.L. (1987). The stigma of bankruptcy: Spoiled organizational image and its management. *Academy of Management Journal*, 30(3), 405–436.

The Lancet. (2020). The plight of essential workers during the COVID-19 pandemic. *The Lancet*, 395, 1587.

Vogel, D. (2006). *The Market for Virtue*. Washington, DC: Brookings Institute.

Waldman, D.A. and Galvin, B.M. (2008). Alternative perspectives of responsible leadership. *Organizational Dynamics*, 37(4), 327–341.

Wanderley, L.S.O., Lucian, R., Farache, F. and de Sousa Filho, J.M. (2008). CSR information disclosure on the web: A context-based approach analysing the influence of country of origin and industry sector. *Journal of Business Ethics*, 82(2), 369–378.

West, L.A. (2001). Negotiating masculinities in American drinking subcultures. *Journal of Men's Studies*, 9(3), 371–392.

Wickert, C. (2021). Corporate social responsibility research in the Journal of Management Studies: A shift from a business-centric to a society-centric focus. *Journal of Management Studies*, 58(8), E1–E17.

Yoon, Y., Gürhan-Canli, Z. and Schwarz, N. (2006). The effect of corporate social responsibility (CSR) activities on companies with bad reputations. *Journal of Consumer Psychology*, 16(4), 377–390.

Zennie, M. and Tsai, G. (2021). How a false sense of security, and a little secret tea, broke down Taiwan's COVID-19 defenses. Available at: https://time.com/6050316/taiwan-covid-19-outbreak-tea/

Part 2

CSR – Challenges in Developing and Least Developed Countries

7 The Role of NGOs in CSR

A Comparison of NGOs' Practices of and Influences on CSR in Developing and Developed Countries

Anisur R. Faroque, Esnaina Quader, Mohammad Osman Gani, and Sina Mortazavi

Introduction

The term "corporate social responsibility" (CSR) was coined by the American economist Howard R. Bowen in his 1953 book *Social Responsibilities of the Businessman* (Bowen, 2013). Bowen stated that businesses are responsible not only for maximizing profit or value for shareholders but also for the interests of the workers, consumers, and communities who are their stakeholders (Bowen, 2013). In the 1960s and 1970s, conflicts between and contrasting interests of different stakeholder groups severely jeopardized the core operations of some Western corporations. In response to these conflicts, the firms involved turned to CSR to demonstrate their social and environmental concerns and began integrating social responsibilities into their corporate agendas. In the ensuing decades, CSR has attracted considerable attention from scholars, who have redefined Bowen's concept from various perspectives. It has become a comparatively common yet complex concept that lacks a single accepted definition or established facilitation criterion (Carroll and Shabana, 2010). For example, Milton Friedman's (2007) very popular view suggests that a firm's social responsibilities are its long-term commitment to increasing profit for its shareholders rather than its legal obligations to societal, environmental, and economic development. Carroll (1991) and other scholars with similar perceptions of CSR contradicted Friedman's argument, positing CSR as the assorted social, economic, legal, ethical, and philanthropic obligations businesses must undertake.

Today, managers of businesses of all different sizes vary in how they address their CSR activities. They use a variety of terms to refer to their CSR activities, including corporate social responsiveness, corporate responsibilities, corporate citizenship, stakeholder management, corporate sustainable business practice, and others (Carroll and Shabana, 2010; Sharma and Kiran, 2013). Thus, due to the lack of a universal description of CSR, the modern definition of the term is based on an informal consensus that corporations have legal, ethical, and moral responsibilities for both their shareholders and their stakeholders, who have the power to affect a business and are affected by that business's operations (Freeman, 1984; Trevino and Nelson, 2011).

DOI: 10.4324/9781003274575-9

Government organizations, nongovernmental organizations (NGOs), and interest groups have become great sources of support and resources pertaining to CSR for corporate organizations of various sizes and forms (Kotler and Lee, 2005). NGOs in particular have become key partners in corporations' implementation of CSR, motivated by many strategic points of view. Their knowledge of local development issues and network of local talent has been beneficial for corporations to address these needs through CSR projects. NGOs' role as nonprofit socioeconomic development agents of marginalized populations (Lewis and Kanji, 2009) has undergone many shifts and alterations from the conventional form. NGOs are now active participants in the development of policies, income-generating social enterprise models, and small- and large-scale nonprofit development projects. This activity has overshadowed the role of ineffective governments of many developing nations and influenced leaders of developed countries to build and maintain cordial relationships with them (Doh and Gauy, 2006).

Previous research has documented that NGOs play two roles in CSR: they are both confrontational development agents and cooperative development partners. NGOs either lead corporations toward voluntary development initiatives through coercion or collaborate with firms of various sizes and types to facilitate CSR projects that support socioeconomic development goals (Fiedler and Deegan, 2007; Arenas et al., 2009). NGOs have demonstrated a great influence on CSR culture in both developing and developed nations for a long time (Jamali and Neville, 2011).

Shared Value

The new paradigm of shared value has added new dimensions to CSR and produced new means for corporations and NGOs to perform CSR in both developing and developed nations. Whereas a lack of sustainable financial support has been an inherent reason for NGOs to engage in CSR, "acceptance as a socially responsible business" influenced firms and corporations to see CSR as a strategic competitive benefit. The United Nations' (UN) Sustainable Development Goals (SDGs) have also fueled global development movements over the last decade and highlighted firms that have worked to mitigate global development challenges through sustainable operations. An increasing number of businesses are now building strategic alliances with external partners such as NGOs to integrate sustainable operations and thereby support social, economic, and environmental progress. The UN's SDGs have prompted businesses to use CSR activities to combine their corporate agendas with social, environmental, and economic goals.

In recent years, the implementations and implications of CSR have evolved drastically, drawing attention from both the public and private sectors. According to Kotler and Lee (2005), companies have gained strategic benefits in implementing CSR activities through partnerships with key CSR agents (NGOs). However, the impact of NGOs' structural, managerial, and operational changes on the parameters for evaluating the effectiveness of CSR and the relationships and partnerships between key CSR agents requires more in-depth analysis. This chapter is an attempt to meet that need by critically analyzing the impact of NGOs' operations and strategies on CSR and its primary agents—corporations—on different levels of economies. Partnerships and cooperation with NGOs ease the corporate process of combining social development goals with business agendas. Firms' inclination to build strategic alliances with stakeholders (specifically NGOs) to enhance the legitimacy and transparency of their sustainable operations was one of the precursors of CSR (Kurucz et al., 2008).

How NGOs Practice and Facilitate CSR at Different Economic Levels

Due to the lack of a universal definition and practice of CSR, NGOs practice and facilitate CSR in different ways around the world. Not all NGOs demonstrate a strong foothold or interest in CSR in both developed and developing nations; small NGOs tend to restrict their focus to local humanitarian concerns (Jamali and Neville, 2011). However, some NGOs in both developed and developing nations have become, whether coincidentally or deliberately, key players in global and regional governance through cross-sectoral strategic associations (Arenas et al., 2009). These NGOs are mostly medium to large in size and have well-organized managerial structures, operational strategies, and development programs, which enable them to practice CSR and cooperate in implementing it with other players in different parts of the world.

Over the last decade, NGOs' roles and goals as secondary stakeholders have clearly evolved in developing and developed nations (Doh and Guay, 2006; Jamali and Neville, 2011). How NGOs practice and perceive CSR has been shaped by the national and regional contexts in which they operate, so this chapter is focused on the underlying forces that impact the roles of NGOs in CSR. A series of these organizations has been deeply analyzed to elucidate how NGOs have transformed from mere supporters to major partners of corporations in the practice of CSR. The NGOs discussed in this chapter were selected from four different countries: Bangladesh, China, the United States, and the United Kingdom. After a rigorous evaluation to determine eligibility for the intended study, NGOs with a strong global and national presence were carefully selected from these four nations. Comprehensive research was conducted to understand how CSR is perceived and practiced by NGOs as key agents in these countries, which are strikingly different from each other in terms of their social, cultural, economic, and government policies and legal structures. A qualitative research method based on secondary data was used to support the study, as sufficient and reliable information was already available from multiple sources. Throughout the research, several attempts were made to scrutinize the application and utilization of relevant data collected from the internet, NGO websites, research journals, articles, and books. The following sections provide detailed descriptions of the selected NGOs and the nations in which they operate to scrutinize, compare, and shed light on the similarities, key differences, and driving factors influencing their performance as servers and advocates of CSR.

The Case of Bangladesh

Bangladeshi NGOs played a vital role in the reformation of the country after its liberation in 1971. BRAC, Grameen Bank, ASA, and Care Bangladesh were some of the first NGOs to support the reconstruction of sustainable humanitarian development models and economic welfare for the underprivileged people of the country (Muhammad, 2009). Besides BRAC, the largest and fastest-growing development NGO in the world (*The Economist*, 2010), Bangladesh is home to the pioneer of the concepts of microcredit and microfinance, Grameen Bank, which was founded by Nobel Peace Laureate Muhammad Yunus (Yunus, 2010). Bangladesh is expected to graduate from the United Nation's least developed country list and become a developing country by 2026. It is a lower-middle-income country with a population of approximately 165 million, 24 million of whom live under the poverty line (World Bank, 2021). Bangladesh has outperformed many other low-income countries with its remarkable progress in human development. Much of its progress in this regard has been possible due to the social, economic, and environmental development projects conducted by national and international NGOs. The CSR activities of multinational corporations (MNCs) have also driven Bangladesh's growth in the right direction.

The seed of CSR was first planted by early MNCs through their philanthropic charitable work as part of the corporate culture in Bangladesh. Over the years, the dynamics of CSR have transformed due to globalization. Exposure to global CSR standards now directs how CSR is practiced by MNCs in Bangladesh. A majority of the combined CSR initiatives of MNCs in Bangladesh are focused on local development projects rather than simple charitable initiatives. For instance, MNCs like Grameen Phone and Chevron Bangladesh include healthcare, education, poverty, job creation, women's empowerment, etc., as key development areas to focus on in their CSR activities (Alam et al., 2010; Parveen, 2016).

MNCs' cross-sectoral collaborations with NGOs focusing on the local humanitarian and development crisis in Bangladesh have increased dramatically over the last decade. The desire to be perceived as socially and environmentally responsible business entities has influenced and secured global market access for many MNCs, including Unilever, British American Tobacco (BAT), Standard Chartered Bank (SCB), Grameen Phone, and Chevron Bangladesh (Parveen, 2016). CSR in the form of collaboration with local communities and national and international NGOs has also brought these MNCs strategic benefits. The knowledge of and networks with local communities have increased the influence of national and international NGOs, which are now partnering with large corporations to facilitate CSR.

Escalating competition for national and international donations and the dearth of adequate government policies and constitutional laws favoring NGOs' operations in Bangladesh have strengthened NGOs' interest in collaborating with MNCs. As a result, many NGOs have developed alternative means for their survival; in particular, they have formulated strategies for sustainable social enterprise models to reduce their dependency on formal and informal donors and government bodies. NGOs such as BRAC and Grameen Bank earned global accolades for their unique social enterprise, microcredit, and microfinance models. These NGOs create social, environmental, and economic value by combining their nonprofit development programs with income-generating social enterprises and investment projects. The inclusion of the bottom-of-the-pyramid market in supply chains as both consumers and suppliers in the income-generating social enterprises of Grameen Foundation (Grameen Danone, Grameen Shakti, Grameen Check, Grameen Phone) has been used as an alternative sustainability strategy for local community development programs in many developing and underdeveloped nations (Balasundaram et al., 2009; Yunus et al., 2010).

NGOs supporting and facilitating development-oriented CSR activities through social enterprises are a rising trend in Bangladesh. BRAC, for instance, has established multiple social enterprises and investment projects that support the social, economic, and environmental goals of the NGO (BRAC, n.d). BRAC Aarong, one of Bangladesh's largest clothing brands, operates as a social enterprise at home and abroad. With over 16 outlets across the country, it advances its social and economic goals by connecting poor artisans to the market. BRAC Bank, BRAC University are social investment projects and BRAC Cold Storage, BRAC Dairy, BRAC Seed and Agro, and BRAC Fisheries are separate social enterprise units of BRAC NGO (BRAC, n.d). Because most of BRAC's social enterprises operate as income-generating ventures and contribute a portion of their income to help BRAC become a self-financed NGO (Cho and Sulatana, 2015), their CSR initiatives are handled separately from BRAC's development projects.

The Case of China

Home to the world's largest national population, China has become a key emerging economy. Driven by rapid economic growth and the transformation of social and environmental regulation policies, China's private sector is gradually becoming dominant, although the government still holds substantial power and controls most of the country's firms and corporations. Most Chinese businesses are either state-run or state-led, and they use CSR as a defensive mechanism alongside the government to tackle international criticism over factors such as human rights violations, environmental degradation, social discontent, etc. (Zhang et al., 2019). CSR in China lacks clarity in definition and practice. Although the Chinese government is vocal about firms' CSR practices, there are no structured guidelines or parameters to measure their contribution to productive CSR initiatives. Chinese firms' CSR is perceived as ornamental rather than genuine efforts to promote social, environmental, and economic development (Lin, 2010).

Until the late 1970s, CSR in China was strictly managed by the state and was limited to simple activities to support economic development and social benefits initiated for the people by state-owned enterprises. In 1978, however, the government slightly withdrew its influence over CSR practices as it entered an open-market economy. Through foreign direct investments and MNCs' entering the Chinese market, privately owned and state-led enterprises were introduced to global CSR standards. The emergence of China as a key player in the global supply chain influenced many Chinese firms to embrace international CSR standards, although China's complex political and institutional settings retained invisible control over the operation of firms in the Chinese market (Yin and Zhang, 2012). The inequalities and disparities in social justice and trading facilities in China have attracted international attention in the ensuing decades.

International NGOs and advocates of human and social rights also struggle to operate freely in China due to the new law governing foreign NGOs imposed on January 1, 2017, which prohibits national and international NGOs from conducting development activities in the country without government involvement. This law essentially relegated NGOs in China to the role of silent observers with regard to CSR and sustainable corporate operations and restricted their ability to protect social, economic, environmental, and humanitarian rights. Foreign NGOs are now required to report periodically to government sponsors and public security authorities regarding their activities and their utilization of funds. These policies and regulations have impacted the freedom of both national and international NGOs, so the CSR practiced in China is now designed to facilitate and support the interests of the government (Yang and Webber, 2014). It is now the Chinese government that works as the main promoter of CSR (Zhang et al., 2019); regardless of any desire on their part to meet international CSR standards, Chinese companies' first obligation is to comply with the CSR practices and strategies designed by the state.

Such state-influenced CSR practices do not present a favorable platform for NGOs to provide support for the implementation of CSR by corporations (Whitehead, 2014). While CSR is implemented as a corporate sustainable strategy that merges societal, economic, and environmental goals with business agendas in most parts of the world, in China, CSR is perceived as a tool by which to obey and satisfy government needs. The increasing volumes of NGOs, media coverage, and consumer interest are still insufficient to enforce and legitimize CSR as a core responsibility of Chinese firms seeking to ensure that their operations are sustainable (Sarkis et al., 2011). However, in the last few years, a few national and international NGOs have succeeded in shifting China's policy slightly by building partnerships with Chinese firms. They are promoting CSR activities designed to mitigate environmental concerns resulting from maintaining textile companies' supply chains (Davis and Moosmayer, 2015). Nevertheless, these partnerships remain subject to China's complex institutional setting (She and Bo, 2014; Whitehead, 2014).

The Case of the United Kingdom

Before CSR emerged formally, a group of businesspeople in the United Kingdom were already practicing CSR back in the 19th century with their missions to provide better living conditions, proper social security, and healthcare for their employees (Reddy, 2020). Modern CSR in the United Kingdom was established based on these early efforts, which became the foundation and shaped the structure of CSR in the United Kingdom. As interest in and the practice of CSR spread globally, the United Kingdom developed legislative rules to legalize and formalize CSR for its businesses (UK Government, 2020). For instance, the UK government once made it mandatory for companies to provide information on their CSR activities in annual reports produced for stakeholders (Rangan et al., 2015). Over the past few decades, various initiatives have been undertaken to strengthen connections between business goals and social and environmental concerns (Allen-Gil et al., 2005). Associations and communities of business organizations have designed long- and short-term programs to bridge the gap between business and socioeconomic development agendas. For instance, in 1982, over 700 companies created a network known as Business in the Community, which was based on a program that supports social issues with new business development (Sofidel, 2018).

The UK government has also played a major role in establishing a fundamental system that facilitates corporate CSR practices. The incorporation of strategies for fulfilling the social responsibilities of both profit-oriented and nonprofit businesses is rigorously promoted by the government (Doh and Guay, 2006). The United Kingdom took a step toward the serious implementation of CSR by appointing Kim Howells as the first CSR minister at the beginning of the 21st century (Reddy, 2020). Since this dramatic step, the government has reached new heights in its involvement in CSR implementation and adoption by companies of all sizes and types in the United Kingdom.

The UK government relaxed its focus on CSR following the country's formal withdrawal from the European Union (Brexit) on January 31, 2020. The financial service and retail sectors were among the important industries deemed to be capable of redefining the British economy. The United Kingdom has maintained its focus on social expectations, environmental needs, and economic empowerment through CSR practices despite the tensions created by Brexit. The government has continued encouraging corporations to promote community and environmental development-oriented CSR.

Large companies are seen as the major practitioners of CSR in the United Kingdom (Jones et al., 2005), even though the country's standardized CSR policy does not target any specific size or type of organization. Companies such as Tesco, Aldi, Morrisons, and Marks and Spencer facilitate and practice CSR through a variety of activities, including pure charity work (Jones et al., 2005; Reynold et al., 2005). NGOs' role in CSR practice in the context of the United Kingdom is, similar to their position in China, that of a voluntary or silent spectator. In recent years, they have initiated no noteworthy initiatives as important development agents to support the CSR activities of British companies (Brewis, 2013). The British government's decision to change the reporting of CSR activities for firms from a mandatory to a voluntary action also impacted the dynamics for NGOs in CSR. As the UK government is very transparent and active regarding the CSR initiatives of British organizations, NGOs' role is for the most part limited to fundraising and community and environmental development activities. The UK government's well-designed formal policies, institutional agreements, and awareness of employees and consumers are some of the key factors responsible for NGOs taking a backseat in the CSR practices of British companies (Păceşilă and Colesca, 2020).

The Case of the United States

The United States's CSR journey began in 1953 with Bowen's formal conceptualization and definition of CSR (Bowen, 2013). US corporations thus have a long history of facilitating and practicing CSR through their core business operations. The growth of interest in sustainable business operations has made CSR a vital corporate strategy due to fierce national and global competition in almost every sector. CSR affects the internal and external environments that shape and control American businesses' operations and ability to achieve their goals. It also has a clear impact on how companies demonstrate their social and environmental concerns through the operational strategies applied in US markets (Snider et al., 2003). As has been observed in other developed parts of the world, CSR is highly appreciated and is now expected from US corporations.

Organizations are expected to be transparent in their practice of CSR, as the perceptions of both stakeholders and shareholders depend on the execution of CSR activities in the United States (Doh and Guay, 2006). Due to the increasing interest in CSR and sustainable corporate strategies, US companies are now improvising strategies to improve their national and international CSR performance. However, there have been incidents in the United States of firms making false claims and engaging in unethical practices in the name of CSR. To ensure that companies are held accountable for corporate misconduct, the US government has implemented legislative regulations at the federal and state levels (Camilleri, 2017). Even though these US government initiatives were considered appropriate and pertinent by government regulatory bodies at the time of their promulgation, there have since been questions about and debates over the systematic regulation of education, healthcare, agriculture, tech-based industries, etc. In the United States, national and international organizations, civil society, and NGOs are important agents, but their motives for engaging in CSR are usually driven by federal measures.

Cross-sectoral alliances between corporations and NGOs have been a common form of practicing CSR in the United States for a very long time. American companies' performance and profitability are associated with how they uphold social and environmental values. As a result, CSR is often used to maintain companies' market value and favorable image. Donating to NGOs and local communities as part of CSR initiatives has also become a common corporate practice in the United States. For instance, every year corporate giants such as Amazon, Coca-Cola, Microsoft, Starbucks, Apple, Google, General Electronics, and Bank of America donate millions of dollars through their in-house CSR programs to national and international NGOs, including UNICEF USA, Path, Save the Children, USAID, Doctors without Borders, etc. After federal and state government grants, donations made in the form of CSR by corporations are thus a significant funding stream for NGOs in the United States.

NGOs' contributions to CSR in the context of the United States have been shaped by the pressing issues affecting the nation. Their role in CSR has been most evident through their direct and indirect participation in different sectoral policymaking and environmental and social movements (Doh and Guay, 2004). Institutional, political, and social settings are considered major drivers that strengthen or weaken the impact of NGOs on CSR (Păceşilă and Colesca, 2020).

Factors Shaping Regional Variations in the Role of NGOs in CSR

Institutional Variation

Institutional settings and dynamics play a critical role in shaping CSR in different parts of the world (Aguilera et al., 2006; Miska and Mendenhall, 2015). According to Tolbert and Zucker (1996), how a company legitimizes its operation in an institutional environment and strategizes to integrate into that environment is a concern of institutional theory. North (1990) suggested that there are three main types of institutional settings. The first is influenced by formal settings that are built upon formal institutions, constitutional laws, legitimate government policies, and verdicts. The second is influenced by informal settings that emphasize political beliefs, cultural patterns, and voluntary institutions such as the United Nations. The last is influenced by individualistic traits, religious and family values, etc. Among these settings, CSR and its agents fall into the first two institutional settings in a general sense. Variations in the regulations and settings of institutions lead to variations in how NGOs and corporations adopt and adapt to the drivers of such changes (Yin and Zhang, 2012). For instance, in developed nations such as the United States and the United Kingdom, governments have stable systematic national and state policies supported by formal institutions to ensure the sustainable operation of corporations (Albareda et al., 2006; Moon, 2007). NGOs in developed nations are thus perceived as strategic partners by large corporations such as Coca-Cola, Marks and Spencer, Gap, Costco, etc., in their implementation of sustainable CSR activities. In developing nations such as Bangladesh, due to the lack of concrete government policies and initiatives to formalize corporate CSR, informal institutional settings are the important drivers of CSR activities. National and international NGOs such as the World Bank, the United Nations, BRAC, ASA, NRC, USAID, and Grameen collaborate with corporations to support and enable development-oriented CSR for social, environmental, and economic progress on the national level. In contrast, China has an unusual institutional arrangement that advocates conditional political CSR and restricts the CSR activities of corporations and NGOs. In China, domestic environmental NGOs, as well as international NGOs like Greenpeace and API, have made little progress in CSR practices in the apparel sector over the past decade. Despite having the resources and knowledge to support the formal and unhindered practice of CSR (Zhang et al., 2019), NGOs in China downplay their role largely due to the constraining NGO regulatory laws imposed by the Chinese government.

Organizational Legitimacy

The core value of CSR is corporations' interest in social, environmental, and economic concerns and their ability to address these concerns through their business operations and strategies (Bowen, 2013). The legitimacy and transparency of corporate actions and operations must therefore acknowledge that the social, economic, and environmental needs of different stakeholders can be achieved through cooperation with NGOs (Doh and Gauy, 2006; Kotler and Lee, 2005). Corporate operations and structure must strive to ensure a firm's survival through profitable business, so when such organizations publicize their sustainable operations, stakeholders who are influenced by that company's image and brand value require proper proof and evidence of their CSR activities (Păceşilă and Colesca, 2020). This is where NGOs come into play. For example, the Coca-Cola Company collaborated with the World Wildlife Fund, the leading independent natural resource conservation NGO, to support global water neutrality (The Coca-Cola Company, n.d.). Through this collaboration, Coca-Cola strove to improve its corporate image and legitimize its initiative to conserve water resources and replace the water used in the production of drinks to maintain global water neutrality. As NGOs are perceived as selfless nonprofit-oriented development agents in most parts of the world (Austin et al., 2012), collaboration with nonprofit and nongovernmental organizations diminishes barriers and legitimizes corporations' social, environmental, and economic development goals. This collaborative approach with corporations also offers strategic benefits to NGOs. NGOs thus often devise strategies to pursue associations with corporations that legitimize profit-oriented business ventures under a nonprofit NGO structure (Selsky and Parker, 2005). For instance, BRAC NGO was associated with HSBC Bank as part of the bank's CSR project, which increased the financial benefits of running social enterprises such as BRAC Aarong.

Access to Local Communities

NGOs' access to local communities, knowledge, and resources is utilized differently in developing and developed nations (Bocken et al., 2016). While NGOs in developed countries use local knowledge to assist government bodies in forming national policy, in developing countries they focus on mitigating local needs through utilizing resources as a means of targeting social and economic development goals for marginalized populations (Jamali et al., 2008). NGOs are also a great source of resources and networks that connect corporations practicing CSR and communities thriving on the CSR activities of corporations. NGOs' expertise in developing fruitful social, economic, and environmental development programs enables many MNCs to meet their SDGs. For instance, Unilever Bangladesh Limited (UBL) collaborated with a local NGO, Friendship, to facilitate a CSR project called the Lifebuoy Friendship Hospital (LFH). LFH is a floating hospital that provides primary and secondary healthcare services to underprivileged people in seven remote subdistricts of northern Bangladesh (Sharmin et al., 2018). UBL finances a major share of the operation for LFH, while Friendship provides a broad range of information on the healthcare needs of local communities; together, these two efforts facilitate the CSR project. Some corporate–NGO partnerships have even advanced strategic collaborations in more innovative ways by using nonprofit development activities to initiate sustainable business models.

Over the last few decades, NGOs, both independently and through collaboration with local and international organizations, have embraced profit-generating social enterprise models to target bottom-of-the-pyramid markets in developing economies. These new strategic moves have influenced how NGOs practice and facilitate CSR for themselves and their corporate partners. For example, the Grameen Foundation and BRAC in Bangladesh run multiple social enterprises and investment projects that have distinct groups of customers, suppliers, and distributors. These NGOs target social and economic value creations for marginalized and disadvantaged individuals through their social enterprises (Cho and Sulatana, 2015; Yunus et al., 2010), which operate as market-oriented business units that support and follow CSR guidelines provided by the parent NGO. For example, BRAC Bank, one of the leading commercial banks in Bangladesh, is also a part of the social investment projects of BRAC NGO. Thus, the lion's share of BRAC Bank's CSR activities is guided by BRAC NGO.

Commitment to Financial Sustainability

The operation and activities of NGOs as development agents have always depended on the funds donated by external sources such as government, national and international donors, corporations, philanthropists, etc. (Lewis and Kanji, 2009). Financial sustainability and solvency are thus important drivers that influence NGOs' concerns regarding the establishment of sustainable flows of resources. Corporations also reap strategic benefits from CSR activities that require collaboration with NGOs. These strategic collaborations to sustainably operate corporations in developed nations are often initiated by NGOs to comply with government regulations, market drivers, and company policies. For example, in developed countries such as the United States and the United Kingdom, government initiatives and market drivers (e.g., consumers, shareholders, and key business partners) influence the sustainable operation of corporations. These factors also directly or indirectly revolve around policies concerning the financial sustainability of NGOs in these nations. Developed nations emphasize having a well-designed and well-articulated system that reduces disruptions in the distribution of funds and influences the CSR of corporations that support the financial needs of national and international NGOs.

However, in recent years, shortages of funds and increasing competition for donations have raised concerns among NGOs regarding their financial well-being, especially Bangladesh and other developing countries. National and international agencies and donors have become skeptical about releasing funds to an NGO without scrutinizing its development agenda (Doherty et al., 2020). Therefore, NGOs, especially those in developing nations, consider CSR to be a potential means of securing funding. For instance, most local NGOs in Bangladesh endure rigorous competition to secure government donations due to the lack of transparent and reliable fund distribution policies on the part of the government; thus, they solicit international NGOs and MNCs for financial assistance in Bangladesh. In the case of Chinese NGOs, the situation is quite severe: local NGOs often struggle to find financial backing for their activities because they must rely on the Chinese government's development funds. The Chinese government has recently compounded these NGOs' difficulties with new laws that hinder their ability to receive donations from international NGOs and MNCs.

Discussion

The CSR literature in recent decades has emphasized the influence of key agents (e.g., governments, NGOs, interest groups, MNCs, etc.) that catalyzed the evolution of CSR into an essential strategy for many private and public organizations across the world (Barkemeyer, 2009; Blowfield and Dolan, 2014; Jamali, 2010). Prominent researchers in this field have identified several factors that impact how CSR is practiced at different economic levels (Bhatia and Makkar, 2019; Doh and Guay, 2006; Jamali and Neville, 2011). A significant amount of research has documented the relationships and impacts on the CSR of key agents in both developing and developed nations (Aguilera et al., 2006; Rafael, 2010; Welford, 2005). Factors such as government interference (Fifka and Pobizhan, 2014), corruption, availability of resources (Baughn et al., 2007), institutional settings (Doh and Guay, 2006), the willingness of corporate leaders (Jizi et al., 2014), and the influence of civil society (Hamann and Acutt, 2003) are considered major drivers of how CSR is perceived and practiced in different parts of the world. These factors also influence the adoption and adaptation of novel strategic moves to maintain the sustainable operation of key CSR agents such as corporations and NGOs in developed and developing nations. For instance, many NGOs that were formerly considered secondary stakeholders to corporations have collaborated with MNCs over the past decade to develop income-generating social enterprise models as a means of achieving SDGs (Cho and Sulatana, 2015; Doherty et al., 2014, 2020; Fontana, 2017; Hackett, 2016; Suykens et al., 2018). Thus, this research focuses on the variety of roles NGOs play in supporting and enabling CSR practices in different parts of the world.

This research shows that NGOs support and facilitate CSR in both developed and developing nations. They transform corporate strategies and operational methods by influencing external factors such as government regulations, relationships with corporations, availability of funds, and sustainable social, environmental, and economic development agendas. NGOs' role as key agents of CSR has become more visible, especially in developing economies (Jamali et al., 2008; Burgos, 2013; Cho and Sulatana, 2015). For instance, the absence of government support and formal regulation of CSR in developing countries often jeopardize NGOs' development activities, so NGOs devise alternative strategies to enhance their productivity and associate with potential development agents to ensure a stable flow of resources. Some NGOs collaborate with corporations to foster CSR as a means of securing financial stability and the sustainability of corporate operations, while others view corporate–NGO collaborations as a means of making their voices heard and strengthening their position as they pursue SDGs.

NGOs have long played an active role in reinforcing national development policies in developed nations such as the United States and the United Kingdom. Despite their actions generating questionable and negative publicity, the governments and regulatory bodies of these nations have also on occasions guarded the interests of large corporations. Therefore, NGOs in both developed and developing countries campaign against corporate misconduct, government corruption, environmental abuse, human rights violations, conflicts over natural resources, etc.

As CSR agents, NGOs can act as either supportive agents or coercive forces to ensure the fruitful implementation of sustainable corporate operations in both developed and developing nations. For instance, when the collapse of the Rana Plaza building in 2013 injured more than 2,500 garment workers and killed at least 1,132 in Bangladesh, the brutal incident highlighted the disregard of workplace safety guidelines in garment factories and spurred a global movement on the part of national and international NGOs to punish incidents of misconduct in Bangladesh's readymade garment sector (International Labor Organization, 2017).

This study also highlights that NGOs' roles in the field of CSR vary depending on whether they advocate for strategic, development-oriented, or political CSR. How NGOs directly and indirectly contribute to CSR by accomplishing their own goals and supporting the agendas of other CSR agents is influenced by the type of CSR they support at different economic levels. The outcomes of this research showcase a small but important part of the larger CSR ecosystem, which can be intriguing for policymakers, practitioners, and managers of NGOs as well as businesses, especially those working in developing countries and that are striving for development-oriented CSR.

References

Aguilera, R., Williams, C., Conley, J. and Rupp, D. (2006). Corporate governance and social responsibility: A comparative analysis of the UK and the US. *Corporate Governance: An International Review*, 14(3), 147–158.

Alam, S.M.S., Hoque, S.M.S. and Hosen, M.Z. (2010). Corporate social responsibility of multinational corporation in Bangladesh: A case study on Grameen Phone. *Journal of Patuakhali Science and Technology University*, 2(1), 51–61.

Albareda, L., Tencati, A., Lozano, J.M. and Perrini, F. (2006). The government's role in promoting corporate responsibility: A comparative analysis of Italy and UK from the relational state perspective. *Corporate Governance: The International Journal of Business in Society*, 6(4), 386–400.

Allen-Gil, S., Walker, L., Thomas, G., Shevory, T. and Elan, S. (2005). Forming a community partnership to enhance education in sustainability. *International Journal of Sustainability in Higher Education*, 6(4), 392–402.

Austin, J.E. and Seitanidi, M.M. (2012). Collaborative value creation: A review of partnering between nonprofits and businesses: Part 1. Value creation spectrum and collaboration stages. *Nonprofit and Voluntary Sector Quarterly*, 41(5), 726–758.

Arenas, D., Lozano, J.M. and Albareda, L. (2009). The role of NGOs in CSR: Mutual perceptions among stakeholders. *Journal of Business Ethics*, 88(1), 175–197.

Balasundaram, N. (2009, July 26). Social responsibility of business: A case study of Grameen Phone in Bangladesh. Available at: https://papers.ssrn.com/sol3/papers.cfm?abstract_id=2117904

Barkemeyer, R. (2009). Beyond compliance: Below expectations? Cross-border CSR, development, and the UN Global Compact. *Business Ethics: A European Review*, 18(3), 273–289.

Baughn, C.C., Bodie, N.L. and McIntosh, J.C. (2007). Corporate social and environmental responsibility in Asian countries and other geographical regions. *Corporate Social Responsibility and Environmental Management*, 14(4), 189–205.

Bocken, N.M.P., Fil, A. and Prabhu, J. (2016). Scaling up social businesses in developing markets. *Journal of Cleaner Production*, 139, 295–308.

Bhatia, A. and Makkar, B. (2019). CSR disclosure in developing and developed countries: A comparative study. *Journal of Global Responsibility*, 11(1), 1–26.

BRAC. (n.d.). BRAC enterprises and investments: An overview. Available at: http://www.brac.net/sites/default/files/Overview-BRAC-enterprises-and-investments.pdf

Blowfield, M. and Dolan, C. (2014). Business as a development agent: Evidence of possibility and improbability. *Third World Quarterly*, 35(1), 22–42.

Brewis, G. (2013). Towards a new understanding of volunteering in England before 1960? University College London working paper. Available at: http://discovery.ucl.ac.uk/10018258/1/IVR_working_paper_two_history_of_volunteering.Pdf

Bowen, H.R. (2013). *Social Responsibilities of the Businessman*. Iowa City, IA: University of Iowa Press.

Burgos, S. (2013). Corporations and social responsibility: NGOs in the ascendancy. *Journal of Business Strategy*, 34(1), 21–29.

Camilleri, M.A. (2017). Corporate social responsibility policy in the US of America. In Idowu, S., Vertigans, S. and Schiopoiu Burlea, A. (Eds.), *Corporate Social Responsibility in Times of Crisis: CSR, Sustainability, Ethics and Governance*. Cham: Springer Nature.

Carroll, A. and Shabana, K. (2010). The business case for corporate social responsibility: A review of concepts, research, and practice. *International Journal of Management Reviews*, 12(1), 85–105.

Carroll, A.B. (1991). The pyramid of corporate social responsibility: Toward the moral management of organizational stakeholders. *Business Horizons*, 34, 39–48.

Cho, S. and Sulatana, R. (2015). Journey from NGO to sustainable social enterprise: Acceleratory organizational factors of BRAC. *Asian Social Work and Policy Review*, 9(3), 293–306.

Davis, S.M. and Moosmayer, D.C. (2015). Greening the field? How NGOs are shaping corporate social responsibility in China. *Journal of Current Chinese Affairs*, 43(4), 75–110.

Doh, J.P. and Guay, T.R. (2004). Globalization and corporate social responsibility: How non-governmental organizations influence labor and environmental codes of conduct. *Management International Review*, 44(2), 7–29.

Doh, J.P. and Guay, T.R. (2006). Corporate social responsibility, public policy, and NGO activism in Europe and the US: An institutional-stakeholder perspective. *Journal of Management Studies*, 43(1), 47–72.

Doherty, B., Haugh, H. and Lyon, F. (2014). Social enterprises as hybrid organizations: A review and research agenda. *International Journal of Management Reviews*, 16(4), 417–436.

Doherty, B., Haugh, H., Sahan, E., Wills, T. and Croft, S. (2020). Creating the new economy: Business models that put people and planet first. Available at: http://eprints.whiterose.ac.uk/155977/

Fiedler, T. and Deegan, C. (2007). Motivations for environmental collaboration within the building and construction industry. *Managerial Auditing Journal*, 22(4), 410–441.

Fifka, M.S. and Pobizhan, M. (2014). An institutional approach to corporate social responsibility in Russia. *Journal of Cleaner Production*, 82(1), 192–201.

Fontana, E. (2017). Corporate social responsibility as stakeholder engagement: Firm-NGO collaboration in Sweden. *Corporate Social Responsibility and Environmental Management*, 25(4), 327–338.

Freeman, R.E. (1984). *Strategic Management: A Stakeholder Approach*. London: Pitman.

Friedman, M. (2007). The social responsibility of business is to increase its profits. In Zimmerli, W.C., Holzinger, M. and Richter, K. (Eds.), *Corporate Ethics and Corporate Governance*. Heidelberg: Springer.

Hackett, M. (2016). Solving 'social market failures' with social enterprises? Grameen Shakti (village energy) in Bangladesh. *Journal of Social Entrepreneurship*, 7(3), 312–341.

Hamann, R. and Acutt, N. (2003). How should civil society (and the government) respond to "corporate social responsibility"? A critique of business motivations and the potential for partnerships. *Development Southern Africa*, 20(2), 255–270.

International Labor Organization. (2017, December 21). The Rana Plaza accident and its aftermath. Available at: https://www.ilo.org/global/topics/geip/WCMS_614394/lang--en/index.htm

Jamali, D. (2010). The CSR of MNC subsidiaries in developing countries: Global, local, substantive or diluted? *Journal of Business Ethics*, 93(S2), 181–200.

Jamali, D. and Neville, B. (2011). Convergence versus divergence of CSR in developing countries: An embedded multi-layered institutional lens. *Journal of Business Ethics*, 102(4), 599–621.

Jamali, D., Safieddine, A.M. and Rabbath, M. (2008). Corporate governance and corporate social responsibility synergies and interrelationships. *Corporate Governance: an International Review*, 16(5), 443–459.

Jizi, M.I., Salama, A., Dixon, R. and Stratling, R. (2014). Corporate governance and corporate social responsibility disclosure: Evidence from the US banking sector. *Journal of Business Ethics*, 125(4), 601–615.

Jones, P., Comfort, D. and Hillier, D. (2005). Corporate social responsibility and the UK's top ten retailers. *International Journal of Retail and Distribution Management*, 33(12), 882–892.

Kotler, P. and Lee, N. (2005). *Corporate Responsibility: Doing the Most Good for Your Company and Your Cause.* Hoboken, NJ: Wiley.

Kurucz, E., Colbert, B. and Wheeler, D. (2008). The business case for corporate social responsibility. In Crane, A., McWilliams, A., Matten, D., Moon, J. and Siegel, D. (Eds.), *The Oxford Handbook of Corporate Social Responsibility.* Oxford: Oxford University Press.

Lewis, D. and Kanji, N. (2009). *Non-governmental Organizations and Development.* Abingdon: Routledge.

Lin, L.-W. (2010). Corporate social responsibility in China: Window dressing or structural change. *Berkeley Journal of International Law*, 28(1), 64–100.

Muhammad, A. (2009). Grameen and microcredit: A tale of corporate success. *Economic and Political Weekly*, 44(35), 35–42.

Moon, J. (2007). The contribution of corporate social responsibility to sustainable development. *Sustainable Development*, 15(5), 296–306.

North, D.C. (1990). *Institutions, Institutional Change, and Economic Performance.* Cambridge: Cambridge University Press.

Miska, C. and Mendenhall, M.E. (2015). Responsible leadership: A mapping of extant research and future directions. *Journal of Business Ethics*, 148(1), 117–134.

Păceşilă, M. and Colesca, S.E. (2020). Insights on social responsibility of NGOS. *Systemic Practice and Action Research*, 33(3), 311–339.

Parveen, H.A. (2016). Corporate social responsibility (CSR) practices of MNCs in Bangladesh: A case study on Chevron Bangladesh. *Global Journal of Management and Business Research*, 16(5-A). Available at: https://journalofbusiness.org/index.php/GJMBR/article/view/1982/1884

Sharma, A. and Kiran, R. (2013). Corporate social responsibility: Driving forces and challenges. *International Journal of Business Research and Development*, 2(1), 18–27.

Sarkis, J., Ni, N. and Zhu, Q. (2011). Winds of change: Corporate social responsibility in China. *Ivey Business Journal*, 75, 1–4.

Selsky, J.W. and Parker, B. (2005). Cross-sector partnerships to address social issues: Challenges to theory and practice. *Journal of Management*, 31(6), 849–873.

Shen, D. and Bo, J.J. (2014). Corporate social responsibility and emancipatory accounting: Roles of non-governmental organisations in transformative change in China. *Economy and Business Journal*, 8(1), 96–110.

Suykens, B., De Rynck, F. and Verschuere, B. (2018). Nonprofit organizations in between the nonprofit and market spheres: Shifting goals, governance and management? *Nonprofit Management and Leadership*, 29(4), 623–636.

Rafael, L. (2010). How we see them versus how they see themselves: A cognitive perspective of firm-NGO relationships. *Business and Society*, 49(1), 116–139.

Rangan, V.K., Chase, L. and Karim, S. (2015). The truth about CSR. *Harvard Business Review*, 93(1/2), 40–49.

Reddy, S.S. (2020). Comparing the CSR regulations in India and the UK. *Legal Maxim*, August 20. Available at: https://www.legalmaxim.in/comparing-the-csr-regulations-in-india-and-the-uk/

Reynolds, J., Howard, E., Dragun, D., Rosewell, B. and Ormerod, P. (2005). Assessing the productivity of the UK retail sector. *International Review of Retail, Distribution and Consumer Research*, 15(3), 237–280.

Sharmin, S., Khan, N.A. and Belal, A.R. (2018). Governance capabilities and sustainability concerning "corporate-NGO" collaboration: The case of Lifebuoy Friendship Hospital in Bangladesh. *Global Social Welfare*, 5(4), 277–286.

Snider, J., Hill, R.P. and Martin, D. (2003). Corporate social responsibility in the 21st century: A view from the world's most successful firms. *Journal of Business Ethics*, 48(2), 175–187.

Sofidel. (2018, January 26). CSR in the United Kingdom. Available at: https://www.sofidel.com/en/softandgreen/circular-economy-and-industry/csr-in-the-united-kingdom/

The Coca-Cola Company. (n.d.). Water conservation and stewardship. Available at: https://www.coca-colacompany.com/sustainable-business/water-stewardship#:~:text=policies%20and%20practices

The Economist. (2010). BRAC in business. *The Economist*, February 18. Available at: https://www.economist.com/node/15546464

Tolbert, P.S. and Zucker, L.G. (1996). The institutionalization of institutional theory. In Clegg, S.R., Hardy, C. and Nord, W.R. (Eds.), *Handbook of Organization Studies*. Thousand Oaks, CA: Sage.

Trevino, L.K. and Nelson, K.A. (2011). *Managing Business Ethics*, 5th edition. London: John Wiley.

UK Government. (2020). Our commitment to corporate social responsibility (CSR). Available at: https://www.gov.uk/government/news/our-commitment-to-corporate-social-responsibility-CSR

Welford, R. (2005). Corporate social responsibility in Europe, North America, and Asia. *Journal of Corporate Citizenship*, 17(17), 33–52.

Whitehead, D. (2014). Chinese NGO–firm partnerships and CSR from an institutional perspective. *Journal of Current Chinese Affairs*, 43(4), 41–74.

World Bank. (2021). Overview. Available at: https://www.worldbank.org/en/country/bangladesh/overview#1

Yang, J. and Webber, J. (2014). Empowering corporate social responsibility in Chinese nongovernmental organizations. *Journal of Psychological Issues in Organizational Culture*, 5(1), 16–39.

Yin, J. and Zhang, Y. (2012). Institutional dynamics and corporate social responsibility (CSR) in an emerging country context: Evidence from China. *Journal of Business Ethics*, 111(2), 301–316.

Yunus, M. (2010). *Building Social Business: The New Kind of Capitalism that Serves Humanity's Most Pressing Needs*. New York: Public Affairs.

Yunus, M., Moingeon, B. and Lehmann-Ortega, L. (2010). Building social business models: Lessons from the Grameen experience. *Long Range Planning*, 43(2–3), 308–325.

Zhang, D., Morse, S. and Ma, Q. (2019). Corporate social responsibility and sustainable development in China: Current status and future perspectives. *Sustainability*, 11(16), 4392.

8 The Process Model of Inclusive Innovation from an MNE Perspective

A Case Study of India

Sina Mortazavi, Anisur R. Faroque, Markus Raatikainen, and Pirooz Tohidi Khiavi

Introduction

Four billion people globally live under the poverty line (Prahalad, 2012) and earn less than the income necessary to survive. Even though these communities have fewer resources to purchase products and services, they nevertheless have purchasing power and demand for goods (Prahalad and Mashelkar, 2010). Multinational enterprises (MNEs) or small and medium enterprises (SMEs) from developed countries support low-income communities through corporate social responsibility (CSR), aiming to relieve poverty and build community empowerment (Mousiolis et al., 2015). However, Western companies often lack the motivation to operate in impoverished regions at the bottom-of-the-pyramid (BOP) due to the many constraints they face as these markets lack resources and infrastructures. BOP refers to people who live on less than USD 4 a day or who cannot afford the necessities to survive (Prahalad, 2009).

For companies to operate comfortably in low-income markets, they must be capable of fostering sustainable innovation that cultivates demand in the market (Prahalad, 2012; Prahalad and Krishnan, 2008). In the past decade, several types of sustainable innovation have emerged aiming to offer affordable goods and services to the impoverished. Sustainable innovation approaches include frugal, reverse, inclusive, and Gandhian, to name a few—most of these terms originated in developing countries (Prahalad and Mashelkar, 2010; Rosca et al., 2017). However, to create social empowerment and build capabilities for impoverished societies, MNEs or SMEs need to act beyond charity-based CSR practices and engage with local people in their business activities (Halme et al., 2012; Prahalad and Krishnan, 2008; Prahalad and Mashelkar, 2010). Inclusive innovation (ININ) is a type of sustainable innovation that aims to offer a mechanism for MNEs to tailor their CSR activities so that they not only offer affordability to the people but also build capabilities and social empowerment, leading to sustainable long-term solutions. ININ is defined as any innovation that serves low-income people who are excluded from the market (Foster and Heeks, 2013a). As the concept of ININ is very new in the sustainable innovation stream, theorizing

DOI: 10.4324/9781003274575-10

this notion is crucial. Theoretical perspectives such as dynamic capability (DC) theory and the resource-based view (RBV) are seen as essential and insightful concepts that may facilitate the understanding of ININ from a theoretical perspective (George et al., 2012).

So far, scholars have studied ININ conceptually (Heeks et al., 2014; Foster and Heeks, 2013c) and conducted case studies to understand how ININ is translated into organizations (Pansera and Owen, 2018). However, researchers have not focused on the nature of the process of ININ for MNEs and the constraints along the way. It is essential to understand the constraints MNEs encounter when aiming to sell their offerings in imperfect markets. Likewise, ININ experts have defined ININ (Foster and Heeks, 2013b) but have not offered any explanation on the nature of the process of this type of innovation from start to finish from an international business (IB) point of view or MNE perspective. To explore the ININ concept through IB lenses and understand the capabilities and resources MNEs must utilize, we see DC theory as highly insightful and relevant. In this context, we intend to conduct our research and extend the ININ literature via DC theory to understand the constraints and processes relevant to ININ in MNEs.

To understand the process of ININ and the constraints in fostering it, this study aims to investigate the link between innovations from the products/services of MNEs all the way to the social development it brings to impoverished societies. Accordingly, we have formulated two research questions presented below:

RQ1: How is the process of fostering ININ?
RQ2: How to overcome the constraints to fostering ININ?

The rest of this chapter unfolds as follows. In the next chapter, we conduct a literature review on ININ and DC theory regarding the various challenges that MNEs face in emerging markets. There follows the "Methodology" section, followed by the research findings from our case firm, Nokia. In the Discussion section, we link our findings with existing theories and offer propositions and a conceptual process model for ININ. We conclude by highlighting our theoretical contributions, managerial implications, study limitations, and future research directions.

Literature Review

Inclusive Innovation in Multinational Enterprises

The concept of ININ has its roots in the BOP literature (Prahalad, 2012). However, the term itself was defined only recently (Foster and Heeks, 2013b). ININ refers to innovative models and tools to contribute to the marginalized members of society by involving people and new technology (Heeks et al., 2014). Even though ININ has received attention from the research community, the concept remains bound to the context of the BOP literature and not on MNEs' activities in other low-income markets other than the BOP (Hart, 2005; Hart and Christensen, 2002; Prahalad and Mashelkar, 2010). Studies of ININ have been published in well-known journals (e.g., *Journal of Management Studies*, *Journal of Innovation and Development*) and have emerged as an essential topic in the recently established *Journal of Frugal Innovation* (see, e.g., George et al., 2012; Heeks et al., 2014). Similarly, the United Nations and governing bodies in developing nations have highlighted the vital role of ININ in the fight against poverty in developing economies (Planning Commission, 2013; Prahalad and Mashelkar, 2010; United Nations, 2015).

Unilever decided to sell its products to BOP markets in smaller quantities, making them more affordable for target markets. According to Rajan (2007), the MNE used a pricing strategy and sold goods in packets (e.g., shampoo and instant coffee) with affordable prices while meeting the standards of the developing market. General Electric (GE) has also strived to implement frugal and innovative changes that result in affordable products for developing markets while overcoming competition barriers (Immelt et al., 2009). The Indian government has played an important role in the growth of GE. Such initiatives have resulted in the inclusive growth and employment of 12,000 people in India (Dossani and Kenney, 2007). Already in 2009, GE announced $3 billion in investments over the following six years to finance about 100 health-care innovations for the BOP in the rural areas of China and India (Immelt et al., 2009). These two different cases demonstrate that MNEs are tailoring their strategies to provide the innovation demanded by low-income markets. However, the above cases represent a minority of MNEs; the majority faces challenges when entering these markets; moreover, they often focus solely on the affordability of goods and not primarily on social empowerment (Karnani, 2007). Prahalad (2009) argues that MNEs lack the motivation and incentive to invest in developing countries where a substantial number of people belong to the BOP. At the same time, he asserts that low-income markets are no different from markets consisting of people with buying power and access to distribution channels who demand quality products and services at an affordable price (Prahalad, 2009). CSR programs aim to offer sustainable solutions to less privileged communities in developing countries. However, a lack of inclusive strategies can slow down their effectiveness. For example, Reliance Industries Limited (RIL), one of the largest MNEs in India, encountered challenges in offering inclusive solutions in its CSR strategies that facilitate community growth (Amaladoss and Manother, 2013). Moreover, charity-based fundraising as a CSR program is not a long-term strategy unless MNEs and SMEs commit to educate, provide manpower, and facilitate the growth of entrepreneurs among the local people (Romero et al., 2014).

Only with appropriate strategies and production can MNEs achieve profitability in low-income markets in developing countries. MNEs need a strategy that will result in affordably priced goods while encouraging inclusive growth at the BOP (Sinha et al., 2017; Jones, 2010). While previous studies have outlined some of the challenges in emerging markets and sustainable business models for frugal innovation, the literature has stopped short of suggesting an effective process model for fostering ININ, thus neglecting innovation that can promote sustainability in developing countries (Amit and Zott, 2001; Bock et al., 2012; Hart, 2005; Prahalad, 2004; Rosca et al., 2017; Zeschky et al., 2014).

Many emerging markets have attracted the attention of international business scholars during the past ten years (see, e.g., Peng et al., 2008). However, the link between MNEs' innovation and the internationalization process in the emerging economy context is not yet understood. From a managerial perspective, MNEs have already been active for decades in many developing countries where they sell products and services (Nijhof et al., 2002). However, when MNEs aim to incorporate ININ into their strategic repertoire for developing markets, managers must deal with various barriers to profitability (Prahalad and Ramaswamy, 2004). Additionally, MNEs must be conscious of the primary objective of ININ—addressing poverty issues and creating livelihood opportunities for local people. This objective implies a primary goal not only of achieving profitability but also of promoting livelihood opportunities for otherwise socially and economically excluded people (George et al., 2012; Prahalad and Ramaswamy, 2004). Selling products and services to lower-income developing markets must also be accomplished through frugal approaches that allow the maximization of value amid resource scarcity (Hossain et al., 2016). Accordingly, the firm has to move beyond its comfort zone and develop products and services (or a combination of both) that are inexpensive, sustainable, and user-friendly.

As outlined by Prahalad (2009), MNEs can attain both ININ and profitability by networking with partners, such as government bodies. MNEs' networking strategies in emerging markets like India have brought about promising growth with government assistance, making the target markets more attractive through subsidies and flexible taxation for investors (Caldwell et al., 2017; Patil and Laishram, 2016). Despite partnerships between MNEs and local entrepreneurs and governments in developing nations, the topic has remained an uncharted territory for scholars.

Nevertheless, practical approaches that MNEs should implement to successfully utilize hidden innovative potential in developing countries by pursuing ININ remain an overlooked but promising area of study. To address the above-outlined complexities of the focal concept in the context of developing economies, by drawing from the current literature on strategy, we will discuss the role of DC theory in facilitating the constraints related to the ININ process.

Dynamic Capabilities Fostering Inclusive Innovation Process

The RBV suggests that firms perform in the same industry differently because of their resource and capability pool differences (Wernerfelt, 1984). The research literature on RBV focuses on firm-specific resources that are static in nature, whereas the knowledge-based view (KBV) and DC theory extend the RBV to examine those resources that are more dynamic in nature (Kuivalainen and Bell, 2004). Therefore, the KBV overlaps with the DC view (Teece et al., 1997). The KBV and DC perspectives have been used interchangeably in the literature because both approaches focus on knowledge inventories, capabilities, and resources as sources of competitive advantage and firm growth. The difference lies in how the DC view suggests the need to distinguish capabilities from resources, stressing the importance of the dynamic processes of capability building in gaining competitive advantage (Weerawardena et al., 2007).

In contrast to the RBV, DC theory suggests that firms are required to develop new knowledge and skills to identify international market opportunities and to respond quickly to them (Jarvenpaa et al., 1998). Therefore, it considers firms as the primary source of competitive resources by which managers integrate, build, and reconfigure internal and external competencies to address rapidly changing environments (Teece et al., 1997, 380). In our view, DCs tend to play a more critical role in emerging market and BOP contexts. These markets are more demanding from a strategic perspective, and MNEs are required to shape and expand both their existing knowledge and resource pool to operate successfully.

In successful international business, the firm's capability to acquire, allocate, and possess unique capabilities plays an important role. These unique resources are vital resources, knowledge, or capabilities that are firm-specific, difficult to imitate, and can generate an economic return and competitive advantage in foreign markets. Here, the firm's ability to create, transfer, assemble, integrate, and exploit these resources becomes essential. These unique resources are used to drive market-specific strategies and fund continual development of new capabilities needed for international expansion. When firms invest and operate internationally, they must develop specific strategic and organizational capabilities to counteract the natural advantages unique to local businesses (Luo, 2000). In our view, the MNE's ability to build new capabilities, transform its resource base, and reconfigure its organizational processes and structures to succeed in ININ development in the developing market context plays a critical role. Overcoming the resource constraints would, therefore, be facilitated by combining the existing internal and external resources and creating new ones.

MNEs often prefer to exploit their unique resources through expansion (i.e., foreign direct investment through joint ventures or wholly owned subsidiaries) rather than by leasing or licensing. Such resources are often information intensive, tacit, and organizationally embedded and thus cannot be transmitted through markets by leasing or licensing (Teece, 1982). Therefore, more organizationally embedded resources require greater organizational control over transactions, necessitating more hierarchical governance structures, such as wholly owned subsidiaries or majority joint ventures. A firm with such a governance structure has institutional capabilities that allow it to protect knowledge from expropriation and imitation more effectively than would leasing or licensing contracts. With well-developed systems to control and integrate these operations, MNEs can internalize and transfer these resources successfully (Luo, 2000). In our view, such managerial and organizational capabilities are essential in BOP and developing economy contexts.

Eisenhardt and Martin (2000) suggest that a firm can be seen as a bundle of resources (financial, know-how, production), with the implication that RBV notions could be beneficial for scholars investigating MNEs under challenging market conditions. The authors also suggest that an excellent approach to utilizing resources is through DCs; this approach focuses on strategy for resource integration and resource use for MNEs. In line with Eisenhardt and Martin (2000), we argue that DCs are fostered when a company adjusts its resources with market changes (e.g., market turbulence, evolution, expansion, splitting, and collisions).

Teece (2014) developed a robust conceptual article in the *Journal of International Business Studies* where he advances and develops the DC-based theory of MNEs in the IB literature. In the article, he argues that MNEs need the process of internationalization to sustain long-term survival in the market. However, the internationalization phase has its ups and downs for many MNEs and requires further study. Consequently, Teece (2014) builds the motivation for his research based on the lack of sufficient research on failures of MNEs and the role of differential firm performance in these failures.

Throughout the research, the author provides several examples of MNE market failures and holds responsible certain internationalization elements that can cause risks for MNEs. Among these actions are contracting out intermediaries, transaction costs, resource-transfer costs, and learning issues. The core finding of Teece (2014) shows that MNEs need to foster internationalization in the global market through DCs and appropriate strategies.

Research on DCs has focused on MNEs and entrepreneurship (Augier and Teece, 2007), DCs and RBV (Eisenhardt and Martin, 2000), DCs and market expansion (Luo, 2000), and the review of DCs (Barreto, 2010), while others have begun studying emerging markets (Ludwig and Pemberton, 2011). However, research has explored neither DCs in developing economy contexts nor with ININs, which invites us to explore the commonalities between these two concepts, understand the ININ process of MNEs, and obtain a holistic understanding of the types of challenges MNEs must overcome when operating in these markets under high uncertainty. In the following section, we explain the research method selected to study the phenomenon and seek answers to our two research questions.

Research Methodology

As the aim of this study was to examine ININ-building processes, a case study method was the chosen strategy (Eisenhardt, 1989; Yin, 1994). One way of capturing processes is through case studies of firms, which are useful ways of understanding why things are as they are (Spender, 1996). Many authors (e.g., Chetty, 1996; Fletcher, 2009; Ghauri, 2004) have advocated the use of cases in research on internationalization. One key advantage of the case over survey research is the former's role in facilitating the study of the internationalization process from several perspectives and thereby facilitating a more thorough analysis of each firm. A single case study design was adopted to gain a holistic, in-depth understanding of the ININ process in an MNE (Yin, 1994). When the research problem demands rich, in-depth information, a single case is appropriate; as long as generalizability is not expected, meaningful findings can be found (Coviello and Jones, 2004).

Data Collection and Analysis

In preparing for data collection, secondary data for the selected case firm (industry reports, secondary documentation, Nokia's telecom and IT technology websites) were reviewed before the interviews. Interviews of 60–90 minutes were conducted (in 2019) with the sales, country, and marketing managers of the case firm. Data were gathered from the telecom equipment and software service branch of Nokia. Our case company operates in the B2B sector; however, our primary data included both B2B and B2C aspects as our interviewees talked about their relations with local operators, companies, and local end users. Three of the interviewees were regional, sales, and country managers with more than 25 years of B2B and B2C business experience in India. Moreover, one interviewee located in India was the designated portfolio manager for Nokia India. The interviews were semi-structured and open-ended so the interviewees could reply freely in their own words without limitations. The senior managers were involved in all aspects of the business; consequently, they had first-hand knowledge of the firm's strategy, operations, and administration in particular developing markets.

We chose a case study approach via abductive theory-building for this study. The case study methodology was adopted with the aim to analyze the notion of ININ and later theorize this concept. Qualitative case study methodology is suitable for exploring and clarifying the interplay of logic between theoretical constructs and complex empirical phenomena (Eisenhardt and Graebner, 2007). The chosen method underlines the explanatory nature of our study (Piekkari et al., 2010). It is particularly appropriate for this investigation as there has been little research on innovation in BOP market contexts. Furthermore, this methodology provides an opportunity to investigate how the process of ININ is operationalized in multinational organizations.

Focusing on a variety of data sources, we followed typical methodological decisions for case studies (Yin, 1994) concerning the incremental innovation process of Nokia in a developing market context. The case study approach enabled us to investigate the innovation process in a particular context where the phenomenon and context actively support each other and, hence, are interconnected (Yin, 2009). Incremental innovation is an understudied field in the literature. A clearer understanding of the phenomenon is required, especially in the IB literature; therefore, a qualitative case study method was selected.

We firstly collected four personal interviews with the senior executives from the case firm. These interviews were further corroborated by secondary data. The secondary data consisted of annual reports, press releases, and interviewees' notes and documents supporting the primary data. Hence, data triangulation was used to validate the research and strengthen the interview data by considering multiple sources of evidence (Miles and Huberman, 1994).

In the analysis, we used abductive logic and qualitative content analysis (Miles and Huberman, 1994) to identify context-specific meanings (Brown, 2006) of our empirical data based on this phenomenon. Three researchers analyzed the data, a chain of evidence was built, and explanation-building logic was followed in the case analysis. Reliability was ensured by careful data collection and the formation of a case database. Interviewees reviewed the transcribed data, and the coded data were cross-checked (Piekkari et al., 2010).

During the face-to-face interviews, we used a digital voice recorder to record and store the data to ensure dependability and repeatability (Sinkovics et al., 2008). The coding process was conducted during the case analysis through a cyclic process of axial, selective, and open coding (Miles and Huberman, 1984; Sinkovics et al., 2008, 704; Sobh and Perry, 2006, 1204) to capture both emerging themes and themes related to our theoretical framework.

To ensure quality in the case study research approach, we emphasized (1) ontological appropriateness, (2) contingent validity, (3) multiple perceptions of individuals/researchers, (4) methodological trustworthiness, (5) analytic generalization, and (6) construct validity (Healy and Perry, 2000; Yin, 1994). By ontological appropriateness, we ensured that the research problem is approached using the appropriate research method (Healy and Perry, 2000). The research question is exploratory as it seeks to find answers to an understudied phenomenon. Contingent validity was achieved via theoretical sampling (Healy and Perry, 2000, 125). We ensured many perceptions of participants had converged by triangulating peer researchers' interpretations (Healy and Perry, 2000; Patton, 2002). The interview data were transcribed separately by two authors and then compared and discussed between them. Methodological trustworthiness was ensured by the establishment of a case study database (Healy and Perry, 2000, 123) involving the development of conceptual constructs, operationalization, application, confirmation and disconfirmation of the theory, and a final model for future empirical testing. We ensured construct validity by using a priori theory (Healy and Perry, 2000, 124).

Findings

Table 8.1 illustrates the core structure of the primary data from the interviews. The data show the process of ININ from product attributes through innovation constraints and social empowerment. The process of ININ extracted from the data was seen in three dimensions: affordable products/services, ININ constraints, and social empowerment. The first dimension includes part of Nokia's offerings that are designed to be affordable for low-income customers in India. This was seen as the first step in the process of ININ as the intention and aim of the product/service must be targeted to this demographic. Thus, with the first dimension, it is evident that the offerings suit the nature of ININ, although they face several innovation constraints along the way. These constraints were coded as the second dimension within the ININ process, which consists of the constraints as well as solutions that the companies devised (for some constraints,

Table 8.1 The Case Findings

Product/service characteristic of affordability	*Constraints that impact the inclusive innovation process*	*Themes*	*Quotes*
Scaling up telecom equipment and telecom software with affordable plans (voice over Long Term Evolution (LTE), voice over Internet Protocol (IP)). Scaling up telecom equipment and telecom software with affordable plans (voice over LTE, voice over IP). Scaling up telecom equipment and telecom software with affordable plans (voice over LTE, voice over IP)	Inclusive innovation constraints	Cannibalization and spillover effect: Legitimacy: Personal relationship/ corruption: Price and competition:	• Selling voice over IP software was not successful as clients thought it would cannibalize other offerings. • Leaking ideas too early is no good since competitors can imitate. However, in the modern age, it is difficult to protect knowledge. • Air interface in phones can be used for phones, military, TV, and so on. Therefore, regulations are tough in the telecom business. • Taxation was very high and we did not receive aid or subsidies from government. • One rule can be interpreted differently for others. • In developing countries, it is mostly about personal relationships. Lack of access to the right organizations and resources can be problematic. • Corruption exists in the market and can slow down the operations. Emerging MNEs (EMNEs) can perform better in these situations as they are more familiar with these contexts.

		• The government and locals ask for favors that are not ethical sometimes. This means that the country asks the company to sell their products but also helps them trade (sell something) with Europe as well as buying other things from Europe in bundles. • Price wars are now present in Indian markets. • Huawei is aggressive in pricing, meaning that they can offer very low prices. • Price wars are now present with a local network operator Reliance JIO. This local company has very low prices that result in price wars. • Indian market is highly price sensitive, which is very difficult to operate in.
Overcoming inclusive innovation constraints	Inclusive resource management for price constraint:	• In the so-called upsell approach, the firm removes the additional features and sells the basic feature of the phones, by selling the core basic function according to the demand. Then they have to pay extra for the additional.
	Legitimacy constraint: Inclusive embeddedness for personal relationship and spillover effect: Competition:	• Selling offerings that have existed in the market for some time and now have dropped in value. • Using local people's ideas to innovate and create offerings that suit the poor people.

(*Continued*)

Table 8.1 (Continued)

Product/service characteristic of affordability	*Constraints that impact the inclusive innovation process*	*Themes*	*Quotes*
			• Offering loans to people and organizations in India so that they can gain more buying power. • Government can be a big moderator in helping Nokia through subsidies, taxation, and waiving regulation challenges.
			• Educating the locals can help Nokia in two ways. They can help us handle technical issues in the local market. They can help us produce knowledge and innovation that can be used in India or in Europe. • Educating the community is important as the people in the community can become competitive employees. Nokia uses a global training program to train local people.
			• Patenting is, of course, how we protect, and we have a strong patent department. • Learning from local entrepreneurs and how they operate in these markets. • People in India have a good image of Nokia and trust its offerings. • Nokia is the market leader in India and has over 70% of the market.

Social empowerment	Inclusive innovation aimed at:	• Offer cheap and affordable phone call solutions for the poor people. • People can have access to products and services that they could not afford in the past. • Building skills for locals and offering education. • Locals are engaged in R&D and innovations that help Nokia to sell to the people. • Local operators gain profit and offer jobs, leading to localization. • Taxation money from Nokia offers social empowerment for the locals.

Nokia offered solutions). The third dimension was coded as social empowerment, which is the core principle of ININ. At this stage, the company must demonstrate localization through engaging the community of people in its business operations to offer locals the necessary value to empower their community.

Discussion

Firms are seen as the main source of competitive resources, and their managers shape their intra- and inter-organizational resources and competencies by integrating, building, and reconfiguring them to meet the market dynamics (Teece et al., 1997). When MNEs enter developing markets and start to develop innovation to improve local social empowerment and the local economy, they face constraints that can slow or even prevent the ININ process. Therefore, DCs are required to reshape the internal and external strategies based on market-specific needs and to overcome the challenges that firms meet in developing economies.

Our case firm Nokia utilized multiple strategies to overcome the constraints related to Indian market entry. Firstly, the managers experienced concerns from local customers who feared that Nokia's innovation could replace and thus cannibalize the main products of the local operator.

Respectively, our case firm feared that their local partners might imitate their innovation and, therefore, that the cooperation could lead to the loss of the innovation through the spillover effect. Another constraint was related to the target market's rules and regulations, such as taxation and subsidies within the developing economy. Legitimacy constraints, relationship, and price were among other issues that prevented Nokia from expanding into the markets. According to Eisenhardt and Martin (2000), firms need to customize their capabilities regarding strategic decisions to expand into markets despite the related constraints. Our data show that Nokia is in line with the DC point of view since they are changing their strategies according to the constraints of the market. To overcome the ININ constraints, Nokia used inclusive resource management, followed their code of conduct to overcome legislation constraints, and used an inclusive embeddedness mechanism. However, while interpreting the primary data from Nokia, we noticed that the so-called inclusive embeddedness school of thought may offer more help to Nokia in overcoming relationship innovation constraints.

Several scholars (Burt, 2004; Möller and Halinen, 1999) argue that for companies to utilize their resources, such as knowledge, capital, and human resources, they need to work with traditional (e.g., governmental and formal institutions) and non-traditional actors (e.g., not-for-profit organizations, community groups) in low-income markets (Hart and London, 2005). For instance, Levin and Cross (2004) affirmed that linkages between traditional and non-traditional actors can ease diminution and production activities.

While the network method remains common in IB and entrepreneurship research (Hansen, 1995; Johanson and Mattsson, 1988), it also can be particularly accommodating in developing economies by bringing growth and stability to these markets (Khayesi and George, 2011). We see that working with non-traditional actors can create more jobs and social empowerment for the people as well as help Nokia to overcome relationship and regulatory constraints. In this regard, we offer the following propositions, as we believe MNEs can benefit from a more robust relationship mechanism.

Proposition a: Inclusive embeddedness by MNEs operating in developing countries helps MNEs to overcome relationship constraints for ININ.

Proposition b: Inclusive embeddedness by MNEs operating in developing countries increases social empowerment leading to ININ.

Conclusion

As mentioned in the Introduction, this study was developed based on two research questions constructed while identifying the research gap. Below, RQs 1 and 2 are recapitulated and answered according to the findings from the primary and secondary data.

RQ1: How is the process of fostering ININ?

The chapter establishes that for an MNE to foster ININ, it must follow the three-phase process. The first phase is the intention to make affordable products to create market inclusion for low-income individuals. We show the first step in the conceptual model with three drivers (intention for inclusion, scaling up the production, and mutual benefit for the company and the people). Later, the company must overcome the innovation constraints that it faces (as elaborated in the "Findings" section). Later, social empowerment needs to be created for the market to enter the third and last step in the process model. What we understand from Nokia is that ININ is a strategy that can have more impact than a traditional fundraising CSR strategy. Nokia did not label their operation in India as a CSR operation but rather as a business operation that helps localization of the communities in India such that both locals and the company itself profit. The findings from Nokia (as indicated in the "Discussion" section and presented in Table 8.1 and Figure 8.1) show that Nokia did not just focus on selling but also on educating, hiring, and engaging with the local people in India to contribute to a more sustainable business practice.

RQ2: How to overcome the constraints to fostering ININ?

Nokia has faced challenges such as legitimacy, cannibalization, price, competition, and corruption constraints (highlighted in Table 8.1 and Figure 8.1). To overcome these innovation constraints, solutions such as inclusive resource management and inclusive embeddedness are highly effective. Inclusive resource management allowed Nokia to generate better results from its internal resources to overcome pricing constraints. Inclusive embeddedness will help Nokia in extending its relationships and partnership abilities to traditional and non-traditional actors. It is essential that Nokia should have access to grassroots-level knowledge to overcome innovation constraints.

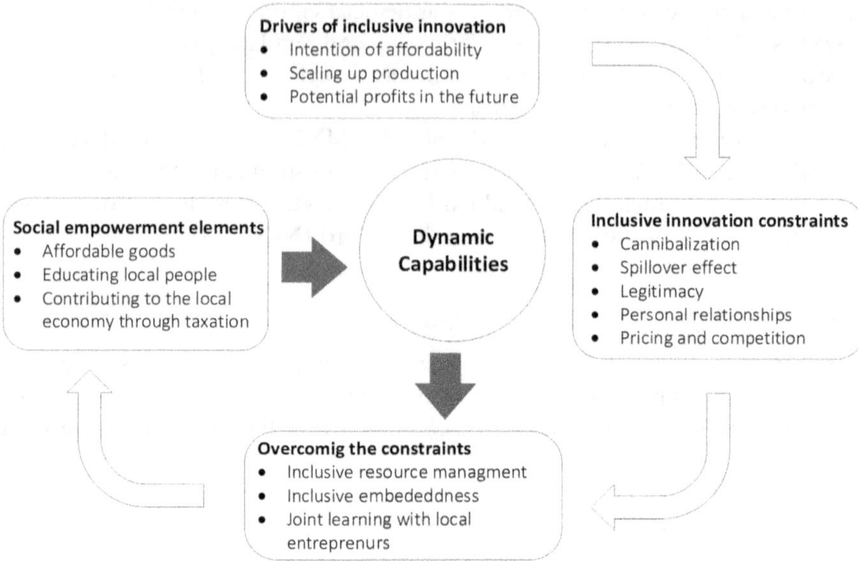

Figure 8.1 The Process of Inclusive Innovation

To illustrate all the ININ processes and constraints, we present the following conceptual model in Figure 8.1.

Theoretical Contributions

In this chapter, we have made a number of theoretical contributions that we outline and discuss in greater detail in this section. We used DC theory in the context of ININ and showed how this perspective can be insightful in overcoming the constraints to ININ. Teece et al. (1997) argue that MNEs need to customize their internal and external strategies according to the market in which they operate. We noticed the scope of Nokia's DC as they operate differently in low-income markets in India compared to higher-income markets. Nokia has both external strategies for overcoming ININ constraints as well as internal strategies. However, external strategies are more prevalent as ININ is the result of processes and linkages between Nokia and other actors in the markets. Internal strategies, such as price and production constraints, are solved through external strategies, such as inclusive embeddedness and inclusive resource management (as explained in the "Findings" section). In this regard, we have modified the DC from Teece et al. (1997) into a process model for ININ and used the model to show the logic of Nokia's market expansion behavior.

We have also extended the social innovation and innovation constraint literature from an IB perspective. These streams of literature have not looked into ININ constraints and processes from IB and MNE perspectives (Sharma and Lyer, 2012; Enderwick, 2009; McDonough et al., 2008; Prahalad and Mashelkar, 2010).

Moreover, we have extended the notional repertoire of the sustainable innovation literature by conceptualizing ININ in terms of DC theory and developing a process model. This model illustrates three phases (intention of affordability, ININ constraints, and social empowerment) that need to be applied by MNEs to foster ININ. Moreover, this chapter has developed two propositions that can be tested in the future. Lastly, this chapter advanced the IB literature since it focuses on the role of MNEs with respect to ININ. Regarding theoretical contributions, we have also extended the following issues. We have developed the term inclusive resource management to help support MNEs in overcoming ININ constraints. Moreover, we have modified the concept of embeddedness into inclusive embeddedness, which is a facilitator for the ININ process model. In this regard, inclusive embeddedness and inclusive resource management can be labeled as early-phase theoretical constructs that facilitate the ININ model, leading to mechanisms that overcome ININ constraints.

Managerial Implications

In this study, we have identified several managerial implications that might help practitioners understand the role of innovation for successful businesses in low-income markets in India. Fostering ININ is not only about making products affordable for the people; it is also about engaging with local communities and understanding their needs. ININ can help companies not only to understand low-income markets and their mechanisms better but also to observe the role of innovation. It is essential for managers to include local people in the process of innovation as they can offer many solutions to help companies overcome innovation constraints. For instance, in the Nokia case, it was noticed that local people clearly show the company what they require and how a product or service is going to work in the market. Furthermore, hiring and training locals, as well as engaging them in R&D, is a strategy that needs to be implemented. Many ideas and products have emerged from R&D departments in India that are also used in Europe or the US market. This means that engaging the locals creates a win–win scenario from which both MNEs and host countries can benefit.

Lastly, working with non-traditional actors, such as local startups and local business partners, can be more helpful compared to working with the government. Mechanisms of inclusive embeddedness and inclusive resource management should therefore be studied by managers to allow for a better business experience in low-income markets in India.

Future Research

We identified several limitations to our research that could open avenues of inquiry to future researchers. During the research process, we thought of several future research opportunities for the disciplines of IB and social innovation that we shall elucidate below. For example, researchers could modify and examine the model via qualitative tools by employing multiple cases in different regions. Additionally, we encourage scholars to challenge and test the model through quantitative scholarly investigation. They could use different theoretical underpinnings of DC and conceptualize ININ and its process from a different perspective. Scholars might also develop additional propositions and test the existing propositions to validate. Future research could also determine whether NGOs play any supporting role vis-à-vis MNEs in low-income markets and whether they help MNEs in the process of ININ. Studying the role of ININ for MNEs in regions other than India would also be appreciated as this study only focuses on the Indian market. Scholars might also focus on the role of social entrepreneurship and ININ in low-income markets rather than looking at the phenomena solely from an IB perspective. Future researchers could engage in scale development for inclusive resource management and inclusive embeddedness constructs in a more robust manner, both from an MNE and entrepreneurship standpoint. Lastly, scholars in the field of CSR should investigate the notion of ININ to see if the ININ mechanism can be utilized as an impactful element in CSR practices, both conceptually and empirically. Researchers see the notion of CSR as a very broad concept with various dimensions (Choi and La, 2013), and this could be a promising research avenue to understand if ININ can be conceptualized as an element within the mechanism of CSR.

References

Amaladoss, M.X. and Manohar, H.L. (2013). Communicating corporate social responsibility–A case of CSR communication in emerging economies. *Corporate Social Responsibility and Environmental Management*, 20(2), 65–80.

Amit, R. and Zott, C. (2001). Value creation in e-business. *Strategic Management Journal*, 22(6–7), 493–520.

Barreto, I. (2010). Dynamic capabilities: A review of past research and an agenda for the future. *Journal of Management*, 36(1), 256–280.

Bock, A.J., Opsahl, T., George, G. and Gann, D.M. (2012). The effects of culture and structure on strategic flexibility during business model innovation. *Journal of Management Studies*, 49(2), 279–305.

Brown, A.D. (2006). A narrative approach to collective identities. *Journal of Management Studies*, 43(4), 731–753.

Burt, R.S. (2004). *Structural Holes: The Social Structure of Competition*. Cambridge, MA: Harvard University Press.

Caldwell, N.D., Roehrich, J.K. and George, G. (2017). Social value creation and relational coordination in public-private collaborations. *Journal of Management Studies*, 54(6), 906–928.

Choi, B. and La, S. (2013). The impact of corporate social responsibility (CSR) and customer trust on the restoration of loyalty after service failure and recovery. *Journal of Services Marketing*, 27(3), 223–233.

Coviello, N.E. and Jones, M.V. (2004). Methodological issues in international entrepreneurship research. *Journal of Business Venturing*, 19(4), 485–508.

Dossani, R. and Kenney, M. (2007). The next wave of globalization: Relocating service provision to India. *World Development*, 35(5), 772–791.

Eisenhardt, K.M. and Graebner, M.E. (2007). Theory building from cases: Opportunities and challenges. *Academy of Management Journal*, 50(1), 25–32.

Eisenhardt, K.M. and Martin, J.A. (2000). Dynamic capabilities: What are they? *Strategic Management Journal*, 21(10–11), 1105–1121.

Enderwick, P. (2009). Responding to global crisis: The contribution of emerging markets to strategic adaptation. *International Journal of Emerging Markets*, 4(4), 358–374.

Foster, C. and Heeks, R. (2013a). Analyzing policy for inclusive innovation: The mobile sector and base-of-the-pyramid markets in Kenya. *Innovation and Development*, 3(1), 103–119.

Foster, C. and Heeks, R. (2013b). Conceptualising inclusive innovation: Modifying systems of innovation frameworks to understand diffusion of new technology to low-income consumers. *European Journal of Development Research*, 25(3), 333–355.

Foster, C. and Heeks, R. (2013c). Innovation and scaling of ICT for the bottom-of-the-pyramid. *Journal of Information Technology*, 28(4), 296–315.

George, G., McGahan, A.M. and Prabhu, J. (2012). Innovation for inclusive growth: Towards a theoretical framework and a research agenda. *Journal of Management Studies*, 49(4), 661–683.

Halme, M., Lindeman, S. and Linna, P. (2012). Innovation for inclusive business: Intrapreneurial bricolage in multinational corporations. *Journal of Management Studies*, 49(4), 743–784.

Hansen, E.L. (1995). Entrepreneurial networks and new organization growth. *Entrepreneurship: Theory and Practice*, 19(4), 7–19.

Hart, S.L. (2005). Innovation, creative destruction and sustainability. *Research-Technology Management*, 48(5), 21–27.

Hart, S.L. and Christensen, C.M. (2002). The great leap: Driving innovation from the base of the pyramid. *MIT Sloan Management Review*, 44(1), 51–56.

Healy, M. and Perry, C. (2000). Comprehensive criteria to judge validity and reliability of qualitative research within the realism paradigm. *Qualitative Market Research: An International Journal*, 3(3), 118–126.

Heeks, R., Foster, C. and Nugroho, Y. (2014). New models of inclusive innovation for development. *Innovation and Development*, 4(2), 175–185.

Hossain, M., Simula, H. and Halme, M. (2016). Can frugal go global? Diffusion patterns of frugal innovations. *Technology in Society*, 46, 132–139.

Immelt, J.R., Govindarajan, V. and Trimble, C. (2009). How GE is disrupting itself. *Harvard Business Review*, 87, 10–18.

Jarvenpaa, S.L., Knoll, K. and Leidner, D.E. (1998). Is anybody out there? Antecedents of trust in global virtual teams. *Journal of Management Information Systems*, 14(4), 29–64.

Johanson, J. and Mattson, L. (1988). Internationalization in industrial systems—A network approach. In Hood, N. and Vahlne, J.-E. (Eds.), *Strategies in Global Competition*. Kent: Croom Helm.

Jones, G.J. (2010). Multinational strategies and developing countries in historical perspective. Harvard Business School Working Paper 10-076. Available at: https://ssrn.com/abstract=1568086.

Karnani, A. (2007). The mirage of marketing to the bottom of the pyramid: How the private sector can help alleviate poverty. *California Management Review*, 49(4), 90–111.

Khayesi, J. and George, G. (2011). When does socio-cultural context matter? Communal orientation and enterpreneurs' resource accumulation in Africa. *Journal of Organization and Occupartional Psychology*, 84(3), 471–492.

Kuivalainen, O. and Bell, J. (2004). Knowledge-based view of the firm and small firm internationalisation. In *The Proceedings of the 4th Biennial McGill Conference on International Entrepreneurship (CD-ROM)*, September.

Levin, D.Z. and Cross, R. (2004). The strength of weak ties you can trust: The mediating role of trust in effective knowledge transfer. *Management Science*, 50(11), 1477–1490.

Ludwig, G. and Pemberton, J. (2011). A managerial perspective of dynamic capabilities in emerging markets: The case of the Russian steel industry. *Journal for East European Management Studies*, 16(3), 215–236.

Luo, Y. (2000). Dynamic capabilities in international expansion. *Journal of World Business*, 35(4), 355–378.

McDonough, E.F., Zack, M.H., Lin, H.E. and Berdrow, I. (2008). Integrating innovation style and knowledge into strategy. *MIT Sloan Management Review*, 50(1), 53–58.

Miles, M.B. and Huberman, A.M. (1984). *Qualitative Data Analysis: A Sourcebook of New Methods*. Thousand Oaks, CA: Sage.

Miles, M.B. and Huberman, A.M. (1994). *Qualitative Data Analysis: An Expanded Sourcebook*. Thousand Oaks, CA: Sage.

Möller, K.K. and Halinen, A. (1999). Business relationships and networks: Managerial challenge of network era. *Industrial Marketing Management*, 28(5), 413–427.

Mousiolis, D.T., Zaridis, A.D., Karamanis, K. and Rontogianni, A. (2015). Corporate social responsibility in SMEs and MNEs: The different strategic decision making. *Procedia-Social and Behavioral Sciences*, 175, 579–583.

Nijhof, A., Fisscher, O. and Looise, J.K. (2002). Inclusive innovation: A research project on the inclusion of social responsibility. *Corporate Social Responsibility and Environmental Management*, 9(2), 83–90.

Pansera, M. and Owen, R. (2018). Framing inclusive innovation within the discourse of development: Insights from case studies in India. *Research Policy*, 47(1), 23–34.

Patil, N.A. and Laishram, B. (2016). Public–private partnerships from sustainability perspective – A critical analysis of the Indian case. *International Journal of Construction Management*, 16(2), 161–174.

Patton, M.Q. (2002). *Qualitative Research and Evaluation Methods*, 3rd edition. Thousand Oaks, CA: Sage.

Peng, M.W., Wang, D.Y. and Jiang, Y. (2008). An institution-based view of international business strategy: A focus on emerging economies. *Journal of International Business Studies*, 39(5), 920–936.

Piekkari, R., Plakoyiannaki, E. and Welch, C. (2010). "Good" case research in industrial marketing: Insights from research practice. *Industrial Marketing Management*, 39(1), 109–117.

Planning Commission. (2013). *Draft Compendium of PPP Projects in Infrastructure*. New Delhi: Planning Commission.

Prahalad, C.K. (2009). *The Fortune at the Bottom of the Pyramid, Revised and Updated 5th Anniversary Edition: Eradicating Poverty through Profits.* Upper Saddle River, NJ: FT Press.

Prahalad, C.K. (2012). Bottom of the pyramid as a source of breakthrough innovations. *Journal of Product Innovation Management*, 29(1), 6–12.

Prahalad, C.K. and Krishnan (2008). T*he New Age of Innovation: Driving Cocreated Values through Global Networks.* New York, NY: McGraw-Hill.

Prahalad, C.K. and Mashelkar, R.A. (2010). Innovation's Holy Grail. *Harvard Business Review*, 88, 7–8.

Prahalad, C.K. and Ramaswamy, V. (2004). Co-creating unique value with customers. *Strategy and Leadership*, 32(3), 4–9.

Rajan, R. (2007). Unilever's business in India's subsistence economies. In Rosa, J.A. and Viswanathan, M. (Eds.), *Product and Market Development for Subsistence Marketplaces (Advances in International Management, Vol. 20)*. Bingley: Emerald Group Publishing Limited.

Romero, K.C.C. and Lamadrid, L.R. (2014). Rethinking corporate social responsibility within the sustainability agenda: Issues and challenges for Asian-based companies. *Journal of Global Responsibility*, 5(2), 180–202.

Rosca, E., Arnold, M. and Bendul, J.C. (2017). Business models for sustainable innovation – An empirical analysis of frugal products and services. *Journal of Cleaner Production*, 162, S133–S145.

Sharma, A. and Iyer, G.R. (2012). Resource-constrained product development: Implications for green marketing and green supply chains. *Industrial Marketing Management*, 41(4), 599–608.

Sinha, P.K., Gupta, S. and Rawal, S. (2017). Brand adoption by BOP retailers. *Qualitative Market Research*, 20(2), 181–207.

Sinkovics, R.R., Penz, E. and Ghauri, P.N. (2008). Enhancing the trustworthiness of qualitative research in international business. *Management International Review*, 48(6), 689–714.

Sobh, R. and Perry, C. (2006). Research design and data analysis in realism research. *European Journal of Marketing*, 40(11/12), 1194–1209.

Teece, D.J. (1982). Towards an economic theory of the multiproduct firm. *Journal of Economic Behavior and Organization*, 3(1), 39–63.

Teece, D.J. (2014). A dynamic capabilities-based entrepreneurship theory of the multinational enterprises: A theory model-knowledge based view. *Journal of International Business Studies*, 45(1), 8–37.

Teece, D.J., Pisano, G. and Shuen, A. (1997). Dynamic capabilities and strategic management. *Strategic Management Journal*, 18(7), 509–533.

United Nations. (2015). Transforming our world: The 2030 Agenda for Sustainable Development. *General Assembly Resolution 70/1, 25 September 2015* (Vol. 16301, pp. 1–40). Available at: http://unctad.org/meetings/es/SessionalDocuments/ares70d1_es.pdf

Weerawardena, J., Mort, G.S., Liesch, P.W. and Knight, G. (2007). Conceptualizing accelerated internationalization in the born global firm: A dynamic capabilities perspective. *Journal of World Business*, 42(3), 294–306.

Wernerfelt, B. (1984). A resource-based view of the firm. *Strategic Management Journal*, 5(2), 171–180.

Yin, R.K. (1994). *Case Study Research: Design and Methods.* Thousand Oaks, CA: Sage.

Yin, R.K. (2009). *Case Study Research: Design and Methods, Essential Guide to Qualitative Methods in Organizational Research*. Thousand Oaks, CA: Sage.

Zeschky, M.B., Winterhalter, S. and Gassmann, O. (2014). From cost to frugal and reverse innovation: Mapping the field and implications for global competitiveness. *Research-Technology Management*, 57(4), 20–27.

9 CSR by Regulators

The Case of Sustainable Villages for Development (SV4D) in Mozambique

Pedro Verga Matos, Paulo Almeida Gonçalves, and Nadine Chorão

Introduction

According to the most current reports regarding the importance of information and communication technologies (ICT) for human development (UNDP, 2019), internet access is an important tool that enhances development and contributes to increasing household income, and seems to have gained a prominent place in international agendas (UN, 2018; ITU, 2018). The implementation of broadband access infrastructure is at the top of the nations' priorities, and is considered to promote the development of societies. This objective is highlighted in SDG 9 – Industry, Innovation, and Infrastructure – of the United Nations 2030 Agenda for Sustainable Development (UN, 2018).

This research aims to analyse the implementation of the Sustainable Villages for Development (SV4D) project in Mozambique, a project developed by ARCTEL-CPLP and Fraunhofer AICOS, Portugal. ARCTEL-CPLP is a private association that promotes information sharing and exchange of experiences between telecommunication and communication regulators of the Portuguese-speaking countries (CPLP – Comunidade dos Países de Língua Oficial Portuguesa) towards the sector's improvement and market growth. The Fraunhofer Portugal is a non-profit private association founded by Fraunhofer-Gesellschaft, the largest organization for applied research in Europe, now working through the Research Center for Assistive Information and Communication Solutions (AICOS), located in Porto (Portugal), following a partnership among the Fraunhofer Society (Fraunhofer-Gesellschaft), the Foundation for Science and Technology (FCT-Portugal), and the University of Porto (UP).

Corporate social responsibility (CSR) has been gaining increasing relevance in recent decades (Carroll, 1999; Ali et al., 2017). It has become a very relevant factor in the analysis of corporate behaviour, particularly from the perspective of the stakeholders (Porter and Kramer, 2006). The various studies of CSR have identified different types of initiatives (e.g., social, environmental, or philanthropic), their impact on consumers (Luo and Bhattacharya, 2006; Miller and Merrilees, 2013), as well as their relevance for companies (Lee, 2008; Maon et al., 2010; Hildebrand et al., 2011). But the impacts of CSR actions may vary across countries (Hammad et al., 2014; Bauman et al., 2018; Davidson and Yin,

DOI: 10.4324/9781003274575-11

2019). However, very little has been studied when these actions are carried out by business associations (or other types of associations) in emerging markets. In this context, this work is innovative by studying an intervention of an association of regulators from different countries (that share the same national language) to support the development of an emerging market.

The theoretical framework is built around two concepts, namely ICT (in this case applied by an association of regulators) and social innovation. Then a review of the Sustainable Villages for Development (SV4D) case is done by presenting its objectives, its relevance to Mozambique, its implementation, and some preliminary results. We analyse whether this project can be designated as a development project, according to the current understanding of the concept of "development", as well as whether it is a "social innovation" project. The project requires a multidimensional and interdisciplinary perspective, based on participatory and empowerment dynamics, suggesting new territorial levels of action, and the co-responsibility of the partners. It is also expected to potentiate behavioural changes and bring about unity of the communities around a network of common interests and to work as a driving agent of social innovations which can only be generated by collective actions.

Theoretical Framework

Information and Communication Technologies (ICT)

Internet connectivity is at the heart of the digital economy and although access to the internet seems to be a basic right for many people, it is no less true that there is still a large majority of the world population, including young people, for whom the word "internet" is completely unknown. Connectivity is vital for individuals and for businesses and "must be improved for the internet to be globally inclusive and beneficial" (Pepper and Jackman, 2019, 29). Internet access is understood to be a tool for human development (UN, 2018) and is being considered by several nations as a fundamental right. This relates to universal access to the internet, to the need to decrease digital divides, and also to the right to privacy and freedom of expression online (UNDP, 2019).

This new concern of the 21st century has been considered by the United Nations (UN) that passed a resolution stressing the importance of thinking about a broad and integrated approach to human rights, which also includes access to the internet and its expansion (UN, 2018). The UN recognize that ICT, as well as the possibility of achieving global interconnectivity, have the potential to accelerate human development, with a view to overcoming the digital divides and digital gender gap (gender inequality in access to internet) problems and promoting the development of a knowledge society (UN, 2018).

In 2018, according to the International Telecommunication Union (ITU), 58% of the world's households had access to the internet at home (ITU, 2018). Such value reveals that more than half of the world's households have access to the internet which can be translated into a world increasingly closer to a more global and inclusive information society. However, in developing countries, the total percentage of internet users is only 45%, and in less developed countries it drops to 20% (ITU, 2018). In terms of broadband, for low human development countries, such as Mozambique, there is less than one subscription per 100 inhabitants, compared to 28 subscriptions per 100 inhabitants in high human development countries (UNDP, 2019).

The 2019 Human Development Report (UNDP, 2019), considers that another significant issue for low-income communities is the cost of internet access. This barrier is just one more way to perpetuate a cycle in which groups with lower human development indices have difficulty. The report considers that two children born in the year 2000, in countries with different levels of development, will have completely different perspectives on life, largely due to their economic and social contexts, which means that these inequalities can accumulate over a lifetime.

There is a global trend towards an increase in the use of ICT, with all indicators – mobile telephone, mobile and fixed broadband – registering sustainable increases between 2007 and 2018, with the exception of the landline. One of the reasons for this trend was the general decline in communications prices (ITU, 2018). Nevertheless, apart from the fact that not everybody can afford the communications cost, it is necessary to educate those who have access to make profitable use of the internet. It is also necessary to take into consideration the culture and context of the local community, not only for the implementation of the project to increase ICT use, but to guarantee its sustainability as well.

The digitization of the economy and the associated services require skills and resources that not all people have, which can result in a new form of inequality in work areas that is likely to become central in the coming decades. While there are improvements in equal opportunities for men and women, the same progress proves more difficult when one considers acquiring more advanced skills (UNDP, 2019). More than half of the world's population lacks the necessary basic information and communication skills (UNDP, 2019) and this marginalizes even those who can afford internet access (Deen-Swarray, 2016). The ITU (2018) report states that as digital activities become more complex, fewer people have the skills to perform them.

One of the ways to reduce the effects of digital divides and digital illiteracy can be through the implementation of technological tools. Another is through the joint effort of governments, the private sector, and civil society who must ensure that, in addition to training in digital skills in English (the most commonly used technological language), content is created and made available in local languages (Deen-Swarray, 2016). This issue is particularly important in isolated rural areas far from urban centres, where the information is inaccessible or non-existent and the majority of people do not speak the same language.

Furthermore, even if the next generations are empowered with the digital skills necessary for this global internet environment, if they do not have the opportunity to apply them, they will end up abandoning their communities searching for a better future. Many African countries aspire to become information and knowledge societies themselves, allowing them to participate as equal partners in this information-based global economy (Ponelis and Holmner, 2015).

Social Innovation

The concept of social innovation referring to experimental research in the social and human sciences emerged in the 1960s (Caulier-Grice et al., 2012). From that time on it has been associated with social entrepreneurship, technological innovation, corporate social responsibility, and open innovation. According to Bignetti (2011), the term "social innovation" refers to new or greatly improved ideas, actions, and knowledge whose purpose is to overcome social needs in a wide variety of fields, through the cooperation and participation of all those involved. Mulgan et al. (2007) argue that social innovations underlie new ideas through which individuals organize interactions and develop interpersonal relationships to achieve certain goals or overcome social obstacles. As such, any form of innovation results in some form of social innovation. Murray et al. (2010) define social innovation as a set of new ideas (products, services, and models) that simultaneously meet social needs and create new social relationships or collaborations. In other words, social innovations are innovations that simultaneously bring benefits to society and increase its capacity to act. Besides the goal of satisfying social needs, André and Abreu (2006) present that promoting social innovation includes enabling and empowering the actors involved and creating value according to the interests of social groups, rather than the appropriation of values for individual interests. Social innovations are therefore planned and coordinated for the specific goal to achieve social change through new social practices (Howaldt and Schwarz, 2010). Buchegger and Ornetzeder (2000) distinguish two perspectives on goals. From a micro perspective, they argue that the goals of social innovation concern meeting unmet social needs, continuous improvement of living standards, and increasing the capacity of groups and individuals to act. From a macro perspective, social innovation aims to achieve a general change in society by reducing inequalities and promoting sustainable development. Finally, Pol and Ville (2008) point out that for an innovation to be considered "social", it must improve both the economic and social performance of the society in which it is developed.

There is, therefore, a diversity of approaches to the concept, although they all have in common the need to articulate innovation with shared benefits. Social innovation is considered differently according to its context, geography, or industry and is mainly related to actions, and people doing new things in different ways (Caulier-Grice et al., 2012). Cichorzewska and Cholewa-Wiktor (2015) consider two points in common – the objective must always aim to contribute to social change and common wellbeing, and there is a joint participation of several entities through partnership cooperation. Until today, the concept definition, characteristics, and use still raise many doubts and questions as no one has managed to produce a unique definition so far (Neumeier, 2012).

Grimm et al. (2013) emphasize the existence of a growing link between social and technological innovation, especially in the current digital age. Regarding the concept of technological innovation associated with social innovation, Ionescu (2015) warns about the use of the term "social", in the sense that the word implies the creation of new relationships or the change of existing ones. It thus implies the disintegration or reorganization of social institutions that prevent people from satisfying their basic needs and consumption practices.

The understanding of technological innovation as social innovation is thus limited to "it is obvious that technological innovations can support social innovation, but only if it acts as a mechanism to transform social relationships so that excluded groups could improve their living conditions" (Ionescu, 2015, 59). Technological innovations should only be considered as social innovations if they are addressed to the community as a whole and not just to less privileged groups. Ionescu (2015) also emphasizes the importance of the feeling of empathy as a means to change power relations and the way of thinking and acting, fundamental for growth, to be reflected in human development, just as economic growth only makes sense if it results in social development.

Social innovation seems particularly relevant to fill the gaps that existing political structures cannot fill and can be accomplished by intensifying the will of society and governments to seek alternatives that reduce, for example, the levels of poverty of the population (Ionescu, 2015). Howaldt et al. (2016) corroborate the idea that it is necessary to create a new model for innovation policies, which shifts the focus from technologies to social innovations, and to the creation of systemic solutions with the corresponding training of its actors, thus complementing the new understanding of social innovation with a consistent policy.

An inductive approach for data analysis and a descriptive method for the presentation of results have been applied for this research, following the recommendations of Yin (2015). The methodology adopted in this work can be classified as qualitative, considering that it is a suitable way to understand the nature of a social phenomenon. With this case study, we intend to demonstrate the importance of ICT projects and social innovations for assuring sustainable development and improving living conditions in developing countries. The conceptual framework used is presented in Figure 9.1.

Case Study

Introduction

The Project SV4D – Sustainable Villages for Development – is a social project aimed to reduce inequalities in internet access. It was conceived to be implemented in rural or isolated areas, targeting the facilitation of broadband internet access, free of charge, through the implementation of internet infrastructure and Wi-Fi in public areas. The availability of Wi-Fi technology as an internet access technology stimulates the development of governmental, commercial,

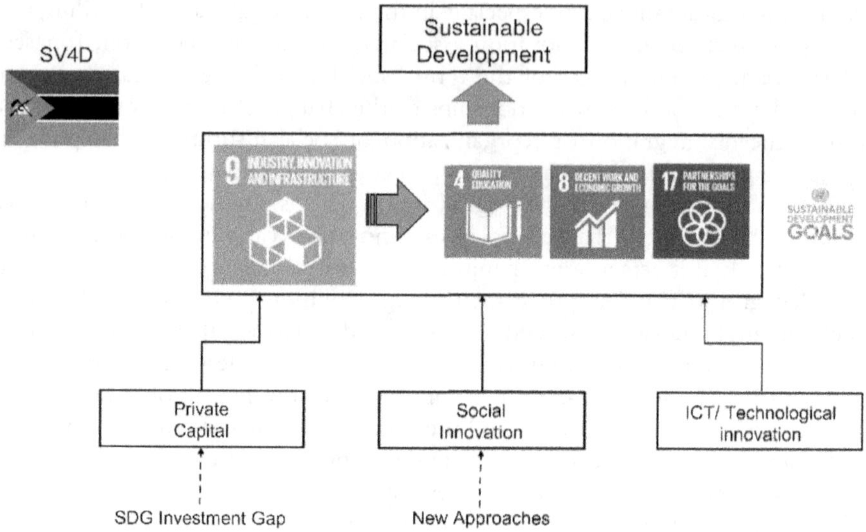

Figure 9.1 Conceptual Framework

and even community initiatives for the creation and availability of local services (Song et al., 2019).

In addition to the implementation of the infrastructure, the SV4D project also intends to promote training of the population to use the internet properly and to contribute to the development of digital skills. Such skills will allow the population to obtain more information and further training and will enable the development of small businesses. Consequently, the increase in family income will allow the population not to be left behind in the race towards digital transformation. In developing countries, there is a great demand for digital skills that are still not satisfied, and these skills are directly linked to higher financial income potential (ITU, 2018). The project is then directly linked to SDG 9, by building resilient infrastructure to promote sustainable industrialization and innovation. In addition, it contributes to strengthening quality and lifelong education (SDG 4), and promotes sustainable economic growth and new employment opportunities (SDG 8). Finally, it is a good example of a partnership for sustainable development (SDG 17), by bringing together in the same project private entities (with know-how and resources) and central and local government.

Overview

The SV4D is a project that aims at the development of local communities through broadband internet access as a way of enhancing the population's education; but also, with a view to improving their quality of life through the development of the local economy, and with the objective of providing recreational moments for the population. Hilbert (2016) notes that there is a relationship between broadband and population income – mobile phone subscriptions follow the population, but fixed broadband subscriptions relate to where there is higher income. There is also a strong consensus in the existing literature towards the positive impact of ICT on economic growth in Africa (Adams and Akobeng, 2021; Adeleye and Eboagu, 2019; David and Grobler, 2020).

The partners of this project came together to create SV4D, to enhance the economic and social development of local communities, through the research and development of ICT solutions aimed at meeting some of the needs of these countries. The SV4D project was designed and developed by the Community of Portuguese Language Countries (CPLP) and the Association of the Regulators of Communications and Telecommunications of the Community of Portuguese-Speaking Countries (ARCTEL-CPLP). ARCTEL was created in 2008 and represents the interests of the following Portuguese-speaking countries – Angola, Cape Verde, Brazil, Guinea-Bissau, Equatorial Guinea, Mozambique, Portugal, São Tomé and Principe, and East Timor. The mission of ARCTEL is to reinforce the sharing of information among the nine regulatory authorities that constitute it, thus contributing to the development of the market and the communications sector of these countries.

This project is implemented by ARCTEL-CPLP in partnership with the Fraunhofer AICOS (Research Center for Assistive Information and Communications Solutions), Portugal, which brings to the project the communications infrastructure and the skills to develop technological solutions focused on development. In Mozambique, the project is implemented by the Mozambique Communications Regulatory Authority (ARECOM), with the support of the District Governments of Alto Molocué and Mocuba, and financed by the Universal Access Service Fund of Mozambique. Universities, hospitals, governmental buildings, and central public squares of the localities were the places chosen for the implementation of this project in the villages of Alto Molocué and Mocuba, in the Zambézia Province of Mozambique (CPLP, 2018)

The SV4D project has a three-layer goal. The first layer targets the promotion for access to broadband internet, alongside the universalization of the use of ICT tools aiming at digital inclusion. The second layer's goal focuses on the creation of 20 living labs in 15 rural villages to conduct R&D for a sub-project called ICT solutions for Development (ICT4D). Such living labs will foster the implementation of digital services to address problems in the following domains – knowledge, health, education, economic situation, commerce, freedom, environment, security, and government. The aim of the third and last goal is to promote and enable data and information exchange between the different villages or labs to accelerate the deployment of R&D proofs of concept and enable big data and analytics concepts (SV4D, 2017).

It is expected that the long-term results of the SV4D project will take a few years to be visible. It is a complex project and, above all, dependent on transversal interactions such as (a) training the population, (b) raising awareness of entrepreneurship, and (c) spreading the use of technology to promote the improvement of the living conditions of communities. Thus, there is a need for the concerted efforts and involvement of government authorities in the countries where the project is implemented, and international entities (such as the ITU or Fraunhofer) and, above all, the local community.

The project is only feasible when solid partnerships are established with local authorities (whether they are municipalities, ministries, or regulatory authorities) and operators capable of guaranteeing the financing or co-financing of the project, monitoring the needs assessment phase and identifying the locations, monitoring the implementation (through the availability of technicians who know the territory and who act as a point of contact for interaction with communities), and who are responsible for the monitoring and sustainability of the project (CPLP, 2018). The first phase of the project was the implementation of the infrastructure, after which the project partners organized a meeting with the aim of clarifying the characteristics of the network. They also aimed to raise the awareness of the community to understand the potentialities of the project in an attempt to share mutual information, which also made room for ARCTEL-CPLP and Fraunhofer to collect data on the needs of the population for the second phase of the project (CPLP, 2018).

The second phase of the project assumes the resolution of a specific need of the local community, identified by the population, addressable through the implementation of a specific technological solution. In this sense, the SV4D project has the capability to adapt to various economic and cultural contexts. This second phase was carried out by Fraunhofer, with the support of ARCTEL-CPLP and the local authorities. The architecture of the SV4D project is presented in Figure 9.2.

The SV4D project faces several major challenges, namely the terrain, the lack of sustainability, the cultural issues, and the administrative bureaucracy. The

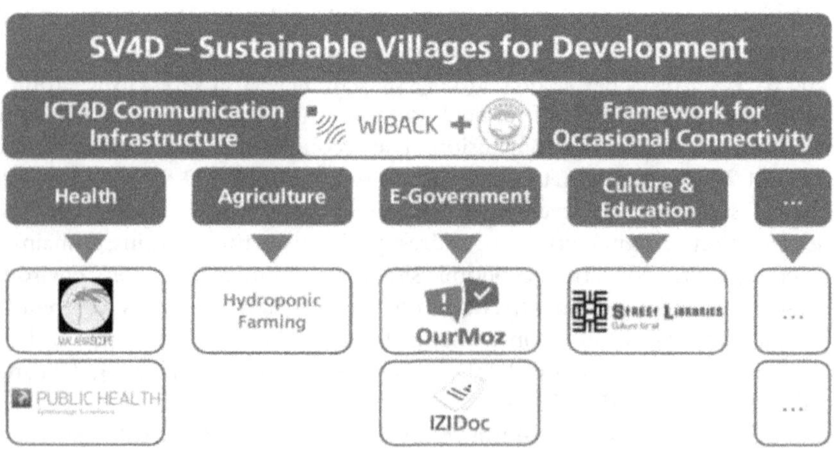

Figure 9.2 SV4D Project Architecture (SV4D, 2017)

terrain poses several challenges, not only in terms of accessibility to the places where the technological components will be deployed, but also in terms of where exactly those components will be installed. In addition, the fact that in most of the countries the rainy season is usually quite demanding. The lack of sustainability is related to the lack of means to make use of the technology that is being made available. Some of the existing hardware and software are either obsolete, or suffering from lack of proper maintenance, or with malfunctions, or installed in buildings with poor conditions, or with frequent power shortages. The cultural issues refer to the lack of knowledge and proper training to deal with and to handle technical components, which sometimes results in poor use of the resources made available.

Last, but not least, the administrative bureaucracy in the participating countries has several common characteristics – complex hierarchies associated with the several entities involved, communication issues related to lack of complete information, poor process handling and loss of documents, and many delays as a result of a reactive than a proactive approach (SV4D, 2017).

Mozambique

Mozambique is a country in East Africa, with an area of 801,590 km^2, and a population of 27,909,797 million people, with 66.6% of the population living in rural areas (INE, 2017). The official language is Portuguese.

Mozambique occupies the 180th position (out of 189 countries considered) in the Human Development Index (HDI). The HDI is a measure that analyses long-term development in three basic dimensions of human development, namely a long and healthy life (average life expectancy), access to knowledge (average years of effective schooling), and standard of living conditions (measured by the national gross domestic product (GDP)). The country's position at 180 places Mozambique on the list of low human development countries (UNDP, 2019).

In the communications sector, Mozambique is making progress in the development of ICT. The arrival of a third communication operator in 2012, Movitel, made room for greater competitiveness in the sector. Mozambique currently has three mobile telephone operators, namely Mcel, Vodacom, and Movitel. The connection to the first submarine cable, SEACOM in 2009, and to EASSy in 2010, provided considerable improvements in internet quality which has also led to a drop in communications prices (ITU, 2018).

In 2018, Mozambique had a 3G network coverage of about 40%, and about 20.8% of internet users. Fixed broadband subscription was only 0.1 in every 100 inhabitants (ITU, 2018). This was driven by high fixed broadband prices. The 3G network package offers are cheaper than fixed broadband offers, and for this reason, most of the internet access in the country is through mobile broadband (ITU, 2018).

Mozambique has two more submarine cables planned, which will contribute to improving network coverage, better quality of infrastructure, and lower prices. Additionally, the new Mozambican telecommunications law reinforces the need for infrastructure sharing, thus aiming to avoid duplication of investment in rural areas (ITU, 2018). The focus on projects such as SV4D, combined with the improvement of communications infrastructure and the development of the sector, will contribute to greater digital inclusion.

SV4D Project Infrastructure and Implementation

The system adopted to implement the SV4D project was the WiBack system, a Wi-Fi network that uses point-to-point direct beam connections (antenna to antenna). The maximum distance between two WiBack antennas is 20 km (line of sight required) and a maximum of ten antennas in a row can be deployed. On all WiBack antennas, Wi-Fi Hotspots can be installed and the WiBack Controller connects to the internet via the network of a mobile telecom operator. The operator that provides the signal for the project becomes a partner in the project.

In 2018, the first infrastructure of the SV4D project was implemented in the districts of Mocuba and Alto Molocué, in the Zambézia Province, in Mozambique (CPLP, 2018). The implementation was requested by the Mozambique Communications Regulatory Authority (ARECOM) and financed by the Universal Access Service Fund (FSAU). FSAU is a public service fund managed by ARECOM.

The places where internet hotspots were implemented were called "digital squares", and these were implemented, in two phases, in the following locations:

- Mocuba – City Hall, Instituto Agrário de Mocuba, Hospital Rural de Mocuba, Universidade da Zambézia, Escola Secundária Geral de Mocuba, Administração do Distrito;
- Alto Molocué – Governo do Distrito de Alto Molocué, Instituto de Formação de Professores, Escola Secundária Pista Nova, Conselho Municipal da Vila de Alto Molocué, Mercado Central.

After both implementations, training in the functioning of the network was provided to representatives of all institutions where the WiBack system was implemented. Afterwards, the implementation team made up of members from Fraunhofer, ARCTEL-CPLP, and ARECOM, had the opportunity to directly contact the local population and understand the conditions in which the project was being implemented, the level of proximity to the new technologies, and what were the expectations regarding the project.

It was found was that a young population close to new technologies made the biggest references to the ease of researching school contents. They were students from the University of Zambézia, the Agrário Institute, and the Pista Nova Secondary School. However, the population in an older age group should not to be disregarded, users of social networks such as Facebook or WhatsApp and YouTube who search for informative contents. Several references were made to the use of YouTube to view news content, even by the older population with less schooling.

During the official launching of the SV4D project in 2019, the "Orera" application (which means "clean" in the local dialect) was announced. It was developed by Fraunhofer, with the support of ARECOM, FSAU, and the local government of Mocuba, to help with the problem of garbage collection in the city. This application allows the population to alert and interact with local authorities for failures in the cleaning of common spaces, thus providing a cleaner and healthier city for the entire community.

SV4D Project Outcomes

The impact evaluation of projects is essential to analyse the results, identify deviations from the forecasts, and, if necessary, correct errors and mistakes for future projects (Epstein and Yuthas, 2017; Cohen, 2020). In a context of severe resource constraints, these elements are even more relevant, although they are difficult to implement and are often replaced by assessments of short-term outputs rather than impact.

In order to understand the outcomes of the SV4D project, Fraunhofer and ARCTEL-CPLP, prepared a network usage report preserving the privacy and anonymity of users (INCM, 2019). The report analysed the traffic generated by the users of the digital squares in both districts, along with data related to the traffic volume, profiles of usage schedules, and types of protocols used.

The top four categories with the most traffic in digital squares alternated between webs (which included http, SSL, and Wikipedia), media (which included Netflix, SoundCloud, Spotify, and YouTube), Virtual Private Networks (VPNs) and Privacy (which included Open VPN, SOCKS, SSL, and Tor), and Services (Apple, Google, and Microsoft). As expected, the media category, due to the type of content available (videos, music, etc.), normally generated a higher volume of data than the other categories whose content is generally available on a text basis.

The use of VPNs and Privacy in all digital squares was around 13–20%. We can deduce from this a more conscious use of the internet regarding browsing safety, as well as protecting the privacy of searches and the users' identities. Social networks, on the other hand, registered relatively low usage data, when compared to the other categories, ranging between 6% and 11% in Mocuba, and between 2% and2.8% in Alto Molocué.

Due to the type of data collected, which are based only on experience and usage times, and the absence of previous impact studies, it was not possible to assess the economic impact of using these networks. Also contributing to this difficulty in the analysis was the occurrence of recurring technical problems of the internet connection, which did not allow a direct comparative analysis of the data generated by the users of the two networks. However, from the data available, everything shows that, from a macro perspective, the general profiles of the users of the two networks are similar. The collected data were not enough to outline the specific profiles of the users. Other data would have to be considered as well, such as education level, income, age, socioeconomic conditions, ease of access to information technologies, among others.

Despite considering that the implementation of this project was successful, as it provides internet access available free of charge and allows it to be used in a very diversified way, thus democratizing access to information, some technical difficulties were experienced. Among these, there were failures in the internet connection by the service provider, power failures, and signal failures (due to equipment failure, for example) by the institutions where the service was installed.

Other difficulties perceived included the lack of disclosure of the project (at the time of preparation of the report, the official inauguration of the project had not yet taken place), some issues related to digital literacy, such as the lack of knowledge of the word "internet" when citizens were asked about the use of the internet, and the lack of knowledge about the mechanisms for reporting failures within the institutions of the project. Another difficulty felt by the SV4D project team was the language issue. Although Portuguese is the official language in Mozambique, the locations where the project was installed are rural areas where the prevailing languages are still the local dialects. In addition, the language of the technology used today is either in English or derived from English, a fact that makes it difficult to use questionnaires, especially for the population with less schooling. However, this was not an issue for university students, who mastered ICT technologies and concepts without difficulty.

Conclusion

The SD4S project is a pilot and innovative project, both in its design (by a consortium of telecommunications regulators) and content (internet access in rural communities), and in the area of implementation (Mozambique). The mobilization of funds and materials and its execution was carried out by a partnership between diverse entities, aggregated by the historical links between the Portuguese-speaking countries, and its implementation was done in a community in one of the very low HDI countries. There is certainly a greater need for this type of projects.

It is clearly a social innovation project, according to the dimensions identified by Gerometta et al. (2005): (1) it aims to meet human needs (a collective social problem, of low levels of digital literacy and internet access, with an impact on employment opportunities, income level, and the creation of projects); (2) it leads to a change in social relations (by allowing new forms of participation and integration of people involved in the community and the economy, by improving their level of information and knowledge); (3) it leads to an increase in sociopolitical capacity and access to resources (project beneficiaries can have a more social and political active position).

Although, as mentioned above, the measurement of outcomes was very limited, the project had an impact on a large number of people (scale), on various levels – knowledge, employability, etc. (coverage) and allowed the acquisition of knowledge for its implementation in other countries, such as São Tomé and Principe (resonance). Therefore, according to Nilsson (2003), considering its scale, scope, and resonance, the project is considered a success.

The reported results are very preliminary, but the increase in the use of the internet can be considered a proxy for the creation of local economic initiatives, an improvement in digital skills, which is associated with a higher level of employability and, in general, an increase in the living conditions of the communities and greater empowerment.

Acknowledgement

The authors acknowledge Fundação para a Ciencia e Tecnologia (FCT-Portugal) for the support with the multi-year research funding UIDB/04521/2020 (ADVANCE/CSG).

References

Adams, S. and Akobeng, E. (2021). ICT, governance and inequality in Africa. *Telecommunications Policy*, 45(10), 10, 102198.

Adeleye, N. and Eboagu, C. (2019). Evaluation of ICT development and economic growth in Africa. *Netnomics: Economic Research and Electronic Networking*, 20(1), 31–53.

Ali, W., Frynas, J.G. and Mahmood, Z. (2017). Determinants of corporate social responsibility (CSR) disclosure in developed and developing countries: A literature review. *Corporate Social Responsibility and Environmental Management*, 24(4), 273–294.

André, I. and Abreu, A. (2006). Dimensões e espaços da inovação social. *Finisterra: Revista Portuguesa de Geografia*, 41(81), 121–141.

Baumann, C., Winzar, H. and Fang, T. (2018). East Asian wisdom and relativity. *Cross Cultural and Strategic Management*, 25(2), 210–230.

Bignetti, L.P. (2011). As inovações sociais: Uma incursão por ideias, tendências e focos de pesquisa. *Ciências Sociais Unisinos*, 47(1), 3–14.

Buchegger, B. and Ornetzeder, M. (2000). Social innovations on the way to sustainable development. ESEE Conference in Vienna. May 2000.

Carroll, A.B. (1999). Corporate social responsibility: Evolution of a definitional construct. *Business and Society*, 38(3), 268–295.

Caulier-Grice, J., Davies, A., Patrick, R. and Norman, W. (2012). Defining social innovation. In: *The Young Foundation (2012) Social Innovation Overview: A Deliverable of the Project: "The Theoretical, Empirical and Policy Foundations for Building Social Innovation in Europe" (TEPSIE)*. European Commission – 7th Framework Programme. Brussels: European Commission, DG Research.

Cichorzewska, M. and Cholewa-Wiktor, M. (2015). *The Influence of Social Innovation upon the Development of Regions and Organizations. Research Papers of the Wroclaw University of Economics/Prace Naukowe Uniwersytetu Ekonomicznego We Wroclawiu, 387.*

Cohen, R. (2020). *Impact: Reshaping Capitalism to Drive Real Change*. New York, NY: Random House.

CPLP (2018). Agenda digital para a CPLP 2018. Community of Portuguese Language Countries. Available at: https://arctel-cplp.org/wp-content/uploads/2022/01/Agenda-Digital-para-a-CPLP.pdf

David, O.O. and Grobler, W. (2020). Information and communication technology penetration level as an impetus for economic growth and development in Africa. *Economic Research-Ekonomska Istraživanja*, 33(1), 1394–1418.

Davidson, D.K. and Yin, J. (2019). Corporate social responsibility (CSR) in China: A contextual exploration. In Information Resources Management Association (USA) (Ed.) *Corporate Social Responsibility: Concepts, Methodologies, Tools, and Applications*. Derry Township, PA: IGI Global.

Deen-Swarray, M. (2016). Toward digital inclusion: Understanding the literacy effect on adoption and use of mobile phones and the internet in Africa. *Information Technologies and International Development*, 12(2), 29–45.

Epstein, M.J. and Yuthas, K. (2017). *Measuring and Improving Social Impacts: A Guide for Nonprofits, Companies, and Impact Investors*. London: Routledge.

Gerometta, J., Haussermann, H. and Longo, G. (2005). Social innovation and civil society in urban governance: Strategies for an inclusive city. *Urban Studies*, 42(11), 2007–2021.

Grimm, R., Fox, C., Baines, S. and Albertson, K. (2013). Social innovation, an answer to contemporary societal challenges? Locating the concept in theory and practice. *Innovation: the European Journal of Social Science Research*, 26(4), 436–455.

Hilbert, M. (2016). The bad news is that the digital access divide is here to stay: Domestically installed bandwidths among 172 countries for 1986–2014. *Telecommunications Policy*, 40(6), 567–581.

Hildebrand, D., Sen, S. and Bhattacharya, C.B. (2011). Corporate social responsibility: A corporate marketing perspective. *European Journal of Marketing*, 45(9-10), 1353–1364.

Howaldt, J. and Schwarz, M. (2010). *Social Innovation: Concepts, Research Fields and International Trends*. Aachen: IMA/ZLW IfU Aachen.

Howaldt, J., Domanski, D. and Kaletka, C. (2016). Social innovation: Towards a new innovation paradigm. *RAM. Revista de Administração Mackenzie*, 17(6), 20–44.

INCM (2019). Relatório de Regulação das Comunicações 2019. *Autoridade Reguladora das comunicações de Moçambique*. Available at: https://www.incm.gov.mz/index.php/sala-de-imprensa/postal-2/224-relatorio-de-regulacao-das-comunicacoes-2019-1

INE (2017). *Estatísticas de Moçambique*. Instituto Nacional de Estatísticas de Moçambique. Available at: www.ine.gov.mz

Ionescu, C. (2015). About the conceptualization of social innovation. *Theoretical and Applied Economics*, 22(3), 53–62.

ITU (2018). *Measuring the Information Society Report Volume*. Available at: https://www.itu.int/en/ITU-D/Statistics/Pages/publications/misr2018.aspx, *1. ITU* Publications. International Telecommunication Union

Lee, M.-D.P. (2008). A review of the theories of corporate social responsibility: Its evolutionary path and the road ahead. *International Journal of Management Reviews*, 10(1), 53–73.

Luo, X. and Bhattacharya, C.B. (2006). Corporate social responsibility, customer satisfaction, and market value. *Journal of Marketing*, 70(4), 1–18.

Maon, F., Lindgreen, A. and Swaen, V. (2010). Organizational stages and cultural phases: A critical review and a consolidative model of corporate social responsibility development. *International Journal of Management Reviews*, 12(1), 20–38.

Miller, D. and Merrilees, B. (2013). Linking retailer corporate brand and environmental sustainability practices. *Journal of Product and Brand Management*, 22(7), 437–443.

Mulgan, G., Tucker, S., Ali, R. and Sanders, B. (2007). *Social Innovation. What It Is, Why It Matters and How It Can Be Accelerated.* Oxford Said Business School - Skoll Centre for Social Entrepreneurship.

Murray, R., Caulier-Grice, J. and Mulgan, G. (2010). *The Open Book of Social Innovation.* The Young Foundation/ National Endowment for Science, Technology and the Arts (NESTA).

Nilsson, W.O. (2003). Social innovation: An exploration of the literature. McGill-Dupont Social Innovation Initiative, Montreal. McGill University.

Neumeier, S. (2012). Why do social innovations in rural development matter and should they be considered more seriously in rural development research? - Proposal for a stronger focus on social innovations in rural development research. *Sociologia Ruralis*, 52(1), 48–69.

Hammad, H., El-Bassiouny Paul, P. and Mukhopadhyay, K. (2014). Antecedents and consequences of consumers' attitudinal dispositions toward cause- related marketing in Egypt. *Journal of Islamic Marketing*, 5(3), 414–445.

Pepper, R. and Jackman, M. (2019). A data-driven approach to closing the internet inclusion gap. In: *Digital Economies at Global Margins* Graham, M. (Ed.). Cambridge, MA: MIT Press.

Pol, E. and Ville, S. (2008). Social innovation: Buzz or enduring term? Working paper 08-09. Department of Economics, University of Wollongong. Available at: https://ro.uow.edu.au/commwkpapers/194.

Ponelis, S.R. and Holmner, M.A. (2015). ICT in Africa: Building a better life for all. *Information Technology for Development*, 21(2), 163–177.

Porter, M.E. and Kramer, M.R. (2006). Strategy and society: The link between competitive advantage and corporate social responsibility. *Harvard Business Review*, 84(12), 78–92.

Song, S., Rey-Moreno, C. and Jensen, M. (2019). Innovations in spectrum management: Enabling community networks and small operators to connect the unconnected. Internet Society. Available at: https://www.internetsociety.org/wp-content/uploads/2019/03/InnovationsinSpectrum

SV4D (2017). In: Lagos. *SV4D: The Project, the Reality Observed and the Challenges to Be Addressed. Presentation by Fraunhofer AICOS – Portugal in the International Workshop on Affordable Wireless Connectivity Solutions (AWCS).* Available at: https://www.slideshare.net/WaldirJunior1/sv4d-the-project-the-reality-observed-and-the-challenges-to-be-addressed. Nigeria

UN (2018). The promotion, protection and enjoyment of human rights on the Internet. Human Rights Council (38th sess. : 2018 : Geneva). United Nations. Available at: https://digitallibrary.un.org/record/1639840#record-files-collapse-header

UNDP (2019). *Human Development Report 2019.* Available at: http://hdr.undp.org/sites/default/files/hdr2019.pdf. United Nations Development Programme

Yin, R.K. (2015). *Qualitative Research from Start to Finish.* 2nd edition. New York, NY: Guilford Publications.

10 Using "Actor–Network Theory and Friends" to Explore CSR Reporting in the Information and Communication Technology Sector under the Belt and Road Initiative

Carlos Noronha and Ruopiao Zhang

Introduction

The international business literature (Bansal and Roth, 2000; Muller and Kolk, 2010) provides compelling evidence of the global diffusion of corporate social responsibility (CSR) practices and the critical role of multinational enterprises (MNEs) in this process (Brammer et al., 2012; Marano et al., 2017). Foreign direct investment (FDI) and MNEs' international trade activities are regarded as conduits for cross-border development of CSR (Belal and Owen, 2015; Husted and Allen, 2006). Are MNEs makers or breakers of the rules on global CSR practices in host countries? Recent CSR literature offers lively debates on this question. Faced with growing demands to be socially accountable to host-country communities, MNEs may use their global influence in leading the way by connecting CSR initiatives with their core business activities to promote sustainable development (Kolk and Van Tulder, 2010; Van Zanten and Van Tulder, 2018). Previous studies have identified various benefits for MNEs that derive from superior CSR performance, including increased international reputation and competitive advantage (Porter and Kramer, 2006), enhanced operational legitimacy (Reimann et al., 2012; Tai and Chuang, 2014) and reduced liability of foreignness (Boubakri et al., 2016; Campbell et al., 2012). However, the lack of comprehensive international regulation on social and environmental issues poses challenges for MNEs (Aguilera-Caracuel and Guerrero-Villegas, 2018; Husted and Allen, 2007; Rhee et al., 2021).

While MNEs from developed countries are already commonplace, MNEs from emerging economies (EMNEs), known for their less efficient markets, active government participation, broad commercial networking and high levels of unpredictability, are attracting greater academic attention (Ervits, 2021; Gugler and Shi, 2009; Miska et al., 2016). When operating abroad, EMNEs bear the liability of "emergingness", which refers to the increased costs of foreign expansion resulting from the nature of their home countries (Cuervo-Cazurra, 2012; Miska et al., 2016; Gammeltoft et al., 2010). While Chinese MNEs have been increasing their impact in the international arena with their presence on

DOI: 10.4324/9781003274575-12

the Fortune Global 500 list (135 companies in 2021), China has experienced dramatic structural change over the last few decades. It is an emerging market, with a peculiar institutional framework marked by government intervention (Miska et al., 2016; Tashman et al., 2019). The Silk Road Economic Belt and 21st Century Maritime Silk Road Development Strategy proposed in 2013, which subsequently became the Belt and Road Initiative (BRI – from China to Central Asia, Eurasia, Western Asia, Russia, Southeast Asia, South Asia and Europe, the BRI aims to facilitate trade, investment, infrastructure, cultural and other forms of connectedness in a global manner (Huang, 2016)), are two substantial government-led initiatives which injected vitality into the globalization process of Chinese enterprises.

The major goal of the BRI is to promote socioeconomic growth by developing land and maritime trade routes (Fang and Nolan, 2019; Huang, 2016; Hurley et al., 2019). A substantial proportion of BRI projects is linked with investments in ports, roads, railways and airport infrastructure, as well as power plants and telecommunication networks. As an important part of the overall BRI strategy, the Chinese government launched the Digital Silk Road (DSR) policy in 2015. This promotes the building of bilateral cable networks, transcontinental submarine cable projects and satellite passageways along the BRI. Globally, mergers in the telecommunications and computing industries and the relevant sectors have resulted in a broader definition of information and communications technologies (ICT). In this paper, the ICT industry is defined as producing "equipment and services connected to broadcasting, computers, and telecommunications, all of which capture and display information electronically" (UNSEC, 2004, 2).

However, a number of BRI-related projects have been widely criticized by the world community in relation to the environment and biodiversity and have triggered research on CSR responses to such concerns (Gu and Qiu, 2019; Hong and Shuai, 2020; Renwick, 2019). The World Wildlife Fund warns of significant overlap between BRI projects and vulnerable ecosystems. Using data from international organizations, it identifies 1,739 Important Bird Areas and Key Biodiversity Areas as being endangered. Over 265 threatened species, including rare tigers and the severely endangered saiga antelope, may be harmed (WWF, 2017). Relatively few studies have examined how digital infrastructures in BRI countries may have impacted social concerns (Bernal-Conesa et al., 2017; Calero et al., 2019).

CSR reporting, which refers to public disclosure of firms' social responsibility and corporate governance practices, is a globally legitimating activity (Muller and Kolk, 2015; Li et al., 2010). It is important to understand the substance, objectives and targets of CSR in context, and to tailor theory to firms from both developed and developing countries (Gugler and Shi, 2009; Marano et al., 2017). Recent studies have highlighted the need to examine the context-dependence of EMNEs' CSR in host countries and to pay greater attention to these countries' unique institutional constellations and national business configurations, which may result in diverse expressions of CSR (Dam and Scholtens, 2013; Jamali and Neville, 2011). EMNEs must associate themselves with global "meta" institutions such as CSR mechanisms that set "guidelines and expectations for MNE behavior on a global basis" to overcome or work around their liabilities of origin (Kostova et al., 2008, 998).

The Digital Silk Road policy under the BRI (abbreviated as BRI-DSR) provides a precious opportunity to examine how MNEs from China establish and maintain legitimacy across their global operations, especially since many countries participating in the BRI are developing or emerging economies (Ramasamy and Yeung, 2019; Yang et al., 2020). Furthermore, given that the concept of CSR is still new and Chinese MNEs' CSR management mechanisms are relatively immature (Fang and Nolan, 2019; Yang et al., 2020), the unique setting of the BRI-DSR allows investigation of the CSR reporting of Chinese ICT-MNEs and their contribution to economic and social development in host-country communities while addressing home-country concerns. Furthermore, the interplay among human and non-human actors in the global ICT industry serves as an excellent demonstration of how actor–network theory (ANT), originally developed from a "sociotechnical" background, can be elevated to an all-encompassing interpretation toward "theory emancipation".

The major research objectives of this study are: (1) to explore the CSR approach of Chinese ICT-MNEs, (2) to identify the industry-specific external factors influencing the contents of CSR reporting and (3) to identify the industry-specific contents of CSR reporting in BRI host countries. These objectives will be crafted into research questions after the theoretical approach is specified in detail.

Theoretical Consideration

Actor–Network Theory in Accounting Research

The current study is influenced by ANT based on two important considerations as raised by Justesen and Mouritsen (2011). Firstly, they pointed out that most ANT-inspired accounting research is based on single case studies, making such research difficult to generalize (p. 162). Secondly, as in Latour's own works, ANT itself is a body of knowledge which is changing ("in action") over time, and new theoretical formulations may become relevant to accounting research (p. 126).

According to Justesen and Mouritsen's (2011) detailed description of the development of ANT in the accounting literature, it mainly started with Burrell and Morgan's (1979) book on organizational theory that offered new perspectives for accounting researchers to engage in a more sociological approach toward the subject. ANT, in particular the works of Bruno Latour, has since received rigorous attention by the accounting academia. Although ANT was not developed solely by Latour (Callon, Law and others are also pioneers), his work *Science in Action* (Latour, 1987) is the main reference accounting researchers draw upon.

Probably due to ANT's original roots from studies involving science, technology and laboratories (sociotechnology), a number of landmark studies in accounting using ANT were based on single case studies in mining/aluminum rolling (Briers and Chua, 2001), clinics/healthcare (Lowe, 2000), hospitals (Llewellyn and Northcott, 2005), and telecommunications (Hopper and Major, 2007). These are only a few examples from the myriad of ANT-inspired accounting projects. For further examples, Justesen and Mouritsen (2011) and Lukka and Vinnari (2014) provide comprehensive reviews. However, all of the above attempts are field studies related to management accounting (especially activity-based costing, budgeting and benchmarking) and there is a lack of ANT-inspired research in other accounting-related areas (e.g., non-financial (CSR) reporting as in the current study) and at a more "general level" as underscored by Justesen and Mouritsen (2011).

In relation to Justesen and Mouritsen's (2011) call above, two studies are particularly highlighted here. MacKenzie (2009) has examined, from an ANT perspective (drawing mainly from Callon), the political aspects of gas emissions and carbon markets. Carbon accounting is currently highly topical, and carbon market trading and related matters (e.g., COP26) are enthusiastically being debated under the sustainable development goals (SDGs). MacKenzie (2009) has brought a much bigger accounting issue into international awareness through the perspective of ANT. He argued that "to conclude that carbon markets must fail may be unduly pessimistic ... If carbon markets are here to stay, can they be improved?" (p. 452). A few important considerations may be pointed out here. Firstly, MacKenzie (2009) emphasized the pluralistic nature of the market (Callon, 1998). Secondly, he raised the importance of "bottom lines" (p. 448) in his analysis of carbon trading under IFRIC3 (mainly on accounting for emission rights). Thirdly, he has also emphasized that carbon markets is only one tool to fight global warming from the sub-political tools (p. 453) such as direct legal requirements, carbon taxes and R&D. These important messages gleaned from MacKenzie (2009) are reflective of the ontology of ANT proposed as an alternative foundation in this current study.

Other research conducted by Vosselman (2014) concerning the elevation of ANT-inspired accounting research to a more "general level" warrants attention here. Vosselman (2014) has compared interfirm transactions through an ostensive perspective (transaction cost economics) and a performative perspective (ANT) and emphasized that transaction cost economics can be viewed in terms of a "translation" focal point and that both transaction cost economics and ANT can both generate or create knowledge, and they have interactions, although from different ontological viewpoints (pp. 13–14). These two studies now lead us to the discussion of the ontology of "ANT and friends".

Ontology of "ANT and Friends"

Based on Law's (1999) notion of "after ANT", Lowe (2001) discussed the nature of qualitative accounting research "after ANT". He has systematically listed out Latour's "rules of ANT" (Lowe, 2001, 334–335, largely taken from *Science in Action*) which later served as the standard in other ANT-inspired accounting studies, although he stressed that there be should no prescription for interpretative research (p. 346).

As pointed out earlier, ANT is a changing and living body of knowledge and as such, the way that ANT is applied in research is also "fluid" (Latour, 2005). Many authors have been adhering to ANT's original "flat ontology", that every "actor" and "actant" should be laid on a flat plain for analyses of their "translations". Translation is used in the sense of association but not necessarily having causality (Latour, 2005). It is also in the sense of "transforming" but not "transporting" (Vosselman, 2014), as Latour (2005) has differentiated between "intermediaries" and "mediators". Lukka and Vinnari (2014) have compared and contrasted "domain theory" and "method theory" in accounting research, where domain theory can be accounting theory itself while method theory is often borrowed from other disciplines such as sociology. ANT is a good example of method theory. Here, we also borrow the concept of theory from "within" and theory from "without" in the management literature. In other words, we propose a contemporary and all-embracing interpretation of ANT's flat ontology.

In a recent critique of ANT, Modell (2020) suggested that a critical realism approach to accounting research may have advantages over the traditional flat ANT ontology. Since Latour's original flat ontology concept was supposed to contrast with the concept of "social structure" (hierarchies, humans and non-humans, micro and macro, etc.), Modell (2020) was critical of ANT as it may conflict with the conventional "social construction of reality" (Berger and Luckmann, 1966) and thus conflict with many structural theories, including institutional theory (DiMaggio and Powell, 1983) often deployed in accounting research (Latour has actually emphasized the difference between fabrication/constructionism and social construction, see Lukka and Vinnari (2014)). Interestingly, two "ants", namely Baxter and Chua (2020, 655) refuted Modell's (2020) criticism and his "Mexican standoff" and suggested that methodological diversity is to be explored; they acknowledged the ontological preferences of researchers.

This serious debate has opened the way for more liberal approaches to the application of ANT in accounting research. For example, Bussular et al. (2020, 177, 186) have recently applied ANT both as a theory as well as a methodology (semiotic material tools, sensibilities and methods of analysis for the engagement to the world) in studying an environmental catastrophe in Brazil. The above storyline has paved the way toward an all-encompassing and fluid way of applying ANT to accounting. In fact, Lowe (2001, 337) had already used the term "*Latour's version of ANT*" in his paper. In other words, we are trying to make Latour's Janus talk to himself.

Figure 10.1 shows the original flat ontology of ANT as insisted by "hardcore" ants, and Figure 10.2 our suggested "ANT and friends" in which an embracement of the blending of the flat field approach with the unavoidable social structuralism of the real world can be seen. A pile (or layers) of coins on the flat field represents the actors as well as the actants. They can be aligned according to

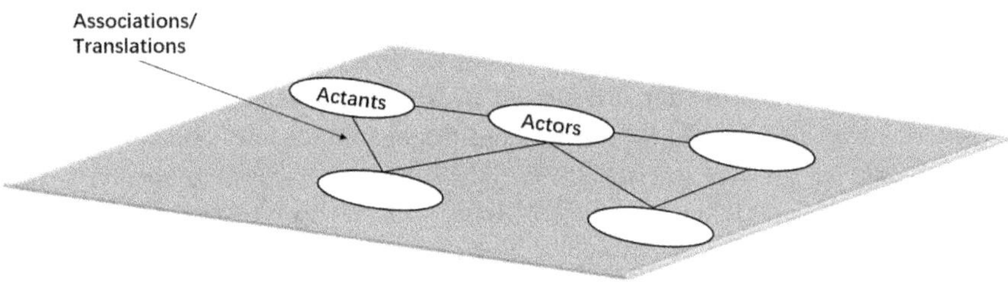

Figure 10.1 The Flat Ontology of ANT (a 2D Perspective)

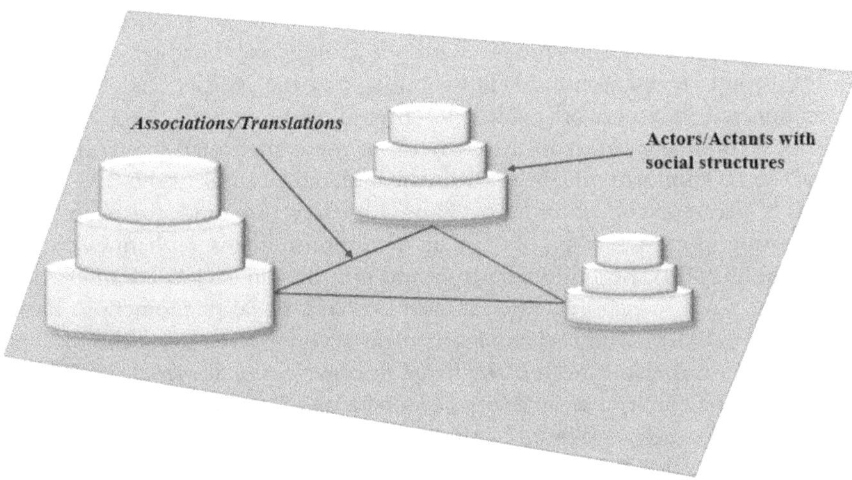

Figure 10.2 "ANT and Friends" Ontology (a 3D Perspective)

hierarchical associations as well as micro and macro relationships. The associations or translations are still represented by straight lines among the elements within the network. Imaginative readers can also replace straight lines by "snake lines" to indicate the fluid nature of associations in ANT.

The openness to interpretations of ANT has also recently been acknowledged by Gautier and Bonneveux (2021). In studying successful CSR diffusion (levels of interaction, conceptualization of CSR, initiating actor for change, stakeholders, innovation diffusion processes and conditions (p. 53)) in French IT (French Association of Digital Clusters), they used both neo-institutional theory (NIT) and ANT as complementary lenses to explore the phenomenon. They concluded that it is appropriate to use both NIT and ANT in the context of diffusion of CSR (p. 61). Furthermore, Rautiainen and Scapens (2013) had already indicated the compatible nature of neo-institutional sociology (NIS) and ANT in understanding accounting change and stability.

In another study by Gond and Nyberg (2017), the material context of CSR and the conceptualization of power to materialize CSR were firstly discussed from the classical market-centered approach, the political approach and the critical approach. The authors then articulated an ANT approach to fill in the void left by current progressive CSR (based on traditional market and political-centered foci) and critical CSR (e.g., Marxism). ANT-inspired CSR (agencement, performativity, etc.) can tackle existing problems such as those related to materiality of the needs of different stakeholders. The notion of a hybrid forum (p. 1140) which proposes a space for heterogeneous actors to collectively define problems in which they are all implicated is an excellent example of ANT.

Preparing "ANT and Friends" for the Current Research

Latour (2005) has redefined the meaning of sociology as "the tracing of associations" (through translations). ANT is about tracing the associations of all things interconnected in a network which "re-assembles the social". ANT therefore lends itself to an analysis of all the elements in the complicated interconnectedness of the ICT industry under government-initiated auspices of the BRI-DSR.

ANT's greatest contribution to knowledge creation and discovery is in its bypassing of the duality of humans and non-humans (Johannesson and Baerenholdt, 2000). Both human actors and non-human actants are interwoven into the network, which generates an ever-evolving social phenomenon. Barter and Russell (2013) have provided an excellent account concerning the machine versus organism metaphor often employed in organizational theory. While they pointed out the conceptual similarity of humans as cogs in the machine versus a form of resource to be exploited by the organization (p. 151), they (p. 148) also referred to Morgan (2011) and Lakoff and Turner (1987), who assert that the "great chain" implies dominance by humans. Humans, animals, plants, inanimate objects and other objects constitute a chain in a similar way. While humans dominate the earth in their impact upon sustainable development, the earth also acts as a life support system for humans. Barter and Russell's (2013) notion provides support to the application of ANT not only at the organizational level, but also at the more macro institutional level or even beyond, such as the BRI-DSR setting in this study.

In the context of the ICT industry, Cresswell et al. (2010) have underscored the usefulness of ANT in understanding the implementation of healthcare IT. ANT provides a lens through which to view the role of technology in shaping social processes contributing to a more holistic appreciation of the complexity of introducing technology. ANT has been applied as a sociotechnical approach (Walsham, 1997) in understanding workplace relations, but it has not been used to explain the interconnections among actors and actants of industrial sectors, MNEs and official policies. This chapter contributes to accounting studies, especially in the CSR reporting area, while proposing an in-action and all-embracing approach to the theory/method itself. Also, we are trying to break away from the conventional application of ANT to the perusal of isolated cases concerning accounting change only. This study fills this void through the proposed "ANT and friends" framework.

Calling the Actors to Stage

Now let us identify the actors and actants and other essential elements in this study. They are interconnected, influence each other and function together in line with the core concept of ANT. The theory advocates treating human and non-human actors in a completely equal manner, eliminating the binary division between them (Barter and Russell, 2013).

Table 10.1 attempts to name the major participants in the actor–network, acting in the spotlight of the BRI. In this case, we designate Chinese MNEs (the investors) and the BRI host countries (the investment recipients) as the human actors. Actants usually refer to non-human objects which have a role in the entire actor–network. Here under the BRI-DSR, there are many; however, we emphasize investments. There are intermediaries between the actors, such as Macau which acts as an organizer of opportunities and conventions to promote the BRI between China and Portuguese-speaking countries. Since Portuguese-speaking African countries play an important role in the BRI as host countries, Macau, a former Portuguese enclave now returned back to Chinese sovereignty, acts as an active "intermediary" between China and Portuguese-speaking Africa, Portugal as well as Brazil. The "Forum" set up by the Macau government is an example of a platform to facilitate trade and cultural exchange under the BRI.

The token or quasi-object overseeing the entire network is the initiative itself, the BRI, as well as the DSR policy under it. And translations refer to that which actors consider to be worthy of building the entire stage, or the actor–network. Here we simply use technology transfer (although all non-human actants such as infrastructure, technology, hardware and the like play important roles in the entire actor–network). By using our suggested "ANT and friends" perspective, all actors and actants are laid on the flat field for analysis. However, they can also be interpreted in terms of NIT/NIS which incorporate structures and institutional hierarchies and settings. For example, DSR is a sub-set of BRI,

Table 10.1 Actors, Actants and Related Essential Elements

Actors	*Actants*	*Intermediaries*	*Quasi-objects/ Tokens*	*Translations*
ICT-MNEs	Investments	Forums/conventions	BRI-DSR	Technology transfers
BRI host countries	Investment receipts	Forums/conventions	BRI-DSR	Technology receipts

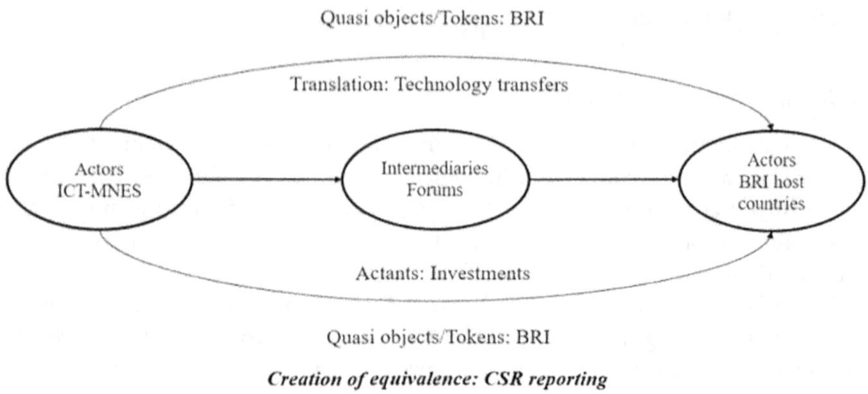

Figure 10.3 The ANT Framework

while technology transfers and CSR practices also have various layers (the pile of coins analogy).

ANT posits that in a network, each actor has the ability to act and has its own interests. The stability of the network is therefore dependent on the continuous coordination (translations) of the interests of the actors (Murdoch, 1998). Callon (1986) suggested that for the sociology of translation to be expressed and maintained so that the actor–network can be sustained, one of the elements is the creation of equivalence (interessement can also be used here which refers to the strategies by which the focal actor attempts to enroll others according to the roles defined for them (Callon, 1986)). Therefore, technology transfer refers not only to the give and take of hard knowledge but also to important soft issues such as sustainability, business and moral ethics and social responsibility. In this study, we focus on all these elements using the existence of "accounting" as evidence; that is to say, proper CSR reporting. We shall further explore the interconnectivities of all the players in Figure 10.3. For simplicity, we exhibit a 2D perspective here.

Research Questions and Methodology

Hassan et al. (2021, 4) highlighted that the absence of a comprehensive theoretical framework to explain the networking between human and non-human elements can be a reason behind the lack of coherent reporting of non-financial elements by companies (e.g., CSR and sustainability performance). Therefore, based on ANT, this paper aims to analyze and answer "how" and "why" Chinese ICT-MNEs engage in CSR with the BRI host countries by examining their CSR reporting. In this study, we use the published information of Huawei to explore the Chinese ICT-MNEs and their activities under the BRI-DSR policy. The major research questions are below.

1. What is the CSR approach taken by Chinese ICT-MNEs (actors), focusing on the involvement of CSR both in the company's strategy (missions, visions and activities) and in the network (structure, roles and management systems of CSR) (actants and translations)?
2. What are the industry-specific external factors (token or quasi-object) influencing the content of CSR reporting (creation of equivalence) by Chinese ICT-MNEs?
3. What is the content of industry-specific CSR reporting (creation of equivalence) by Chinese ICT-MNEs in BRI host countries (actors)?

Note that in the ANT literature, "black boxes" or "immutable mobiles" (Callon, 1991) have also been identified. They represent frozen actor elements that often have properties of irreversibility (Walsham, 1997, 468). In our study, we will also pay attention to such frozen elements which may be derived from the ICT-MNEs' endeavors in host countries. That is to say, the inability to conserve equivalence might be due to failure to achieve true CSR (e.g., mere window-dressing or greenwashing or even improperly disposed wastages).

Three selection criteria were utilized in choosing the target firm. First, the selected ICT-MNE needed to be a CSR frontrunner within its industry and believed to have the most comprehensive set of CSR strategies. The GoldenBee CSR reporting award list was used to determine the CSR reporting champion in the Chinese ICT sector. Second, the selected company needed to be the industry leader in terms of operating profit and production scale, as CSR reporting in overseas markets requires extensive resources, and strong commitment and dedication. Thirdly, the chosen company needed to be actively participating in the BRI, and clearly indicate its involvement in its annual/CSR reports and corporate websites over the selected period (2014–2019, since the BRI was promulgated in 2013).

Huawei was chosen as the specific case which satisfies all the requirements above. It represents one of the most successful Chinese ICT-MNEs with the highest operating revenue among all private Chinese enterprises. It has had significant expansion in recent years, from a tiny manufacturer of telephone exchange switches to a global leader in the technology business. Currently, Huawei has about 197,000 employees, with operations in more than 170 countries and regions, serving more than 3 billion people worldwide. Furthermore, as a case study, Huawei provides a rich source of publicly available data and case materials, offering a comprehensive understanding of the entire process of the company's CSR strategy and its evolution. As a result, Huawei is an exemplar case for investigating how an ICT-MNE embraces the challenges and opportunities of CSR and sustainable development within the context of BRI.

Documents published by Huawei including annual reports, CSR/sustainability reports, COP reports and information disclosed in corporate websites were collected and reviewed to establish a baseline narrative of its CSR approach in the BRI context. The in-depth analysis of these documents provides insight into how CSR reporting can be used as a tool of translation and to create equivalence among the actors and actants in the actor–network. Qualitative data analysis (Silverman, 2001) was employed to extract different CSR themes from the documents, and to follow their emergence over the six-year time span. By analyzing the documents and recordings during the chosen period, this paper sheds light on how CSR is embedded in the social reporting of Huawei and examines how its CSR goals are set and developed in the BRI host countries. The study thus contributes to the literature on EMNEs as well as CSR reporting.

The Tool for Analysis and the Industry Background

In studying the inter-relationships among the various actors and actants within the actor–network, we need to define our meaning of CSR based on an established framework; that is to say, an operationalization tool in the translation process or the creation of equivalence. We have chosen to conduct our qualitative data analysis mostly founded on Elkington's (1994) Triple Bottom Line (TBL). As widely known, TBL is the very origin of many subsequent CSR concepts and a compelling advancement in the pursuit of accountability. TBL's accounting framework is evaluated based on the three most significant dimensions namely, social, environmental and economic performances, or the 3Ps (people, planet and profit) (Elkington, 2013). The paradigm assumes that the company is a member of the community and has social duties. The choice of using TBL is also supported by MacKenzie's (2009) emphasis on bottom lines.

The Chinese ICT sector, particularly the export-oriented ICT manufacturing subsector, has suffered from a decrease in external market demand, precipitated by the 2008 economic crisis (Ambalov and Heim, 2020). Meanwhile, China's low-consumption home market, which is a result of its low-wage and labor-repressing economic strategy, has proven insufficient to absorb the huge quantity of ICT-related items it has produced at home (Naughton, 2020). For example, by the end of 2015, China's optical fiber and cable industry had reached 50% overcapacity, necessitating a search for external markets (Vila Seoane, 2020). Meanwhile, with the growing importance of IT in global economies after the 2008 crisis (Shen, 2016, 2018), Chinese ICT firms have been assigned a new role in the second round of the Going Out policy. The State Council (2016) issued an action plan for the new Internet Plus policy in July 2015, which elevated the development of the ICT industry as one of the top national strategies (Sen and Bingqin, 2019). Therefore, sector-specific CSR challenges have emerged in addition to generic CSR issues (Fox, 2004; Fox et al., 2002). The particular TBL concerns related to the ICT industry are listed in Table 10.2, unpacked into four dimensions.

The Case of ICT-MNEs

The ICT Sector and CSR Challenges

ICT has emerged as one of the world's fastest-growing markets, marked by significant liberalization and globalization processes, as well as high levels of

Table 10.2 TBL Dimensions for the ICT Industry and Sources

CSR dimensions	*CSR concerns in the ICT industry*	*Literature*
Economy	• Unemployment due to improved technology and efficiency improvements • Increased competition for local ICT companies	Dunning and Fortanier (2007); Dunning and Lundan (2008); Meyer (2004); Narula and Pineli (2017)
Social–labor practices	• Equal treatment for women and minorities • Health and working conditions • Human rights protection	Briscoe et al. (2012); McDonnell et al. (2011); Shen and Darby (2006)
Social–local community	• Direct and indirect impacts on local living standards • Knowledge sharing and transfer to local employees	Amiri and Woodside (2017); Floridi (2007); Hernandez (2017); Venturini (2009)
Environment	• Environmental concerns over product design, manufacturing, use of materials, and waste disposal along the full product life cycle • Boosted energy consumption/ emissions due to short product life cycles	Haini (2021); Hankel et al. (2018); Ollo-López and Aramendía-Muneta (2012)

innovation, albeit with varying waves and shocks (such as the advent of 5G) (Jones et al., 2017). As a result, severe rivalry has emerged, requiring ICT companies to focus heavily on customer retention and innovation in order to profit (Hung and Lu, 2007).

The ICT sector is a significant actor in sustainable development since it provides a wide range of solutions to environmental and social issues (Ernst and Young, 2013). Digitalization of information, dematerialization of transportation and reductions in warehouse and office spaces are only a few examples. This industry has been playing an important role in addressing climate change over the years, compensating for the massive amount of greenhouse gas emissions produced by other industries (Azadnia et al., 2017). Paradoxically, it has to cope with both direct and indirect CSR concerns related to its own production and delivery of ICT services (Hilty and Hercheui, 2010). The industry has been identified as one of the most polluting industries representing a threat to public health (Hilty et al., 2011). The main environmental implications of its products include e-waste, hazardous compounds, electromagnetic radiation and resource consumption during hardware manufacturing and disposal. As a result, ICT companies must take further steps to reduce pollution, decrease waste production and eliminate dangerous products (Latif et al., 2017).

Despite the positive scenarios advocated under the DSR incentives such as lofty national goals like "Made in China 2025" and "China Standards 2035", Chinese ICT-MNEs also face many challenges in the field of sustainability, including the geographical and social digital divide, protection of privacy, cybercrime, poor work conditions (e.g., mining of substances, recycling and disposal of e-wastes) as well as employment conditions in overseas sites.

Push Factors of ICT-MNEs' CSR

The "Vision and Actions on Jointly Building the Silk Road Economic Belt and the 21st-Century Maritime Silk Road" (2015) and the "Belt and Road Ecological and Environmental Cooperation Plan" (2017) which stated that Chinese MNEs need to emphasize ecological progress in investment and trade, improve environmental, biodiversity and climate change cooperation (Yang et al., 2020), highlight the importance of ecological progress, green development, eco-environmental protection (Fang and Nolan, 2019) and the attainment of UNSDGs by 2030 (Scott and Rajabifard, 2017). In addition, financial organizations like the Asian Infrastructure Investment Bank (AIIB), Silk Road Fund and others have identified and strengthened CSR requirements in their investment rules (Volz, 2018).

The construction of railroads and power plants under the BRI policy is extremely important in developing countries that lack key infrastructure (Fung et al., 2018). Nonetheless, there are concerns that when Chinese ICT-MNEs assert themselves globally, DSR can be instrumental in forcing recipient countries to follow China's technology-enabled model. Another major issue is that, if Chinese ICT-MNEs are not well regulated, they could lead to increased control and surveillance as well as harm to local IT enterprises (Vila Seoane, 2020).

To elucidate the "why" of ICT-MNEs' CSR reporting, we summarize the "push factors". Firstly, the Chinese ICT sector, particularly the export-oriented ICT manufacturing subsector, has suffered from a decline in external market demand. Under the government's policy, massive financial aid, political support and other assistance are given to Chinese ICT-MNEs. Thus, public scrutiny from both home and host countries, as well as international stakeholders, has become greater. For example, Huawei has built more than half of the wireless towers, 70% of the Long-Term Evolution mobile broadband network, and more than 60,000 km of optical cable networks in over 50 African countries (Huawei, 2019). Chinese enterprises are primarily responding to, and profiting from, demands for additional telecommunications infrastructure and technological products in BRI host countries (Triolo et al., 2020). Of relevance here is the economic dimension of CSR which is concerned with the direct and indirect economic impact of a company's operations on the local community and other stakeholders (Uddin et al., 2008). Long-term sustainable and socially responsible businesses can be profitable and cost-effective and are more likely to avoid negative social repercussions while enhancing positive social outcomes. Companies cannot operate without their employees, customers or supply chain participants, and economic growth must be accompanied by social development. Furthermore, large corporations will be affected just as much as anything else on earth if their actions harm the environment and push the planet to destruction (Gupta and Kumar, 2018). Therefore, an important consideration regarding Chinese ICT-MNEs is striking a balance among the 3Ps, with the overarching goal of sustainability.

Secondly, the UNSDGs highlight worldwide difficulties such as poverty and inequality. For example, as stated in SDG 4, ICT-MNEs play a critical role in achieving high-quality education and opportunities for lifelong learning on a global basis. The availability of free online learning platforms demonstrates how knowledge (even specialized) may be made available to a broad audience (Wu et al., 2018; Jones et al., 2017). In addition, ICT-MNEs are expected to promote digital equity, which ensures that everyone has the same access to resources they need to fully participate as a citizen in today's digitally powered society. Digital equity is the state of being able to bridge both the digital divide and the participation gap (Rothe, 2020). For example, Huawei has introduced two flagship CSR programs, "Bridging the Digital Divide" and "Seeds of Future Communications". These programs are committed to contribute to the social development of the host countries and cultivate communication talents. Huawei's initiatives have been accepted and recognized by local stakeholders and have contributed toward soothing local legitimacy pressures. Although the ICT sector may have negative consequences to sustainability, such as the generation of e-waste, it is unquestionably an enabler of more effective resource utilization, education and corporate cooperation, which are major success elements in attaining SDGs (Kostoska and Kocarev, 2019).

Thirdly, various international regulatory bodies have set requirements for ICT-MNEs to shoulder their CSR. The various European and international standardization bodies such as European Telecommunications Standards Institute (ETSI), International Telecommunications Union-Telecommunication Standardization Sector (ITU-T), International Electrotechnical Commission (IEC), International Organization for Standardization (ISO) and others are developing methodologies to assess the environmental impact of operations which is currently focused on energy management, including energy consumption and greenhouse gas emissions. Many international treatises in specific areas (Watson et al., 2010; Vyas-Doorgapersad, 2014; Wu et al., 2018) have provided motivation for Chinese ICT-MNEs to engage actively in CSR and sustainability.

CSR Approach and Strategy

By analyzing Huawei's contextual information from its various company reports, we can better understand the CSR strategies of the ICT-MNEs in the BRI-DSR (the "why" (Table 10.3: push factors), "how" (Tables 10.4 and 10.5: approach and strategy), and "what" (Table 10.6: CSR reporting)). The tables can also be read in conjunction with Figure 10.4 which depicts the major players (the actors and actants, the token/quasi-object, the translations and possible black box elements) in the entire network. The theoretical framework of "ANT and friends" helps us understand how the various actors and actants form the complex actor–network incorporating social/institutional structures and engaging in

Table 10.3 The "Push" Factors (the Why) of Chinese ICT-MNEs' CSR Reporting

External factors	*The why of CSR disclosure by Chinese ICT-MNEs*
BRI proposed in 2013	Ecological and environmental protection has been prioritized, making CSR an inevitable requirement under the BRI context.
DSR policy launched in 2015 as part of BRI	Financial aid, political and other support to Chinese ICT-MNEs with massive scope of global interest in DSR: Stronger public scrutiny from home and host countries.
UNSDGs on the ICT sector	SDGs with high relevance to ICT: SDG 4: Quality Education; SDG 3: Good Health and Well-Being; SDG 9: Industry, Innovation and Infrastructure; SDG 5: Gender equality; SDG 11: Sustainable Cities and Communities; SDG 12: Responsible Consumption and Production; SDG 15: Life on Land.
International regulations for ICT enterprises	Various laws and regulations governing environmental preservation in the ICT sector.

a flat but 3D ontology. For example, the CSR approaches and strategies of social inclusion, bridging the digital divide and adherence to international conventions are illustrations of actants, translations/associations, and creation of equivalences involving social structuralism (micro/macro, hierarchical relations and so on).

Final Remarks

The research objective of the current study is to describe and explain Chinese ICT-MNEs' participation in the BRI-DSR program (the why, the how, and the what). The theoretical contribution of the study is that ANT ("ANT and friends" in this case when interpreted from an emancipated perspective embracing social structuralism) can be deployed as a useful tool to help explain a network phenomenon at the international business level. Furthermore, CSR and sustainability reporting (e.g., TBL accounting) has become an important tool for the creation of equivalence and translations in the actor–network.

In summary, we have used ANT to explain an international business phenomenon, the BRI-DSR. The actors (Chinese ICT-MNEs and the host countries' enterprises), the actants (FDI, technology, knowledge transfer and CSR), act closely through the creation of elements of equivalence (CSR reporting). All these players, human and non-human, are under the auspices of the token of BRI-DSR. As remarked by Latour (1996, 2005), ANT guides us into a world of associations and relations, thus has enhanced our understanding of the BRI-DSR in an institutional context. Furthermore, Cressman (2009) (cited in Costa and da Cunha, 2015, 5) stated that ANT cannot be reduced to a standard approach

Table 10.4 CSR Approach (the How) of Huawei

CSR approach	*CSR management*
• Huawei follows the principle of combining economic growth, social inclusion and environmental sustainability in BRI host countries. • Huawei uses SDGs as a basis for setting its goals and plans for sustainability and aims to proactively influence the entire industry to contribute to SDGs. The CSR strategy of Digital Inclusion is related to SDG 3: Good Health and Well-Being; SDG 4: Quality Education; SDG 5: Gender Equality; SDG 8: Decent Work and Economic Growth; SDG 9: Industry, Innovation and Infrastructure; SDG 13: Climate Action; SDG 14: Life Below Water; SDG 15: Life on Land; SDG 17: Partnerships for the Goals. • Huawei establishes a sustainability management system based on international standards and guidelines.	• CSR Disclosure (CSD) Committee: Over ten senior executives from diverse areas, including human resources, manufacturing, administration, procurement, and research and development, constitute the CSD Committee. • Sustainability management system: Incorporating internal and external environments and various stakeholders' needs. The management system operates in six areas: leadership, planning, organization and skills support, process operations, performance appraisal and continuous improvement. • The Ethics and Compliance Office (ECO): In charge of overseeing ethics and compliance throughout the corporation, as well as promoting an organizational culture dedicated to doing business lawfully, ethically and with integrity.

that can be universally applied. Costa and da Cunha borrow ANT's ideas, further developing them by integration into their own approach, thus molding them to their own needs.

Barter and Bebbington (2013) point out that ANT emphasizes work, movement and flow and thus does not assume a solid fixed base and does not require a specific research method ("fluid"). Therefore, in a similar fashion and taking into account the fluidity of ANT's ideas, CSR reporting from the leading company (Huawei) in the Chinese ICT industry are presented to understand how Chinese ICT-MNEs report their CSR activities in both home and host countries and how they interact with other actors.

In our introduction on the theoretical implication of ANT, we mentioned the metaphor examples (Barter and Russell, 2013; Morgan, 2011). The case of Huawei serves as a good example. It showcases and reflects the reality of the Chinese ICT-MNEs' participation in the global token of the BRI. Although the CSR reporting of Huawei mainly illustrates the more positive aspects of their CSR activities, black box issues such as overcapacity, e-waste and political dominance are not disclosed and not mentioned, even conservatively. As critically analyzed in the "why" factors in this paper, it is apparent that window-dressing

Table 10.5 CSR Strategy (the How) of Huawei

Year	*CSR vision and mission*	*CSR strategy*
2014	To bridge the digital divide and promote harmonious and sustainable development of the economy, the environment and society. To establish a leading sustainability management system, operate with integrity and in compliance with applicable laws and regulations, continuously enhance communication with stakeholders, promote a harmonious business ecosystem, ensure sustainable development and contribute to our customers and society.	• Bridging the Digital Divide • Supporting Stable and Secure Network Operations • Promoting Environmental Protection • Seeking Win–Win Development
2015	Bridging the digital divide and promoting harmonious and sustainable development of the economy, environment and society.	• Bridging the Digital Divide • Supporting Stable and Secure Network Operations and Protecting User Privacy • Promoting Environmental Protection • Seeking Win–Win Development
2016	To bring digital capability to every person, home and organization for a fully connected, intelligent world.	• Bridging the Digital Divide • Supporting Stable and Secure Network Operations and Protecting User Privacy • Promoting Environmental Protection • Building a Healthy Industry Ecosystem
2017	To bring digital capability to every person, home and organization for a fully connected, intelligent world.	• Bridging the Digital Divide • Supporting Network Stability and Security and Protecting Privacy • Promoting Environmental Protection • Building a Healthy Ecosystem
2018	Huawei's vision and mission is to bring digital capability to every person, home and organization for a fully connected, intelligent world.	• Digital inclusion • Security and trustworthiness • Environmental protection • Healthy and harmonious ecosystem
2019	Huawei's vision and mission is to bring digital capability to every person, home and organization for a fully connected, intelligent world. Based on the company's vision and mission, Huawei has developed its sustainability strategy, considering sustainability to be one of its priorities and incorporating it into the company's overall development strategy.	• Digital inclusion • Security and trustworthiness • Environmental protection • Healthy and harmonious ecosystem

Table 10.6 Industry-Specific CSR Reporting Contents (the What) of Huawei

Major CSR strategy in BRI countries	*Industry-specific CSR reporting topics*
Digital inclusion (TECH4ALL)	Driving Equity and Quality in Education Protecting the Environment Enabling Inclusion and Equity in Health Driving Balanced Development
Security and trustworthiness	Intellectual Property Rights (IPR) and Trade Secret Protection Data Privacy and Security E-waste recycling program
Environmental protection	Reducing Carbon Emissions Promoting Renewable Energy Contributing to a Circular Economy Conflict Minerals Management
Healthy and harmonious ecosystem	Supply Chain Responsibilities Community Responsibilities Business Ethics

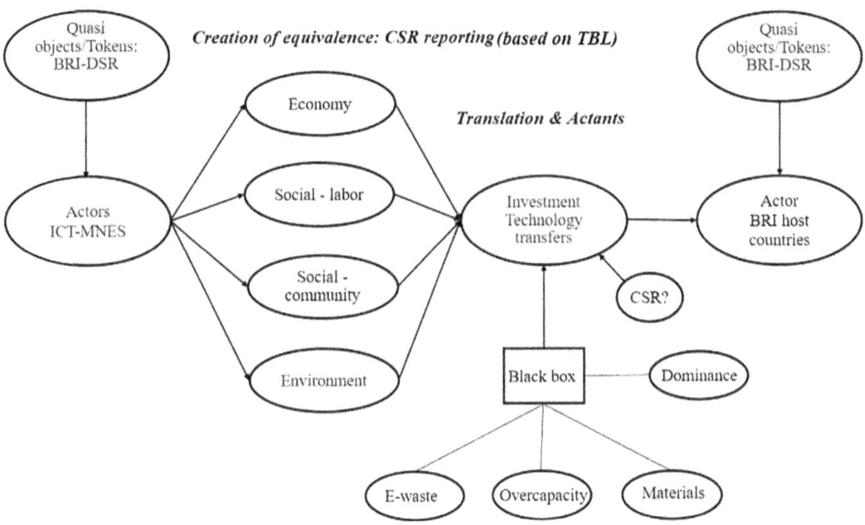

Figure 10.4 Actor–Network in the BRI-DSR

using CSR reporting is not surprisingly prevalent. Consequently, ANT can help to systematically and critically explain the roles of all the human and non-human actors, actants and artifacts in the entire actor–network.

Nevertheless, we still conclude that the participation of the Chinese ICT-MNEs in the BRI is of great importance in transferring not only "hard" digital technology to host countries, but also CSR and sustainability knowledge, and messages to other developing or less developed nations. In terms of practical implications, it can be said that the BRI-DSR policy can create equivalence in the ANT sense to both China and host countries. However, sustainability issues ought to be resolved without resulting in China being a creator of overcapacity and an e-waste "dumper" to the BRI host countries. Adherence to international conventions is of utmost importance. Furthermore, the ICT industry's policies could be tailored to each country's political and economic ideologies, while cooperation and collaboration should prove effective in promoting global prosperity. Competition can be healthy, but dominance is not; it will only create more and more black box elements.

Finally, from the publicly disclosed information analyzed, we can still observe some hints of CSR reporting being used as a kind of window-dressing or impression management tool (Lu and Abeysekera, 2014). This can be interpreted as a black box issue in ANT which draws our attention to the significance of third-party assurance of CSR reports, both from academic and professional viewpoints. In the case of Huawei, although its CSR reports were verified independently, adverse reporting has obviously been avoided. It should be emphasized here that third-party verification only assures that certain clauses have been disclosed or not; for example, whether the Global Reporting Initiative (GRI) standards have or have not been mentioned in the reports, or the percentage of achievement toward sustainability goals. Third-party assurance can only ensure conformity but academic research through triangulation can go beyond that.

The study inevitably suffers from some drawbacks of classic single case-based studies. Zawawi (2018, 227) also pointed out that it is a common perception that a case study involves a single setting, which is unique in terms of factors such as operation, culture and structure, and the concern is whether the findings are applicable to other settings. Furthermore, she borrows from Yin (2003) and Eisenhardt (1989) to explain that a case study is not intended to represent samples and to enumerate frequencies (or statistical generalizations). Instead, it is used to expand and generalize existing and emerging theories (analytic generalizations). In any case, within the token of the BRI, which is at the global cross-institutional level, the current study has attempted to provide further motivation for researchers to apply ANT with an all-encompassing and more open approach to explain macro social accounting phenomena.

References

Aguilera-Caracuel, J. and Guerrero-Villegas, J. (2018). How corporate social responsibility helps MNEs to improve their reputation: The moderating effects of geographical diversification and operating in developing regions. *Corporate Social Responsibility and Environmental Management*, 25(4), 355–372.

Ambalov, V. and Heim, I. (2020). Investments in the digital silk road. In Heim, I. (Ed.), *Kazakhstan's Diversification from the Natural Resources Sector.* Cham: Palgrave Macmillan.

Amiri, S. and Woodside, J.M. (2017). Emerging markets: The impact of ICT on the economy and society. *Digital Policy, Regulation and Governance*, 19(5), 383–396.

Azadnia, M., Zahedi, S. and Pourabedy, M.R. (2017). Analysis of the impact of ICT on sustainable development using sustainability indicators. *International Journal of Computer and Applications*, 169(6), 975–987.

Bansal, P. and Roth, K. (2000). Why companies go green: A model of ecological responsiveness. *Academy of Management Journal*, 43(4), 717–736.

Barter, N. and Bebbington, J. (2013). Actor-network theory: A briefing note and possibilities for social and environmental accounting research. *Social and Environmental Accountability Journal*, 33(1), 33–50.

Barter, N. and Russell, S. (2013). Organizational metaphors and sustainable development: Enabling or inhibiting? *Sustainability Accounting, Management and Policy Journal*, 4(2), 145–162.

Baxter, J. and Chua, W.F. (2020). Using critical realism in critical accounting research: A commentary by two ants. *Accounting, Auditing and Accountability Journal*, 33(3), 655–665.

Belal, A. and Owen, D.L. (2015). The rise and fall of stand-alone social reporting in a multinational subsidiary in Bangladesh. *Accounting, Auditing and Accountability Journal*, 28(7), 1160–1192.

Berger, P.L. and Luckmann, T. (1966). *The Social Construction of Reality: A Treatise in the Sociology of Knowledge*. Garden City, NY: Anchor.

Bernal-Conesa, J.A., de Nieves Nieto, C. and Briones-Peñalver, A.J. (2017). CSR strategy in technology companies: Its influence on performance, competitiveness and sustainability. *Corporate Social Responsibility and Environmental Management*, 24(2), 96–107.

Boubakri, N., El Ghoul, S., Wang, H., Guedhami, O. and Kwok, C.C. (2016). Cross-listing and corporate social responsibility. *Journal of Corporate Finance*, 41(1), 123–138.

Brammer, S., Jackson, G. and Matten, D. (2012). Corporate social responsibility and institutional theory: New perspectives on private governance. *Socio-Economic Review*, 10(1), 3–28.

Briers, M. and Chua, W.F. (2001). The role of actor-networks and boundary objects in management accounting change: A field study of an implementation of activity-based costing. *Accounting, Organizations and Society*, 26(3), 237–269.

Briscoe, D., Schuler, R. and Tarique, I. (2012). *International Human Resource Management: Policies and Practices for Multinational Enterprises*. London: Routledge.

Burrell, G. and Morgan, G. (1979). *Sociological Paradigms and Organisational Analysis: Elements of the Sociology of Corporate Life*. London: Heinemann.

Busslar, C.Z., Burtet, C.G. and Antonelo, C.S. (2020). Actor-network theory as a method in the analysis of Samarco disaster in Brazil. *Qualitative Research in Organizations and Management: An International Journal*, 15(2), 176–191.

Calero, C., García-Rodríguez De Guzmán, I., Moraga, M.A. and García, F. (2019). Is software sustainability considered in the CSR of software industry? *International Journal of Sustainable Development and World Ecology*, 26(5), 439–459.

Callon, M. (1986). Some elements of a sociology of translation: Domestication of the scallops and the fishermen of St Brieuc Bay. In Law, J. (Ed.), *Power, Action and Belief: A New Sociology of Knowledge*. London: Routledge and Kegan Paul.

Callon, M. (1991). Techno-economic networks and irreversibility. In Law, L. (Ed.), *A Sociology of Monsters: Essays on Power, Technology and Domination*. London: Routledge.

Callon, M. (Ed.). (1998). *The Laws of the Markets*. Oxford: Blackwell.

Campbell, J.T., Eden, L. and Miller, S.R. (2012). Multinationals and corporate social responsibility in host countries: Does distance matter? *Journal of International Business Studies*, 43(1), 84–106.

Costa, C.C. and da Cunha, P.R. (2015). The social dimension of business models: An actor-network theory perspective. Paper presented at the Twenty-first Americas Conference on Information Systems, Puerto Rico, 2015.

Cressman, D. (2009). A brief overview of actor-network theory: Punctualization, heterogeneous engineering and translation. Available at: http://www.sfu.ca/cprost/docs/A%20Brief%20Overview%20of%20ANT.pdf

Cresswell, K.M., Worth, A. and Sheikh, A. (2010). Actor-network theory and its role in understanding the implementation of information technology developments in healthcare. *BMC Medical Informatics and Decision Making*, 10, 67.

Cuervo-Cazurra, A. (2012). Extending theory by analyzing developing country multinational companies: Solving the Goldilocks debate. *Global Strategy Journal*, 2(3), 153–167.

Dam, L. and Scholtens, B. (2013). Ownership concentration and CSR policy of European multinational enterprises. *Journal of Business Ethics*, 118(1), 117–126.

DiMaggio, P.J. and Powell, W.W. (1983). The iron cage revisited: Institutional isomorphism and collective rationality in organizational fields. *American Sociology Review*, 48(2), 147–160.

Dunning, J.H. and Fortanier, F. (2007). Multinational enterprises and the new development paradigm: Consequences for host country development. *Multinational Business Review*, 15(1), 25–46.

Dunning, J.H. and Lundan, S.M. (2008). *Multinational Enterprises and the Global Economy*. Cheltenham: Edward Elgar Publishing.

Eisenhardt, K.M. (1989). Building theories from case study research. *Academy of Management Review*, 14(4), 532–550.

Elkington, J. (1994). Towards the sustainable corporation: Win-win-win business strategies for sustainable development. *California Management Review*, 32(2), 90–100.

Elkington, J. (2013). Enter the triple bottom line. In Henriques, A. and Richardson, J. (Eds.), *The Triple Bottom Line*. London: Routledge.

Ernst and Young. (2013). Inside telecommunications. Issue 10, EYGM Limited.

Ervits, I. (2021). CSR reporting by Chinese and Western MNEs: Patterns combining formal homogenization and substantive differences. *International Journal of Corporate Social Responsibility*, 6(1), 1–24.

Fang, C. and Nolan, P. (Eds.). (2019). *Routledge Handbook of the Belt and Road*. New York: Routledge.

Floridi, L. (2007). A look into the future impact of ICT on our lives. *The Information Society*, 23(1), 59–64.

Fox, T. (2004). Corporate social responsibility and development: In quest of an agenda. *Development*, 47(3), 29–36.

Fox, T., Ward, H. and Howard, B. (2002). *Public Sector Roles in Strengthening Corporate Social Responsibility: A Baseline Study*. Washington, DC: World Bank.

Fung, K.C., Aminian, N., Fu, X. and Tung, C.Y. (2018). Digital silk road, Silicon Valley and connectivity. *Journal of Chinese Economic and Business Studies*, 16(3), 313–336.

Gammeltoft, P., Pradhan, J.P. and Goldstein, A. (2010). Emerging multinationals: Home and host country determinants and outcomes. *International Journal of Emerging Markets*, 5(3/4), 254–265.

Gond, J.-P. and Nyberg, D. (2017). Materializing power to recover corporate social responsibility. *Organization Studies*, 32(8), 1127–1148.

Gu, J. and Qiu, S. (2019). The Belt and Road Initiative and Africa's sustainable development: A case study of Kenya. *IDS Bulletin*, 50(4), 89–109.

Guatier, A. and Bonneveux, E. (2021). The diffusion of corporate social responsibility within an organizational field: An analysis through the complementary lenses of neo-institutional theory and actor-network theory. *M@n@gement*, 24(2), 48–65.

Gugler, P. and Shi, J.Y. (2009). Corporate social responsibility for developing country multinational corporations: Lost war in pertaining global competitiveness? *Journal of Business Ethics*, 87(1), 3–24.

Gupta, M. and Kumar, M. (2018). Impact of ICT usage on productivity of unorganised manufacturing enterprises in India. *The Indian Journal of Labour Economics*, 61(2), 411–425.

Haini, H. (2021). Examining the impact of ICT, human capital and carbon emissions: Evidence from the ASEAN economies. *International Economics*, 116, 116–125.

Hankel, A., Heimeriks, G. and Lago, P. (2018). A systematic literature review of the factors of influence on the environmental impact of ICT. *Technologies*, 6(3), 85.

Hassan, A., Alamer, A.A., Lodh, S., Roberts, L. and Nandy, M. (2021). The future of non-financial businesses reporting: Learning from the Covid-19 pandemic. *Corporate Social Responsibility and Environmental Management*, 28(4), 1231–1240.

Hernandez, R.M. (2017). Impact of ICT on education: Challenges and perspectives. *Journal of Educational Psychology - Propositos Representaciones*, 5(1), 337–347.

Hilty, L.M. and Hercheui, M.D. (2010). ICT and sustainable development. In Berleur, J., Herchehi, M.D. and Hilty, L.M. (Eds.), *What Kind of Information Society? Governance, Virtuality, Surveillance, Sustainability, Resilience.* Heidelberg: Springer.

Hilty, L., Lohmann, W. and Huang, E.M. (2011). Sustainability and ICT-an overview of the field. *Notizie di Politeia*, 27(104), 13–28.

Hong, W. and Shuai, D. (2020). Research on the social responsibility of Chinese enterprises along the 'Belt and Road'. In Cowther, D. and Quoquab, F. (Eds.), *CSR in an Age of Isolationism.* Bingley: Emerald Publishing Limited.

Hopper, T. and Major, M. (2007). Extending institutional analysis through theoretical triangulation: Regulation and activity-based costing in Portuguese telecommunications. *European Accounting Review*, 16(1), 59–97.

Huang, Y. (2016). Understanding China's Belt and Road Initiative: Motivation, framework and assessment. *China Economic Review*, 40, 314–321.

Huawei. (2014, 2015, 2016, 2017, 2018, 2019). Annual CSR Report. Available at: https://www.huawei.com/cn/sustainability/sustainability-report

Hung, S.W. and Lu, W.M. (2007). A comparative study of the performance measurement in global telecom operators. *Total Quality Management*, 18(10), 1117–1132.

Hurley, J., Morris, S. and Portelance, G. (2019). Examining the debt implications of the Belt and Road Initiative from a policy perspective. *Journal of Infrastructure, Policy and Development*, 3(1), 139–175.

Husted, B.W. and Allen, D.B. (2006). Corporate social responsibility in the multinational enterprise: Strategic and institutional approaches. *Journal of International Business Studies*, 37(6), 838–849.

Husted, B.W. and Allen, D.B. (2007). Corporate social strategy in multinational enterprises: Antecedents and value creation. *Journal of Business Ethics*, 74(4), 345–361.

Jamali, D. and Neville, B. (2011). Convergence versus divergence of CSR in developing countries: An embedded multi-layered institutional lens. *Journal of Business Ethics*, 102(4), 599–621.

Johannesson, G.T. and Baerenholdt, J.O. (2000). Actor-network theory. In Kobayashi, A. (Ed.), *International Encyclopedia of Human Geography*. New York: Elsevier.

Jones, P., Wynn, M., Hillier, D. and Comfort, D. (2017). The sustainable development goals and information and communication technologies. *Indonesian Journal of Sustainability Accounting and Management*, 1(1), 1–15.

Justesen, L. and Mouritsen, J. (2011). Effects of actor-network theory in accounting research. *Accounting, Auditing and Accountability Journal*, 24(2), 161–193.

Kolk, A. and Van Tulder, R. (2010). International business, corporate social responsibility and sustainable development. *International Business Review*, 19(2), 119–125.

Kostoska, O. and Kocarev, L. (2019). A novel ICT framework for sustainable development goals. *Sustainability*, 11(7), 1961.

Kostova, T., Roth, K. and Dacin, M.T. (2008). Institutional theory in the study of multinational corporations: A critique and new directions. *Academy of Management Review*, 33(4), 994–1006.

Lakoff, G. and Turner, M. (1987). *More Than Cool Reason: A Field Guide to Poetic Metaphor*. Chicago, IL: University of Chicago Press.

Latif, Z., Xin, W., Khan, D., Iqbal, K., Pathan, Z.H., Salam, S. and Jan, N. (2017). ICT and sustainable development in South Asian countries. *Human Systems Management*, 36(4), 353–362.

Latour, B. (1987). *Science in Action: How to Follow Scientists and Engineers Through Society*. Cambridge, MA: Harvard University Press.

Latour, B. (1996). On Actor-Network theory: A few clarifications. *Soziale Welt*, 47(4), 369–381.

Latour, B. (2005). *Reassembling the Social: Introduction to Actor-Network-Theory*. New York: Oxford University Press.

Law, J. (1999). After ANT: Complexity, naming and topology. In Law, J. and Hassard, J. (Eds.), *Actor-Network Theory and After*. Oxford: Blackwell.

Li, S., Fetscherin, M., Alon, I., Lattemann, C. and Yeh, K. (2010). Corporate social responsibility in emerging markets. *Management International Review*, 50(5), 635–654.

Llewellyn, S. and Northcott, D. (2005). The average hospital. *Accounting, Organizations and Society*, 30(1), 555–583.

Lowe, A. (2000). The construction of a network at Health Waikato: 'The towards clinical budgeting' project. *Accounting, Auditing and Accountability Journal*, 13(1), 84–114.

Lowe, A. (2001). After ANT: An illustrative discussion of the implications for qualitative accounting research. *Accounting, Auditing and Accountability Journal*, 14(3), 327–351.

Lu, Y. and Abeysekera, I. (2014). *Social and Environmental Disclosure by Chinese Firms*. London: Routledge.

Lukka, K. and Vinnari, E. (2014). Domain theory and method theory in management accounting research. *Accounting, Auditing and Accountability Journal*, 27(8), 1038–1338.

MacKenzie, D. (2009). Making things the same: Gases, emission rights and carbon markets. *Accounting, Organizations and Society*, 34(3–4), 440–455.

Marano, V., Tashman, P. and Kostova, T. (2017). Escaping the iron cage: Liabilities of origin and CSR reporting of emerging market multinational enterprises. *Journal of International Business Studies*, 48(3), 386–408.

McDonnell, A., Stanton, P. and Burgess, J. (2011). Multinational enterprises in Australia: Two decades of international human resource management research reviewed. *Asia Pacific Journal of Human Resources*, 49(1), 9–35.

Meyer, K.E. (2004). Perspectives on multinational enterprises in emerging economies. *Journal of International Business Studies*, 35(4), 259–276.

Miska, C., Witt, M.A. and Stahl, G.K. (2016). Drivers of global CSR integration and local CSR responsiveness: Evidence from Chinese MNEs. *Business Ethics Quarterly*, 26(3), 317–345.

Modell, S. (2020). A critical realist critique of the use of actor-network theory in critical accounting research. *Accounting, Auditing and Accountability Journal*, 33(3), 621–640.

Morgan, G. (2011). Reflections on images of organization and its implications for organization and environment. *Organization and Environment*, 24(4), 459–478.

Muller, A. and Kolk, A. (2010). Extrinsic and intrinsic drivers of corporate social performance: Evidence from foreign and domestic firms in Mexico. *Journal of Management Studies*, 47(1), 1–26.

Muller, A. and Kolk, A. (2015). Responsible tax as corporate social responsibility: The case of multinational enterprises and effective tax in India. *Business and Society*, 54(4), 435–463.

Murdoch, J. (1998). The spaces of actor-network theory. *Geoforum*, 29(4), 357–374.

Narula, R. and Pineli, A. (2017). Multinational enterprises and economic development in host countries: What we know and what we don't know. In Giorgioni, G. (Ed.), *Development Finance: Challenges and Opportunities*. London: Palgrave Macmillan.

Naughton, B. (2020). Chinese industrial policy and the Digital Silk Road: The case of AliBaba in Malaysia. *Asia Policy*, 27(1), 23–39.

Ollo-López, A. and Aramendía-Muneta, M.E. (2012). ICT impact on competitiveness, innovation and environment. *Telematics and Informatics*, 29(2), 204–210.

Porter, M.E. and Kramer, M.R. (2006). Strategy and society: The link between corporate social responsibility and competitive advantage. *Harvard Business Review*, 84(12), 78–92.

Ramasamy, B. and Yeung, M.C. (2019). China's one belt one road initiative: The impact of trade facilitation versus physical infrastructure on exports. *The World Economy*, 42(6), 1673–1694.

Rautiainen, A. and Scapens, R.W. (2013). Path-dependencies, constrained transformations and dynamic agency: An accounting case study informed by both NIS and ANT. *Qualitative Research in Accounting and Management*, 10(2), 100–126.

Reimann, F., Ehrgott, M., Kaufmann, L. and Carter, C.R. (2012). Local stakeholders and local legitimacy: MNEs' social strategies in emerging economies. *Journal of International Management*, 18(1), 1–17.

Renwick, N. (2019). The Belt and Road Initiative: Infrastructure and sustainable development. In Paladini, S. and George, S. (Eds.), *Sustainable Economy and Emerging Markets*. London: Routledge.

Rhee, Y.P., Park, C. and Petersen, B. (2021). The effect of local stakeholder pressures on responsive and strategic CSR activities. *Business and Society*, 60(3), 582–613.

Rothe, F.F. (2020). Rethinking positive and negative impacts of 'ICT for development' through the holistic lens of the sustainable development goals. *Information Technology for Development*, 26(4), 653–669.

Scott, G. and Rajabifard, A. (2017). Sustainable development and geospatial information: A strategic framework for integrating a global policy agenda into national geospatial capabilities. *Geo-Spatial Information Science*, 20(2), 59–76.

Sen, G. and Bingqin, L. (2019). The digital silk road and the sustainable development goals. In Sen, G., Leach, M. and Gu, J. (Eds.), *The Belt and Road Initiative and the SDGs: Towards Equitable, Sustainable Development*. Brighton: IDS.

Shen, H. (2016). China and global internet governance: Toward an alternative analytical framework. *Chinese Journal of Communication*, 9(3), 304–324.

Shen, H. (2018). Building a digital silk road? Situating the internet in China's belt and road initiative. *International Journal of Communication*, 12, 19.

Shen, J. and Darby, R. (2006). Training and management development in Chinese multinational enterprises. *Employee Relations*, 28(4), 342–362.

Silverman, D. (2001). *Interpreting Qualitative Data: Methods for Analyzing Talk, Text and Interaction*, 2nd edition. Thousand Oaks, CA: Sage.

State Council. (2016). Notice of the State Council on Issuing the National Informatization Plan for the 13th five-year Plan. Available at: http://www.gov.cn/zhengce/content/2016-12/27/content_5153411.htm

Tai, F.M. and Chuang, S.H. (2014). Corporate social responsibility. *iBusiness*, 6(3), 117.

Tashman, P., Marano, V. and Kostova, T. (2019). Walking the walk or talking the talk? Corporate social responsibility decoupling in emerging market multinationals. *Journal of International Business Studies*, 50(2), 153–171.

Triolo, P., Allison, K., Brown, C. and Broderick, K. (2020). *The Digital Silk Road: Expanding China's Digital Footprint, Eurasia Group*, April, 8.

Uddin, M.B., Hassan, M.D. and Tarique, K.M. (2008). Three dimensional aspects of corporate social responsibility. *Daffodil International University Journal of Business and Economics*, 3(1), 199–212.

UNSEC. (2004). *Report of the International Telecommunication Union on Information and Communication Technologies Statistics*. Available at: https://unstats.un.org/unsd/statcom/doc04/2004-16e.pdf

Van Zanten, J.A. and Van Tulder, R. (2018). Multinational enterprises and the sustainable development goals: An institutional approach to corporate engagement. *Journal of International Business Policy*, 1(3), 208–233.

Venturini, F. (2009). The long-run impact of ICT. *Empirical Economics*, 37(3), 497–515.

Vila Seoane, M.F. (2020). Alibaba's discourse for the Digital Silk Road: The electronic world trade platform and 'inclusive globalization'. *Chinese Journal of Communication*, 13(1), 68–83.

Volz, U. (2018). Fostering green finance for sustainable development in Asia. ADBI Working Paper 814, March 2018. Available at: https://ssrn.com/abstract=3198680

Vosselman, E. (2014). Approaching control in interfirm transactional relationships: Contrasting and connecting a transaction cost economics perspective with actor-network theory perspective. *Quantitative Research in Accounting and Management*, 9(1), 4–12.

Vyas-Doorgapersad, S. (2014). Gender, ICT and millennium development goals for sustainable development in West Africa. *Mediterranean Journal of Social Sciences*, 5(21), 405.

Walsham, G. (1997). Actor-Network Theory and IS research: Current status and future prospects. In Lee, A.S., Liebenau, J. and DeGross, J.I. (Eds.), *Information Systems and Qualitative Research*. Boston, MA: Springer.

Watson, R.T., Boudreau, M.C. and Chen, A.J. (2010). Information systems and environmentally sustainable development: Energy informatics and new directions for the IS community. *MIS Quarterly*, 34(1), 23–38.

Wu, J., Guo, S., Huang, H., Liu, W. and Xiang, Y. (2018). Information and communications technologies for sustainable development goals: State-of-the-art, needs and perspectives. *IEEE Communications Surveys and Tutorials*, 20(3), 2389–2406.

WWF. (2017). The belt and road initiative - WWF recommendations and spatial analysis. Available at: https://awsassets.panda.org/downloads/the_belt_and_road_initiative___wwf_recommenThe%20Belt%20and%20Road%20Initiative%20-%20WWF%20Recommendations%20and%20Spatial%20Analysisations_and_spatial_analysis___may_2017.pdf

Yang, N., Wang, J., Liu, X. and Huang, L. (2020). Home-country institutions and corporate social responsibility of emerging economy multinational enterprises: The belt and road initiative as an example. *Asia Pacific Journal of Management*. https://doi.org/10.1007/s10490-021-09770-0

Yin, R.K. (2003). *Case Study Research: Design and Methods*, 3rd edition. Thousand Oaks, CA: Sage.

Zawawi, N.H.M. (2018). Actor-Network Theory and inter-organizational management control. *International Journal of Business and Society*, 19(2), 219–234.

Part 3

CSR – Greenwashing and Window-Dressing

11 Corporate Green Initiatives as Real Circular Economy or Window-dressing?

Limin Fu

What Are Corporate Green Initiatives and How Do They Serve in the Real Circular Economy?

Spurred on by the increasing global discussion over climate change, green initiatives have become a hot topic. Green initiatives refer to all individual and organizational practices aimed at protecting the environment, including reducing emissions and waste, increasing recycling, developing, and adopting green innovation (Marco-Fondevila et al., 2021). Stakeholders' increasing awareness of firms' green initiatives is part of the wider concept of environmental, social, and governance (ESG) strategy. ESG is a relatively recent development, stemming from the more established concept of corporate social responsibility (CSR), the basis of which is businesses taking ownership of their impact on society.

The circular economy model has recently gained a lot of attention as an effective way to cope with climate change and sustainability. Restorative and regenerative by design, a circular economy minimizes waste and optimizes the efficiency through value chains. It aims to redefine growth, focusing on positive society-wide benefits that entail decoupling economic activity from the consumption of finite resources (Geissdoerfer et al., 2017). The principles of the circular economy include designing out waste and pollution, keeping products and materials in use, and regenerating natural systems (MacArthur, 2013). The European Union (EU) has launched a series of reports, plans, and activities known as the Circular Economy Package, the main goal of which is to expand the circular economy model throughout Europe, with large firms leading the initiative (European Commission, 2015).

Under the influence of circular economy policies, many businesses are progressively adopting circular practices in the form of green initiatives. These green initiatives mainly focus on cleaner production, emissions reduction, material recycling, sourcing strategies, circular product design, business model design, and so on (Marco-Fondevila et al., 2021; Urbinati et al., 2017). These practices have been demonstrated as contributing to the circular economy and the sustainable development of society at large. For instance, the green supply chain, such as the adoption of recycling technologies by the automobile sector in many countries, has significantly reduced carbon emissions (Kushwaha and Sharma, 2016). In

DOI: 10.4324/9781003274575-14

addition to environmental benefits stemming from the circular economy, green initiatives can produce a wide range of economic and social benefits (Korhonen et al., 2018; Moraga et al., 2019). For example, recycling materials not only reduces waste and cuts emissions, but also lowers the costs of raw materials and creates employment opportunities through new uses of the value embedded in resources. Through technological and market innovation in developing and implementing green initiatives, business organizations are viewed as one of the most effective contributors to the circular economy (Borghesi et al., 2015; Garnaut, 2008). Recognizing the crucial role of corporate green initiatives, the United Nations calls on business leadership in applying creativity and innovation in building a better, more sustainable future (United Nations, 2015).

The Business Case for Green Initiatives

With the mounting stakeholder pressure on businesses, the cost of doing nothing may be more expensive than practicing green initiatives (Fu et al., 2019; Helmig et al., 2016; Kassinis and Vafeas, 2006). Customers care more about whether their products are made from recycled materials, and investors are increasingly scrutinizing firms' performance and efforts with regard to environmental issues. Firms' concern for the environment and green initiatives are beneficial for their reputation, stakeholder relations, employee engagement and, ultimately, their business profitability, and better equity returns (Ameer and Othman, 2012; Flammer, 2013, 2021; Hawn et al., 2018; Pucker, 2021). Moreover, practicing green initiatives provides businesses an opportunity to discover a source of significant value creation (e.g., innovation), which will create sustained competitive advantage. Therefore, it is evident that incorporating sustainability and green initiatives into business strategy and embedding them into organizational processes has become a compelling business case.

Green Initiatives and Innovation

Because of the embeddedness of green initiatives in other organizational activities, green initiatives require the deployment of other supporting organizational activities (Aguinis and Glavas, 2013; Zerbini, 2017). Particularly, green initiatives addressing environmental demands often require organizational learning from key environmental issues, relevant stakeholders, and the translation to product and process developments. The quest for sustainability also propels firms to innovate products, technologies, processes, and business models. As such, green initiatives act as an important driver for firms' innovation, which provides solutions that are both environmentally viable and financially sensible.

For example, emissions trading and CO_2 abatement motivate firms to redesign their production processes to reduce emissions and build a more sustainable value chain (Borghesi et al., 2015; Nidumolu et al., 2009). Stakeholders provide invaluable resources, knowledge, collaboration, and network capital essential to firms' innovation (Surroca et al., 2010). Public policies such as green innovation tax relief incentivize firms to innovate for green solutions. All of these help build firms' green core competency and learning capacity, leading to a greater green innovation (Chen, 2008). Broadly, green innovation plays a key role in reducing environmental impact and moving industries towards sustainable production. As a virtuous cycle, stakeholders reciprocate firms' environmental innovation and further incentivize firms' innovative inputs (O'Brien and David, 2014).

In turn, firms' green initiatives are also, to a large extent, enabled and determined by a firm's existing effort in innovation, which typically manifests in its R&D capacity (Fu et al., 2020; Surroca et al., 2010). R&D-intensive firms have greater learning capability to identify, assimilate, and exploit new knowledge from the environment and stakeholders, and apply it to their organizational activities (Cohen and Levinthal, 1989; Lee, 2010). As such, R&D-intensive firms are better equipped to acquire stakeholder knowledge and build connections with their current R&D knowledge stock to improve their green initiatives. Further, firms' R&D activities and stakeholder demands to share relevant knowledge can spur synergies with their green initiatives (Fu et al., 2020; Tanriverdi and Venkatraman, 2005). For instance, firms' R&D capacity for process development can both increase resource use efficiency and reduce waste emission demanded by customers, investors, and the general public's demand for sustainability (Borghesi et al., 2015; Cainelli and Mazzanti, 2013; Fu et al., 2020). In exploiting this knowledge relatedness, R&D-intensive firms are more capable of developing cost-efficient green initiatives (Fu et al., 2020; Surroca et al., 2010).

In an era of transformation, high learners are most likely to be also "high performers", as they see the "value of values" and have an open mind and flexible agenda to adapt and adopt. Continuous organizational learning and innovation will play an integral role in creating business solutions to the ongoing environmental and societal challenges. Recognizing these business solutions, the United Nations and the OECD both call for a technological transformation to build a more sustainable future (OECD, 2021; United Nations, 2015).

Green Initiatives as Window-dressing: "Talk the Talk, Not Walk the Walk"

Despite the compelling business case for green initiatives, critics argue that some firms may only "talk the talk, but not walk the walk" (Perez-Batres et al., 2012; Schoeneborn et al., 2020). Some firms simply use green initiatives as a window-dressing technique to alter public perception and to curry favor from their key stakeholders, but do not intend to make a substantial impact on the environment (Bowen and Aragon-Correa, 2014). This is known as "greenwashing", whereby firms demonstrate poor environmental performance while actively engaging in positive communication about their environmental initiatives (Delmas and Cuerel Burbano, 2011; Marquis et al., 2016). One well-known greenwashing example is the Volkswagen diesel car emission scandal. Volkswagen's installation of "defeat devices" deliberately deceived the public about its environmental performance—it claimed it was undertaking measures that would benefit the environment, when the opposite was the case (Partridge, 2015; Plungis, 2015).

Although not as serious as greenwashing, some firms also engage in window-dressing, or symbolic environmentalism. Different from greenwashing, which deliberately deceives stakeholders, symbolic environmentalism refers to green initiatives with no implemented actions, or only partially undertaken as a separate activity, largely disconnected from everyday business policies, processes, and routines (Bowen, 2014). That is, they may adopt some green practices in some of their internal activities; however, this adoption is not implemented at the firm level (Urbinati et al., 2017). In these firms, their green initiatives make no difference to the organization's "business as usual", creating no substantial impact (Easter et al., 2021; Wright and Nyberg, 2017). For instance, a firm that promotes itself as "reducing plastics" may still use disposable plastic cups in its employee lunchroom. In a similar vein, a company that recycles waste may still emit a large amount of carbon dioxide.

There are multiple underlying factors as to why firms use green initiatives as window-dressing. One of the key reasons is that many businesses choose not to incorporate the environment into their business purpose or principles; rather, they merely do so to respond to stakeholder pressure (Bowen, 2014; Crilly et al., 2012). In doing so, they falsely signal their prosocial intentions and capabilities to the public and investors to gain stakeholder support or avoid stakeholder sanction (Fu et al., 2021a). Some firms may be committed to green initiatives but do not have sufficient resources and capabilities to support substantial green initiatives, because these normally require significant investment in technology or a large-scale overhaul of current processes (Delmas and Cuerel Burbano, 2011; Fu et al., 2019). The biggest difficulty perhaps is that firms have little knowledge on how to integrate costly environmental and social challenges within the organizational goal of short-term profit maximization. The causal complexity between actions of green initiatives and the intended financial and environmental performance poses great challenges for firms to materialize the business case for green initiatives. This is what promotes regressive reliance on "business as usual" (Wright and Nyberg, 2017). To successfully engage with green initiatives, firms need to develop innovative business models that align environmental challenges with profitability. But no consensus has been reached so far as to how to achieve this. Hence, firms either muddle through or "talk the talk, but not walk the walk" (Crilly et al., 2012; Tashman et al., 2019).

Inevitably, window-dressing makes it more difficult for stakeholders to discern the genuineness and actual impact of a firm's green initiatives. One of the consequences is that this creates noise in the stock market. Investors may form widely differing opinions of the same company based on window-dressing information: some pro-environment investors may be swayed by greenwashing to buy more shares; others may interpret greenwashing as a failure of trust and sell their shares (Fu et al., 2021a). Large-scale trading of buying and selling consequently results in a higher stock price volatility (Fu et al., 2021a; Fu et al., 2020; Orlitzky, 2013). For the firm, window-dressing is likely to erode their stakeholder relationship, thereby diminishing trust and their future stakeholder influence capacity (Chen and Chang, 2013; Connors et al., 2017). Should this happen, even if firms undertake genuine and credible green initiatives in the future, stakeholders may not trust and reward firms' good green initiatives.

Collectively, window-dressing wastes social resources and may cause more environmental problems. At the firm level, firms have to spend resources and time on advertising to promote their symbolic green initiatives that could have been used in more meaningful environmental actions. Broadly, at the society level, "green solutions" promoted by businesses may attract social attention, reducing awareness of environmental damage caused by industrial activity, particularly in other economies. For instance, firms that window dress may transfer their environmentally damaging activities to developing countries or "pollution havens", exacerbating the already seriously pressing environmental problems. This may eventually result in environmentalism being hijacked in a discourse in which business plays a central role, whereby the real complex, interconnected, and dynamic environmental challenges are reduced to corporate rhetoric in which business is placed at the center of the narrative about managing environmental challenges (Bowen, 2014). These window-dressing practices with empty pledges will become corporate distractions that will eventually cost the world dearly.

Therefore, it is evident that corporate "green solutions" do not necessarily translate to actual solutions. Firms that commit to proactive green solutions may not be substantially improving the environment (Bowden et al., 2021), especially when these green solutions are largely disconnected from their organizational processes and mainly based on sustainability certifications and voluntary disclosure programs (Blackman and Rivera, 2011; Pucheta-Martínez and Gallego-Álvarez, 2020). Rampant window-dressing, in particular, suggests that there remains a significant grey area in which green initiatives promise some environmental benefits, but apparently deliver more reputational and legitimacy benefits for businesses than actual substantive environmental improvements (Bowen, 2014). Even worse, it is likely to result in major social waste, ultimately inhibiting society-wide progress in addressing environmental challenges. As a result, while businesses are capable of resolving environmental challenges through their technological and market innovation, they are often complicit in causing the very problems they claim to resolve (Wright and Nyberg, 2017).

How to Tell the Difference?

As green initiatives can take the form of both circular economy and window-dressing, how can we tell the differences? Drawing on past research, this chapter proposes three methods that should help to make appropriate judgments.

All Elements Should Be Examined in Conjunction

As green initiatives are normally interconnected to, and supported by, other organizational activities (Aguinis and Glavas, 2013; Wood, 1991), one way to distinguish genuine green initiatives is to judge to what extent green initiatives are connected to a firm's principles, processes, and actions in relation to environmental responsibility

(Wood, 1991). Adopting genuine green initiatives requires firms to not only initiate and develop technology, but also reflect firms' principles in assuming environmental responsibility. Moreover, it also requires innovating business models that are based on longevity, renewability, reuse, repair, upgrades, refurbishment, capacity sharing, and dematerialization (Urbinati et al., 2017). This means that firms must take cost management and control into consideration and start rethinking products and services as well as end-user propositions that increase efficiency, effectiveness, and performance (Esposito et al., 2018). Integrating green initiatives into a firm's operating routines and search activities can best signal to stakeholders that the focal firm is indeed genuinely committed to its environmental responsibility (Fu et al., 2021b; Fu et al., 2020).

Thus, to assess a firm's green initiatives, as recommended by Wood (1991), stakeholders should examine all elements in conjunction, namely, principles, processes, and outcomes. Specifically, stakeholders should examine the degree to which principles of environmental responsibility motivate green actions taken by the firm, the degree to which the firm makes use of green processes, the existence and nature of policies and programs designed to manage the firm's environmental relationships, and the environmental impacts (i.e., observable outcomes) of the firm's actions, programs, and policies. Most importantly, stakeholders should assess the degree to which the firm integrates green initiatives into its core business. In contrast, if a firm's green initiatives are largely standalone activities or merely lip service, it may suggest that the firm is simply using green initiatives as a symbolic gesture to gain legitimacy. For instance, some firms claim green initiatives that are merely donations made or some temporary token programs, rather than any substantial long-term actions or organizational changes undertaken. Because these activities are separate from their core operation, they can easily dispense with these so-called green initiatives when stakeholder pressure declines, or when they face intense competitive pressure or lack of resources (Campbell, 2007). Understandably, however, sometimes firms using such initiatives may also mark an incremental process of assuming environmental responsibility from superficial to integrated approach.

In making these recommendations, it is important to acknowledge that it is not always easy for stakeholders to judge the credibility of firms' green initiatives. This is because many of these criteria (principles, processes, and actions) are not always quantifiable, nor readily available to outsiders. Much of the ratings provided by data agents can at best capture the outcomes of green initiatives, but not the firms' processes and principles (Delmas et al., 2013). However, compared with window-dressing firms, research shows that green firms are generally more active on social media and produce more sustainability reports in detailing their efforts and tangible outcomes (Reilly and Hynan, 2014).

Motives

A second method is to evaluate to what extent a firm's green initiatives are driven by instrumental or altruistic motives. The CSR literature features a lengthy debate in this regard about instrumental and normative CSR. Previous studies of environmental responsibility, typically in the form of green initiatives, predominately take an instrumental approach, finding that it is implemented primarily to gain profits, legitimacy, and competitive advantage (e.g., El Ghoul et al., 2018; Jayachandran et al., 2013; Orlitzky et al., 2011). However, critics argue that instrumental CSR is mostly practiced as window-dressing and should be abandoned (Crane and Matten, 2021), with studies identifying green initiatives as a form of virtue signaling that makes no real impact on the environment and society (Delmas and Montes-Sancho, 2010). Hence, opponents of instrumental CSR strongly advocate for normative CSR. They argue for the implementation of ethical principles that support CSR as meeting all stakeholder needs without trade-offs and genuinely committing to the betterment of the environment and society.

Both sides of this debate seem to assume that the motives for, and purpose of, green initiatives are key to differentiating instrumental versus normative CSR (Bridoux et al., 2016; Chen et al., 2020). However, motive relies heavily on stakeholder perception and is almost impossible for those outside the firm to verify, making it very difficult to ascertain the real purpose of firms' green initiatives (Bridoux and Stoelhorst, 2014; Chen et al., 2020). In particular, as green initiatives entail interconnected elements of principles, processes, and outcomes, sound motives but poor translation via processes are also likely to result in negative outcomes (Wood, 1991). For instance, a survey conducted by McKinsey demonstrates that 30% of managers pointed to the complexity of consistent implementation, including the absence of clear objectives or metrics for green initiatives, difficulties in effectively engaging employees, and a lack of thorough understanding of green initiatives. All of which are all likely to disintegrate the well-intended green programs (McKinsey, 2021).

The broader literature also sheds light on the complexities surrounding firms' green initiatives, outlining how organizational decision-making processes can cause organizations to deviate from their initial purpose and motive, resulting in unintentional outcomes, or even opposite outcomes (Brunsson, 1982; March, 1994). For instance, even firms with genuine commitment can unintentionally engage in "symbolic" or "window-dressing" due to a lack of experience, knowledge, and capability in implementing certain green initiatives. DesJardine et al. (2020) highlight that firms with the best intentions and motives in implementing social responsibility initiatives can still be considered to be "wasting resources".

An equally likely scenario is that good outcomes come from bad motives. Many firms that engage in green initiatives or integrate greenness into their processes are not necessarily motivated by their concerns for the environment but rather driven by economic gains or external pressures (Kassinis and Vafeas, 2006; Perez-Batres et al., 2012). For example, some firms practice green initiatives to gain a license to pollute (Ormiston and Wong, 2013; Panwar, 2021). Notwithstanding these instrumental motives, through adopting cost-efficient synergies with their business routine, some firms may almost inadvertently create highly effective and visible green initiatives that are deemed as "substantial" or "genuine" (Fu et al., 2020). A case in point is that of Country Garden (a Fortune 500 property development company), which, following media coverage of construction accidents, decided to redeploy robots, simultaneously cutting labor costs and reducing construction injuries and accidents considerably (Thomson Reuters, 2020).

Perhaps more often than not, green initiatives represent a combination of genuine commitments and window-dressing driven by both ethical principles and instrumental motives. This mixed motives argument is supported by evolutionary biology, which suggests that pure altruism is almost impossible; that is, all altruistic motives have some instrumental motives (Dawkins, 1976). For instance, firms driven by concerns for the environment may still want to capitalize on their green initiatives for a better reputation and greater stakeholder support. Such mixed motives may result in firms adopting simultaneous trade-offs and synergies in their green initiatives, depending on how the motives may evolve or outweigh each other under different conditions. In particular, when firms are under resource constraints posed by an extreme external environment such as COVID-19 and the accompanying economic recession, they may choose to only focus on a selective few green initiatives at the expense of other environmental issues and stakeholders. This makes such challenging market conditions a real test ground for the genuineness of firms' green initiatives.

COVID-19 as a Real Test Ground for Green Initiatives

The COVID-19 crisis has brought on an economic recession, severely threatening the survival of businesses (Amankwah-Amoah, 2020). When a firm is running short of resources and struggling to limit financial losses, the long-term outlook is, at best, a couple of weeks into the future. Without a long-term outlook and sufficient resources supporting their green initiatives, these firms find it difficult to keep their green promises, because pursuing a sustainability agenda runs counter to the wishes of their shareholders during this extreme economic stress. Consequently, over 50% of businesses reportedly opted to scale back their green initiatives during the COVID-19 pandemic (Sandhu, 2021). For instance, automakers spending billions of dollars to make transportation cleaner and safer have delayed or cancelled green programs in autonomous vehicle, electrification, and car-sharing. Numerous firms that in recent years have promoted efforts to innovate for the environment have had to pause or terminate their green innovation projects (Stoll, 2020). Although there is no telling whether these cutbacks will become permanent, the mounting stakeholder pressure will likely propel businesses to resume corporate green initiatives and environmentalism when the good times return. But these cutbacks undoubtedly demonstrate that in the hierarchy of subjects, firms care about survival and shareholders trump higher-minded ideals and commitment to the environment.

Paradoxically, the COVID-19 pandemic has stressed the critical importance of the relationships between the environment, society, and our livelihoods at an unprecedented level (Crane and Matten, 2021; Kramer, 2020; OECD, 2021). Amidst the pandemic, many governments have pushed ahead with more decisive policies and regulations in addressing environmental challenges (Vince, 2020).

For instance, the Australian Government announced its plan to reach a "net-zero" target by 2050 (The Australian Government, 2021). Across the board, net-zero emissions require rapid economic, social, and technological transformation (OECD, 2021). Such government-led policies and initiatives are echoed by the society at large and call for more business solutions and more sustained commitment to such challenges than the pandemic.

In genuinely committing to meeting environmental challenges, businesses have reached a major turning point. It is time for them to reconsider their roles in environmental and social challenges and their capability in creating sustainable value to meet society's expectations. Inevitably, this creates a dilemma for all businesses: while firms are under pressure to invest more in green initiatives and meet the expectations of stakeholders more broadly, they are also struggling to survive and fulfill the expectations of shareholders. Under this dual pressure and conflicting demands, firms naturally face a new paradoxical challenge: improve their green initiatives to respond to the heightened expectations created by COVID-19 whilst at the same time surviving the threats posed by COVID-19.

Hence, more than ever, firms' green initiatives are being put to the test. Some may choose to jettison their green initiatives or suspend them, unsurprisingly, given that green initiatives require significant resources, managerial capabilities, and coordination (Dowell and Muthulingam, 2017). When firms' survival is threatened, they are very likely to resort to trade-offs and withdraw their investments in green initiatives (Campbell, 2007; Fu et al., 2019); whereas for some firms, the threats posed by COVID-19 present a unique opportunity to further explore and exploit the synergies between green initiatives, market opportunities, and organizational processes (Berrone et al., 2013; Fu et al., 2020). High learning firms tend to have a stronger capacity to take an innovative approach to exploit such opportunities, integrating external challenges into their internal processes to implement organizational change (Antonioli et al., 2013). For instance, Facebook uses its R&D in AI algorithms for predicting COVID-19 conditions (Shead, 2021). Microsoft, Oracle, and other technology giants have utilized their R&D expertise to co-build digital COVID-19 vaccine records (Duffy, 2021).

Naturally, public policymaking also has an indispensable role to play in incentivizing firms to continue their green initiatives and innovations during COVID-19. Along with the more restrictive policies introduced by many governments, more support and stimulus packages to business actions from governments are required to actively shape a cleaner economy and a better environment. For instance, R&D tax relief can promote green initiatives by freeing more resources and inducing firms' synergy between R&D with CSR through the extension of firms' processes and new product development (Fu et al., 2020; Yang et al., 2012). A good example is a new policy launched by the Indian Government, wherein firms' investment in R&D activities addressing environmental and societal issues during COVID-19 are considered as CSR supported by the government (Noronha, 2020). More importantly, to shape a greener, more resilient economy and environment, governments need to collaborate and co-create in a way that supports society-wide system transformation through policies on investment, innovation, restructuring of industry, employment support, and beyond. Overall, rather than abandoning environmental initiatives during the pandemic, governments, businesses, and societies should use the pandemic to reset our collective response to environmental and societal challenges.

Conclusion

This chapter has highlighted contemporary issues associated with firms' green initiatives. The compelling business case for green initiatives provides hope that we are no longer solely focused on shareholder primacy. Corporations have been leading the transition to the circular economy with their green initiatives: some are reducing their emissions and others are going further in investing in environmental innovation. However, a sobering truth remains: rampant window-dressing and greenwashing practices suggest that many firms are failing to follow through (Goodman, 2020). Due to firms' mixed motives, the market alone will not address environmental challenges.

The COVID-19 pandemic poses a challenge for corporate green initiatives, yet it also presents invaluable opportunities. Even in this economic downturn, firms are well-positioned to address environmental challenges, and they can make or save money doing it. Therefore, businesses should always consider synergies between business, environment, and society that help develop inclusive business models. To profitably do so requires a corporation to change its value proposition and undertake continuous organizational learning, particularly in innovation. This would potentially call for business model transformation and cooperation with a broad network of partners, including competitors.

Moreover, businesses can move beyond greenwashing and window-dressing toward real substantive change. Specifically, businesses should engage with their critics, act with partners, and integrate green initiatives and environmentalism into managerial decision-making processes and core business connected with other organizational activities. Correspondingly, firms should use metrics and relate environmental impact to day-to-day deliverables to support all value chain activities, even if the results may only manifest over a longer time frame. For stakeholders, their future evaluation and scrutiny of firms' green initiatives should and would also be process-based along with outcome-based.

I call on businesses everywhere to embrace these practices as their own and apply them to their operations. By cultivating credible and sustainable green initiatives integrated into a more inclusive business model, a corporation empowers tomorrow's stakeholders and creates a stronger brand with a more loyal following. It can thereby weather economic downturns, ensure greater long-term profits, and attract more investors. This is especially true in emerging markets, where rapid growth is shrinking the distance between old-fashioned "charity" and smart investment.

Of course, businesses cannot be expected to act alone, or pursue business models that are not profitable. Governments need to do their part to create incentives and foster collaborations. Hence, a new relationship paradigm between businesses and governments should be developed. Transiting to the circular economy and confronting climate changes, businesses and governments should collaborate in green innovation to address environmental challenges. Businesses address environmental challenges through their technology and market innovation, while, in turn, governments' public policy support provides long-term protection to businesses.

Looking forward, sustainable value creation and green innovation will continue to be critical in putting genuine green initiatives into practice where both internal mechanisms within organizations and external support can be established. There are more opportunities for interdisciplinary collaborations between researchers, practitioners, and policymakers to collectively push for green innovation. Therefore, the purpose of this chapter is to connect our understanding of these key issues surrounding green initiatives, to help unlock the great potential of a fully operating business and economic system integrated with sustainability and the circular economy.

References

Aguinis, H. and Glavas, A. (2013). Embedded versus peripheral corporate social responsibility: Psychological foundations. *Industrial and Organizational Psychology*, 6(4), 314–332.

Amankwah-Amoah, J. (2020). Stepping up and stepping out of COVID-19: New challenges for environmental sustainability policies in the global airline industry. *Journal of Cleaner Production*, 271, 123000.

Ameer, R. and Othman, R. (2012). Sustainability practices and corporate financial performance: A study based on the top global corporations. *Journal of Business Ethics*, 108(1), 61–79.

Antonioli, D., Mancinelli, S. and Mazzanti, M. (2013). Is environmental innovation embedded within high-performance organisational changes? The role of human resource management and complementarity in green business strategies. *Research Policy*, 42(4), 975–988.

Berrone, P., Fosfuri, A., Gelabert, L. and Gomez-Mejia, L.R. (2013). Necessity as the mother of "green" inventions: Institutional pressures and environmental innovations. *Strategic Management Journal*, 34(8), 891–909.

Blackman, A. and Rivera, J. (2011). Producer-level benefits of sustainability certification. *Conservation Biology*, 25(6), 1176–1185.

Borghesi, S., Cainelli, G. and Mazzanti, M. (2015). Linking emission trading to environmental innovation: Evidence from the Italian manufacturing industry. *Research Policy*, 44(3), 669–683.

Bowden, V., Nyberg, D. and Wright, C. (2021). "We're going under": The role of local news media in dislocating climate change adaptation. *Environmental Communication*, 15(5), 625–640.

Bowen, F. (2014). *After Greenwashing: Symbolic Corporate Environmentalism and Society*. Cambridge: Cambridge University Press.

Bowen, F. and Aragon-Correa, J.A. (2014). Greenwashing in corporate environmentalism research and practice: The importance of what we say and do. *Organization and Environment*, 27(2), 107–112.

Bridoux, F. and Stoelhorst, J. (2014). Microfoundations for stakeholder theory: Managing stakeholders with heterogeneous motives. *Strategic Management Journal*, 35(1), 107–125.

Bridoux, F., Stofberg, N. and Den Hartog, D. (2016). Stakeholders' responses to CSR tradeoffs: When other-orientation and trust trump material self-interest. *Frontiers in Psychology*, 6, 1992. https://doi.org/10.3389/fpsyg.2015.01992.

Brunsson, N. (1982). The irrationality of action and action rationality: Decisions, ideologies and organizational actions. *Journal of Management Studies*, 19(1), 29–44.

Cainelli, G. and Mazzanti, M. (2013). Environmental innovations in services: Manufacturing–services integration and policy transmissions. *Research Policy*, 42(9), 1595–1604.

Campbell, J.L. (2007). Why would corporations behave in socially responsible ways? An institutional theory of corporate social responsibility. *Academy of Management Review*, 32(3), 946–967.

Chen, Y.-S. (2008). The driver of green innovation and green image–green core competence. *Journal of Business Ethics*, 81(3), 531–543.

Chen, Y.-S. and Chang, C.-H. (2013). Greenwash and green trust: The mediation effects of green consumer confusion and green perceived risk. *Journal of Business Ethics*, 114(3), 489–500.

Chen, Z., Hang, H., Pavelin, S. and Porter, L. (2020). Corporate social (ir) responsibility and corporate hypocrisy: Warmth, motive and the protective value of corporate social responsibility. *Business Ethics Quarterly*, 30(4), 486–524.

Cohen, W.M. and Levinthal, D.A. (1989). Innovation and learning: The two faces of R&D. *The Economic Journal*, 99(397), 569–596.

Connors, S., Anderson-MacDonald, S. and Thomson, M. (2017). Overcoming the "window dressing" effect: Mitigating the negative effects of inherent skepticism towards corporate social responsibility. *Journal of Business Ethics*, 145(3), 599–621.

Crane, A. and Matten, D. (2021). COVID-19 and the future of CSR Research. *Journal of Management Studies*, 58(1), 281–284.

Crilly, D., Zollo, M. and Hansen, M. (2012). Faking it or muddling through? Understanding decoupling in response to stakeholder pressures. *Academy of Management Journal*, 55(6), 1429–1448.

Dawkins, R. (1976). *The Selfish Gene*. Oxford: Oxford University Press.

Delmas, M.A. and Cuerel Burbano, V. (2011). The drivers of greenwashing. *California Management Review*, 54(1), 64.

Delmas, M.A., Etzion, D. and Nairn-Birch, N. (2013). Triangulating environmental performance: What do corporate social responsibility ratings really capture? *Academy of Management Perspectives*, 27(3), 255–267.

Delmas, M.A. and Montes-Sancho, M.J. (2010). Voluntary agreements to improve environmental quality: Symbolic and substantive cooperation. *Strategic Management Journal*, 31(6), 575–601.

DesJardine, M.R., Marti, E. and Durand, R. (2020). Why activist hedge funds target socially responsible firms: The reaction costs of signaling corporate social responsibility. *Academy of Management Journal*, 64(3), 851–872.

Dowell, G.W. and Muthulingam, S. (2017). Will firms go green if it pays? The impact of disruption, cost, and external factors on the adoption of environmental initiatives. *Strategic Management Journal*, 38(6), 1287–1304.

Duffy, C. (2021). Microsoft, Oracle and other tech giants team up Covid-19 vaccine "passports". Available at: https://edition.cnn.com/2021/01/16/tech/coronavirus-vaccine-records-microsoft-salesforce/index.html

Easter, S., Ceulemans, K. and Lynn, M.L. (2021). Moving beyond Sisyphus: Pursuing sustainable development in a business-as-usual world. *Business and Society*, 61(4), 924–963.

El Ghoul, S., Guedhami, O., Kim, H. and Park, K. (2018). Corporate environmental responsibility and the cost of capital: International evidence. *Journal of Business Ethics*, 149(2), 335–361.

Esposito, M., Tse, T. and Soufani, K. (2018). Introducing a circular economy: New thinking with managerial and policy implications. *California Management Review*, 60(3), 5–19.

European Commission. (2015). *Communication form the Commission to the European Parliament, the Council, the European Economic and Social Committee of the Regions - Closing the Loop -An EU Action Plan for the Circular Economy. COM/2015/0614 final.* Bussells: European Commission.

Flammer, C. (2013). Corporate social responsibility and shareholder reaction: The environmental awareness of investors. *Academy of Management Journal*, 56(3), 758–781.

Flammer, C. (2021). Corporate green bonds. *Journal of Financial Economics*, 142(2), 499–516.

Fu, L., Boehe, D. and Orlitzky, M. (2020). Are R&D-intensive firms also corporate social responsibility specialists? A multicountry study. *Research Policy*, 49(8), 104082.

Fu, L., Boehe, D., Orlitzky, M. and Swanson, D.L. (2019). Managing stakeholder pressures: Toward a typology of corporate social performance profiles. *Long Range Planning*, 52(6), 1–13.

Fu, L., Boehe, D.M. and Orlitzky, M. (2021a). Broad or narrow stakeholder management? A signaling theory perspective. *Business and Society*. https://doi.org/10.1177/00076503211053018

Fu, L., Boehe, D. and Akhtaruzzaman, M. (2021b). Culture and mixed signals: Does ESG reduce risk everywhere? *Academy of Management Proceedings*, 1(1), 10306.

Garnaut, R. (2008). *The Garnaut Climate Change Review*. Melbourne: Cambridge University Press.

Geissdoerfer, M., Savaget, P., Bocken, N.M. and Hultink, E.J. (2017). The Circular Economy–A new sustainability paradigm? *Journal of Cleaner Production*, 143, 757–768.

Goodman, P.S. (2020). Stakeholder capitalism gets a report card. It's not good. Available at: https://www.nytimes.com/2020/09/22/business/business-roudtable-stakeholder-capitalism.html

Hawn, O., Chatterji, A.K. and Mitchell, W. (2018). Do investors actually value sustainability? New evidence from investor reactions to the Dow Jones Sustainability Index (DJSI). *Strategic Management Journal*, 39(4), 949–976.

Helmig, B., Spraul, K. and Ingenhoff, D. (2016). Under positive pressure: How stakeholder pressure affects corporate social responsibility implementation. *Business and Society*, 55(2), 151–187.

Jayachandran, S., Kalaignanam, K. and Eilert, M. (2013). Product and environmental social performance: Varying effect on firm performance. *Strategic Management Journal*, 34(10), 1255–1264.

Kassinis, G. and Vafeas, N. (2006). Stakeholder pressures and environmental performance. *Academy of Management Journal*, 49(1), 145–159.

Korhonen, J., Honkasalo, A. and Seppälä, J. (2018). Circular economy: The concept and its limitations. *Ecological Economics*, 143, 37–46.

Kramer, M.R. (2020). Coronavirus is putting corporate social responsibility to the test. *Harvard Business Review*. Available at: https://hbr.org/2020/04/coronavirus-is-putting-corporate-social-responsibility-to-the-test

Kushwaha, G.S. and Sharma, N.K. (2016). Green initiatives: A step towards sustainable development and firm's performance in the automobile industry. *Journal of Cleaner Production*, 121, 116–129.

Lee, C.-Y. (2010). A theory of firm growth: Learning capability, knowledge threshold, and patterns of growth. *Research Policy*, 39(2), 278–289.

MacArthur, E. (2013). Towards the circular economy. *Journal of Industrial Ecology*, 2, 23–44.

March, J.G. (1994). *Primer on Decision Making: How Decisions Happen*. New York: The Free Press.

Marco-Fondevila, M., Llena-Macarulla, F., Callao-Gastón, S. and Jarne-Jarne, J. (2021). Are circular economy policies actually reaching organizations? Evidence from the largest Spanish companies. *Journal of Cleaner Production*, 285, 124858.

Marquis, C., Toffel, M.W. and Zhou, Y. (2016). Scrutiny, norms, and selective disclosure: A global study of greenwashing. *Organization Science*, 27(2), 483–504.

McKinsey. (2021). How companies capture the value of sustainability: Survey findings. Available at: https://www.mckinsey.com/business-functions/sustainability/our-insights/how-companies-capture-the-value-of-sustainability-survey-findings

Moraga, G., Huysveld, S., Mathieux, F., Blengini, G.A., Alaerts, L., Van Acker, K., de Meester, S. and Dewulf, J. (2019). Circular economy indicators: What do they measure? *Resources, Conservation and Recycling*, 146, 452–461.

Nidumolu, R., Prahalad, C.K. and Rangaswami, M.R. (2009). Why sustainability is now the key driver of innovation. *Harvard Business Review*, 87(9), 56–64.

Noronha, G. (2020). Contributions to R&D spends on Covid-related vaccine, drugs to be considered as CSR: Govt. Available at: https://economictimes.indiatimes.com/industry/healthcare/biotech/healthcare/contributions-to-rd-spends-on-covid-related-vaccine-drugs-to-be-considered-as-csr-govt/articleshow/77744246.cms?from=mdr

O'Brien, J.P. and David, P. (2014). Reciprocity and R&D search: Applying the behavioral theory of the firm to a communitarian context. *Strategic Management Journal*, 35(4), 550–565.

OECD. (2021). Focus on green recovery. Available at: https://www.oecd.org/coronavirus/en/themes/green-recovery

Orlitzky, M. (2013). Corporate social responsibility, noise, and stock market volatility. *Academy of Management Perspectives*, 27(3), 238–254.

Orlitzky, M., Siegel, D.S. and Waldman, D.A. (2011). Strategic corporate social responsibility and environmental sustainability. *Business and Society*, 50(1), 6–27.

Ormiston, M.E. and Wong, E.M. (2013). License to ill: The effects of corporate social responsibility and CEO moral identity on corporate social irresponsibility. *Personnel Psychology*, 66(4), 861–893.

Panwar, R. (2021). Optimism amid despair: How to avoid a net-zero debacle. *Business and Society*. https://doi.org/10.1177/00076503211053816

Partridge, K. (2015). VW scandal just the tip of the greenwashing iceberg. Available at: https://www8.gsb.columbia.edu/articles/ideas-work/vw-scandal-just-tip-greenwashing-iceberg

Perez-Batres, L.A., Doh, J.P., Miller, V.V. and Pisani, M.J. (2012). Stakeholder pressures as determinants of CSR strategic choice: Why do firms choose symbolic versus substantive self-regulatory codes of conduct? *Journal of Business Ethics*, 110(2), 157–172.

Plungis, J. (2015). Volkswagen emissions scandal: Forty years of greenwashing - The well-travelled road taken by VW. Available at: https://www.independent.co.uk/news/business/analysis-and-features/volkswagen-emissions-scandal-forty-years-of-greenwashing-the-welltravelled-road-taken-by-vw-10516209.html

Pucheta-Martínez, M.C. and Gallego-Álvarez, I. (2020). Corporate environmental disclosure practices in different national contexts: The influence of cultural dimensions. *Organization and Environment*, 33(4), 597–623.

Pucker, K.P. (2021). Overselling sustainability reporting. *Harvard Business Review*, 99(3), 134–143.

Reilly, A.H. and Hynan, K.A. (2014). Corporate communication, sustainability, and social media: It's not easy (really) being green. *Business Horizons*, 57(6), 747–758.

Sandhu, S. (2021). Risky business: 54% of Australian companies plan to slow "green" initiatives due to COVID. Available at: https://theconversation.com/risky-business-54-of-australian-companies-plan-to-slow-green-initiatives-due-to-covid-158532

Schoeneborn, D., Morsing, M. and Crane, A. (2020). Formative perspectives on the relation between CSR communication and CSR practices: Pathways for walking, talking, and t (w) alking. *Business and Society*, 59(1), 5–33.

Shead, S. (2021). Facebook develops A.I. to predict likelihood of worsening Covid symptons. Available at: https://www.cnbc.com/2021/01/15/facebook-develops-ai-to-predict-likelihood-of-worsening-covid-symptoms.html

Stoll, J.D. (2020). Airbnb aimed to practice stakeholder capitalism. Coronavirus complicated its goals. Available at: https://www.wsj.com/articles/airbnb-aimed-to-practice-stakeholder-capitalism-coronavirus-complicated-its-goals-11588726267

Surroca, J., Tribó, J.A. and Waddock, S. (2010). Corporate responsibility and financial performance: The role of intangible resources. *Strategic Management Journal*, 31(5), 463–490.

Tanriverdi, H. and Venkatraman, N. (2005). Knowledge relatedness and the performance of multibusiness firms. *Strategic Management Journal*, 26(2), 97–119.

Tashman, P., Marano, V. and Kostova, T. (2019). Walking the walk or talking the talk? Corporate social responsibility decoupling in emerging market multinationals. *Journal of International Business Studies*, 50(2), 153–171.

The Australian Government. (2021). Australia's plan to reach our net zero target by 2050. Available at: https://www.minister.industry.gov.au/ministers/taylor/media-releases/australias-plan-reach-our-net-zero-target-2050

Thomson Reuters. (2020). Chinese property firm Country Garden plans mass production of construction robots. Available at: https://www.reuters.com/article/us-country-garden-robots-idUSKBN1ZG0XG

United Nations. (2015). Transforming our world: The 2030 Agenda for Sustainable Development. Available at: https://sdgs.un.org/2030agenda

Urbinati, A., Chiaroni, D. and Chiesa, V. (2017). Towards a new taxonomy of circular economy business models. *Journal of Cleaner Production*, 168, 487–498.

Vince, G. (2020). After the Covid-19 crisis, will we get a greener world? Available at: https://www.theguardian.com/environment/2020/may/17/after-the-covid-19-crisis-will-we-get-a-greener-world

Wood, D.J. (1991). Corporate social performance revisited. *Academy of Management Review*, 16(4), 691–718.

Wright, C. and Nyberg, D. (2017). An inconvenient truth: How organizations translate climate change into business as usual. *Academy of Management Journal*, 60(5), 1633–1661.

Yang, C.-H., Huang, C.-H. and Hou, T.C.-T. (2012). Tax incentives and R&D activity: Firm-level evidence from Taiwan. *Research Policy*, 41(9), 1578–1588.

Zerbini, F. (2017). CSR initiatives as market signals: A review and research agenda. *Journal of Business Ethics*, 146(1), 1–23.

12 Why Are Japanese Companies Publishing Integrated Reports?

Perceiving through the Lens of Institutional Theory

Md Tapan Mahmud

Introduction

Communicating entities' environmental, social and governance (ESG) positions through non-financial platforms—sustainability reporting (SR), integrated reporting (IR), various forms of environmental reporting—are becoming institutionalized in most countries (Khan et al., 2020; Shabana et al., 2017); this institutionalization process stems largely from voluntary drives. Non-financial initiatives in varied forms are mandated in some countries, such as France, Denmark, the Netherlands and the United Kingdom. However, when it comes to IR, except for South Africa, it is considered a voluntary disclosure platform (Maroun, 2019). Interestingly, even if disclosing ESG information is not mandatory, it is now widely considered an additional tool for comprehending company performances and financial reporting (Higgins and Coffey, 2016). Hence, companies recognize the importance of ESG-based disclosures and publish corporate social reports (CSRs) (Greenwood et al., 2019). Approximately 85% of S&P-500 companies are reporting through various forms of CSRs lately (Governance and Accountability Institute, 2017). Intriguingly, publishing CSRs warrants a considerable amount of resource consumption, and the motivation behind such herculean efforts may be credited to three potential sources: interest-based motivation, corporate responsibility-based motivation and institutionalized (irrational) compulsion-based motivation. Furthermore, three fundamental theories are popular in explaining the motivational sources for publishing CSRs: legitimacy theory, stakeholder theory and institutional theory (Mahmud, 2020).

Legitimacy theory holds that companies search for social approval to survive by publishing CSRs; (managerial) stakeholder theory posits that companies determine the most influential stakeholders and design disclosures for them; and institutional theory operates from an irrational ground stating that firms pursue "isomorphism", imitate numerous aspects of the society and industry and ESG disclosure is one of those aspects (Deegan, 2014). Notably, greenwashing—selective positive disclosure regarding the environmental and social performance—is a legitimacy management technique (De Freitas Netto et al., 2020; Marquis et al., 2016). Following the idea of legitimacy management—greenwashing—is the "go-to" path to explain the motivations for CSR reporting practices (Mahmud, 2019);

DOI: 10.4324/9781003274575-15

in this case, a rational, that is, an interest-based motivational angle is referred to. Logically, there remain alternative sources of motivation that drive the publications of CSRs. Addressing this gap, this study opts for an institutional compulsion-based path focusing on the non-economically attached (irrational but befitting (see Mahmud, 2020)) isomorphic mechanisms of the institutional theory (DiMaggio and Powell, 1983) to explain the motivation behind Japanese IR publication.

Several researchers (e.g., Ho and Taylor, 2007; Kokubu et al., 2003; Saka and Burritt, 2003) have studied Japanese contextual factors. Moreover, Kawahara (2017) did an excellent review of the Japanese literature and mentioned institutional factors along with trends and challenges in the Japanese CSR arena. Komura (2009) highlighted institutional factors that may improve CSRs quality, and a recent study from Madein (2020) unearthed institutional issues in the Japanese CSRs context by referring to various mechanisms of institutional theory. Intriguingly, using institutional theory's components to highlight contextual determinants and employing those to explain the motivation behind publishing Japanese IRs is an uncharted research path; and the specific contribution of this study is coming from this angle.

Logically, the objective of this study is to explain the motivational sources for publishing CSRs/IRs in the unique contextual setting of Japanese CSR based on the three isomorphic mechanisms of institutional theory. The rest of the chapter is structured as follows. The second section of this chapter holds the logic for locking institutional theory and the Japanese IR context. The third section enumerates the methodology for this study. The fourth section puts up the pragmatic dynamism of the isomorphic mechanisms. The fifth section arranges the institutional determinants of the CSR context in the mold of the isomorphic mechanisms and the remaining two sections offer the related discussion and conclusion of this study, respectively.

The Rationality of Selection: Institutional Theory and Japanese IRs

Why Institutional Theory is a Befitting Choice for Explaining the Motivations for Publishing CSRs/IRs?

Institutional theory holds that organizational structure and behaviors are driven more by contextual factors rather than economic objectives (Moll et al., 2006). Moreover, institutions and structural determinants lead transformations in an organizational field and economic rationality is ruled out as the leading force (DiMaggio and Powell, 1983; Meyer and Rowan, 1977). This theory is implemented based on the seminal works by DiMaggio and Powell as well as Scott (see Table 12.1). It is one of the mainstream theories that is utilized when explaining numerous issues related to CSR (Mata et al., 2018). Interestingly, this theory can complement both legitimacy theory and stakeholder theory by covering the explanatory angles of these alternatives. It has all the potential to be an allrounder theory.

Table 12.1 Bases of Institutional Theory (Adapted from Higgins and Larrinaga (2014) and Mahmud (2020))

DiMaggio and Powell (1983, 1991)		*Scott (1995, 2008)*	
3 Isomorphic mechanisms		**3 Pillars**	
Coercive mechanism		**Regulative structure**	
Regulatory authority, professional body, powerful stakeholder	Avoiding sanctions and negative consequences of not following the lines	Rules, laws, related sanctions	Enforced mainly by government and other influential coalitions
Normative mechanism		**Normative structure**	
Social values, norms, professionalism, formal education, networks	Filling in for social and network (peer) related expectations	Values, norms, collective expectations	Influenced by morality, educational and professional background
Mimetic mechanism		**Cultural–cognitive structure**	
Leading organization, uncertainty	Following mainstream (model) practices for legitimacy	Taken-for-granted systemic symbol/ meaning,	Constructed through subjective psychological reconciliation

Higgins and Larrinaga (2014) state that legitimacy theory is a specific case of institutional theory's regulative pillar. Furthermore, three forms of isomorphic mechanism bring legitimacy-related organizational forms and processes to the table (Deegan, 2014; DiMaggio and Powell, 1983). Unerman and Bennett (2004) connect the idea of "mimetic isomorphism" to CSR and competitiveness. According to them, companies follow a leading entity's innovative reporting practices and operation strategies to sustain and extend organizational legitimacy. Interestingly, "decoupling" is a crucial concept of institutional theory that covers another idea of legitimacy. That is, managers pursue symbolic management to show off their attachment towards approved practices by publishing positive ESG disclosures. Decoupling behavior is synonymous with greenwashing (Ashforth and Gibbs, 1990; Dillard et al., 2004; De Freitas Netto et al., 2020). Therefore, it can be safely stated that institutional theory covers the rational—social approval, competitive advantage and symbolic management—grounds of legitimacy theory. Additionally, stakeholder theory's (managerial branch) position of identifying influential stakeholders and aligning organizational practices according to their demands can be complemented by the idea of "coercive isomorphism". In other words, influential stakeholders can coerce an organization to follow a specific institutionalized practice (DiMaggio and Powell, 1983). In addition, managers may pursue "mimetic isomorphism" by copying various practices to maintain and enhance external stakeholders'—both economically powerful and marginalized groups—interests (Unerman and Bennett, 2004).

Speaking from the perception of the relationship between institutional theory and ESG disclosures, CSRs can be interpreted as an aftermath of three forms of isomorphisms (Higgins and Larrinaga, 2014), namely ESG disclosures' responses to coercion, which are sourced from regulations, and capital providers' and consumers' demands (coercive isomorphism). Such disclosures are also an output of voluntary efforts backed by social responsibility (normative isomorphism). Finally, these are sometimes identical reflections of model organizations' reporting practices (mimetic isomorphism).

Hence, it can be concluded that institutional theory (originally) is based on an irrational ground. However, it also covers the rational explanatory angles of legitimacy theory, stakeholder theory and the dynamism of various CSR patterns. It is the most suitable theory to explain the motivations for publishing CSRs/IRs. Lately, institutional theory has been opted for in explaining varied phenomena of CSRs (IRs, SRs and similar platforms) by researchers such as Arul et al. (2021), Bhatia and Makkar (2018), Comyns (2018), Dumitru et al. (2017), El-Bassiouny and El-Bassiouny (2019), Khan et al. (2020), Kılıç et al. (2020), Oware and Mallikarjunappa (2022) and Shabana et al. (2017).

Why the Japanese IRs?

Japan has a rich history of environmental reporting. Since 2002, Japan has been among the top countries that publish CSRs and currently is ranked second in publishing IRs (Reporting Exchange, 2019; Schrader, 2019). Facts support exceptional growth of Japanese IRs. In 2010, only 23 listed companies published IRs but this figure rose to 513 in 2019 (KPMG, 2019). Despite having such a remarkable record and history related to IRs, Japan is almost ruled out in the related research arena. In contrast, Anglo-Saxon countries, such as the United States, the United Kingdom and Australia have received immense attention from scholars (Mata, et al., 2018). Intriguingly, Japan has a unique business culture with a tight ethical code driving a social responsibility-based corporate philosophy (Mahmud, 2022). Additionally, an institutional setting featured with a *J-firm* (or modified version of it) corporate governance (Aoki, 2007) and voluntary corporate social reporting setup (Lewin et al., 1995; Choi and Aguilera, 2009) make Japan an immensely interesting subject to understand the managerial motivation behind publishing IRs utilizing institutional theory.

Research Methodology

This study aims to investigate the motivational sources for publishing IRs in the unique Japanese CSR context. Commonly, the researchers embrace a rational explanatory angle to explain the said motivational sources. Nonetheless, this study adheres to an irrational angle to do the same. To conclude, an exploratory qualitative research method is opted for. And to find out the information related to the aim of the study, a thematic analysis is conducted. In this case, a theory-driven thematic analysis (Boyatzis, 1998; Miles et al., 2013) is utilized, pillared on institutional theory. Two seminal works are related to this theory, namely DiMaggio and Powell (1983) and Scott (1995). The former focused on three mechanisms (coercive, normative and mimetic) to explain institutional theory and the latter referred to three elements (regulative, normative and cultural–cognitive) to do the same. The ideas mostly overlap one another. However, DiMaggio and Powell's ideas have more explanatory power than those of Scott (Miner, 2006). Hence, the contents of the three mechanisms are preferred to create the related themes in this study.

Data sources are secondary which include guidelines, website information, surveys from the Ministry of Environment (MOE), Ministry of Economy Trade and Industry (METI), Financial Services Agency (FSA), Japan Exchange Group (JPX), Tokyo Stock Exchange (TSE), websites of various Japanese environmental groups, related Japanese acts and scholarly outputs. Consequently, the information found was attached to the themes to create a logical and thematic platform that enabled the researcher to enumerate the motivation of the Japanese IR preparers based on the three mechanisms of institutional theory.

Many researchers have studied CSR phenomena in different institutional settings with numerous variables and research objectives. Each of the studies unearths alternative implementations of isomorphic mechanisms based on the ideas of DiMaggio and Powell (1983, 1991). Table 12.2 presents some selected studies focusing on the three mechanisms' elements.

How Do Isomorphic Mechanisms Pan Out in Various Pragmatic Scenarios?

All the factors under the umbrella of the three mechanisms aid us in understanding the reasons for which CSR practices differ among companies in varied institutional settings (Gauthier, 2013). Interestingly, the extent of pressure resulting from the institutional components of the three mechanisms varies distinguishably. Pressures from the coercive and mimetic mechanisms are high and those from the normative counterpart are considerably low (Ali and Rizwan, 2013). According to Dumitru et al. (2017), as a part of the mimetic mechanism, state ownership may improve reporting quality and normative isomorphism becomes forceful in a matured system. Moreover, even if legislation/regulation happens to be the strongest coercive drive—especially at a macroeconomic level—it can exert both positive and negative impacts on CSR quality; and the determinant factor is the process through which such bindings are enforced.

Moreover, there are different stages of CSR depending on the legitimacy status and sustainability strategy of a given company and the overall perception of CSR of a specific industry. Table 12.3 depicts three isomorphic mechanisms that motivate corporate reporting practices in three different stages.

Therefore, it can be assumed that the impact of the isomorphic mechanism on environmental institutions and CSR is not straightforward. It takes different shapes depending on varied institutional settings. Similarly, the mainstream

Table 12.2 Various Implementations of Isomorphic Items in Different Research Settings

Coercive isomorphism	
Ali and Rizwan (2013)	Governments, trade unions, customer associations, media, employees, investors/financial institutions
Dumitru et al. (2017)	Legislation, stakeholders
Khan et al. (2020)	Cultural expectations, government regulations, corporate governance code
Amran and Devi (2007)	Stock exchange listing requirements, standard operating procedures (parent-subsidiary relationship), investment agencies
Normative isomorphism	
Ali and Rizwan (2013)	Company characteristics, CSR frameworks, NGOs, CSR labels, standard-setting and academic institutions
Dumitru et al. (2017)	CSR frameworks/guidelines, auditors
Depoers and Jerome (2020)	professional (accounting) associations
Kılıç et al. (2020)	Employee turnover, industry trade associations, consulting firms
Amran and Devi (2007)	Socialization among top management, association memberships, coalitions, unions, workshop enrollment, government contracts, reporting award requirements
Mimetic isomorphism	
Ali and Rizwan (2013)	Multinationals, industry standards, competitors
Dumitru et al. (2017)	Industry sensitivity (environmentally sensitive and non-sensitive), ownership
Legendre and Coderre (2013)	High-risk industries (high levels of political risk, high media visibility or concentrated competition)
Amran and Devi (2007)	Symbolic uncertainty, consultancy firms (agency)

perception regarding a particular item of a given mechanism and the strategical context of a firm determine the degree of impact or implementation.

Can Institutional Theory Explain the Motivation of the Japanese IR Preparers?

Institutional factors force the homogenization of corporate reporting practices and the integrated reporting adoption (pattern) can also be explained by such factors (Depoers and Jerome, 2020). According to the Eco Survey of the MOE, the (claimed) primary purpose of disclosing environmental information for the Japanese companies is to discharge social responsibility rather than following

Table 12.3 Isomorphic Mechanism's Impact on Corporate Social Reporting in Three Different Stages (Adapted from Ashforth and Gibbs (1990); DiMaggio and Powell (1983); Shabana et al. (2017))

Reporting phases Criteria	*Defensive reporting (Stage 1)*	*Proactive reporting (Stage 2)*	*Imitative reporting (Stage 3)*
Context	There is a big gap between major stakeholder groups' expectations and firm performance	CSR practice becomes normatively sanctioned and reaches a tipping point	CSR becomes mainstream, non-reporters feel insecure and there is a potential net benefit from reporting
Objective	Filling up the gap between expectation and firm performance	Using CSR to capitalize on fresh opportunities and goal attainment	Imitating model firms to mitigate insecurity and reporting without a goal
Determinants	Membership in hazardous industry, controversial product/services providers, stakeholder concerns	Advertising intensity, high media coverage, high stakeholder strength	Firm-size, internationalization (disparity in social issues)
Isomorphism in play	Coercive isomorphism	Normative isomorphism	Mimetic isomorphism

self-interest-based (economically led rational choice) paths, such as communicating with stakeholders, promoting environmental conservation efforts and educating employees. This context justifies the irrational (non-economic) isomorphic pressure on the Japanese CSR arena (Madein, 2020). Hence, institutional theory is well-poised to clarify the motivation of the Japanese IRs preparers.

Scott's (1995, 2008) three pillars and DiMaggio and Powell's (1983, 1991) three isomorphic mechanisms construct the bases of institutional theory (see Table 12.1). Most of these ideas overlap. However, Scott is more about elements while DiMaggio and Powell are more concerned about processes and the isomorphic processes of DiMaggio and Powell are preferred as representative of institutional theory to dissect the motivations of the Japanese IRs publishers. The three processes also cover almost all the elements of Scott's three pillars and stretch to other associated ideas too (Miner, 2006). Laine (2009), Contrafatto (2014) and Madein (2020) analyzed Finnish, Italian and Japanese institutional contexts of CSRs, respectively, by referring to institutional theory's pillars or mechanisms. The following items in Table 12.4 are utilized to explain the managerial motivation behind publishing IRs based on institutional theory.

Table 12.4 Mechanism Items that Influence the Context of Japanese CSRs/IRs

Coercive isomorphism	*Normative isomorphism*	*Mimetic isomorphism*
Laws and sanctions TSE listing requirements	Major guidelines and Government Pension and Investment Fund (GPIF) Awards, ratings and networks Environmental and social Awareness of Japanese Companies Corporate philosophy and culture Societal values of Japanese people	Globalized corporate practices Model companies

Coercive Isomorphism

Laws and Sanctions

In Japan, different types of acts influence corporate social reporting practices and there is no one dedicated act for such practices. Most of these acts are associated with ministry notification protocols and sanctions (see Table 12.5 for a list of these acts).

It is worth noting that not all the acts have sanctions associated with them and there lies an option of providing notification (explanation) when an entity fails to report. Specifically, Act No. 77 of 2004 imposes a sanction on the executive officers of some specific corporations to issue an environmental report; however, article 11 of this act encourages (does not force) large corporations to disclose the same without a particular sanction for failure. This act also recommends assurance reporting; following this act, Matsushita Electric reported a third-party assurance for its environmental report in 2006; Fujitsu and Sony Corporation have also been doing the same since 2000 and 2001. Notably, the other acts in Table 12.5 (except Act No. 77 and 25) demand that the companies notify related authorities only. However, CSRs of Sony Corporation, Panasonic Corporation and Fujitsu offer this information voluntarily (Madein, 2020).

Interestingly, Japan is classified as a code law country with a weak institutional setting that offers less investor protection than common law countries, such as the United Kingdom and the United States (Aman et al., 2021; Ball et al., 2000). Additionally, the Japanese Company Act (Act No. 86, 2005) does not press on any specific ESG issue-based disclosure. There is only a couple of corporate governance-based requirements regarding director numbers and committee members in articles 373 and 400 and the annexed detailed statements for a separate business report in article 435. Furthermore, the Order for Enforcement of the Companies Act (Cabinet Order No 364, 2005) asks for company officers' names, positions, remuneration amounts/policies/methods and so on in the business reports. According to the substitution hypothesis, companies that lie in a weak institutional setup-based country function as a substitute of the system (in

Table 12.5 Acts Influencing Japanese CSR Practice and Related Sanctions (Adapted from Mahmud (2022))

Year	*Act*	*Reporting focus*	*Penalty*
2020	Act on Improving Transparency and Fairness of Digital Platforms	Refusal criteria to a deal, search ranking factors, terms and conditions to acquire data about sellers' items and consumers' buying behavior	Up to 500,000 JPY
2015	Act on Promotion of Women's Participation and Advancement in the Workplace, Act No. 64	Rates of newly hired female employees, gender gap, working hours, female manager rates and gender equality action plan	N/A
2004	Act on the Promotion of Business Activities with Environmental Consideration, Act No. 77	Environmental information	Up to 200,000 JPY
1999	Act on Confirmation, etc. of Release Amounts of Specific Chemical Substances in the Environment and Promotion of Improvements to the Management Thereof, Act No. 86	Disclosures related to the Pollutant Release and Transfer Register' (PRTR), management of chemical substance	Up to 200,000 JPY
1998	Act on Promotion of Global Warming Countermeasures, Act No. 117	Carbon dioxide equivalent greenhouse gas emission	200,000 JPY
1986	Railway Business Act, Act No. 92	Safety reports: management of safety challenges	N/A
1979; amended in 2008	Act on the Rational Use of Energy, Act No. 49	Efficient usage of energy in factories and business areas	Up to 500,000 JPY
1970; amended in 2010	Act on Waste Management and Public Cleansing, Act No. 137	Waste management status and process	Financial sanction
1952	Civil Aeronautics Act, Act No. 231	Safety reports: management of safety challenges	N/A
1948; amended in 2006 and 2019	Financial Instrument and Exchange Act, Act No. 25	Numbers of females in managerial and executive positions, corporate management strategy, directors' remuneration, cross-shareholdings and corporate governance	N/A

the voluntary aspect) and are more likely to publish integrated reports to make up for the weak links (Vaz et al., 2016).

TSE Listing Requirements

The Tokyo Stock Exchange (TSE) requires the companies that wish to be listed to follow specific disclosure requirements that were in effect from June 11, 2021. The requirements are: (a) disclosing board independence and a skill-matrix of the board members, (b) disclosing policies and voluntary measurable targets to promote diversity—engaging non-Japanese, female and aged professionals—in senior management, (c) disclosing human resource development policies focusing on diversity along with their implementation, (d) disclosing basic policies and sustainability-initiatives of the company, (e) enriching the quality and quantity of climate-based disclosures referring to Task Force on Climate-Related Financial Disclosures (TCFD) recommendations or other similar international frameworks, (f) providing disclosures in English along with Japanese.

Furthermore, as a listing rule, companies' material environmental and social information must be immediately disclosed using TDnet (Timely Disclosure Network). Changes to this information must also be filed with a material change report. Moreover, a report containing comparable corporate governance information is also expected.

Normative Isomorphism

Guidelines

There are four guidelines from the Ministry of Environment (MOE), Ministry of Economy, Trade and Industry (METI), Financial Services Agency (FSA) and Japan Exchange Group (JPX) that make a flexible and alternatively interpretable framework for the CSRs/IRs preparers of Japan. The guidelines have various versions pertaining to different years. The older versions hinged more towards the idea of environmental reporting; however, the new versions hanker after broad coverage of sustainability issues and disclosure transparency and tilt towards corporate social reporting (see Table 12.6 for more detail).

In addition to the mentioned guidelines, the Government Pension and Investment Fund (GPIF) under the Minister of Health, Labour and Welfare plays an influential role in guiding the ESG-elements of the Japanese CSRs/IRs. The GPIF was founded in 2006 and currently has the largest pool of investment funds in the world, accumulating Japan's pension reserve. It has its ESG-themed indexes as benchmarks for passive investment. These indexes and the preferred ESG-indicators guide Japanese CSR practitioners to select certain disclosure items in their reports (Reporting Exchange, 2019).

Awards, Ratings and Networks

Two Japanese environmental reporting awards are top-rated, namely the Environmental Communication Award (ECA) and Environmental Reporting

Table 12.6 Four Major Guidelines, Contents and Latest Revisions (Adapted from Mahmud (2022))

Guidelines and year	*Focus*	*Reporting requirements*	*Latest addition/ revision*
Environmental Reporting Guideline by Ministry of Environment (MOE) 2000, 2012, 2018	Integrated environmental reporting with an attachment to international regulation and practical trends. It pushes entities to report their unique context of materiality	Basic information related to environmental reporting, major environmental issues along with performance indicators	Forward-looking non-financial data, financial impact of environmental issues
Guidance for Integrated Corporate Disclosure and Company–Investor Dialogue for Collaborative Value Creation, 2017 by Ministry of Economy, Trade and Industry (METI)	Facilitating collaborative value creation integrating the demands of both the managers and investors which is centered on the idea of the entity's unique value creation process and constructive engagement of these parties	Corporate values, business model, sustainability/growth, strategy, performance and KPIs, governance	2017 version is the only one so far
Stewardship Code by Financial Services Agency (FSA) 2014, 2017, 2020	Ensuring that the institutional investors are aware of their stewardship responsibilities and discharge related tasks	Clarified stewardship responsibilities and related degree of fulfillment, policy of managing conflict of interests, sustainable growth-related issues, voting policy and related activity	Broad ESG issues, reasons for voting on agenda items, principles regarding institutional investors' service providers
Corporate Governance Code by Japan Exchange Group (JPX) 2015, 2018, 2021	Setting fundamental principles for effective corporate governance and items for engagement for the investors and entities	Rights of the shareholders, stakeholder cooperation, board responsibilities, stakeholder dialogue	Increased board independence, diversity promotion, more attention to ESG issues

Award (ERA). These two award platforms have a single goal to improve CSR quality in Japan. The first one was established in 1997 and supported by the Ministry of Environment and Global Environmental Forum and the second one was initiated jointly by Toyo-Keizai Inc. and Green Reporting Forum in 1998. The Environmental Communication Award platform has interesting criteria. For example, it gives more points for negative disclosures, economic impact-based environmental management and accounting information, and biodiversity facts; since 2009, it has declared special awards for biodiversity and environmental financial reports.

In Japan, independent research institutes, universities and newspapers collect information on environmental conservation efforts of various firms and publish the results. Nikkei Business Publication's Environmental Brand Survey—introduced in 2000—happens to be one of the pioneers in the Japanese environmental ranking arena. It started to rate Japanese companies' environmental communication by awarding points and ranking them since 2004.

The Network for Environmental Reporting (NER) was established by various entities in 1998. Government (MOE), companies, numerous organizations, academic institutions and even citizens caring for environmental reporting are contributing to this initiative. This network was mainly led by the Japanese society. With the help of its members, this network collaborates with various stakeholders and dispatches information widely to improve CSR quality. Interestingly, some of its members received awards from the two reporting award platforms mentioned in the last paragraph (MOE, 2000).

Environmental and Social Awareness of Japanese Companies

Comprehension of the Japanese companies' environmental and social awareness warrants the understanding of Japan's influential economic associations and Japanese companies' eagerness to earn environmental management-related certification. These two aspects influence the disclosures of CSRs considerably.

Japan has three major economic coalitions such as *Keizaidoyukai*, *Nihon Shokokaigisho* and *Keidanren*. Among them, *Keidanren* (Japan Business Federation) is the most influential body mainly consisting of listed companies. It was initially established in 1946. However, the current *Keidanren* was modified in 2002 by merging with *Nikkeiren* (Japan Federation of Employers' Associations). Now, it has 1,461 Japanese companies as members and 109 nation-wide industry associations. Its core approach to CSR is that such an activity should be voluntary and should not be forced by anybody. In 1991, it established the "Corporate Behavior Charter" to guide corporations regarding their social role. Presently, it is preaching sustainable capitalism through green growth, supply chain reformation aligned with Society 5.0, work style reform, diversity promotion, revitalization of local society, social security reform, and innovation reformation (Tanimoto, 2013; Keidanren, 2021). Since almost 1,500 listed companies are partners to the initiatives of *Keidanren*, it impacts their social activities and corporate social reporting immensely.

Japanese companies are also keen to earn Environmental Management System (EMS) certification from the ISO authority. In terms of achieving EMS—ISO 14001—certification, they are one of the top performers in the world (ISO, 2017). Additionally, the contents of the Japanese CSRs almost always depict adherence to EMS certification. Hence, the ISO 14001 certification is very much part and parcel of the ESG disclosure mechanism. The sustainability report of Canon (Canon, 2019) and the integrated report of Maxwell Holdings Ltd (Maxwell, 2019) serve as good examples of CSRs with such certification. Other certifications worth mentioning include Forest Management Certification from Forest Stewardship Council (FSC) and Eco Mark Certification from Japan Environmental Association (JEA). The former is related to how a company interacts with natural resources, such as wood, and the latter is aligned with ISO 14020 and ISO 14024 that certify environmental conservation-related attributes of products.

Corporate Philosophy and Culture

The Japanese ethical business code is attached to the idea of *kyosei*. This term is synonymous with the notion of fair business practice and corporate responsibility towards society (Boardman and Kato, 2003). According to Wokutch and Shepard (1999), the concept of *kyosei* can be expanded to include the ideas of environmental protection, humanization of the workplace, embracing diversity, broadening the coverage of stakeholders—customers, staff, shareholders, suppliers, competitors—other than shareholders and the macro view of business ethics along with social responsibility that embed local and regional communities. On top of it, Japanese entities are more likely to embrace the idea of *jishukisei* (self-regulation) than other countries. Self-regulation denotes a configuration of formal and informal boundaries adhered to by a specific group (Porter and Ronit, 2006). It also encompasses companies' voluntary approach toward environmental performance in an institutional setting featured with a dearth of government standards (Volden and Wiseman, 2012).

Japanese employees have a tight internal relationship with each other. They work the hardest, respect their seniors, accept seniority-based payment and promotion, assist others in time of need, are always ready for additional responsibilities and believe in long-term tenure. All these features contribute towards an internally collaborative and cohesive culture (Japan Intercultural Consulting, 2021; Miroshnik and Basu, 2014), creating a specific kind of norm inside the workspace.

Societal Value of the Japanese People

Japanese citizens care about the environment and they are active in initiating various groups and networks to trigger environmental care in communities and companies. In 1993, the Japan Center for a Sustainable Environment and Society (JACSES) was established. This group is headed by academics and experts from society and their mission is to achieve environmental and social justice through policy research and advocacy. They were instrumental in constructing NER—Network for Environmental Reporting—in 1998, promoting research to improve environmental reporting quality (MOE, 2000). Moreover, Japanese people are accustomed to follow a complex garbage disposal system, which reconfirms their attention to nature. Their environmental care is noted by both the governments and companies. According to MOE (2000), local inhabitants are enthusiastic to note the environmental impacts of businesses on their neighborhood because they are skeptical about the potential consequences which may be caused by those businesses. For example, Canon (2019) disclosed the initiative of a local community that signed a business continuity plan (BCP) agreement with them to share local knowledge regarding natural disasters. They also collaborated in biodiversity conservation activities.

Two typical terms—*tatemae* and *honne*—define psychological standpoints of mutual harmony and care of the Japanese people. *Tatemae* denotes an individual's adherence to social norms and *honne* means personal motivation and opinions. Traditionally, the Japanese people are ready to sacrifice their *honne* to accept and maintain social norms leading towards harmonious interpersonal relationships and camaraderie. Wagatsuma and Rosett (1983) and Sato et al. (2018) postulate that this is still the case with Japanese individuals.

Mimetic Isomorphism

Globalization of Corporate Practices

In the 1980s, the Japanese financial market gradually opened itself to the world and international investors started to grab ownership of Japanese firms (Fujiyama, et al., 2019). In the 1990s, these outlandish investors progressively became a large part of the ownership chunk and emphasized detailed corporate disclosures (Desender et al., 2016) and non-financial information. On this note, positive impacts of globalization on CSR were evidenced by Tanimoto and Suzuki (2005) and Fukukawa and Teramoto (2009). In the late 1990s, the United States and EU countries were the major markets for Japan. These regions were the frontrunners in practicing CSR. Gradually, Japanese companies started to follow their non-financial reporting benchmarks, even if not explicitly warranted by them (Madein, 2020). As additional evidence, eco-fund managers from the United States and the European Union regions started to show attention to Japanese companies around the late 1990s, which fast-forwarded the current growth of CSR practices in Japan (Kawamura, 2003). Consequently, the Eco Survey from 1998 to 2003 confirms that in publishing environmental reports, Japanese companies used to follow the practices of other countries, especially the European Union and the United States (Madein, 2020).

Following this overseas influence, Japanese companies refer to multiple international frameworks. Currently, the most popular global framework in Japan is GRI

(PWC, 2020); other popular international frameworks include Environmental Reporting Guidelines, Guidance for Integrated Corporate Disclosure and Company–Investor Dialogue for Collaborative Value Creation, ISO 14000 and 26000, and the UN Global Compact (Ali et al., 2015; Albrecht and Greenwald, 2014; Tanaka, 2015).

Model Companies

Fortune 500 companies are considered models of innovation, and they utilize their IRs to mitigate the negative impacts of their environment-damaging actions. Hence, their adoption and presentation of IRs are pursued by other firms (Kılıç et al., 2020).

The two environmental reporting awards mentioned in the last section (ECA and ERA) consistently chose Fujitsu, IBM Japan, Matsushita Electric and Sony Corporation as top environmental reporting firms from 1997 to 2000. These companies are pioneers in setting up quality CSR practices by showing the path for the inclusion of proper contents, scope of topics, methods of reporting and presentation. Sony Corporation defined a proper scope of CSR. IBM Japan was the first of its kind to include environmental financial information. Fujitsu was among the first generation of companies that obtained assurance for environmental accounting information. Matsushita Electric was a master in depicting information through graphical illustration. In addition, two series of Eco Survey in 2014 and 2015 confirmed that 39% and 33%, respectively, of the companies used these model companies' environmental reports as reference. Hence, it can be assumed that the top companies selected by ECA and ERA have shown model paths for the pursuant firms (Madein, 2020).

Discussion

Coercive Isomorphism

Coercion is primarily sourced from the regulatory authority and their boundaries (DiMaggio and Powell, 1983). The acts mentioned in the "laws and sanction" section refer to various reporting (notification) requirements of specific entities to different authorities. They also demonstrate the financial sanction related to a "false report" or "no report" scenario. This context exerts formal pressure on the specific entities and coerces them to follow a certain path of reporting or notification through CSR or other forms of communication channels. Moreover, similar sort of studies in other regions also found that legislation leads toward extended reporting, including Chelli et al. (2014) in France, Dumitru et al. (2017) in Poland and Romania, Fallan and Fallan (2009) in Norway, Frost (2007) in Australia, Luo et al., (2017) in China and Weber (2014) in developing countries. Furthermore, TSE's listing requirements for disclosures related to diversity, board independence, sustainability and human resource development add another source of coercion to the report preparers since getting listed is related to the long-term survival of firms. Amran and Devi (2007) were on the same page studying the impact of Bursa Malaysia's requirements on the motivation for publishing CSRs in Malaysia.

However, in addition to the coercive sources, one must bear in mind the code law adherence and flexible (comply or explain) mindset of the Japanese government in setting and implementing boundaries for companies (Aman et al., 2021; Choi and Aguilera, 2009). Although this context is congenial for developing integrated reporting (Vaz et al., 2016), it weakens the position of coercive isomorphism a little bit.

Normative Isomorphism

Japanese citizens are environmentally aware individuals who sponsor and participate in various environmental initiatives. In addition, they adapt *tatemae* to follow social norms and harmony. Consequently, they expect the companies to report on their environmental and social performance and reward the firms with quality reporting practices. Similarly, the Japanese government wants companies to report their material ESG issues. However, the government does not always coerce companies to do so. Rather, it is flexible enough to give companies room for alternative interpretations and presentations (Lewin et al., 1995; Choi and Aguilera, 2009), hence the government expects them to behave like responsible corporate citizens. Logically, normative mechanisms are attached to values that lead toward desirable behaviors (DiMaggio and Powell, 1983) and the desired behaviors from the perceptions of the society and government pave a path for the advancement of corporate social reporting/integrated reporting (Bebbington et al., 2012).

Corporate philosophy is dependent on shared values (Picken, 1987) which is an essential vibrator of normative mechanism (DiMaggio and Powell, 1983). On this note, Japanese companies follow *kyosei* that vouches for CSR and care for others. This creates a positive vibe for social reporting. Furthermore, a strong culture creates employees' distinctive version of reality or norm, which is difficult to alter (Ledford et al., 1995). Japanese companies have a robust internally collaborative culture that is congenial for adopting and developing integrated reporting (García-Sánchez et al., 2013). Additionally, they participate in the *Keidanren*'s Voluntary Action Plan and are keen enough to pursue various environmental management and conservation-related certifications. This confirms that Japanese firms are ready to sacrifice their *honne* (personal motivation) and practice corporate social reporting by accepting *tatemae* (compliance with norms) pursuing *jishukisei* (self-regulation) (Schaede, 1999).

Furthermore, normative isomorphism is dependent on two attributes of professionalization: (a) resting education and legitimation on a cognitive base and (b) diffusing the legitimate ideas rapidly through professional networks (DiMaggio and Powell, 1983). Four guidelines (Environmental Reporting Guidelines, Guidance for Integrated Corporate Disclosure and Company–Investor Dialogue for Collaborative Value Creation, Stewardship

Code, Corporate Governance Code) along with ESG-index preference of Government Pension and Investment Fund, projects and publications of *Keidanren*, certification requirements, award criteria, and scoring rule of rating rest on a cognitive base and form a norm regarding the dissemination of ESG information. Subsequently, *Keidanren*'s network of almost 1,500 listed companies, Network of Environmental Reporting and reporting awards aid the diffusion of norms matured in cognitive base. In this way, normative isomorphism triggers a specific pattern of reporting corporate social activities. Some related studies found a positive relationship between normative mechanisms and the quality or expansion of corporate social reporting (e.g., Dumitru et al., 2017; Amran and Haniffa, 2011).

Mimetic Isomorphism

According to DiMaggio and Powell (1983), when a firm does not have a clear connection between its means and ends, its goal becomes vague, leading itself to an uncertain terrain. This uncertainty forces it to find a model or leading companies and mime their organizational practices to be consistent with the top firms (Shabana et al., 2017). Uncertainty of the Japanese firms can primarily be linked to the flexibility of guideline interpretation (Choi and Aguilera, 2009), the influence of global corporate practice and leading companies (Komura, 2009), as well as the emergence of model companies through an award or rating culture (Madein, 2020).

When firms follow flexible guidelines and assume multiple interpretations in preparing CSRs, they are most likely to become confused regarding the content, format and types of information. According to MOE (2017), environmental disclosure practice in around 2015 was reduced by a significant margin due to the voluntary nature of reporting (thus creating uncertainty) and a number of companies were requesting a specific disclosure framework.

Additionally, Japanese firms were influenced by foreign ownership and reporting practices of their major markets, that is, the United States and EU countries. These two regions were leading the idea of corporate social reporting in the 1990s and Japanese entities were in an uncertain territory regarding CSR and tried to mimic the reporting patterns of these model regions. Interestingly, they still mimic them, and therefore their preference towards various international CSR frameworks. Nowadays, South Africa is the only territory that has a mandate for IR and is considered as one of the leading IR-practicing countries. At present, Japanese firms are also replicating the IR practices of South Africa (Arul et al., 2021; Maroun, 2019). Moreover, there have been some consistent toppers in receiving environmental reporting awards and ratings in Japan and these companies are perceived as model companies. The others mimic their reporting practices to be on the same apex footing. The impact of mimetic forces on CSR is documented by various researchers, such as Aerts et al. (2006), Kannenberg and Schreck (2019) and Martínez-Ferrero and García-Sánchez (2017).

Conclusion

The motivations of report preparers to publish IRs vary. Some may try to defend themselves against reputation loss, some may want to take advantage of a special opportunity, or some may just desire to follow the frontrunning CSR practitioners in an uncertain state. Regardless of the scenario, institutional theory is well-posed to explain the motivation behind IR publication by utilizing three mechanisms, namely coercive, normative and mimetic. Furthermore, the institutional setting of Japanese CSR comprises flexible laws and guidelines, harmony-centered societal values and a social responsibility-based business code. These features constitute a suitable setup for the development of integrated reporting practice.

The Japanese CSR arena is coerced by a few laws and listing requirements. Some of these laws apply to specific entities and provide a "comply or explain" based flexibility for the companies. Therefore, Japanese companies enjoy a voluntary terrain of CSR/IR. Hence, it can be concluded that, by "texts", Japanese report preparers are coerced to disclose through IRs. In reality, "norms" can explain better regarding their primary motivation toward IR practices. Mimetic isomorphism has a voice in interpreting the managerial motivation of IR publications. Due to the high degree of flexibility, Japanese companies face uncertainties while reporting; therefore, they simply mimic the model domestic or foreign companies.

Finally, it can be concluded that the strength of the coercive mechanism in explaining the managerial motivation for publishing Japanese IRs is low. In contrast, normative and mimetic mechanisms have the strongest and most moderate influences, respectively, in rationalizing the same. Interestingly, these mechanisms are primarily based on the sources of irrational motivation. However, rational legitimacy-based motivation of managers can be directly tied up to mimetic isomorphism and indirectly to the other types. The results of this research may vary marginally due to the subjectivity of the coding and theme creation process as well as the uniqueness of the Japanese CSR context. This study will benefit researchers and standard-setters of the CSR domain who may draw value from the institutional theory-based contextual frameworks. Future research lies in empirically understanding the impacts of the framed contextual determinants on published CSRs/IRs.

References

Aerts, W., Cormier, D. and Magnan, M. (2006). Intra-industry imitation in corporate environmental reporting: An international perspective. *Journal of Accounting and Public Policy*, 25(3), 299–331.

Albrecht, P. and Greenwald, C. (2014). Financial materiality of sustainability–The Japanese context. *Journal of Corporate Citizenship*, 22(56), 31–52.

Ali, M., Haider, M.B. and Islam, M.T. (2015). Revisiting corporate social disclosure in Japan. In Noronha, C. (Ed.), *Corporate Social Disclosure: Critical Perspectives in China and Japan*. Basingstoke: Palgrave Macmillan.

Ali, W. and Rizwan, M. (2013). Factors influencing Corporate Social and Environmental Disclosure (CSED) practices in the developing countries: An institutional theoretical perspective. *International Journal of Asian Social Science*, 3(3), 590–609.

Aman, H., Beekes, W. and Brown, P. (2021). Corporate governance and transparency in Japan. *International Journal of Accounting*, 56(1), 1–40.

Amran, A. and Haniffa, R. (2011). Evidence in development of sustainability reporting: A case of a developing country. *Business Strategy and the Environment*, 20(3), 141–156.

Amran, A. and Devi, S.S. (2007). Corporate social reporting in Malaysia: An institutional perspective. *World Review of Entrepreneurship, Management and Sustainable Development*, 3(1), 20–36.

Aoki, M. (2007). Conclusion: Whither Japan's corporate governance? In Aoki, M., Jackson, G. and Miyajima, H. (Eds.), *Corporate Governance in Japan*. New York: Oxford University Press.

Arul, R., De Villiers, C. and Dimes, R. (2021). Insights from narrative disclosures regarding integrated thinking in integrated reports in South Africa and Japan. *Meditari Accountancy Research*, 29(4), 720–739.

Ashforth, B.E. and Gibbs, B.W. (1990). The double-edge of organizational legitimation. *Organization Science*, 1(2), 177–194.

Ball, R., Kothari, S.P. and Robin, A. (2000). The effect of international institutional factors on properties of accounting earnings. *Journal of Accounting and Economics*, 29(1), 1–51.

Bebbington, J., Kirk, E.A. and Larrinaga, C. (2012). The production of normativity: A comparison of reporting regimes in Spain and the UK. *Accounting, Organizations and Society*, 37(2), 78–94.

Bhatia, A. and Makkar, B. (2018). Cross-country comparison of CSR reporting practices – Evidenced from institutional theory in India and China. *International Journal of Sustainable Strategic Management*, 6(2), 117–144.

Boardman, C. and Kato, H. (2003). The Confucian roots of business kyosei. *Journal of Business Ethics*, 48(4), 317–333.

Boyatzis, R.E. (1998). *Transforming Qualitative Information: Thematic Analysis and Code Development*. Thousand Oaks, CA: Sage.

Canon. (2019). Canon Sustainability Report 2019. Available at: https://global.canon/en/csr/report/index.html

Chelli, M., Durocher, S. and Richard, J. (2014). France's new economic regulations: Insights from institutional legitimacy theory. *Accounting, Auditing and Accountability Journal*, 27(2), 283–316.

Choi, S. and Aguilera, R.V. (2009). Corporate social responsibility dynamics in South Korea and Japan: A comparative analysis. In Mallin, C.A. (Ed.), *Corporate Social Responsibility: A Case Study Approach*. Cheltenham: Edward Elgar.

Comyns, B. (2018). Climate change reporting and multinational companies: Insights from institutional theory and international business. *Accounting Forum*, 42(1), 65–77.

Contrafatto, M. (2014). The institutionalization of social and environmental reporting: An Italian narrative. *Accounting, Organizations and Society*, 39(6), 414–432.

De Freitas Netto, S.V., Sobral, M.F.F., Ribeiro, A.R.B. and Soares, G.R.D.L. (2020). Concepts and forms of greenwashing: A systematic review. *Environmental Sciences Europe*, 32(1), 19.

Deegan, C. (2014). An overview of legitimacy theory as applied within the social and environmental accounting literature. In Unerman, J., Bebbington, J. and O'Dwyer, B. (Eds.), *Sustainability Accounting and Accountability*. New York: Routledge.

Depoers, F. and Jérôme, T. (2020). Coercive, normative, and mimetic isomorphisms as drivers of corporate tax disclosure: The case of the tax reconciliation. *Journal of Applied Accounting Research*, 21(1), 90–105.

Desender, K.A., Aguilera, R.V., Lopezpuertas-Lamy, M. and Crespi, R. (2016). A clash of governance logistics: Foreign ownership and board monitoring. *Strategic Management Journal*, 37(2), 349–369.

Dillard, J.F., Rigsby, J.T. and Goodman, C. (2004). The making and remaking of organization context: Duality and the institutionalization process. *Accounting, Auditing and Accountability Journal*, 17(4), 506–542.

DiMaggio, P.J. and Powell, W.W. (1983). The iron cage revisited: Institutional isomorphism and collective rationality in organizational fields. *American Sociological Review*, 48(2), 147–160.

DiMaggio, P.J. and Powell, W.W. (1991). Introduction. In Powell, W.W. and DiMaggio, P.J. (Eds.), *The New Institutionalism in Organizational Analysis*. Chicago, IL: University of Chicago Press.

Dumitru, M., Dyduch, J., Guşe, R. and Krasodomska, J. (2017). Corporate reporting practices in Poland and Romania – An ex-ante study to the new non-financial reporting European directive. *Accounting in Europe*, 14(3), 279–304.

El-Bassiouny, D. and El-Bassiouny, N. (2019). Diversity, corporate governance and CSR reporting: A comparative analysis between top-listed firms in Egypt, Germany and the USA. *Management of Environmental Quality*, 30(1), 116–136.

Fallan, E. and Fallan, L. (2009). Voluntarism versus regulation: Lessons from public disclosure of environmental performance information in Norwegian companies. *Journal of Accounting and Organizational Change*, 5(4), 472–489.

Frost, G.R. (2007). The introduction of mandatory environmental reporting guidelines: Australian evidence. *Abacus*, 43(2), 190–216.

Fujiyama, K., Gray, S.J. and Koga, Y. (2019). Transitioning from a bank towards an equity financing system in Japan: The impact on income smoothing practices over 40 years. *Proceedings of the Korean Accounting Association*, 1, 1–37.

Fukukawa, K. and Teramoto, Y. (2009). Understanding Japanese CSR: The reflections of managers in the field of global operations. *Journal of Business Ethics*, 85(S1), 133–146.

García-Sánchez, I.-M., Rodríguez-Ariza, L. and Frías-Aceituno, J.V. (2013). The cultural system and integrated reporting. *International Business Review*, 22(5), 828–838.

Gauthier, J. (2013). Institutional theory and corporate sustainability: Determinant versus interactive approaches. *Organization Management Journal*, 10(2), 86–96.

Governance and Accountability Institute. (2017). Flash report: 85% of S&P 500 Index® companies publish sustainability reports in 2017. Available at: https://www.ga-institute.com/press-releases/article/flash-report-85-of-sp-500-indexR-companies-publish-sustainability-reports-in-2017.html

Greenwood, M., Jack, G. and Haylock, B. (2019). Toward a methodology for analyzing visual rhetoric in corporate reports. *Organizational Research Methods*, 22(3), 798–827.

Higgins, C. and Coffey, B. (2016). Improving how sustainability reports drive change: A critical discourse analysis. *Journal of Cleaner Production*, 136, 18–29.

Higgins, C. and Larrinaga, C. (2014). Sustainability reporting: Insights from institutional theory. In Unerman, J., Bebbington, J. and O'Dwyer, B. (Eds.), *Sustainability Accounting and Accountability*. New York: Routledge.

Ho, L.C.J. and Taylor, M.E. (2007). An empirical analysis of triple bottom line reporting and its determinants: Evidence from the United States and Japan. *Journal of International Financial Management and Accounting*, 18(2), 123–150.

ISO. (2017). The ISO survey of management system standard certifications: ISO 14001. *Environmental Management Systems - Requirements with Guidance for Use*. Available at: https://www.iso.org/the-iso-survey.html

Japan Intercultural Consulting. (2021). *Japanese Business Keywords*. Available at: https://japanintercultural.com/category/free-resources/articles/japanese-business-keywords

Kannenberg, L. and Schreck, P. (2019). Integrated reporting: Boon or bane? A review of empirical research on its determinants and implications. *Journal of Business Economics*, 89(5), 515–567.

Kawahara, N. (2017). Current trends and challenges in sustainability reporting practices in Japan - Literature review. *Journal of Business Studies*, 64(2), 353–382.

Kawamura, M. (2003). *Japanese Companies Launch a New Era of CSR Management in 2003*. Tokyo: NLI Research.

Keidanren. (2021). *Keidanren Annual Report 2021*. Available at: https://www.keidanren.or.jp/en/profile/ Keidanren_Annual_Report2021.pdf

Khan, M., Lockhart, J. and Bathurst, R. (2020). A multi-level institutional perspective of corporate social responsibility reporting: A mixed-method study. *Journal of Cleaner Production*, 265, 121739.

Kılıç, M., Uyar, A., Kuzey, C. and Karaman, A.S. (2020). Does institutional theory explain integrated reporting adoption of Fortune 500 companies? *Journal of Applied Accounting Research*, 22(1), 114–137.

Kokubu, K., Nashioka, E., Saio, K. and Imai, S. (2003). Two governmental initiatives on environmental management accounting and corporate practices in Japan. In Bennett, M., Rikhardsson, P.M. and Schaltegger, S. (Eds.), *Environmental Management Accounting—Purpose and Progress*. Dordrecht: Springer.

Komura, K. (2009). Consider the spread of sustainability report in Japan. *Journal of the Japan Association for Social and Economic System Studies*, 30, 89–95.

KPMG. (2019). *Survey of Integrated Reports in Japan*. Available at: https://home.kpmg/jp/en/home/insights/2020/03/integrated-reporting.html

Laine, M. (2009). Ensuring legitimacy through rhetorical changes? A Longitudinal interpretation of the environmental disclosures of a leading Finnish chemical company. *Accounting, Auditing and Accountability Journal*, 22(7), 1029–1054.

Ledford, G.E., Wendenhof, J.R. and Strahley, J.T. (1995). Realizing a corporate philosophy. *Organizational Dynamics*, 23(3), 5–19.

Legendre, S. and Coderre, F. (2013). Determinants of GRI G3 application levels: The case of the Fortune Global 500. *Corporate Social Responsibility and Environmental Management*, 20(3), 182–192.

Lewin, A.Y., Sakano, T., Stephens, C.U. and Victor, B. (1995). Corporate citizenship in Japan: Survey results from Japanese firms. *Journal of Business Ethics*, 14(2), 83–101.

Luo, X.R., Wang, D. and Zhang, J. (2017). Whose call to answer: Institutional complexity and firms' CSR reporting. *Academy of Management Journal*, 60(1), 321–344.

Madein, A. (2020). The institution of environmental reporting in Japan: An exploratory study. *Asia-Pacific Management Accounting Journal*, 15(3), 189–218.

Mahmud, M.T. (2019). Legitimacy theory and its relationship to CSR disclosures: A literature review. *The Keizai Ronkyu*, 163, 1–16.

Mahmud, M.T. (2020). Quest for a single theory to explain managerial motivations for sustainability disclosures: Legitimacy theory, stakeholder theory or institutional theory. *Bulletin of Japanese Association for International Accounting Studies*, 1–2, 135–159.

Mahmud, M.T. (2022). History and institutional setting of corporate social reporting (CSR): The Japanese context. *Journal of Innovation in Business Studies*. Accepted and Forthcoming.

Maroun, W. (2019). Does external assurance contribute to higher quality integrated reports? *Journal of Accounting and Public Policy*, 38(4), 106670.

Marquis, C., Toffel, M. and Zhou, Y. (2016). Scrutiny, norms, and selective disclosure: A global study of greenwashing. *Organization Science*, 27(2), 483–504.

Martínez-Ferrero, J. and García-Sánchez, I.-M. (2017). Coercive, normative and mimetic isomorphism as determinants of the voluntary assurance of sustainability reports. *International Business Review*, 26(1), 102–118.

Mata, C., Fialho, A. and Eugénio, T. (2018). A decade of environmental accounting reporting: What we know? *Journal of Cleaner Production*, 198, 1198–1209.

Maxwell. (2019). *Maxwell Holdings Ltd. Integrated Report 2019*. Available at: https://www2.maxell.co.jp/ir/pdf/MHD_IR19_E.pdf

Meyer, J.W. and Rowan, B. (1977). Institutionalized organizations: Form structure as myth and ceremony. *American Journal of Sociology*, 83(2), 340–363.

Miles, M.B., Huberman, A.M. and Saldaña, J. (2013). *Qualitative Data Analysis: A Methods Sourcebook*. Thousand Oaks, CA: Sage.

Miner, J.B. (2006). *Organizational Behavior 2: Essential Theories of Process and Structure*. New York: Routledge.

Miroshnik, V.W. and Basu, D. (2014). *Corporate Culture in Multinational Japanese Companies – A Japanese Perspective*. Basingstoke: Palgrave Macmillan.

MOE. (2000). Environmental reporting guidelines – Guidance for publishing environmental reporting. Available at: https://www.env.go.jp/en/policy/ssee/erg2000.pdf

MOE. (2017). 2015 results of the survey of environmentally friendly corporate behavior (in Japanese). Japan: Ministry of the Environment.

Moll, J., Burns, J. and Major, M. (2006). Institutional theory. In Hoque, Z. (Ed.), *Methodological Issues in Accounting: Theories and Methods*. London: Spiramus.

Oware, K.M. and Mallikarjunappa, T. (2022). CSR expenditure, mandatory CSR reporting and financial performance of listed firms in India: An institutional theory perspective. *Meditari Accountancy Research*, 30(1), 1–21.

Picken, S.D.B. (1987). Values and value related strategies in Japanese corporate culture. *Journal of Business Ethics*, 6(2), 137–143.

Porter, T. and Ronit, K. (2006). Self-regulation as policy process: The multiple and criss-crossing stages of private rule-making. *Policy Sciences*, 39(1), 41–72.

PWC. (2020). Sustainability reporting in Japan and Sweden - A brief comparison. Available at: https://www.pwc.com/jp/en/knowledge/column/sustainability-reporting-in-japan-and-sweden.html

Reporting Exchange. (2019). *Corporate and Sustainability Reporting Trends in Japan*. Available at: https://docs.wbcsd.org/2019/02/Corporate_and_sustainability_reporting_trends_in_Japan.pdf

Saka, C. and Burritt, R. (2003). Environmental accounting in Japan – Recent evidence. *Journal of the Asia Pacific Centre for Environmental Accountability*, 9(4), 4–10.

Sato, E., Matsuda, K. and Carducci, B.J. (2018). A factor analytical investigation of the Japanese translation of the Cheek-Buss Shyness Scale in support of the three-component model of shyness. *Personality and Individual Differences*, 124, 160–167.

Schaede, U. (1999). Self-regulation and the sanctuary strategy: Competitive advantage through domestic cooperation by Japanese firms. Center on Japanese Economy and Business, Working Paper 157, New York: Columbia University.

Schrader, A. (2019). Sustainability reporting across Asia: Trends and challenges. Available at: https://www.conference-board.org/blog/sustainability/Asia-Sustainability-Reporting-Trends

Scott, W.R. (1995). *Institutions and Organizations: Ideas, Interests and Identities.* Thousand Oaks, CA: Sage Publications.

Scott, W.R. (2008). Institutions and organizations: Ideas and interests. Los Angeles, CA: Sage Publications.

Shabana, K.M., Buchholtz, A.K. and Carroll, A.B. (2017). The institutionalization of corporate social responsibility reporting. *Business and Society*, 56(8), 1107–1135.

Tanaka, G. (2015). Corporate social disclosure practice in Japanese corporations: The case of Meiko Electronics. In Noronha, C. (Ed.), *Corporate Social Disclosure: Critical Perspectives in China and Japan.* Basingstoke: Palgrave Macmillan.

Tanimoto, K. and Suzuki, K. (2005). Corporate social responsibility in Japan: Analyzing the participating companies in global reporting initiative. European Institute of Japanese Studies, Working Paper 208, Stockholm: European Institute of Japanese Studies.

Tanimoto, K. (2013). Keidanren. In Idowu, S.O., Capaldi, N., Zu, L. and Gupta, A.D. (Eds.), *Encyclopedia of Corporate Social Responsibility.* Heidelberg: Springer.

Unerman, J. and Bennett, M. (2004). Increased stakeholder dialogue and the internet: Towards greater corporate accountability or reinforcing capitalist hegemony? *Accounting, Organizations and Society*, 29(7), 685–707.

Vaz, N., Fernandez-Feijoo, B. and Ruiz, S. (2016). Integrated reporting: An international overview. *Business Ethics: A European Review*, 25(4), 577–591.

Volden, C. and Wiseman, A.E. (2012). Governmental regulation and self-regulation. Available at: http://www.vanderbilt.edu/csdi/events/prvtgov_wiseman.pdf

Wagatsuma, H. and Rosett, A. (1983). Cultural attitudes towards contract law: Japan and the United States compared. *UCLA Pacific Basin Law Journal*, 2(1–2), 76–96.

Weber, O. (2014). Environmental, social and governance reporting in China. *Business Strategy and the Environment*, 23(5), 303–317.

Wokutch, R.E. and Shepard, J.M. (1999). The maturing of the Japanese economy: Corporate social responsibility implications. *Business Ethics Quarterly*, 9(3), 527–540.

13 Conceptualizing CSR Avoidance and Engagement

Duane Windsor

Introduction to CSR Avoidance and Engagement

This chapter provides a conceptual framework for defining corporate social responsibility (CSR) avoidance and engagement in contrast to corporate social irresponsibility (CSIR). The framework is a more precise formulation than the extant distinction between CSR and CSIR, as examined in Windsor (2013b). The current framework identifies a set of four general strategies for business executives in addressing responsibilities of the profit-seeking business sector toward society. These four strategies are located along a simple continuum from socially "bad" (CSIR) to socially "good" (CSR engagement) as defined externally to the firm. CSR engagement is good corporate citizenship. Bad and good define motives, actions, and outcomes as interlinked dimensions of corporate social performance (CSP), which is the impact of business activities on society (Wood, 1991, 2010). CSR, CSIR, and CSP form the key constructs for business responsibility reasoning.

The four strategic options take their definitions from assigned values for CSIR and CSR. Two options "avoid" CSR differently; two options "engage" with CSR differently. The pure avoidance options are CSIR (a negative value and combined logically with zero CSR) and strict neutrality (zero CSIR and zero CSR). In strict neutrality, the firm avoids both CSIR and CSR engagement. CSIR is when a business imposes social harm (a negative impact on social welfare) to generate profit. The violation might be ethical or legal (Friedman, 1970). Strict neutrality is the actual position advocated by Friedman (1970) for publicly traded corporations. Strictly speaking, Friedman (1970) exempts privately owned businesses from this position (a private business is the same as a household for philanthropy or altruism).

The two engagement options are public policy requirements for CSR and good corporate citizenship. In either engagement option, CSIR remains zero; however, CSR must be positive rather than zero (that is, neutral). Positive CSR actions can arise from two sources. Public policy imposes mandatory requirements on businesses. Typically, such requirements prohibit CSIR actions. However, public policy might also require CSR expenditures (illustrated by the 2013 Indian CSR law) or minimum conditions for the composition of the board of directors (as

DOI: 10.4324/9781003274575-16

by gender or race). Such requirements extend the idea of compliance with laws by mandating positive actions by businesses as distinct from prohibiting negative actions (CSIR). Good corporate citizenship undertakes voluntary actions and investments to improve social welfare and environmental sustainability. Voluntary actions (not required by public policy) can arise from responsiveness, profitable or competitive advantage opportunity, or virtue (principles and values). Virtue is the defining quality of good corporate citizenship. The continuum of strategic options can be understood as follows.

First, reckless misconduct (CSIR) is found at the socially harmful end. It is defined as harming any or all of society, stakeholders, or the natural environment. The irresponsibility may lie in legal violations or ethical violations permitted by law. However, the essence of irresponsibility is the harm that is difficult to conceal. A fundamental feature of such irresponsible misconduct is that business executives typically conceal and deny the actions involved.

Second along the continuum is avoidance of CSR. This strategy is, in effect, neutrality. Ideally, the business obeys law and ethics in the sense of strict compliance (avoidance of generating harm as defined by society in some way). Friedman (1970) rested his case against discretionary CSR by the executives of publicly traded firms on this neutrality. For example, businesses obey laws and basic principles of ethics for conducting business (like honesty and absence of fraud), but businesses do not engage in philanthropy.

Third is an expansion of mandatory public policy. The firm's strategy remains neutral in the form of strict compliance. However, in addition to defining bad and good for the firm, society increases requirements and expectations for prosocial contribution labeled CSR. This expansion is different from anti-CSIR requirements.

Fourth, at the socially good end, is an expansive conception of CSR engagement. Businesses undertake this expansion to make social contributions beyond the effects of reasonably neutral market operations. CSR engagement involves trying to solve the world's problems through market operations or nonmarket activities.

The remainder of the chapter is organized as follows. The second section provides a formal exposition of the conceptual framework, aiming to address the adoption of CSR engagement both empirically and normatively. Figure 13.1 demonstrates the conceptual framework in terms of the four strategies. The section amplifies the problem of authenticity vs. hypocrisy and "washing" for purposes of improving reputation without real contribution. The section provides examples of businesses to illustrate the strategies. The third section explains the social impact as emphasized by the chapter. Table 13.1 explains four general relationships between business and society regarding logical combinations of win and loss. The fourth section discusses the difference between instrumental corporate social responsiveness and moral CSR (CSRM). This chapter borrows the idea and acronym from Mitnick et al. (2022). The conclusion explains the implications of the approach developed in this chapter.

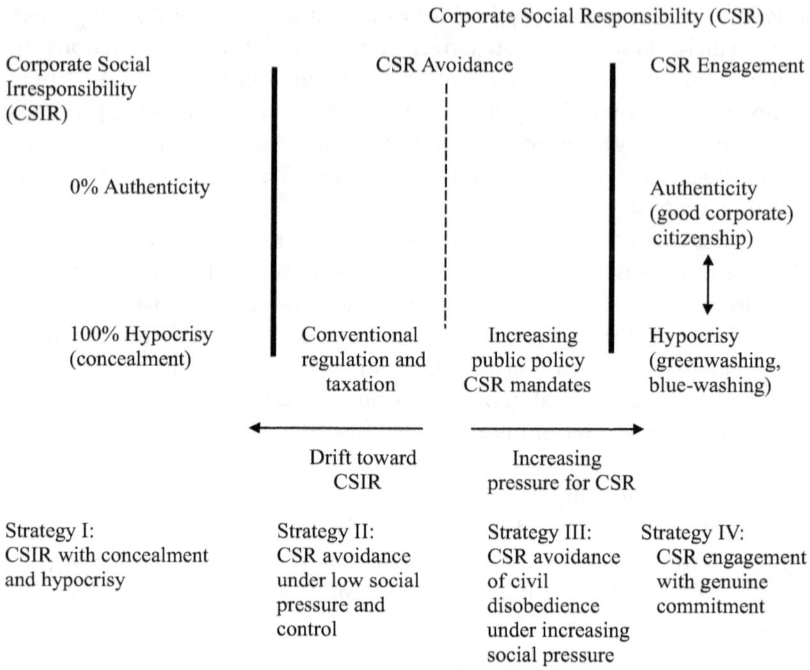

Figure 13.1 The Conceptual Framework for Four Strategic Options (Author's Development)

Exposition of the Conceptual Framework

The idea of CSR and how to construct a theory of CSR motives, actions, and impacts (see Aguinis and Glavas, 2012) is "essentially contested" (a term deriving from Gallie, 1955–56). Windsor (2006) noted that CSR is "contestable" and that the contest is unlikely to yield a theoretical synthesis. Okoye (2009) developed the notion of such a contest over all the basics of CSR (see Gond and Moon, 2011). Mitnick et al. (2021) further argued that what characterizes the CSR field is this contest, which results in over-theorization or competing theories grounded in different perspectives and disciplines. Economic, strategic, and institutional approaches to CSR are instrumental (what is good for the firm) and morally neutral (society is not necessarily superior to business). The economic approach (Friedman, 1970) is hostile to voluntary CSR, arguing that such activities should be a government responsibility. The strategic approach is that a firm should assess CSR activities in terms of advantages to the business. The institutional approach emphasizes the role of external pressures on the firm to adopt CSR practices (Campbell, 2007; Matten and Moon, 2008). A cross-country empirical study of formal

Table 13.1 Relationships between Business and Society (Author's Development)

	Society	
Business	*Gains*	*Losses*
Gains	*Ideal win–win outcome* • Competition • Efficiency • Effectiveness • Equity • Innovation • Sustainability (business, social, and environmental) • Welfare growth	*CSIR* • Monopolization • Negative externalities such as pollution and other harmful effects on common resources • Dishonesty and fraud • Corruption
Losses	*Social overreach* • Over-regulation • Over-taxation • Socialism or communism	*Lose–lose outcome* • For example, continuous pandemic with lockdowns and high casualty rates • For example, accelerating climate deterioration

and informal institutional pressures is available (Tolmie et al., 2020). These approaches are generally instrumental in the following sense (Husted and Allen, 2006; Husted et al., 2015): the firm maximizes something for its owners (e.g., profit, competitive advantage and strategic position, and social legitimacy); institutional pressures determine whether the firm can avoid CSR entirely or must invest (or pretend to invest) in CSR. Both the local institutional setting and the local social issues may affect the content of CSR engagement (Husted et al., 2016). Windsor (2006, 93) differentiated among three approaches as follows:

> Ethical responsibility theory advocates strong corporate self-restraint and altruism duties and expansive public policy strengthening stakeholder rights. Economic responsibility theory advocates market wealth creation subject only to minimalist public policy and perhaps customary business ethics. … Corporate citizenship language invokes a political metaphor providing neither true intermediate positioning nor theoretical synthesis.

A fundamental unresolved question concerns the adoption of CSR engagement. One can think of Friedman's CSR neutrality position as at least a rejection of CSIR. Relatively few scholars and managers are likely to embrace and defend explicitly wrong CSIR motives, actions, and outcomes. The problematic debate is about businesses moving beyond CSR avoidance to CSR engagement. This fundamental question separates into three issues.

1. Empirical: Why and where does an organization adopt CSR? Campbell (2007) proposed an institutional framework in which external pressures shape the adoption of CSR postures (Matten and Moon, 2008).
2. Normative: Why and where should an organization prescriptively adopt CSR? Friedman (1970) answered the question negatively: the answer is no CSR beyond compliance with laws and basic ethics. Much of the extant CSR literature is a debate with Friedman about this question. Mitnick et al. (2021) criticized the effort to be neutral, grounded in economic or strategic rationales, and formulated a case for CSRM. In essence, CSRM argues that a business must be anti-CSIR and pro-CSR engagement. Mere avoidance, whether in the form of compliance only with conventional regulation or expansive CSR public policy requirements, is not sufficient to qualify as CSRM. The moral responsibilities of business are high rather than low (see Epstein, 1999; Frederick, 1986). CSRM draws on the older foundations in Epstein and Frederick.
3. How to separate between businesses and governments: Business adoption might be voluntary (involving discretion permitted by public policy) or mandatory (explicitly or implicitly required by public policy). This question involves the selection of a perspective on CSR from the viewpoint of business or from the viewpoint of government (which might or might not correctly represent the viewpoint and interest of society).

Figure 13.1 provides a sketch of the conceptual framework. The conception comprises a definitional continuum with four general zones that correspond to the four strategic options identified at the beginning of the chapter. CSIR is at the negative end of the continuum. The opposite of CSIR, CSR, is at the positive end of the continuum. The two thick vertical lines separate different conceptions. CSIR is fundamentally different from any form of CSR avoidance or engagement. CSR engagement is, in turn, fundamentally different from any form of CSR avoidance. Avoidance can combine with compliance to social control. Engagement involves going beyond compliance to good corporate citizenship. The dashed vertical line around the center of the figure reflects a weaker differentiation between the two forms of CSR avoidance. Avoidance involves doing neither CSIR on one side nor CSR engagement on the other side. However, there can be a profound difference in the content of public policy requirements for business. This difference is between conventional public policy and expanding CSR requirements.

Negative and positive signs take meaning as harm to social welfare and improvement to social welfare, respectively. The essence of CSIR is harm to stakeholders, the natural environment, and, thus, society. Harm has a negative sign. In contrast, the essence of CSR engagement is intentional improvement in the welfare of stakeholders, the natural environment, and, thus, society. Social gain (beyond market outcomes) has a positive sign. CSR avoidance is the middle zone between these polar-opposite definitions (CSIR vs. CSR). A business neither harms nor improves social welfare beyond the outcomes of legally and ethically acceptable market actions. CSR avoidance is neutral concerning negative and positive signs associated with CSIR and CSR engagement. CSR avoidance has no sign; therefore, this zone is effectively the zero "point" between harm (i.e., negative sign) and improvement (i.e., positive sign). This definitional continuum forms the upper part of the framework in Figure 13.1.

Strategy I: CSIR Concealment

The essence of CSIR is the concealed imposition of harm on society, stakeholders, or the natural environment to make a profit. An illustration is an allegation against DuPont that, for an extended period, it concealed pollution and health risks associated with the production and consumption of Teflon coating, especially in West Virginia (Kourabas, 2016). Shapira and Zingales (2017), based on a study of DuPont documents released due to civil lawsuit, concluded that the DuPont CSIR concealment was rational so long as the likelihood of discovery and penalty was relatively low (see Dizik, 2018 for a summary).

Strategy II: CSR Avoidance

Classical CSR avoidance proceeds from Friedman's (1970) case against corporate philanthropy by the executives of publicly traded firms. These executives are agents of the shareholders rather than owners of the firm. The essence of this classical avoidance strategy is that (in principle) firms obey laws and basic ethics while avoiding CSR engagement.

A step beyond the Friedman position is to posit "creating social value" (Porter and Kramer, 2011). In CSV, the business finds profitable opportunities in solving social problems. The market mechanism can help with social problems; "doing well by doing good" operates effectively. This CSV approach is subject to criticism in the literature (see Lynn, 2021). The CSV approach can function in the ideal win–win cell of Table 13.1; however, it is limited to that cell. There are two empirical questions about CSV. First, CSV conditions, when they exist, are they, in fact, sufficiently profitable to attract business interest (Trudel and Cotte, 2009)? Second, regarding the scope of such CSV conditions, should there be many opportunities for profitable CSV investments?

CSV is a subset of the more general argument concerning a business case for CSR and environmental sustainability (Whelan and Frank, 2016). The basic idea of a business case approach is that the firm can find either short-term profit or long-term advantage and opportunity likely to generate future profit in a CSR investment option (Carroll and Shabana, 2010). For example, investing in CSR may generate value for customers and increase customer support for the business (Noked, 2011). McWilliams and Siegel (2001) formulated a business case model in which a firm does not undertake any CSR investment unless some stakeholder other than the shareholders is prepared to pay for the additional cost. For instance, if customers want green products, they should pay for the additional cost and maintain constant profit for the shareholders. Barnett (2019) pointed out that the business case typically amounts to stakeholder management and tends to omit what happens to society more broadly. The Noked and McWilliams-Siegel proposals illustrate stakeholder management rather than CSR.

The drift toward CSIR may include schemes for avoiding or evading public policy. There may be variations across countries or loopholes in legislation and regulation that permit such schemes to function. For example, businesses can evade taxation by various legal schemes (Windsor, 2015, 2017, 2018b). The correction for such a situation is some international agreement on minimum taxation of multinational enterprises. Such international agreement is in process. Nevertheless, concurrence ignores whether governments should tax businesses and capital for redistribution of wealth or regulation of perceived monopoly power (also subject to fines and breakup) as distinct from benefit taxation to cover costs of delivering government services to business. Progressive taxation may suit households, but the extension to businesses is a different policy issue.

Strategy III: Avoidance of Civil Disobedience

While Strategy III may seem to be a simple extension of Strategy II, two crucial differences exist. First, Strategy II addresses conventional regulation and taxation, illustrated by antimonopoly and anticorruption laws and control of negative externalities. Strategy III deals with a considerable expansion of social control to compel positive CSR contributions by a business. The Indian CSR statute 2013 requiring CSR spending is a step in this direction, as are legal requirements in some countries and the state of California specifying diversity in business governance boards. Strategy III, thus, deals with a fundamental change in the firm's external environment.

Second, businesses can only comply with laws everywhere by avoiding civil disobedience when there is a fundamental conflict between legal conceptions. The JPMorgan Chase and Co. Code of Conduct states:

> The Code of Conduct is a collection of rules and principles intended to assist employees and directors in making decisions about their conduct in relation to the firm's business. The Code is based on the fundamental understanding that we are all responsible for conducting business ethically and in compliance with the law everywhere we operate. No one should ever sacrifice integrity—or give the impression that they have—even if they think it would help the firm's business.
>
> (JPMorgan, n.d., para. 1)

JPMorgan and Chase is a globally operating financial institution of considerable size and importance (for a critique, see Strong, 2015). This neutrality involves a difficulty concerning civil disobedience. A neo-totalitarian dictatorship determines "law" and requires compliance just as much as does a constitutional democracy. A business cannot obey the law everywhere unless law everywhere is just. Civil disobedience involves making a moral judgment about compliance. One option is to exit from an unsatisfactory setting. However, a large country like the People's Republic of China (the PRC) is too large and financially crucial for a significant banking institution to exit voluntarily (although that institution must weigh the decision). JPMorgan is not a citizen of the PRC; however, even a citizen of the PRC must judge legal compliance within a moral framework.

Civil disobedience places a different perspective on corporate political activity (CPA), particularly for lobbying elected and appointed officials (Gregor, 2011; Schuler et al., 2019). One view of lobbying is that the process provides information, distinct from pressure, concerning the socially desirable content of public policy (Segal, 2021). Lobbying may concern private benefits to business. It can also concern social benefits. Government policy is not necessarily a socially desirable policy. Friedman (1970) was clear that businesses can lobby the government if such lobbying is part of the understanding for the political process.

Strategy IV: Authentic CSR Engagement

Authentic CSR engagement is the opposite of CSIR. Generally, the firm attempts to address social issues and make social contributions. Unilever promotes a strategic posture of CSR engagement as a sustainable business (Matsangou, 2016). Nestlé (n.d.) positioned its approach in terms of CSV.

Strategy IV is an interaction between executive values and capacity to design and executive CSR initiatives. How to do CSR is as important as why to do CSR (see Barnett et al., 2020). The strategy requires an orientation toward addressing social issues, even at cost to the business. The issue is the limit to such cost. For instance, virtually all countries prohibit bribery by foreign businesses. There is both a United Nation (UN) convention and regional multinational accords for prohibition. The next step beyond the refusal to pay bribes is direct anticorruption action by multinational enterprises (Windsor, 2019).

Authenticity, Hypocrisy, and Washing

The lower part of the Figure 13.1 framework provides an amplification of the basic idea. A difficulty is that a business may use CSR engagement as "greenwashing" or camouflage for doing nothing while pretending to do something approved as legitimate by society.

Figure 13.1, therefore, provides in the CSR engagement zone a distinction between "authenticity" and "hypocrisy". Authenticity means that CSR engagement reflects genuine values, beliefs, and norms concerning the desirability of positive social contributions by a business. The distinction appears as a continuum between authenticity and hypocrisy within the CSR engagement zone. CSIR typically involves concealment or a bet concerning the likelihood and timing of discovery. Therefore, the CSIR zone is synonymous with hypocrisy. Figure 13.1

characterizes this CSIR zone as 0% authenticity and 100% hypocrisy through intentional concealment.

There may be a difference between greenwashing (or blue-washing) to camouflage the reality of no CSR engagement generating no improvement (but not necessarily generating harm) and concealment to camouflage the reality of CSIR misconduct resulting in harm. At some location within the CSR avoidance zone, there is a tipping point beyond which the intentional avoidance of CSR engagement is likely to drift toward CSIR. This potential drift occurs because of the incentives in businesses for profit maximization without regard to laws and ethics. The drift might be intentional as a matter of business strategy or might occur through the deviant behavior of individuals or groups within the business. For the convenience of exposition, Figure 13.1 shows this tipping point as a line around the center of the continuum (within the CSR avoidance zone).

For example, Mackenzie (2021) argued that oil companies use carbon capture efforts (if undertaken) as a means of sidestepping the real problems in investing in net-zero emissions. Oil companies continue to generate emissions while trying to recapture those emissions technologically. The result might claim to be net-zero; however, there is damage and repair without resolving the continuing damage.

Figure 13.1 distinguishes between concealment as hypocrisy associated with CSIR and either greenwashing (Delmas and Burbano, 2011) or blue-washing as forms of hypocrisy associated with CSR engagement. CSIR's hypocrisy attempts to conceal misconduct. However, the effort is about concealment rather than the most general sense of whitewashing. Hypocrisy concerning CSR engagement involves distorting nonperformance to obtain public reputation benefits at the lowest cost. Greenwashing technically refers to environmental (i.e., green) concerns (Seele and Gatti, 2017); blue-washing technically refers to human rights concerns. Blue-washing refers to the blue color of the UN emblem, with a specific focus on the UN Global Compact's human rights principles (Zosso, 2019).

Washing is the effort to control business reputation by pretending to do something good or pretending not to be doing something bad. Haack et al. (2021) formulated a model in which CSR operates as bait-and-switch. Bogus CSR claims seek to attract stakeholders, such as customers and employees.

Authenticity is when business judgments, which may reflect self-interest, do not involve greenwashing or blue-washing (see Windsor, 2018a). Ting (2021) tested for hypocrisy by examining the CSR reports of businesses. One should find confirming evidence of genuine CSR efforts in those reports. However, it is difficult to assess CSR reporting because businesses are likely to under-report CSIR while emphasizing CSR. How to balance CSR good against CSIR bad is not resolved theoretically. The information in CSR reports may not fully disclose the company's actions.

Natural disasters may create an experimental condition to examine business CSR reactions. Fernando (2010) studied how two firms in Sri Lanka responded to the Boxing Day Asian tsunami. The author used interviews conducted in two phases, at 11 months and then at 35 months following the disaster date. The idea of the interview process was to capture information closer to and further away from the disaster. The first firm was Unilever Sri Lanka, a consumer goods company owned by Unilever, UK. The second firm, Brandix Apparel Limited, was headquartered in Sri Lanka. Although owned by a foreign multinational, Unilever Sri Lanka had operated since 1938. Brandix was an important local firm. Fernando (2010, 68) looked at "human impact, moral goodness, and unconditionality of social benefit" as dimensions of "organizational virtuousness".

The Social Impact Setting

The chapter proceeds from a social impact perspective for defining CSR (Windsor, 2022). A business CSR profile has negative, neutral, or positive impacts on social welfare and environmental sustainability in a social impact approach. Two more perspectives in the literature are instrumental and ethical. From an instrumental perspective, the business assesses CSR in terms of its economic effect on business. From an ethical perspective, the business assesses CSR based on its moral duties (a Kantian view) or its values and principles (a virtue theory view). The approach here is consequentialist regarding impacts on social welfare and environmental sustainability. All three issues in CSR adoption identified earlier come ultimately to the impact analysis.

Table 13.1 depicts the social impact perspective. The table is a simple two-by-two display. The horizontal stub involves impacts on society. The vertical stub involves impacts on business. Society gains or losses occur from a business action. Business gains or losses occur from its action, social action, or reaction.

The ideal situation is that both society and business gain from the interaction. This ideal situation most likely involves a political economy with a well-functioning market economy and constitutional democracy. The outcome is profitability and CSP (Husted and Salazar, 2006). The Friedman position rests on the first welfare theorems of neoclassical economics. For example, markets outperform governments over the long run, despite market failures and considering governmental failures.

The worst (and opposing) situation is that both society and business suffer from the interaction. One possibility faced today is a continuing pandemic with catastrophic consequences. Another possibility is accelerating climate deterioration. Table 13.1 restructures a continuum from best to worst joint outcomes. There are two intervening situations in this continuum before arriving at the worst situation of social and political chaos. Businesses can gain, at least temporarily, by misconduct (CSIR). There can be monopolization (whether through intentional actions or as an unintended result of conditions), negative externalities (defined as unpriced harms imposed on others by actions of the business), dishonesty and fraud, and corruption. A business might lose through social overreach because society over-regulates or over-taxes businesses in ways that damage the market economy. The most extreme example would be socialism (illustrated by Cuba and Venezuela) or communism (illustrated by China, North Korea, or Vietnam) practiced in ways that cripple the productive capacity of the economy.

Society may gain relative to business temporarily; however, the long-term effect is to move toward the lose–lose outcome. China experiments, on one interpretation, with combining a more market-oriented and partly privatized economy with a neo-totalitarian single-party communist regime in some way that obtains reasonable benefits of the market economy while maintaining social control by the party. Scholars, managers, and politicians can disagree on the characterization of each of the four relationships defined in Table 13.1. The design of the table is a movement away from the ideal. Businesses can act in the direction of CSIR, harming society. Society can overreact toward social overreach, harming business in the short term and society in the long term.

Instrumental Corporate Social Responsiveness vs. Moral CSR

The fundamental choice for a business and its executives is whether to be irresponsible in pursuit of profits, responsive to society, or voluntarily initiate prosocial benefit actions beyond social responsiveness. Responsiveness is an instrumental strategy. A problem for conceptual exposition is that social control separates into two forms. One form is conventional regulation, mainly focused on deterring and punishing CSIR. The other form is expansive CSR requirements or suggestions.

Frederick (1994/1978) differentiated in 1978 between responsibility (labeled CSR1) and responsiveness (labeled CSR2). Subsequently, Frederick (1986) identified ethical analysis (labeled CSR3) explicitly. Then, Frederick (1998) also identified environmental responsibility (labeled CSR4). Responsiveness is when the business elects to make changes due to external pressure. A group might announce a boycott or institutional investors could make demands. Profitable or competitive advantage opportunities might arise in CSV social issues (Porter and Kramer, 2011) or "bottom of the pyramid" market segments (Prahalad, 2004). The business benefits from the opportunity in a direct financial or strategic sense. It might elect to take a minor (but not significant) financial loss to improve social welfare and environmental sustainability in a virtue judgment. A key constraint on business judgment is that a business cannot undertake significant losses for social benefit (Strine, 2012), although an individual household or a privately owned business can benefit (Friedman, 1970). The flip side is that a business cannot make gains by generating social harm. Strine's (2014) proposed solution is to rely more on statutory changes, such as the Delaware B Corporation, that relieves executives of the profit-seeking emphasis in favor of a more significant social contribution (Strine, 2014). The publicly traded corporation is a capital-raising device rather than a requirement of the market economy. The combination of considerations may tend to cluster businesses close to strict neutrality (avoid legal or ethical violations and do not engage in opportunities to lose money). Laws and ethics govern detailed judgments.

In *The Theory of Moral Sentiments*, Adam Smith (1759) distinguished between citizenship and good citizenship. A citizen complies with laws and public policies. A good citizen seeks to promote social welfare, which goes beyond compliance:

> He is not a citizen who is not disposed to respect the laws and obey the civil magistrate; and he is certainly not a good citizen who does not wish to promote, by every means in his power, the welfare of the whole society of his fellow-citizens.
>
> (Smith, 1759, 210)

Authentic CSR engagement is necessary for good corporate citizenship (Moon et al., 2005; Wood et al., 2006). By inference, washing disguised as claiming good citizenship means that actual promotion of social welfare is not occurring, and actions are undertaken only for low-cost (or cheap) reputation gain.

Kaptein (2021) provided a VBN conception for thinking about values (V), beliefs (B), and norms (N). Kaptein's thesis is that a business should adopt a new norm (or extend an existing norm) to protect a value. A value is presumably the worth of something as ascribed by an individual or community or, in economic terms, as set by demand and supply. A norm governs action and behavior. Beliefs influence the relationship between values and norms:

> After more than two decades of searching, the holy grail of integrating norms into management and organization research remains elusive. Researchers still lack a clear framework that explains value creation in relation to normative values and, in turn, a means to incorporate values into research methods and generate value-based practical insights. (Donaldson, 2021, 1)

Donaldson's proposed solution for solving this "holy grail" search problem emphasizes an epistemological framework grounded in practical reasoning. The reasoning activity depends on intrinsic values, as illustrated by "social-economic welfare and fairness" (Donaldson, 2021, 2). In simple terms, everyone can appreciate increased individual and social welfare, as well as the general principle of fairness in dealing with people (in business, customers, employees, and suppliers especially).

Bennis and Nanus (1985) promoted transformational leadership theory as a "leader" transforms the organization through people motivation. They argued for four qualities of the transformational leader: (1) clear, future-oriented vision; (2) organizational architecture developer through the communication of direction and structure; (3) trustworthiness through clarity and consistency; and (4) self-awareness of and emphasis on personal strengths (relative to personal weaknesses).

The transformation of business enterprises and philosophies may involve "moral wayfinding" by executives and organizations (Valentinov and Pérez-Valls, 2021). Such moral wayfinding may depend on the moral character and philosophical orientations of the executives, employees, and other stakeholders. The present author has proposed a typology of moral exemplars in business (Windsor,

2013a), as well as a comparison of calculation, responsiveness, and conscience in executives and entrepreneurs (Windsor, 2021).

Conclusion

CSR and CSIR go to the very heart of the relationship between business and society in the 21st century. While no firm should engage in CSIR, CSR avoidance is insufficient, whether in conventional regulation or CSR public policy expansion. CSRM means that a firm moves to CSR engagement to improve society and the natural environment to the extent feasible under prevailing business conditions. The significant differentiation between Strategy II and Strategy III is that the latter involves moral judgments concerning civil disobedience. Wickert (2021, E15) expressed the role for CSR scholarship as follows:

> [W]e need to make CSR research a scholarly enterprise that is about the big questions that are worth asking. In the 21st century and in light of the vast challenges we face, this does not mean asking how CSR can benefit business, but rather how business can benefit society through CSR.

Wickert (2021) argued that CSR is and should shift from a business-centric to a society-centric perspective. The business-centric approach has dominated the CSR literature. That approach concerns what works for the business. The society-centric approach asks what happens for and to society. Wickert's argument requires addressing several important questions. First, what are the "big questions" and "vast challenges"? Second, what business actions benefit society and offer the most social benefit. More precisely, what can business do to benefit society? Third, how do business executives choose a strategy concerning the relationship among private benefits, business benefits, and social benefits. Does this choice involve instrumental CSR (what benefits the firm as well as society) or CSRM (what is most important for society as a moral judgment, even if at the expense of the firm)?

Business, including international business, is confronting what Cavusgil et al. (2021) characterize as "an accelerated VUCA world". VUCA is an acronym, originally military in origin and derived from Bennis and Nanus (1985), for the combined conditions of volatility (V), uncertainty (U), complexity (C), and ambiguity (A) in a decision-maker's external environment. These combined conditions predict the future and make current decisions difficult. VUCA imposes additional considerations on CSR behavior. One possible result is to cause business executives to be prudent about making social contributions at any high cost to the business or themselves.

Additionally, multinational businesses operate across national jurisdictions, which raises the reality of conflicts in legal and ethical systems across countries. A firm may be able to navigate variations up to some extent, but a flat conflict between antithetical standards or requirements is a very different matter. For instance, suppose Country A requires X and Country B requires not-X (the polar-opposite action). The firm's executives must choose between X and not-X.

There is movement in the direction of more robust CSR engagement. The Business Roundtable (2019) and Larry Fink, CEO of the BlackRock investment management company (Fink, 2019) have issued statements favoring broader conceptions of corporate purpose. A fundamental difficulty remains that it is awkward to differentiate between stakeholder relationships and social contribution. Improving consumer welfare or improving the natural environment while holding constant the welfare of other stakeholders improves social welfare. CSR engagement becomes more complicated when there are conflicts between the interests of various stakeholders. Freeman (2017) argued that the job of executives and entrepreneurs is to innovate in ways that obviate tradeoffs.

References

Aguinis, H. and Glavas, A. (2012). What we know and don't know about corporate social responsibility: A review and research agenda. *Journal of Management*, 38(4), 932–968.

Barnett, M.L. (2019). The business case for corporate social responsibility: A critique and an indirect path forward. *Business and Society*, 58(1), 167–190.

Barnett, M.L., Henriques, I. and Husted, B.W. (2020). Beyond good intentions: Designing CSR initiatives for greater social impact. *Journal of Management*, 46(6), 937–964.

Bennis, W. and Nanus, B. (1985). *Leaders: The Strategies for Taking Charge*. New York: Harper and Row.

Business Roundtable. (2019). Business roundtable redefines the purpose of a corporation to promote "an economy that serves All Americans", August 19. Available at: https://www.businessroundtable.org/business-roundtable-redefines-the-purpose-of-a-corporation-to-promote-an-economy-that-serves-all-americans

Campbell, J.L. (2007). Why would corporations behave in socially responsible ways? An institutional theory of corporate social responsibility. *Academy of Management Review*, 32(3), 946–967.

Carroll, A.B. and Shabana, K.M. (2010). The business case for corporate social responsibility: A review of concepts, research and practice. *International Journal of Management Reviews*, 12(1), 85–105.

Cavusgil, S.T., van der Vegt, S., Dakhli, M., De Farias, S., Doria, E.F., Eroglu, S., Liu, L.A. and Wang, E.Y. (2021). International business in an accelerated VUCA world: Trends, disruptions, and coping strategies. *Rutgers Business Review*, 6(3), 219–243.

Delmas, M.A. and Burbano, V.C. (2011). The drivers of greenwashing. *California Management Review*, 54(1), 64–87.

Dizik, A. (2018). When it makes sense to pollute—And how to change the equation: A trove of documents reveals the corporate decision-making that led to an environmental disaster, and could lead to other bad behavior. *Chicago Booth Review*, August 28. Available at: https://review.chicagobooth.edu/economics/2018/article/when-it-makes-sense-pollute-and-how-change-equation

Donaldson, T. (2021). How values ground value creation: The practical inference framework. *Organization Theory*, 2(4), 1–27.

Epstein, E.M. (1999). The continuing quest for accountable, ethical, and humane corporate capitalism: An enduring challenge for social issues in management in the new millennium. *Business and Society*, 38(3), 253–267.

Fernando, M. (2010). Corporate social responsibility in the wake of the Asian tsunami: Effect of time on the genuineness of CSR initiatives. *European Management Journal*, 28(1), 68–79.

Fink, L. (2019). Larry Fink's 2019 letter to CEOs: Purpose and profit. Available at: https://www.blackrock.com/corporate/investor-relations/2019-larry-fink-ceo-letter

Frederick, W.C. (1986). Toward CSR3: Why ethical analysis is indispensable and unavoidable in corporate affairs. *California Management Review*, 28(2), 126–141.

Frederick, W.C. (1994/1978). From CSR1 to CSR2: The maturing of business-and-society thought. *Business and Society*, 33(2), 150–164.

Frederick, W.C. (1998). Moving to CSR4: What to pack for the trip. *Business and Society*, 37(1), 40–59.

Freeman, R.E. (2017). The new story of business: Towards a more responsible capitalism. *Business and Society Review*, 122(3), 449–465.

Friedman, M. (1970). The social responsibility of business is to increase its profits. *New York Times Magazine*, September 13.

Gallie, W.B. (1955–56). Essentially contested concepts. *Proceedings of the Aristotelian Society (New Series)*, 56, 167–198.

Gond, J.-P. and Moon, J. (2011). Corporate social responsibility in retrospect and prospect: Exploring the life-cycle of an essentially contested concept. In Gond, J.-P. and Moon, J. (Eds.), *Corporate Social Responsibility: A Reader Volume 1*. London: Routledge.

Gregor, M. (2011). Corporate lobbying: A review of the recent literature. Institute of Economic Studies (IES) Working Paper No. 32/2011, Faculty of Social Sciences, Charles University, Prague. Available at: http://doi.org/10.2139/ssrn.1978724

Haack, P., Martignoni, D. and Schoeneborn, D. (2021). A bait-and-switch model of corporate social responsibility. *Academy of Management Review*, 46(3), 440–464.

Husted, B.W. and Allen, D.B. (2006). Corporate social responsibility in the multinational enterprise: Strategic and institutional approaches. *Journal of International Business Studies*, 37(6), 838–849.

Husted, B.W. and Salazar, J. (2006). Taking Friedman seriously: Maximizing profits and social performance. *Journal of Management Studies*, 43(1), 75–91.

Husted, B.W., Allen, D.B. and Kock, N. (2015). Value creation through social strategy. *Business and Society*, 54(2), 147–186.

Husted, B.W., Jamali, D. and Saffar, W. (2016). Near and dear? The role of location in CSR engagement. *Strategic Management Journal*, 37(10), 2050–2070.

JPMorgan and Chase Co. (n.d.). Code of conduct. Available at: https://www.jpmorganchase.com/about/governance/code-of-conduct with full content available at https://www.jpmorganchase.com/content/dam/jpmc/jpmorgan-chase-and-co/documents/code-of-conduct.pdf

Kaptein, M. (2021). Issue-driven progress in business ethics: When the responsibility to protect values requires companies to introduce new norms. Available at: http://doi.org/10.2139/ssrn.3943915

Kourabas, M. (2016). The case of DuPont's pollution and the importance of CSR. *Triple Pundit*, January 11. Available at: https://www.triplepundit.com/story/2016/case-duponts-pollution-and-importance-csr/29241

Lynn, A. (2021). Why "doing well by doing good" went wrong: Getting beyond "good ethics pays" claims in managerial thinking. *Academy of Management Review*, 46(3), 512–533.

Mackenzie, K. (2021). Too many oil companies using carbon capture as a net-zero crutch. *TEXAS INC. (Houston Chronicle)*, January 18, Monday, 120(97), B16.

Matsangou, E. (2016). Unilever CEO Paul Polman is redefining sustainable business. *EuropeanCEO*, April 15. Available at: https://www.europeanceo.com/business-and-management/unilever-ceo-paul-polman-is-redefining-sustainable-business/

Matten, D. and Moon, J. (2008). "Implicit" and "explicit" CSR: A conceptual framework for a comparative understanding of corporate social responsibility. *Academy of Management Review*, 33(2), 404–424.

McWilliams, A. and Siegel, D. (2001). Corporate social responsibility: A theory of the firm perspective. *Academy of Management Review*, 26(1), 117–127.

Mitnick, B.M., Windsor, D. and Wood, D.J. (2021). CSR: Undertheorized or essentially contested? *Academy of Management Review*, 46(3), 623–629.

Mitnick, B.M., Windsor, D. and Wood, D.J. (2022). Moral CSR. *Business and Society*. https://doi.org/10.1177/00076503221086881

Moon, J., Crane, A. and Matten, D. (2005). Can corporations be citizens? Corporate citizenship as a metaphor for business participation in society. *Business Ethics Quarterly*, 15(3), 427–451.

Nestlé. (n.d.). Our approach: Our long-term success depends on creating value both for our shareholders and for society. Available at: https://www.nestle.com/csv/what-is-csv

Noked, N. (2011, February 28). Investing in corporate social responsibility to enhance customer value. Available at: https://corpgov.law.harvard.edu/2011/02/28/investing-in-corporate-social-responsibility-to-enhance-customer-value/

Okoye, A. (2009). Theorising corporate social responsibility as an essentially contested concept: Is a definition necessary? *Journal of Business Ethics*, 89(4), 613–627.

Porter, M.E. and Kramer, M.R. (2011). Creating shared value: How to reinvent capitalism—And unleash a wave of innovation and growth. *Harvard Business Review*, 89(1/2), 62–77.

Prahalad, C.K. (2004). *The Fortune at the Bottom of the Pyramid: Eradicating Poverty Through Profits*. Philadelphia, PA: Wharton School Publishing.

Schuler, D.A., Rehbein, K. and Green, C.D. (2019). Is corporate political activity a field? *Business and Society*, 58(7), 1376–1405.

Seele, P. and Gatti, L. (2017). Greenwashing revisited: In search of a typology and accusation-based definition incorporating legitimacy strategies. *Business Strategy and the Environment*, 26(2), 239–252.

Segal, E. (2021, January 26). How and why corporate lobbying will continue to matter during the Biden administration. Available at: https://www.forbes.com/sites/edwardsegal/2021/01/26/how-and-why-corporate-lobbying-will-continue-to-matter-during-the-biden-administration/

Shapira, R. and Zingales, L. (2017). Is pollution value-maximizing? The DuPont case. Available at: https://www.law.northwestern.edu/research-faculty/colloquium/law-economics/documents/Spring18Zingales.pdf

Smith, A. (1759). *The Theory of Moral Sentiments*, 6th edition. London: A. Millar.

Strine, L.E. (2012). Our continuing struggle with the idea that for-profit corporations seek profit. *Wake Forest Law Review*, 47, 135–172.

Strine, L.E. (2014). Making it easier for directors to “do the right thing?” *Harvard Business Law Review*, 4, 235–253.

Strong, D. (2015, September 10). JPMorgan Chase: Code of ethics and revisions since the 2008 financial crisis. Available at: https://sevenpillarsinstitute.org/jpmorgan-chase-code-of-ethics-and-revisions-since-the-2008-financial-crisis/

Ting, P.-H. (2021). Do large firms just talk corporate social responsibility? The evidence from CSR report disclosure. *Finance Research Letters*, 38(January), 101476.

Tolmie, C.R., Lehnert, K. and Zhao, H. (2020). Formal and informal institutional pressures on corporate social responsibility: A cross-country analysis. *Corporate Social Responsibility and Environmental Management*, 27(2), 786–802.

Trudel, R. and Cotte, J. (2009). Does it pay to be good? *MIT Sloan Management Review*, 50(2), 61–68.

Valentinov, V. and Pérez-Valls, M. (2021). A conception of moral wayfinding for business managers: The obligation for a sustainable corporation. *Journal of Cleaner Production*, 284, 124771.

Whelan, T. and Fink, C. (2016). The comprehensive business case for sustainability. *Harvard Business Review*, October 21. Available at: https://hbr.org/2016/10/the-comprehensive-business-case-for-sustainability

Wickert, C. (2021). Corporate social responsibility research in the Journal of Management Studies: A shift from a business-centric to a society-centric focus. *Journal of Management Studies*, 58(8), E1–E17.

Windsor, D. (2006). Corporate social responsibility: Three key approaches. *Journal of Management Studies*, 43(1), 93–114.

Windsor, D. (2013a). A typology of moral exemplars in business. In Schwartz, M. and Harris, H. (Eds.), *Moral Saints and Moral Exemplars, Research in Ethical Issues in Organizations*, 10. Bingley: Emerald.

Windsor, D. (2013b). Corporate social responsibility and irresponsibility: A positive theory approach. *Journal of Business Research*, 66(10), 1937–1944.

Windsor, D. (2015). Public policy avoidance: Economic patriotism and social responsibility in corporate inversion, other tax avoidance, and regulatory haven decisions. Proceedings of the International Association for Business and Society, vol. 26, annual IABS Conference, Guanacaste, Costa Rica, March 12–15.

Windsor, D. (2017). The ethics and business diplomacy of MNE tax avoidance. In Ruël, H. (Ed.), *International Business Diplomacy: How Can Multinational Corporations Deal with Global Challenges?* Bingley: Emerald.

Windsor, D. (2018a). Hypocrisy, cynicism, and non-limited altruism needs. Proceedings of the International Association for Business and Society, vol. 29, annual IABS Conference, Hong Kong, June 6–10.

Windsor, D. (2018b). Responsible capitalism: Legal tax liability minimization versus socially responsible tax. Proceedings of the International Association for Business and Society, vol. 29, annual IABS Conference, Hong Kong, June 6–10.

Windsor, D. (2019). Influencing MNC strategies for managing corruption and favoritism in Pacific Asia countries: A multiple-theory configurational perspective. *Asia Pacific Business Review*, 25(4), 501–533.

Windsor, D. (2021). Calculation, responsiveness, and conscience in CSR and social entrepreneurship. In Marques, J. (Ed.), *Business with a Conscience: A Research Companion*. London: Routledge.

Windsor, D. (2022). The ethical dimension of impact-oriented corporate social responsibility (CSR). In Kudlak, R., Preuss, L., Heikkinen, A. and Barkemeyer, R. (Eds.), *The Impact of Corporate Social Responsibility: Corporate Activities, the Environment and Society*. London: Routledge.

Wood, D.J. (1991). Corporate social performance revisited. *Academy of Management Review*, 16(4), 693–718.

Wood, D.J. (2010). Measuring corporate social performance: A review. *International Journal of Management Reviews*, 12(1), 50–84.

Wood, D.J., Logsdon, J.M., Lewellyn, P.G. and Davenport, K. (2006). *Global Business Citizenship: A Transformative Framework for Ethics and Sustainable Capitalism*. Armonk, NY: M.E. Sharpe.

Zosso, M. (2019). After greenwashing, blue-washing? *Mabucom*, November 15 Available at: http://www.mabucom.ch/after-greenwashing-blue-washing/

Part 4

CSR – New Underlying Assumptions

14 CSR and the Orbital Theory of Accountability

Gabriel Donleavy

Introduction

Corporate social responsibility (CSR) is the notion that firms both ought to be, and increasingly actually are, good citizens of the societies in which their activities reside. Responsibility entails accountability. Legitimacy theory postulates that a corporate entity will be allowed a degree of self-regulation as long as it behaves in a way that takes the public interest into account (Dowling and Pfeffer, 1975; Lindblom, 1993). This exchange between society and organizations is the so-called social contract. Maintenance of the social contract requires accountability for its enforcement. That requires a shared understanding of what accountability actually is. It is an easy concept to appreciate loosely but its operational or concrete definition is subject to considerable variation between the scholars cited most in the academic business literature reviewed inter alia by Bansall and Kistruck (2006).

Institutional theory is widely used in the accountability literature. Di Maggio and Powell (1983) posit therein that firms will converge in shape, structure, and governance over time in response to a range of contextual forces – a process they term isomorphism. An even more widely used creature of their theory is what they call decoupling – a notion very important in discussing whether or not any one instance of CSR reporting is authentic or hypocritical (or worse). Decoupling refers to a significant gap between what is said and what is done. It is a serious accountability disease, subverting trust between a firm and its stakeholders, and this chapter makes frequent use of this concept.

Business ethics literature is heavily endowed with normative theories and papers, but very short of positive, descriptive, and/or analytic ones. Positive theories are necessary to gain real and useful insight into the causes and effects of real-world behaviour (including CSR) and of the processes of accountability that circulate within it. The orbital theory of accountability (Donleavy, 2012) is an attempt to provide such insight.

The Ethical Frameworks of Accountability

The ethical root of accountability, and of CSR alike, is acceptance of the existence of a human *community*. It is more than an aggregation of individual people,

DOI: 10.4324/9781003274575-18

and it needs cementing forces to turn a bunch of individuals, a crowd, a mob, or a neighbourhood into a single social organism. Accountability is one such cementing force and comprises not only the proposition that community requires us to have others in mind when we take action or omit to take action, but also the matching proposition that we are to explain our actions and omissions to the community. Accountability thus begins with the ethical stance that every person who lives in anything that can validly be seen as a community is obliged to act and account with full awareness of his/her membership in that community.

CSR has a similar point of departure to that of accountability, the existence of a community in which corporate actions, omissions, and words take place. Since the privileges awarded to corporate structures from the legal construct of corporate personhood are real and generally accepted, CSR is the expectation normatively, and the manifestation positively, that corporate persons have no less a range of accountability obligations than individual flesh and blood human persons have. The notion of CSR would make no sense if the corporation was regarded as no more than a kind of machine or a set of contracts having a validity and enforceability strictly constrained by its constituent contracts. The Universal Declaration of Human Rights proclaims its "recognition of the inherent dignity and of the equal and inalienable rights of all members of the human family [as] the foundation of freedom, justice and peace in the world" (Weston, 2012).

Influential ethical postulates and maxims of the twentieth century have proceeded from the points of departure just described to specify further what should properly be expected, but some have done so by stepping away from experienced social reality to an imaginary realm, idealized and with unbounded rationality. Rawls (1971) postulates his influential theory of justice in such a realm where people would not know into what situation they are to be born but he nonetheless purports to stipulate that they would require strict equality of opportunity and would tolerate only such differences of rank, status, wealth, etc. as would be generally agreed to be good for the whole community. He applies this to time as well as to space, so that people in the imaginary realm do not even know when in history or in the future they will be born. What is wrong with this is that not only can no such state exist, even in Eastern religions or in reports of "the Afterlife" found in such places as YouTube, but also that it cannot possibly be reconciled with Hume's Law which states that you cannot derive a prescription from a description or vice versa. Rawls (1971) offers a *description* of the imaginary land beyond the so-called veil of ignorance, then draws very *prescriptive* inferences from it, empirical evidence being precluded by the very act of loading the imaginary realm with such a "heavy lifting" ethical job. Economics and politics also fall into this fallacy. Walter Lippman's (1955, 42) much-quoted definition of the public interest, for example, holds that the public interest "may be presumed to be what ... [people] would choose if they saw clearly, thought rationally, acted disinterestedly and benevolently".

It is submitted, however, that any proposition about the real world, whether normative or prescriptive, cannot *validly be derived from imaginary worlds*. To the extent that such derivations do resonate with us, they are invoking feelings, convictions, or beliefs sourced in our real-world experience. Accordingly, ethical frameworks likely to be capable of being *effective* in manifesting the they behaviours seek to induce will be frameworks derived from the real world. Arguably the frameworks both of care theory and of virtue ethics have such a foundation, but Posner, inter alia, asserts the root of ethics empirically is *actual intuition*. Rawls (1971, 34) defined Intuitionism as "the doctrine that there is an irreducible family of first principles which have to be weighed against one another by asking ourselves which balance, in our considered judgment, is the most just". Posner (1998, 1642) justified his own belief that only human beings are the proper subject of morality by invoking intuitionism in this declaration: "If the moral irrelevance of humanity is what philosophy teaches, so that we have to choose between philosophy and the intuition that says that membership in the human species is morally relevant, philosophy will have to go". A less dogmatic approach is taken by Birch (1993, 382–383) who defined an ethic of duty as being sourced in "deontic experience ... the experience, in response to something or someone, that one must do something, that one is called upon to do something". Generally, in deontic experience, duty is prior to value (Lacey, 1986, 67). It is arguable that CSR is anchored in such deontic experience, itself grown in the soil of intuition. If so, we are delivered from the temptation to attribute its validity to goings on by imaginary people in imaginary realms.

The Public Interest

All three orbits of accountability rate very highly the claim of the public interest to restrain, guide, and disclose behaviour. The public interest concept is similar to the notion of human community, and at a helicopter level is unproblematic. Descending from the abstract to the concrete or operational levels of the idea, however, is to drive uncertainly through a denser veil of foggy ignorance than the one created by Rawls (1971). The notion of "a", or "the", public interest provides no operational decision rule or test, and thus little guidance to public administrators juggling compound and often conflicting criteria in discharging their duties (Lewis, 2006). Some see the public interest as an effort to confound particular interests with general interests and thereby to camouflage self-interested advocacy. Among those so frustrated by driving in this fog, some are tempted to take refuge in heuristic oversimplification. Frederickson (1994), for instance, declares that in an elected democratic country like the United States, the public interest is whatever the majority in Congress or the president say it is. Back then the word "or" was not the problem it has since become for US democracy. Claiming to represent the public good, some public officials and technical experts may confound the public interest by confusing it with their own preferences and biases (Lewis, 2006). This is a problem of greater concern in the inner orbits than the other two, as politicians are especially apt to appropriate to their own agency the claim to be representing "the" public interest. Indeed, the agency itself sources an array of malfeasance, misfeasance, non-feasance, and breaches of trust.

Others assert that a major barrier to clear thinking about the public interest is our prioritization of rights over obligations. Thus Schneider (1988, 163–164), for example, argues,

> thinking in terms of rights encourages us to ask what we may do to free ourselves, not to bind ourselves. It encourages us to think about what constrains us from doing what we want, not what obligates us to do what we ought. Obligations create relationships, connections and bonding between individuals and communities.

Moreover, the common good could be seen as not merely the sum of individual goods (as liberal and other individualistic theories of society would have it), but rather "a state of equilibrium in the interplay of individual goods" that resides in all of humankind – which may be understood as the good of humankind as a whole, including past, present, and future generations (Weston, 2012).

A facet of guarding the public interest is stewardship, which Kass (1990, 113) defines as the "administrator's willingness and ability to earn the public trust by being an effective and ethical agent in carrying out the republic's business". Stewardship as the major point of accounting was trumped when the United States' Trueblood Report (Trueblood and Stevens, 1973) told users and preparers of accounting reports that the *purpose* of accounting was to produce information useful to decision makers. Subsequent scholars such as Dellaportas and Davenport (2008) have taken "public" in the public interest to mean the investing public, as they are the ones who make resource allocation decisions which can be affected by reading accounts. This "appropriation of the commons" seized from the general public is a sophisticated decoupling of the public interest in favour of factional interest. It supports the findings of such scholars as Walker (1987) who find the accounting profession, in Australia at least, exemplifies well the phenomenon of regulatory capture. Even for the inner orbit, regulatory capture renders ineffective the regulatory framework alleged to have been erected in the public interest. Lobbying and revolving doors between government and corporate boards are principal means by which such capture occurs and they both dilute and subvert firms from showing authentic CSR.

Inner Orbit Accountability

In the inner orbit reside the laws, regulations, and national policies that a state has in its regulatory portfolio.

In many countries, constitutions are the basis both of law and of public policy, for they embody a society's fundamental assumptions about law and legitimacy (Kennedy, 2017). As part of the orbital theory, it is postulated that constitutions which prioritize individual rights and freedoms over community obligations will display rarer and weaker CSR actions and correspondingly greater decoupling of deeds from words than those jurisdictions placing obligations over rights and those jurisdictions which have no constitution at all. This raises a ticklish question of whether rights-based constitutions tend to be used in democracies and obligation-based ones in autocracies. In the latter, however, kleptocratic acts are easily decoupled from communitarian words.

CSR in the inner orbit is directed by the State, through statutes, regulations, and direct state pressure. The enforcement through statute is often a matter of black letter law and strict liability. From traffic offences, such as parking in an unauthorized place up to causing death by dangerous driving, are offences for which motive and excuse are quite irrelevant to being found guilty (though they may mitigate the severity of any sentence). Truck drivers may be under pressure from the employer to take on excessive loads, to work longer than the legally permitted hours, and to break speed limits in order to minimize the employer's costs; but the State holds the driver responsible for any breaches of its strict liability regulations, and thereby pressures the trucking company to display a statutory minimum degree of CSR. Regulations based on an enabling statute, sometimes indirectly rather than directly, are likewise usually concerned with testing whether compliance did or did not occur, irrespective of motive, mental state, or allegedly mitigating circumstances. Countries which have Independent Commissions Against Corruption exemplify this focus well and regard mitigating circumstances (such as medical expenses of ill spouses) as evidence in favour of pursuing a suspect, rather than regard the suspect as suffering from an understandable though unfortunate lapse of ethical standards.

Payment of taxes duly assessed is a slightly different case, as here the boundary that accountants and tax lawyers have blurred between tax evasion and tax avoidance means that strict liability can only be applied when someone has broken the letter of any tax rule rather than the spirit (unless, as with the Enron case, the number and style of avoidances was so consistently egregious that a prosecution was able to succeed). Avoidance of tax is "only" a failure of CSR, whereas evasion of tax is also a crime by way of fraud and/or theft. This exemplifies how state pressure can induce CSR in the inner orbit without here being a direct line from a statute or regulation to enforce it. Finally, there are food safety and workplace regulations, where it is sometimes a defence to show the defendant could not reasonably have known of the harm done by their product in the light of the state of science at the time. This defence worked well for tobacco companies until the 1960s and for multinational producers of toxic weedkiller right up to the end of the last century.

The price society pays for enforcing CSR through strict liability is a moral hazard (Herlin, 2017). For instance, the British comedian, Jimmy Carr, was charged by the English tax authority with international tax evasion, but he went on to an even more successful career after he said it was a "fair cop" but he expected the State to stop him doing it and it was not up to him to do without the State's firm guidance. He was pleading external locus of control to the point of addiction, and wanting even stronger laws and their enforcement so he would thereby be absolved of responsibility. Such is the moral hazard of strong law enforcement.

Despite its imperative form and its binding character, a law is on its own not sufficient to change behaviour. De Benedetto (2018) asserts that failures occur for one or more of three reasons: (a) failure to detect non-compliance, (b) failure to sanction detected non-compliance, and (c) lack of enforcement by relevant officials.

Tort is the principal subset of law ruling CSR and accountability. In tort, regard for one's "neighbour" is given legal authority and force. Arguably, its most famous encapsulation was in *Donoghue v Stephenson*, [1932] A.C. 562:

> You must take reasonable care to avoid acts or omissions which you can reasonably foresee would be likely to injure your neighbour. Who, then, in law is my neighbour? The answer seems to be persons who are so closely and directly affected by my act that I ought reasonably to have them in contemplation as being so affected when I am directing my mind to the acts or omissions which are called in question.
>
> (Kumaralingam, 2007, 580–581)

The neighbour of that 1932 case has morphed through the midwifery of Eddie Freeman (1984) into the stakeholder. His normative stakeholder theory asserts that firms prosper more if they manage to resolve conflicts between stakeholder groups rather than focus exclusively on the maximization of the present value of shareholder wealth. He says seeing any business situation as a zero-sum game is self-defeating in the long run and the point is to generate new values for all parties involved. In this theory, the board is sovereign, arbitrating between the claims of various stakeholder groups, whereas in the still very influential agency theory, it is the shareholder in the general meeting who is sovereign and is accordingly minded to monitor and to bond the directors to act in the shareholders' interests first and foremost. Milton Friedman aligns with agency theory, Eddie Freeman does not. Normative stakeholder theory has been very influential in the analysis of CSR, increasingly so as environmental issues have come to play a central role in mediating between corporate self-interest and CSR. It is, at the time of writing in 2022, embodied in the struggle to dominate sustainability accounting internationally with the International Financial Reporting Standards (IFRS) and its new Sustainability Accounting Standards Board (SASB) representing the investor class and the GRI representing the multistakeholder approach. Neither body has asked Freeman to mediate and both bodies claim to be committed to be working toward a convergence of regulatory approach. Things have moved a very long way since Milton Friedman (1970) declared, "the corporate social responsibility of business is to increase its profits".

Middle Orbit Accountability

The middle orbit is the residual space of the orbital theory. It includes all accountability behaviours *not* driven by national regulations *and not* concerned with future generations or non-human beings. The most concrete and most common form of accountability here is the contract. Both in common law and in civil law jurisdictions, the existence of a valid contract requires offer, acceptance, specific details of the performance required, and the payment or other exchange to be given in return. Accountability governed by a contract is mutual. There is no such thing as a contract imposing responsibility and accountability on one party only. Such a document or agreement would not be a contract. Breaches of contract are subject to legal sanction, and like all other aspects of the law, enforcement is an important empirical variable.

The middle orbit is also the space where an activity is undertaken to move items from the middle to the inner orbits. That is an area where stakeholder salience, lobbying, and pressure group campaigns play a significant role.

CSR has been widely argued to be chiefly a tool to enhance corporate legitimacy (Bansal and Kistruck, 2006; Campbell, 2007; Castello and Lozano, 2011; Laufer, 2003; Schultz and Wehmeier, 2010). Within the realm of CSR especially, firms are alleged to decouple actions from words, to meet minimum reporting requirements (Aguinis and Glavas, 2012, 941). In the environmental sphere, decoupling displays as greenwashing (Bansal and Kistruck, 2006; Ramus and Montiel, 2005). Despite being spruiked by Freeman (1984) and his followers as a vision of a new flourishing of capitalism, multistakeholder models do not trespass on the ownership rights of shareholders. Rather, by inviting asset managers to voluntarily adopt more long-term behaviour, they serve to keep in alignment shareholder and managerial interests (Bailey, 2020/2021). Many studies doubt the authenticity and sincerity of self-reporting claims by companies to exemplify good CSR. For example, Roberts (2003) argues that CSR reporting is a "narcissistic concern" by corporations to appear responsible, an act of corporate egoism (Messner, 2009), a legitimation device (Patten, 1991, 1992; Cho and Patten, 2007), a greenwashing strategy to revamp a business image (Gotsi and Wilson, 2001; Seele and Gatti, 2015, Wu, 2019), a "carefully tailored public relations documents" (Lock and Seele, 2016, 87), little more than self-laudatory public relations (Seele and Knebel, 2015), and an opportunity for corporations to engage in impression management (Merkl-Davies and Brennan, 2007). Enoch (2007) argues that the discourse of CSR operates to legitimize the status quo, since by the logic of CSR, engagement by the public in matters of ecological concern is unnecessary. We merely need to put our faith in the beneficence of corporate capital to solve the problem for us. In this regard, CSR acts as an individualizing tactic. It encourages fatalism toward political action by framing substantive social change as the sole province of managers and other elites. CSR embodies a neoliberal rationality in that it responds to demands for addressing the social and environmental effects of capitalist production through the individualized mechanism of the market, thereby reframing and reorganizing social actors as "stakeholders" positioned within the corporate orbit. CSR, then, is viewed by some encouraging voluntaristic, individualized strategies as a *sufficient* means to respond to ecological crisis while eschewing more collective and more radical means of political engagement.

It is not the investing public only that drives firms toward CSR. Mohr et al. (2001) found that consumers prefer to purchase from companies that behave responsibly toward the environment. Environmental legitimacy, as a concept, has been defined as "the generalized perception or assumption that a firm's corporate environmental performance is desirable, proper, or appropriate" (Bansal and Kistruck, 2006).

A significant concern in modern administrative states is agency capture, in which industries influence regulation to cater to their interests at the expense of the public interest (Kwak, 2014). Capture can occur when new public officers come from the same private sector now within their purview. Based on public officers' allegiance to their former industry, lobbying is *de facto* exerted, "from within" (Tai, 2017; Yates and Cardin-Trudeau, 2021).

Social Network Theory (SNT) analyses the characteristics of networks and their influences on people's behaviours (Phiri and Guven-Uslu, 2019). One of the main purposes of SNT is to identify the most influential powerful members of a social network and their *modi operandi.* Three key concepts underline the nature of social networks: network density, centrality, and brokerage (Burt, 2001, 2004). Network density is a measure of the number of connections between actors compared with the maximum possible number of connections that could exist between the actors; network centrality measures the extent to which an actor occupies a central position within the network. Centrality encompasses the idea of popularity or access to resources under the influence or command of the person who has many connections to other people. Brokerage entails the extent to which the focal actor bridges other actors who are themselves not connected with each other (Phiri and Guven-Uslu, 2019). SNT has been used to analyse the effectiveness of lobbying by pressure to achieve the changes they seek. For orbital accountability theory, SNT can be used to predict the effectiveness of government resistance to lobbying and to corruption, and the prospects of success for any proposal to change state policy or law. Lobbying groups and factions seeking to benefit from corruption will be likely to fail; unless their network density exceeds that of government supporters, and their centrality and brokerage approach those on the government side. It is posited that density has greater salience than centrality and brokerage.

Virtually all sociologists and political scientists publishing in the top journals hypothesize that … interest groups … influence public policy, and it is safe to assume that they generally expect the impact to be substantial. This hypothesis is not as well supported by the data as we might expect. The impact of political organizations is significantly different from zero, by conventional statistical tests, *only about half the time*, and important in policy terms (as assessed by the authors) in just over a fifth (Lowery, 2013). This may be explained by relatively low density or weak centrality and brokerage, but as an alternative explanation, agency factors may apply.

Agency is another class of relation that some deny fully attracts fiduciary accountability. Flannnigan (2002, 2009) posits that agents who are not actually trusted, or who have no discretion or advisory function, and only execute completely defined transactions, are not accountable. Agency problems affect lobbying in three ways. First, lobbying is unlike many other goods and services, given its ambiguity of outcomes. Indeed, defining goals against which to evaluate lobbying success is difficult, given the complex set of interests of lobby organizations

(Godwin et al., 2008; Lowery, 2013). Second, lobbyists often have multiple clients (Schiff et al., 2015). Third, there is asymmetry of information between the principal and the agent (Kersh, 2000, 2002; Miller, 2005; Stephenson and Jackson, 2010).

In contrast to the evidence gathered over the last two decades or so that CSR is more often honoured in the decoupling breach than the costly observance, the Putin invasion of Ukraine has generated overwhelming evidence that large corporations can act like good corporate citizens when the human community calls to them. The wave of revulsion in the West was so great that virtually all the Western multinational companies in Russia abruptly stopped doing business in and with that country. This is the most dramatic empirical evidence to date that CSR is not mostly greenwashing, decoupling, or a public relations exercise, but is an authentic characterization of the contemporary business community in those parts of the world that practise liberal democracy and free market economics – still called the West though the group includes Australia, New Zealand, Japan, South Korea, ASEAN, south of Myanmar and, up to a point, the Indian sub-continent too.

Outer Orbit Accountability

The contractarian view of obligations is that even if we feel attachment toward the next generations and feel we owe something to them, one could not talk about an obligation because future generations have no reciprocal duties toward us (Arenas and Rodrigo, 2016).

There is a contractarian flavour to the middle orbit but it extends beyond the frontiers of even implied agreements to include trusts, fiduciarity, tort liability, and socially imposed or expected obligations to account for actions and omissions. The outer orbit behaves quite differently from the other two. Here one party is assigned, or at least imputed, an accountability obligation, but there is no reciprocal duty or accountability on the other party, chiefly because such a reciprocal accountability is impossible as at times the arrow moves only in one direction. Accordingly, the duty argued to be owed to posterity is a strictly one-way accountability and some argue no such accountability exists as no unborn child can voice any claim on those now alive. New concepts of accountability have arisen in this realm.

The outer orbit is where responsibility does not depend on the law nor on reciprocity. It has several aspects. One aspect is the responsibility for non-human life and the natural environment in general. Another is the responsibility to future generations. The area of the law which sources much discussion on the outer orbit is tort.

It is argued within contractarianism that an act cannot be wrong unless there is, or will be, someone whom this act wronged. Human extinction itself could only be wrong insofar as it negatively impacts currently, or at least necessarily, existing people (Finneron-Burns, 2017, 338; Kaczmarek and Beard, 2020). Wellman (1995, 156) on the other hand, posits the idea of surviving *duties* thus: “Our claim is that, so far as we have a duty to realize the value of others’ sacrifices, these duties survive the death of the person who performed this sacrifice. Nor does their strength depreciate". As Baier observed, however, "the ontological precariousness of future generations that some see as a reason for not recognizing any rights of theirs is not significantly greater than that of the future states of present persons" (Weston, 2012).

Immanuel Kant's categorical imperative does not presuppose temporal limitations. Time is irrelevant in moral philosophy (Rawls, 1971). If justice or equality are imperative principles of conduct in one place and at one time, they are imperative in another place and at another time (Frederickson, 1994). This is the "just savings principle", a capital accumulation in one generation for the next, and so forth.

Empirical studies have found that people reciprocate the good and evil done to them by previous generations by behaving similarly toward the next generation (Wade-Benzoni, 2010). Some scholars have talked about an intergenerational version of the Golden Rule, which would exhort the present generation to treat future generations as they would like to have been treated by the preceding generation (Richards, 1982; Wade-Benzoni, 2010; Arenas and Rodrigo, 2016).

Brown-Weiss (1989) argues that future generations have a legal right to a clean, healthy, ecologically balanced and sustainable environment, and that the living are legally obligated to provide it. Brown-Weiss argues that each generation receives a "natural and cultural legacy" in legal trust from previous generations; and that this legacy it holds in trust for future generations. Brown (1989, 38) advances three basic principles of our obligations for future generations. First, each generation should be required to conserve the diversity of the natural and cultural resource base, so that it does not unduly restrict the options available to future generations in solving their problems. Second, each generation should be required to maintain the quality of the planet so that it is passed on in no worse condition than the present generation received it. Third, each generation should provide access to the legacy from past generations to future generations. These basic principles can be satisfied if we consider every generation as equal and do not presuppose anything about the value-preferences of future generations.

Jonas (1979, 1984) argues that the nature of human action has changed so dramatically in our times that it calls for a radical change in ethics as well. Jonas (1984, 90) extends traditional notions of fiduciarity to future generations thus. The first and most general condition of responsibility is causal power, that is, that acting makes an impact on the world; the second, that such acting is under the agent's control; and the third, that he can foresee its consequences to some extent. Jonas (1984, 95) differentiates between natural and contractual responsibility: It is the distinction between natural responsibility, where the immanent "ought-to-be" of the object claims its agent *a priori* and quite unilaterally, and contracted or appointed responsibility, which is conditional *a posteriori* upon the fact and the terms of the relationship actually entered into (Zsolnai, 2006). The parent and the statesman are presented as ideal types of natural responsibility and contractual responsibility, respectively. The parent is responsible for his or her child not because of the child's own will or even contrary to it. But the responsibility of the statesman comes from the political contract that he or she has established with his or her constituencies (Zsolnai, 2006).

A rare example of an outer orbit issue being pushed into the inner orbit is Hungary's appointment of an Ombudsman for Future Generations who is empowered by the Ombudsman Act to foster the interests and needs of future generations and is accountable only to the Parliament. The primary mission of the Ombudsman for Future Generations is to remind the state, including all the state organs and levels, of this task and responsibility (Bandi, 2020). It will be interesting to see if this innovation results in Hungary displaying significantly more outer orbit CSR relative to its population, its GDP, or other relevant indices than other countries at a comparable state of legal and economic development, over the next five years or more.

A vivid illustration of the worldwide recognition of the legacy obligation to future generations is the international reaction to the looting of Iraq's National Museum of Antiquities during the spring of 2003. When the news broke, the media, international and professional associations, and museum and archaeology sites on the Internet blazed with concern and condemnation of the United States' failure to safeguard the museum. Initially, 170,000 artifacts and art treasures were reported lost; one archaeologist described it as "a rape of civilization" (Booth and Gugliotta, 2003). In May 2003, UN Security Council Resolution 1483 imposed a worldwide ban on illicit trade in Iraqi cultural property (UNESCO, 2003 cited in Booth and Gugliotta, 2003; Lewis, 2006).

A strong empirical case for giving salience to future generations as regards accountability and CSR in word and deed is found in decision theory. "It takes time for decisions to have their effect (therefore) all obligations in principle concern the future. Indeed the entire rational significance of the present is in its contribution to the future good" (Hartshorne, 1981, 103). If a decision, however instinctive or calculated, is the predicate of an action, then the processes of decisions and actions are *always inclined toward the future.* The question is the extent of the future – the next minute? the next day? year? generation? or remote generations of possible people? Decision processes, by definition, cannot affect the past. We know that the cycle of decisions and actions is partly a process of informed predictions – as the future gets more distant, our predictions are less well informed and our decisions and actions are less reliable. In addition, we are not only more confident in the short term, but are also more subject to pressure to serve short-term interests (Harmon and Mayer, 1986; Harmon, 1995; Frederickson, 1994). In other words, since all decisions assume the existence and validity of the future, there is already fertile ground for giving salience to the claims of future generations. And this view can be argued to trump contractarianism's objections to granting rights to people who cannot benefit us in return. Indeed, it may be argued that morality and ethics themselves begin where contractarianism ends.

Ethical precepts rooted both in respect for individual dignity and in consciousness of a sense of belonging to the human community justify including posterity within the scope of CSR, if it is accepted that posterity is (not just will be) part of the human community. It is another manifestation of the ubiquity of the public interest, as opposed to its appropriation by a faction, autocrat, political party, or family mafia. The orbital theory posits that CSR will manifest in the outer orbit to the extent that:

(a) firms internalize the sense that posterity is part of the human community;
(b) firms are affected by isomorphism with salient stakeholders rating highly the need to protect posterity; and
(c) the costs and risks of disregarding obligations to posterity are material.

Directions for Future Research

The orbital theory of accountability is a positive theory with postulates about CSR that can be tested in future research. The research questions arising from the theory can be expressed as hypotheses as below. They are given in substantive rather than null form, to retain clarity about what is predicted from the theory at an operational level and to indicate the predicted direction of cause and effect – which would be lost if they were to be expressed in null form.

1 Countries with constitutions that prioritize rights over obligations significantly will manifest a larger rate of decoupling in their public documents than other countries. (This is a first postulate of inner orbit accountability)
2 CSR will occur more often and more significantly in countries verified for low corruption (e.g., by Transparency International) than in countries verified as high corruption ones. (This is a quite easily testable proposition in the inner orbit)
3 Lobbying will be more successful in affecting legislation for agencies that display stronger SNT factors than their opponents do. (The three SNT factors are essential components of operationalizing middle orbit accountability)
4 Appointment of state officials, such as Hungary's Commissioner for Future Generations, will result in a measurable increase in CSR actions and a decrease in public document decoupling. (This tests the implicit assumption of the theory that inner orbit institutions are more effective in generating CSR than are outer or middle ones)
5 CSR for future generations is not associated with any particular age profile distribution in a population. (This tests an assumption that the outer orbit activity will be positively associated with a high proportion of younger people in a population since they are closer to posterity than the rest of the population)
6 Voluntary disclosure through GRI is associated with greater CSR activity and less decoupling than voluntary disclosure through integrated accounting reports. (This tests the middle orbit assumption that CSR activity will be greater by firms demonstrating a commitment to the stakeholder theory enshrined in GRI than to the agency theory and conventional corporate governance assumptions enshrined in investor-focused integrated accounting.)

References

Aguinis, H. and Glavas, A. (2012). What we know and don't know about corporate social responsibility: A review and research agenda. *Journal of Management*, 38(4), 932–939.

Arenas, D. and Rodrigo, P. (2016). On firms and the next generations: Difficulties and possibilities for business ethics inquiry. *Journal of Business Ethics*, 133(1), 165–178.

Bailey, K.H. (2020/2021). Stakeholder capitalism against democracy: Relegitimising global neoliberalism. *The Journal of Australian Political Economy*, 86, 85–121.

Bándi, G. (2020). Principles of EU environmental law including (the objective of) sustainable development. In Markan, P. and Eliantino, M. (Eds.) *Research Handbook on EU Environmental Law*. Elgaronline. Available at: https://doi.org/10.4337/9781788970679

Bansal, P. and Kistruck, G. (2006). Seeing is (not) believing: Managing the impressions of the firm's commitment to the natural environment. *Journal of Business Ethics*, 67(2), 165–180.

Birch, T.H. (1993). Moral considerability and universal consideration. *Environmental Ethics*, 15(4), 313–332.

Booth, W. and Gugliotta, G. (2003). All along, most Iraqi relics were "safe and sound". *Washington Post*, June 9, A12.

Brown, W.E. (1989). *In Fairness to Future Generations: International Law, Common Patrimony, and Intergeneration Equity*. Tokyo: The United Nations University and Dobbs Ferry, NY/New York: Kaczma Transnational Publishers, Inc.

Burt, R.S. (2001). The social capital of structural holes. In Guillen, M.F., Collins, R., England, P. and Meyer, M. (Eds.), *New Directions in Economic Sociology*. New York: Russell Sage Foundation.

Burt, R.S. (2004). Structural holes and good ideas. *American Journal of Sociology*, 110(2), 349–399.

Campbell, J.L. (2007). Why would corporations behave in socially responsible ways? An institutional theory of corporate social responsibility? *Academy of Management Review*, 32(3), 946–967.

Castello, I. and Lozano, J.M. (2011). Searching for new forms of legitimacy through corporate responsibility rhetoric. *Journal of Business Ethics*, 100(1), 11–29.

Cho, C.H. and Patten, D.M. (2007). The role of environmental disclosures as tools of legitimacy: A research note. *Accounting, Organizations and Society*, 32(7/8), 639–647.

De Benedetto, M. (2018). Effective law from a regulatory and administrative law perspective. *European Journal of Risk Regulation*, 9(3), 391–415.

Dellaportas, S. and Davenport, L. (2008). Reflections on the public interest in accounting. *Critical Perspectives on Accounting*, 19(7), 1080–1098.

Di Maggio, P. and Powell, W. (1983). The iron cage revisited: Institutional, isomorphism and collective rationality in organizational fields. *American Sociological Review*, 48(2), 146–160.

Donleavy, G.D. (2012). Floodgates and accountability: Issues in an orbital theory. *International Journal of Economics and Accounting*, 3(2), 101–114.

Dowling, J. and Pfeffer, J. (1975). Organizational legitimacy, social values and organizational behavior. *Pacific Sociological Review*, 18(1), 122–136.

Enoch, S. (2007). A greener Potemkin Village? Corporate social responsibility and the limits of growth. *Capitalism, Nature, Socialism*, 18(2), 79–90.

Finneron-Burns, E. (2017). What's wrong with human extinction? *Canadian Journal of Philosophy*, 47(2–3), 327–343.

Flannigan, R. (2002). Fiduciary control of political corruption. *Advocates' Quarterly*, 26, 252–258.

Flannigan, R. (2009). The core nature of fiduciary accountability. *New Zealand Law Review*, 375, 376–385.

Frederickson, H.G. (1994). Can public officials correctly be said to have obligations to future generations? *Public Administration Review*, 54(5), 457.

Freeman, E.R. (1984). *Strategic Management: A Stakeholder Approach.* Minneapolis, MN: Pitman.

Friedman, M. (1970). The social responsibility of business is to increase its profits. *The New York Times Magazine*, September 13. Available at: https:inlink.springer.com/chapter/10.1007/978-3-540-70818-6_14

Godwin, R.K., Lopez, E.J. and Seldon, B.J. (2008). Allocating lobbying resources between collective and private rents. *Political Research Quarterly*, 61(2), 345–359.

Gotsi, M. and Wilson, A.M. (2001). Corporate reputation: Seeking a definition. *Corporate Communications: an International Journal*, 6(1), 24–30.

Harmon, M.M. (1995). *Responsibility as Paradox: A Critique of Rational Discourse on Government.* Thousand Oaks, CA: Sage Publications.

Harmon, M.M. and Mayer, R.T. (1986). *Organization Theory for Public Administration.* Boston, MA: Little, Brown and Company.

Hartshorne, C. (1981). The ethics of contributionism. In Partridge, E. (Ed.), *Responsibility to Future Generations.* Buffalo, NY: Prometheus Books.

Herlin, H. (2017). Corporate social responsibility as relief from responsibility. *Critical Perspectives on International Business*, 13(1), 2–22.

Jonas, H. (1979). *Das Prinzip Verantwortung.* Frankfurt am Main: Insel Verlag.

Jonas, H. (1984). *The Imperative of Responsibility: In Search of an Ethics for the Technological Age.* Chicago, IL: University of Chicago Press.

Kaczmarek, P. and Beard, S.I. (2020). Human extinction and our obligations to the past. *Utilitas*, 32(2), 199–208.

Kass, L.R. (1990). Applied ethics. *The Hastings Center Report*, 20(1), 5–12.

Kennedy, S.S. (2017). Thirty years of public management scholarship: Plenty of "how", not enough "why". *International Journal of Public Sector Management*, 30(6–7), 566–574.

Kersh, R. (2000). State autonomy and civil society: The lobbyist connection. *Critical Review*, 14(2–3), 237–258.

Kersh, R. (2002). The well-informed lobbyist: Information and interest group lobbying. In Cigler, A. and Loomis, B. (Eds.), *Interest Group Politics*, 7th edition. Washington, DC: Congressional Quarterly Press.

Kumaralingam, A. (2007). Lord Atkin and the philosopher's stone: The search for a universal test for duty. *Singapore Journal of Legal Studies*, December, 350–360.

Kwak, J. (2014). Cultural capture and financial crisis. In Carpenter, D. and Moss, D.A. (Eds.) *Preventing Regulatory Capture: Special Interest Influence and how to Limit it.* Cambridge: Cambridge University Press.

Lacey, A.R. (1986). *A Dictionary of Philosophy.* London: Routledge and Kegan Paul.

Laufer, W.S. (2003). Social accountability and corporate greenwashing. *Journal of Business Ethics*, 43(3), 253–261.

Lewis, C.W. (2006). In pursuit of the public interest. *Public Administration Review*, 66(5), 694–701.

Lindblom, C. (1993). Theoretical implications of organisational legitimacy for corporate social performance and disclosure. Critical Perspectives on Accounting Conference Presentation, New York.

Lippman, W. (1955/1989). *Essays in the Public Philosophy*. Boston, MA/New Brunswick, NJ: Little Brown and Company/Transaction Publishers.

Lock, I. and Seele, P. (2016). The credibility of CSR reports in Europe. Evidence from a quantitative content analysis in 11 countries. *Journal of Cleaner Production*, 122(3), 186–200.

Lowery, D. (2013). Lobbying influence: Meaning, measurement and missing. *Interest Groups and Advocacy*, 2(1), 1–26.

Merkl-Davies, D.M. and Brennan, N.M. (2007). Discretionary disclosure strategies in corporate narratives: Incremental information or impression management? *Journal of Accounting Literature*, 26, 116–196.

Messner, M. (2009). The limits of accountability. *Accounting, Organizations and Society*, 34, 918–939.

Miller, D. (2005). Reasonable partiality towards compatriots. *Ethical Theory and Moral Practice*, 8(12), 63–81.

Mohr, L.A., Webb, D.J. and Harris, K.E. (2001). Do consumers expect companies to be socially responsible? The impact of corporate social responsibility on buying behavior. *The Journal of Consumer Affairs*, 35(1), 45–72.

Patten, D.M. (1991). Exposure, legitimacy, and social disclosure. *Journal of Accounting and Public Policy*, 10(4), 297–308.

Patten, D.M. (1992). Intra-industry environmental disclosures in response to the Alaskan oil spill: A note on legitimacy theory. *Accounting, Organizations and Society*, 17(5), 471–475.

Phiri, J.G.A. and Guven-Uslu, P. (2019). Social networks, corruption and institutions of accounting, auditing and accountability. *Accounting, Auditing and Accountability Journal*, 32(2), 508–530.

Posner, R.A. (1998). The problematics of moral and legal theory. *Harvard Law Review*, 111(7), 1637, 1642–1646.

Ramus, C.A. and Montiel, I. (2005). When are corporate environmental policies a form of greenwashing? *Business and Society*, 44(4), 377–414.

Rawls, J. (1971). *A Theory of Justice*. Cambridge, MA: Belknap Press of Harvard University Press.

Richards, D.A.J. (1982). Contractarian theory, intergenerational justice, and energy policy. In MacLean, D. and Brown, P.G. (Eds.), *Energy and the Future*. Totowa, NJ: Rowman and Littlefield.

Roberts, J. (2003). The manufacture of corporate social responsibility: Construction corporate sensibility. *Organization Ethics, Politics and Organizing*, 10(2), 135–149.

Schiff, E.L., Seufer, K., Whitesell, A. and Lowery, D. (2015). Agency problems and interest representation: An empirical analysis of the costs of lobbying. *Interest Groups and Advocacy*, 4(3), 225–248.

Schneider, S.C. (1988). National vs. corporate culture: Implications for human resource management. *Human Resource Management*, 27(2), 231–246.

Schultz, F. and Wehmeier, S. (2010). Institutionalization of corporate social responsibility within corporate communications: Combining institutional, sense making and communication perspectives. *Corporate Communications*, 15(1), 929.

Seele, P. and Gatti, L. (2015). Greenwashing revisited: In search of a typology and accusation-based definition incorporating legitimacy strategies. *Business Strategy and the Environment*, 26(2), 239–252.

Seele, P. and Knebel, S. (2015). Quo vadis GRI? A (critical) assessment of GRI 3.1 A+ non-financial reports and implications for credibility and standardization. *Corporate Communications: an International Journal*, 20(2), 196–212.

Stephenson, M. and Jackson, H.E. (2010). Lobbyists as imperfect agents: Implications for public policy in a pluralist system. *Harvard Journal on Legislation*, 47(1), 1–20.

Tai, L. (2017). Regulatory capture and quality. *Journal of Public Policy*, 37(3), 261–286.

Trueblood, R.M. and Stevens, R. (1973). Trueblood on the Trueblood report. *Tempo*, 19(1), 1–5.

UNESCO. (2003). Resolution 1483. The Situation between Iraq and Kuwait. Available at: http://unscr.com/en/resolutions/1483

Wade-Benzoni, K.A., Sondak, H. and Galinsky, A.D. (2010). Leaving a legacy: Intergenerational allocations of benefits and burdens. *Business Ethics Quarterly*, 20(1), 734.

Walker, R.G. (1987). Australia's ASRB: A case study of political activity and regulatory "capture". *Accounting and Business Research*, 17(67), 269–286.

Wellman, C. (1995). *Real Rights*. Oxford: Oxford University Press.

Weston, B.H. (2012). The theoretical foundations of intergenerational ecological justice: An overview. *Human Rights Quarterly*, 34(1), 251–266.

Wu, D. (2019). Information overload in CSR reports in China: An exploratory study. *Australasian Accounting, Business and Finance Journal*, 13(3), 3–28.

Yates, S. and Cardin-Trudeau, L. (2021). Lobbying "from within": A new perspective on the revolving door and regulatory capture. *Canadian Public Administration*, 64(2), 301–319.

Zsolnai, L. (2006). Extended stakeholder theory. *Society and Business Review*, 1(1), 37–44.

15 Companies' Responsibilities and Political Dissent

The New Frontier of Corporate Social Responsibility?

Denis De Castro Halis

Introduction

Multinational companies need to be aware of an indeterminate multitude of markets and their governments and peoples' political sensitivities. When trying to please one of these, they might face a backlash from others. "Money or high moral ground?" is the core question in media reports about the rift between the US National Basketball Association (NBA), the Chinese Basketball Association (CBA), and Chinese companies and the Chinese government that started in 2019 (Smith, 2019; White, 2019b). The rift was triggered by a tweet by Daryl Morey, then general manager of the Houston Rockets (an NBA team), expressing support for the massive and continuing demonstrations of political dissent in Hong Kong in 2019. The tweet contained an image with the message "Fight for freedom, stand with Hong Kong" (Agnew, 2019). The long-lasting demonstrations in Hong Kong turned increasingly violent, with repeated clashes between the police and protesters, and became a politically sensitive issue in China and a divisive one in Hong Kong. The NBA was, then, the most popular sports league in China (McNicol, 2017; Perper, 2019) but, nevertheless, the CBA, Chinese companies, and government officials pulled the plug on NBA events, revoked sponsorships, ceased the broadcasting of games in the country, and even delisted Rockets products from online shopping platforms (Blennerhassett, 2019; Kharpal, 2019; Toh and He, 2019; White, 2019a).

Some of these media reports underscore what was arguably a dilemma faced by the NBA: either to try to get back into the good graces of China, the NBA's largest overseas market, to maintain the profitable business relationship, or to adopt a principled stand on behalf of individual freedom of expression. As one report stated,

> Nevermind [sic] that this was a tweet from an individual, not the Houston Rockets and certainly not the NBA as a whole. Nevermind [sic] that decades of laying the foundations of a relationship, where the NBA has become the foreign sports league most enmeshed in China, stand to be undone. It has been said that 30 years have gone in 30 seconds while a message shared on

DOI: 10.4324/9781003274575-19

> Chinese social media read, "US–China people-to-people exchanges started with ping pong, and ended with basketball".
>
> (White, 2019b)

Morey later backtracked, apologizing somehow, and deleted his tweet (Agnew, 2019). However, this was not sufficient to end the rift. People in China, including the spokesperson for China's Foreign Ministry, continued to maintain that his and the NBA's conduct had been provocative, offensive, and insensitive. Tilman Fertitta, the team's owner, later posted a tweet saying that Morey did not speak for the Rockets and that the team was not a political organization (Sielski, 2019). In a public statement about the rift, the NBA's commissioner and spokesperson, Adam Silver, mentioned free speech for individuals who did not speak on behalf of the league, and explained that his role was not to adjudicate on differences of opinion. He then became the center of attention, receiving pressure from all sides to take one of two extreme and antagonistic options: to punish and make an example of Morey in order to satisfy the Chinese government, or to unquestionably affirm NBA's defense of free speech, which was demanded by audiences and other people (i.e., politicians, media broadcasters, and companies with US headquarters) within the United States and elsewhere. US lawmakers got involved and formed a bipartisan group. They issued a statement saying that it was outrageous that the NBA had to cave in to pressure from the Chinese government "to suppress the speech of Americans inside the United States" (Lane, 2019).

This chapter explores this and other examples of the actions of well-known for-profit organizations and companies when they have become involved in events that resulted in controversial repercussions of a political nature. It is hoped that this investigation about what companies have effectively done highlights the importance of the theme for scholars, and sheds light on the choices available to corporate decision makers and spokespeople when facing dilemmas involving choices of morality, legal principles, and profit. The investigation draws on the author's theoretical and empirical socio-legal investigations into the concept of dissent, the various types and forms of dissent, and the reactions to dissent (Halis, 2020, 2022). Thus, it benefits from the author's effort to categorize the manifestations of dissent, to address the importance of dissent, and to formulate a comprehensive concept. Moreover, the investigation advances the argument that corporate social responsibility (CSR) is no longer just linked to the marketing strategies of companies (i.e., to build their image and sell their products or services), but is becoming increasingly regulated via enforceable legal rules.

This investigation relies, in particular, on the method of induction, in which information and insights are extracted from the analysis of paradigmatic cases that attracted worldwide media coverage. Giants of the digital industry, such as Apple, Facebook, WhatsApp, Tencent, and Twitter, have been at the forefront of the discussion on the political and legal responsibilities of companies concerning dissent. Others, however, from various industries, such as the transportation industry (e.g., Hong Kong's international airline Cathay Pacific and the Italian carmaker Fiat), the food industry (e.g., Starbucks), the accommodation industry (e.g.,

Airbnb), for-profit sports organizations (e.g., the NBA and the National Football Association/NFL, both in the United States), and even the steel industry (e.g., Brazil's largest steel producer Gerdau) have also taken a stand with regard to initiatives of dissent. Some cases involving some of these companies will be explored here. The cases highlight contemporary political and legal responsibilities of companies that go beyond the issues that are commonly linked to the idea of CSR, such as the environment, labor relations, poverty, and education. The investigation uses media reports from well-known media broadcasting outlets, as well as reports from academic and other organizations, to obtain and offer details about those cases.

Concept of Dissent and Political Dissent

To succeed in addressing what political dissent is, one first needs to engage in a broader effort of conceptualizing "dissent". There are a multitude of different uses of the term, accompanied by a general lack of a clear definition. A search for the term "dissent" in the titles of publications in the Web of Science databases in the period between 1980 and 2019 resulted in 4,469 records which show that the term is used in the literature of diverse fields of inquiry, including religion, political science, economics, international relations, philosophy, and law. The search, and a review of the literature connected to law and social theory, suggests that the term has become a comprehensive label, a catch-all term, comprising very different phenomena, including disobedience, conflict, social movements, disagreement, deviance, transgression, rebellion, free speech, freedom of demonstration, resistance, and protest. The non-rigorous use of the term adds to its ambivalence and makes it indistinguishable from several of those other concepts, which are only coincidentally equivalent.

The opacity of the term complicates debates about the importance and the legal regulation (for both protection and restriction) of different types and forms of the manifestation of political dissent. Work has been done on the reasons behind the conceptualization of dissent:

> The need to conceptualize dissent is linked to several relevant questions. What constitutes manifestations of dissent? When democracies should not endure dissent (e.g., what or when forms of political dissent expressed by public protest are not acceptable)? What is it about dissent that makes it valuable (e.g., when can it transform societies for the better)? Who are dissenters (e.g., Nobel laureates, but not religious terrorists?) and what to do with them?
>
> (Halis, 2022, 6)

Collins and Skover (2013, xviii) add other questions to the previous ones: "Can a commercial for-profit corporation ever be a dissenter? Does the profit motive change the analytical equation? If so, why? If not, why not?". They quote from their interviews with prestigious contemporary scholars who offer opposing views and, thus, their questions remain without definite answers.

All the above are relevant questions that need to be addressed in order to help CSR-committed companies to act when faced with political controversies related to people's rights and freedoms. There are a variety of ways to answer them, depending on the chosen perspective (e.g., one of the various shades pertaining to a more liberal or a more authoritarian perspective), on who is behind the manifestation of dissent (e.g., a segregated and discriminated against minority, or the majority of a population under an authoritarian government controlled by a political elite), on the form in which it is expressed (e.g., violent or peaceful dissent), and on various other criteria. Legal scholars who have written on dissent, including Harvard's Sunstein and Tushnet, have tried to answer those questions using dualistic and moral labels: good and bad dissent, dissent of the right and wrong kind, or positive and negative dissent. Tushnet (2012) seeks to argue against the depiction by Sunstein (2003) by contending that societies need dissent of the right kind, rather than dissent as such. Sunstein, however, had already made that point and had been cautious not to be seen as a supporter of dissent in all cases and at all costs: "What we want to encourage is not dissent as such but reasonable dissent, or dissent of the right kind" (2003, 91). This sort of moral and dualistic label poses new difficulties for well-intentioned companies: Who is to define what is positive or negative dissent? How is that to be practically defined? Governments may adopt and promote such labeling to encourage or, on the other hand, to suppress particular dissenting perspectives, selecting one over others. Political leaders can instrumentalize those labels in pursuit of their goals within power struggles and institutions, using them as propaganda for either the promotion or the silencing of voices of dissent.

To dissent implies having the possibility of speaking out or behaving differently when faced with other people's opinions or conduct, and making the choice to do so. That different voice or behavior needs to be manifested (externally expressed or articulated). Thus, within this concept, there is no such a thing as a person who dissents in silence, without anyone knowing about it. Such a person, who holds a different view for herself, is not to be considered a dissenter. The manifestation of dissent, either by action (active) or by omission (passive, when an action was the expected behavior) brings the dissent to life and produces reactions. The different thoughts, feelings, or beliefs of dissatisfied but silent people are relevant if they are manifested, but otherwise these silent people are no different from the conformists. Silent dissatisfaction, however, can be useful for popular action or for follow-up actions, and require a leader or a first dissenter to catalyze the silent divergence in a society (Halis, 2020, 2022). Further, the concept of dissent offered here goes beyond mere rejection or non-acceptance, as these neither propose something new nor disclose new information. Dissent has a propositional nature, which reflects non-conformist thought and action. It is not equal to criticism, and it does not even imply divergence (i.e., contrary views or antagonism), but, rather, it is a view from elsewhere (Daube, 1971, 784ff) that offers another sense, another meaning, another feeling, or another reason that is different from the existing ones (i.e., is a holding otherwise), but is not necessarily divergent (Halis, 2020, 2022). An alternative view to usual or majoritarian beliefs can merely be different from, rather than contrary to, them. Dissent may strengthen the grounds of existing views when it questions common but thoughtless assumptions. Rejected or even hated dissenting behaviors can encourage conformists to reflect upon their own choices and reassess their ideas and postures, and can, perhaps, strengthen them at the individual or collective level. Dissent is a relational and contextual concept, and its manifestations are potential catalysts of societal change. A behavior becomes dissenting behavior when it occupies a position that challenges a feature within the expected order of things (political, social, cultural, and so on) in a given time and context (Halis, 2020). The usual assessment of specific manifestations of dissent and the changes it provokes, which considers them as positive or negative, depends more on the results achieved by the dissent and the reactions it produces than on any evaluation of its actual substance or form (Halis, 2022).

Halis (2020, 2022) has offered a framework, with ideal-type categories, to classify actual manifestations of dissent according to their predominant nature and other factors such as their forms of expression, motivations, goals, promoters, outcomes, and the reactions they provoke. Dissent of a political nature, or political dissent, is one of these broad types of dissent. It is not equal, for example, to judicial or religious dissent, although there might be overlaps between these categories. Likewise with environmental dissent. When Greta Thunberg started demonstrating in favor of the preservation of the environment and against perceived inaction by her government, her protest was initially carried out in front of the parliament building in Stockholm (Kraemer, 2021). Hers was environmental as well as political dissent. Moreover, her dissent provoked reactions around the globe and gained many followers, in a move that shows how political dissent in one place can fire similar initiatives in many other places:

> Dissent has become a significant transnational phenomenon, reflecting and shaping various aspects of global politics. In fact, dissent has become what could be called a transversal phenomenon – a political practice that not only transgresses national boundaries, but also questions the spatial logic through which these boundaries have come to constitute and frame the conduct of international relations.
>
> (Bleiker, 2000, 2)

Political dissent occurs across the whole of the political spectrum, from the extreme left-wing to the extreme right-wing. It can be represented by manifestations against one given reality while favoring another. In this way, it is both negative (denies something) and positive (proposes something else) (Buela, 2004, 77–78). In Halis' framework, political dissent may be violent or peaceful, and it does not need to be public (overt) as it can be concealed or anonymous. It may be motivated by egoistic or by altruistic (principled) interests and values. Altruistic and principled dissenters aspire to be right and are willing to sacrifice themselves for the benefit of others, while egoistic dissenters do not have such aspirations and willingness. Thus, political dissenters are not necessarily martyrs or morally correct. Political dissent can favor innovations (being innovative or progressive) or, conversely, favor the maintenance of the status quo or the return to a previous status quo (being either conservative or reactionary). It does not need to be promoted by single individuals or minorities, by outsiders, or by disadvantaged people. There can be collective and institutional political dissent, as well as dissent by majorities, by insiders, and by those with or in power. Hence, individuals behind or in control of companies can lead their organizations to undertake dissenting actions (e.g., through marketing campaigns or the financial sponsorship of causes) in favor of political issues in a way that confronts government policies or a feature of society that they would like to change. Google may be an example of this. The company is reported to have left its operations in China, closing its office in the country in 2010, because of its resistance and objections to caving in to the government's pressure to add political censorship filters to its search engines and to share information with officials that could be used against political dissenters (Fannin, 2010; Johnson, 2010).

Companies that get involved with the protection or the promotion of political dissent can become important agents of societal change. These changes, however, can be considered to be for the better or for the worse, according to distinct perspectives and interests. Such a judgment is complex, however, and its detailed discussion is beyond the scope of this chapter. There are, however, extreme cases already foreseen in laws throughout the world that involve dissent that is punishable, such as the dissent of violent terrorists on behalf of religious or race-supremacist beliefs. My argument here is that companies should not support or attempt to protect this sort of dissenting initiative that undoubtedly violates laws aimed at advancing human rights. If a company did so, its behavior would be incompatible with the idea of CSR in its new interface with political dissent. Many cases are not as extreme as those mentioned, however, and it would not be possible to address them in such a straightforward way. As mentioned above, this discussion is not going to be undertaken here; the important point being made is that even a single articulated politically dissenting view can enable a debate or other actions that might not exist otherwise and, thus, can trigger or enhance discussions over matters of great social relevance. Political dissent can provoke reflection on the ways societies and organizations are structured and function. It can also provoke debates regarding the limits and clashes inherent in fundamental rights and freedoms, which are needed to reach a balance between societal unity and diversity, as well as between conformity and dissent. As Collins and Skover (2013, xii) put it, "democracy is diversity, and diversity of views is often born out of dissent".

Digital technology companies do have a special responsibility concerning political dissent, both to protect it and to make sure that their platforms do not become places of homogeneous debate based on intolerance and false and wrongful information. As with any other causes, such as sustainable development, the task needs to be carried out as a common effort between companies, civil society, and government officials from the three branches of political power. This is a task some of them have become aware of and taken measures against. Moreover, parliamentary hearings in various countries have summoned and heard company executives, to debate how their businesses are regulating themselves and how to regulate them further. The result is the passing of laws throughout much of the world to protect personal data, to tackle fake news, and to impose sanctions on companies that do not comply with national legislation and judicial orders. Scholarship has underscored the fact that, by challenging social conformity, dissent has the potential to correct errors, break up wrongful informational cascades (e.g., fake news), and combat polarization and extremism (Sunstein, 2003, v, 2009), all of which have been facilitated by the popularization of digital means of communication. Other works maintain that, by encouraging channels of dissent alongside heterogeneity and exchanges of views, institutions can improve deliberation processes, allowing the maximum disclosure of information, and this can result in sound policy decisions (de Melo-Martín and Intemann, 2013).

CSR and Contemporary Political Controversies Over Rights and Freedoms in Digitalized Contexts

Controversy over the responsibility of companies has acquired new dimensions. This has been true for multinational companies (i.e., mega corporations) and for for-profit organizations operating in various industries that are as important and well known as those in Table 15.1.

All of these have taken stands on one or more of the political causes, stances, and movements that have gained visibility across the world and that include those in Table 15.2.

The limits and aim of this chapter mean that it is impossible to explore all these political controversies involving these multinational companies. The controversies have involved not only multinational companies and for-profit organizations

Table 15.1 Examples of Companies Involved in Controversial Political Issues

Airbnb	NBA
Apple	NFL
Cathay Pacific	Nike
Facebook	Starbucks
Fiat	Twitter
Gerdau	WhatsApp
Google	YouTube

Table 15.2 Examples of Political Causes, Stances, and Movements

2019 Hong Kong Protests
Black Lives Matter
Covid-19 Antivaccine Positions of US and Brazilian Presidents
LGBTQ Rights
Me Too
Stop Asian Hate

but also small companies with local customer bases. A notable contemporary example of the latter is the bakery shop whose owner, a practicing Christian, refused to accept an order for a custom-made cake for the wedding ceremony of a same-sex couple (Hurley, 2018; Satta, 2019). This took place in the state of Colorado, United States, and the details were reviewed by the Colorado Civil Rights Commission. The Commission found that the bakery had discriminated against the couple and, thus, violated Colorado's Anti-Discrimination Act. After losing some appeals, the bakery took the case to the US Supreme Court, where it was heard in December 2017 (*Masterpiece Cakeshop v Colorado Civil Rights Commission*, 584 U.S. Sup. C.2018). The two sides' arguments concerned free speech and the free exercise of religion against the law ensuring non-discrimination. In June 2018, the Court reached its decision, with a 7–2 majority, and reversed the Commission's decision. Despite the Court's decision, the case continues to provoke wide controversy on the arguments of the Justices and on whether the bakery shop did indeed have the right to do what it did. This took place in a political context marked by strong advances in the recognition and exercise of the rights of LGBTQ communities, whose voices are being increasingly often heard.

The *Business and Human Rights Journal* (*BHRJ*) offered an assessment of past and emerging business and human rights (BHR) issues, including various types of responsibility of companies, in its editorial "Business and Human Rights Scholarship: Past Trends and Future Directions" (Deva et al., 2019). The editorial notes that "treating corporations as political institutions with political responsibilities more generally is not a new idea" (p. 209). Further, "the fact that many corporations, especially large multinationals, yield [sic] enormous power and influence is not a new insight. However, the BHR debate has engaged relatively rarely with it at a conceptual level" (p. 208). The editorial cites referential works (Ulrich, 2008; Votaw, 1961) that signal that companies have a political nature or a political dimension to their policies and practices (i.e., a power to interfere in societal affairs, public opinion, and public policies). The term "political" used here refers, however, to politics in its broad meaning, which remains closely attached to that of CSR (i.e., concern for the environment and the interests of workers and the larger community of stakeholders rather than those of shareholders only). This is different from what this chapter aims to highlight, which is related to a narrower meaning of the expression "political responsibility of companies", one that is connected to the notion of political dissent.

The expression "political CSR" tends to be used in a general sense, as a comprehensive label, even within scholarship focusing on it as a field of research (e.g., Frynas and Stephens, 2015, 483). This label can be attached to the activities of companies when exerting political pressure in relation to a wide range of societal issues (e.g., the environment, labor, and social equality), when providing or contributing to community services (e.g., health and education), and when considering codes of conduct applicable to their subsidiaries and their production chains, which can complement or fill gaps in domestic legislation. Additionally, the label is used to discuss the "political aspects" or "political impacts" of CSR without a precise consideration of what that means.

The *BHRJ* editorial refers to the expression "political CSR" as a new research paradigm:

> These and other works led to the emergence of a new research paradigm labelled 'political CSR' in the mid-2000s, whose aim has been to conceptualize the political stature of multinationals and their role in new, polycentric global governance schemes. Further research on positive lobbying or 'lobbying for the good' as well as on 'corporate political advocacy' has explored political responsibility of corporations within and beyond formal political processes and their role in tackling global problems.
>
> (Deva et al., 2019, 209)

Yet again, the editorial refers to BHR strands of research that have underscored the economic, social, and political nature or role of companies, but they do not give special attention to, and offer no empirically based practical advice for companies caught up in polarized societies where there are new ways in which political dissent is formed, takes place, and is disseminated. Hence, there is work to be done concerning the involvement of companies in events related to manifestations of political dissent. That involvement, forced or voluntary, has gained visibility because of the digitization of social life and the rapid circulation of information via social media and communication apps.

Indeed, digital developments implemented by public and private entities have changed people's interactions, the formation of public opinion, governance, and companies' responsibilities. New ways to do ordinary things (e.g., to shop, order and have food delivered, communicate, or pass through immigration departments) have made life convenient to many, but leave digital traces. artificial intelligence (AI), biometrics, and big data are now used in combined processes. Massive data can be and is now collected. It can be used to track and control people and dissenting behavior. Hence, digital technologies have opened new channels for the expression of ideas and behavior, but also new forms of monitoring, censorship, and ways of reacting to dissenting behavior – all provided for by digital technology companies. Further, mass and social media have the potential to turn localized acts of dissent almost immediately into events of global importance, provoking reactions in distant places (Bleiker, 2000, 1). The impact of digitization on dissent is, however, mediated differently in different contexts and legal cultures. The adoption and use of surveillance cameras and biometrics, for example, is seen as natural and is easily accepted in some contexts, while it is not even considered in others (Halis, 2020, 2022).

The *BHRJ* editorial notes a trend that demands from corporations and their leaders' proactive postures and engagement are in favor of human rights ideals and causes, so that their products and services can advance, rather than restrict them:

> Business leaders are expected not only to do what it takes to respect human rights throughout their business operations in all types of environments, but

> also to proactively engage in defending human rights against the movements actively undermining them. Increasingly, they are called on to resist damaging policies, oppose harmful speech and the repeal of human rights instruments more generally. Furthermore, they are increasingly expected to take a stand on social issues, engage in human rights advocacy and actively support human rights defenders. Corporations, in other words, are expected to become 'corporate human rights defenders' themselves.
>
> (Deva et al., 2019, 208–209)

The editorial cites works that have addressed and sustained this sort of political advocacy in favor of human rights (e.g., marriage equality in Wettstein and Baur, 2016; Wettstein, 2010) and even in favor of specific human rights defenders (Ineichen, 2017). The heart of the matter, however, is not whether companies should defend human rights and freedoms, but how to decide practical dilemmas when those rights clash with each other, as seen in the case of the US bakery. Among other arguments, the bakery affirmed the freedom of religion and conscience, while the other party affirmed the right not to be discriminated against (Satta, 2019). Was the company defending the religious rights of Christians, or was it discriminating against people based on their sexual orientation? Further, this case involves the classic discussion of the nature and scope of the legal personality of companies. This means, for example, reflecting on the view that the company's owner (the bakery's owner) may have his own religious beliefs and act in accordance with them, but the company is a distinct and separate legal person from the owner, being a legal fiction to conduct business, rather than an actual living and conscious natural person.

CSR, Political Rights, and National Governments

The concept and the ideas related to CSR have been continuously developing in a movement that goes from the field of business to that of law. CSR has moved from marketing strategies that develop brands, to accounting obligations (such as the obligation of a company to report on the CSR-related activities it conducts), to national and international guidelines and directives (e.g., soft law and the UN's Guiding Principles on Business and Human Rights), and to domestic and international legally enforceable rules.

Furthermore, pieces of legislation on a range of issues related to CSR, such as labor relations, the environment, consumer rights, and human rights, were kept separate from each other, and separate from company, trade, investment, and business laws. Deva (2011, 80) has used the term "traditional landscape" to describe the situation in which the laws and governing institutions that had an impact, or that should have had an impact, on the businesses and the functioning of companies were like "isolated islands". More recently, that landscape is being transformed: "winds of change" have favored the integration of all those "islands" (Deva, 2011, 85). The regulation on that first range of issues (i.e., labor, the environment, etc.) is becoming a part of the regulation of the second range of issues (i.e., company, trade, etc.). CSR has entered company- and business-related laws and has been strengthened in confrontations with traditional approaches that only emphasize the profit motive of companies or define them as legal bodies conducting business for profit.

China and India are among the pioneers among countries that have company laws that expressly mention CSR. India's current Company Act entered into force in 2013 and China's current Company Law entered into force in 2014. However, many previous movements of integration between CSR and company laws had already occurred in other jurisdictions, including the United Kingdom, Australia, Indonesia, South Africa, and various countries in continental Europe (Deva, 2011). These initiatives of integration between different areas of law have all been based on the initial views of CSR, which are narrower than the view proposed here in which it is connected to the political responsibilities of companies.

The theme of the responsibility of companies regarding political rights and freedoms becomes increasingly topical in the context of populist governments carrying out practices and discourses that criticize human rights or their underpinning ideals. The actions of such governments have repeatedly put the spotlight on companies, obliging them to take positions concerning a range of essentially political and controversial issues. In Brazil, under the presidency of Bolsonaro (whose term is due to last from January 2019 to December 2022), there have been many public calls in favor of additional powers for the executive branch of the government (i.e., in favor of a strong government), as well as advocacy of torture, the death penalty, and the freedom for "good citizens" to use guns. These calls have gained space and followers among the population and are blended with anti-corruption, anti-crime, anti-system, nationalistic, and religious-based discourses. The president has not only learned to ride that wave and benefit from those sentiments, but has also encouraged them. In many ways, he has shamelessly tried his utmost to mimic the former US president Donald Trump's controversial arguments, decisions, and practices (Morrison, 2021). He has done this since his presidential campaign (Phillips, 2018). He has gone beyond it, however, continuously complementing those rhetorical and behavioral elements with praise for authoritarianism and military power.

After the start of the COVID-19 pandemic, Bolsonaro also became one of the world leaders who adopted recalcitrant, antiscientific, and antivaccine approaches to address the menace of the virus (Nicas, 2021; Saad Filho and Feil, 2021). Through discourses, interviews, posts on his social media, behaviors at public events, and the policies and legal norms that were enacted, Bolsonaro dissented from the course of action recommended by most scientists, respectful leaders, health personnel, and officials from the World Health Organization. He even dissented from his own health ministers, who were continuously replaced. His postures and comments became known worldwide and led to investigations by Brazil's parliament and several accusations of crime, including crimes against humanity (Nicas, 2021).

Despite much controversy, Bolsonaro's leadership of his base remains in place. A notable reason for this is that messages are created and circulated in WhatsApp groups – extremely popular in Brazil – and other social media networks, which contribute to the spread of misinformation and fake news among his supporters (Daniels, 2021). In trying to address the use of its platform to disseminate wrong information and false news, WhatsApp has limited the number of people to whom a message can be forwarded (Hamilton, 2019). In many and important ways, Bolsonaro has tried to mimic and even amplify the discourse and postures of the former US president Trump regarding the pandemic. As happened with Trump, Twitter, Facebook, and YouTube have censored some of the president's actions that have spread wrongful or misleading information about the virus and the pandemic.

Today's reality of Brazil is, however, not an isolated example of the current situation in the world regarding national political leaders. The *BHRJ* editorial notes:

> The recent backlash against human rights and the rise of right-wing populist movements and anti-democratic sentiments around the globe have led to new political demands for corporations to use their power and influence in defense of human rights. As a result, human rights activists increasingly look to corporations to fill the void left by political leadership. Business leaders are expected not only to do what it takes to respect human rights throughout their business operations in all types of environments, but also to proactively engage in defending human rights against the movements actively undermining them. Increasingly, they are called on to resist damaging policies, oppose harmful speech and the repeal of human rights instruments more generally.
>
> (Deva et al., 2019, 208)

Under mounting pressure from different forces, and acknowledging their current role as major digital platforms for the dissemination of information, YouTube, Twitter, and Facebook have more than once taken down videos, tweets, and posts and suspended people's accounts, including those of Trump and Bolsonaro – even though some of those companies have made their rules more flexible in the case of posts by high-level politicians (Morrison, 2021). Some of the actions by these technology companies were said to be the first to be taken against high-level elected leaders. This may seem remarkable to many people, as these are leaders of important nations, widely considered to have democratic institutional structures and traditions. Bolsonaro has had his social media accounts suspended or his posts taken down, in particular, due to false and antiscientific news related to the COVID-19 pandemic (Fonseca, 2021; Palau, 2021; The Cube, 2021).

These strategies, in which digital technology companies interfere with the circulation of information and dissenting views by elected leaders, do, however, have a worrying side. The suspension of the communication of elected politicians with their audiences could represent a new form of defending, or imposing, private corporate interests and views in the disguise of defensible goals or democratic ideals. The *BHRJ* editorial also notes that:

> Despite the calls for harnessing corporate power for the advancement and realization of human rights, dangers loom in the distortion of public and political processes through private interests when corporations enter the policy space … Corporate capture denotes the undermining of public space and processes by private corporate interests.
>
> (Deva et al., 2019, 209–210)

Indeed, rather than standing up for the rights and freedoms of individuals and groups, corporations could advance strategies to use BHR discourse to expand their own corporate rights and freedoms, avoiding government regulation and societal interference in their affairs:

> Court rulings granting unprecedented power to corporations (including the ability to claim human rights) and the use of strategic lawsuits against public participation (SLAPP) by corporations, among other things, show that the takeover of public, judicial and policy space by corporations is ongoing today. The difference may be that it is happening not secretly and in silence anymore, but noisily and in plain sight. In regard to such problematic aspects of corporate political activity in the BHR space and the negative impact this may have on the realization of human rights, publication of more systematic research in forums such as BHRJ is needed.
>
> (Deva et al., 2019, 210)

The jury remains out on what the corporate responsibilities related to manifestations of political dissent by politicians, individuals, organizations, and institutions might be in practice. When do such responsibilities require action, and when do they require inaction? What changes, in terms of companies' responsibilities, and what new roles of corporate private actors regarding political dissent have gained relevance because of the advance of digital technologies that is changing societies? How do companies want to be perceived, and how are they likely to be perceived, after engaging on one side of a political power struggle? These doubts remain, and the matter is arguably a new frontier for CSR that is not yet clearly regulated, if it is regulated at all.

Further Examples of Companies and Their Dilemmas Related to CSR and Political Dissent

The previous sections refer to cases that provide contemporary evidence about the way that companies and for-profit organizations are being called on to take a stand in the face of issues that are not clearly regulated and that polarize societies. This section seeks to supply additional evidence, either by providing further elaboration about the companies and cases already mentioned, or by offering new cases.

The beginning of this chapter has referred to the tension in 2019 between the NBA and the Chinese government and other parties, which was triggered by a tweet of Daryl Morey. The NBA and the Rockets lost hundreds of millions of dollars because of the incident (MacMahon, 2020). Even though Morey stepped down from his general manager position at the Rockets, the offended parties in China did not forget him. This became evident when he took up a new position as president of the basketball operations of another NBA team, the Philadelphia 76ers. Tencent then stopped putting out live broadcasts of that team's games (*The Guardian*, 2020). The NBA came under strong criticism in the United States, which weakened the various efforts it was making to construct the image of "a force for positive social change" by supporting domestic causes against discrimination and in favor of rights and freedoms (Novak, 2019; Tensley, 2019).

In 2021, when business between the different Chinese and US parties was appearing to improve, an important new round of controversy occurred. The NBA player Enes Kanter started wearing shoes with political images and phrases during games in which his team – the Boston Celtics – was playing, with the aim of criticizing the Chinese government. Some of these controversial shoes contained messages in favor of the freedom of regions in China with large minority populations. Some of the designs of the shoes were said to have been created by Badiucao, a Chinese artist and political dissident based in Australia. Tencent, the large digital company that owns WeChat – China's largest messaging app and one of the country's biggest payment services – which held exclusive streaming rights for NBA games in China, stopped streaming Boston Celtics games online, as did the Chinese television broadcaster CCTV. Further reactions were seen on Chinese social media platforms, which were flooded with demands for Kanter to apologize, to be dismissed, and to be banned from the NBA altogether (Blennerhassett, 2021a).

Kanter went further and called out Nike, one of the NBA's most important sponsors, on its alleged silence on rights issues in China and alleged forced labor of Uyghurs in the Chinese region of Xinjiang. He accused Nike of having contradictory stands:

> Nike remains vocal about injustice [in the US], but when it comes to China, Nike remains silent. … You do not address police brutality in China, you do not speak about discrimination against the LGBT community, you do not say a word about the oppression of minorities in China, you are scared to speak up.
>
> (Blennerhassett, 2021b)

Forced to reply to Kanter's accusations, Nike issued a statement saying that it was committed to ethical and responsible manufacturing and that it upheld international labor standards. The Boston Celtics president of basketball operations affirmed the team's support for all their players and their right to freedom of speech (Blennerhassett, 2021b).

The relationship between sports leagues or associations and individual or collective political dissent by their athletes is not, however, restricted to issues happening internationally. Political dissent by various athletes of the NBA and the NFL has happened often, with the athletes protesting and calling for changes related to racial discrimination and inequality in the United States, provoking both supportive and suppressive reactions. A recent illustration is the protests by athletes against the deaths of black citizens at the hands of members of police forces in the United States. These manifestations gained momentum with the rise of the Black Lives Matter movement, which is a political movement founded in response to perceived injustices, systemic racism, and institutional brutality against black citizens in the United States. Its official website (https://blacklivesmatter.com/about/) states that the movement started in 2013 and is now a Global Network Foundation "whose mission is to eradicate white supremacy and build local power to intervene in violence inflicted on Black communities by the state and vigilantes".

This movement gained worldwide visibility and support after the murder of George Perry Floyd Jr., a black man, in May 2020. His murder was another of several instances of police brutality against black citizens in the United States. George Floyd was murdered by police officers in Minneapolis during an arrest over a suspicion that he had used a counterfeit 20-dollar bill (Bailey, 2021; Fernandez and Burch, 2021). The images of his murder were captured and widely disseminated (E. Murphy, 2020), triggering multiple protests across the United States and the world against police brutality towards black people, and underscoring the cause of the Black Lives Matter movement (Donaghue, 2020; The Economist, 2020). "I can't breathe" were Floyd's dying words, and they became a slogan of the protests. Athletes of both the NBA and the NFL started wearing "I can't breathe" shirts at public events, to show support for the cause and solidarity with the ongoing protests at the time. The movement was, and is, not uncontroversial, however. Many of the protests became violent, with clashes with the police and the destruction of private and public property. Also, its critics commonly affirm that "all lives matter". Even Mike Pence, the US vice president at the time, echoed those words by saying "I really believe all lives matter" (Capatides, 2020).

After Floyd's death, not only high-level athletes but also many ordinary people started wearing shirts and other symbols of the Black Lives Matter movement. Among these were some Starbucks employees. It then became known that the company had issued an internal memo prohibiting its staff from wearing such garments and accessories (Beer, 2020; Bowden, 2020). The company initially claimed that this position was necessary to avoid misunderstandings and the potential incitement to violence. Moreover, it invoked its dress code policy that forbids accessories that advocate a political, religious, or personal issue, maintaining that the policy was necessary and was in place "to create a safe and welcoming" environment for customers and staff. It did not take long for many to accuse the company of being hypocritical, as it had manifested support for racial equality on other occasions, and of also being contradictory, as it exempted from its dress code – and even handed out – buttons and attire celebrating LGBTQ rights and marriage equality (Bowden, 2020; Sacks and Samaha, 2020). As a result of the strong backlash, criticism, and general calls for the chain to be boycotted, the company announced the reversal of its original position, which meant not only that employees were allowed to wear Black Lives Matter apparel, but also that the company produced its own Black Lives Matter shirts for baristas who wanted them (Adams, 2020; Denham, 2020; H. Murphy, 2020).

At the time, other companies, such as Airbnb that operates in the accommodation industry, quickly took different stands on the movement. Airbnb had previously had its own issues concerning accusations that people using its platform, which links those wanting to be lodged with those wanting to rent their space, were being discriminated against. The company took a public stand in support of the movement, which included having a Black Lives Matter symbol on its website and stepping up its efforts to remove customers with discriminatory behavior from its platform, while also launching or strengthening initiatives against racial discrimination (Airbnb, 2022).

These are examples of companies taking a stand on a cause – racial discrimination and police violence – which can be considered to be grounded in legal norms, including norms of a constitutional stature. Such norms do not stand alone, though, and their content is the object of continuous interpretation and doubts about what exactly they mean and how they should be applied in practice in different situations. Further, these are divisive and very controversial issues that polarize the members of communities and can thus impact the business of companies for better or worse. There are other examples of cases, though, in which governments themselves invoke legal norms to tackle political dissent. Such cases should facilitate the decision of companies caught in the political struggles within a society, as their apparent choice is to side with the law or to break it. The reality can, however, show how far this assumption is from the truth.

In 2019, mass demonstrations in Hong Kong led companies as big as Apple, Twitter, and Facebook to take measures that received praise or, on the other hand, criticism from antagonistic social and political forces, both domestically and externally, within the context of developments related to the broad principle of "One Country, Two Systems" (Chan, 2019). This principle is the important political–legal foundation that allowed Hong Kong to become a Special Administrative Region (SAR) of China and retain a high degree of autonomy from the mainland since the 1997 handover. It was agreed that this arrangement with Hong Kong as a SAR was to last for a period of 50 years, until 2047 (Halis, 2015).

The 2019 mass demonstrations in Hong Kong are a recent example of the widespread use of digital resources having a heavy impact on political polarization and dissent. If media reports have referred to the demonstrations as leaderless, they have also underscored how well they were coordinated (Ag, 2019; Frosina, 2021; Shao, 2019). The protesters used new means to channel and organize their dissent. Those means include social media, digital apps, and encrypted communication platforms offered by technology companies. Furthermore, the convenient circulation of images and videos and the exchange of information have strengthened dissent and created a support network of people who either could not, or chose not to, participate directly in the demonstrations, but who provided food and other necessary means for protesters. On the other hand, the government also relied on DNA collection and testing, artificial intelligence, and digital means, including facial recognition, to surveil, track, and tackle the protesters and their demonstrations (Halis, 2020; Lo and Mok, 2019). Fake social media accounts and internet "warriors and robots" have entered the digital environment, with counter-information and "patriotic" activism in favor of government views (Zhang and Chen, 2019). Social media companies, including Twitter and Facebook, revealed that the Chinese government and its proxies created fake social media accounts to undermine the protest movement and the calls for change in Hong Kong (Frier, 2019). Those companies decided to delete thousands of such accounts and bring the matter to the public eye.

The reality in Hong Kong has shown how the use of new digital technologies and means of communication configure a two-way road in which ideas and distinct points of view have additional channels of dissemination while also registering the traces of the people using them, who can then be tracked and sanctioned. As techniques by the security forces evolved, so did the defensive strategies of the protesters (Halis, 2020). An example of that is found in the rise of camera surveillance with facial recognition, which can be used to track or deter potential dissenters. Companies started developing means to protect people's facial identities, bypassing those AI technologies (Holmes, 2020). During the 2019 protests in Hong Kong, people moved from well-known social media platforms to others, not so widespread, that had better guarantee of encrypted communication. The end of the cycle cannot be seen at this point.

Among the digital apps used by the protesters, there was one available from Apple's digital apps store that indicated the real-time location of police squads on a map of Hong Kong (Deng, 2019). By using the app, protesters could quickly relocate and avoid the police force, in a sort of contemporary guerrilla warfare (Wood, 2019). When government officials learned about the use of the app by protesters, they demanded that Apple take it down from its online store. The government argued that the app was helping criminals and others to commit legal offenses. Apple complied with that demand, only to see itself under intense criticism from other social and political forces not only within Hong Kong but also elsewhere. Fearing the impact of that backlash, Apple decided to put the app back in its store, accepting arguments that these were popular demonstrations of political dissent in favor of democratic goals. Criticism and opposing arguments, along with threats of consumer boycotts and legal action, continued from all sides, and the app kept being taken down and put back up in the online store (Deng, 2019; Wood, 2019).

Conclusion

This chapter argues that there is a new frontier of CSR, and it is the result of a study about companies and political dissent. It uses typical cases of companies and other for-profit organizations, most of them with operations beyond national borders, to demonstrate how these have become the center of attention and controversy because of distinct manifestations of dissent related to divisive political and social issues. Besides that, the study reveals the different reactions of these organizations in the face of these manifestations of dissent. The presentation of the cases shows the stands taken by those companies: either to protect and promote or, on the other hand, to restrain collective or individual manifestations of dissent.

Some of the companies reacted, voluntarily or because they were forced to do so, to manifestations of dissent that gained media visibility and caused controversy, intensifying previously existing polarization. It is not uncommon today for companies to find themselves and their businesses at the crossroads of legal, moral, and monetary considerations and dilemmas. The cases illuminate the decisions of some well-known companies at those crossroads.

The chapter's discussion, and its offer of concepts of dissent as well as of political dissent, help to answer the question of whether commercial for-profit bodies can be political dissenters. The fact is that they can, both from a theoretical point of view and from a pragmatic one. Not only can they be important agents of dissent, catalyzing important progressive (i.e., innovative), conservative (i.e., aiming to keep the status quo), or reactionary (aiming to return to a previous status quo that no longer exists) changes or impacts on societies, but they can also support or undermine other political dissenters. These adjectives (progressive, conservative, etc.) are not to be used in their usual senses in political disputes, with a content that is evaluated from moral points of view, but rather in their literal sense as indicated. The exact ways in which companies can or should behave remain in dispute, though, as laws and situations involving fundamental rights and freedoms need to be and are constantly interpreted. Also, dissent and political dissent are contextual and relational concepts that are complex enough for one to talk about good and bad, or negative and positive, dissent. Except in clear-cut and extreme examples, one cannot truly determine at this point which criteria should be followed by companies that are committed to taking their CSR obligations seriously regarding all types and forms of political dissent. It is hoped that this chapter offers a step towards reaching that broad goal.

Acknowledgment

The author acknowledges and thanks UNESA, Rio de Janeiro and its Post-Graduation Program of Law (PPGD) for the partial funding of his investigations through its Scholarship Programs. The author would also like to thank Prof. Hiroshi Fukurai of the University of California, Santa Cruz and Prof. Hanne Petersen of the Faculty of Law of the University of Copenhagen for their continuous support and intellectual exchange, which have greatly enriched his work in the recent years. Finally, the author thanks the editors for their insightful and careful comments.

References

Adams, P. (2020). Starbucks' stumble on Black Lives Matter shows rising stakes for brands in addressing race. *Marketing Dive*, 22 June. Available at: https://www.marketingdive.com/news/starbucks-stumble-black-lives-matter-rising-stakes-race/580131/

Ag, M. (2019). Inside Hong Kong's leaderless uprising. *The Diplomat*, 24 October. Available at: https://thediplomat.com/2019/10/inside-hong-kongs-leaderless-uprising/

Agnew, M. (2019). Houston Rockets' Daryl Morey backtracks after 'stand with Hong Kong' backlash, saying he did not intend to offend China. *South China Morning Post*, 7 October. Available at: https://www.scmp.com/sport/basketball/article/3031797/houston-rockets-daryl-morey-backtracks-after-stand-hong-kong

Airbnb. (2022). Combating discrimination on Airbnb, 5 February. Available at: https://www.airbnb.com.br/against-discrimination

Bailey, H. (2021). 'George Floyd died of low level of oxygen', medical expert testifies; Derek Chauvin kept knee on his neck 'majority of the time'. *The Washington Post*, 8 April. Available at: https://www.washingtonpost.com/nation/2021/04/08/derek-chauvin-trial-2/

Beer, T. (2020). Starbucks bans employees from wearing Black Lives Matter attire. *Forbes*, 11 June. Available at: https://www.forbes.com/sites/tommybeer/2020/06/11/starbucks-bans-employees-from-wearing-black-lives-matter-attire/?sh=6749c2856dd6

Bleiker, R. (2000). *Popular Dissent, Human Agency, and Global Politics*. Cambridge: Cambridge University Press.

Blennerhassett, P. (2019). Brooklyn Nets' NBA community event in Shanghai abruptly cancelled by government as China political storm rages on. *South China Morning Post*, 8 October. Available at: https://www.scmp.com/sport/basketball/article/3031957/nba-cancels-shanghai-brooklyn-nets-event-political-storm-china

Blennerhassett, P. (2021a). NBA player Enes Kanter wears 'Free China' shoes featuring image of Winnie the Pooh during game. *South China Morning Post*, 25 October. Available at: https://www.scmp.com/sport/china/article/3153576/nba-player-enes-kanter-wears-free-china-shoes-featuring-image-winnie

Blennerhassett, P. (2021b). NBA's Enes Kanter calls out Nike's 'silence' on China and alleged forced labour of Uygurs, wears 'modern day slavery' shoes. *South China Morning Post*, 26 October. Available at: https://www.scmp.com/sport/china/article/3153670/nbas-enes-kanter-calls-out-nikes-silence-china-and-alleged-forced

Bowden, J. (2020). Starbucks bans employees from wearing anything in support of Black Lives Matter. *The Hill*, 11 June. Available at: https://thehill.com/business-a-lobbying/502252-starbucks-bans-employees-from-wearing-anything-in-support-of-black-lives

Buela, A. (2004). Teoría del disenso. *Utopía y Praxis Latinoamericana*, 9(27), 75–85.

Capatides, C. (2020). Why saying 'all lives matter' communicates to Black people that their lives don't. *CBS News*, 8 July. Available at: https://www.cbsnews.com/news/all-lives-matter-black-lives-matter/

Chan, C. (2019). Demise of 'One country, Two Systems?' Reflections on the Hong Kong rendition saga. *Hong Kong Law Journal*, 49(2), 447–458.

Collins, R.K.L. and Skover, D.M. (2013). *On Dissent: Its Meaning in America*. New York: Cambridge University Press.

Daniels, J.P. (2021). Health experts slam Bolsonaro's vaccine comments. *The Lancet*, 30 January. Available at: https://www.thelancet.com/journals/lancet/article/PIIS0140-6736(21)00181-1/fulltext

Daube, D. (1971). Dissent in Bible and Talmud. *California Law Review*, 59(3), 784–794.

De Melo-Martín, I. and Intemann, K. (2013). Scientific dissent and public policy: Is targeting dissent a reasonable way to protect sound policy decisions? *EMBO Reports*, 14(3), 231–235.

Deng, I. (2019). Apple allows Hong Kong protest map app that can track police and protester locations. *South China Morning Post*, 8 October. Available at: https://www.scmp.com/tech/apps-social/article/3032001/apple-allows-hong-kong-protest-map-app-can-track-police-and

Denham, H. (2020). In reversal, Starbucks will allow employees to wear 'Black Lives Matter' T-shirts. *The Washington Post*, 12 June. Available at: https://www.washingtonpost.com/business/2020/06/12/starbucks-black-lives-matter/

Deva, S. (2011). Sustainable development: What role for the company law? *International and Comparative Corporate Law Journal*, 8, 76–102.

Deva, S., Ramasastry, A., Wettstein, F. and Santoro, M. (2019). Business and human rights scholarship: Past trends and future directions. *Business and Human Rights Journal*, 4(2), 201–212.

Donaghue, E. (2020). Mayor makes emotional call for peace after violent protests: 'I believe in Minneapolis'. *CBS News*. Archived from the Original May 29. Available at: https://www.cbsnews.com/news/minneapolis-george-floyd-protests-mayor-jacob-frey-peace/

Fannin, R. (2010). Why Google is quitting China. *Forbes*, 15 January. Available at: https://www.forbes.com/2010/01/15/baidu-china-search-intelligent-technology-google.html?sh=7b607cb18844

Fernandez, M. and Burch, A.D.S. (2021). George Floyd, from 'I want to touch the world' to 'I can't breathe'. *The New York Times*, 20 April 20. Available at: https://www.nytimes.com/article/george-floyd-who-is.html

Fonseca, P. (2021). Facebook, YouTube take down Bolsonaro video over false vaccine claim. *Reuters*, 26 October. Available at: https://www.reuters.com/world/americas/facebook-takes-down-bolsonaro-video-over-false-vaccine-claim-2021-10-25/

Frier, S. (2019). Twitter says China used fake accounts on Hong Kong protests. *Bloomberg*. Available at: https://www.bloomberg.com/news/articles/2019-08-19/twitter-says-china-used-fake-accounts-to-manipulate-hong-kong

Frosina, S. (2021). Digital revolution: How social media shaped the 2019 Hong Kong protests. *ISPI*, 9 June. Available at: https://www.ispionline.it/en/pubblicazione/digital-revolution-how-social-media-shaped-2019-hong-kong-protests-30756

Frynas, J.G. and Stephens, S. (2015). Political corporate social responsibility: Reviewing theories and setting new agendas. *International Journal of Management Reviews*, 17(4), 483–509.

Halis, D.D.C. (2015). 'Post-colonial' legal interpretation in Macau, China: Between European and Chinese influences. In Miyazawa, S., Ji, W., Fukurai, H., Chan, K.-W. and Vanhullebusch, M. (Eds.), *East Asia's Renewed Respect for the Rule of Law in the 21st Century: The Future of Legal and Judicial Landscapes in East Asia*. Leiden: Brill.

Halis, D.D.C. (2020). Digitalization and dissent in legal cultures: Chinese and other perspectives. *Naveiñ Reet: Nordic Journal of Law and Social Research*, 9, 127–152.

Halis, D.D.C. (2022). Law and dissent. In Sellers, M.N.S. and Kirste, S. (Eds.), *Encyclopedia of the Philosophy of Law and Social Philosophy*. Dordrecht: Springer.

Hamilton, I.A. (2019). WhatsApp will only let people forward messages 5 times to fight fake news. *Insider*, 21 January. Available at: https://www.businessinsider.com/whatsapp-limits-the-number-of-messages-users-can-forward-to-fight-fake-news-2019-1

Holmes, A. (2020). These clothes use outlandish designs to trick facial recognition software into thinking you're not human. *Business Insider*, 17 January. Available at: https://www.businessinsider.com/clothes-accessories-that-outsmart-facial-recognition-tech-2019-10

Hurley, L. (2018). U.S. Supreme Court backs Christian baker who rebuffed gay couple. *Reuters*, 4 June. Available at: https://www.reuters.com/article/us-usa-court-baker-idUSKCN1J01WU

Ineichen, M. (2017). Protecting human rights defenders: A critical step towards a more holistic implementation of the UNGPs. *Business and Human Rights Journal*, 3(1), 97.

Johnson, B. (2010). Google stops censoring Chinese search engine: How it happened. *The Guardian*, 22 March. Available at: https://www.theguardian.com/technology/blog/2010/mar/22/google-china-live

Kharpal, A. (2019). Alibaba shopping sites appear to have de-listed Houston Rockets products in China. *CNBC*, 8 October. Available at: https://www.cnbc.com/2019/10/08/houston-rockets-china-fallout-alibaba-de-lists-products-broadcasters-cut-ties.html

Kraemer, D. (2021). Greta Thunberg: Who is the climate campaigner and what are her aims? *BBC News*, 5 November. Available at: https://www.bbc.com/news/world-europe-49918719

Lane, S. (2019). Ocasio-Cortez, Ted Cruz join colleagues blasting NBA for 'outrageous' response to China. *The Hill*, 9 October. Available at: https://thehill.com/policy/finance/465111-lawmakers-blast-nba-for-outrageous-response-to-chinese-boycott

Lo, C. and Mok, D. (2019). First arrest as Hong Kong police prepare citywide raids to hunt down protesters who stormed and vandalised Legislative Council complex. *South China Morning Post*, 3 July. Available at: https://www.scmp.com/news/hong-kong/law-and-crime/article/3017166/hong-kong-police-prepare-citywide-raids-hunt-down-and

MacMahon, T. (2020). Daryl Morey stepping down as Houston Rockets GM. *ESPN*, 15 October. Available at: https://www.espn.com/nba/story/_/id/30120824/daryl-morey-stepping-houston-rockets-gm-sources-say

McNicol, A. (2017). How the NBA became China's most popular sports league, with a boost from tech giants such as Weibo and Tencent. *South China Morning Post*, 27

September. Available at: https://www.scmp.com/sport/china/article/2112972/how-nba-became-chinas-most-popular-sports-league-boost-tech-giants-such

Morrison, S. (2021). Facebook and Twitter Made Special World Leader Rules for Trump. What Happens Now? *Vox. Recode*, 20 January. Available at: https://www.vox.com/recode/22233450/trump-twitter-facebook-ban-world-leader-rules-exception

Murphy, E. (2020). 'I Can't Breathe!': Video of fatal arrest shows Minneapolis officer kneeling on George Floyd's neck for several minutes. *KSTP-TV*, 26 May. Available at: https://minnesota.cbslocal.com/2020/05/26/george-floyd-man-dies-after-being-arrested-by-minneapolis-police-fbi-called-to-investigate/

Murphy, H. (2020). Starbucks will allow employees to wear Black Lives Matter Apparel. *The New York Times*, 12 June. Available at: https://www.nytimes.com/2020/06/12/business/starbucks-blm-ban-reversed.html

Nicas, J. (2021). Brazilian leader accused of crimes against humanity in pandemic response. *The New York Times*, 19 October. Available at: https://www.nytimes.com/2021/10/19/world/americas/bolsonaro-covid-19-brazil.html

Novak, J. (2019). China's heavy-handed reaction to the NBA is just the wake-up call the world needed. *CNBC*, 8 October. Available at: https://www.cnbc.com/2019/10/08/chinas-reaction-to-the-nba-is-the-wake-up-call-the-world-needed.html

Palau, M. (2021). The battle over fake news: Inside Brazil's dangerous battle over fake news. *Americas Quarterly*, 19 October. Available at: https://www.americasquarterly.org/article/inside-brazils-dangerous-battle-over-fake-news/

Perper, R. (2019). China and the NBA are coming to blows over a pro-Hong Kong tweet. Here's why. *Insider*, 22 October. Available at: https://www.businessinsider.com/nba-china-feud-timeline-daryl-morey-tweet-hong-kong-protests-2019-10

Phillips, T. (2018). Trump of the tropics: The 'dangerous' candidate leading Brazil's presidential race. *The Guardian*, 19 April. Available at: https://www.theguardian.com/world/2018/apr/19/jair-bolsonaro-brazil-presidential-candidate-trump-parallels

Saad Filho, A. and Feil, F. (2021). *Covid-19 in Brazil: How Jair Bolsonaro Created a Calamity*. King's College London, 27 April. Available at: https://www.kcl.ac.uk/covid-19-in-brazil-how-jair-bolsonaro-created-a-calamity

Sacks, B. and Samaha, A. (2020). Starbucks won't let employees wear gear that supports Black Lives Matter because it is political or could incite violence. *Buzz Feed News*, 10 June. Available at: https://www.buzzfeednews.com/article/briannasacks/starbucks-is-now-very-pro-black-lives-matter-but-it-wont

Satta, M. (2019). Why you can't sell your cake and control it too: Distinguishing use from design in Masterpiece Cakeshop v. Colorado. *Harvard Civil Rights – Civil Liberties Law Review*, 10 July. Available at: https://harvardcrcl.org/why-you-cant-sell-your-cake-and-control-it-too-distinguishing-use-from-design-in-masterpiece-cakeshop-v-colorado/

Shao, G. (2019). Social media has become a battleground in Hong Kong's protests. *CNBC*, 15 August. Available at: https://www.cnbc.com/2019/08/16/social-media-has-become-a-battleground-in-hong-kongs-protests.html

Sielski, M. (2019). Sixers have a chance to show some guts about the NBA and China. They're passing it up. *Philadelphia Inquirer*, 7 October. Available at: https://www.inquirer.com/sixers/philadelphia-76ers-china-daryl-morey-nba-tweet-loong-lions-20191007.html

Smith, J. (2019). The NBA chooses China's money over Hong Kong's human rights. *Rolling Stone*, 7 October. Available at: https://www.rollingstone.com/politics/politics-news/daryl-morey-nba-hong-kong-houston-rockets-895706/

Sunstein, C.R. (2009). *Going to Extremes: How Like Minds Unite and Divide*. New York: Oxford University Press.

Sunstein, C.R. (2003). *Why Societies Need Dissent*. Cambridge, MA: Harvard University Press.

Tensley, B. (2019). NBA's response to China backlash at odds with league's history. *CNN*, 8 October. Available at: https://edition.cnn.com/2019/10/07/politics/nba-politics-china-analysis/index.html

The Cube. (2021). Bolsonaro sanctioned by social media companies for COVID vaccine misinformation. *Euronews*, 26 October. Available at: https://www.euronews.com/my-europe/2021/10/26/jair-bolsonaro-sanctioned-by-social-media-companies-for-covid-vaccine-misinformation

The Economist. (2020). The power of protest and the legacy of George Floyd, 11 June. Available at: https://www.economist.com/leaders/2020/06/11/the-power-of-protest-and-the-legacy-of-george-floyd

The Guardian. (2020). China drops Philadelphia 76ers broadcasts as Hong Kong row continues. 30 December. Available at: https://www.theguardian.com/sport/2020/dec/30/china-drops-76ers-broadcasts-daryl-morey

Toh, M. and He, L. (2019). NBA's official Chinese partners have suspended ties with the league. *CNN Business*, 9 October. Available at: https://edition.cnn.com/2019/10/09/business/nba-china-partners/index.html

Tushnet, M. (2012). Why societies don't need dissent (as such). In Sarat, A. (Ed.), *Dissenting Voices in American Society: The Role of Judges, Lawyers, and Citizens*. New York: Cambridge University Press.

Ulrich, P. (2008). *Integrative Economic Ethics: Foundations of a Civilized Market Economy*. Cambridge: Cambridge University Press.

US Supreme Court. (2018). Masterpiece Cakeshop, Ltd. v. Colo. Civil Rights Commission, 138, 1719, 1724.

Votaw, D. (1961). The politics of a changing corporate society. *California Management Review*, 3(3), 105–118.

Wettstein, F. (2010). The duty to protect: Corporate complicity, political responsibility, and human rights advocacy. *Journal of Business Ethics*, 96(1), 33–47.

Wettstein, F. and Baur, D. (2016). Why should we care about marriage equality? Political advocacy as a part of corporate responsibility. *Journal of Business Ethics*, 138(2), 192–213.

White, J. (2019a). CCTV pulls NBA China Games broadcast in response to Adam Silver's support for Houston Rockets GM Daryl Morey's right to free speech. *South China Morning Post*, 8 October. Available at: https://www.scmp.com/sport/basketball/article/3031997/cctv-pulls-nba-china-games-broadcast-response-adam-silvers-support

White, J. (2019b). Money or moral high ground? NBA's China crisis shows it can't cave both – Adam Silver has to pick a side in a game he might not win. *South China Morning Post*, 9 October. Available at: https://www.scmp.com/print/sport/china/article/3032112/money-or-moral-high-ground-nbas-china-crisis-shows-it-cant-have-both

Wood, C. (2019). Apple has approved an app which lets Hong Kong protesters track the police after initially rejecting it. *Insider*, 8 October. Available at: https://www

.businessinsider.com/apple-approves-app-that-lets-protestors-track-hong-kong-police-2019-10

Zhang, P. and Chen, L. (2019). The emergence and evolution of China's internet warriors going to battle over Hong Kong protests. *South China Morning Post*, 4 September. Available at: https://www.scmp.com/print/news/china/society/article/3024223/emergence-and-evolution-chinas-internet-warriors

16 Do Businesses Have a Responsibility or an Obligation to Society?

Setting Out the Terms for Business Engagement

Sam Sarpong

Introduction

"Responsibility" and "obligations" are two key concepts that underlie the relationship between business and its stakeholders. These two concepts have been used interchangeably without any recourse to delineating them. As such, many people, so it seems, do not realize the meanings that can be attached to them or the differences, if any, between them. This has often led to conflictual situations in some societies as those who prey upon the two concepts tend to interpret them in ways to suit their caprices (Bain, 2010; Ruland, 1984).

The chapter believes having a better understanding of these concepts can offer a means by which we could have a better perspective of what business ought to do in its relationship with society; more so, when the role of business in society and the accompanying responsibilities that transpire from that role, remain a highly contentious and debated topic. This inquisition is fuelled by the delineation of responsibility and obligations as core areas of business' involvement in society and, yet, the bewildering oscillation of their constituents has obfuscated their characters along the way. Therefore, the chapter makes an important contribution by detailing the interplay between these two concepts and their applications within the business–society nexus.

The chapter will first attempt to look at the social context of business. It will then look at the features of responsibility and obligations and the implied objectives of their use. It will then reflect on how responsibility relates to ethics and morality and analyse the conditions that are commonly named for the ascription of responsibility. From there, it will delve into the determinants of responsibility and obligations. Aside that, it will look at the nature and implications of the two concepts and also provide a means to address the issues they constitute.

The Social Context of Business

Many firms are today operating in an environment which seems to be quite uncertain, complex, and demanding (FitzGerald and Cormack, 2006). They

DOI: 10.4324/9781003274575-20

face organizational and societal challenges that they are, perhaps, not best placed to address (Idowu et al., 2017). As central to the development of many countries, they are expected to bring in capital investment, job creation, skill transfer, knowledge sharing, and social responsibility programs (Visser et al., 2017). For these reasons, their scope of operations impacts on society in so many ways. Some companies have assisted their communities in positive ways, whilst the actions or inactions too of others have also been quite negative as their support for and engagement with society have remained quite minimal and distorted (Malesky, 2009; Mosley and Uno, 2007; Rudra, 2005).

Societies have had huge expectations of businesses for years. A growing challenge to this is that in recent years these expectations have been changing, and changing fast, thanks to big trends like demographic shifts, technological advances, instantaneous information flows, and many others (PwC, 2021). From environmental footprints to social impacts to investor demands and everything in between, businesses are expected to exhibit responsible behaviours in more areas and be accountable to an ever-wider array of stakeholders (Sarpong, 2021). A more responsible and pronounced role for business continues to be assigned by society (Miller, 2008).

Society does not exist without some form of an economy and businesses are what make up the economic system of the world (Rabie, 2016). Society gives firms the resources they require for them to fulfil their business mission, whilst these firms, in turn, ought to fulfil the needs of society (Davis and Blomstrom, 1971). The principle behind this is that companies can improve their opportunities whilst they provide benefits to the social context in which they operate (Heslin and Ochoa, 2008).

In order to fulfil the broader expectations of society, therefore, business has to make a leadership contribution based on authority and responsibility within society (FitzGerald and Cormack, 2006). It has to meet its responsibilities and obligations in a manner that leads to the creation of a bond with society.

Theoretical Considerations: Setting Out the Terms

The Concept of Responsibility

The concept of responsibility seems to be an important one in our social life, in our personal relations at home, at play, sport and leisure, at work; in our relations to various institutions, society in general; and in any spiritual beliefs we may hold (Martin, 2007). Responsibility is of increasing importance in order to assess and guide individual and collective actions, in particular with respect to large-scale issues such as sustainable development (Baumgärtner et al., 2018). It is also adverbial, in that, doing something responsibly means doing something with due care and attention and can be contrasted with irresponsible actions, actions that might lead to some sort of error or problem (Martin, 2007). It is about the actions, and their consequences, that a person executes out of free will. People would indeed want to know who is responsible for certain actions and who is accountable for the consequences of those actions (Bivins, 2006).

Outside the scholarly discussion, the term "responsibility", according to Baumgärtner et al. (2018) is often used in a sloppy, diffuse, and unspecific manner, so that it remains unclear what it actually means. But responsibility, when properly specified, shows the scope and the limitations of what some general norm implies for some concrete action of a concrete person in a concrete action context (Baumgärtner et al., 2018). It has become a key term of modernity because it explains man's behaviour towards himself and others (Stahl, 2006). More so, being responsible for someone or something can ease uncertainty concerning one's behaviour and one's self.

People are said to be responsible for the consequences of their actions if they could have acted otherwise (Ruland, 1984). One takes responsibility for a particular outcome, whenever one accepts the burden associated with achieving or preventing that outcome (Baumgärtner et al., 2018). Responsibility can also be viewed as a bundle of obligations associated with a job or function (Bivins, 2006). If one is responsible in any way for an action, then one must also accept some degree of accountability. According to Bivins (2006), whilst tracing the lines of responsibility and accountability can be difficult, in the end, if responsibility and accountability are not equitably shared and if the process by which they are assigned is not transparent, then problems would arise.

A responsible actor may be seen as one whose job involves a predetermined set of obligations that must be met in order for the job to be accomplished. Hence, responsibility entails the status of morally deserving praise, blame, reward, or punishment for an act or omission in accordance with one's moral obligations (Klein, 2005). Whereas responsibility in an elementary sense means that an action and its consequences can be ascribed to the perpetrator in a normative sense, responsibility means that the perpetrator of the action ought to take care that the action and its consequences are of a certain quality (Baumgärtner et al., 2018).

Being responsible evokes considerations about moral competence. Entities or people who have moral responsibility for an action are seen as moral agents. Therefore, moral agency follows from an individual or an entity's ability to make moral judgements which is much needed in a state of responsibility (Barret, 2004). For instance, corporations can in principle be understood as moral agents, a precondition for the ascription of responsibility (Werhane, 1985). Although arguments can be made for and against this position, Donaldson (1982) recognizes the need for us to see corporations as moral agents because they can make ethical decisions and have the duty to acknowledge standards that transcend laws.

The role of moral agency can arrogate to a business, the capability of being concerned and accountable (French, 1979). In order to carry out such a role, the moral agent should have good impulses to assess a situation and to take the appropriate actions immediately to rectify any problem (Andreou and Thalos, 2007). The view that accords organizations as either persons or as aggregations of people is based on philosophical assumptions which stress that organizations share the normative status of persons (Dan-Cohen, 1986). This also makes an organization accountable for the outcome of its actions (Bain, 2010).

Social Responsibility

Responsibility to society, on the part of corporate bodies, entails showing both social awareness and self-management skills, an awareness of how one's decisions affect others and doing business in a manner that can benefit the society (Latapí-Agudelo et al., 2019; Freeman, 2010). It also implies the obligations of the management of a business enterprise to adhere to social norms and expectations (Suchman, 1995). This reinforces the idea that the objective of managers for taking business decisions is not merely to maximize profits or shareholders' value but also to serve and protect the interests of other members of a society such as workers, consumers, and the community at large (Freeman, 2010). Freeman's stakeholder theory accounts for the multiple constituencies that are impacted by business activities and to which businesses should be responsible.

Social responsibility can be appropriately marked by Howard R. Bowen's (1953) landmark book, *Social Responsibilities of the Businessman*, which was published in 1953. He defined social responsibilities as the obligations of businessmen to pursue those policies, to make those decisions, or to follow those lines of action that are desirable in terms of the objectives and values of our society. Following from Bowen's (1953) definition, we can today speak of numerous definitions for this concept. We can also make references to the many constructs of corporate social responsibility (CSR) in modern times with various scholars outlining what they believe constitutes the key responsibilities of businesses to society. Caroll's (1991) depiction of CSR, for instance, comes in handy here with his CSR pyramid (Figure 16.1).

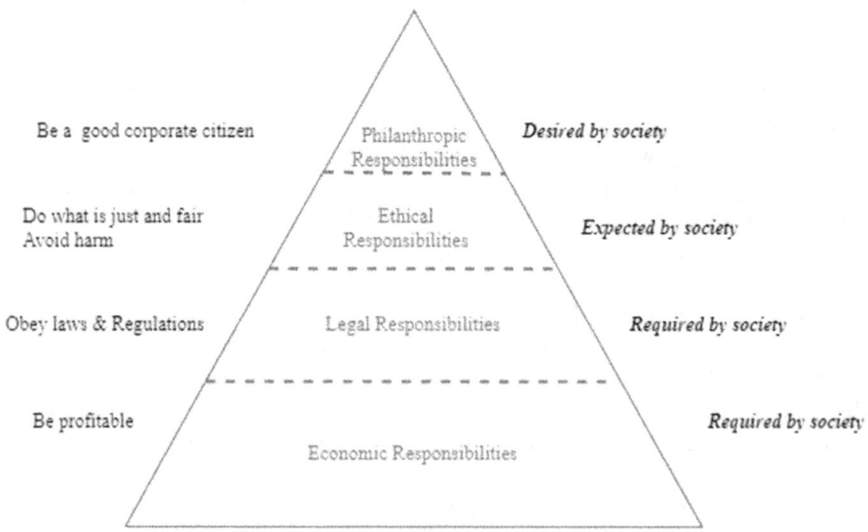

Figure 16.1 Caroll's Pyramid (Caroll, 1991)

The CSR pyramid holds that the social responsibility of business entails the concurrent fulfilment of a firm's economic, legal, ethical, and philanthropic responsibilities required or desired by society. Stated in more practical and managerial terms, the CSR-driven firm should strive to make a profit, obey the law, engage in ethical practices, and be a good corporate citizen. The basis for this is that the economic responsibility is "required" of business by society; the legal responsibility also is "required" of business by society; the ethical responsibility is "expected" of business by society; and the philanthropic responsibility is "expected/desired" of business by society.

It is gratifying to note that responsibility has become a role or behaviour that ought to be put up by someone towards the other. Making judgements about whether a person is morally responsible for one's behaviour, and holding others and ourselves responsible for actions and the consequences of actions, is a fundamental and familiar part of our moral practices and our interpersonal relationships (Talbert, 2019). Lukes' (2005) investigation of the relationship between power and responsibility in the field of political theory, presents some influential contributions towards understanding organizations from a moral perspective. He finds that the realization of an exercise of power by either an individual or an organization is at the same time an ascription of responsibility. Meanwhile, as argued by Donaldson (1982), a clear distinction exists between a corporation's formal power, its authority to act *intra vires*, which flows from its rights as defined by law or charter, and its practical power, which derives from its special role in society. As such, large corporations are capable of influencing mainstream societal events and this power is not only economic but also social and political.

The Concept of Obligation

Philosophers like John Stuart Mill (1998), Richard Brandt (1979), and Allan Gibbard (1990) have argued that moral obligation, duty, right, and wrong are conceptually tied to moral responsibility. In many instances, philosophers use "moral obligation" as a synonym for "moral requirement" or "moral duty", to signify acts that can be morally appropriate to do (Ogien, 2016). "Obligation" has also been used to denote the ties that exist between moral agents and groups or individuals to whom they are obligated. Obligations denoting ties are sometimes called "relational" (Gilbert, 2004). Theories of moral obligation bring to the fore certain difficulties as many scholars have different interpretations of what the scope of an obligation entails (Owens, 2012). Incidentally, the nature of moral obligation is best understood against a conception of moral goodness.

An obligation can be deemed as a course of action that is required of someone to take, and this can either be legal or moral (Owens, 2012). The term "obligation" insinuates that it is a tie that exists between at least two individual persons which enables one person (the obligor) to carry out a task in favour of the obligee (Thompson, 2004). Obligation can also be seen in other normative contexts such as social obligations, religious obligations amongst others, where there are requirements to be fulfilled.

In ordinary discourse, we sometimes use the language of right and wrong to morally evaluate our actions (Ogien, 2016). We also categorize actions as being morally required or obligatory, other actions are deemed as permissible, and still others are seen as forbidden or wrong (Ross, 1970). The ability to insist on some forms of behaviour provides us with a means by which we can create and maintain conditions and services that tend to regulate and benefit all members of the society. Ultimately, this would have been impossible without any direction being given.

Dissecting the Concepts

For quite some time now, a good deal of scholarship has been devoted to articulating and justifying the responsibilities of business enterprises and their relationship with society (Hsieh, 2017). With the reduced role of state in many countries, and as the private sector expands, the spotlight has increasingly turned onto what firms could and should do in their communities (Chang, 2004; Lodge and Wilson, 2006). How these responsibilities are defined, how they are discharged and how performance is measured and reported on, are issues that are rapidly getting on the agenda for businesses and particularly so for leading companies around the world (Sarpong, 2010).

Consequently, the debate around corporate social responsibility (CSR) has evolved rapidly as organizations begin to appreciate that non-financial returns to their stakeholders are equally as important as financial returns to shareholders (Freeman, 2010). As noted by Latapí-Agudelo et al. (2019), the social responsibilities placed upon firms have evolved from being merely acknowledged in the early publications over the years to being explicitly defined. For example, during the 1990s, society placed broader responsibilities upon businesses when the international community adopted agreements with regard to sustainable development. To this end, there was a massive advocacy for a CSR push to address the social concerns of the time.

Meanwhile, in the early part of the 2000s, new roles and responsibilities were placed on corporations by the international community in addressing the United Nations Millennium Development Goals (MDGs) which ended in 2015. After that, in came the Sustainable Development Goals (SDGs), which serve as the blueprint to achieve a better and sustainable future for all by the year 2030. Whilst ultimately it is governments that are being asked to deliver the SDGs, the simple fact is that this critical agenda cannot be realized without an effective engagement with business. The World Business Council for Sustainable Development (WBCSD) points out that business has a critical role to play as a source of finance, a driver of innovation and technology, and an engine of economic growth and employment.

More recently, with COVID-19, businesses have been urged to navigate the financial and operational challenges of the pandemic whilst rapidly addressing the needs of their people, customers, and suppliers (PwC, 2021). In all these, business has had to play a pivotal role. Such is the state in which business finds itself, as it is expected to play certain roles in respect of any occurrences that happen.

In spite of the key role that business plays in society today, recent scandals have led the world to become more critical of some business practices (Carson, 2003). Several firms, along with managers and accountants, have over the past years been accused of corrupt and deceitful practices. The scandals devastated the market values and credit ratings of companies such as Enron (2001), Volkswagen (2015), BP (2010), among others, which were found to have acted fraudulently (Child, 2002). Enron, for instance, was found to have hidden billions of dollars in liabilities through special-purpose entities (companies it controlled), which enabled it to appear profitable even though it was actually haemorrhaging cash. Meanwhile, Volkswagen (VW) reportedly cheated emission tests. This discovery led to investigations worldwide, with some estimates suggesting the scandal affected up to 11 million cars.

These scandals, as well as other related cases, have severely led to a crisis of confidence in corporations (Child, 2002). As such, there are now unprecedented levels of scrutiny of large corporations and their actions with those falling foul of the law facing a more severe backlash than before (Marquis et al., 2016; Adegbite, 2010). This is breathing new life into the debate around good corporate governance, corporate moral responsibility, and the extent to which business organizations can be said to have moral responsibilities and obligations (Davis et al., 1997). Firms that have acted irresponsibly have incurred the wrath of society in many parts of the world (Omotola, 2009). Shell's operations in Nigeria, for instance, have come under scrutiny at various times because of the incidence of pollution. Its ability to operate effectively has been marred in Nigeria, where community members feel left out from the benefits of the oil exploitation (Frynas, 2000).

Community unrest and agitation has been recorded too in places like Papua New Guinea, India, and the Philippines where communities' interests are being sacrificed in the name of "development" (Sarpong, 2010). Some of these communities now represent a veritable picture of areas where ecological concerns are side-stepped for economic gains. Contrary to what Blunden (1985) asserts, that the exploitation of any resource must inevitably lead to increased employment opportunities and economic growth for areas in which it is exploited, such communities seem to be bereft of such opportunities. Major disagreements and conflicts have subsequently occurred as a result of the lack of opportunities in these areas. Key to this instability in such areas is the incompatibility between the distribution of power and the institutional structure of benefit or rent distribution and the unequal relationships among political actors (North et al., 2007).

The Issue with Legitimacy

It is generally known that when society grants business the privilege of operating in it, then that endeavour obliges business to avoid doing anything that is undesirable from the point of view of society. It also legitimizes the role of business in society. Legitimacy is, therefore, considered vital for the survival of organizations and a prerequisite for stakeholder support (Palazzo and Scherer, 2006). It can be seen as "a process whereby organizations seek approval for their acts from groups in society" (Kaplan and Ruland, 1991, 320). In view of that, society can effectively revoke an organization's "contract" to continue its operations if it is dissatisfied with it (Deegan, 2002). So, obtaining legitimacy by aligning corporate behaviour with stakeholder expectations is necessary to guarantee the corporation's continued existence (Dawkins, 2004).

In many parts of the world, the issue of legitimacy has been quite delicate for large corporations especially those involved in major mining ventures. There, communities and non-governmental organizations ferret out business operations to see whether the firms are abiding by their claims of responsibility (Saenz, 2018). If a firm is unable to provide what the society really needs, then protests or the assignation of blame might come in, irrespective of whether the company has the wherewithal to provide the request or not (Sarpong, 2010). In such places, the idea of responsibility and the related concept of accountability become deeply entangled with judgements that interrogate conduct in the light of expectations (Darwall, 2006).

There is a strong basis for the present thrust that assumes that businesses have the responsibility of providing for communities that host them. Some scholars (Scott, 2008; Campbell, 2007; DiMaggio and Powell, 1983) have argued that since companies are embedded in a larger social environment, it is important for them to be part of what goes on in these societies. This cause has been championed by governments and communities alike, which to some extent, has led to the neglect of the equally important and crucial role expected of governments in creating sustainable governance (Sarpong, 2021).

In some jurisdictions, especially in developing countries, far and remote communities tend to depend on firms because of less government involvement or what Lodge and Wilson (2006) describe as the state's "fragility" in these places. Numerous studies have found similar expectations from many remote areas (Downing et al., 2002; Thomson and Joyce, 2000). The companies, by virtue of their position, are often well positioned to provide assistance to such communities in view of their economic status and social standing (Kline, 2006). Such an assistance is deemed to be an obligation and in the context of CSR.

What is quite notable though is that the relationship between business and society often bodes well for both parties. However, it also gives rise to the numerous expectations about each other. The relationship also creates societal expectations about how people in a certain role should act (Falgelson, 1999). Oftentimes, the onus rests with businesses to perform certain functions to the community. The desired part expected to be played by business towards society is often defined by the role differentiation assigned to the parties – with business being the patron (Lodge and Wilson, 2006).

Situational Analysis

What Does Responsibility Entail?

What emerges from our discussion so far is that since society grants business the opportunity to operate within it, such a privilege assumingly entails that business would act in seeing to the welfare of society. Such a role can be revoked for dereliction or for an abuse of privilege. Hence, society has a means of withdrawing this social licence which it grants to business, if and when it finds that businesses are doing things that they are not supposed to do. The social licence refers to the perceptions of stakeholders that a company operating in a given region is socially acceptable or legitimate (Thomson and Boutilier, 2011). In this regard, the role privilege is directly correlated with role duties and it is on this basis that businesses assume certain responsibilities to the society.

Crucially, responsibility does not require the actual commission of harm for evaluative statements to be made, and the expectation that businesses ought to conduct themselves in a good way leaves them liable to blame when they fail to do so (Barrett, 2004). The idea of responsibility also discloses a "retrospective" indulgence whereby praise or blame is assigned in relation to an evaluation of specific actions and the consequences in which they result (Bivins, 2006). Considerations of blame can arise when a company's actions directly or indirectly lead to deaths, as the case was when more than 1,000 garment workers died following the collapse of the Rana Plaza building in Bangladesh in 2013. In the light of that, questions were raised about the seeming complicity of international retail companies in that tragedy as the factory was producing for them (Sarpong, 2018).

Complicity may arise in terms of certain responsibilities. A mining company, for instance, can retrospectively be responsible for causing harm if it fails to cover abandoned mined-out tunnels which might have led to the death of people. Besides, acting without any knowledge that one's act could contribute to wrongdoing is sufficient to make one morally complicit in it and culpable ignorance is no excuse, as the major international retailers found out in 2013 (Sarpong, 2018). The recent conflict between Russia and Ukraine has also placed a lot of moral issues on businesses and their responsibilities. Many companies have had to pull out of Russia because of the notion that their continuous stay in that country might constitute an irresponsible act and a gross violation of humanity. These companies had to consider whether their commercial activities are aiding the Russian military, directly or indirectly, and whether they ought to cease operations in Russia as part of the broader opposition to the invasion (Prosner, 2022).

Certain situations and our moral responsibility might lead us to think something more like shared intentions are required. The extent and nature of these responsibilities, however, can be contentious at times and that often reflects on the conflictual situations experienced by the firms in some communities (Stierle, 1994). Sometimes, the harm for which organizations are responsible can be avoided if greater care is taken by the responsible authorities (Cullinan et al., 2008). People want more than vague excuses or insincere apologies, hence the need for and insistence on firms to be more responsible (Sarpong, 2010; Campbell, 2007).

In spite of the aforementioned issues, there appear to be two factors that may contribute to the overall strength of a responsibility. They are the quality of responsibility present and, in some circumstances, its depth as measured by the magnitude of the consequences involved (Ruland, 1984). It is the notion of quality of responsibility that is of main concern here. What matters here too is the extent of proactiveness that a firm could show in terms of helping its stakeholders, how deeply ingrained this cause of service is and then the extent to which such favours can be carried out (Darwall, 2006; French, 1979). The depth of responsibility details the best possible consequences that such a responsibility could have (Ruland, 1984).

Even with our attempt at attributing responsibility as a key point for business, there is often a lack of clarity pertaining to that, as there are different notions of what responsibilities entails. As Stierle (1994) explains, different people or parties have different opinions of what responsibilities should be. Notwithstanding that, one thing that ought to be realized is that a responsible actor may be seen as one whose job involves a predetermined set of obligations that must be met in order for the job to be accomplished (Dan-Cohen, 1986).

Obligation: To What Extent Can Businesses Be Obligated?

The foundational assumption of obligation is that there exists a moral imperative to assist the structurally dispossessed and functionally abused (FitzGerald and Cormack, 2006; French, 1979). The belief in the public good is at the heart of this. A party should be impelled by common gratitude to alleviate the other's misfortune, which is a kind of humanitarian act. So, for businesses, that requires them to do things in standing with the power they wield, the privilege they have and the profit they make (Sarpong, 2010). This supposed role that businesses have is the obligation they have towards the society. As Freeman (2010) contends, business has an obligation towards different segments of the society and all these need to be accounted for during any business deliberation.

Unlike the idea of responsibility, which designates a locus of accountability, the idea of obligation does enjoin action. It embraces the idea that something must be done independently of what considerations of interest or advantage might recommend. The obligations to which these duties relate to are standards of behaviour which imply a certain ethical consideration. Primarily, an obligation is something which a person is bound or obliged to do. It arises out of a sense of duty or results from something that is to be done for some particular reasons. It could be a binding promise, contract, sense of duty, etc. Obligations are generally granted in return for an increase in an individual's rights or power. For instance, adults have more obligations and are held to higher standards of accountability than children are. The same applies to businesses in their relationship with society.

Indeed, the demand that businesses act to prevent poverty in their areas of operation, emanates from the assumption that they have voluntarily assumed an obligation to do so (Campbell. 2007). This is more so when the central government, perhaps, is less endowed or inclined to undertake projects of that nature (Kline, 2006). It is only then that the issue of responsibility comes up. Ruland (1984) for instance, has indicated that certain circumstances give rise to an obligation. He projects certain relations as the foundation of prima facie obligations.

Examples of such relations are those of promisee–promisor, debtor–creditor, and child–parent. For instance, an implicit promise is recognizable through a moral obligation and if someone owes someone, then the person who owes is obliged to pay the one who is owed.

Two issues often come to the fore when promises are made. There is the expectation that usually comes with it and also the reliance on the said promise. A promise creates expectations in the promisee as well as a reliance upon the promise (Patterson, 1992). Hence, it would be morally wrong to disappoint the entity or person who has been promised because of the huge expectations that come with that. These two positions, the so-called expectation and reliance theories, have traditionally been thought to be incommensurable. A promise, thus, commits the promiser to a certain course of action which is an obligation to act (Austin, 1975). Breaking the promise is then tantamount to deceiving those who have been once promised, and since one has a moral duty not to deceive, one has a moral duty to keep one's promises too.

If, for instance, a company promises to build a school for a community, it would be important to fulfil this promise or else the community would feel let down. Like any promise, it would entail a commitment, hence an obligation arises from that. An obligation also arises from the understanding that something needs to be done for someone at a particular point in time. Let us say, the firm becomes aware of the need to do something for a community in which it operates. Ultimately, the firm is aware it has to do something and the community also becomes expectant as a result of that. If this is not attended to, it can affect the firm in a number of ways and perhaps its relationship with the community. Hence, obligations are owed to others which, in effect, also leads others to stand in to demand their compliance (Patterson, 1992).

Aside from that, if the company fails to abide by its promise, it can be blamed for being unreliable, uncaring, and perhaps deemed as only interested in profit-making to the detriment of the society. Another aspect of this is the normative force of obligation. To say that a company is obligated to do something is to say, among other things, that it must do it, irrespective of whether it has the means to do it or not. Sometimes fulfilling one's obligations is in a company's own best interest, as it could lead to admiration from the community, meanwhile failure to do so could spell the doom for many businesses (Darwall, 2006). Besides, obligations provide a means by which a party can act in accordance with some expectations. For example, companies have an obligation to take care of people within their catchment areas, and not everyone else. A business can offer scholarship opportunities to people in the community in which it operates first before venturing out to help others elsewhere. Such an obligation is relative to its immediate environments.

Admittedly, a business enterprise is an important part of the society, hence it should ensure it does its business in line with societal demands and the objectives of the business (Rabie, 2016; Heslin and Ochoa, 2008). As such, when we talk of social responsibility of a business, our reference point here should be the obligations the firm has to take in order to perform those actions which are desirable in terms of the objectives and values of society and also in accordance with the objectives of the firm (Idowu et al., 2017). It is the idea that businesses should balance profit-making activities with activities that benefit society. It also involves developing business enterprises with a positive relationship with the society in which they operate (Visser et al., 2017).

Despite the fact that business has assorted obligations, it is not always clear what these obligations amount to. Key questions have often engaged our thoughts and inspired considerable debate over the years in connection with this. For instance, who defines what these obligations are? Do obligations make sense in situations where there is no risk of sanction for not performing one's duty? Can one be obligated to cultivate particular character traits or to believe specific things, even as these characteristics seem to be out of our control? Are there obligations so strong that no circumstance can override them? The ambiguity of obligation is that it draws in a contractual relationship. But it would be superfluous to specify that business and society are under "contractual obligations" when both seek their best interests, i.e., the business wants to have a good image among the people whilst the society wants developmental projects. The obligations to which these duties or aspirations relate simply imply a degree of solidarity between business and society.

What emerges from our discussion so far is that obligation and responsibility are two terms that are often considered to be similar, yet at the same time quite different. There are probably subtle differences in common usage of both responsibility and obligation. The key difference between obligation and responsibility is that obligation refers to actions that must be fulfilled or performed, whereas responsibility refers to a duty or task that you are required or expected to do.

Conclusion

The chapter has put forward the argument that responsibilities and obligations are important concepts to address in the organizational world. The emphasis here is that what business stands for is ultimately relational, hence a caring attitude is demanded of business since that serves as a fundamental position of what business should condition itself for. In such a state, a business has to emphasize virtues that would be important to this relationship, such as compassion, sympathy, empathy, loyalty, and responsibility, among others. The rationality of having a responsibility ultimately depends on the concept of obligation, hence the need to realize the huge roles these concepts play in the business–society relationship.

Meanwhile, the shifts between the language of "responsibility" and the language of "obligation" underscore the need to bring a degree of clarity to both terms in order for business to appreciate much better the obligations and the responsibilities placed on them. Although some businesses seemingly ignore certain obligations, being conscious of businesses' role in society remains an important part of running an ethical, trustworthy, and sustainable business these days. Responsibility is the building block of all moral behaviours (Bauman, 1989) and moral capacity is fostered, cultivated, and exercised within the social environment (Vetlesen, 1993).

In as much as people in a society are morally obligated to follow its rules, it is just as appropriate too for businesses to operate by their expected moral tenets. So, as well as being *responsible*, business must also be *responsive* to society's fast-changing expectations and achieving this comes down to: first, having the right leadership and understanding the evolving needs and expectations of society; second, being aware of how those collective and individual expectations are shifting; third, having the right personnel who understand and can take into account the wider impacts and implications of their actions, words, and decisions. Put together, these three priorities can help organizations enhance trust and build the ability for agility and sustainability and ensure society accords them their due.

References

Adegbite, E. (2010). A scrutiny of corporate governance. *Journal of Corporate Governance*, 2(1), 242–265.

Andreou, C. and Thalos, M. (2007). Sense and sensibility. *American Philosophical Quarterly*, 44(1), 71–80.

Austin, J.L. (1975). *How to Do Things with Words*. Cambridge, MA: Harvard University Press.

Bain, W. (2010). Responsibility and obligation in the 'Responsibility to Protect'. *Review of International Studies*, 36(S1), 25–46.

Barrett, W. (2004). Responsibility, accountability and corporate activity. *Online Opinion: Australia's E-journal of Social and Political Debate*, August 25. Available at: http://www.onlineopinion.com.au/print.asp?article=2480#

Bauman, B. (1989). *Modernity and the Holocaust*. Cambridge: Polity Press.

Baumgärtner, S., Petersen, T. and Schiller, J. (2018). The concept of responsibility: norms, actions and their consequences. *SSRN Electronic Journal*. https://doi.org/10.2139/ssrn.3157667.

Bivins, T. (2006). Responsibility and accountability. In Fitzpatrick, K. and Bronstein, C. (Eds.), *Ethics in Public Relations: Responsible Advocacy*. Thousand Oaks, CA: Sage Publications.

Blunden, J. (1985). *Mineral Resources and their Management*. London: Longman.

Bowen, H.R. (1953). *Social Responsibilities of the Businessman*. Iowa City, IA: University of Iowa Press.

Brandt, R. (1979). *A Theory of the Good and the Right*. Oxford: Oxford University Press.

Campbell, J. (2007). Why would corporations behave in socially responsible ways? An institutional theory of corporate social responsibility. *Academy of Management Review*, 32(3), 946–967.

Caroll, A.B. (1991). The pyramid of corporate social responsibility: Toward the moral management of organizational stakeholders. *Business Horizons*, 34(4), 39–48.

Carson, T.L. (2003). Self–interest and business ethics: Some lessons of the recent corporate scandals. *Journal of Business Ethics*, 43(4), 389–394.

Chang, H.-J. (2004). *Globalisation, Economic Development and the Role of the State*. London: Zed Books.

Child, J. (2002). The international crisis of confidence in corporations. *Academy of Management Executive*, 16(3), 145–147.

Cullinan, C., Bline, D., Farrar, R. and Lowe, D. (2008). Organization-harm vs. organization-gain ethical issues: An exploratory examination of the effects of organizational commitment. *Journal of Business Ethics*, 80(2), 225–235.

Dan-Cohen, M. (1986). *Rights, Persons, and Organizations*. Berkeley, CA: University of California Press.

Darwall, S. (2006). *The Second-Person Standpoint: Morality, Respect, and Accountability*. Cambridge, MA: Harvard University Press.

Davis, J., Schoorman, F.D. and Donaldson, L. (1997). Towards a stewardship theory of management. *Academy of Management Review*, 22(1), 20–48.

Davis, K. and Blomstrom, R.L. (1971). *Business, Society, and Environment: Social Power and Social Response*. New York: McGraw-Hill.

Dawkins, J. (2004). Corporate responsibility: The communication challenge. *Journal of Communication Management*, 9(2), 108–119.

Deegan, C. (2002). The legitimizing effect of social and environmental disclosures – A theoretical foundation. *Accounting, Auditing and Accountability Journal*, 15(3), 282–311.

DiMaggio, P. and Powell, W. (1983). The iron cage revisited: Institutional isomorphism and collective rationality in organizational fields. *American Sociology Review*, 48(2), 147–160.

Donaldson, T. (1982). *Corporations and Morality*. Englewood Cliffs, NJ: Prentice Hall.

Downing, T.E., Moles, J., McIntosh, I. and Garcia-Downing, C. (2002). Indigenous peoples and mining encounters: Strategies and tactics. No 57. *Mining, Minerals and Sustainable Development*. London: IIED and WBCSD.

FitzGerald, N. and Cormack, M. (2006). *The Role of Business in Society: An Agenda for Action*. John F. Kennedy School of Government, Harvard University and the Prince of Wales International Leaders Forum.

Freeman, R.E. (2010). *Strategic Management: A Stakeholder Approach*. Cambridge: Cambridge University Press.

French, P.A. (1979). The corporation as a moral person. *American Philosophical Quarterly*, 16(3), 207–215.

Frynas, J.G. (2000). *Oil in Nigeria: Conflict and Litigation between Oil Companies and Village Communities*. Münster: LIT Verlag.

Gibbard, A. (1990). *Wise Choices, Apt Feelings*. Cambridge, MA: Harvard University Press.

Gilbert, M. (2004). Scanlon on promissory obligation: The problem of promisees' rights. *Journal of Philosophy*, 101(2), 83–109.

Heslin, P.A. and Ochoa, J.D. (2008). Understanding and developing strategic corporate social responsibility. *Organizational Dynamics*, 37(2), 125–144.

Hsieh, N. (2017). The responsibilities and role of business in relation to society: Back to basics? *Business Ethics Quarterly*, 27(2), 293–314.

Idowu, S., Vertigans, S. and Burlea, A.S. (2017). Introduction. In Idowu, S., Vertigans, S. and Burlea, A. S. (Eds.), *Corporate Social Responsibility in Times of Crisis – Practices and Cases from Europe, Africa and the World*. Cham: Springer.

Kaplan, S.E. and Ruland, R.G. (1991). Positive theory, rationality and accounting regulation. *Critical Perspectives on Accounting*, 2(4), 361–374.

Klein, M. (2005). Responsibility. In Honderich, T. (Ed.), *Oxford Companion to Philosophy*. Oxford: Oxford University Press.

Kline, J.M. (2006). MNCs and surrogate sovereignty. *The Brown Journal of World Affairs*, 13(1), 123–133.

Latapi Agudelo, M.A., Jóhannsdóttir, L. and Davídsdóttir, B. (2019). A literature review of the history and evolution of corporate social responsibility. *International Journal of Corporate Social Responsibility*, 4(1), 1. https://doi.org/10.1186/s40991-018-0039-y

Lodge, G. and Wilson, C. (2006). *A Corporate Solution to Global Poverty; How Multinationals Can Help the Poor and Invigorate Their Own Legitimacy*. Princeton, NJ: Princeton University Press.

Lukes, S. (2005). *Power: A Radical View*, 2nd edition. New York: Palgrave Macmillan.

Marquis, C., Toffel, M.W. and Zhou, Y. (2016). Scrutiny, norms, and selective disclosure: A global study of greenwashing. *Organization Science*, 27(2), 483–504.

Martin, D. (2007). Responsibility: A philosophical perspective. In Dewsbury, G. and Dobson, J. (Eds.), *Responsibility and Dependable Systems*. Cham: Springer.

Malesky, E.J. (2009). Foreign direct investors as agents of economic transition: An instrumental variables analysis. *Quarterly Journal of Political Science*, 4(1), 59–85.

Mill, J.S. (1998). Utilitarianism. In Crisp, R. (Ed.), *Oxford Philosophical Texts*. Oxford: Oxford University Press.

Miller, D. (2008). National responsibility and global justice. *Critical Review of International Social and Political Philosophy*, 11(4), 383–399.

Mosley, L. and Uno, S. (2007). Racing to the bottom or climbing to the top? Economic globalization and collective labour rights. *Comparative Political Studies*, 40(8), 923–948.

North, D.C., Wallis, J.J., Webb, S.B. and Weingast, B.R. (2007). Limited access orders in the developing world: A new approach to the problems of development, policy. Research Working Paper No. 4359.Washington, DC: World Bank Publications.

Ogien, A. (2016). Obligation and impersonality: Wittgenstein and the nature of the social. *Philosophy of the Social Sciences*, 46(6), 1–20.

Omotola, S.J. (2009). Liberation movements and the rising violence in the Niger Delta: The new continuous site of oil and environmental politics. *Studies in Conflict and Terrorism*, 33(1), 36–54.

Owens, D. (2012). *Shaping the Normative Landscape*. Oxford: Oxford University Press.

Palazzo, G. and Scherer, A.G. (2006). Corporate legitimacy as deliberation: A communicative framework. *Journal of Business Ethics*, 66(1), 71–88.

Patterson, D.M. (1992). The value of a promise. *Law and Philosophy*, 11(4), 385–402.

Posner, M. (2022). The Ukraine Crisis: How corporations should respond to Russia's invasion. *Forbes*, 10 March. Available at: https://www.forbes.com/sites/michaelposner/2022/03/10/the-ukraine-crisis-how-corporations-should-respond-to-russias-invasion/?sh=7daf94c74829

PwC. (2021). The geometry of sustainability: Progressing from linear to circularity, 19 August. Available at: https://www.pwc.com/my/en/perspective/esg/210820-geometry-of-sustainability.html

Rabie, M. (2016). *A Theory of Sustainable Sociocultural and Economic Development*. New York: Palgrave Macmillan.

Ross, R. (1970). *Obligation*. Ann Arbor, MI: The University of Michigan Press.
Rudra, N. (2005). Globalization and the strengthening of democracy in the developing World. *American Journal of Political Science*, 49(4), 704–730.
Ruland, R.G. (1984). Duty, obligation, and responsibility in accounting policy making. *Journal of Accounting and Public Policy*, 3(3), 223–237.
Saenz, C. (2018). Building legitimacy and trust between a mining company and a community to earn social license to operate: A Peruvian case study. *Corporate Social Responsibility and Environmental Management*, 26(4), 1–11.
Sarpong, S. (2010). *Multinationals and the Social Perspectives: An Assessment of the Mining Communities in Western Ghana*. Unpublished PhD thesis. Cardiff University.
Sarpong, S. (2018). Sweatshops and a duty of care – To what extent? The case of Bangladesh. In Seifi, S. and Crowther, D. (Eds.), *Stakeholders, Governance and Responsibility*. Bingley: Emerald.
Sarpong, S. (2021). Why have we forgotten 'government social responsibility'? Charting the course for sustainability in governance. In Idowu, S. (Ed.), *Current Global Practices of CSR - In the Era of Sustainable Development Goals*. Cham: Springer.
Scott, W.R. (2008). *Institutions and Organizations: Ideas and Interests*, 3rd edition. Los Angeles, CA: Sage Publications.
Stahl, B.C. (2006). Responsible computers? A case for ascribing quasi-responsibility to computers independent of personhood or agency. *Ethics and Information Technology*, 8(4), 205–213.
Stierle, K. (1994). Interpretations of responsibility and responsibilities of interpretation. *New Literary History*, 25(4), 853–867.
Suchman, M.C. (1995). Managing legitimacy: Strategic and institutional approaches. *Academy of Management Journal*, 20(3), 571–610.
Talbert, M. (2019). Moral responsibility. *Stanford Encyclopaedia of Philosophy*. Available at: https://plato.stanford.edu/entries/moral-responsibility/
Thompson, M. (2004). What is it to wrong someone? A puzzle about justice. In Wallace, R.J., Pettit, P., Scheffler, S. and Smith, M. (Eds.), *Reason and Value: Themes from the Philosophy of Joseph Raz*. Oxford: Oxford University Press.
Thomson, I. and Boutilier, R.G. (2011). Social license to operate. In Darling, P. (Ed.), *SME Mining Engineering Handbook*. Littleton, CO: Society for Mining, Metallurgy and Exploration.
Thomson, I. and Joyce, S.A. (2000). Mineral exploration and the challenge of community relations. *The PDAC Communiqué*, 1, 1–9.
Vetlesen, A.J. (1993). Why does proximity make a moral difference? Coming to terms with lessons learned from the Holocaust. *Paxis International*, 12, 371–386.
Visser, W., McIntosh, M. and Middleton, C. (2017). Introduction and overview. In Visser, W., McIntosh, M. and Middleton, C. (Eds.), *Corporate Citizenship in Africa: Lessons from the Past; Paths to the Future*. London: Routledge.
Werhane, P. (1985). *Persons, Rights, and Corporations*. Englewood Cliffs, NJ: Prentice-Hall.

17 Managing Stakeholder Relationships within Corporate Social Responsibility Communication

Teresa Burguete, Cristina Sales Baptista, and Idalina Dias Sardinha

Introduction

Organizations that have significant social, economic, and environmental impacts are shifting from merely business purposes to responsible management, given they need a social license to operate and to achieve sustainability goals. The change is being developed under the realm of corporate social responsibility (hereafter known as CSR) and business sustainability where shareholders are no longer the most important stakeholder. In the current context, organizations must be accountable to stakeholders and engage them to get their support and work together towards mutually agreed sustainability goals (Schultz and Wehmeier, 2010). Thus, stakeholder participation is a determinant factor in achieving lasting social, economic, and environmental development (Schädler et al., 2011; Sardinha et al., 2013).

Corporate social responsibility communication (hereafter known as CSRC) is paramount for managing stakeholder relationships. CSRC is not only a vehicle for organizations to disseminate their values and beliefs (Schultz et al., 2013; Brennan et al., 2013) but also a way to influence stakeholders, manage relationships, and attain legitimacy (Hooghiemstra, 2000; Van Riel and Fombrun, 2007; Brennan et al., 2013).

This study introduces a conceptual framework that enables the analysis of stakeholder relationships through the principal dimensions of sensemaking, sensegiving, exchange, adaptation, and coordination. A new interdisciplinary approach is put forward, by bringing together marketing and economic and social organizational theories regarding interaction processes (hereafter known as IP) and CSRC, which complement each other in terms of the understanding of stakeholder relationships.

The industrial marketing purchase approach (hereafter known as the IMP approach) focuses on business relationships but aims to enlarge the span of business relationships (Esse et al., 2012) to all stakeholders' groups. There is a growing awareness that the current call for socially accountable and transparent businesses gives potential to the value of stakeholder relationships (Andriof et al., 2017). In their research on relationships, Esse et al. (2012) pointed out that the

DOI: 10.4324/9781003274575-21

stakeholder management approach can increase return and company rankings. These authors brought together stakeholder theory and the IMP approach to study expectations in stakeholder relationships.

The stakeholder approach is closely related to CSR as a means to implement its principles (Freeman et al., 2010). The stakeholder relationship is closely related to the CSRC strategies, and the business relationship is closely related to the IP within the IMP approach. Based on the literature review, CSRC processes within responsible strategies and the IP are jointly analyzed, focusing on relationships. The authors incorporate the IMP approach and its conceptualization of the IP, as these capture the development of the relationships between actors and lead to results that are relevant for stakeholder relationship management.

This study aims to develop a conceptual framework to understand the relationships between organizations and their stakeholders. This understanding will contribute to the development of stakeholder relationship management that can provide legitimacy and contribute to the achievement of sustainability goals.

The theory reveals that there are gaps when trying to gain a clear picture of how CSRC occurs (Tuan et al., 2019). Some scholars conclude that the existing literature misinterprets and misunderstands the complex processes of interaction and negotiation between business and its stakeholders (Brennan et al., 2013). Others go even further, stating there is a limitation of knowledge with regard to matters such as the impact of CSRC on management (Crane and Glozer, 2016). Esse et al. (2012) brought a new discussion by putting together stakeholder and business networks, however still with a focus on customers, buyers, and suppliers. Hence, there is still the need to focus on other salient stakeholders' groups for the company. So, several research questions remain to be developed. This implies the need for more research on the management of relationships between organizations and their stakeholders. Globally, the findings of this research intend to fill gaps concerning the CSRC and IMP approaches.

The chapter now proceeds to examine more thoroughly the relationship between CSRC and IP. Next, a theoretical framework is proposed for researching stakeholder relationships and the potential operationalization of the model is described. To conclude, the authors will comment on the purpose of this study and its expected contribution to society. Finally, some methodological considerations are drawn regarding further lines of research and the approach.

Corporate Social Responsibility Communication and Stakeholder Relationship

The most cited initial definition of CSR refers to "the obligations of businessmen to follow the lines of action which are desirable in terms of values and objectives for our society" (Bowen, 1953, 44) and this remains the core of the definitions that were to follow. In 1991, Carroll (1999) constructed the "Pyramid of Corporate Social Responsibilities", whereby the socially responsible organization must seek to make a profit, albeit complying with the law, according to the principles of ethics and behaving like a good corporate citizen. Over the years, the

CSR concept has been discussed, adapted, and complemented, leading to differing and more complete definitions. According to both Dahlsrud's (2008) and our understandings, a unique definition of CSR is irrelevant. What matters is the ability to contextualize CSR and integrate its evolving principles, implement support and frequently improved tools, and continually expand responsible business management in all sectors.

Mostly, CSR approaches are closely related to guarantee stakeholder interaction (e.g., European Commission, 2001; McBarnet, 2009; Gond et al., 2011), suggesting that management strategies should entail relationship development with all related actors (Savage et al., 1991; Du et al., 2010). Each of these actors – a stakeholder – has been defined in the seminal work of Freeman – *Strategic Management: A Stakeholder Approach* – as "any group or individual who can affect and be affected by the achievement of the organization's objectives" (Freeman, 1984, 25). The stakeholder approach, later known as stakeholder theory, can be seen as a means to implement the principles of CSR and advocate that organizations should evolve from social responsibility to accountability to their stakeholders (Freeman et al., 2010). Thus, the relevance of the stakeholder influence is highlighted, making it crucial for organizations to involve stakeholders to achieve their sustainability goals (Schultz and Wehmeier, 2010; Sardinha et al., 2013).

CSRC was initially guided by principles of transparency to gain trust, and has mainly consisted of communicating and reporting CSR policies and activities (Chaudhri, 2016). Thus, accountability is common between CSRC and the stakeholder approach. However, CSRC is not only communicating CSR policies and activities but is also about stakeholder engagement (Crane and Glozer, 2016). It can strategically involve stakeholders so that organizations can get their support and obtain legitimacy.

Through the lens of stakeholder management, CSRC is mainly perceived as a way of disseminating the values and beliefs that are inherent to an organization's identity, enhancing the way an organization addresses stakeholders' concerns and expectations (Schultz et al., 2013; Brennan et al., 2013; Chaudhri, 2016). The organizational identity within CSR focuses on external stakeholders, resulting in the paradigm of how to best manage CSRC and transmit corporate identity to external stakeholders to obtain legitimacy (Crane and Glozer, 2016).

Sensegiving and sensemaking processes are essential within CSRC, as they are a common denominator in a multiplicity of studies (e.g., Cornelissen, 2012; Maitlis and Christianson, 2014). Morsing and Schultz (2006) developed a model of stakeholder relationship strategies anchored on the processes of sensemaking and sensegiving. Their model elaborates three categories as below:

(1) the "stakeholder information strategy" – the organization informs the stakeholder about its identity and corporate CSR decisions and actions in such a way that it may have stakeholders' acceptance and benefit the organization's image. It is a one-way communication involving a sensegiving process;
(2) the "stakeholder response strategy" – the organization tries to find out what the stakeholders want and then tries to make sense of its decisions and

actions. The goal is to demonstrate to stakeholders that the organization has made adaptations to comply with stakeholders' expectations. It is a two-way asymmetric communication involving a process of sensemaking followed by sensegiving;

(3) the "stakeholder involvement strategy" – the organization builds sound relationships with stakeholders, and both actors influence one another. Actors communicate frequently, establish agreements, and have mutual influences. It is a two-way symmetric communication holding processes of sensemaking and sensegiving to and from organizations and stakeholders.

To achieve sound results, long-term relationships must be developed (Sonpar, 2011) and these relationships are created according to the organization's legitimacy (Mitchell et al., 1997). A responsible organization protects the interests of stakeholders, focusing on two issues, namely the identification of legitimate stakeholders and the management of stakeholder's demands (Greenwood, 2007). Stakeholders identification can be a hard task and stakeholder theory presents multiple options, such as primary and secondary; owners and non-owners of the firm; owners of capital or owners of less-tangible assets; actors or those acted upon; those who have a voluntary or an involuntary relationship with the firm; rights-holders, contractors, or moral claimants; resource providers or dependents of the firm; risk-takers or influencers, and finally, "legal principles which result in a fiduciary duty for agents/managers" (Mitchell et al., 1997, 854).

Corporate Social Responsibility Communication and Interaction Processes

Communication, through sensegiving and sensemaking processes, enhances stakeholder relationships and leads to better results in terms of trust and engagement with the organization (Schultz and Wehemeir, 2010; Capriotti, 2011).

Sensemaking happens when stakeholders interpret and make sense of the organization's actions and issues (Cornelissen, 2012; Maitlis and Christianson, 2014). Stakeholders try to check whether the organization's actions are transparent and consistent with its identity and line it up with their expectations. Sensegiving is the dissemination of an organization's vision to its stakeholders, to influence how the stakeholders perceive or make sense of the organization's identity and behavior (Morsing and Schultz, 2006). Sensemaking and sensegiving lead to better results within a context of consistency and transparency (Kim, 2019). Consistency, under the lens of CSR, is conceptualized as being the absence of discrepancy between the organization's CSR identity and its CSR activities (Basu and Palazzo, 2008), whereby the organization is continually communicating its CSR goals (Kim and Ferguson, 2018). Transparency is about telling the whole story regardless of favors or penalties to the organization (Kim and Ferguson, 2018). Thus, it ensures that organizations act visibly and properly communicate their activities to the stakeholders.

Stakeholder relationships that entail participation and involvement can promote trust (Pomeroy and Douvere, 2008; Röckmann et al., 2015). In such relationships, transparency and trust have a mutual influence, whereby transparency leads to trust (Morsing and Schultz, 2006) and more transparency is evident when there is trust (Scandelius and Cohen, 2016). Definitions of trust within CSR and CSRC are not common. Carroll and Shabana (2010, 101) quote Pivato et al. (2008) in their definition of trust as "a mediating variable which shapes the relationship between CSR activities and firm performance". Du et al. (2010) regard trust to be an outcome within their proposed communication framework. In this study, the authors adopt an IMP approach's definition that trust is to rely on the idea that the other actor is reliable and just (Palmatier et al., 2007).

CSRC is related to stakeholder relationships and so is the IMP approach, except the latter focuses on business relationships. It is accepted that relationships consist of an interaction where at least two parties influence and are affected by each other (e.g., Canning and Hanmer-Llyod, 2002; Ford et al., 2008). This definition also fits the concept of stakeholder relationship in a context where the stakeholder is one actor and the organization the other actor.

To develop an understanding of industrial business relationships, the IMP approach focuses on the interaction between organizations, that is, within the scope of their relationships (Perna et al., 2012). From this perspective, studying relationships necessarily involves studying interaction processes (IP). Interaction is typified by characteristics such as exchange (Håkansson, 1982; Medlin, 2004; Ford et al., 2008; Baptista, 2013; Håkansson and Ford, 2016), adaptation (Håkansson and Snehota, 1995; Ford et al., 2008; Baptista, 2013; Johanson and Mattsson, 2015; Håkansson and Ford, 2016), and coordination (Ford and Håkansson, 2013). Furthermore, the exchange processes can be divided into the exchange of resources and the exchange of social resources (Möller and Wilson, 1995). An interaction of exchange would tend to evolve into adaptation when one or both actors are willing to strengthen the relationship and adapt by changing resources, activities, and mutual dependence (Metcalf et al., 1992; Ford et al., 2008).

Relationships may also develop to the extent that both actors cooperate to achieve effectiveness (Baptista, 2013). This coordination is regarded as the degree of institutionalization of the relationships established (e.g., Håkansson, 1982; Baptista, 2013), thus enabling the ability to capture the more formal aspects of the relationship development between the organization and its stakeholders (e.g., contractual arrangements, protocols, agreements). Coordination can only be achieved if there is stakeholder involvement. This CSRC strategy involves processes of sensemaking and sensegiving in both ways where both actors coordinate their decisions and tasks. If adaptation and coordination are present, together they lead to cooperation and the two parties work to accomplish their respective or mutual goals and one cannot succeed without the other (Ford and Håkansson, 2013).

Albeit CSRC stakeholder strategies seem to imply that the company is the main actor of the relationship and IP processes consider actors as equal. The authors have managed to find interconnectedness between CSRC strategies and IP processes. The CSRC stakeholder information strategy happens when the company merely informs the stakeholder. There is no dialogue, it is a sensegiving process. Similarly, in the information exchange process, the company informs the stakeholder and the stakeholder informs the company. Both processes are one-way communication. The stakeholder response strategy holds processes of sensemaking followed by sensegiving. The company seeks to demonstrate to stakeholders that their concerns matter. The company, based on stakeholder information, may adapt its decisions and activities to meet what the company assumes stakeholders' expectations are. The process also refers to adaptation, in the sense that both actors wish to adapt to one another. In the stakeholder involvement strategy, the company fosters stakeholder engagement to build a relationship, and finally, there is a two-way symmetric communication holding processes of sensegiving and sensemaking. In the corresponding process of IP, both actors coordinate to achieve effectiveness.

The Outcomes of CSRC and IP

Legitimacy is an outcome of CSRC. It has been introduced in social theory by Weber (1978), and the most widely quoted definition of legitimacy is that proposed by Suchman (1995, 574) "a generalized perception or assumption that the actions of an entity are desirable, proper, or appropriate within some socially constructed system of norms, values, beliefs and definitions".

Palazzo and Scherer (2006) advocate that legitimacy is the main purpose of CSRC and the way to build legitimacy through CSRC is by developing stakeholder relationships based on trust (Crane and Glozer, 2016). Organizations that have significant social and environmental impacts require legitimacy, which implies ongoing acceptance of the organization's practices by its stakeholders. Together with trust, legitimacy assigns them a social license to operate (Thomson and Joyce, 2008; Carroll and Shabana, 2010; Gillespie et al., 2016).

Cooperation is an IP outcome, being an indicator of relationship performance (Palmatier et al., 2007) and results from the combination of adaptation and coordination processes, in the sense of achieving mutual goals (Håkansson and Ford, 2016). Together with trust and commitment, cooperation enables the establishment of long-term relationships that can evolve into partnerships (Håkansson and Ford, 2016).

Trust is to rely on your business partner and commitment is the will to maintain the relationship (Palmatier et al., 2007) and strengthen the relationship (Ford et al., 2008). This means the actors work together towards a long-term relationship to get results such as trust and commitment. This study adopts the definition of relationship as the continuous interaction between at least two actors that are willing to maintain long-lasting relationships based on common interests (Baptista, 2013).

Trust is an outcome shared by both CSRC and IP. The processes of sensegiving and sensemaking lead to trust, especially when consistency and transparency are involved. But these processes are limited to the assignment of legitimacy and trust. When stakeholders and organizations share the same sustainability goals, legitimacy and trust need to be complemented by cooperation and commitment to achieve those mutual goals. The authors argue that CSRC theory and IP can have mutual benefits concerning the management of stakeholder relationships.

A Conceptual Framework for Researching Stakeholder Relationships

The proposed conceptual framework (Figure 17.1) allows the analysis of stakeholder relationships under the principal dimensions of sensegiving, sensemaking, exchange, adaptation, and coordination. The focus of the framework is on the relationships between the organization and its external key stakeholders, under the realm of CSRC.

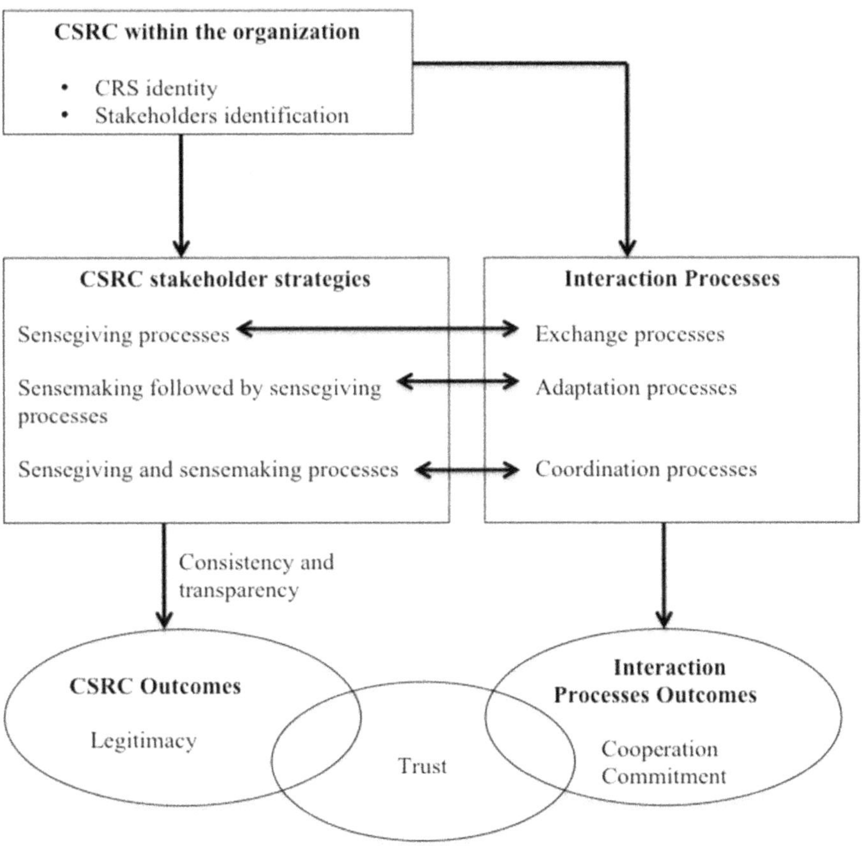

Figure 17.1 Proposed Conceptual Framework on Stakeholder Relationships

The company's CSR identity is relevant to identify the values and beliefs of the organization, to understand how it is disseminated through the CSRC processes, and to further the evidence of consistency and transparency of those values and beliefs. Stakeholder identification and analysis can be done based on three core attributes such as power, legitimacy, and urgency (Mitchell et al.,1997).

CSRC stakeholder strategies involve incorporating the sensemaking and sensegiving processes (Morsing and Schultz, 2006). These are adequate to understand what kind of relationship exists between the company and stakeholders and how stakeholders make sense of what the company communicates. Within these processes, consistency and transparency are looked for within CSR communication and activities. The same relationships are studied under the IP processes of exchange, adaptation, and coordination to understand the maturity of the relationship.

This conceptual framework also permits the study of CSRC strategic approaches to stakeholder relationships devised by Morsing and Schultz (2006), namely the stakeholder information strategy, the stakeholder response strategy, and the stakeholder involvement strategy. Outcomes of cooperation, commitment, trust, and legitimacy are expected. These are crucial for assigning the company with a license to operate and contribute to reinforcing long-term stakeholder relationships management that fosters sustainability achievements.

Conceptualization and Operationalization of the Proposed Framework

In this section, the authors present, for each dimension, the conceptualization and potential operationalization. The CSRC dimensions in Table 17.1 are studied through the main concepts of identity and stakeholder strategies, with the seminal work of Crane and Glozer (2016) being the basis for this study. CSR identity is based on the company's CSR policy and its values and beliefs. The key stakeholders are identified as those that matter in decision-making towards sustainability goals. Stakeholder strategies identification is based on the analysis of information regarding CSR decisions and activities, on how the company integrates stakeholders' expectations in management, and the frequency of meetings with key stakeholders and the subjects discussed.

Sensegiving and sensemaking processes are essential within CSRC, as they are a common denominator in a multiplicity of studies (e.g., Cornelissen, 2012; Maitlis and Christianson, 2014; Morsing and Schultz, 2006). The studies of both Weick (1993) and Basu and Palazzo (2008) are used as the definition is grounded on the widely defined concept of sensemaking. Accordingly, a broad definition is adopted that incorporates external stakeholders (Morsing and Schultz, 2006). These processes are studied by finding out how stakeholders make sense of the organization's identity and what the company decides, says, and does according to its identity.

Consistency and transparency are key for achieving trust within interactive CSRC (Kim, 2019). Thus, they are crucial to go along with the processes of

Table 17.1 Conceptualization and Potential Operationalization of CSRC

Dimension	*Concept*	*Definition*	*Relevant studies*	*Indicators/ Potential operationalization*
CSRC within the organization	CSR Identity	Manage CSRC and transmit corporate identity to external stakeholders	Crane and Glozer (2016)	Values and beliefs
	Stakeholder's identification	Can be done based on three core attributes such as power, legitimacy, and urgency	Mitchell et al. (1997)	Who matters in decision-making towards sustainability goals
CSRC strategies	Stakeholder information strategy	The organization informs the stakeholder (one-way communication) about favorable CSR decisions and tasks	Morsing and Schultz (2006)	Favorable CSR decisions and tasks
	Stakeholder response strategy	The organization demonstrates to stakeholders (two-way asymmetric communication) how the company integrates their concerns		Evidence on how the company integrates stakeholder's expectations
	Stakeholder involvement strategy	The organization builds relationships and establishes frequent, systematic, and pro-active dialogues with stakeholders (two-way symmetric communication)		Frequency of contacts and pro-active dialogue
CSRC processes	Sensegiving	It is the dissemination of the company's vision by the company to its stakeholders, with the intention of influencing the way stakeholders understand or make sense of their identity	Morsing and Schultz (2006)	How others make sense of the organization's identity and behavior Transparency and consistency between the organization's overall strategy and its CSR activities
	Sensemaking	Sensemaking is grounded in identity construction. The company chooses and decides what to do to have an influence on its relationships with stakeholders, based on company identity and aiming for legitimacy	Weick (1993); Basu and Palazzo (2008)	What the company decides, says, and does according to its identity Transparency and consistency of CSR activities during a given period

sensegiving and sensemaking. Consistency and transparency must be detected in the organization's overall strategy and its CSR activities. Consistency can also be evaluated through the reliability of CSR activities during given periods of time (Basu and Palazzo, 2008). Transparency ensures that the organization acts visibly and communicates its activities to the stakeholders, whether activities are favorable or unfavorable (Kim and Ferguson, 2018), and hold the organization accountable to stakeholders (Transparency International, 2018).

To achieve the objective of this study, another key dimension is crucial: the IP processes. The IP (see Table 17.2) are commonly conceptualized through the processes of exchange, adaptation, and coordination (e.g., Ford and Håkansson, 2013; Baptista, 2013; Håkansson and Ford, 2016).

Table 17.2 Conceptualization and Potential Operationalization of IP

Dimension	*Concept*	*Definition*	*Relevant studies*	*Indicators/ Potential operationalization*
Interaction processes	Exchange/ Information exchange	Information exchange involves distinct width and depth of technical, economic, or organizational issues, which can be performed by impersonal or personal communication in different formality degrees	Håkansson et al. (1982)	Frequency of contacts between parties
	Adaptation	Both actors are willing to strengthen the relationship and adapt by changing resources, activities, and mutual dependence	Metcalf et al. (1992); Ford et al. (2008)	Adapt by changing resources, activities, and planning or scheduling systems
	Coordination	Both actors coordinate to achieve effectiveness	Baptista (2013)	Degree of institutionalization of the relationships

Within the scope of this study, exchange processes focus on information exchange, and the frequency of contacts between the company and stakeholders. From a wide perspective, the adaptation processes are defined by Metcalf et al. (1992) and Ford et al. (2008). This perspective is adopted, as it enables identifying the way organizations and stakeholders can mutually adapt. It is relevant to look for companies' adaptations that meet stakeholders' expectations and further perceive whether stakeholders also adapt to the companies' requests. Coordination is regarded to be the degree of institutionalization (e.g., contractual arrangements, protocols, agreements) of the relationships established within CSRC (e.g., Håkansson, 1982; Baptista, 2013), enabling the capture of the more formal aspects of the relationship between the organization and its key stakeholders. The understanding of relationships involves disentangling how they develop towards outcomes that can: (1) assign acceptance on how the company operates, and (2) contribute to sustainability outputs. Therefore, these outcomes are a result of the mutual influence of CSRC and IP processes and they are legitimacy, cooperation, commitment, and trust (see Table 17.3).

The authors adopted Suchman's (1995) broad-based definition of legitimacy. Stakeholders must accept the way the company operates. Cooperation is conceptualized based on the IP perspective, where the company and stakeholders work together to achieve goals (Håkansson and Ford, 2016). Commitment focuses on the will to establish lasting relationships. Trust is present as an outcome in most studies (e.g., Morsing and Schultz, 2006; Palmatier, 2007; Pomeroy and Douvere, 2008; Schultz and Wehemeir, 2010; Röckman et al., 2015; Chaudhri, 2016; Scandelius and Cohen, 2016). The aim is to ascertain whether stakeholders consider the company reliable and just and whether the company trusts stakeholders.

Concluding Remarks and Further Research

The objective to build an interdisciplinary conceptual framework to understand the relationships between organizations and their key stakeholders is achieved through the adoption of IMP and CSRC. The authors also propose its potential operationalization. Some of the elements, such as CSRC strategies (Morsing and Schultz, 2006), are more stabilized for operationalization, while the others may need further proxies, no matter whether the future research is quantitative or qualitative in nature.

The interconnectedness of CSRC and IP is found in the similarities and differences within the processes of CSRC and the processes of IP. CSRC brings the legitimacy for organizations to operate. Both CSRC and IP find trust crucial for successful relationships. Together with the outputs of cooperation and commitment from IP, legitimacy and trust contribute to sustainability results.

Further research may contribute to disentangling the relationships that occur between organizations and their key stakeholders, showing that legitimacy, cooperation, commitment, and trust can be achieved for mutual benefit towards sustainable outcomes.

Table 17.3 Conceptualization and Potential Operationalization of Outcomes

Dimension	*Concept*	*Definition*	*Relevant studies*	*Indicators/ Potential operationalization*
Outcomes	Legitimacy	A generalized perception that the actions of an entity are desirable, proper, or appropriate within some socially constructed system of norms, values, beliefs, and definitions	Suchman (1995)	Social license to operate – ongoing acceptance of company's practices
	Cooperation	Processes of coordination and adaptation; both participants try to achieve something and one cannot succeed without the other	Håkansson and Ford (2016)	Goals achieved by both the company and stakeholders when working together
	Commitment	The will to maintain the relationship	Palmatier et al. (2007)	Relationship soundness
	Trust	Rely on the idea that the other actor is reliable and just	Palmatier et al. (2007)	Confidence between company and stakeholders

This conceptual framework is intended for application to dyads within stakeholder relationships and provide an improved understanding of the relationships between organizations and their stakeholders. The framework also contributes to achieving organizational goals within responsible management. Particularly, we propose research settings of industries that have relevant social, economic, and environmental impacts. Regarding the theoretical contribution, the interdisciplinary approach taken unravels new insights towards the understanding of stakeholder relationships.

Although this chapter is conceptual, some methodological insights to further test the conceptual framework hereby developed are put forward. The focus is on organizations that have huge social, economic, and environmental impacts.

The sectors that are assumed to be useful to test the framework are mining and brownfield redevelopment. These are rather good examples, as they generate both significant "good and bad" impacts. The mining industry provides key resources to important commodities people need in their current lifestyle and contributes to leveraging economic and social growth. However, it also promotes significant and negative local social and environmental impacts (Baptista, 2013).

The mine life cycle has nine stages, namely exploration, pre-feasibility, feasibility, construction, operations, decommissioning, closure, post-closure, and relinquishment (ICMM, 2009). The balance of positive and negative impacts may indicate that positive ones prevail during the operations stage and negative impacts increase in the post-closure stage. After mine closure, mine sites often evolve to brownfield sites "where environmental contamination is an obstacle to the beneficial use and redevelopment of such properties" (Swickard, 2008, 122).

Both in the case of mine life cycle management and the case of brownfield redevelopment, organizations often face problems of decision-making due to the lack of effective communication with their stakeholders, namely the local community, the local authority and regulators, among others. To ensure that stakeholders trust the organization and are engaged in sustainable solutions, it is of primordial importance to study the development of their relationships, with communication being critical for this process (Cornelissen, 2020).

Facing pressures from international organizations and locally exposed communities, mining companies are recognizing their responsibility towards society. Some are willing to embrace responsible mining to address social, economic, and environmental impacts more effectively (Sonesson et al., 2016). Mine brownfields are a distressing reality all over the world and far from being solved. Thus, the test of the framework within this sector seems to be highly suitable.

From a social constructivist perspective, a qualitative approach to understand how the stakeholders' relationships evolve over time would be suggested. Based on multiple case studies, the approach enables the study of contemporary phenomena in their real-life settings (Eisenhardt, 1989; Yin, 1994). This perspective also enables the study of the dynamics of events that provide multidimensional views (Easton, 1995; Eisenhardt, 1989; Bernardi et al., 2012).

The unit of analysis is the development of two-party relationships between the organization and its key stakeholders. Furthermore, the authors suggest looking at the process as being a "sequence of events that describes how things change over time" (Van de Ven, 1992, 169), and combining real-time studies and the historical reconstruction of relationships. Pre-understanding and prolonged involvement with the research setting facilitates the comprehension of how and why things appear, develop, grow, or terminate over time; which is the purpose of process studies (Langley et al., 2013).

The data collection methods would comprise documentation analyses, interviews, as well as observations. Potter (2013) argues that these evidence-gathering methods are appropriate for a qualitative approach. Informal conversational interviews should be held with some stakeholders (Patton, 2014); however, semi-structured interviews (Saunders et al., 2016) might be the main source for primary data. Interview guides would be developed based on the conceptual framework. Non-participant observations could also be used in visits to mines as a complementary method of data collection. Direct observations can range from formal to casual data collection (Yin, 1994). Content analysis should then be implemented following Miles and Huberman (1994) using the cross-case analysis logic.

References

Andriof, J., Waddock, S., Husted, B. and Rahman, S.S. (2017). *Unfolding Stakeholder Thinking: Theory, Responsibility and Engagement.* Sheffield: Greenleaf.

Baptista, C. (2013). Interaction processes in long-term relationships in the metal mining industry: Longitudinal case studies of capital equipment buying. *Industrial Marketing Management*, 42(6), 969–982.

Basu, K. and Palazzo, G. (2008). Corporate social responsibility: A process model of sensemaking. *Academy of Management Review*, 33(1), 122–136.

Bernardi, C., Boffi, M. and Snehota, I. (2012). Living the innovation space without pre-existing relationships. *The IMP Journal*, 6(1), 69–84.

Bowen, H.R. (1953). *Social Responsibility of the Businessman.* New York: Harper.

Brennan, N., Merkl-Davies, D. and Beelitz, A. (2013). Dialogism in corporate social responsibility communications: Conceptualising verbal interaction between organisations and their audiences. *Journal of Business Ethics*, 115(4), 665–679.

Canning, L. and Hanmer-Llyod, S. (2002). Modelling the adaptation process in interactive business relationships. *Journal of Business and Industrial Marketing*, 17(7), 615–636.

Capriotti, P. (2011). Communicating corporate social responsibility through the internet and social media. In Ihlen, Ø., Bartlett, J. and May, S. (Eds.), *The Handbook of Communication and Corporate Social Responsibility.* New York: Wiley.

Carroll, A.B. (1999). Corporate social responsibility: Evolution of a definitional construct. *Business and Society*, 38(3), 268–295.

Carroll, A.B. and Shabana, K.M. (2010). The business case for corporate social responsibility: A review of concepts, research and practice. *International Journal of Management Reviews*, 12(1), 85–105.

Chaudhri, V. (2016). Corporate social responsibility and the communication imperative: Perspectives from CSR managers. *International Journal of Business Communication*, 53(4), 419–442.

Cornelissen, J.P. (2012). Sensemaking under pressure: The influence of professional roles and social accountability on the creation of sense. *Organization Science*, 23(1), 118–137.

Cornelissen, J. (2020). *Corporate Communication: A Guide to Theory and Practice*, 6th edition. London: Sage.

Crane, A. and Glozer, S. (2016). Researching corporate social responsibility communication: Themes, opportunities and challenges. *Journal of Management Studies*, 53(7), 1223–1252.

Dahlsrud, A. (2008). How corporate social responsibility is defined: An analysis of 37 definitions. *Corporate Social Responsibility and Environmental Management*, 15(1), 1–13.

Du, S., Bhattacharya, C.B. and Sen, S. (2010). Maximizing business returns to corporate social responsibility (CSR): The role of CSR communication. *International Journal of Management Reviews*, 12(1), 8–19.

Easton, G. (1995). Methodology and industrial networks. In Möller, K. and Wilson, D.T. (Eds.), *Business Marketing: An Interaction and Network Perspective*. Norwell, MA: Kluwer Academic Publishers.

Eisenhardt, K.M. (1989). Building theories from case study research. *Academy of Management Review*, 14(4), 532–550.

Esse, B., Szántó, R. and Wimmer, A. (2012). Business relationships and relationships with stakeholders – Perception of Hungarian executives. *IMP Journal*, 6(2), 98–108.

European Commission Directorate-General for Employment. (2001). *Promoting a European Framework for Corporate Social Responsibility: Green Paper*. Brussels: Office for Official Publications of the European Communities.

Ford, D., Gadde, L.E., Håkansson, H., Snehota, I. and Waluszewski, A. (2008). Analysing business interaction. 24th IMP Conference, September, Uppsala.

Ford, D. and Håkansson, H. (2013). Competition in business networks. *Industrial Marketing Management*, 42(7), 1017–1024.

Freeman, R.E. (1984). *Strategic Management: A Stakeholder Approach*. Boston, MA: Pitman.

Freeman, R.E., Harrison, J.S., Wicks, A.C., Parmar, B.L. and Colle, S. (2010). *Stakeholder Theory: The State of the Art*. Cambridge: Cambridge University Press.

Gillespie, N., Bond, C.J., Downs, V. and Staggs, J. (2016). Stakeholder trust in the Queensland CSG industry. *The APPEA Journal*, 56(1), 239–246.

Gond, J.P., Kang, N. and Moon, J. (2011). The government of self-regulation: On the comparative dynamics of corporate social responsibility. *Economy and Society*, 40(4), 640–671.

Greenwood, M.R. (2007). Stakeholder engagement: Beyond the myth of corporate responsibility. *Journal of Business Ethics*, 74(4), 315–327.

Håkansson, H. (Ed.). (1982). *Industrial Marketing and Purchasing of Industrial Goods: An Interaction Approach*. Chichester: John Wiley.

Håkansson, H. and Ford, D. (2016). The managerial challenge of business interaction: Behind the market façade. *IMP Journal*, 10(1), 154–171.

Håkansson, H. and Snehota, I. (Eds.). (1995). *Developing Relationships in Business Networks*. London: Routledge.

Hooghiemstra, R. (2000). Corporate communication and impression management – New perspectives why companies engage in corporate social reporting. *Journal of Business Ethics*, 27(1–2), 55–68.

ICMM (International Council on Mining & Metals) (2009). *Human Rights in the Mining & Metals Industry: Handling and Resolvong Local Level Concerns & Grievances*. London: ICMM.

Johanson, J. and Mattsson, L.G. (2015). Internationalisation in industrial systems—A network approach. In Holm, U., Forsgren, M. and Johanson, J. (Eds.), *Knowledge, Networks and Power*. Basingstoke: Palgrave Macmillan.

Kim, S. (2019). The process model of corporate social responsibility (CSR) communication: CSR communication and its relationship with consumer's CSR knowledge, trust, and corporate reputation perception. *Journal of Business Ethics*, 154(4), 1143–1159.

Kim, S. and Ferguson, M.T. (2018). Dimensions of effective CSR communication based on public expectations. *Journal of Marketing Communications*, 24(6), 549–567.

Langley, A.N.N., Smallman, C., Tsoukas, H. and Van de Ven, A.H. (2013). Process studies of change in organization and management: Unveiling temporality, activity, and flow. *Academy of Management Journal*, 56(1), 1–13.

Maitlis, S. and Christianson, M. (2014). Sensemaking in organizations: Taking stock and moving forward. *Academy of Management Annals*, 8(1), 57–125.

McBarnet, D. (2009). Corporate social responsibility beyond law, through law, for law: The new corporate accountability. In McBarnet, D., Voiculescu, A. and Campbell, T. (Eds.), *The New Accountability: Corporate Social Responsibility and the Law*. Cambridge: Cambridge University Press.

Medlin, C.J. (2004). Interaction in business relationships: A time perspective. *Industrial Marketing Management*, 33(3), 185–193.

Metcalf, L.E., Frear, C.R. and Krishnan, R. (1992). Buyer–seller relationships: An application of the IMP interaction model. *European Journal of Marketing*, 26(2), 27–46.

Miles, M.B. and Huberman, A.M. (1994). *Qualitative Data Analysis*, 2nd edition. Thousand Oaks, CA: Sage Publications.

Mitchell, R.K., Agle, B.R. and Wood, D.J. (1997). Towards a theory of stakeholder identification and salience: Defining the principle of who and what really counts. *Academy of Management Review*, 22(4), 853–886.

Möller, K. and Wilson, D.T. (1995). Business relationships - An interaction perspective. In Möller, K. and Wilson, D.T. (Eds.), *Business Marketing: An Interaction and Network Perspective*. Norwell, MA: Kluwer Academic Publishers.

Morsing, M. and Schultz, M. (2006). Corporate social responsibility communication: Stakeholder information, response and involvement strategies. *Business Ethics: A European Review*, 15(4), 323–338.

Palazzo, G. and Scherer, A.G. (2006). Corporate legitimacy as deliberation: A communicative framework. *Journal of Business Ethics*, 66(1), 71–88.

Palmatier, R.W., Dant, R.P. and Grewal, D. (2007). A comparative longitudinal analysis of theoretical perspectives of interorganisational relationship performance. *Journal of Marketing*, 71(4), 172–194.

Patton, M.Q. (2014). *Qualitative Research and Evaluation Method: Integrating Theory and Practice*, 3rd edition. Thousand Oaks, CA: Sage Publications.

Perna, A., Baraldi, E. and Gregori, G.L. (2012). Exploring the conditions for marketing an innovative and unique customized solution: Mexus case study. *The IMP Journal*, 6(1), 1–16.

Pivato, S., Misani, N. and Tencati, A. (2008). The impact of corporate social responsibility on consumer trust: The case of organic food. *Business Ethics: A European Review*, 17(1), 3–12.

Pomeroy, R. and Douvere, F. (2008). The engagement of stakeholders in the marine spatial planning process. *Marine Policy*, 32(5), 816–822.

Potter, W.J. (2013). *An Analysis of Thinking and Research about Qualitative Methods*. New York: Routledge.

Röckmann, C., van Leeuwen, J., Goldsborough, D., Kraan, M. and Piet, G. (2015). The interaction triangle as a tool for understanding stakeholder interactions in marine ecosystem-based management. *Marine Policy*, 52, 155–162.

Sardinha, I., Craveiro, D. and Milheiras, S. (2013). A sustainability framework for redevelopment of rural brownfields: Stakeholder participation at São Domingos mine, Portugal. *Journal of Cleaner Production*, 57, 200–208.

Saunders, M., Lewis, P. and Thornhill, A. (2016). *Research Methods for Business Students*, 7th edition. Harlow: Prentice Hall.

Savage, G., Nix, T.W., Whitehead, C.J. and Blair, J.D. (1991). Strategies for assessing and managing organisational stakeholders. *The Executive*, 5(2), 61–75.

Scandelius, C. and Cohen, G. (2016). Achieving collaboration with diverse stakeholders - The role of strategic ambiguity in CSR communication. *Journal of Business Research*, 69(9), 3487–3499.

Schädler, S., Morio, M., Bartke, S., Rohr-Zänker, R. and Finkel, M. (2011). Designing sustainable and economically attractive brownfield revitalization option using an integrated assessment model. *Journal of Environmental Management*, 92(3), 827–837.

Schultz, F. and Wehmeier, S. (2010). Institutionalization of corporate social responsibility within corporate communications: Combining institutional, sensemaking and communication perspectives. *Corporate Communications: An International Journal*, 15(1), 9–29.

Schultz, F., Castelló, I. and Morsing, M. (2013). The construction of corporate social responsibility in network societies: A communication view. *Journal of Business Ethics*, 115(4), 681–692.

Sonesson, C., Davidson, G. and Sachs, L. (2016). *Mapping Mining to the Sustainable Development Goals: An Atlas*. Geneva: World Economic Forum.

Sonpar, K. (2011). Book review on Freeman et al. (2010). Stakeholder Theory: The State of the Art. *M@n@gement*, 14(3), 209–220.

Suchman, M.C. (1995). Managing legitimacy: Strategic and institutional approaches. *Academy of Management Review*, 20(3), 571–610.

Swickard, T.J. (2008). Regulatory incentives to promote private sector brownfield remediation and reuse. *Soil and Sediment Contamination*, 17(2), 121–136.

Thomson, I. and Joyce, S. (2008). The social licence to operate: What it is and why does it seem so difficult to obtain. Paper presented at Prospectors and Developers Association of Canada (PDAC) Convention, 2–5 March, Toronto.

Transparency International. (2018). Transparency International – The global anti-corruption coalition. Available at: https://www.transparency.org/what-is-corruption#what-is-transparency

Tuan, A., Dalli, D., Gandolfo, A. and Gravina, A. (2019). Theories and methods in CSRC research: A systematic literature review. *Corporate Communications: An International Journal*, 24(2), 212–231.

Van de Ven, A.H. (1992). Suggestions for studying strategy process: A research note. *Strategic Management Journal*, 13(5), 169–188.

Van Riel, C. and Fombrun, C. (2007). *Essentials of Corporate Communication: Implementing Practices for Effective Reputation Management*. New York: Routledge.

Weber, M. (1978). *Economy and Society: An Outline of Interpretive Sociology* (Vol. 1). Berkeley, CA: University of California Press.

Weick, K.E. (1993). Sensemaking in organization: Small structures with large consequences. In Murnighan, J.K. (Ed.), *Social Psychology in Organizations: Advances in Theory and Research*. Englewood Cliffs, NJ: Prentice Hall.

Yin, R.K. (1994). *Case Study Research, Design and Methods*. London: Sage.

Part 5

CSR – Sustainability Goals and ESG

18 The Road Towards an Internationalized Sustainable Development Goals Disclosure (SDGD) practice in China

Jieqi Guan, Sandy Hou In Sio, and Cindia, Ching Chi Lam

Introduction

In January 2020, the United Nations Sustainable Development Goals Disclosure (SDGD) Recommendations (hereinafter referred to as the Recommendations) were jointly issued by six international associations. These associations included the Association of Chartered Certified Accountants (ACCA), Chartered Accountants Australia and New Zealand (ANZ), the Institute of Chartered Accountants of Scotland (ICAS), the International Federation of Accountants (IFAC), the International Integrated Reporting Council (IIRC), and the World Benchmarking Alliance (WBA) (Adams et al., 2020). The Recommendations aim to guide enterprises to accurately identify significant risks and opportunities related to sustainable development, and encourage enterprises to adjust their development mode to contribute to the realization of the 17 SDGs promoted by the United Nations in 2015. The Recommendations serve as a blueprint to achieve a global sustainable future.

Creating long-term value for all stakeholders and the society, maintaining transparent and effective communication, and helping the realization of SDGs have become the basis for enterprises to win social credibility and achieve sustainable operations (Rosati and Faria, 2019a). Among them, transparent and effective information disclosure is an important way for society to understand the operations of enterprises, and for the enterprises to gain trust from their stakeholders (Izzo et al., 2020a). As a conceptual framework, the Recommendations embody the best practices of SDGs' information disclosure. They advocate and support more comprehensive, transparent, and practical reporting and communications, and are conducive to enhancing the effectiveness and credibility of a firm's sustainability reporting. Furthermore, they guide companies to take sustainable operations and long-term value creation as their goal by fully considering the needs of governments, investors, consumers, the public, media, and other stakeholders, and also to integrate SDGs with the company's development strategy (Izzo et al., 2020b).

Since the Recommendations were published, they have been translated into different languages, so that enterprises, organizations, and stakeholders worldwide could read and apply them. The simplified Chinese version of the Recommendations was launched in China in June 2020. It was then embraced

DOI: 10.4324/9781003274575-23

and implemented widely in China by both the government and commercial enterprises (GoldenBee, 2021). By the end of 2020, the Chinese government declared its victory in eliminating extreme poverty across the country. It has then pledged another goal by setting the "3060" target to achieve the carbon peak by 2030 and carbon neutrality by 2060 (ICCST, 2021). Considering the increasing concern in such areas surrounding the SDGs and their relevant disclosures, this study is conducted to explore the development status of SDGD in China since the release of the Recommendations. It also aims to extend the previous country-level SDGD studies from the West to China, a large potential contributing country for the planet's sustainable development.

Interviews were conducted with experts from Big 4 accounting firms and consultancy companies, managers from enterprises adapting SDGs, scholars from well-known higher education institutes, and key persons from important associations. Content analysis was applied to investigate the situation of SDGD development in China, and the results have revealed the problems and challenges encountered by the stakeholders. The findings have provided constructive references for future developmental directions to strengthen sustainability reporting practices in China.

The Historical Evolution of SDGs in Corporate Sustainability Reporting

Prior to the launch of the UNSDGs, enterprises that voluntarily engaged in corporate sustainability and social responsibility initiatives mostly aimed to enhance their corporate image and reputation, or to comply with the explicit requirements of regulators and the implicit expectations of stakeholders as a passive response. In 2000, the UN mobilized the Global Compact, which established ten global principles of corporate sustainability that aimed to support business organizations worldwide to meet fundamental responsibilities in the areas of human rights, labor, environment, and anti-corruption. These ten fundamental principles were set to let companies uphold, at the minimum, the primary responsibilities to people and the planet. In 2006, the UN Principles for Responsible Investment (PRI) were launched to further reinforce corporate sustainability and responsibility.

The PRI aligned an international group of institutional investors towards the commitment of incorporating environmental, social, and governance (ESG) objectives into their investment strategies. Besides the PRI, the United Nations Environment Programme Finance Initiative (UNEP FI) has supported the creation of numerous frameworks, such as the Sustainable Stock Exchanges Initiative (SSEI). These frameworks set out the norms and provide the basis for standard-setting among the private finance sector and global stock markets to achieve the Paris Agreement on Climate Change. With the efforts of the UN-related bodies, the importance of corporate responsibilities leading to sustainable development has been materialized through enterprise investments, and is integrated into the ESG reporting framework to fulfill the requisites of the global financial markets and their industry regulators.

As a result of the initiatives, the level of enterprise involvement in ESG has gradually become an influential factor in corporate decision-making. Enterprises have shifted the paradigm of corporate sustainability reporting from qualitative measures addressing ethical and philanthropic concerns of stakeholders to the integration of quantitative ESG factors on top of meeting the conventional performance indicators. This current approach of integrated ESG reporting is adopted by enterprises to present their management of risks and opportunities with respect to factors that are deemed material to financial prospects, like environmental issues, human capital, human rights, supply chain management, and corporate governance. When the 2030 Agenda for Sustainable Development was announced, more and more enterprises worldwide proactively addressed the SDGs through various innovative practices and reported their efforts invested. Meanwhile, investors and other stakeholders are getting more acquainted with using the SDGs as references to associate their investments with impact goals.

In view of the general acceptance of SDGs among the national governments, they have rapidly become a popular benchmark undertaken by enterprises to attest to their ESG performance. Governments, financial market regulators, and investors refer to the SDGs when devising their standards to ensure the enterprises' commitment to their financial and non-financial obligations. Since then, the global sustainable development journey has led to the creation of multifold investment opportunities aligned to the potential impact and return from the SDGs, *inter alia*, the investment in sustainable infrastructure, green finance, and community support projects. According to Credit Suisse (2020), achieving the SDGs requires an estimated investment of USD 5–7 trillion per year. This investment volume implies a remarkable financial opportunity and a need for more comprehensive ESG management and oversight.

Notwithstanding the concerns from investors, regulators, and other stakeholders, a universally credible mechanism of monitoring and reporting an enterprise's SDG strategies and performance was absent. To fill this gap, the Recommendations were developed and published in 2020. During the consultation stage, stakeholders' feedback suggested that the level of disclosure by enterprises on sustainable development issues was insufficient to support the achievement of SDGs and the long-term net value creation. This situation has triggered the increasing demand for the enterprises' rigorous data to back up their tangible actions so as to ensure that they are committed to the SDGs and have integrated them into daily operations (Adams, 2020). Therefore, the Recommendations also aim at realizing the spirit of SDG 17 (partnership for the goals) through collaboration with various parties, and revitalizing a global partnership through establishing the best practice for SDGs reporting (Adams et al., 2020).

SDGD Compared with Other Sustainability Reporting Frameworks

As mentioned, sustainability measures were implemented by some enterprises before the UNSDGs were introduced. These enterprises may have already adopted some mainstream sustainability standards/frameworks other than the 17 SDGs (see Appendix 1) when planning for and reporting on their CSR activities for their stakeholders' interests and/or for statutory filings, regulatory, and financing purposes. In contrast to other sustainability reporting standards/frameworks that often have overlapping focuses and approaches (Adams and Abhayawansa, 2021) such as heavy reliance on exhaustive guidelines and technical indicators, the SDGs are expected to become the guiding vision for sharing long-lasting prosperity (Bebbington and Unerman, 2018; Hajer et al., 2015). Thus, when the Recommendations were proposed, they called for consolidating sustainable development considerations into strategy, management approach, governance oversight, disclosure of performance, and targets. They are now set to focus on the materiality of sustainability reporting on long-term value creation, the impact (both positive or negative) of the enterprises on sustainable development, and their achievements on SDGs (Adams et al., 2020; Adams and Abhayawansa, 2021). The main objective is to complement the organizations' strategic focus and report on the global level in alignment with other sustainability reporting standards/frameworks, such as Integrated Reporting (IR), GRI Standards, and the Task Force on Climate-related Financial Disclosures (TCFD) recommendations.

Prior Research on Corporate SDG Disclosures

The widespread promotion of SDGs has led to scholarly research to examine the role of SDGs under the umbrella of CSR and sustainability reporting and how sustainability accounting and reporting could be effectively managed and conducted. In the literature, SDGs have been criticized for being broadly framed, vague, inconsistent, and difficult to quantify, implement, and monitor (Arena et al., 2015). Moreover, some researchers found problems in reconciling SDGs concerns with the goal of creating shareholder value, as they noted that the win–win situation for enterprises is not precise in terms of contributing to some of the goals, such as SDG 1 (no poverty), SDG 2 (zero hunger), and SDG 16 (peace and justice) (Van der Waal and Thijssens, 2020). These difficulties have contributed to skepticism surrounding SDGs reporting on its lack of substance (García-Meca and Martínez-Ferrero, 2021).

Contrariwise, based on a study of European companies, the findings from García-Meca and Martínez-Ferrero (2021) confirmed that SDG reporting could play a substantive role for firms in controversial and environmentally sensitive industries. Through reporting on global sustainable goals, the enterprises in these sectors can improve their public image and frame themselves as legitimate firms with social, ethical, and green targets (Aherns, 2004; Deegan and Gordon, 1996). This situation enables enterprises to reduce risk and information asymmetry, attract investors, and enhance their market reputation for stakeholders. Despite the seemingly increasing level of commitment by enterprises around the world, an analysis of 1,370 organizations from 97 countries conducted by Heras-Saizarbitoria et al. (2022) scrutinized that enterprises engaged in SDGs as a way to strengthen their social legitimacy and as a mode of impression management (Macellari et al., 2021; Van der Waal and Thijssens, 2020), and were suspected of SDG-washing and "cherry-picking" the SDGs.

SDGs are perceived as having the potential to inform and advance research and practice on sustainability accounting (Bebbington and Unerman, 2018). This is attributable to their features of representing a sufficiently radical, coherent, generally accepted definition of sustainable development (Bebbington et al., 2017) and a compelling call for sustainability action (Shoaf et al., 2018; Thorlakson et al., 2018; Verdolini et al., 2017). However, whether companies can realize the benefits for their reputation and credibility by integrating SDGs in sustainability reporting, and whether they will deliver the disclosures that their stakeholders find legitimate are also subject to the extent to which countries concretely formalize their commitments to the goals and by their ability to turn such challenges into national issues (Biermann et al., 2017). A study by Rosati and Faria (2019b) suggested that organizations reporting on SDGs are more likely to be in countries with higher levels of climate change vulnerability, national CSR, spending on tertiary education, indulgence, and individualism, and lower levels of market coordination, employment protection, power distance, and long-term orientation. Although China is known to have a higher level of collectivism, it is transitioning to a country with advanced education and innovation, climate risk awareness, and national CSR commitment.

Development of the SDGs and SDGD in China

From the execution of the country's 13th five-year plan (2016--2020) to the 14th five-year plan (2021–2025), China has determined to set a series of significant goals and targets to achieve its ultimate state of sustainable development. The first goal to eradicate extreme poverty in 2020 and create a moderately prosperous society in all respects by 2021 was accomplished despite the COVID-19 pandemic. The second goal to build a modern socialist country that is prosperous, strong, democratic, culturally advanced, and harmonious is targeted to be achieved in 2049, the centennial year of the founding of the People's Republic of China, via a midpoint objective set for 2035. To reach the second goal, China will need to double its economic output by 2035 (China Today, 2021). Further to these footsteps of economic development goals, China also stresses realizing various environmental goals. These include the "dual carbon" goal (the "3060" target) to combat climate risks and take the lead in the global biodiversity commitment via the Kunming Declaration, which was signed by over 100 countries in October 2021.

The time and extent of how these sustainability goals will be achieved will depend on the efforts of the central government, the municipal governments, enterprises, the civil society, and many other stakeholders in the country. Over the last 40 years since the "Open Door Policy", China has made significant contributions to sustainable development, in particular, ending poverty (SDG 1), improving education (SDG 4) and health (SDG 3). As a result of these efforts,

China achieved the eradication of extreme poverty in 2020, has increased the average year of schooling from 8.8 to 13.9 since 1990, and increased life expectancy from 69 years to 76 years during the same time span. More remarkably, China is the only country that has moved from the low to high human development category, as measured by the Human Development Index (HDI) of UNDP (PwC, 2020). Now there is less than a decade to go before the point of delivering the SDGs and the 2030 agenda. To carry on the SDG journey in the post-2020 stage, the United Nations and the Chinese government have together identified three strategic priorities in the 2021–2025 United Nations Sustainable Development Cooperation Framework (UNSDCF), aiming at six outcomes (see Appendix 2). These strategic priorities mainly address the remaining development gaps in China, such as the urban–rural and inter-regional divides, and further progress on income equality and gender equality (United Nations, 2020).

Following the initiatives of the Chinese government and international organizations, there has been a notable growth in SDGs disclosure by companies in China in recent years. According to the 2021 report published by GoldenBee, a CSR consultant firm in China, 343 CSR reports with SDGs information released in 2021 were studied and analyzed. The reports were compared with similar reports collected during the period 2019–2020. The results showed that companies in China had focused more on SDGD, of which the respective proportion of CSR reports increased from 13.70% in 2019 to 23.49% in 2021, a growth rate of approximately 60% (see Figure 18.1).

Meanwhile, the companies' interpretation and adaptation of the SDGs can be reflected in the presentation formats of the companies' CSR reports. The results show that approximately 80% of the companies disclosed in their CSR reports how they executed the SDGs and included the SDGs index. On the other hand, they did not address SDGs so much in their senior management's sustainability

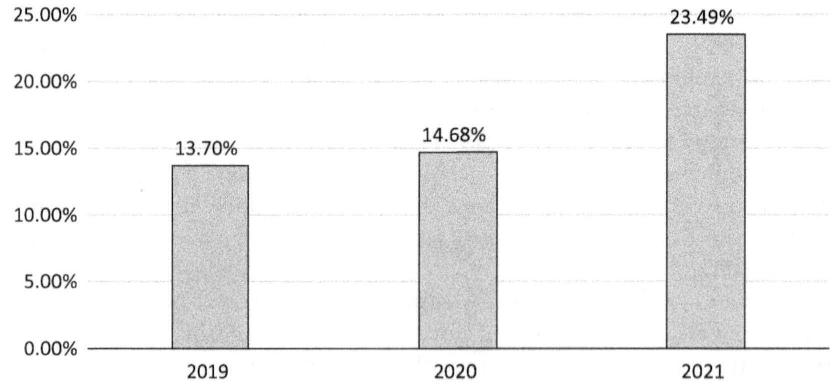

Figure 18.1 Percentage of SDGs Disclosure in Chinese Companies' CSR Reports (GoldenBee, 2021)

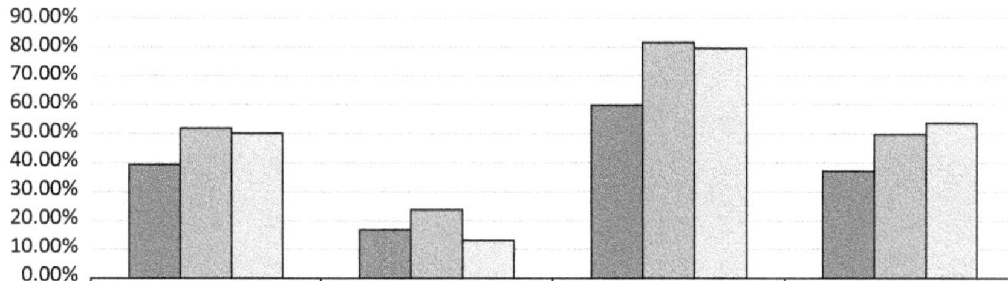

	Referenced to SDGs when preparing CSR reports	SDGs were mentioned in senior management's message or sustainability reporting background analysis	Disclosure on the execution of SDGs in CSR report	SDGs index included in CSR report
2019	39.27%	16.89%	59.82%	36.99%
2020	51.88%	23.85%	81.59%	49.79%
2021	50.15%	13.12%	79.59%	53.64%

Figure 18.2 Presentation Formats of SDGs Disclosure among Chinese Companies (GoldenBee, 2021)

messages and their analyses of their corporate sustainability backgrounds (see Figure 18.2).

Among the 17 SDGs, SDG 3 (good health and well-being), SDG 8 (decent work and economic growth), SDG 12 (responsible consumption and production), and SDG 13 (climate action) had the highest disclosure rate in the CSR reports of Chinese companies. Each of these goals had accumulated over 500 CSR reports coverage during 2019–2021 (see Figure 18.3). These SDGs had higher coverage because they were very closely related to the top concerns in the sustainable development policy address of the Chinese government. The top concerns included climate change, "dual carbon" goals, pandemic control, and post-COVID recovery in economic and social aspects. As the government is currently the most critical stakeholder in driving the commitment among Chinese companies (see Figure 18.4), the resulting SDGD focuses are consistent with the government's agenda of concerns. After fulfilling the government's primary SDG targets, the disclosure pattern would then address other stakeholders' targets and objectives, such as brand and image building, improving competitive advantages, and compliance with existing provisions (see Figure 18.5).

The literature to date focuses on the contextual information on the disclosure of SDGs and the driving factors of their application based on the high-level agenda of the country. The challenges and obstacles during implementation are, however, rarely discussed. Now the study will investigate the challenges in adopting SDGD in China and identify feasible solutions for future success. Qualitative research using in-depth interviews was conducted to examine the perspectives of

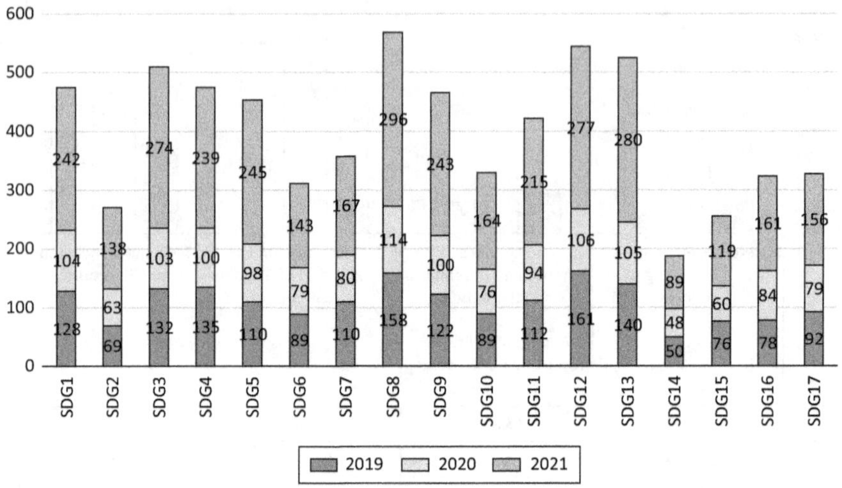

Figure 18.3 Number of Chinese Companies Reporting Each SDG (GoldenBee, 2021)

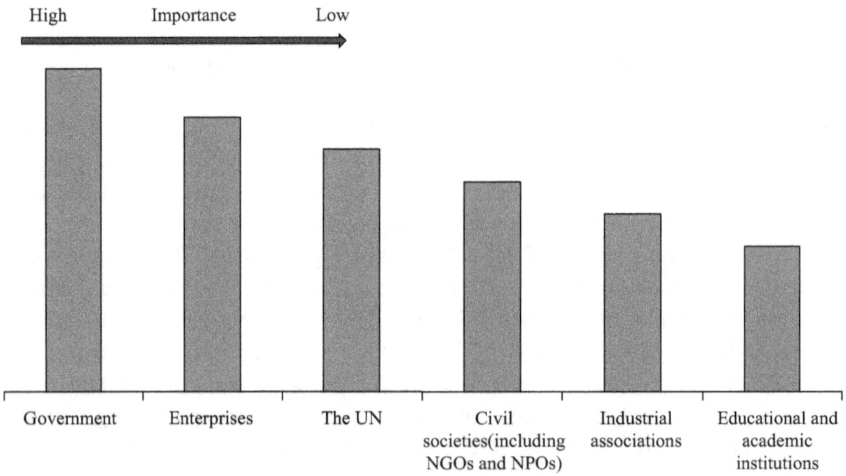

Figure 18.4 Major Stakeholders Driving SDGs for Chinese Companies (PwC, 2020)

industry practitioners, scholars, and key opinion leaders. The interview methodology and findings are presented in the following sections.

Methodology

The in-depth interviews were conducted from December 2021 to March 2022. Eight purposefully selected informants from reputable organizations were

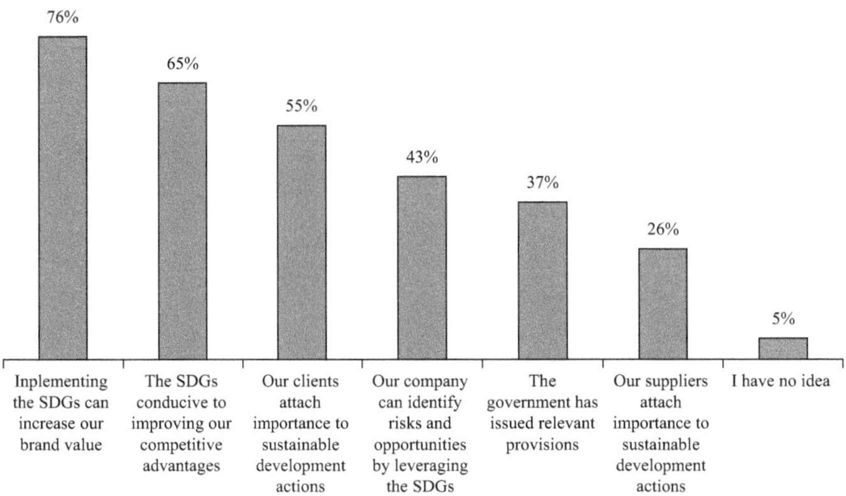

Figure 18.5 Key Driving Factors for Chinese Companies to Promote SDGs (PwC, 2020)

approached. The informants represent key stakeholders of SDGD development in China. They include scholars, professionals, practitioners, and leaders of NGOs and industry associations (see Table 18.1). In this study, the informant recruitment focused on looking for variations and contexts of their viewpoints rather than enrolling a large number of participants (Hennink et al., 2011). The number of informants recruited for this qualitative research was guided by the theoretical principle of "saturation" (Saunders et al., 2018). Two more interviews were arranged to verify the saturation when the collected information became redundant.

The interview questions were open-ended and designed based on the research objectives. Due to the diverse backgrounds of the informants, the conversations leaned towards their respective areas of expertise to understand the development status of SDGD in China. In general, the questions revolved around the following areas:

1) Development status and trend;
2) Key challenges and obstacles;
3) Feasible solutions.

Inductive content analysis was applied by creating small chunks of data and assigning a code for each chunk. The codes were then placed into similar groupings. Prior to coding, familiarity with the qualitative data was gained through a thorough overview of all the data. Initial labels/codes were devised based on phrases or sentences relating to the above chunks. All data were collated into groups identified by a code, which helped to provide a condensed overview of

Table 18.1 List of Informants

#	*Stakeholder*	*Organization*	*Position of interviewees*	*Gender*	*Age (years)*
1	Scholars specializing in CSR/ sustainability reporting	A top university in mainland China	Professor in accounting	Female	40–50
2		A top university in mainland China	Professor in business management	Male	60–70
3	Professionals/ practitioners	A leading consultancy company	Director	Male	50–60
4		One of the Big 4 accounting firms	Partner	Male	40–50
5		One of the largest property companies in mainland China	Senior manager from sustainable development department	Male	40–50
6		One of the four largest banks in mainland China	Branch president	Female	50–60
7	NGO	A relevant international organization (Beijing office)	Representative	Male	60–70
8	Association	One of the enterprise alliances in mainland China	Vice president	Male	50–60

commonly recurring topics in the qualitative data. These patterns were reviewed and several codes were combined into single themes. Finally, each theme was given a succinct and easily understandable name to describe the main results.

Findings and Discussion

The main findings extracted from the interview transcripts are presented in Table 18.2. They were arranged in three tiers, starting from the current status and development trend, followed by the exploration of key challenges and obstacles, and finally the feasible solutions suggested by the informants. The proposed solutions provide valuable suggestions for the government and regulatory bodies.

Development Status and Trend

It was mentioned by Informant #6 that China has made many attempts and great progress in sustainability reporting. More than 1,000 companies listed on the

Table 18.2 Highlights of the Findings

Dimensions	*Findings*
Development status and trend	• Level of awareness is getting higher • More attention on ESG related disclosure is attached • Increasing trend of disclosure on carbon emissions • SDGD practice is gradually being implemented • Disclosure guidelines are improving continuously
Key challenges and obstacles	• Information disclosure is still relatively fragmented • Comparability of information disclosed is not strong enough • Disclosure is arbitrary and selective • Disclosure quality is an issue of concern • Need to accelerate the implementation of disclosure standards in line with national conditions • Lack of verification and supervision
Feasible solutions	• Develop an internal mechanism of disclosure for playing a positive "incentive and restraint" role • Measurement and disclosure methods should be standardized • Need to pay attention to the connection with financial accounting standards • Need to be in line with international standards while developing domestic initiatives • Strengthen training and supervision

Shanghai Stock Exchange and the Shenzhen Stock Exchange (SSE and SZE) and nearly 90% of the constituent companies of the Shanghai and Shenzhen 300 Index have issued standalone reports. Many of these reports follow the GRI, ESG guidelines, or other related domestic/international initiatives, but not necessarily the exact 17 UNSDGs. This provides a very good practical basis for China to actively adopt an internationally unified reporting framework of sustainable development, such as the one mentioned in the Recommendations (Informant #1).

With this trend, the disclosure of carbon emissions has attracted great attention. At present, companies are encouraged to disclose more quantitative emission information in order to achieve the goal of "carbon peaking and carbon neutrality" set by the central government. On the one hand, the disclosure can help enterprises to improve their awareness and ability of climate risk management and actively implement carbon emission reduction policies. On the other hand, it is beneficial for the emission trading market to play its pricing function and promote the society to achieve emission reduction in the most cost-effective way (Informant #5 and Informant #8). In addition, high-quality carbon emission disclosure is also an important channel for the public to understand and monitor companies to achieve the emission reduction targets (Informant #8).

Therefore, the Recommendations will become an important foundation to help enterprises to meet the requirements of regulatory agencies, the decision-making criteria of investment institutions, and the improvement needs of the enterprises themselves (Informant #3 and Informant #7).

Key Challenges and Obstacles

There are still many difficulties and challenges on the practical side. Compared with the adoption of the International Financial Reporting Standards (IFRS) and accounting standards, the disclosure of SDGs is still relatively fragmented in China. Although the Recommendations can provide guidance and reference to companies, a set of standardized reporting guidelines or a framework is still needed in China. It can be developed based on generally accepted international initiatives (Informant #2) because the existing problem is that the comparability of disclosed SDG information among different industries and companies is not strong enough. It is common that disclosures are arbitrary and selective. Companies tend to disclose more qualitatively and less quantitatively, and with more "good news" and less "bad news" (Informant #4).

At the same time, the availability of public data is still relatively low in the domestic market. The willingness for voluntary disclosure needs to be improved. In addition, SDGD is commonly conducted on an annual basis in the form of standalone reports, which leads to significant time lag and information asymmetry between companies and their stakeholders (Informant #2 and Informant #3). Besides, data verification is another key obstacle. Much SDG information disclosed by listed companies is difficult to trace, verify, and supervise (Informant #1 and Informant #4).

Feasible Solutions

To cope with the aforementioned challenges and obstacles, it is suggested the government and related regulatory bodies be stricter with the listed companies and reinforce their quality of SDGD (Informants #1, #2, #4, and #7). Considering that the international community has begun to gradually formulate unified guidelines, such as the Recommendations, China should also take the initiative to become a participant, contributor, and developer (Informants #3, #4, and #7). It is also pointed out that regulatory bodies need to emphasize the principles of materiality, integrity, and consistency of SDGD and highlight the connection with financial information and accounting standards (Informant #1 and Informant #4).

In this aspect, Informant #8 proposed a micro viewpoint. It is mentioned that industry associations can initiate a set of internal SDGD mechanisms to play a positive "incentive and restraint" role in companies from different sectors. In this process, measurement standards and relevant information disclosure requirements are needed. It can be implemented together with a pricing mechanism or other relevant subsidies, rewards, or punishment. Only when the measurement standards and information disclosure requirements are clear can the corresponding internal mechanism be targeted and implemented fairly to truly play a positive "incentive and restraint" role.

Further Discussion and Conclusion

In summary, based on the interview results, the Recommendations are beneficial to the development of sustainability reporting in China. Practitioners and stakeholders do recognize their importance and value. However, in practice, they still encounter some problems and challenges. Reporting entities, especially listed companies, hope that regulators can provide a standard framework that can be specifically implemented and provide guidance for their SDG disclosure. Institutional asset owners expect China to have a relatively uniform information disclosure standard that suits national conditions, so that asset managers can effectively compare different targets when making investment decisions. Local third-party rating agencies and index companies also need regulators to establish standard guidelines for information disclosure to help public companies to disclose consistent, comparable, and substantive information that can facilitate their data collection, integration, and use.

In view of the aforementioned solutions proposed by the informants, it is emphasized that a set of generally accepted sustainability accounting and reporting standards is urgently needed. Indeed, at the current stage, no clear accounting measurement standards for rights and responsibilities related to SDG is available. For example, the existing international accounting standards exclude most environmental issues from the scope of accounting recognition. Only the accounting treatment for biological assets and liability recognition requirements related to environmental damage has been covered. In addition, there is still no consensus on the accounting measurement of carbon emission rights.

On November 3, 2021, the International Financial Reporting Standards (IFRS) Foundation announced the establishment of the International Sustainability Standards Board (ISSB) to develop the International Sustainability Disclosure Standards (ISDS). The ISSB is the counterpart to the International Accounting Standards Board (IASB) and the ISDS is the counterpart to the IFRS. It is expected that this set of sustainable development reporting standards is parallel to international accounting and financial reporting standards, and will have a sound technical foundation and international credibility under the auspices of the IFRS Foundation.

The development of ISDS provides an excellent opportunity for China to actively support and participate in the formulation process of international standards. Obviously, China and its enterprises have made great efforts in the reform and development of SDGs in the past decade. As shown in Figure 18.6, the disclosure of SDGs in the CSR reports released by different types of enterprises has demonstrated a continuously increasing trend since 2018. Therefore, it is suggested that the Chinese government or regulatory bodies can take more active actions on the existing foundation of SDGD and initiate its own domestic guidelines or standards suitable for the national macro conditions and environment. At the same time, China also needs to focus on "docking" with the IFRS and ISDS systems and to become a firm "practitioner" of the standards in the future.

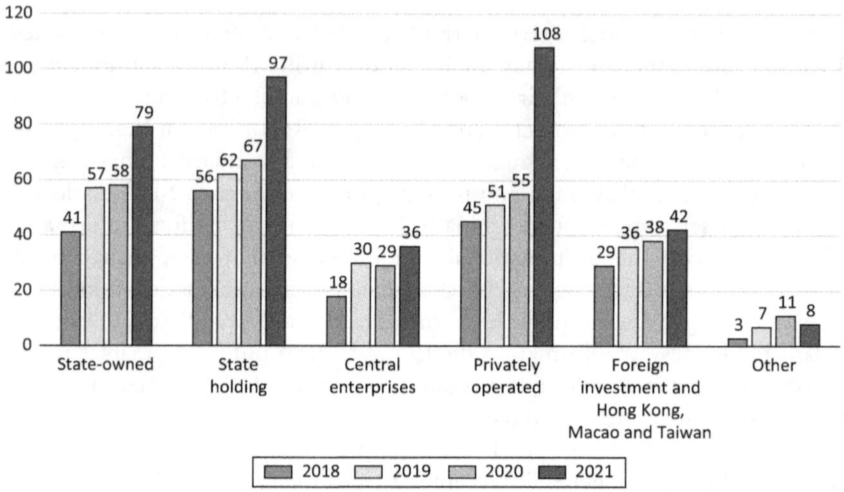

Figure 18.6 SDGs Disclosure in CSR Reports Released by Different Types of Enterprises (GoldenBee, 2020 and GoldenBee, 2021)

This study reviews and investigates the development status and trend of SDGD in China. The results show that aside from the Recommendations, many listed companies and investment institutions also refer to other international guidelines and initiatives. However, due to the respective development histories and different perspectives, these international standards or frameworks bring difficulties to the disclosing party and inconvenience to the information user. Most of the informants interviewed agree that this problem is due to the lack of specific and unified information disclosure standards suitable for China's national conditions. Therefore, within the formulation process of ISDS, the country can incorporate local features into the domestic guidelines to ensure consistency and smooth connection with international requirements while maintaining applicability. The findings of this study provide valuable insights for the recent development of sustainability reporting in China. The results have identified the challenges and obstacles during implementation and proposed feasible solutions for the consideration of the government and regulatory bodies.

Acknowledgement

This research is extended from the research project granted by the Specialized Subsidy Scheme for the Tourism Education and Training for the Guangdong-Hong Kong-Macao Greater Bay Area of Higher Education Fund, Education and Youth Development Bureau (Project No. TET-IFT-2021-05).

References

Adams, C.A. (2020). *Sustainable Development Goals Disclosure (SDGD) Recommendations: Feedback on the Consulation Responses.* ACCA, IIRC, WBA. Available at: https://www.ifac.org/system/files/publications/files/Adams_2020_Feedback-on-the-consultation.pdf

Adams, C.A., Druckman, P.B. and Picot, R.C. (2020). *Sustainable Development Goals Disclosure (SDGD) Recommendations.* ACCA, ANZ, ICAS, IFAC, IIRC. Available at: https://www.ifac.org/knowledge-gateway/contributing-global-economy/publications/sustainable-development-goals-disclosure-sdgd-recommendations

Adams, C.A. and Abhayawansa, S. (2021). Connecting the COVID-19 pandemic, environmental, social and governance (ESG) investing and calls for "harmonisation" of sustainability reporting. *Critical Perspectives on Accounting.* https://doi.org/10.1016/j.cpa.2021.102309

Ahrens, D. (2004). *Investing in Vice.* New York: St Martin's Press.

Arena, C., Bozzolan, S. and Michelon, G. (2015). Environmental reporting: Transparency to stakeholders or stakeholder manipulation? An analysis of disclosure tone and the role of the board of directors. *Corporate Social Responsibility and Environmental Management*, 22(6), 346–361.

Bebbington, J. and Unerman, J. (2018). Achieving the United Nations sustainable development goals: An enabling role for accounting research. *Accounting, Auditing and Accountability Journal*, 31(1), 2–24.

Bebbington, J., Russeli, S. and Thompson, I. (2017). Accounting and sustainable development: Reflections and propositions. *Critical Perspectives on Accounting*, 48, 21–34.

Biermann, F., Kanie, N. and Kim, R. (2017). Global governance by goal-setting: The novel approach of the UM Sustainable Development Goals. *Current Opinion in Environmental Sustainability*, 26–27, 26–31.

China Today. (2021). China 2035: Achieving socialist modernization basically. Available at: http://www.chinatoday.com.cn/ctenglish/2018/commentaries/202106/t20210625_800250626.html

Credit Suisse. (2020). From ESG to the SDGs: The shift from process and policies to delivering positive contribution. Available at: https://www.credit-suisse.com/media/assets/microsite/docs/responsibleinvesting/esg-to-sdgs-2020.pdf

Deegan, C. and Gordon, B. (1996). A study of the environmental disclosure practices of Australian corporations. *Accounting and Business Research*, 26(3), 187–199.

García-Meca, E. and Martínez-Ferrero, J. (2021). Is SDG reporting substantial or symbolic? An examination of controversial and environmentally sensitive industries. *Journal of Cleaner Production*, 298, 126781.

GoldenBee. (2020). The latest progress of SDGs information disclosure in the CSR reports of Chinese companies in 2020 (in Chinese). Available at: https://new.qq.com/omn/20201126/20201126A0DH7500.html

GoldenBee. (2021). The latest progress of SDGs information disclosure in the CSR reports of Chinese companies in 2021 (in Chinese). Available at: https://www.sohu.com/a/434519465_370262

GRI. (2021). Our mission and history. Available at: https://www.globalreporting.org/about-gri/mission-history/

Hajer, M., Nilsson, M., Raworth, K., Bakker, P., Berkhout, F., De Boer,Y., Rockström, J., Ludwig, K. and Kok, M. (2015). Beyond cockpit-ism: Four insights to enhance the transformative potential of the sustainable development goals. *Sustainability*, 7(2), 1651–1660.

Hannink, M.M., Hutter, I. and Bailey, A. (2011). *Qualitative Research Methods*. London: Sage.

Heras-Saizarbitoria, I., Urbieta, L. and Boiral, O. (2022). Organizations' engagement with sustainable development goals: From cherry-picking to SDG-washing? *Corporate Social Responsibility and Environmental Management*, 29(2), 316–328.

ICCST. (2021). China and US can cooperate to build a climate community: International communication center for science and technology. Available at: http://www.stdaily.com/English/ChinaNews/2021-06/02/content_1149911.shtml

IIRC. (2021). *International <IR> Framework*. London: International Integrated Reporting Council.

Izzo, M.F., Alberto, D.S. and Fabrizio, G. (2020a). Learning from the best: New challenges and trends in IR reporters' disclosure and the role of SDGs. *Sustainability*, 12(14), 5545.

Izzo, M.F., Mirella, C. and Riccardo,T. (2020b). The challenge of sustainable development goal reporting: The first evidence from Italian listed companies. *Sustainability*, 12(8), 3494.

Macellari, M., Yuriev, A., Testa, F. and Boiral, O. (2021). Exploring bluewashing practices of alleged sustainability leaders through a counter-accounting analysis. *Environmental Impact Assessment Review*, 86, 106489.

PwC. (2020). *Private Sector Awareness of the Sustainable Development Goals: A Survey Report on Business and Sustainability in China*. Available at: https://www.pwccn.com/en/consulting/private-sector-awareness-of-the-sustainable-development-goals-jul2020.pdf

Rosati, F. and Faria, L.G. (2019a). Business contribution to the sustainable development agenda: Organizational factors related to early adoption of SDG reporting. *Corporate Social Responsibility and Environmental Management*, 26(3), 588–597.

Rosati, F. and Faria, L.G. (2019b). Addressing the SDGs in sustainability reports: The relationship with institutional factors. *Journal of Cleaner Production*, 215, 1312–1326.

Saunders, B., Sim, J., Kingstone, T., Baker, S., Waterfield, J., Bartlam, B., Burroughs, H. and Jinks, C. (2018). Saturation in qualitative research: Exploring its conceptualization and operationalization. *Quality and Quantity*, 52(4), 1893–1907.

SASB. (2021). About us. Available at: https://www.sasb.org/about/

Shoaf, V., Jermakowicz, E.K. and Epstein, B.J. (2018). Toward sustainability and integrated reporting. *Review of Business*, 38, 1–15.

Thorlakson, T., de Zegher, J.F. and Lambin, E.F. (2018). Companies' contribution to sustainability through global supply chains. *Proceedings of the National Academy of Sciences*, 115(9), 201716695.

United Nations. (2020). United Nations sustainable development cooperation framework for the People's Republic of China 2021–2025. Available at: https://unsdg.un.org/sites/default/files/2021-06/UNSDCF-China-2021-2025.pdf

Van der Waal, J. and Thijsseens, T. (2020). Corporate involvement in sustainable development goals: Exploring the territory? *Journal of Cleaner Production*, 252, 119625.

Verdolini, E., Bak, C., Ruet, J. and Venkatachalam, A. (2017). Innovative green-technology SMEs as an opportunity to promote financial de-risking. *Economics: The Open-Access, Open-Assessment E-Journal*, 12(1), 1–12.

Appendix 1 Characteristics and Influence of Main Sustainability Standards/Framework Setters before the Launch of UNSDGs (Adams and Abhayawansa, 2021)

Sustainability standards/framework setter	*Foundation date*	*Purpose*	*Approach*	*Materiality focus*
Global Reporting Initiative (GRI)	1997 (the first version of GRI guidelines launched in 2000)	Promote transparency and open dialogue about impacts and create a future in which reporting on impacts is common practice by all organizations (GRI, 2021).	• Principles based • External reporting and organizational change	Double materiality
International Integrated Reporting Council (IIRC)	2010 (the first version of the International Integrated Reporting Framework was issued as a prototype in 2012)	Promote communication about value creation, preservation, and erosion to improve the quality of information available to providers of financial capital to enable more efficient and productive allocation of capital (IIRC, 2021).	• Principles based • External reporting and organizational change	Financial materiality
Sustainability Accounting Standards Board (SASB)	2012	"to establish and improve industry specific disclosure standards across financially material environmental, social, and governance topics that facilitate communication between companies and investors about decision-useful information" (SASB, 2021, p. 1).	• Rules based • External reporting only	Financial materiality
Climate Disclosure Standards Board (CDSB)	2007 (the first edition of the CDSB Framework was published in 2010)	Provide investors with decision-useful environmental information via the mainstream corporate report, enhancing the efficient allocation of capital (CDSB, 2019).	• Rules based • External reporting only	Financial materiality

Appendix 2 The Three Strategic Priorities and the Six High-Level Outcome Results under the 2021–2025 UNSDCF for China (United Nations, 2020)

Priority 1 – People and Prosperity: Achieving Innovation-driven, Coordinated and Shared Development. Equitable and high-quality economic, social, and human development for all throughout the life course.	Outcome 1: Relative poverty and multidimensional poverty are reduced, and more coordinated development leads to reduction in gaps between rural and urban areas and among regions, as more people in China, including left-behind groups, benefit from sustainable, innovation-driven, and shared high-quality economic development, with enhanced access to economic opportunities arising through innovation, entrepreneurship, and rural revitalization, enjoying decent work, sustainable livelihoods, and the right to development equally for both women and men. Outcome 2: People's lives in China are improved further as headway is made in ensuring access to childcare, education, healthcare services, elderly care, housing, and social assistance, and more people in China, including left-behind groups, benefit from equitable and high-quality public services and social protection systems as well as accelerated efforts to reduce gender inequality and other forms of social inequality throughout the life course.
Priority 2 – Planet: Achieving Green Development towards a more sustainable and resilient environment.	Outcome 3: People in China and the region benefit from a healthier and more resilient environment. Outcome 4: China accelerates its transition to a people-centered, inclusive, low-carbon, and circular economy.
Priority 3 – Partnerships: Realizing the full potential of China's international engagement to promote its open development and partnerships to accelerate achievement of the SDGs across the world.	Outcome 5: China's international financing, investments and business engagements, including through connectivity initiatives, programs, and projects, contribute to SDG attainment in partner countries. Outcome 6: Through South–South cooperation and humanitarian cooperation, China makes greater contributions to SDG attainment and the principles of the 2030 Agenda, including leaving no one behind.

19 The General Overview of Environmental, Social, and Governance (ESG) Guidelines in Hong Kong

Past, Present, and Future

Tiffany Cheng-Han Leung and You Shi Xiang

Introduction

Environmental, social, and governance (ESG) reports describe how a company addresses these issues. They function as practical tools for issuers to communicate with stakeholders (PricewaterhouseCoopers, 2021). The first corporate environmental report was issued in 1989. Since then, an increasing number of companies have disclosed information on their ESG issues. Current ESG reporting standards address environmental protection, social relationships, and standards for business operations (CFA Institute, 2021). ESG matters may evolve over time and differ among sectors or regions (Eccles et al., 2012; UNPRI, 2020).

Issuers choose to disclose ESG information for many reasons. Some companies issue ESG reports to improve corporate reputation, brand value, and employee motivation (Cornell and Shapiro, 1987; HKEX, 2011; Turban and Greening, 1997). ESG performance indicates that management (Waddock and Graves, 1997) and stakeholders require disclosures for transparent information on companies' ESG risk management (HKEX, 2011; KPMG, 2020).

ESG can be regarded as non-financial information that will positively or negatively affect a company's financial performance depending on how the issues are managed (NASDAQ, 2019; WBCSD, 2010). For companies pursuing better economic performance, ESG integration can be considered as a financial opportunity (Amir and Serafeim, 2018; UNPRI, 2020). The rapid growth of responsible investment may account for this situation. In 2020, global sustainable investment reached USD 35.3 trillion, an increase of 15% since 2018. In addition, sustainable investment assets under management accounted for 35.9% of total assets under management, an increase of 2.5% compared to 2018 (GSIA, 2020).

ESG reporting standards have been established to deal with prevailing responsible investment practices and to ensure that the information provided by each company is comparable (WBCSD, 2010). ESG reporting standards or guidelines released by non-governmental organizations, such as the Global Reporting Initiative (GRI), United Nations Global Compact (UNGC), ISO 26000 Guidance on Social Responsibility, and Carbon Disclosure Project (CDP), have been widely adopted.

DOI: 10.4324/9781003274575-24

Table 19.1 ESG Guidelines from Governments and Stock Exchanges

Year of release	*Country/region*	*Reporting standard*	*Obligation level*
2003	Japan	Environmental Reporting Guidelines	Voluntary
2006	China–Shenzhen Stock Exchange (SZSE)	SZSE Social Responsibility Guidelines to Listed Companies	Mandatory for specific issuers, while voluntary for the rest.
2008	China–Shanghai Stock Exchange (SSE)	Guidelines on Environmental Information Disclosure	
2010	Thailand	Guidelines for Sustainability Reporting	Voluntary
2012	Hong Kong SAR, China	ESG Reporting Guide	Comply or explain
2016	Singapore	Sustainability Reporting Guide	Comply or explain
2017	The European Commission	Guidelines on Non-financial Reporting	Voluntary
2017	United States (NASDAQ)	ESG Reporting Guide	Voluntary
2018	United Kingdom	LSE Group Guide to ESG Reporting	Voluntary

Furthermore, regulators (i.e., governments and stock exchanges) take measures to standardize ESG reporting practices (HKEX, 2011; NASDAQ, 2019).

Table 19.1 indicates that some regional regulators have established ESG regulations with varying obligation levels. In 2017, the European Commission issued the Guidelines on Non-financial Reporting and in the United States, the National Association of Securities Dealers Automated Quotations (NASDAQ) launched a voluntary ESG reporting guide. The London Stock Exchange (LSE) Group followed in 2018 with the release of the LSE Group Guide to ESG Reporting to improve the ESG reporting practice in the United Kingdom (LSE, 2020; NASDAQ, 2019).

The Asian market is increasingly engaged in improving ESG reporting performance (GSIA, 2020; Leung, 2021). With the best ESG performance in Asia, Japan released environmental reporting guidelines in 2003 to encourage companies to quantify and report environmental performance (Yook et al., 2017). In mainland China, the Shenzhen Stock Exchange (SZSE) released the SZSE Social Responsibility Guidelines to Listed Companies in 2006, and the Shanghai Stock Exchange (SSE) issued Guidelines on Environmental Information Disclosure in 2008. Both stock exchanges in mainland China provide issuers with guidance on sustainability reporting and have developed sustainability indexes, such as the SSE Corporate Governance

Index, SSE Sustainable Development Industry Index, SSE Social Responsibility Index, and SZSE SME CSR Index. In addition, the SSE requires that listed companies in the SSE Corporate Governance Index, cross-listed companies, and listed companies in the financial industry provide mandatory disclosures on ESG issues, while other listed companies issue voluntary sustainability reports. Constituents of the Shenzhen 100 Index are mandated to issue annual sustainability reports by SZSE (Sustainable Stock Exchanges Initiative, 2019).

Hong Kong is recognized as Asia's top global financial centre (FSDC, 2013; Leung, 2021), but the Hong Kong Stock Exchange was only ranked 27th of 47 international stock exchanges measuring sustainability disclosure in 2019 (Corporate Knights, 2019). Although the gap has narrowed compared to what it was in 2017, the ranking does not match the status of Hong Kong as a global financial centre. As a result, Hong Kong Exchanges and Clearing Limited (HKEX) decided to establish an ESG reporting framework based on international ESG reporting standards to improve local listed companies' ESG performance and increase the competitiveness of the exchange.

This chapter is structured as follows. After the introduction, a review of the development of ESG reporting standards in Hong Kong is presented. This section is followed by a discussion about the HKEX's emphasis on the ESG Guide and the comply or explain approach, materiality assessment, stakeholder engagement, board involvement, third-party assurance, and connection with the contemporary global market. The final section summarizes and concludes the chapter.

General Review on the ESG Guide in Hong Kong

The Evolution of the ESG Guide

Hong Kong was a former British colony for over 150 years. When Hong Kong was handed back to China in 1997, it became a Special Administrative Region (SAR) within the People's Republic of China (PRC). Hong Kong has positioned itself as the gateway to mainland China and its offshore financial centre with free trade, a low tax rate, and free flow of capital (HKMA, 2021; Lai, 2012; Lu, 2016).

The development of Corporate Social Responsibility (CSR) reporting in Hong Kong can be traced back to the 1990s (Lynn, 1992). Prior studies show that Hong Kong listed companies appear to disclose social rather than environmental information in their CSR reporting and the level of environmental reporting among Hong Kong listed companies is relatively low between 1990 and 2005 (Lynn, 1992; Jaggi and Zhao, 1996; Chan and Welford, 2005; Gao et al., 2005). During the observed period, the CSR reporting in Hong Kong tended to be voluntary rather than mandatory. One year later, the SSE and SZSE launched several CSR reporting requirements and regulations for listed companies in 2006 and 2008 in China. In particular, all major Chinese State-owned enterprises (SOEs) under the State-owned Assets Supervision and Administration Commission (SASAC), published a CSR or sustainability report by 2011.

Table 19.2 illustrates the recent development of the ESG Guide in Hong Kong. In December 2011, the HKEX published a consultation paper on its proposed

Table 19.2 Timeline of the ESG Guide (HKEX, 2011, 2012, 2015a, 2015b, 2018, 2019b)

Date	*Events*	*Obligation level*			*Effective time*
		Environmental	*Social*	*Governance*	
Dec 2011	Consultation Paper on the ESG Guide	Recommended	Recommended		
Aug 2012	Consultation conclusion				
July 2015	Consultation Paper on the ESG Guide				
Dec 2015	Consultation conclusion				
Jan 2016	The first update	Comply or explain: General disclosures and KPIs	Comply or explain: General disclosures Recommended: KPIs		The updates of General disclosures and "Environmental" KPIs take effect on 1 January 2016 and 1 January 2017, respectively.
May 2018	First periodic review				
May 2019	Consultation Paper on the ESG Guide				
Dec 2019	Consultation conclusion				
	Second periodic review				
	The second update	Comply or explain: General disclosures and KPIs	Comply or explain: General disclosures and KPIs	Mandatory: Board statement; Application of reporting principles; Reporting boundaries	1 July 2020

ESG Reporting Guide. The ESG Guide was divided into four major areas: (i) Workplace Quality, (ii) Environment Protection, (iii) Operating Practices, and (iv) Community Involvement. Each area consisted of three sections: (i) Aspects, (ii) General Disclosure Recommendations, and (iii) Key Performance Indicators (KPIs). The Guide was appended to the Listing Rules in August 2012. At this stage, ESG disclosure was voluntary for issuers and they were allowed to report selected KPIs (HKEX, 2011; HKEX, 2012).

In January 2016, the HKEX released the first update on the ESG Guide. The initial four areas were reclassified as two main areas: (i) "Environmental" subject with three aspects and (ii) "Social" subject with eight aspects. The obligation level of the general disclosures for both subject areas and the KPIs under "Environmental" was raised to "comply or explain" (HKEX, 2012; HKEX, 2015b).

In December 2019, the HKEX announced the second update on the ESG Guide after conducting two consecutive periodic reviews. In this update, "comply or explain" applied to "Social" KPIs and a statement on board involvement in ESG issues was mandatory for all listed companies. Issuers must adopt the reporting principles of "materiality, quantitative, and consistency" and explain the reporting boundaries. The HKEX added KPIs on climate change due to global concern and the risks from negative impacts of climate change (Environment Bureau, 2017; TCFD, 2017). With these amendments, the ESG reports would become conclusive and cater to the global trends of ESG reporting standards or benchmarks (HKEX, 2019b). Thus, the implementation of ESG reporting in Hong Kong has gone through an open consultation process over ongoing stakeholder dialogue and engagement which is different from that of the CSR reporting in China (Ng and Leung, 2020).

Discussion

Current ESG Reporting Rate in Hong Kong

According to a Bloomberg's survey (HKEX, 2015a), 46.4% of the sampled issuers reported ESG performance under the voluntary ESG reporting framework. In particular, H-share issuers, which are either state-owned enterprises or private companies in mainland China but traded on the HKEX, had an overall ESG reporting rate of 83% (HKEX, 2015a). The divergence in the overall reporting rate may arise from the liability of foreignness (LOF), which refers to all the additional costs generated by a company's overseas operation compared to a local company (Zaheer, 1995; Bell et al., 2012). Although Hong Kong is located in the southern part of the mainland, China-related companies may still suffer from LOF due to significant institutional differences under the "one-country-two-systems" approach. ESG disclosures can mitigate LOF in foreign capital markets since institutional investors tend to prioritize ESG factors in their investment decisions (Liu et al., 2019; Yu and Luu, 2021).

The ESG reporting rate varies greatly depending on firm size. Around 80% of the largest market capitalization issuers reported ESG, whereas the reporting rate for middle-sized capitalization companies was only 34% (HKEX, 2015a). According to Hörisch et al. (2015), small and medium-sized enterprises (SMEs) utilize sustainability tools less than large capitalization companies due to less professional knowledge on sustainability management. Furthermore, larger firms usually offer available resources for generating information to reflect ESG performance to meet broad stakeholders' expectations (Baldini et al., 2018; Drempetic et al., 2020). After the first update on the ESG Guide, every listed company in the HKEX needs to disclose ESG information but in a flexible way (HKEX, 2015b).

ESG Reporting Quality in Hong Kong

Although the "comply or explain" framework allowed a high overall ESG reporting rate, the reporting quality remains relatively low and varies among listed companies. The HKEX (2019a) found that listed companies tend to adopt a box-ticking approach while compiling ESG reports, with neither detailed explanations nor informative descriptions on how they conformed to the ESG Guide or why they did not report certain aspects. According to Liu et al. (2019), the Hong Kong market is dominated by SMEs, but sustainability reporting is valued by Western institutional investors who mainly aim at large capitalization companies. Therefore, some listed companies in Hong Kong may view ESG disclosures as legitimacy-seeking tools to comply with the ESG Guide from the local stock exchange (Tang and Demeritt, 2018).

One reason for the low quality of reporting could be that issuers appear not to have sufficient professional ESG knowledge (Hörisch et al., 2015; PingAn, 2020). Some issuers may not understand the rationale behind specific KPIs, while others do not know the calculation method required for certain ESG data. For example, KPI B5.1 requires issuers to report suppliers by geographical region (HKEX, 2015b). Apart from listed companies, weak regulations and insufficient guidance from the regulators may contribute to the problem of low-quality reporting. Although Article 109 of the Basic Law (2021) requires that the Hong Kong SAR (HKSAR) government should promote the region as an international financial centre, the government's power is limited due to the market-dominant economy in Hong Kong. This situation may result from Hong Kong's "big market, small government" capitalism and the inability of the government to engage stakeholders with divergent ideologies (Lu, 2016; Ng and Leung, 2020; Tsang, 2006). Therefore, although the Chinese government is both the regulator of ESG performance and its audience (Noronha et al., 2015), it is less likely for the HKSAR government to release mandatory regulations for ESG reporting practice due to Hong Kong's different political and economic system. In addition, based on PingAn's (2020) report, the HKEX provided only limited guidance on the materiality of indicators, which may lead to listed companies' misunderstanding of certain KPIs.

In general, the stepwise changes indicate that the HKEX continually refines the ESG Guide and maintains dialogue with stakeholders (Ng and Leung, 2020). However, the performance of ESG reporting is somewhat unsatisfactory due to many companies' limited professional ESG knowledge, and relatively weak enforcement by the government and the local stock exchange. Thus, the HKEX, as the financial regulator for Hong Kong, has further included board governance, stakeholder engagement, materiality assessment, and other refinements, such as third-party assurance to the Guide, to help listed companies assess and evaluate their ESG risks and improve the overall reporting quality (HKEX, 2018; HKEX, 2019a).

"Comply or Explain"

The basic ESG reporting framework in Hong Kong is "comply or explain". This was firstly proposed by the Cadbury Committee (1992) in the United Kingdom. "Comply or explain" works as a practical approach for companies to flexibly disclose their corporate governance performance, preventing reporters from adhering to the rigid "one size fits all" method (Rose, 2016; Seidl et al., 2013). Reporting companies can either implement the codes' provisions or provide detailed and reasonable explanations as to why they do not follow the provision (Financial Reporting Council, 2006; Ho, 2017). Only companies that do not use either method are considered in breach of the "comply or explain" rule. Therefore, issuers often adopt this liberal mechanism to legitimize (Thanasas et al., 2018).

Ho (2017) suggests that the "comply or explain" framework could be transferred to ESG reporting out of cost–benefit considerations since some issuers are concerned about the additional cost of reporting on KPIs (HKEX, 2012). They can choose to disclose only specific KPIs and explain why they do not disclose the others. In this way, companies can save costs and not deviate from the listing rules.

The Financial Reporting Council (2006) claims that the "comply or explain" framework is flexible and benefits both companies and investors. However, research demonstrates that sometimes "comply or explain" rules may not achieve the anticipated effects or even become counterproductive as a "soft law". First, some issuers choose to fully comply with the reporting codes to avoid deviation from listing rules without an understanding of the principle itself, while others provide weak explanations. Second, companies in the same industry may behave mimetically in compiling ESG disclosures due to their unfamiliarity with stakeholders' expectations (Hahn and Kühnen, 2013; Torelli et al., 2020). Third, managerial capture can occur in the absence of effective board involvement and stakeholder engagement (Farooq et al., 2021).

Overall, the "comply or explain" framework is sometimes vulnerable due to its gentle nature. To achieve the goal of improving the quality of reporting, regulators need to increase their efforts to make "comply or explain" more convincing. The ESG Guide may include penalties for insufficient explanations and cases where companies improperly claim to be complying with specific provisions.

Materiality Assessment

Materiality originates from financial reporting and has been applied to ESG reporting (Ortar, 2016) in the recent decade. To meet stakeholders'

Table 19.3 Different Definitions of Materiality (GRI, 2016; IIRC, 2015; SASB, 2018)

Reporting standards	*Definitions of materiality*
Global Reporting Initiatives (GRI)	Material topics bring: • significant impacts on economics, the environment, and society; • substantive influence on stakeholders' assessments and decisions.
International Integrated Reporting Framework (the (IR) Framework)	Material topics substantively affect the organization's ability to create value.
Sustainability Accounting Standards Board (SASB) Framework	Material issues have a significant impact on corporate financial performance and business operations.

expectations, materiality requires companies to report issues that are most material to their ESG risks based on priority (Torelli et al., 2020). Table 19.3 presents various definitions of materiality according to international ESG reporting standards.

The GRI standards focus on ESG issues that are material to a wide range of stakeholders and are not limited to investors. The impacts of material ESG issues are multidimensional in the GRI standards, indicating comprehensive stakeholder engagement and evaluation of ESG-related risks (GRI, 2016). The IR Framework integrates various corporate reports into a reporting system to demonstrate business value creation, and its definition of materiality reflects the concept (IIRC, 2015). The Sustainability Accounting Standards Board (SASB) Framework is an investor-based ESG reporting standard, so it mainly highlights the impact of materiality issues on corporate financial performance, which is critical for investment decisions (SASB, 2018).

In Hong Kong, the ESG Guide states that materiality can be expressed for strategic, operational, and financial consideration. Material issues are sufficiently important to investors and other stakeholders and should be determined by the board of directors (HKEX, 2019b). The HKEX encourages listed companies to refer to the Materiality Map released by SASB, which specifies the interpretation of sector-specific material ESG issues (HKEX, 2019a; SASB, 2018). In general, the definition of materiality differs due to the focus of certain reporting standards. Currently, the Hong Kong ESG Guide's definition focuses on investors' interests more than the general stakeholders' interests.

Issuers are supposed to conduct a materiality assessment to determine material aspects carefully. The assessment identifies, chooses, and prioritizes a company and its relevant stakeholders' most critical topics (Calabrese et al., 2016). A proper materiality assessment and ensuing enforcement can contribute to a company's superior performance (Khan et al., 2016). The quality of materiality assessment varies among companies. Some ESG reports are reasonably detailed and based on assessment that includes the stakeholder engagement process and a materiality matrix, which graphically describes firms' orientation to ESG issues, while others only offer vague descriptions (Ortar, 2016; Pizzi et al., 2021).

An inexplicit materiality assessment could mislead companies to evaluate their ESG risks and stakeholders' interests (Sepúlveda-Alzate et al., 2022; Torelli et al., 2020). As mentioned above, some companies comply with all the provisions rather than explain them (HKEX, 2019a), which implies that issuers strictly abide by the "comply or explain" provisions. However, this situation could infer that listed companies do not fully implement materiality assessments, so that they are not aware of whether an aspect is material and choose to conform to every provision rather than explain it directly. In the case of a provision being deemed immaterial, the materiality assessment does not provide supporting evidences.

Stakeholder Engagement

Stakeholders are individuals or groups that affect or are affected by an organization's decisions and activities (Deloitte, 2014; HKEX, 2011). They may include shareholders, employees, suppliers, regulators, and the public. Each group has unique characteristics and engagement levels and, in some cases, conflicting interests. According to stakeholder theory, issuers are required to provide transparent and timely information to stakeholders on the major impact of their business operations (Calabrese et al., 2016; Dubbink and Liederkerke, 2008).

Stakeholder engagement is the process in which a company engages all relevant stakeholders for a mutual purpose to achieve satisfactory outcomes (AccountAbility, 2015). Due to stakeholder diversity and resource scarcity, a company should select the key stakeholder groups, communicate with them, and prioritize their claims based on their importance when compiling ESG reports (Guenther et al., 2016). Consequently, stakeholders with different priority levels can all obtain valuable information from the disclosure.

Some senior managers believe that a firm's survival depends on stakeholder approval and support, which is essential for companies' long-term economic success (Hart and Sharma, 2004). Thus, companies need to manage their stakeholders based on their ESG strategies (Romero et al., 2019). Stakeholder engagement is vital to materiality assessment, as it obliges listed companies to prioritize the ESG issues and to allocate resources and time for disclosing specific KPIs accordingly (HKEX, 2018; BDO, 2019).

The low level of stakeholder engagement may cause misinterpretation of stakeholder expectations, leading to information asymmetry between issuers and stakeholders (Romito and Vurro, 2021). Moreover, some companies appear to avoid reporting unfavourable issues and drawbacks to stakeholders, resulting in an outwardly good but unbalanced ESG report and leaving the judgement of actual ESG performance to stakeholders themselves (BDO, 2019). To tackle this problem, Romero et al. (2019) state that ESG reports can be treated as strategic tools to manage stakeholder engagement rather than a communication intermediary between companies and stakeholders, so companies may carefully consider the bi-directional relationship when they disclose ESG information.

Board Involvement

In corporate governance, a company's board is responsible for its management and operation, including ESG (HKEX, 2015b). The ESG Guide specifies that "the board is responsible for evaluating and determining the issuer's ESG-related risks and ensuring that appropriate and effective ESG risk management and internal control systems are in place" (HKEX, 2015b, 40). Consequently, the board should show its ESG commitment, how it manages ESG matters, and how these issues relate to its business operation (HKEX, 2018). The evaluation, determination, and assurance of ESG risks should be included in board involvement.

Active involvement in a firm's strategic processes allows the board to understand and support all ESG initiatives and signal that the board values their reporting (Amran et al., 2014; HKEX, 2018). The efforts of the board of directors and senior management contribute to a company's transformative growth and value creation. The board of directors takes the overall responsibility for ESG strategy and reporting but is not required to compile the reports directly. The task can be delegated to employees, a team, or a committee that reports to the board (HKEX, 2011).

A high level of board involvement in ESG contributes to ESG performance. First, board involvement could mitigate agency problems (Broadstock et al., 2019; Galletta et al., 2021), thus reducing agency costs and enhancing information symmetry. The board of directors must be actively involved in ESG issues to prevent managers from opportunistic behaviour. Hence, senior managers cannot leverage their position for self-interest at the cost of shareholders. Second, board involvement tends to increase a board's sensitivity and attention to stakeholder concerns. Kassinis and Vafeas (2002) explain that directors may not represent any specific stakeholders. If the number of environmentally friendly directors increases, the board of directors will be entrusted with more ESG responsibilities, in turn exerting more pressure on the senior management to align with stakeholders' ESG interests. Other board characteristics, such as board size, board independence, and board gender diversity could be considered as contributing factors to affect ESG performance (Amran et al., 2014; Husted and Sousa-Filho, 2019; Rathnayaka Mudiyanselage, 2018).

Next Step: Third-Party Assurance

Companies would like to have their ESG reports assured to enhance credibility and build brand reputation (Sìmnett et al., 2009). Information asymmetry arises from separate ownership and control between internal managers and external stakeholders. Asymmetry usually refers to financial information, but can be extended to non-financial information (Fan et al., 2021). The responsible party for compiling ESG disclosures acquires professional knowledge and private information that is difficult for external stakeholders to obtain. Thus, relevant stakeholders may consider ESG disclosures as management's responsibilities and require open access to the information. In this regard, external assurance can be viewed as a moderator to the credibility problem, reducing information asymmetry between management and stakeholders (Watts and Zimmerman, 1983).

External third-party assurance can be provided by auditing or non-auditing professions, as both offer the same credibility to the assurance (Dutta and Dutta, 2020; Sìmnett et al., 2009). Third-party assurance on ESG reports of Hong Kong listed companies is mainly offered by the Hong Kong Quality Assurance Agency and qualified accounting firms. It is clear that external assurance will enhance transparency and accountability for stakeholders as the assurance process may also involve rigorous management control and evaluation (O'Dwyer and Owen, 2005). According to the ESG Guide, issuers must not intervene in the independence of third-party assurance providers.

Seeking external assurance can be costly, so an issuer should consider whether adopting independent third-party assurance is a cost–beneficial decision (Sìmnett et al., 2009). In addition, listed companies need to consider who their stakeholders are when seeking external assurance (Liu et al., 2019). If investors, shareholders, or senior management do not consider third-party assurance as important, issuers should reconsider whether to adopt it.

Connection to Contemporary Global Markets

Table 19.4 shows climate change disclosure was included in the environmental KPIs in the ESG Guide in 2019. The definition of ESG continues to evolve, so regulators should constantly update the ESG Guide by integrating with mainstream global reporting guidelines in order to meet global macroeconomic forces. Therefore, Hong Kong market regulators could enhance further development of an ESG reporting guideline to cope with the growth of global sustainability with three main approaches (FSDC, 2018).

First, more detailed climate change KPIs could be added to the current ESG Guide due to green finance promotion worldwide. Furthermore, regulators could release supplementary regulations to improve the reporting practice on

Table 19.4 KPIs of Climate Change (HKEX, 2019b)

KPIs	*General description*
KPI A1.2	Greenhouse gas (GHG) emissions and intensity
KPI A1.5	Emission targets and steps to achieve them.
KPI A4.1	The impact of significant climate-related issues on the listed companies and the measures to address them.

green finance issues. In 2021, the Singapore Exchange (SGX) and the Japan Exchange Group (JPX) announced that listed companies must issue mandatory climate reports (SGX, 2021; JPX, 2021). On 5 November 2021, the HKEX published the Guidance on Climate Disclosures (the Climate Guide) to align with the Task Force on Climate-Related Financial Disclosures (TCFD), a reporting guidance focusing on the impacts of climate change on corporate financial performance (TCFD, 2017). The HKEX aims to achieve ESG excellence through this comprehensive reporting system (HKEX, 2021).

Second, the ESG Guide could be sector-specific. In 2021, the Global Sustainability Standards Board (GSSB) revised the GRI standards and planned to add specific reporting guidance according to sectors, the first of which is the oil and gas sector (GRI 2021). Carbon Disclosure Project (CDP) evaluates organizations' ESG performance based on their industry characteristics through their questionnaires (CDP, 2021). TCFD has extra reporting guidance for issuers in the financial sector, namely banks, insurance companies, asset managers, and asset owners (TCFD, 2017). Since the HKEX encourages listed companies to adopt global reporting standards (HKEX, 2011), it could adjust the ESG Guide to focus on the distribution of listed companies in different industries, following international reporting guidelines.

Third, regulators could add a section evaluating the financial impact of listed companies' ESG performance. The SASB releases reporting standards that rely on a process modelled for financial accounting standards which provides cost-effective reporting guidance for companies, and brings decision-useful information to the market (SASB, 2020). Some listed companies in Hong Kong have already adopted SASB reporting standards in 2021. Listed companies may raise awareness of ESG performance and reporting practice when they realize its impact on their corporate financial performance.

Conclusion

This chapter provides a general overview of the development of the ESG Guideline in Hong Kong over the past decade. After analysing the evolution of the ESG Guide, the following findings reveal how Hong Kong listed companies have learned, adopted, and made gradual changes.

First, the ESG Guide was released due to the global ESG reporting standards and guidelines, the special connection between Hong Kong and mainland China, and the growing environmental problems in Hong Kong. Although the HKSAR government fulfils its obligation to promote Hong Kong as an international financial centre and regional green finance hub (Basic Law, 2021; FSDC, 2018), its role is limited due to three main institutional factors.

First, ESG reporting is mainly driven by the HKEX rather than the HKSAR government due to the absence of coercive governmental pressure (Leung, 2021). Thus, the HKEX launched the ESG Guide to improve overall ESG performance in the market. Second, the "comply or explain" principle is flexible but has some drawbacks in relation to materiality assessment, stakeholder engagement, and board involvement as mentioned above. Third, the current ESG Guide could be further improved through the promotion of independent external assurance for sustainability reports. This would ensure each report is a true representation of reality and that global ESG reporting standards are met so that comparisons with other companies or industries across different periods are possible (Crane et al., 2019). Thus, the issuers could continuously improve their ESG performance and enhance the process to currently unassessed areas (Crane et al., 2019).

This study provides some limitations and insights for further research. First, this chapter has been confined to reviewing the ESG Guide in Hong Kong. The coexisting ESG reporting standards at local, industry, and international levels may have a joint effect on the quality of ESG reports. Future empirical research could examine the effectiveness of the ESG Guide at three different levels to assess the quality of ESG disclosure. Second, some companies are cross-listed in the HKEX and other stock exchanges, such as the SSE and the SZSE in mainland China, where ESG reporting is mandatory and has been driven by both stock exchanges and the central government since 2009 (Yin and Zhang, 2012; Yu and Rowe, 2017). Cross-listed companies may be affected by the ESG reporting standards in their home markets and overcome the liability of foreignness in capital markets (Yu and Luu, 2021). Cross-listed companies may have higher compliance levels than companies listed only in Hong Kong due to stricter ESG regulations from another stock exchange. Future research could examine whether specific institutional factors contribute to how effective the ESG Guide is for cross-listed companies in Hong Kong. Finally, whether the promotion of green finance by the major cities in the Greater Bay Area (GBA) contributes to continuous improvement in ESG performance for Hong Kong listed companies (HKGFA, 2020) is another avenue for further exploration.

References

AccountAbility. (2015). AAA1000 stakeholder engagement standard. Available at: https://www.accountability.org/static/940dc017198458fed647f73ad5d47a95/aa1000ses_2015.pdf

Amir, A.Z. and Serafeim, G. (2018). Why and how investors use ESG information: Evidence from a global survey. *Financial Analysts Journal*, 74(3), 87–103.

Amran, A., Lee, S.P. and Devi, S.S. (2014). The influence of governance structure and strategic corporate social responsibility toward sustainability reporting quality. *Business Strategy and the Environment*, 23(4), 217–235.

Baldini, M., Maso, L.D., Liberatore, G., Mazzi, F. and Terzani, S. (2018). Role of country- and firm-level determinants in environmental, social, and governance disclosure. *Journal of Business Ethics*, 150(1), 79–98.

Basic Law. (2021). Article 109. Available at: https://www.basiclaw.gov.hk/en/basiclaw/chapter5.html

BDO. (2019). Third-year ESG reports showed little improvement in overall disclosure and ESG practices. Available at: https://www.bdo.com.hk/en-gb/news/2019/bdo-survey-third-year-esg-reports-showed-little-improvement-in-overall-disclosure-and-esg-practices

Bell, R.G., Filatotchev, I. and Rasheed, A.A. (2012). The liability of foreignness in capital markets: Sources and remedies. *Journal of International Business Studies*, 43(2), 107–122.

Broadstock, D.C., Managi, S., Matousek, R. and Tzeremes, N.G. (2019). Does doing "good" always translate into doing "well"? An eco-efficiency perspective. *Business Strategy and the Environment*, 28(6), 1199–1217.

Cadbury Committee. (1992). *Report of the Committee on the Financial Aspects of Corporate Governance.* Available at: https://www.frc.org.uk/getattachment/9c19ea6f-bcc7-434c-b481-f2e29c1c271a/The-Financial-Aspects-of-Corporate-Governance-(the-Cadbury-Code).pdf

Calabrese, A., Costa, R., Levialdi, N. and Menichini, T. (2016). A fuzzy analytic hierarchy process method to support materiality assessment in sustainability reporting. *Journal of Cleaner Production*, 121, 248–264.

CDP. (2021). Guidance for companies. Available at: https://www.cdp.net/en/guidance/guidance-for-companies

CFA Institution. (2021). ESG investing and analysis. Available at: https://www.cfainstitute.org/en/research/esg-investing

Chan, J.C.H. and Welford, R. (2005). Assessing corporate environmental risk in China: An evaluation of reporting activities of Hong Kong listed enterprises. *Corporate Social Responsibility and Environmental Management*, 12(2), 88–104.

Cornell, B. and Shapiro, A.C. (1987). Corporate stakeholders and corporate finance. *Financial Management*, 16(1), 5–14.

Corporate Knights. (2019). *Measuring Sustainability Disclosure: Ranking the Worlds' Stock Exchanges.* Available at: https://www.aviva.com/content/dam/aviva-corporate/documents/socialpurpose/pdfs/corporate-knights-stock-exchange-ranking-2020.pdf

Crane, A., Matten, D., Glozer, S. and Spence, L. (2019) *Business Ethics: Managing Corporate Citizenship and Sustainability in the Age of Globalization.* Oxford: Oxford University Press.

Deloitte. (2014). Stakeholder engagement. Available at: https://www2.deloitte.com/content/dam/Deloitte/za/Documents/governance-risk-compliance/ZA_StakeholderEngagement_04042014.pdf

Drempetic, S., Klein, C. and Zwergel, B. (2020). The influence of firm size on the ESG score: Corporate sustainability ratings under review. *Journal of Business Ethics*, 167(2), 333–360.

Dubbink, W., Graafland, J. and van Liedekerke, L. (2008). CSR, transparency and the role of intermediate organizations. *Journal of Business Ethics*, 82(2), 391–406.

Dutta, P. and Dutta, A. (2020). Impact of external assurance on corporate climate change disclosures: New evidence from Finland. *Journal of Applied Accounting Research*, 22(2), 252–285.

Eccles, R.G., Krzus, M.P., Rogers, J. and Serafeim, G. (2012). The need for sector-specific materiality and sustainability reporting standards. *Journal of Applied Corporate Finance*, 24(2), 65–71.

Environment Bureau. (2017). Hong Kong's climate action plan 2030+. Available at: https://www.enb.gov.hk/sites/default/files/pdf/ClimateActionPlanEng.pdf

Fan, H., Tang, Q. and Pan, L. (2021). An international study of carbon information asymmetry and independent carbon assurance. *British Accounting Review*, 53(1), 100971.

Farooq, M.B., Zaman, R., Sarraj, D. and Khalid, F. (2021). Examining the extent of and drivers for materiality assessment disclosures in sustainability reports. *Sustainability Accounting, Management and Policy Journal*, 12(5), 965–1002.

Financial Reporting Council. (2006). The combined code on corporate governance. Available at: https://www.frc.org.uk/getattachment/8238c251-5cfe-43b7-abc0-4318ccbdc0fd/Combined-Code-2006-(Oct-version).pdf

Financial Services Development Council (FSDC). (2013). Strengthening Hong Kong as a leading global international financial centre. Available at: https://www.fsdc.org.hk/media/nkukypnh/rev-strengthening-hong-kong-as-leading-english.pdf

Financial Services Development Council (FSDC). (2018). Environmental, social and governance (ESG) strategy for Hong Kong. Available at: https://www.fsdc.org.hk/media/yawlfqwd/esg-paper-eng-_final_0.pdf

Gao, S.S., Heravi, S. and Xiao, J.Z. (2005). Determinants of corporate social and environmental reporting in Hong Kong: A research note. *Accounting Forum*, 29(2), 233–242.

Galletta, S., Mazzù, S. and Naciti, V. (2021). Banks' business strategy and environmental effectiveness: The monitoring role of the board of directors and the managerial incentives. *Business Strategy and the Environment*, 30(5), 2656–2670.

Global Reporting Initiative (GRI). (2016). GRI 101: Foundation. Available at: https://www.globalreporting.org/standards/media/1036/gri-101-foundation-2016.pdf

Global Reporting Initiative (GRI). (2021). Available at: https://www.globalreporting.org/

Global Sustainable Investment Alliance (GSIA). (2020). Global sustainable investment review 2020. Available at: http://www.gsi-alliance.org/wp-content/uploads/2021/07/GSIR-2020.pdf

Guenther, E., Guenther, T., Schiemann, F. and Weber, G. (2016). Stakeholder relevance for reporting: Explanatory factors of carbon disclosure. *Business and Society*, 55(3), 361–397.

Hahn, R. and Kühnen, M. (2013). Determinants of sustainability reporting: A review of results, trends, theory, and opportunities in an expanding field of research. *Journal of Cleaner Production*, 59, 5–21.

Ho, V. (2017). Comply or explain and the future of nonfinancial reporting. *Lewis and Clark Law Review*, 21(2), 317–356.

Hart, S. and Sharma, S. (2004). Engaging fringe stakeholders for competitive imagination. *The Academy of Management Executive*, 18(1), 7–18.

HKEX. (2011). Consultation paper on environmental, social and governance reporting guide. Available at: https://www.hkex.com.hk/-/media/HKEX-Market/News/Market-Consultations/2011-to-2015/December-2011-Consultation-Paper/Consultation-paper/cp201112.pdf

HKEX. (2012). Consultation conclusions on environmental, social and governance reporting guide. Available at: https://www.hkex.com.hk/-/media/HKEX-Market/News/Market-Consultations/2011-to-2015/December-2011-Consultation-Paper/Conclusions/cp201112cc.pdf

HKEX. (2015a). Consultation paper on review of the environmental, social and governance reporting guide. Available at: https://www.hkex.com.hk/-/media/HKEX-Market/News/Market-Consultations/2011-to-2015/July-2015-Consultation-Pape/Consultation-paper/cp201507.pdf

HKEX. (2015b). Consultation conclusions on review of the environmental, social and governance reporting guide. Available at: https://www.hkex.com.hk/-/media/HKEX-Market/News/Market-Consultations/2011-to-2015/July-2015-Consultation-Pape/Conclusions/cp201507cc.PDF

HKEX. (2018). Analysis of environment, social and governance practice disclosure in 2016/2017. Available at: https://www.HKEX.com.hk/-/media/HKEX-Market/Listing/Rules-and-Guidance/Other-Resources/Exchanges-Review-of-Issuers-Annual-Disclosure/ESG Guide/esgreport_2016_2017.pdf?la=en

HKEX. (2019a). Analysis of environmental, social and governance practice disclosure in 2018. Available at: https://www.hkex.com.hk/-/media/HKEX-Market/Listing/Rules-and-Guidance/Other-Resources/Environmental-Social-and-Governance/Exchange-Publications-on-ESG/esgreport_2018.pdf

HKEX. (2019b). Update No. 128: Note to subscribers for the amendments to the rules governing the listing of securities (the "Listing Rules"). Available at: https://en-rules.hkex.com.hk/node/5452

HKEX. (2021). Guidance on climate disclosures. Available at: https://www.hkex.com.hk/-/media/HKEX-Market/Listing/Rules-and-Guidance/Environmental-Social-and-Governance/Exchanges-guidance-materials-on-ESG/guidance_climate_disclosures.pdf?la=en

Hong Kong Green Finance Association (HKGFA). (2020). *HKGFA Sustainable Finance Policy Review 2020.* Available at: HKGFA-Sustainable-Finance-Policy-Review-2020-1.pdf (hkgreenfinance.org)

Hong Kong Monetary Authority (HKMA). (2021). Dominant gateway to China. Available at: https://www.hkma.gov.hk/eng/key-functions/international-financial-centre/hong-kong-as-an-international-financial-centre/dominant-gateway-to-china/

Hörisch, J., Johnson, M.P. and Schaltegger, S. (2015). Implementation of sustainability management and company size: A knowledge-based view. *Business Strategy and the Environment*, 24(8), 765–779.

Husted, B.W. and de Sousa-Filho, J.M. (2019). Board structure and environmental, social, and governance disclosure in Latin America. *Journal of Business Research*, 102, 220–227.

International Integrated Reporting Council (IIRC). (2015). *Materiality in <IR> Guidance for the Preparation of Integrated Reports.* Available at: http://integratedreporting.org/wp-content/uploads/2015/11/1315_MaterialityinIR_Doc_4a_Interactive.pdf

JPX. (2021). Disclosure in line with the TCFD Recommendations. Available at: https://www.jpx.co.jp/english/corporate/sustainability/jpx-esg/environment/index.html

Jaggi, B. and Zhao, R. (1996). Environmental performance and reporting: Perception of managers and accounting professionals in Hong Kong. *The International Journal of Accounting*, 31(3), 333–346.

Kassinis, G. and Vafeas, N. (2002). Corporate boards and outside stakeholders as determinants of environmental litigation. *Strategic Management Journal*, 23(5), 399–415.

Khan, M., Serafeim, G. and Yoon, A. (2016). Corporate sustainability: First evidence on materiality. *Accounting Review*, 91(6), 1697–1724.

KPMG. (2020). The time has come: The KPMG survey of sustainability reporting 2020. Available at: https://assets.kpmg/content/dam/kpmg/be/pdf/2020/12/The_Time_Has_Come_KPMG_ Survey_of_Sustainability_Reporting_2020.pdf

Lai, K. (2012). Differentiated markets: Shanghai, Beijing and Hong Kong in China's financial centre network. *Urban Studies*, 49(6), 1275–1296.

Leung, T.C.H. (2021). Environmental accounting and reporting in South-East Asia. In Bebbington, J., Larrinage, C., O'Dwyer, B. and Thomson, I. (Eds.), *Handbook of Environmental Accounting and Reporting*. New York, NY: Routledge.

Liu, F.H.M., Demeritt, D. and Tang, S. (2019). Accounting for sustainability in Asia: Stock market regulation and reporting in Hong Kong and Singapore. *Economic Geography*, 95(4), 362–384.

LSE. (2020). Guidance for issuers on the integration of ESG into investor reporting and communication. Available at: https://www.lseg.com/sites/default/files/content/GReen/LSEG_Guide_to_ESG_Reporting_2020.pdf

Lu, H. (2016). The "legalisation" of corporate social responsibility: Hong Kong experience on ESG reporting. *Asia Pacific Law Review*, 24(2), 123–148.

Lynn, M. (1992). A note on corporate social disclosure in Hong Kong. *The British Accounting Review*, 24(2), 105–110.

NASDAQ. (2019). *ESG Reporting Guide 2.0. A Support Resource for Companies.* Available at: https://www.nasdaq.com/docs/2019/11/26/2019-ESG-Reporting-Guide.pdf

Ng, A.W. and Leung, T.C.H. (2020). Relevance of SEA to a global financial centre under one country two systems: Engaging stakeholders for sustainability and climate change. *Social and Environmental Accountability Journal*, 40(2), 140–148.

Noronha, C., Leung, T.C.H. and Lei, O.I. (2015). Corporate social responsibility disclosure in Chinese railway companies. *Sustainability Accounting, Management and Policy Journal*, 6(4), 446–474.

O'Dwyer, B. and Owen, D.L. (2005). Assurance statement practice in environmental, social and sustainability reporting: A critical evaluation. *British Accounting Review*, 37(2), 205–229.

Ortar, L. (2016). From flexibility to specificity: Practical lessons from comparing materiality in sustainability reports of the world's largest financial institutions. *International Journal of Corporate Strategy and Social Responsibility*, 1(1), 44.

PingAn. (2020). ESG in China. Available at: http://www.pingan.cn/app_upload/file/official/ESGinChina_EN.pdf

Pizzi, S., Venturelli, A. and Caputo, F. (2021). The "comply-or-explain" principle in directive 95/2014/EU: A rhetorical analysis of Italian PIEs. *Sustainability Accounting, Management and Policy Journal*, 12(1), 30–50.

PricewaterhouseCoopers. (2021). ESG reporting. PwC. Available at: https://www.pwc.com/sk/en/environmental-social-and-corporate-governance-esg/esg-reporting.html

Rathnayaka Mudiyanselage, N.C.S. (2018). Board involvement in corporate sustainability reporting: Evidence from Sri Lanka. *Corporate Governance*, 18(6), 1042–1056.

Romero, S., Ruiz, S. and Fernandez-Feijoo, B. (2019). Sustainability reporting and stakeholder engagement in Spain: Different instruments, different quality. *Business Strategy and the Environment*, 28(1), 221–232.

Romito, S. and Vurro, C. (2021). Nonfinancial disclosure and information asymmetry: A stakeholder view on US listed firms. *Corporate Social Responsibility and Environmental Management*, 28(2), 595–605.

Rose, C. (2016). Firm performance and comply or explain disclosure in corporate governance. *European Management Journal*, 34(3), 202–222.

SASB. (2018). *Materiality Map*. Available at: https://materiality.sasb.org/

SASB. (2020). Proposed changes to the SASB conceptual framework and rules of procedure. Available at: https://www.sasb.org/wp-content/uploads/2021/07/PCP-package_vF.pdf

Seidl, D., Sanderson, P. and Roberts, J. (2013). Applying the "comply-or-explain" principle: Discursive legitimacy tactics with regard to codes of corporate governance. *Journal of Management and Governance*, 17(3), 791–826.

Sepúlveda-Alzate, Y.M., García-Benau, M.A. and Gómez-Villegas, M. (2022). Materiality assessment: The case of Latin American listed companies. *Sustainability Accounting, Management and Policy Journal*, 13(1), 88–113.

SGX. (2021). SGX mandates climate and board diversity disclosures. Available at: https://www.sgx.com/media-centre/20211215-sgx-mandates-climate-and-board-diversity-disclosures

Sìmnett, R., Vanstraelen, A. and Chua, W.F. (2009). Assurance on sustainability reports: An international comparison. *Accounting Review*, 84(3), 937–967.

Sustainable Stock Exchanges Initiative. (2019). *Stock Exchange Database*. Available at: https://sseinitiative.org/exchanges-filter-search/

Tang, S. and Demeritt, D. (2018). Climate change and mandatory carbon reporting: Impacts on business process and performance. *Business Strategy and the Environment*, 27(4), 437–455.

TCFD. (2017). Recommendations of the task force on climate-related financial disclosures. Available at: https://assets.bbhub.io/company/sites/60/2021/10/FINAL-2017-TCFD-Report.pdf

Thanasas, G.L., Kontogeorga, G. and Drogalas, G.A. (2018). Does the "capstone" of the "comply or explain" system work in practice? Evidence from Athens Stock Exchange. *Corporate Governance*, 18(5), 911–930.

Torelli, R., Balluchi, F. and Furlotti, K. (2020). The materiality assessment and stakeholder engagement: A content analysis of sustainability reports. *Corporate Social Responsibility and Environmental Management*, 27(2), 470–484.

Tsang, D. (2006). Big market, small government. Available at: https://www.ceo.gov.hk/archive/2012/eng/press/oped.htm

Turban, D.B. and Greening, D.W. (1997). Corporate social performance and organizational attractiveness to prospective employees. *Academy of Management Journal*, 40(3), 658–672.

United Nations Principles of Responsible Investment (UNPRI). (2020). *Principles for Responsible Investment*. Available at: https://www.unpri.org/download?ac=10948

Waddock, S.A. and Graves, S.B. (1997). The corporate social performance-financial performance link. *Strategic Management Journal*, 18(4), 303–319.

Watts, R. and Zimmerman, J. (1983). Agency problems, auditing, and the theory of the firm: Some evidence. *The Journal of Law and Economics*, 26(3), 613–633.

World Business Council for Sustainable Development (WBCSD). (2010). Translating ESG into sustainable business value. Available at: https://www.unepfi.org/fileadmin/documents/translatingESG.pdf

Yin, J. and Zhang, Y. (2012). Institutional dynamics and corporate social responsibility (CSR) in an emerging country context: Evidence from China. *Journal of Business Ethics*, 111(2), 301–316.

Yook, K.H., Song, H., Patten, D.M. and Kim, I.W. (2017). The disclosure of environmental conservation costs and its relation to eco-efficiency: Evidence from Japan. *Sustainability Accounting, Management and Policy Journal*, 8(1), 2–42.

Yu, E.P. and van Luu, B. (2021). International variations in ESG disclosure – Do cross-listed companies care more? *International Review of Financial Analysis*, 75, 101731.

Yu, S. and Rowe, A.L. (2017). Emerging phenomenon of corporate social and environmental reporting in China. *Sustainability Accounting, Management and Policy Journal*, 8(3), 386–415.

Zaheer, S. (1995). Overcoming the liability of foreignness. *Academy of Management Journal*, 38(2), 341–363.

20 Corporate Social Responsibility and Countries' Reputation

A Study from a Global Strategic Management Perspective

Nataliia Krasnokutska and Taras Danko

Introduction

Problem Description

Since long ago, social responsibility in business has been embedded in many ethically based philanthropic and altruistic practices (Carroll, 1999; Davis et al., 2006; Lantos, 2001), some of which could be traced back even to the Roman Empire and Middle Ages (Chaffee, 2017; Latapí Agudelo et al., 2019). There has always been a society and its institutions that have been actively imposing social norms on businesses and corporations to act in a responsible way (Barrena Martínez et al., 2016; Cochran, 2007; Lantos, 2001).

Eventually, CSR, having gone through a series of evolutionary stages (Stohl et al., 2007), at the dawn of the 21st century arrived on the doorstep of strategic management operationalization, demanding to be integrated as a part of it (Burke and Logsdon, 1996; Lantos, 2001; Latapí Agudelo et al., 2019). The corresponding emergence of the strategic CSR concept focused on the possibilities of systematic alignment of philanthropic contributions with business goals and strategies (Belu and Manescu, 2013; Heslin and Ochoa, 2008; Husted and Allen, 2009; Jamali, 2007; Lantos, 2001; Michelon et al., 2013; Orlitzky et al., 2011; Zhao et al., 2014).

Simultaneously CSR grew across borders as nations and governments worldwide became aware of the pressing unprecedented sustainability issues that were being brought about by frequently irresponsible or simply ignorant business behaviors overseas (Carroll, 2015; Dashwood, 2012; Davis et al., 2006; Hackert et al., 2012; Latapí Agudelo et al., 2019; Park et al., 2019; Roy, 2010; Stohl et al., 2007; Park and Kim, 2011). Moreover, strong pressures for global convergence of a universal CSR framework (Stohl et al., 2007), norms (Dashwood, 2012), and standards (Davis et al., 2006) quickly became evident.

Correspondingly, strategic and global CSR merge as instrumental questions in explaining how to achieve CSR compliance within the global value chain and what external factors influence it (Hackert et al., 2012; Latapí Agudelo et al., 2019; Ponte, 2019b, 2019a, 2020), as well as CSR implementation in the process of cross-border acquisitions (Park et al., 2019).

DOI: 10.4324/9781003274575-25

These developments legitimately called for the study of sustainability practices in emerging economies (Arora and De, 2020; Delai and Takahashi, 2013; Jamali, 2007), as well as their differences from developed ones (Lacy and Hayward, 2011; Lourenço and Branco, 2013) and the challenges of bridging them (Mullerat, 2010; Nkamnebe, 2011). Finally, the subsequent attention of the researchers was drawn toward CSR-related strategies in the emerging markets context (Liu et al., 2014; Roy, 2010; Zhao et al., 2014) and the decoupling phenomena (Bartley and Egels-Zandén, 2016; Dashwood, 2012; Tashman et al., 2019). Within this array of looming research problems and questions, the ultimate but unanswered one is how to manage successfully the transfer of sustainable practices to emerging economies.

Theory and Research Objectives

The challenge of sustainable practices' successful transfer to emerging economies is a strategic one. Essentially, it is about embedding a firm's sustainable behavior in the host country context in alignment with its overall mission and goals. If unsolved, it can lead to the decoupling phenomenon and significant sustainability risks for the international firm.

In its turn, since its beginning, strategic corporate social responsibility research has struggled to synchronize with the mainstream schools of thought on corporate strategy, trying to catch – so to say – the runaway train. To start with, in the golden age of the strategic planning era, it was reasonable to look for ways to internalize CSR policies, programs, and projects into measurable value creation processes inside the firm (Burke and Logsdon, 1996; Husted and Allen, 2009; Latapí Agudelo et al., 2019). Furthermore, it was suggested that the important potential of CSR internalization is hidden within reciprocal stakeholder responsibilities (Arora and De, 2020; Lantos, 2001; Latapí Agudelo et al., 2019; Montiel and Delgado-Ceballos, 2014) and corporate culture (Hawkins, 2006; Lantos, 2001). Eventually, some effort was invested into the identification and validation of the "CSR-inside" strategy development principles and dimensions (Burke and Logsdon, 1996; Heslin and Ochoa, 2008; Husted and Allen, 2009), as well as the exploration of the theoretical background of cost–benefit analysis and transaction costs analysis for the optimization of the firm's level of CSR (McWilliams and Siegel, 2001; Orlitzky et al., 2011). Simultaneously, significant attention of the researchers was assigned to examining the link between strategic CSR and a firm's financial performance (Belu and Manescu, 2013; Burke and Logsdon, 1996; Hawkins, 2006; Lourenço and Branco, 2013; Michelon et al., 2013; Saeidi et al., 2015) in parallel with nurturing the responsible competitiveness concept (McWilliams et al., 2006; Porter and Kramer, 2006; Zadek, 2006). These undertakings were accompanied by occasional allusions to the role of leadership (Orlitzky et al., 2011) and organizational change (Heslin and Ochoa, 2008) in the implementation of strategic CSR. Overall, these studies identified a good enough array of important managerial tools and internalized factors that should be considered in the process of sustainable corporate strategy creation.

The notion of responsible competitiveness brought about awareness of the strong relevance of the resource-based view (RBV) of the firm toward the field of strategic CSR (McWilliams et al., 2006; Orlitzky et al., 2011). In general, the RBV of competitive advantage examines the link between a firm's internal characteristics and its performance (Barney, 1991; Peng, 2001; Peteraf, 1993; Wernerfelt, 1984). Correspondingly, a series of studies revealed, on one hand, the tangible and intangible resources or inputs, including reputation, culture, employees knowledge, and capabilities, owned by the firm and used in the provision of CSR, and assessed, on the other, the mechanisms of how they translate into a firm's performance (Branco and Rodrigues, 2006; McWilliams and Siegel, 2001; Nair and Bhattacharyya, 2019; Sekhar Bhattacharyya, 2010; Xie et al., 2018). In its turn, this discourse prompted a call for comprehensive measurement of corporate sustainability, as well as ratings and rankings of the environmental social performance (Dimson et al., 2020; Giese et al., 2019; Huang, 2021; Montiel and Delgado-Ceballos, 2014; Xie et al., 2018).

A simultaneous appeal from the institution-based perspective on business strategy (Oliver, 1997; Peng, 2002) also found a quick response among strategic CSR scholars (Dashwood, 2012; Doh and Guay, 2006; Husted and Allen, 2009; Zadek, 2006), since it was logically inheriting and building on the well-established and recognized institutional theory of corporate social responsibility (Brammer et al., 2012; Campbell, 2007). This had a notable and fundamental implication for global CSR, as the fact of institutional heterogeneity among nations could hardly be overlooked and had always been among the cornerstone concerns of global strategic thinking (Kolk and van Tulder, 2010). In other words, as institutional theory explains how society and its institutions shape the firm's responsible behavior, from the managerial perspective of the global CSR strategy-making process it becomes of utmost importance and requires first-hand attention. Managers of many multinational corporations (MNCs) face a challenge in identifying and transferring domestic sustainable policies and practices that would be relevant in host country environments (Carroll, 2015). Moreover, they have to keep in mind the global reputation of their corporation, minimize its environmental, social, and governance (ESG) risks, and concurrently attain the desired corporate financial performance indicators.

From an international business perspective, studies confirm the continuum of the sustainability performance of MNCs, from irresponsible and exploitative in host countries to mindful efforts toward the achievement of the UN's sustainable development goals worldwide (Davis et al., 2006; Kolk, 2016; Kourula et al., 2017; Sinkovics et al., 2019). It can be suggested that MNCs which lack responsible competitiveness capabilities and do not have strong economic or institutional incentives to behave responsibly abroad will hardly risk plunging into considerable organizational changes associated with sustainable development concerns simply because of philanthropic or ethical considerations. Perhaps, their natural choice will be to go with sugar-coating and responsibility-blurring strategies in terms of dealing with environmental and social risks abroad.

On the other hand, those MNCs that own strong firm-specific advantages of internalized sustainable practices will tend to seek to transfer them to their overseas locations. For this second type of corporations, an essential question will be how to integrate country-specific CSR context into the strategic planning process and bridge the sustainability gap with their host countries, including emerging and developing economies (Kolk, 2016; Kolk and van Tulder, 2010; Kourula et al., 2017; Sinkovics et al., 2019; Zhao et al., 2014).

The subsequent studies of CSR in emerging and developing economies can be broadly classified into two categories. The first is almost entirely concentrated on distinguishing sustainable performance patterns of MNCs and domestic companies in particular countries (Dashwood, 2012; Delai and Takahashi, 2013; Jamali, 2007; Roy, 2010), while the second contains observations of links between firms' sustainable performance characteristics and their corresponding local institutional context (Husted and Allen, 2009; Lacy and Hayward, 2011; Lourenço and Branco, 2013; Nkamnebe, 2011; Tashman et al., 2019; Zhao et al., 2014). If combined, all the studies suggest that in general MNCs tend to apply the polycentric approach to their CSR strategies in host countries when CSR decision making is decentralized and CSR practices are tailored, sometimes rather chaotically, to local institutional environments. This contradicts the mission centrality principle of strategic CSR (Burke and Logsdon, 1996) and implies the "embryonic" stage of global CSR.

At the same time, the comparably recent development of country-level sustainability performance indexes (Boulouta and Pitelis, 2014; Tajbakhsh and Shamsi, 2019; Xiao et al., 2018) is rather timely and seems to have the potential to become a promising and pretty accurate tool that can help to overcome this constraint of integrating country-specific CSR context into the global strategic planning process.

In conclusion, based on the theoretical assumptions above, our research objectives are (1) to identify appropriate environmental social and governance rankings that can be associated with firm-specific capabilities ownership, and country-level sustainability performance indexes, associated with a country-specific institutional context, and (2) to outline how these indicators can be combined and integrated into the global strategic planning process, enabling sustainable practices transfer, and their successful internalization, to emerging and developing economies.

Research Methodology

According to the above theoretical prerequisites, we have focused on the following tasks: (1) comparative and correlation analyses of global sustainability indexes, and (2) matrix positioning. The first was based on studying the specificity of global sustainable rankings on the institutional and corporate levels and the justification of those that represent the relationship between the firm-level implementation of CSR principles and the country rankings in global ratings of economic and social development that affect a country's overall reputation.

For this purpose, we collected from the databases which contain the most relevant global institutional indexes: (1) Global Sustainable Competitiveness Index (GSCI) provided by Solability, a Swiss–Korean management consultancy company, which is based on 131 quantitative variables from the World Bank, the IMF, and UN agencies (Solability, 2021), and (2) Global Sustainable Development Goals Index (SDG Index), which is a worldwide voluntary assessment of countries' performance on the 17 SDGs and is based on 91 indicators applied for every country in the ranking plus 30 indicators collected additionally for OECD countries, using the latest available data from 2019 to 2021 (Sachs et al., 2021). The countries' sample is derived from the World Bank approach to countries' classification and consists of 19 lower-middle-income (emerging) and 22 high-income (developed) countries. The key requirement for the data was their availability for the whole period of studying, so we did not include the countries that had been represented in rankings for only one or two years. The data collected from the official rankings of the GSCI and SDG Index were processed using correlation tools in Microsoft Excel 365.

The next part of this research required a choice of a proper company-level ESG risk ranking and developing the scale for matrix axes. The corporate sustainability rankings are a matter of numerous scientific debates because of the minimal correlation between ESG metrics from different agencies and funds (Dimson et al., 2020). To make our choice of the corporate ESG ranking we set a range of requirements – transparency of methodology, provider's reputation, and data availability – and analyzed the gaps in meeting them by different agencies.

The matrix method was based on two axes: (1) country sustainability ranking which represents the country's reputation in the field of sustainable development and readiness to support CSR programs and projects, and (2) company ESG ranking which outlines the company's performance toward achieving the SDGs. For matrix positioning, we use the linguistic scale "weak – strong" for both axes.

Analysis and Results

The first phase of this research is devoted to studying the specificity of global sustainable rankings at the institutional level and justification of those that can be used for investigating the relationship between the implementation of CSR principles and the country rankings in global sustainability ratings. Accordingly, we studied different approaches to building institutional sustainable ratings that are mainstream now – namely, the Global Sustainable Competitiveness Index (GSCI), Global Sustainable Development Goals Index (SDG Index), Country Sustainability Ranking (CSR) by Robeco – for the period 2019 to 2021. Before looking deeply into them we checked the accessibility of the data and eliminated from consideration the CSR by Robeco because of lack of transparency (the ranking is available only for the best and the worst 20 countries). The GSCI and SDG Index are totally transparent and easily accessible via their creators' websites. Both are aggregated and comprehensive metrics but based on different methodologies. The main sub-indexes of the GSCI are natural capital (availability of resources and the level of their depletion), social capital (health, security, freedom, equality, life satisfaction), resource efficiency and intensity, intellectual capital and innovation, governance efficiency (infrastructure, market, and employment structure). The SDG Index fully corresponds to the 17 UNSDGs and uses them as a framework without any reorganizing into sub-indexes or categories (Lafortune et al., 2018).

The next step is to justify what rating is worthy to rely on for the purpose of the current research. This justification was made based on the method of pairwise correlation. The results are shown in Figure 20.1 and prove that the SDG Index is strongly correlated with the GSCI ($r^2 = 0.8333$). This means that both metrics are interchangeable and can be used to reliably measure a country's SDG performance.

The second phase of this research is assessing sustainability gaps on the corporate level. Of course, it might have been seen as a concise and clear task that could easily be solved by taking into account the widespread ESG (or CSR) rankings provided by numerous agencies that are designed to assess the firm-level implementation of CSR principles by different corporations and, correspondingly, how weak or strong their CSR capabilities are. But the current practice proves the opposite – the more ESG rankings are developed by different agencies, mutual funds, investment companies, etc., the more ambiguous are their results for the same companies (Diez-Cañamero et al., 2020; Dimson et al., 2020).

The comparative assessment of the most popular approaches to building an ESG ranking system (Dow Jones Sustainability Index and Sustainability Yearbook by S&P; FTSE4GOOD by FTSE Russel; MSCI-ESG by MSCI; Sustainalytics' ESG Risk Rating by Morningstar Co; ESG Ratings by Sustainable Fitch) is shown in Table 20.1.

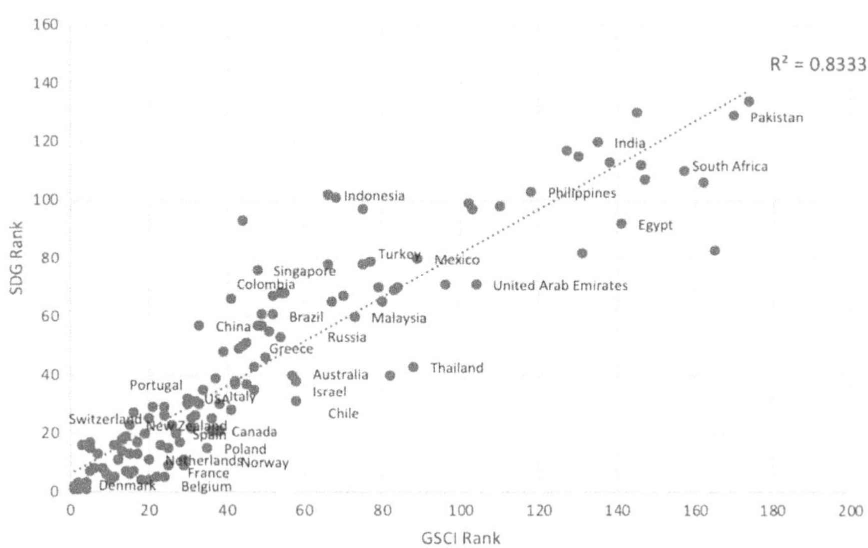

Figure 20.1 Pairwise Correlation of SDG Index with GSCI for Developed and Emerging Countries

Table 20.1 Comparative Assessment of the Most Popular Approaches to Building an ESG Ranking System

ESG ranking	*Provider*	*Criteria*		
		Transparency of methodology	*Providers' reputation*	*Data availability (for a company)*
DJSI	S&P	✓	✓	
Sustainability Yearbook	S&P	✓	✓	✓
FTSE4GOOD	FTSE Russel	✓	✓	
MSCI-ESG	MSCI	✓	✓	
Sustainalytics' ESG Risk Rating	Morningstar Co	✓	✓	✓
ESG Ratings from Sustainable Fitch	Fitch	✓	✓	

For the purpose of the current research, we set three criteria for comparison: (1) transparency of methodology – the description of the applied methodology should be placed on the index developer's website or can be easily accessed via email upon request; (2) provider's reputation – the company that offers its own approach to ranking CSR should be known worldwide and trustworthy; (3) data availability – the ESG score (rank) for any company–participant can be easily checked on the provider's website. The obtained results show that all rankings are methodologically transparent and their providers are trustworthy. But only two ranking systems allow access to any company–participant score – Sustainability Yearbook (SY) by S&P and Sustainalytics' ESG Risk Rating by Morningstar Co. The first is based on the data of 7,000 companies worldwide and awards companies–participants Gold, Silver, Bronze Class, or SY membership. The second represents the ESG risk evaluation for more than 20,000 companies. The comparisons of these two rankings for the sample of companies from different industries demonstrate different results (Table 20.2).

It is considered that all companies listed in SY include ESG projects in their corporate agendas and take important steps for propelling corporate sustainability into the future (SandP Global, 2021). This statement should have been especially true for Gold, Silver, and Bronze Class companies (General Motors, Honda, Cementos Agros in Table 20.2). But at the same time, Sustainalytics' ESG Risk Rating for them varies from medium to high, which proves the ambiguity of rankings and makes it necessary to conduct future research in this field. Since the

Table 20.2 Comparisons of SY 2021 and ESG Risk Rating 2021 for the Sample of Companies

Sample of companies	*Ranking, 2021*		
	Sustainability Yearbook	*ESG risk rating*	*Matching (+/–)*
Puma SE	SY member (78 out of 100)	Low risk (78 out of 185)	+
Adidas AG	SandP Global Bronze Class (82 out of 100)	Low risk (25 out of 185)	+
Skechers U.S.A., Inc.	Non-participating companies (10 out of 100)	Medium risk (164 out of 185)	–
General Motors Company	SandP Global Silver Class (78 out of 100)	High risk (56 out of 82)	–
Honda Motor Co., Ltd.	SandP Global Silver Class (74 out of 100)	Medium risk (45 out of 82)	–
Volvo Car AB	SY member (72 out of 100)	Medium risk (15 out of 82)	–
Cementos Argos S.A.	SandP Global Silver Class (88 out of 100)	High risk (34 out of 128)	–

explanation of such discrepancies between the rankings goes beyond the objectives of this chapter, we consider both of them applicable with limitation for the next stage of our study. Thus, in order to illustrate the suggested matrix approach to global strategic CSR decision making we arbitrarily choose ESG Risk Rating to identify the company's CSR capabilities.

The proposed criteria of ESG risk ranking at the corporate level and country reputation in the SDG context at the institutional level allow us to integrate country-specific CSR context into the strategic decision-making process. For this purpose, we have designed a two-dimensional graphical matrix that permits MNCs' managers to explore strategic options for embedding sustainable behavior in the host country in alignment with the company's mission and goals which depend, on one hand, on the overall strength (or weakness) of the MNC's CSR capabilities, and, on the other, on the host country sustainability-related institutional strength (or weakness) (Figure 20.2).

Each quadrant of the global strategic CSR matrix represents the favorable corporate CSR strategy option in the host country in accordance with the corporate ESG risk ranking and host country sustainability ranking. In order to derive these strategic options, we consider two types of corporations. The first have poor ESG risk ratings associated with their weak firm-level CSR capabilities. We suggest that essentially such corporations should focus their CSR strategy on sustainability risks minimization in countries with weak sustainability-related institutions rankings; while in the countries with high sustainability rankings they should strive

Figure 20.2 Global Strategic CSR Matrix

towards compliance with local institutional pressures. We name the corresponding two quadrants of the global strategic CSR matrix in Figure 20.2 as "Risk Minimization" and "Compliance".

The second type of corporation has strong CSR capabilities. We assume that such a corporation can choose the CSR strategy to transfer its successful responsibility practices to subsidiaries in the countries with a weak level of sustainability institutionalization by applying the change management approaches ("Change Management" quadrant in Figure 20.2). Simultaneously such corporations can benefit from shared value strategies operating in the host countries with high sustainability rankings ("Shared Value Strategies" quadrant in Figure 20.2). We believe that the suggested matrix will allow corporations to systematically avoid inappropriate and reputation-damaging initiatives and behaviors in host countries that do not resonate with their internal capabilities and, at the same time, achieve better performance and manageability of global CSR.

Discussion and Managerial Implications

From the institutional theory perspective, there is one more important dimension that might be added to the global strategic CSR matrix in order to refine its accuracy. This is the MNC's home country's institutional context (Kolk and van Tulder, 2010) and its sustainability ranking. There are several arguments in favor of checking the relationship between the home country context and the firm's environmental social performance. First of all, "MNCs have their own home-based 'administrative heritage' and predisposition toward CSR interpretations"

(Zhao et al., 2014). Next, whilst not homogeneous, there is a confirmed significant degree of similarity in approach and execution of CSR by the MNCs from the same home country, observed for instance in the United Kingdom (Bondy et al., 2012). Finally, institutional differences among developed regions influence the manner in which corporate responsibilities to home country society are shaped (Doh and Guay, 2006).

Based on these assumptions, we develop a strategic analysis tool that will include three dimensions: the firm's ESG risk ranking, the home country's sustainability ranking, and the host country's sustainability ranking. Correspondingly, in order to increase the accuracy of the analysis, we apply a scale of A ("strong") to D ("weak") to each dimension and derive, consistently with the global strategic CSR matrix alternatives (Figure 20.2), the hypothetical situational patterns of possible combinations. Further, as the first attempt to calibrate our tool, we offer the strategic options typology of sustainable practices transfer to host countries for eight extreme patterns (Table 20.3).

We suggest that the ESG risk ranking and home country sustainability ranking will be specific for each MNC. There are four combinations of the extremities of both dimensions that we use to identify the MNC's sustainability type, which is comparably permanent. For instance, the AA MNCs are those with strong CSR capabilities confirmed by the corresponding ESG risk rankings, while their home country also has a strong sustainability ranking. Essentially, they comply with their home country's institutional sustainability context and convert it into the source of their global sustainability competitiveness. Conversely, the DD type of MNCs ranks weak both in their sustainability performance and home country institutional development. The AD MNCs are the ones that, despite their home country's institutional weakness, manage to nurture strong CSR capabilities; while the DA MNCs are, so to speak, "liberal" in terms of their CSR practices implementation despite the strong sustainability reputation of their home country.

Basically, in terms of global strategic CSR, every type of MNC will have to deal with two sets of host countries – those with strong and weak sustainability ranking – and derive specific strategic options for each set, taking into account their own predefined firm-specific sustainability conditions.

For example, the change management option in the AAD case of transferring sustainability/CSR practices by a "strong" MNC from a "strong" home country to a "weak" host country means that the impact of AA-type MNCs' entry into the host country mostly depends on the institutional readiness of the latter. Even the most successful and proven sustainable business models may face a lack of developed market infrastructure, employment barriers, unclear and untransparent regulatory procedures, and poor customer support service culture. Correspondingly, facing such challenges, the AA-type MNCs should be prepared to walk an extra mile in bringing change to their host countries' facilities and counterparts starting at the level of sustainability literacy, attitudes, and behaviors.

In the case of a "weak" home country, we consider that the positive impact of AD-type MNCs with strong CSR performance can be transferred to a weak host

Table 20.3 Strategic Options Typology of Sustainable Practices Transfer to Host Countries

ESG risk ranking	*Home country sustainability ranking*	*MNC type*[1]	*Host country sustainability ranking*	*Pattern code*[2]	*Strategic options*
Weak	Weak	DD	Weak	DDD	Risk minimization
Weak	Weak	DD	Strong	DDA	Compliance. Learning from host countries
Weak	Strong	DA	Weak	DAD	Risk minimization
Weak	Strong	DA	Strong	DAA	Compliance
Strong	Weak	AD	Weak	ADD	Change management with "heavy-weight" support from the headquarters
Strong	Weak	AD	Strong	ADA	Shared value strategies
Strong	Strong	AA	Weak	AAD	Change management in the host country enabling sustainability/ CSR practices transfer
Strong	Strong	AA	Strong	AAA	Shared value strategies

Notes:
1. Two-letter codes in the column "MNC type" are assigned according to scale values of the "ESG risk ranking" column and the "Home country sustainability ranking" column, correspondingly.
2. Three-letter codes in the column "Pattern code" are assigned according to scale values. of the "ESG Risk Ranking" column, the "Home Country Sustainability Ranking" column and the "Host Country Sustainability Ranking" column, correspondingly.

country and it will also require the initiation of institutional changes supported by top management "heavy-weight" leadership.

An interesting aspect is the reciprocal host governments' considerations and policies towards incoming foreign MNCs. We expect that, in terms of sustainability, host countries benefit more from AA- and AD-type MNCs entry, while in the case of DA- and especially DD-type MNCs the host governments should be more cautious. Especially, the probability of risks and vulnerability increases if a "weak" MNC enters a "weak" host country with a low sustainable reputation. Supposedly, the MNC's and host government's interactions and arrangements in the case of DAD- and DDD-patterns might be particularly interesting for the research of global sustainable development's dark sides.

Shared value strategies are possible when the transfer of sustainable business models by "strong" MNCs should strive toward synergy with the institutions of the "strong" host country.

Overall, the identification of the permanent type of the MNC's sustainability, which takes into account both its ESG risk ranking and home country's sustainability ranking, allows to systematically outline the feasible and scalable strategic options of sustainable practices transfer to host countries, depending on their corresponding institutional context.

Conclusions and Future Research Directions

Nowadays, strategic and global CSR merge at the instrumental questions of explaining how to efficiently align the international firm's sustainable behavior in various host countries with its overall mission and goals. Within this broad research problem, the cornerstone is how to successfully manage sustainable practices' transfer to emerging economies. The proper solution will lead to minimizing the decoupling phenomenon and significant reduction of sustainability risks for the international firms.

The recent development of country-level sustainability performance indexes and company-level ESG risk rankings allows the creation of new analytic tools for integrating country-specific CSR contexts into the global strategic planning process. The appropriate ESG rankings, associated with the firm-specific capabilities ownership, and country-level sustainability performance indexes, associated with the host countries' institutional contexts, can be seen as the corresponding axis of the two-dimensional graphical matrix that allows MNCs to explore strategic options for embedding sustainable behavior in the host countries according to the company's mission, goals, and resources. The global CSR strategic options are even more harnessed when the dimension of sustainability-related institutional context ranking of the MNC's home country is added. This allows to identify the type of the MNC's sustainability, which takes into account the comparably permanent parameters of the firm's ESG risk ranking and its home country's sustainability ranking, and to derive the eight extreme patterns of sustainable practices transfer to host countries.

The suggested global strategic CSR matrix and strategic options typology of sustainable practices transfer to host countries are the tools at the conceptual stage of development. The immediate tasks for further research include the study of the corresponding MNCs' cases and validation of the measurements' conversion into the suggested qualitative scales. In addition, there is a clear follow-up question on how the described global strategic CSR analytical tools can be applied to the grand challenge of sustainable global value chains orchestration. One more aspect is the synchronization of the global strategic CSR decision-making process with the mainstream theories of international business strategy, including internalization theory and Dunning's eclectic paradigm of international production. Finally, there is a question of MNCs' resilience in the global turbulent business environment, which is increasingly disrupted by the accelerating pace of technological changes. MNCs are more than ever torn between the urgency of survival when their firm-specific advantages are undermined by new technologies every day and, simultaneously, by the increasing pressure of global stakeholders who are deeply concerned with the piling social and environmental threats worldwide.

References

Arora, P. and De, P. (2020). Environmental sustainability practices and exports: The interplay of strategy and institutions in Latin America. *Journal of World Business*, 55(4), 101094.

Barney, J. (1991). Firm resources and sustained competitive advantage. *Journal of Management*, 17(1), 99–120.

Barrena Martínez, J., López Fernández, M. and Romero Fernández, P.M. (2016). Corporate social responsibility: Evolution through institutional and stakeholder perspectives. *European Journal of Management and Business Economics*, 25(1), 8–14.

Bartley, T. and Egels-Zandén, N. (2016). Beyond decoupling: Unions and the leveraging of corporate social responsibility in Indonesia. *Socio-Economic Review*, 14(2), 231–255.

Belu, C. and Manescu, C. (2013). Strategic corporate social responsibility and economic performance. *Applied Economics*, 45(19), 2751–2764.

Bondy, K., Moon, J. and Matten, D. (2012). An institution of corporate social responsibility (CSR) in multi-national corporations (MNCs): Form and implications. *Journal of Business Ethics*, 111(2), 281–299.

Boulouta, I. and Pitelis, C.N. (2014). Who needs CSR? The impact of corporate social responsibility on national competitiveness. *Journal of Business Ethics*, 119(3), 349–364.

Brammer, S., Jackson, G. and Matten, D. (2012). Corporate social responsibility and institutional theory: New perspectives on private governance. *Socio-Economic Review*, 10(1), 3–28.

Branco, M.C. and Rodrigues, L.L. (2006). Corporate social responsibility and resource-based perspectives. *Journal of Business Ethics*, 69(2), 111–132.

Burke, L. and Logsdon, J.M. (1996). How corporate social responsibility pays off. *Long Range Planning*, 29(4), 495–502.

Campbell, J.L. (2007). Why would corporations behave in socially responsible ways? An institutional theory of corporate social responsibility. *Academy of Management Review*, 32(3), 946–967.

Carroll, A.B. (1999). Corporate social responsibility: Evolution of a definitional construct. *Business and Society*, 38(3), 268–295.

Carroll, A.B. (2015). Corporate social responsibility: The centerpiece of competing and complementary frameworks. *Organizational Dynamics*, 44(2), 87–96.

Chaffee, E.C. (2017). The origins of corporate social responsibility. *University of Cincinnati Law Review*, 85, 353.

Cochran, P.L. (2007). The evolution of corporate social responsibility. *Business Horizons*, 50(6), 449–454.

Dashwood, H.S. (2012). *The Rise of Global Corporate Social Responsibility: Mining and the Spread of Global Norms.* Cambridge: Cambridge University Press.

Davis, G.F., Whitman, M.V.N. and Zald, M.N. (2006). The responsibility paradox: Multinational firms and global corporate social responsibility. SSRN Scholarly Paper ID 899112. https://doi.org/10.2139/ssrn.899112

Delai, I. and Takahashi, S. (2013). Corporate sustainability in emerging markets: Insights from the practices reported by the Brazilian retailers. *Journal of Cleaner Production*, 47, 211–221.

Diez-Cañamero, B., Bishara, T., Otegi-Olaso, J.R., Minguez, R. and Fernández, J.M. (2020). Measurement of corporate social responsibility: A review of corporate sustainability indexes, rankings and ratings. *Sustainability*, 12(5), 2153.

Dimson, E., Marsh, P. and Staunton, M. (2020). Divergent ESG ratings. *The Journal of Portfolio Management*, 47(1), 75–87.

Doh, J.P. and Guay, T.R. (2006). Corporate social responsibility, public policy, and NGO activism in Europe and the United States: An institutional-stakeholder perspective. *Journal of Management Studies*, 43(1), 47–73.

Giese, G., Lee, L.-E., Melas, D., Nagy, Z. and Nishikawa, L. (2019). Foundations of ESG investing: How ESG affects equity valuation, risk, and performance. *The Journal of Portfolio Management*, 45(5), 69–83.

Hackert, A.M., Krumwiede, D., Tokle, J. and Vokurka, R.J. (2012). Global corporate social responsibility practices and cultural dimensions. *S.A.M. Advanced Management Journal*, 77(4), 33–42.

Hawkins, D. (2006). *Corporate Social Responsibility: Balancing Tomorrow's Sustainability and Today's Profitability*. Basingstoke: Palgrave Macmillan.

Heslin, P.A. and Ochoa, J.D. (2008). Understanding and developing strategic corporate social responsibility. *Organizational Dynamics*, 37(2), 125–144.

Huang, D.Z. (2021). Environmental, social and governance (ESG) activity and firm performance: A review and consolidation. *Accounting and Finance*, 61(1), 335–360.

Husted, B.W. and Allen, D.B. (2009). Strategic corporate social responsibility and value creation. *Management International Review*, 49(6), 781–799.

Jamali, D. (2007). The case for strategic corporate social responsibility in developing countries. *Business and Society Review*, 112(1), 1–27.

Kolk, A. (2016). The social responsibility of international business: From ethics and the environment to CSR and sustainable development. *Journal of World Business*, 51(1), 23–34.

Kolk, A. and van Tulder, R. (2010). International business, corporate social responsibility and sustainable development. *International Business Review*, 19(2), 119–125.

Kourula, A., Pisani, N. and Kolk, A. (2017). Corporate sustainability and inclusive development: Highlights from international business and management research. *Current Opinion in Environmental Sustainability*, 24, 14–18.

Lacy, P. and Hayward, R. (2011). A new era of sustainability in emerging markets? Insights from a global CEO study by the United Nations Global Compact and Accenture. *Corporate Governance: International Journal of Business in Society*, 11(4), 348–357.

Lafortune, G., Fuller, G., Moreno, J., Schmidt-Traub, G. and Kroll, C. (2018). SDG index and dashboards detailed methodological paper. Sustainable Development Solutions Network. Available at: https://www.sdgindex.org/reports/sdg-index-and-dashboards-2018/

Lantos, G.P. (2001). The boundaries of strategic corporate social responsibility. *Journal of Consumer Marketing*, 18(7), 595–632.

Latapí Agudelo, M.A., Jóhannsdóttir, L. and Davídsdóttir, B. (2019). A literature review of the history and evolution of corporate social responsibility. *International Journal of Corporate Social Responsibility*, 4(1), 1. https://doi.org/10.1186/s40991-018-0039-y

Liu, Z., Li, J., Zhu, H., Cai, Z. and Wang, L. (2014). Chinese firms' sustainable development—The role of future orientation, environmental commitment, and employee training. *Asia Pacific Journal of Management*, 31(1), 195–213.

Lourenço, I.C. and Branco, M.C. (2013). Determinants of corporate sustainability performance in emerging markets: The Brazilian case. *Journal of Cleaner Production*, 57, 134–141.

McWilliams, A. and Siegel, D. (2001). Corporate social responsibility: A theory of the firm perspective. *Academy of Management Review*, 26(1), 117–127.

McWilliams, A., Siegel, D.S. and Wright, P.M. (2006). Corporate social responsibility: International perspectives. The Journal of Business, 23(1), DOI: 10.2139/ssrn900834.

Michelon, G., Boesso, G. and Kumar, K. (2013). Examining the link between strategic corporate social responsibility and company performance: An analysis of the best corporate citizens. *Corporate Social Responsibility and Environmental Management*, 20(2), 81–94.

Montiel, I. and Delgado-Ceballos, J. (2014). Defining and measuring corporate sustainability: Are we there yet? *Organization and Environment*, 27(2), 113–139.

Mullerat, R. (2010). *International Corporate Social Responsibility: The Role of Corporations in the Economic Order of the 21st Century*. Alphen aan den Rijn: Kluwer Law International B.V.

Nair, A.K. and Bhattacharyya, S.S. (2019). Mandatory corporate social responsibility in India and its effect on corporate financial performance: Perspectives from institutional theory and resource-based view. *Business Strategy and Development*, 2(2), 106–116.

Nkamnebe, A.D. (2011). Sustainability marketing in the emerging markets: Imperatives, challenges, and agenda setting. *International Journal of Emerging Markets*, 6(3), 217–232.

Oliver, C. (1997). Sustainable competitive advantage: Combining institutional and resource-based views. *Strategic Management Journal*, 18(9), 697–713.

Orlitzky, M., Siegel, D.S. and Waldman, D.A. (2011). Strategic corporate social responsibility and environmental sustainability. *Business and Society*, 50(1), 6–27.

Park, J.Y. and Kim, S.W. (2011). Global corporate social responsibility standard, ISO 26000 and its effect on the society. *Asian Journal on Quality*, 12(3), 315–322.

Park, K.M., Meglio, O. and Schriber, S. (2019). Building a global corporate social responsibility program via mergers and acquisitions: A managerial framework. *Business Horizons*, 62(3), 395–407.

Peng, M.W. (2001). The resource-based view and international business. *Journal of Management*, 27(6), 803–829.

Peng, M.W. (2002). Towards an institution-based view of business strategy. *Asia Pacific Journal of Management*, 19(2–3), 251–267.

Peteraf, M.A. (1993). The cornerstones of competitive advantage: A resource-based view. *Strategic Management Journal*, 14(3), 179–191.

Ponte, S. (2019a). *Business, Power and Sustainability in a World of Global Value Chains*. London: Zed Books Ltd.

Ponte, S. (2019b). Sustainability, global value chains and green capital accumulation. In Ponte, S., Gereffi, G. and Raj-Reichert, G. (Eds.), *Handbook on Global Value Chains*. Cheltenham: Edward Elgar Publishing.

Ponte, S. (2020). Green capital accumulation: Business and sustainability management in a world of global value chains. *New Political Economy*, 25(1), 72–84.

Porter, M.E. and Kramer, M.R. (2006). Strategy and society: The link between corporate social responsibility and competitive advantage. *Harvard Business Review*, 84(12), 78–92.

Roy, D.A. (2010). Trends in global corporate social responsibility practices: The case of Sub-Saharan Africa. *International Journal of Civil Society Law*, 8, 64.

Sachs, J., Kroll, C., Lafortune, G., Fuller, G. and Woelm, F. (2021). *Sustainable Development Report 2021*. Cambridge: Cambridge University Press.

Saeidi, S.P., Sofian, S., Saeidi, P., Saeidi, S.P. and Saaeidi, S.A. (2015). How does corporate social responsibility contribute to firm financial performance? The mediating role of competitive advantage, reputation, and customer satisfaction. *Journal of Business Research*, 68(2), 341–350.

Sekhar Bhattacharyya, S. (2010). Exploring the concept of strategic corporate social responsibility for an integrated perspective. *European Business Review*, 22(1), 82–101.

Sinkovics, N., Sinkovics, R.R. and Archie-Acheampong, J. (2019). An overview of social responsibility dimensions in international business. In Leonidou, L.C., Catsikeas, C.S., Samiee, S. and Leonidou, C.N. (Eds.), *Socially Responsible International Business*. Cheltenham: Edward Elgar Publishing.

Solability. (2021). *The Global Sustainable Competitiveness Index 2021*. Available at: http://solability.com/download/the-global-sustainable-competitiveness-index-2021/.

SandP Global. (2021). *The Sustainability Yearbook 2021*. Available at: https://www.spglobal.com/esg/csa/yearbook/

Stohl, M., Stohl, C. and Townsley, N.C. (2007). A new generation of global corporate social responsibility. In May, S., Cheney, G. and Roper, J. (Eds.), *The Debate over Corporate Social Responsibility*. Oxford: Oxford University Press.

Tajbakhsh, A. and Shamsi, A. (2019). Sustainability performance of countries matters: A non-parametric index. *Journal of Cleaner Production*, 224, 506–522.

Tashman, P., Marano, V. and Kostova, T. (2019). Walking the walk or talking the talk? Corporate social responsibility decoupling in emerging market multinationals. *Journal of International Business Studies*, 50(2), 153–171.

Wernerfelt, B. (1984). A resource-based view of the firm. *Strategic Management Journal*, 5(2), 171–180.

Xiao, C., Wang, Q., van der Vaart, T. and van Donk, D.P. (2018). When does corporate sustainability performance pay off? The impact of country-level sustainability performance. *Ecological Economics*, 146, 325–333.

Xie, J., Nozawa, W., Fujii, H. and Yagi, M. (2018). Do environmental, social and governance activities improve corporate financial performance? *Business Strategy and the Environment*, 28(2), 286–300.

Zadek, S. (2006). Responsible competitiveness: Reshaping global markets through responsible business practices. *Corporate Governance: The International Journal of Business in Society*, 6(4), 334–348.

Zhao, M., Park, S.H. and Zhou, N. (2014). MNC strategy and social adaptation in emerging markets. *Journal of International Business Studies*, 45(7), 842–861.

21 Concluding Remarks

Comparative CSR and Sustainability Research – An Axial Analysis

Gabriel Donleavy and Carlos Noronha

Introduction

The concluding chapter to this book is rather unconventional in nature. It is not only a chapter to wrap up the results of the research collection in this book. It also serves several other purposes. First, we look into the research approach, not only the methodology, but the philosophy behind the studies collected in this volume. We assume a horizontal continuum from "conventional" to "critical". Then this continuum will form four axial diagrams against four other vertical continua. These continua are not metric rulers. Here, it is a matter of tendency that we are referring to. They include the issue of whether the studies contribute more toward "theory-building" or "theory-confirming", high or low "non-conformance" toward standards (a rather special topic to address here), the "globalness" or "localness" of the studies and finally how "forward-looking" are the studies; and if "retrospective", what is the value when compared against the research philosophy taken. Importantly, through these four axial diagrams, it is possible to identify possible research gaps to be filled. We firstly go into the issue of the lack of "comparative CSR" research as reflected from a comparative management theory perspective.

Comparative CSR Research and Comparative Management Theory

The paucity of comparative studies in CSR was raised by Williams and Aguilera (2008) who contrasted this field of study to those in comparative governance or comparative law. Williams and Aguilera (2008, 453) attributed the difficulty with comparative CSR studies to the lack of CSR definition, the varieties of units of analysis, geographical locations, as well as socio-political and national differences. The two main "comparative tools" that they have used in shaping their "comparative CSR" are "comparative legal analysis" and "comparative institutional analysis"; and the final destination is to use "comparative CSR" to understand corporate governance systems. Within their analysis, many "actors" (e.g., top management teams, consumers, investors, governments, NGOs, and so on) and "behaviors" (e.g., social and sustainability reporting, socially responsible

DOI: 10.4324/9781003274575-26

investments, MNCs and cross-cultural activities, and so on) were touched on, which demonstrate the diverse nature of CSR as a discipline itself. One very critical message that Williams and Aguilera (2008, 464) brought up is that international diversification of firms can lead to both CSR and corporate irresponsibility (see Chapter 13 Windsor on CSIR); and this point somehow is in line with the central thesis of this book, which has taken a critical and diversified perspective in putting CSR and sustainability under the microscope.

Interestingly, "comparative CSR" has arguably transcended the traditional scope of comparative management; but there are still constraints and boundaries to be dealt with. Chappel and Moon's (2005) seven-Asian country investigation must certainly be cited here. Their study had followed the model of comparative management theory anchored on national/cultural differences and motivated other attempts in "comparative CSR" (e.g., Ramasamy and Hung, 2004; Welford, 2005; Haikos and Antonis, 2016, 2017; Schmidt and Cracau, 2018; etc.). Nevertheless, many experimentations on "comparative CSR" suffered from those weaknesses as pointed out by Williams and Aguilera (2008) above. We would put it this way: many studies were trapped in the country/culture differences mold (*Hofstede-ism*). McSweeney (2002) was probably one of the first scholars to critique Hofstede's model (which was then followed by a plethora of value judgments); but we are not here to repeat the same thing and we state that our position remains neutral. Nevertheless, things have changed a lot since the turn of the millennium, and we will be exemplifying how new social accounting research has brought a new way out of this *cul-de-sac* for "comparative CSR".

If we were to look back to 50 years before, Negandhi (1975) proffered that there is no one way of doing things and there is a principle of equifinality and also there is not a universalistic management style (authoritarian or the other way) though managers may act similarly as well as differently and this is largely a cross-cultural matter. This significance of cultural variables had already been discussed much earlier, in 1965, by Richman (1965) and Farmer and Richman (1964). The cultural approach to comparative management resulted in Ronen and Shenkar's (1985) cultures/countries clusters which, during the early 1980s, were heavily influenced by Hofstede (1980). It should be worth noting that throughout the comparative management expedition (circa 1964–2010, including representative studies such as Redding's (1994) jungle, zoo, and fossil bed, Trompenaars and Hampden-Turner's (2000) waves of culture, Adler's (2002) international organizational behaviors, House et al.'s (2002) GLOBE project, and those beyond such as Tung and Verbeke (2010)), socioeconomic, educational, political, legal, and cultural factors (Negandhi and Prasad, 1971) have been mentioned many times; but Bowen's (1953) corporate social responsibility of the businessmen had almost always been left out.

Therefore, Williams and Aguilera (2008) are right to use legal and institutional factors as the lens to study "comparative CSR". CSR actually started to revive more from the legal and ethical realm of business studies and from institutional theory including the mainstream political economy theory, legitimacy, and stakeholder theories. Halis (Chapter 15) in this volume has also indicated the legal origin of

CSR. But what is important to point out here is that CSR and sustainability studies grew exponentially during the mid-1990s (or earlier), until now mostly in the accounting literature. Highly regarded figures in the CSR arena are accountants (e.g., the late Rob Gray) and many influential papers on CSR, accountability, and sustainability are published in accounting journals (e.g., Gray et al. (1997) *Accounting, Auditing and Accountability Journal*; Gray (2002) *Accounting, Organizations and Society*; Bebbington and Gray (2001) *Critical Perspectives on Accounting*; Patten (2002) *Accounting Forum*). The above are only some examples. There is a myriad of important CSR and sustainability research published in various well-respected accounting and related journals (e.g., *British Accounting Review*, *Journal of Business Ethics*, *Sustainability Accounting, Management and Policy Journal*, *Social and Environmental Accountability Journal*, *Social Responsibility Journal*, just to name a few). A number of contributors to this current volume also possess an accounting background but they are just simply fond of delving into multidisciplinary areas, including law, philosophy, sociology, and the like.

Research Philosophy: The Main Continuum

It may seem that we are swaying a bit from our central discussion of "comparative CSR" and comparative management. No. It is our intention to point out here with confidence that it is the multidisciplinary facet of accounting research that has inspired our "comparative CSR" which has already transcended comparative management as a separate discipline. As mentioned in the introduction, the main continuum used to describe all the essays in this collection is the one that describes the "research philosophy". We have "conventional" at one end and "critical" at the other end of the continuum (see Figure 21.1).

Again, this continuum is not a metric ruler and it is about tendency. It is not also dichotomously about "good" or "bad", "fashionable/posh" or "outdated/unattractive". It is a continuum to help us look at the research philosophy or the "ontology" of a study. Research philosophy is often explained in the standard research methodology textbook as the belief held by the researcher and there are four of them: pragmatism, positivism, realism, interpretivism. From our experience, especially from the social accounting realm, research belief is no longer as it is in the textbooks that one should exclusively believe in one and become suspicious of the others. When we can "emancipate" theory, we are able to embrace and engulf all aspects of research philosophies. Therefore, we understand that, for example, "conventional" may refer to a research based on a positivistic approach of statistical hypotheses-testing; but it can at the same time be of a "controversial" nature, probably exploring a very contentious topic. A "critical" research philosophy needs not to be always qualitative-based and employ profound ideas

Conventional -- Critical

Figure 21.1 The Conventional–Critical Continuum

from classical philosophers. It is still interesting to encounter PhD students in the interpretivist school asking questions like "I didn't use Foucault in my thesis, am I going to fail?" This is as much a cliché as, in the early 1990s, when PhD students who did not learn structural equation modeling had to struggle through the stigma in a world run by positivists.

Conventional–Critical X Theory-Building–Theory-Confirming

We will now approach our essays in this collection through an evaluation of the first axial diagram (Figure 21.2), composed of the conventional–critical x theory-building–theory-confirming continua.

Theory-building or theory-construction is often considered "again" in standard research method manuals as the first step toward theory-testing. Theory-building often involves epistemological processes of linking beliefs and observations until propositions are established to explain a phenomenon. Eisenhardt's (1989) paper is properly still the most widely read theory-construction doctrine in the business research area. The "Eisenhardt method", as many people call it, includes inducting theory using case studies for the development of hypotheses towards the construction of novel, testable, and empirically valid theories (Eisenhardt, 1989, 532). The idea draws heavily from grounded theory and its methodology

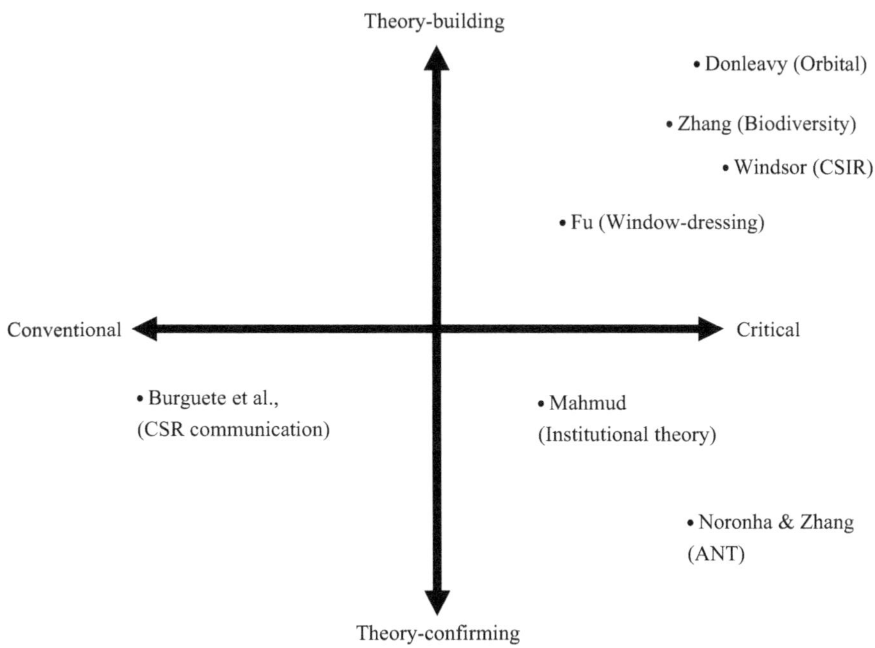

Figure 21.2 Conventional–Critical x Theory-building–Theory-confirming

(Glaser and Strauss, 1967; Strauss and Corbin, 1998). On the other hand, theory-confirming is often derived from the more positivistic aspect of "confirmation theory" (see e.g., Hawthorne, 2011) which is often statistics-oriented; but this is not absolutely the case if we can hold our "emancipated" attitude toward theory as a construct itself. Nevertheless, what we posit here in our Figure 21.2 is not necessarily positivistic or interpretive. What we are trying to present are the quadrants that largely describe the research philosophy in our collection of "comparative CSR" studies.

Within the top right quadrant (theory-building and critical), we position Donleavy's Chapter 14 on Orbital Theory, Zhang's Chapter 2 on biodiversity, Windsor's Chapter 13 on CSIR, and Fu's Chapter 11 on window-dressing at approximately similar locations. The commonalities among these pieces are that they employ a critical perspective on CSR and the theoretical frameworks of these studies are rather new and have further developmental potentials. In particular, the topic on biodiversity and extinction accounting is very much discussed in the field of today's social and environmental accounting and ecological economics with Atkins and Atkins' (2019) book as a representative piece. However, when this idea of extinction accounting is put into a Chinese context, the opportunity for theory development is further intensified (so far, there is probably only Zhao and Atkins' (2021) "panda accounting" in the literature). The other chapters included within this quadrant are all critical in terms of social irresponsibility, window-dressing, and decoupling accountability. From a CSR perspective, they represent tremendous academic resources to add to the institutionalization aspect and theory of CSR.

Mahmud's Chapter 12 on Japanese integrated reporting is regarded as more theory-confirming as the author has used the rather conventional isomorphism (especially the mimetic) theory to explain why Japanese companies produce CSR and sustainability reports, generally known as integrated reports (IRs). However, it still has critical elements as the author has pointed out that it is largely due to some Japanese social and cultural traits (back to the cultural issue in our discussion of comparative management above) that have led Japan to favor the mimetic school. To a certain extent, he has critically pinpointed the Japanese's heavy emphasis on the environmental aspect of CSR. This point echoes Ali et al.'s (2015) findings and it leaves us with an urgent need for the country to become more dynamic in terms of CSR (even though SDGs are almost mundanely promoted in Japan, for example on the national NHK news every day: https://www3.nhk.or.jp/nhkworld/en/ondemand/special/sdgs/). The Fukushima tragedy remains in the hearts of the Japanese but there are many pressing problems such as *karoshi* (overwork death) to deal with.

Noronha and Zhang's Chapter 10 is almost at the far end of the critical side but also near the theory-confirming end. First of all, it must be said that the "ontology" of Latour's actor–network theory (ANT) is not new in the social accounting literature (but it could be quite special in other business-related areas). As we have emphasized, when this ontology could be extended (see e.g., the 3D perspective of ANT's ontology proposed in the chapter), there is critical potential for further development. Furthermore, the setting of the study is China's "Belt and Road Initiative" which heavily involves African countries and is still a novel and less explored topic. We shall come back to this point later when we discuss the other axial diagrams. Nevertheless, Chapter 10 serves as an example of raising a "meso-level" theory to the "macro" level and opens paths for further research in "comparative CSR".

Burguete et al.'s Chapter 17 on CSR communication has been placed in the high conventional but low theory-conformity quadrant. It employs a rather conventional research methodology of literature review to develop a CSR communication framework to be operationalized and tested in further research. However, there is still a lot of space for application as the authors suggest that the framework is particularly suitable for studying the mining industry and the redeveloping of mine brownfields. Thus, there is possibility to combine the framework with critical theories to study highly contentious industries including the extractive industry in a general sense.

Conventional–Critical X High Non-Standard Conformance–Low Non-Standard Conformance

In Figure 21.3 we have our second axial diagram, also with four quadrants. As mentioned, the vertical continuum warrants some explanation. Firstly, what

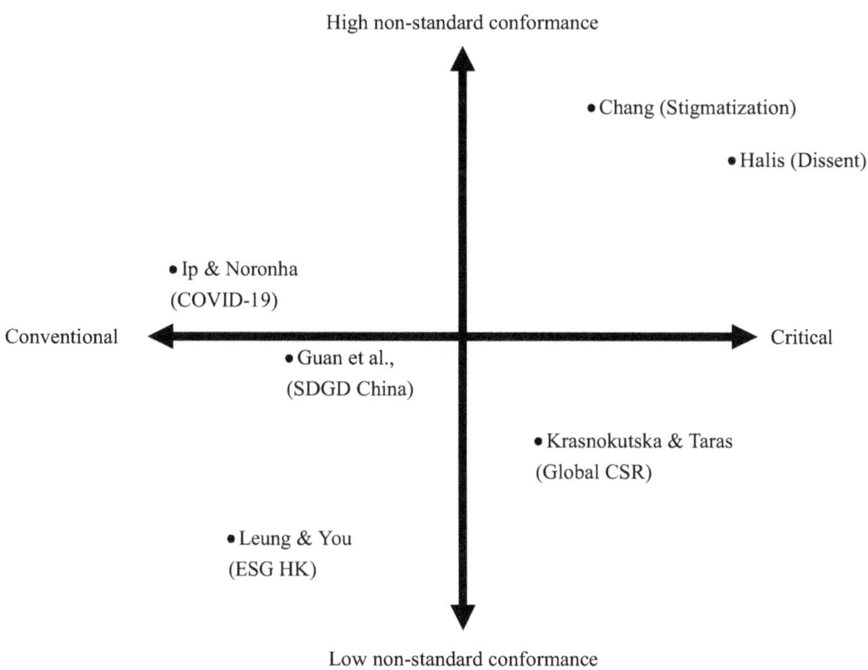

Figure 21.3 Conventional–Critical x High Non-Standard Conformance–Low Non-standard Conformance

is meant by "non-standard conformance" here? We interpret "non-standard conformance" in two aspects in this axial diagram. The first interpretation is related to the rather positivistic and box-checking approach toward CSR and sustainability standards by some people or entities (therefore, low non-standard conformance); in particular, in a place like Hong Kong where the stock exchange requires ESG disclosure to a certain extent. This exercise can be mechanical and, in some instances, even the now famous "comply or explain" principle can also be easily abused. Chapter 19 by Leung and You provides an extensive discussion of how ESG requirements have developed from a box-checking activity to a "comply or explain" phenomenon. The study is located in the conventional and low non-standard conformance quadrant. Nevertheless, the chapter does provide some constructive comments on how the ESG Guide can be improved in the near future. For example, the issue of a market-driven or a government-driven ESG Guide can be a very critical research topic in the Hong Kong SAR where a One-Country Two-System principle is supposed to avail (see, e.g., Ng and Leung, 2020). Following the above reasoning, Guan et al.'s Chapter 18 on sustainability development goals disclosure (SDGD) development in China and Ip and Noronha's Chapter 4 on the effect of COVID-19 on the CSR reporting of the world's major hotel chains are also classified as rather conventional in terms of research method and philosophy.

Now, we would like to explain here our second interpretation of "non-standard conformance", which is in high correlation with the question of research setting and the emergence of the topic under study. Firstly, the concept of SDGD promulgated by Adams et al. (2020) is rather new; but according to Guan et al. China is ready to follow SDGD toward a direction of internationalization just as what had happened with IFRS. We therefore see some rather obvious differences between the studies of Leung and You (Chapter 19) and Guan et al. (Chapter 18) which rest on rather divergent socio-political settings (some may observe the opposite, especially when reading Halis' Chapter 15), while both are claiming to attain a high level of international convergence. As for Chapter 4 on COVID-19's effect on the global hotel industry, we can see that the emergence and controversy (disasters and crises) of the topic position the chapter higher in terms of the level of non-standard conformance but the methodology is obviously conventional.

To a certain extent, Chapter 15 on "CSR dissent" by Halis and Chapter 6 on stigmatization/dirty work and SDGs by Chang are highly controversial. The comparative legal approach employed by Halis reflects Williams and Aguilera's (2008) attempt toward a "comparative CSR" paradigm. Also, the topic of "dissent" is extremely novel in the CSR literature. In a similar vein, Chang's expedition into how work stigmatization in the "special industry" relates to SDG 3 (good health and well-being), SDG 5 (gender equality), SDG 8 (decent work and economic growth), and SDG 10 (reduced inequality), plus the adverse effect of COVID-19, mark the chapter in the high non-standard conformance and critical quadrant.

Finally, Krasnokutska and Taras' Chapter 20 on their multinational study of SDG and Global Sustainable Competitive indices is a neat example of "comparative CSR" pairing with the international business and strategic management schools. Thus, their study leaps out from the country/culture box as elucidated earlier and opens up a wide array of opportunities for international CSR studies.

One may also find it interesting to observe that the three chapters included on the right-hand side of the axial diagram (Figure 21.3) are all non-accounting based (Chapter 15 on law, Chapter 6 on occupational studies, and Chapter 20 on international business); while the other three on the left-hand side of the diagram represent some familiar accounting-based CSR studies, especially in the standard conformance area. This provides further evidence for the idea of "theory emancipation" in "comparative CSR".

Conventional–Critical x Global–Local

Next, we come to Figure 21.4 which is rather self-explanatory. Instead of going through the location of each chapter on the axial diagram, we will firstly review the manifestations by Crane et al. (2016) and Tilt (2016); and then briefly mention the positioning of a few of our chapters. The idea here is to identify further areas of "comparative CSR" which we can possibly work on in the near future.

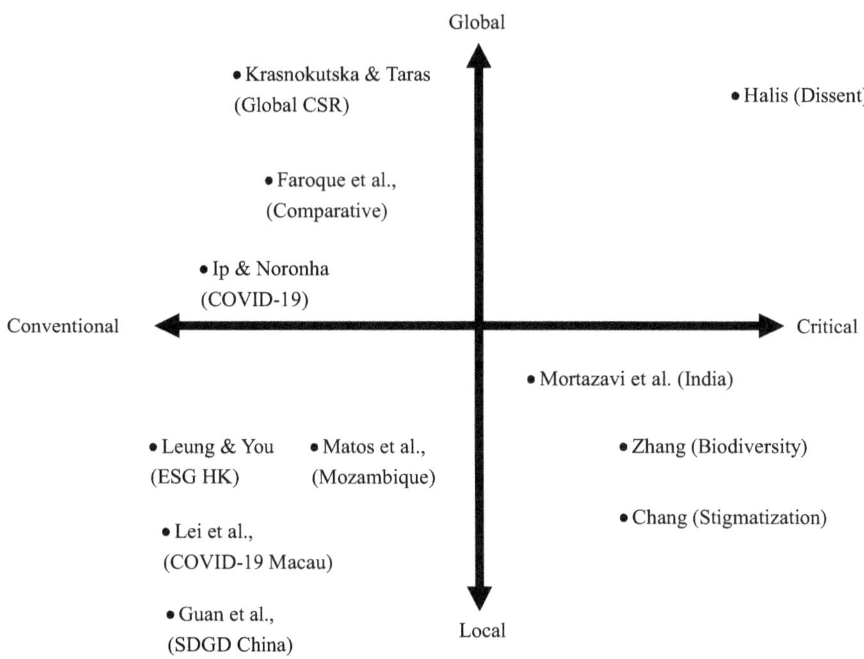

Figure 21.4 Conventional–Critical x Global–Local

The issue of local country CSR studies has been manifested by Crane et al. (2016) in their editorial for which they used an apocryphal article title "Are we interested in CSR in Mongolia?" to demonstrate why country studies of CSR were often desk rejected by prestigious journals like theirs. Probably five or six years later, if the same editorial was to be written, it is likely that the "apocryphal" article title will not be used again. In any case, Crane et al.'s (2016) messages did and still do make sense toward the development of "comparative CSR". In particular, they made three manifestations for local country studies to be significant. First, the country study should develop new theory (p. 4). Second, it should refine a theory (p. 5). Third, it should test a theory (p. 6). In simple, they are referring to theoretical contribution. They have also ascertained that many country studies have been (and are still being) rejected because they simply employ non-Western data to replicate studies or they only apply an existing model in an exotic setting.

We agree with Crane et al.'s concern. For "comparative CSR" to be important, it should embrace a wider view and involve a "phenomenon *grande*" (our term here). In our Figure 21.4, all the chapters that we locate on the left-hand side of the axial diagram, ranging from local to global have all taken a conventional research philosophy. Nevertheless, they have been included in this volume because they represent attempts to embrace some "phenomena *grande*" (COVID-19, China, Africa, etc.). We do not attempt to go into details of the grand, middle-range, or micro-range theories (Mills, 1959; Merton, 1968) here. Our meaning of a "phenomenon *grande*" is simply one which is of wide influence, no matter geographically, politically, methodology-wise, or theory-wise. Hopefully, we shall be discussing more about the details and even the nuances of this notion of "phenomenon *grande*" in another scholastic encounter soon.

Tilt (2016) shared similar concerns with Crane et el. (2016) that there is a lack of context in international CSR studies as many of them preferred to rely on theories and hypotheses developed from studies undertaken in the West, in particular the United States, United Kingdom, and Australasia (Tilt, 2016, 1). In terms of context theorizing, Tilt was actually following up upon a previous call from Adams (2002) and she referred to a wider horizon to include the political (e.g., hegemony and state ownership), socio-cultural (e.g., freedom of press and level of urbanization and secularism), and economic (e.g., industrialization levels, FDI and technology) aspects. These contextual factors are rather concrete and ideal for both local country studies as well as cross-national global studies. Furthermore, she also suggested some solid research agenda such as the need for more in-depth study of CSR in China and Sri Lanka, citing the works of Guan and Noronha (2013) and Beddewela and Herzig (2013), respectively, amongst others.

In particular, we can see the position of Halis' Chapter 15 is at the top right-hand corner of the axial diagram, indicating its global feature plus critical nature. His chapter on examining a "phenomenon *grande*" encompassing digitization, social movements, CSR, and dissent while using examples of events ranging from the 2019 Hong Kong protests to Black Lives Matter and corporations from

Cathay Pacific to Nike is exemplary. We hereby call for more studies which lead to our expectation for eventual "theory emancipation".

Conventional–critical x forward-looking–retrospective

Our last axial diagram (Figure 21.5) examines the forward-looking–retrospective continuum. Firstly, there are indeed in the medical sciences retrospective and prospective studies or analyses. For the former, the outcome is already known, while for the latter, investigators design the study before the subjects develop a particular disease (Elsworth, n.d.). Retrospective studies are also common in historiography and criminology and therefore there is certainly value toward academic enhancement of the field involved. This research approach will often require the analyses of primary sources, including documents, speeches, letters, images, videos, census data, newspaper/magazine articles, interviews, oral transcriptions, and so on (Fraser Hall Library, 2022), which resemble in many aspects the qualitative methodology often applied in organization studies, social accounting, and our subject of CSR in which content analysis is one of the most commonly employed methods.

Some retrospective studies may not employ primary sources (not data), but may be some kind of comprehensive syntheses of important literature reviews in an area of academic interest. In the social accounting field, Gray et al. (2010) and Hoque (2018) are exemplars of retrospective writings in terms of theories

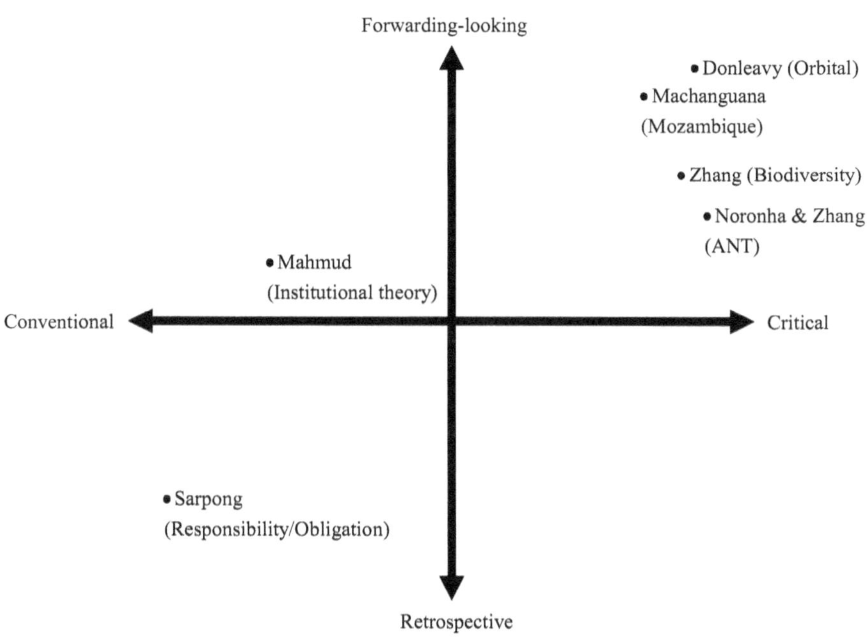

Figure 21.5 Conventional–Critical x Forward-looking–Retrospective

and methodologies. Both represent essential readings for researchers in the social accounting and "comparative CSR" areas. In particular, Gray et al. (2010) provided a comprehensive range of theories (although the authors addressed it as a simple heuristic) which can help social accounting researchers to navigate through. However, the range of theories is extensively interdisciplinary and multidimensional, including three levels, namely meta theory (system level), meso theory (sub-system level) and three micro level theories (organizational, internal to organizations, and individual) (p. 12). Their heuristic has profound influence on the development of social accounting research in the past decade. Some of our essays here are also reflections of their call. For example, Chapter 10 Noronha and Zhang on ANT, Chapter 14 Donleavy on orbital theory/accountability, Chapter 2 Zhang on biodiversity/deep ecology, and Chapter 3 Machanguana on resettlement/social justice in Mozambique. On the other hand, Hoque's (2018) collection of essays has also provided extremely valuable resources for many scholars in the field from how to choose a theory (positivistic, naturalistic, institutional, and contextual perspectives) to the research strategies and data analysis methods that may be employed.

In terms of the chapters in this volume, Sarpong's Chapter 16 on corporate responsibility and corporate obligation and, to a certain extent, Mahmud's Chapter 12 on Japanese IRs can be classified as using conventional research philosophies to review some retrospective theories. Sarpong has reviewed mainly moral theories while Mahmud mainly institutional theory, especially the Japanese mimetic isomorphism. In any case, Mahmud's argument of Japanese traits as a kind of obstacle toward the previously mentioned CSR dynamism provides a more forward-looking perspective and has potentiality to move toward a "phenomenon *grande*".

In the paragraph before the immediate one above, we positioned a few chapters in the quadrant of forward-looking–critical in Figure 21.5. It is necessary to explain here what we refer to as forward-looking research. Lakatos (2015) is famous for his introduction of "scientific research programs" in which he also distinguished between "progressive" research and "degenerative" research (Harman, 2019, 2067). Many may know that Lakatos was greatly influenced by Popper (1992) but he actually refuted his mentor's falsificationism. For instance, Lakatos did not agree with Popper's stance that a theory is scientific only if it is prepared to be falsified and that is why Marxism and psychoanalysis were claimed to be pseudoscientific by Popper (Harman, 2019, 2068). Lakatos believed that his notion of "scientific research programs" should result in progressive research, which many also align the idea with Kuhn's (1996) paradigm shift. Kuhn stressed that there are so-called normal "every-day sciences" as well as core-shaking "paradigm shifts".

Certainly, the collections in this volume are not at the level to cause "Copernican astronomy or relativity and quantum theory" (Harman, 2019, 2068–2069) type of paradigm shifts, but we believe in forward-looking and progressive types of CSR research in our "comparative CSR" which still sees a lot of space for development. We particularly welcome more "phenomena *grande*" to be explored. To sum up, our ideology is in line with Crane et al. (2016), Tilt

(2016), Gray et al. (2010), Hoque (2018), and even Lakatos (1992), though far from an equal footing.

Conclusion: Identifying Research Opportunities

After rather detailed elucidations on our four axial diagrams, we now review each of them. In Figure 21.2, the theory-building–theory-confirming axial diagram, we can identify that an empty quadrant exists on the top left corner (theory-building–conventional). This raises an interesting question. Can a conventional research philosophy help to construct new theory? Frankly speaking, most theory-confirming studies are based on conventional research philosophies, such as positivistic falsification; while most theory-building studies are to a certain extent critical (context or method-wise). However, as in the case of Gray et al. (2010), their comprehensive literature review on theories that they offered has resulted in new research agendas in the social accounting arena. As over a decade has passed since their publication, we believe that it is necessary to have another "decade study" of theory in-use and in-development for the field of "comparative CSR".

Concerning Figure 21.3 the high–low non-standard conformance axial diagram, the distribution of chapters in the four quadrants is comparatively even. In terms of studies of standards conformance, we continue to see many works in the realms of SDGs, GRI, ISO standards, etc. in the current literature and we expect to see more in the upcoming years. For example, the Center for Sustainable Organizations (CSO, 2022), a private organization based in Woodstock, Vermont, has issued the reference model for GAIA (Generally Accepted Integrated Accounting) Principles in 2020 and the latest update was recently released in February 2022. The CSO appears to be rather critical toward the approaches of the "giants" like SASB and IIRC. Therefore, we are expecting more of these comparative studies of standards conformance to appear. They will also proliferate in reports of international organizations (e.g., UN, UNESCO, ILO, WTO, OECD, etc.). What we would want to see more of are those "controversial" (we used this word somewhere above) researches which may not necessarily be talking about standards in "that" standard conformance sense. We wish to see more studies explaining "phenomena *grande*" (Halis' Chapter 15 is a good example).

What about global and local studies? This matter has been discussed in quite some detail already with the help of the ideas of Crane et al. (2016) and Tilt (2016); and we can see from Figure 21.4 that our volume has collected a balanced number of chapters in both the local and global quadrants (the top left quadrant and both quadrants at the bottom). Again, what we need are studies explaining more "phenomena *grande*". The impatient reader may wonder why are we repeating this again. We shall be providing a suggestion soon as we conclude this chapter.

Finally, as to Figure 21.5 the forward-looking–retrospective axial diagram, we seem to have already at least three chapters located at the top right quadrant (forward-looking and critical) but we crave for more. There is an empty quadrant on the bottom right-hand side of the diagram (the retrospective–critical). Similar to our suggestion above, we are in need of a "decade study" of critical researches in CSR so as to reflect and project new research agendas. Examples of critical themes in CSR and social accounting in the past ten years may include zoonosis (Noronha et al., 2021; Schaltegger, 2021), LGBTQ (Ghio et al., 2022), biodiversity (Cuckston, 2018a, 2018b), deep or dark ecology (Vollmer, 2018), extinction accounting (Atkins and Maroun, 2018; Cuckston, 2019), social justice (George et al., 2021), poverty (Danson et al., 2020), and artificial intelligence (Yigitbasioglu et al., 2022). These are topics (and there are many more) that have not been included even in a rather recent Handbook collection by Roslender (2018). Nevertheless, we can see that many emerging topics have been and are being continuously published and debated in journals such as those mentioned earlier in this chapter and other outlets.

To wrap up this chapter, we would like to offer an ongoing proposal for the study of a "phenomenon *grande*" to our readers here. Bruno Latour's ANT has been utilized in social accounting studies, including Noronha and Zhang's Chapter 10 in this volume. But researchers should look beyond ANT. His book *Facing Gaia* (Latour, 2017) has already caught the attention of social and environmental accounting researchers as it investigates deeply a "phenomenon *grande*", that is the new climatic change regime. His attempt to disentangle theology, politics, and nature has developed "the new Anthropocene", something about a paradigmatic change in the relationship between humans and nature. The current interests in deep ecology and biodiversity and extinction accounting are our (humans') accounts of the Anthropocene. Continuing with his discussion on politics and the new climatic regime, Latour published *Down to Earth* (Latour, 2018). Inequalities, deregulation, and globalization are the elements toward a nightmare of global climate change denial (see Halis' Chapter 15 on Bolsonaro). Latour talks about "Trumpism", the Left/Right opposition, the "spell" of nature and many "phenomena *grande*" in this nightmare of ecological evolution. Then came COVID-19 and Latour's (2021) *After Lockdown*, another ground-breaking masterpiece on the new climatic and pandemic regimes that make humans, as inhabitants of the Earth, become more and more difficult to return to their orientation of life as before. These three pieces by Latour have already left us with almost unlimited possibilities for developing new researches in "comparative CSR". The ontology of Latour's ANT (2D or 3D, and how some people dislike it, see Chapter 10) is still needed no matter whether as a theory or a methodology, but "phenomenon *grande*" leading to "theory emancipation" will be essential for the new trajectory of knowledge exploration in the coming decades, if Gaia and the Anthropocene continue to exist.

References

Adams, C.A. (2002). Internal organisational factors influencing corporate social and ethical reporting: Beyond current theorising. *Accounting, Auditing and Accountability Journal*, 15(2), 225–230.

Adams, C.A., Druckman, P.B. and Picot, R.C. (2020). *Sustainable Development Goals Disclosure (SDGD) Recommendations.* ACCA, ANZ, ICAS, IFAC, IIRC. Available at: https://www.ifac.org/knowledge-gateway/contributing-global-economy/publications/sustainable-development-goals-disclosure-sdgd-recommendations

Adler, N. (2002). *International Dimensions of Organizational Behavior.* Cincinnati, OH: South-Western College Publishing.

Ali, M., Haider, M.B. and Islam, M.T. (2015). Revisiting corporate social disclosure in Japan. In Noronha, C. (Ed.), *Corporate Social Disclosure: Critical Perspectives in China and Japan.* Basingstoke: Palgrave Macmillan.

Atkins, J. and Atkins, B. (2019). *Around the World in 80 Species. Exploring the Business of Extinction.* London: Routledge.

Atkins, J. and Maroun, W. (2018). Integrated extinction accounting and accountability: Building an ark. *Accounting, Auditing and Accountability Journal*, 31(3), 750–786.

Bebbington, J. and Gray, R. (2001). An account of sustainability: Failure, success and reconceptualisation. *Critical Perspectives in Accounting*, 12(5), 557–587.

Beddewela, E. and Herzig, C. (2013). Corporate social reporting by MNCs's subsidiary in Sri Lanka. *Accounting Forum*, 32(7), 135–149.

Bowen, H.R. (1953). *Social Responsibilities of the Businessman.* New York: Harper.

Chappel, W. and Moon, J. (2005). Corporate social responsibility (CSR) in Asia: A seven-country study of CSR web site reporting. *Business and Society*, 44(4), 415–441.

Crane, A., Henriques, I., Husted, B.W. and Matten, D. (2016). Publishing country studies in *Business & Society*: Or, do we care about CSR in Mongolia? *Business and Society*, 55(1), 3–10.

CSO. (2022). *Reference Model for Generally Accepted Integrated Accounting (GAIA) Principles: A Working Proposal by the Center for Sustainable Organization.* V. 2.4. February 20, 2022. Woodstock, VT: CSO.

Cuckston, T. (2018a). Making accounting for biodiversity research a force for conservation. *Social and Environmental Accountability Journal*, 38(3), 218–226.

Cuckston, T. (2018b). Making extinction calculable. *Accounting, Auditing and Accountability Journal*, 31(3), 849–874.

Cuckston, T. (2019). Seeking an ecologically defensible calculation of net loss/gain of biodiversity. *Accounting, Auditing and Accountability Journal*, 32(5), 1358–1383.

Danson, M., Galloway, L. and Sherif, M. (2020). From unemployment to self-employment: Can enterprise policy intensify the risk of poverty? *Critical Perspectives on Accounting*, 75, 102164.

Eisenhardt, K.M. (1989). Building theories from case studies research. *Academy of Management Review*, 14(4), 532–540.

Elsworth, S. (n.d.). What is a retrospective analysis? Available at: https://www.theclassroom.com/retrospective-analysis-12033281.html

Farmer, R.N. and Richman, B.M. (1964). A model for research in comparative management. *California Management Review*, Winter, 55–68.

Fraser Hall Library. (2022). What is history research? Available at: https://libguides.geneseo.edu/history/what-is-history-research

George, C., Brown, J. and Dillard, J. (2021). Social movement activists' conceptions of political actions and counter-accounting through a critical accounting dialogue accounting and accountability lens. *Critical Perspectives on Accounting*, https://doi.org/10.1016/j.cpa.2021.102408.

Ghio, A., McGhigan, N. and Powell, L. (2022). The queer accounting manifesto. *Critical Perspectives on Accounting*. https://doi.org/10.1016/j.cpa.2021.102395

Glaser, B. and Strauss, A. (1967). *The Discovery of Grounded Theory: Strategies for Qualitative Research*. Mill Valley, CA: Sociology Press.

Gray, R. (2002). The social accounting project and accounting, organizations and society: Privileging engagements, imaginings, new accounting and pragmatism over critiques? *Accounting, Organizations and Society*, 27(7), 687–707.

Gray, R., Dey, C., Owens, D., Evans, R. and Zadek, S. (1997). Struggling with the praxis of social accounting: Stakeholders, accountability, audits and procedures. *Accounting, Auditing and Accountability Journal*, 10(3), 325–364.

Gray, R., Owen, D. and Adams, C. (2010). Some theories for social accounting? A review essay and a tentative pedagogic categorization of theorisations around social accounting. *Advances in Environmental Accounting and Management*, 4, 1–54.

Guan, J. and Noronha, C. (2013). Corporate social responsibility reporting research in the Chinese academia: A critical review. *Social Responsibility Journal*, 9(1), 35–55.

Haikos, G.E. and Antonis, S. (2016). Cultural dimensions and corporate social responsibility: A cross-country analysis. Munich Personal RePEC Archive (MPRA). Available at: https://mpra.ub.uni-muenchen.de/69222/

Haikos, G.E. and Antonis, S. (2017). Revisiting the nature of corporate social responsibility and national culture: A quantitative assessment. *Management Decision*, 55(3), 595–613.

Harman, G. (2019). On progressive and degenerative research programs with respect to philosophy. *Revista Portuguesa de Filosofia*, 75(4), 2067–2102.

Hawthorne, J. (2011). Confirmation theory. In Bandyopadhyyay, P.S. and Forster, M.C. (Eds.), *Philosophy of Statistics (Volume 7 of the Handbook of the Philosophy of Science)*. Amsterdam: North-Holland.

Hofstede, G. (1980). *Culture's Consequences: International Differences in Work-Related Values*. Beverley Hills, CA: Sage.

Hoque, Z. (Ed.). (2018). *Methodological Issues in Accounting Research*, 2nd edition. London: Spiramus.

House, R., Javidan, M., Hangers, P. and Dorfman, P. (2002). Understanding cultures and implicit leadership theories across the globe: An introduction to project GLOBE. *Journal of World Business*, 37(1), 310.

Kuhn, T. (1996). *The Structure of Scientific Revolution*, 3rd edition. Chicago, IL: University of Chicago Press.

Lakatos, I. (2015). *Proofs and Refutations: The Logic of Mathematical Discoveries*. Cambridge: Cambridge University Press.

Latour, B. (2017a). *After Lockdown: A New Metamorphosis*. Cambridge: Polity.

Latour, B. (2017b). *Facing Gaia: Eight Lectures in the New Climatic Regime*. Cambridge: Polity.

Latour, B. (2018). *Down to Earth: Politics in the New Climatic Regime*. Cambridge: Polity.

Latour, B. (2021). *After Lockdown: A New Metamorphosis*. Translated by J. Rose. Cambridge: Polity.

McSweeney, B. (2002). Hofstede's model of national cultural differences and their consequences: A triumph of faith – A failure of analysis. *Human Relations*, 55(1), 89–112.

Merton, R.K. (1968). *Social Theory and Social Structure*. New York: The Free Press.

Mills, C.W. (1959). *The Social Imagination*. Oxford: Oxford University Press.

Negandhi, A.R. (1975). Comparative management and organizational theory: A marriage needed. *Academy of Management Journal*, 18(2), 334–343.

Negandhi, A.R. and Prasad, S.B. (1971). *Comparative Management*. New York: Appleton Century-Crofts.

Ng, A.W. and Leung, T.C.H. (2020). Relevance of SEA to a global financial centre under one country two systems: Engaging stakeholders for sustainability and climate change. *Social and Environmental Accountability Journal*, 4(2), 140–148.

Noronha, C., Guan, J. and Sio, S.H.I. (2021). Accounting for gaming in the time of plague: COVID-19 in Macau. *Sustainability Accounting, Management and Policy Journal*, 12(5), 943–964.

Patten, D. (2002). Media exposure, public policy pressure, and environmental disclosure: An examination of the impact of tri data availability. *Accounting Forum*, 26(2), 152–171.

Popper, K. (1992). *The Logic of Scientific Discovery*. London: Routledge.

Ramasamy, B. and Hung, W.T. (2004). A comparative analysis of corporate social responsibility awareness. *Journal of Corporate Citizenship*, 13, 109–123.

Redding, S.G. (1994). Comparative management theory: Jungle, zoo or fossil bed? *Organization Studies*, 5(3), 323–359.

Richman, B.M. (1965). Significance of cultural variables. *Academy of Management Journal*, 8(4), 292–308.

Ronen, S. and Shenkar, O. (1985). Clustering countries in attitudinal dimensions: A review and synthesis. *Academy of Management Review*, 10(3), 435–454.

Roslender, R. (Ed.). (2018). *The Routledge Companion to Critical Accounting*. London: Routledge.

Schaltegger, S. (2021). Sustainability learnings from the COVID-19 crisis: Opportunities for resilient industries and business development. *Sustainability Accounting, Management and Policy Journal*, 12(5), 885–897.

Schmidt, M.A. and Cracau, D. (2018). A cross country comparison of the corporate social responsibility orientation in Germany and Qatar: An empirical study among business students. *Business and Professional Ethics Journal*, 37(1), 67–104.

Strauss, A. and Corbin, J. (1998). *Basics of Qualitative Research Techniques and Procedures for Developing Grounded Theory*, 2nd edition. London: Sage.

Tilt, C.A. (2016). Corporate social responsibility research: The importance of context. *International Journal of Corporate Social Responsibility*, 1(1), 2. https://doi.org/10.1186/s40991-016-0003-7

Tung, R.L. and Verbeke, A. (2010). Beyond Hofstede and GLOBE: Improving the quality of cross-cultural research. *Journal of International Business Studies*, 41(8), 1259–1274.

Trompenaars, F. and Hampden-Turner, C. (2000). *Riding the Waves of Culture: Understanding Cultural Diversity in Business*. London: McGraw-Hill.

Vollmer, H. (2018). Dark ecology: For a logic of future coexistence. *Social and Environmental Accountability Journal*, 38(2), 154–156.

Welford, R. (2005). Corporate social responsibility in Europe, North America and Asia. *Journal of Corporate Citizenship*, 17(17), 33–52.

Williams, C. and Aguilera, R.V. (2008). Corporate social responsibility in a comparative perspective. In Crane, A., Matten, D., McWilliams, A., Moon, J. and

Siegel, D.S. (Eds.), *Oxford Handbook of Corporate Social Responsibility*. Oxford: Oxford University Press.

Yigitbasioglu, O., Green, P. and Decca Cheung, M.-Y. (2022). Digital transformation and accountants as advisors. *Accounting, Auditing and Accountability Journal*. https://doi-org.libezproxy.um.edu.mo/10.1108/AAAJ-02-2019-3894

Zhao, L. and Atkins, J. (2021). Assessing the emancipatory nature of Chinese extinction accounting. *Social and Environmental Accountability Journal*, 41(1–2), 8–36.

Index

Note: Page numbers in *italics* indicate figures, **bold** indicate tables in the text.

For Product Safety Concerns and Information please contact our EU
representative GPSR@taylorandfrancis.com
Taylor & Francis Verlag GmbH, Kaufingerstraße 24, 80331 München, Germany

www.ingramcontent.com/pod-product-compliance
Lightning Source LLC
LaVergne TN
LVHW021116300926
849160LV00010B/750

* 9 7 8 1 0 3 2 2 2 8 7 0 9 *